Proton
Service and Repair Manual

Mark Coombs and Spencer Drayton

Models covered (3255-240)

Proton Saloon & Aeroback (Hatchback), including Mpi models and special/limited editions
1.3 litre (1298 cc) & 1.5 litre (1468 cc) 8- & 12-valve petrol engines

Does NOT cover Persona/Compact range

© Haynes Publishing 1997

ABCDE
FGHIJ
KLMNO
PQRST

A book in the **Haynes Service and Repair Manual Series**

All rights reserved. No part of this book may be reproduced or transmitted in any form or by any means, electronic or mechanical, including photocopying, recording or by any information storage or retrieval system, without permission in writing from the copyright holder.

ISBN **1 85960 255 X**

British Library Cataloguing in Publication Data
A catalogue record for this book is available from the British Library.

Printed by **J H Haynes & Co. Ltd, Sparkford, Nr Yeovil, Somerset BA22 7JJ**

Haynes Publishing
Sparkford, Nr Yeovil, Somerset BA22 7JJ, England

Haynes North America, Inc
861 Lawrence Drive, Newbury Park, California 91320, USA

Editions Haynes S.A.
147/149, rue Saint Honoré, 75001 PARIS, France

Haynes Publishing Nordiska AB
Fyrisborgsgatan 5, 754 50 Uppsala, Sverige

Contents

LIVING WITH YOUR PROTON

Introduction	Page	0•4
Safety first!	Page	0•5

Roadside repairs

If your car won't start	Page	0•6
Jump starting	Page	0•7
Wheel changing	Page	0•8
Identifying leaks	Page	0•9
Towing	Page	0•9

Weekly checks

Introduction	Page	0•10
Underbonnet check points	Page	0•10
Engine oil level	Page	0•11
Coolant level	Page	0•11
Brake (and clutch) fluid level	Page	0•12
Screen washer fluid level	Page	0•12
Power steering fluid level	Page	0•13
Wiper blades	Page	0•13
Tyre condition and pressure	Page	0•14
Battery	Page	0•15
Bulbs and fuses	Page	0•15

Lubricants, fluids, capacities and tyre pressures

	Page	0•16

MAINTENANCE

Routine maintenance and servicing

	Page	1•1
Servicing specifications	Page	1•2
Maintenance schedule	Page	1•3
Maintenance procedures	Page	1•6

Contents

REPAIRS & OVERHAUL

Engine and associated systems
Engine in-car repair procedures	Page 2A•1
General engine overhaul procedures	Page 2B•1
Cooling, heating and ventilation systems	Page 3•1
Fuel and exhaust systems- carburettor models	Page 4A•1
Fuel and exhaust systems - fuel-injected models	Page 4B•1
Emission control systems	Page 4C•1
Engine electrical systems	Page 5•1

Transmission
Clutch	Page 6•1
Manual transmission	Page 7A•1
Automatic transmission	Page 7B•1
Driveshafts	Page 8•1

Brakes and suspension
Braking system	Page 9•1
Suspension and steering	Page 10•1

Body equipment
Bodywork and fittings	Page 11•1
Body electrical systems	Page 12•1

Wiring diagrams
Page 12•12

REFERENCE

Dimensions and weights	Page REF•1
Conversion factors	Page REF•2
Buying spare parts	Page REF•3
Vehicle identification	Page REF•3
Jacking and vehicle support	Page REF•3
Tools and working facilities	Page REF•4
MOT test checks	Page REF•6
Fault finding	Page REF•10
General repair procedures	Page REF•17
Glossary of technical terms	Page REF•18

Index
Page REF•23

Introduction

The new Proton was introduced into the UK in early 1989. Both Saloon and Aeroback models were available from launch, with a choice of 1.3 litre (1298 cc) or 1.5 litre (1468 cc) engines. The Proton was based heavily on the Mitsubishi Lancer, Proton having purchased many of the major components and the tooling needed to produce them from the Mitsubishi.

The engine is a well-proven unit which has appeared in many Mitsubishi vehicles. The engine is of four-cylinder overhead camshaft design, mounted transversely at the front of vehicle with the transmission mounted on its right-hand end. The 1.3 litre model was available with only a manual transmission, but the 1.5 litre model was offered with an automatic transmission option

All models have fully-independent front suspension, incorporating MacPherson struts, and trailing arm rear suspension.

A wide range of standard and optional equipment is available within the range to suit most tastes, including central locking, electric windows and an electric sunroof. An air conditioning system was available as an options on certain models.

The model range has remained largely unchanged throughout its life. In early 1991 all models were fitted with 12-valve engines (both 1.3 and 1.5 litre models) to replace the original 8-valve engines, and in late 1992 all models were fitted were fuel-injected to comply with the forthcoming emission regulations. Apart from this, only minor detail changes have been made to the vehicle.

Provided that regular servicing is carried out in accordance with the manufacturer's recommendations, the vehicle should prove reliable and very economical. The engine compartment is well-designed, and most of the items requiring frequent attention are easily accessible.

Proton 1.5 SE Saloon

Proton 1.5 SE Aeroback

The Proton Team

Haynes manuals are produced by dedicated and enthusiastic people working in close co-operation. The team responsible for the creation of this book included:

Authors	Mark Coombs
	Spencer Drayton
Sub-editor	Carole Turk
Editor & Page Make-up	Steve Churchill
	Bob Jex
Workshop manager	Paul Buckland
Photo Scans	John Martin
Cover illustration & Line Art	Roger Healing
Wiring diagrams	Matthew Marke

We hope the book will help you to get the maximum enjoyment from your car. By carrying out routine maintenance as described you will ensure your car's reliability and preserve its resale value.

Your Proton manual

The aim of this manual is to help you get the best value from your vehicle. It can do so in several ways. It can help you decide what work must be done (even should you choose to get it done by a garage). It will also provide information on routine maintenance and servicing, and give a logical course of action and diagnosis when random faults occur. However, it is hoped that you will use the manual by tackling the work yourself. On simpler jobs it may even be quicker than booking the car into a garage and going there twice, to leave and collect it. Perhaps most important, a lot of money can be saved by avoiding the costs a garage must charge to cover its labour and overheads.

The manual has drawings and descriptions to show the function of the various components so that their layout can be understood. Tasks are described and photographed in a clear step-by-step sequence.

Acknowledgements

Thanks are due to Champion Spark Plug, who supplied the illustrations showing spark plug conditions, and to Duckhams Oils who provided lubrication data. Thanks are also due to Sykes-Pickavant Limited, who provided some of the workshop tools, and to all those people at Sparkford and Newbury Park who helped in the production of this manual.

We take great pride in the accuracy of information given in this manual, but vehicle manufacturers make alterations and design changes during the production run of a particular vehicle of which they do not inform us. No liability can be accepted by the authors or publishers for loss, damage or injury caused by any errors in, or omissions from, the information given.

Safety first! 0•5

Working on your car can be dangerous. This page shows just some of the potential risks and hazards, with the aim of creating a safety-conscious attitude.

General hazards

Scalding
• Don't remove the radiator or expansion tank cap while the engine is hot.
• Engine oil, automatic transmission fluid or power steering fluid may also be dangerously hot if the engine has recently been running.

Burning
• Beware of burns from the exhaust system and from any part of the engine. Brake discs and drums can also be extremely hot immediately after use.

Crushing
• When working under or near a raised vehicle, always supplement the jack with axle stands, or use drive-on ramps. *Never venture under a car which is only supported by a jack.*

• Take care if loosening or tightening high-torque nuts when the vehicle is on stands. Initial loosening and final tightening should be done with the wheels on the ground.

Fire
• Fuel is highly flammable; fuel vapour is explosive.
• Don't let fuel spill onto a hot engine.
• Do not smoke or allow naked lights (including pilot lights) anywhere near a vehicle being worked on. Also beware of creating sparks (electrically or by use of tools).
• Fuel vapour is heavier than air, so don't work on the fuel system with the vehicle over an inspection pit.
• Another cause of fire is an electrical overload or short-circuit. Take care when repairing or modifying the vehicle wiring.
• Keep a fire extinguisher handy, of a type suitable for use on fuel and electrical fires.

Electric shock
• Ignition HT voltage can be dangerous, especially to people with heart problems or a pacemaker. Don't work on or near the ignition system with the engine running or the ignition switched on.
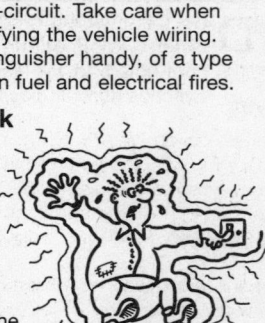
• Mains voltage is also dangerous. Make sure that any mains-operated equipment is correctly earthed. Mains power points should be protected by a residual current device (RCD) circuit breaker.

Fume or gas intoxication
• Exhaust fumes are poisonous; they often contain carbon monoxide, which is rapidly fatal if inhaled. Never run the engine in a confined space such as a garage with the doors shut.
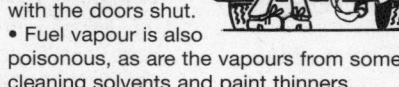
• Fuel vapour is also poisonous, as are the vapours from some cleaning solvents and paint thinners.

Poisonous or irritant substances
• Avoid skin contact with battery acid and with any fuel, fluid or lubricant, especially antifreeze, brake hydraulic fluid and Diesel fuel. Don't syphon them by mouth. If such a substance is swallowed or gets into the eyes, seek medical advice.
• Prolonged contact with used engine oil can cause skin cancer. Wear gloves or use a barrier cream if necessary. Change out of oil-soaked clothes and do not keep oily rags in your pocket.
• Air conditioning refrigerant forms a poisonous gas if exposed to a naked flame (including a cigarette). It can also cause skin burns on contact.

Asbestos
• Asbestos dust can cause cancer if inhaled or swallowed. Asbestos may be found in gaskets and in brake and clutch linings. When dealing with such components it is safest to assume that they contain asbestos.

Special hazards

Hydrofluoric acid
• This extremely corrosive acid is formed when certain types of synthetic rubber, found in some O-rings, oil seals, fuel hoses etc, are exposed to temperatures above 400°C. The rubber changes into a charred or sticky substance containing the acid. *Once formed, the acid remains dangerous for years. If it gets onto the skin, it may be necessary to amputate the limb concerned.*
• When dealing with a vehicle which has suffered a fire, or with components salvaged from such a vehicle, wear protective gloves and discard them after use.

The battery
• Batteries contain sulphuric acid, which attacks clothing, eyes and skin. Take care when topping-up or carrying the battery.
• The hydrogen gas given off by the battery is highly explosive. Never cause a spark or allow a naked light nearby. Be careful when connecting and disconnecting battery chargers or jump leads.

Air bags
• Air bags can cause injury if they go off accidentally. Take care when removing the steering wheel and/or facia. Special storage instructions may apply.

Diesel injection equipment
• Diesel injection pumps supply fuel at very high pressure. Take care when working on the fuel injectors and fuel pipes.

⚠️ *Warning: Never expose the hands, face or any other part of the body to injector spray; the fuel can penetrate the skin with potentially fatal results.*

Remember...

DO
• Do use eye protection when using power tools, and when working under the vehicle.
• Do wear gloves or use barrier cream to protect your hands when necessary.
• Do get someone to check periodically that all is well when working alone on the vehicle.
• Do keep loose clothing and long hair well out of the way of moving mechanical parts.
• Do remove rings, wristwatch etc, before working on the vehicle – especially the electrical system.
• Do ensure that any lifting or jacking equipment has a safe working load rating adequate for the job.

DON'T
• Don't attempt to lift a heavy component which may be beyond your capability – get assistance.
• Don't rush to finish a job, or take unverified short cuts.
• Don't use ill-fitting tools which may slip and cause injury.
• Don't leave tools or parts lying around where someone can trip over them. Mop up oil and fuel spills at once.
• Don't allow children or pets to play in or near a vehicle being worked on.

0•6 Roadside repairs

The following pages are intended to help in dealing with common roadside emergencies and breakdowns. You will find more detailed fault finding information at the back of the manual, and repair information in the main chapters.

If your car won't start and the starter motor doesn't turn

- ☐ If it's a model with automatic transmission, make sure the selector is in 'P' or 'N'.
- ☐ Open the bonnet and make sure that the battery terminals are clean and tight.
- ☐ Switch on the headlights and try to start the engine. If the headlights go very dim when you're trying to start, the battery is probably flat. Get out of trouble by jump starting (see next page) using a friend's car.

If your car won't start even though the starter motor turns as normal

- ☐ Is there fuel in the tank?
- ☐ Is there moisture on electrical components under the bonnet? Switch off the ignition, then wipe off any obvious dampness with a dry cloth. Spray a water-repellent aerosol product (WD-40 or equivalent) on ignition and fuel system electrical connectors like those shown in the photos. Pay special attention to the ignition coil wiring connector and HT leads. (Note that Diesel engines don't normally suffer from damp.)

A Check the condition and security of the battery connections

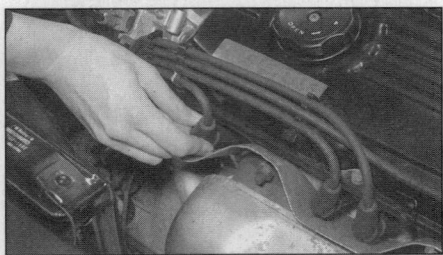

B Check that the spark plug HT leads are securely connected by pushing them onto the plugs

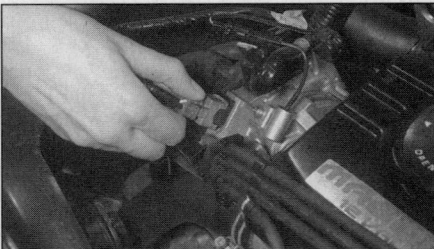

C Check that the HT leads and wiring connectors are securely connected to the distributor (12-valve model shown).

Check that electrical connections are secure (with the ignition switched off) and spray them with a water dispersant spray like WD-40 if you suspect a problem due to damp

D On fuel-injected models check that the wiring connectors are securely connected to the various sensors and switches (throttle position sensor shown).

Roadside repairs 0•7

Jump starting

Jump starting will get you out of trouble, but you must correct whatever made the battery go flat in the first place. There are three possibilities:

1 *The battery has been drained by repeated attempts to start, or by leaving the lights on.*

2 *The charging system is not working properly (alternator drivebelt slack or broken, alternator wiring fault or alternator itself faulty).*

3 *The battery itself is at fault (electrolyte low, or battery worn out).*

When jump-starting a car using a booster battery, observe the following precautions:

✔ Before connecting the booster battery, make sure that the ignition is switched off.

✔ Ensure that all electrical equipment (lights, heater, wipers, etc) is switched off.

✔ Make sure that the booster battery is the same voltage as the discharged one in the vehicle.

✔ If the battery is being jump-started from the battery in another vehicle, the two vehcles MUST NOT TOUCH each other.

✔ Make sure that the transmission is in neutral (or PARK, in the case of automatic transmission).

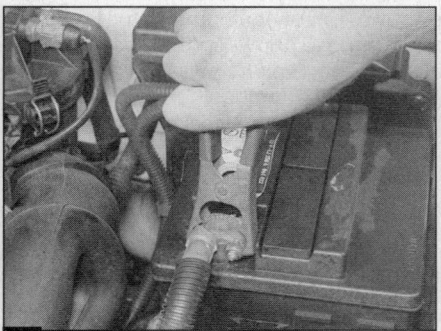

1 Connect one end of the red jump lead to the positive (+) terminal of the flat battery

2 Connect the other end of the red lead to the positive (+) terminal of the booster battery.

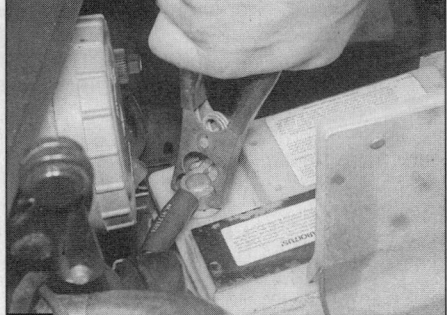

3 Connect one end of the black jump lead to the negative (-) terminal of the booster battery

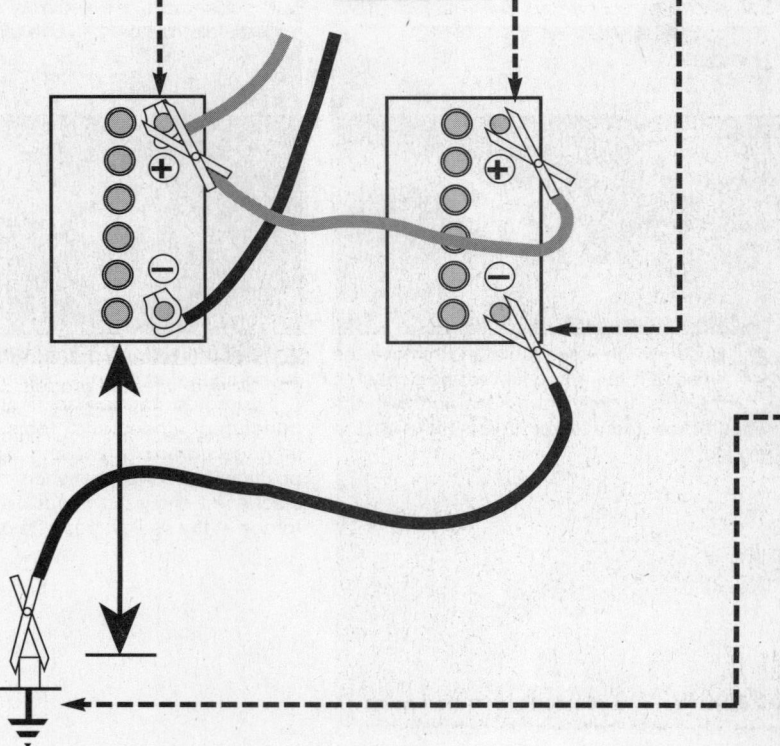

4 Connect the other end of the black jump lead to a bolt or bracket on the engine block, well away from the battery, on the vehicle to be started.

5 Make sure that the jump leads will not come into contact with the fan, drivebelts or other moving parts of the engine.

6 Start the engine using the booster battery, then with the engine running at idle speed, disconnect the jump leads in the reverse order of connection.

0•8 Roadside repairs

Wheel changing

Some of the details shown here will vary according to model. For instance, the location of the spare wheel and jack is not the same on all cars. However, the basic principles apply to all vehicles.

 Warning: Do not change a wheel in a situation where you risk being hit by other traffic. On busy roads, try to stop in a lay-by or a gateway. Be wary of passing traffic while changing the wheel – it is easy to become distracted by the job in hand.

Preparation

- ☐ When a puncture occurs, stop as soon as it is safe to do so.
- ☐ Park on firm level ground, if possible, and well out of the way of other traffic.
- ☐ Use hazard warning lights if necessary.
- ☐ If you have one, use a warning triangle to alert other drivers of your presence.
- ☐ Apply the handbrake and engage first or reverse gear (or Park on models with automatic transmission).
- ☐ Chock the wheel diagonally opposite the one being removed – a couple of large stones will do for this.
- ☐ If the ground is soft, use a flat piece of wood to spread the load under the jack.

Changing the wheel

1 The spare wheel and tools are stored in the luggage compartment. Lift up the carpet and remove the tool kit and jack. Unscrew the retainer and remove the spare wheel from the luggage compartment.

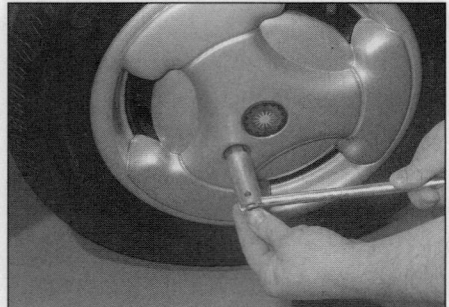

2 Remove the wheel trim/hub cap (as applicable). On models were anti-theft wheel trims are fitted, use the **adapter** in the toolkit to unscrew the retaining screw prior to unclipping the wheel trim.

3 With the vehicle on the ground, slacken each wheel nut by half a turn.

4 Make sure the jack is located on firm ground and engage the jack head correctly with the sill. Raise the jack using the wheelbrace until the wheel is raised clear of the ground.

5 Unscrew the wheel nuts and remove the wheel. Fit the spare wheel and screw on the nuts. Lightly tighten the nuts with the wheelbrace then lower the vehicle to the ground.

6 Securely tighten the wheel nuts in a diagonal sequence then refit the wheel trim/hub cap (as applicable). Stow the punctured wheel and tools back in the luggage compartment and secure them in position. Note that the wheel nuts should be slackened and retightened to the specified torque at the earliest possible opportunity.

Finally...

- ☐ Remove the wheel chocks.
- ☐ Check the tyre pressure on the wheel just fitted. If it is low, or if you don't have a pressure gauge with you, drive slowly to the nearest garage and inflate the tyre to the right pressure.
- ☐ Have the damaged tyre or wheel repaired as soon as possible.

Roadside repairs 0•9

Identifying leaks

Puddles on the garage floor or drive, or obvious wetness under the bonnet or underneath the car, suggest a leak that needs investigating. It can sometimes be difficult to decide where the leak is coming from, especially if the engine bay is very dirty already. Leaking oil or fluid can also be blown rearwards by the passage of air under the car, giving a false impression of where the problem lies.

 Warning: Most automotive oils and fluids are poisonous. Wash them off skin, and change out of contaminated clothing, without delay.

 The smell of a fluid leaking from the car may provide a clue to what's leaking. Some fluids are distinctively coloured. It may help to clean the car and to park it over some clean paper as an aid to locating the source of the leak. Remember that some leaks may only occur while the engine is running.

Sump oil

Engine oil may leak from the drain plug...

Oil from filter

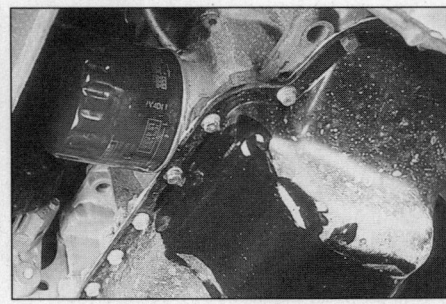

...or from the base of the oil filter.

Gearbox oil

Gearbox oil can leak from the seals at the inboard ends of the driveshafts.

Antifreeze

Leaking antifreeze often leaves a crystalline deposit like this.

Brake fluid

A leak occurring at a wheel is almost certainly brake fluid.

Power steering fluid

Power steering fluid may leak from the pipe connectors on the steering rack.

Towing

When all else fails, you may find yourself having to get a tow home – or of course you may be helping somebody else. Long-distance recovery should only be done by a garage or breakdown service. For shorter distances, DIY towing using another car is easy enough, but observe the following points:
☐ Use a proper tow-rope – they are not expensive. The vehicle being towed must display an 'ON TOW' sign in its rear window.
☐ Always turn the ignition key to the 'on' position when the vehicle is being towed, so that the steering lock is released, and that the direction indicator and brake lights will work.

☐ Only attach the tow-rope to the towing eyes provided.
☐ Before being towed, release the handbrake and select neutral on the transmission.
☐ Note that greater-than-usual pedal pressure will be required to operate the brakes, since the vacuum servo unit is only operational with the engine running.
☐ On models with power steering, greater-than-usual steering effort will also be required.
☐ The driver of the car being towed must keep the tow-rope taut at all times to avoid snatching.
☐ Make sure that both drivers know the route before setting off.

☐ Only drive at moderate speeds and keep the distance towed to a minimum. Drive smoothly and allow plenty of time for slowing down at junctions.
☐ On models with automatic transmission, special precautions apply. If in doubt, do not tow, or transmission damage may result. *On models with automatic transmission, do not tow the vehicle at speeds in excess of 30 mph (50 kmh) or for a distance of greater than 15 miles (25 km). If towing speed/distance are to exceed these limits, then the vehicle must be towed with its front wheels off the ground.*

0•10 Weekly checks

Introduction

There are some very simple checks which need only take a few minutes to carry out, but which could save you a lot of inconvenience and expense.

These "Weekly checks" require no great skill or special tools, and the small amount of time they take to perform could prove to be very well spent, for example;

☐ Keeping an eye on tyre condition and pressures, will not only help to stop them wearing out prematurely, but could also save your life.

☐ Many breakdowns are caused by electrical problems. Battery-related faults are particularly common, and a quick check on a regular basis will often prevent the majority of these.

☐ If your car develops a brake fluid leak, the first time you might know about it is when your brakes don't work properly. Checking the level regularly will give advance warning of this kind of problem.

☐ If the oil or coolant levels run low, the cost of repairing any engine damage will be far greater than fixing the leak, for example.

Underbonnet check points

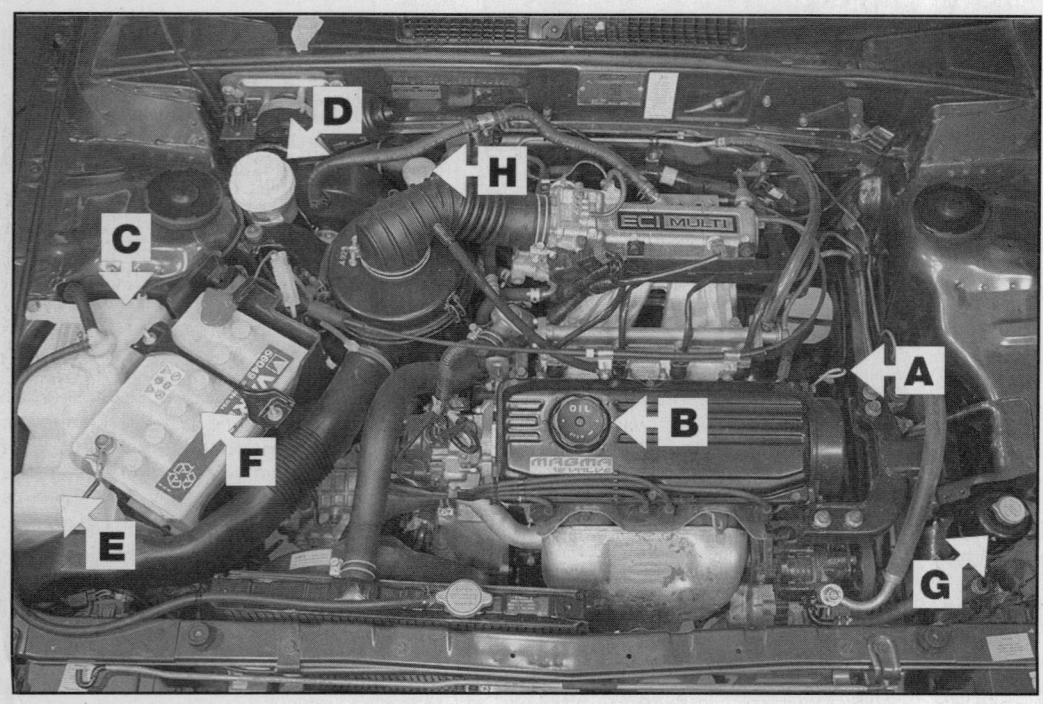

◀ **1.5 litre MPi (others similar)**

A Engine oil level dipstick
B Engine oil filler cap
C Coolant expansion tank
D Brake fluid reservoir
E Screen washer fluid reservoir
F Battery
G Power steering fluid reservoir
H Clutch fluid reservoir (fuel injected models only)

Weekly checks 0•11

Engine oil level

Before you start

✔ Make sure that your car is on level ground.
✔ Check the oil level before the car is driven, or at least 5 minutes after the engine has been switched off.

 *If the oil level is checked immediately after driving the vehicle, some of the oil will remain in the upper engine components, resulting in an inaccurate reading on the dipstick!*

The correct oil

Modern engines place great demands on their oil. It is very important that the correct oil for your car is used (See "Lubricants, fluids and tyre pressures").

Car care

● If you have to add oil frequently, you should check whether you have any oil leaks. Place some clean paper under the car overnight, and check for stains in the morning. If there are no leaks, the engine may be burning oil (see "Fault finding").

● Always maintain the level between the upper and lower dipstick marks (see photo 3). If the level is too low severe engine damage may occur. Oil seal failure may result if the engine is overfilled by adding too much oil.

1 The dipstick is located at the rear of the engine on its left-hand end (refer to "Underbonnet check points" on page **0.10** for exact location). Withdraw the dipstick.

2 Using a clean rag or paper towl remove all oil from the dipstick. Insert the clean dipstick into the tube as far as it will go, then withdraw it again

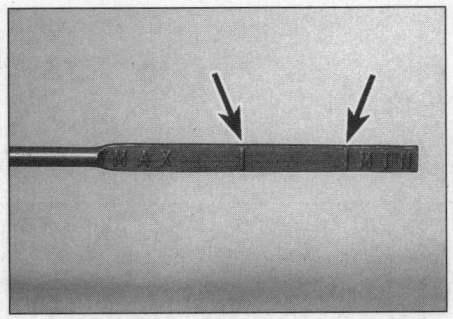

3 Note the oil level on the end of the dipstick, which should be between the upper ("MAX") mark and lower ("MIN") mark.

4 Oil is added through the filler cap. Unscrew the cap and top-up the level; a funnel may help to reduce spillage. Add the oil slowly, checking the level on the dipstick often.

Coolant level

 Warning: DO NOT attempt to remove the expansion tank pressure cap when the engine is hot, as there is a very great risk of scalding. Do not leave open containers of coolant about, as it is poisonous.

Car care

● Adding coolant should not be necessary on a regular basis. If frequent topping-up is required, it is likely there is a leak. Check the radiator, all hoses and joint faces for signs of staining or wetness, and rectify as necessary.

● It is important that antifreeze is used in the cooling system all year round, not just during the winter months. Don't top-up with water alone, as the antifreeze will become too diluted.

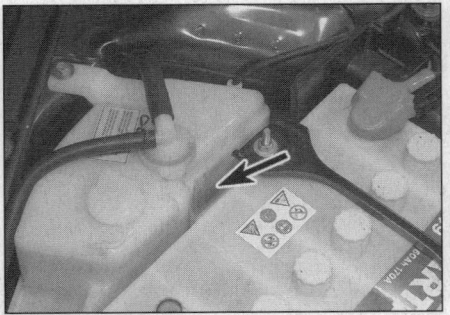

1 The coolant level varies with the temperature of the engine. The level is checked in the expansion tank on the right-hand side of the engine compartment; the expansion tank and washer fluid reservoir are combined in one container, the expansion tank being in the rear section. When the engine is at normal operating temperature, the coolant level should be between the upper (FULL) and lower (LOW) level markings on the side of the expansion tank.

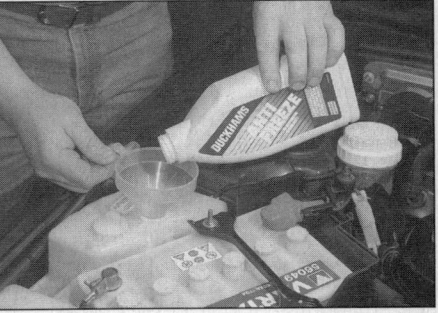

2 If topping up is necessary, remove the (rear) expansion tank cap and add a mixture of water and antifreeze to the expansion tank until the coolant level is between the level marks. Once the level is correct, securely refit the cap.

0•12 Weekly checks

Brake (and clutch*) fluid level

*On fuel-injected models the clutch fluid level should also be checked at the same time as the brake fluid. The reservoir is located just to the left of the brake reservoir and is checked in the same manner.

Warning:
● Brake fluid can harm your eyes and will damage painted surfaces, so use extreme caution when handling and pouring it.
● Do not use fluid that has been standing open for some time, as it absorbs moisture from the air, which can cause a dangerous loss of braking effectiveness.

 Haynes Hint
● Make sure that your car is on level ground.
● The fluid level in the reservoir will drop slightly as the brake pads wear down, but the fluid level must never be allowed to drop below the "MIN" mark.

Safety first!
● If the reservoir requires repeated topping-up this is an indication of a fluid leak somewhere in the system, which should be investigated immediately.
● If a leak is suspected, the car should not be driven until the braking system has been checked. Never take any risks where brakes are concerned.

1 The upper (MAX) and lower (MIN or A) fluid level markings are on the side of the reservoir, which is located in the right-hand rear corner of the engine compartment. The fluid level must always be kept in-between these two marks.

2 If topping up is necessary, first wipe clean the area around the filler cap with a clean cloth then unscrew the cap and remove it along with the rubber diaphragm.

3 Carefully add fluid, avoiding spilling it on the surrounding paintwork. Use only the specified hydraulic fluid. After filling the correct level, refit the cap and diaphragm and tighten it securely. Wipe off any spilt fluid.

4 On fuel-injected models repeat the check on the clutch reservoir (located on the left-hand side of the brake fluid reservoir) and, if necessary, top-up.

Screen washer fluid level

Screenwash additives not only keep the winscreen clean during foul weather, they also prevent the washer system freezing in cold weather - which is when you are likely to need it most. Don't top up using plain water as the screenwash will become too diluted, and will freeze during cold weather. *On no account use coolant antifreeze in the washer system - this could discolour or damage paintwork.*

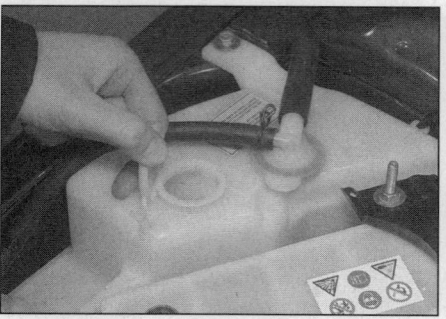

1 The washer fluid reservoir is located on the right-hand side of the engine compartment; the reservoir and expansion tank are combined in one container, the washer reservoir being the front section. The level is visible through the reservoir body and is topped up via the front cap.

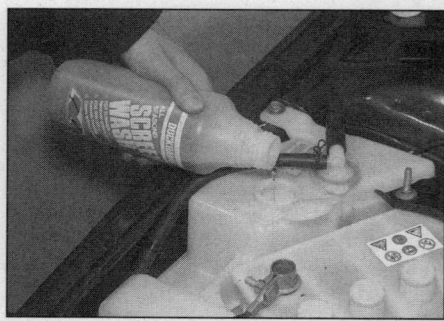

2 If topping up is necessary, add water and a screenwash additive in the quantities recommended by the manufacturer.

Weekly checks 0•13

Power steering fluid level

Before you start:
✔ Park the vehicle on level ground.
✔ Set the steering wheel straight-ahead.
✔ The level should ideally be checked after a journey of at least 5 miles, although this is not essential.

Safety first!
● The fluid level is checked with the engine running - take care to keep loose clothing and long hair out of the way of moving mechanical parts.
● The need for frequent topping-up indicates a leak, which should be investigated immediately.

1 Wipe clean the area around the reservoir cap then remove the cap and withdraw the reservoir filter. Check the filter is clean, if necessary it can be washed solvent and dried, then refit it to the reservoir.

2 Ensure that the front are positioned in the straight-ahead position, then start the engine and allow it to idle. Wipe clean the cap dipstick then insert it fully into the reservoir and withdraw it.

3 Note the fluid level on the end of the dipstick, which should be between the upper (MAX) and lower (MIN) marks.

4 If necessary, top-up the reservoir with the specified type of the fluid. Once the level is between the level marks, securely refit the reservoir cap. Do not overfill the reservoir.

Wiper blades

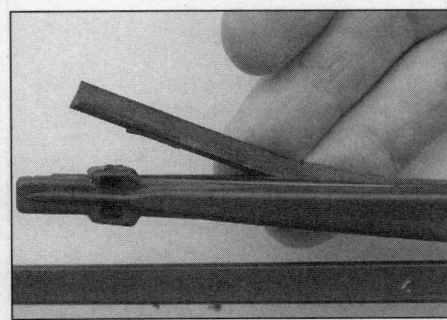

1 Check the condition of the wiper blades: if they are cracked or show signs of deterioration, or if the glass swept area is smeared, renew them. For maximum clarity of vision, wiper blades should be renewed annually.

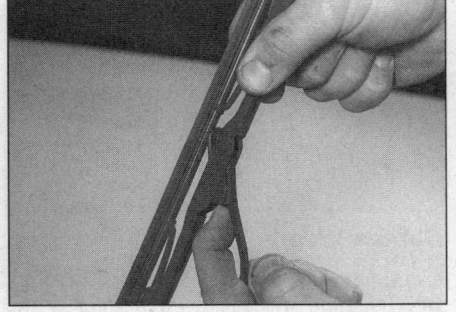

2 To remove a windscreen wiper blade, pull the arm fully away from the screen until it locks. Swivel the blade then depress the locking clip at the base of the mounting block and slide the blade off the arm.

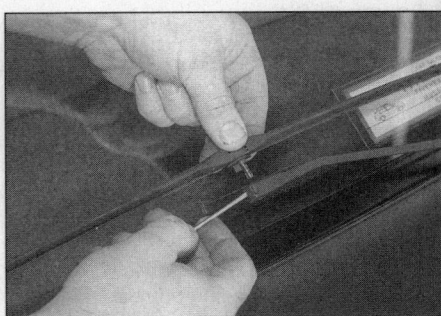

3 To remove a tailgate wiper blade, pull the arm fully away from the screen until it locks in position then depress the retaining clip and pull the blade upwards and away from the arm

Tyre condition and pressure

It is very important that tyres are in good condition, and at the correct pressure - having a tyre failure at any speed is highly dangerous. Tyre wear is influenced by driving style - harsh braking and acceleration, or fast cornering, will all produce more rapid tyre wear. As a general rule, the front tyres wear out faster than the rears. Interchanging the tyres from front to rear ("rotating" the tyres) may result in more even wear. However, if this is completely effective, you may have the expense of replacing all four tyres at once! Remove any nails or stones embedded in the tread before they penetrate the tyre to cause deflation. If removal of a nail does reveal that the tyre has been punctured, refit the nail so that its point of penetration is marked. Then immediately change the wheel, and have the tyre repaired by a tyre dealer.

Regularly check the tyres for damage in the form of cuts or bulges, especially in the sidewalls. Periodically remove the wheels, and clean any dirt or mud from the inside and outside surfaces. Examine the wheel rims for signs of rusting, corrosion or other damage. Light alloy wheels are easily damaged by "kerbing" whilst parking; steel wheels may also become dented or buckled. A new wheel is very often the only way to overcome severe damage.

New tyres should be balanced when they are fitted, but it may become necessary to re-balance them as they wear, or if the balance weights fitted to the wheel rim should fall off. Unbalanced tyres will wear more quickly, as will the steering and suspension components. Wheel imbalance is normally signified by vibration, particularly at a certain speed (typically around 50 mph). If this vibration is felt only through the steering, then it is likely that just the front wheels need balancing. If, however, the vibration is felt through the whole car, the rear wheels could be out of balance. Wheel balancing should be carried out by a tyre dealer or garage.

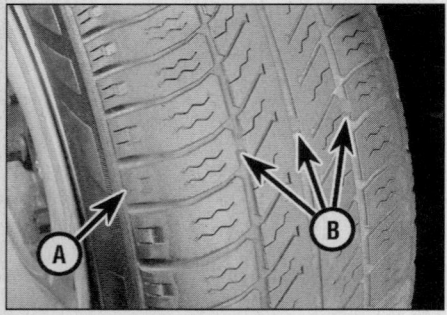

1 Tread Depth - visual check
The original tyres have tread wear safety bands (B), which will appear when the tread depth reaches approximately 1.6 mm. The band positions are indicated by a triangular mark on the tyre sidewall (A).

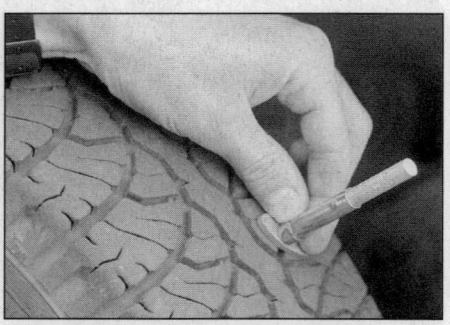

2 Tread Depth - manual check
Alternatively, tread wear can be monitored with a simple, inexpensive device known as a tread depth indicator gauge.

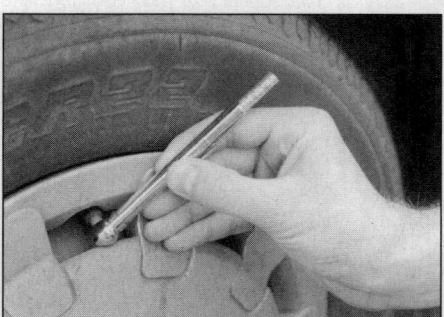

3 Tyre Pressure Check
Check the tyre pressures regularly with the tyres cold. Do not adjust the tyre pressures immediately after the vehicle has been used, or an inaccurate setting will result.

Tyre tread wear patterns

Shoulder Wear

Underinflation (wear on both sides)
Under-inflation will cause overheating of the tyre, because the tyre will flex too much, and the tread will not sit correctly on the road surface. This will cause a loss of grip and excessive wear, not to mention the danger of sudden tyre failure due to heat build-up.
Check and adjust pressures
Incorrect wheel camber (wear on one side)
Repair or renew suspension parts
Hard cornering
Reduce speed!

Centre Wear

Overinflation
Over-inflation will cause rapid wear of the centre part of the tyre tread, coupled with reduced grip, harsher ride, and the danger of shock damage occurring in the tyre casing.
Check and adjust pressures

If you sometimes have to inflate your car's tyres to the higher pressures specified for maximum load or sustained high speed, don't forget to reduce the pressures to normal afterwards.

Uneven Wear

Front tyres may wear unevenly as a result of wheel misalignment. Most tyre dealers and garages can check and adjust the wheel alignment (or "tracking") for a modest charge.
Incorrect camber or castor
Repair or renew suspension parts
Malfunctioning suspension
Repair or renew suspension parts
Unbalanced wheel
Balance tyres
Incorrect toe setting
Adjust front wheel alignment
Note: The feathered edge of the tread which typifies toe wear is best checked by feel.

Weekly checks 0•15

Battery

Caution: *Before carrying out any work on the vehicle battery, read the precautions given in "Safety first" at the start of this manual.*

✔ Make sure that the battery tray is in good condition, and that the clamp is tight. Corrosion on the tray, retaining clamp and the battery itself can be removed with a solution of water and baking soda. Thoroughly rinse all cleaned areas with water. Any metal parts damaged by corrosion should be covered with a zinc-based primer, then painted.

✔ Periodically (approximately every three months), check the charge condition of the battery as described in Chapter 5A.

✔ If the battery is flat, and you need to jump start your vehicle, see **Roadside Repairs**.

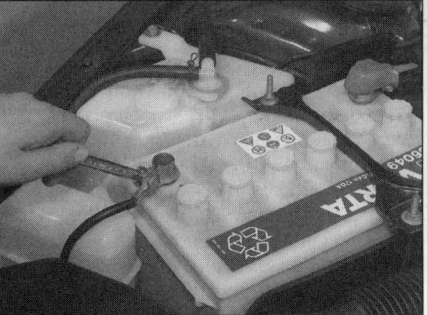

1 Check the battery lead clamps for tightness to ensure good electrical connections.

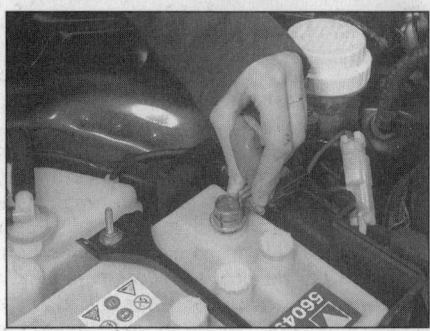

2 Having checked each cable for security, inspect each one for signs of cracks and fraying.

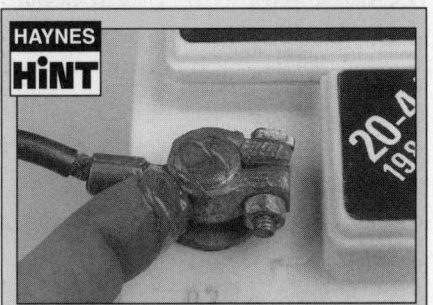

HAYNES HINT

Battery corrosion can be kept to a minimum by applying a layer of petroleum jelly to the clamps and terminals after they are reconnected.

3 If corrosion (white, fluffy deposits) is evident, remove the cables from the battery terminals, clean them with a small wire brush, then refit them. Automotive stores sell a tool for cleaning the battery post.

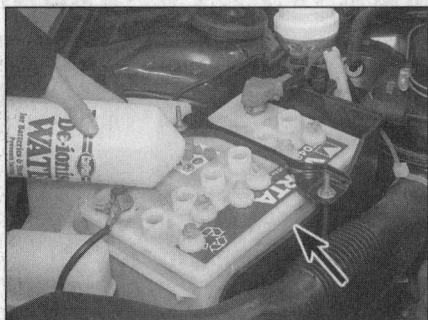

4 Ensure the battery electrolyte level is kept between the upper (MAX) and lower (MIN) level markings (arrowed) on the side of the battery. If topping-up is necessary, remove the cell caps and top-up to the upper level marking using distilled (de-ionised) water **only**. Ordinary tap water may damage the battery. Once the electrolyte level is correct, securely refit the cell caps and wipe off and spilt water.

Bulbs and fuses

✔ Check all external lights and the horn. Refer to the appropriate Sections of Chapter 12 for details if any of the circuits are found to be inoperative.

✔ Visually check all accessible wiring connectors, harnesses and retaining clips for security, and for signs of chafing or damage.

 HAYNES HINT *If you need to check your brake lights and indicators unaided, back up to a wall or garage door and operate the lights. The reflected light should show if they are working properly.*

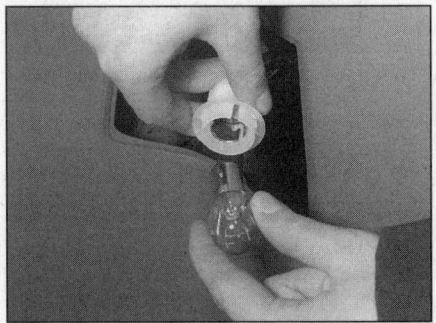

1 If a single indicator light, stop-light or headlight has failed, it is likely that a bulb has blown and will need to be replaced. Refer to Chapter 12 for details. If both stop-lights have failed, it is possible that the switch has failed (see Chapter 9).

2 If more than one indicator light or tail light has failed it is likely that either a fuse has blown or that there is a fault in the circuit (see Chapter 12). The fuses are located behind the fusebox cover on the facia panel.

3 To replace a blown fuse, simply pull it out and fit a new fuse of the correct rating (see the wiring diagrams in Chapter 12). If the fuse blows again, it is important that you find out why - a complete checking procedure is given in Chapter 12.

0•16 Lubricants, fluids, capacities and tyre pressures

Lubricants and fluids

Engine	Multigrade engine oil, viscosity SAE 10W/30 to 10W/40 *(Duckhams QXR, QS, Hypergrade Plus, Hypergrade, or 10W/40 Motor Oil)*
Cooling system	Ethylene glycol based antifreeze *(Duckhams Antifreeze and Summer Coolant)*
Manual transmission	Hypoid gear oil SAE75W to API GL-4 *(Duckhams Hypoid 75)*
Automatic transmission	Dexron type II automatic transmission fluid (ATF) *(Duckhams Uni-Matic)*
Braking system	Hydraulic fluid to SAE J1703F or DOT 3 *(Duckhams Universal Brake and Clutch Fluid)*
Power steering	Dexron type II automatic transmission fluid (ATF) *(Duckhams Uni-Matic)*

Choosing your engine oil

Oils perform vital tasks in all engines. The higher the engine's performance, the greater the demand on lubricants to minimise wear as well as optimise power and economy. Duckhams tailors lubricants to the highest technical standards, meeting and exceeding the demands of all modern engines.

HOW ENGINE OIL WORKS

• **Beating friction**

Without oil, the surfaces inside your engine which rub together will heat, fuse and quickly cause engine seizure. Oil, and its special additives, forms a molecular barrier between moving parts, to stop wear and minimise heat build-up.

• **Cooling hot spots**

Oil cools parts that the engine's water-based coolant cannot reach, bathing the combustion chamber and pistons, where temperatures may exceed 1000°C. The oil assists in transferring the heat to the engine cooling system. Heat in the oil is also lost by air flow over the sump, and via any auxiliary oil cooler.

• **Cleaning the inner engine**

Oil washes away combustion by-products (mainly carbon) on pistons and cylinders, transporting them to the oil filter, and holding the smallest particles in suspension until they are flushed out by an oil change. Duckhams oils undergo extensive tests in the laboratory, and on the road.

Note: It is antisocial and illegal to dump oil down the drain. To find the location of your local oil recycling bank, call this number free.

Engine oil types

Mineral oils are the "traditional" oils, generally suited to older engines and cars not used in harsh conditions. *Duckhams Hypergrade Plus* and *Hypergrade* are well suited for use in most popular family cars.
Diesel oils such as *Duckhams Diesel* are specially formulated for Diesel engines, including turbocharged models and 4x4s.
Synthetic oils are the state-of-the-art in lubricants, offering ultimate protection, but at a fairly high price. One such is *Duckhams QS*, for use in ultra-high performance engines.
Semi-synthetic oils offer high performance engine protection, but at less cost than full synthetic oils. *Duckhams QXR* is an ideal choice for hot hatches and hard-driven cars.

For help with technical queries on lubricants, call Duckhams Oils on 0181 290 8207

Capacities

Engine oil	
Including oil filter	3.5 litres
Cooling system	
All models (approximate)	5 litres
Manual transmission (approximate)	1.8 litres
Automatic transmission (approximate):	
From dry	5.8 litres
At fluid change	4.5 litres
Power-assisted steering	
All models (approximate)	0.9 litre

Tyre pressures

Note: *Recommended tyre pressures are marked on a label attached to the rear of the driver's door. Pressures apply to original-equipment tyres only and may vary if any other make or type of tyre is fitted; check with the tyre manufacturer or supplier for correct pressures if necessary.*
Note: *Tyre pressures must always be checked with the tyres cold to ensure accuracy.*

Up to 4 passengers:		Fully loaded:	
Front	23 psi (1.6 bar)	Front	23 psi (1.6 bar)
Rear	23 psi (1.6 bar)	Rear	28 psi (1.9 bar)

Chapter 1
Routine maintenance and servicing

Contents

Air conditioning system check	7
Air filter element check	13
Air filter element renewal	28
Automatic transmission fluid level check	20
Automatic transmission fluid renewal	31
Auxiliary drivebelt check and renewal	6
Brake and clutch pedal freeplay check	8
Brake fluid renewal	37
Coolant renewal	4
Crankcase emission control system check	17
Driveshaft gaiter check	25
Engine oil and filter renewal	3
Exhaust system check	21
Front brake pad and disc check	10
Front wheel alignment check	27
Fuel filter renewal	29
General information	1
Handbrake check	9
Headlight beam alignment check	33
Hinge and lock lubrication	34
Hose and fluid leak check	22
Idle speed and mixture check and adjustment	18
Ignition system check	14
Ignition timing check	32
Intensive maintenance	2
Manual transmission oil level check	19
Manual transmission oil renewal	30
Rear brake shoe and drum check	23
Rear wheel bearing lubrication	35
Road test	11
Spark plug check	5
Spark plug renewal	12
Suspension and steering check	24
Timing belt check	15
Timing belt renewal	36
Underbody check	26
Valve clearance check and adjustment	16

Degrees of difficulty

| Easy, suitable for novice with little experience | Fairly easy, suitable for beginner with some experience | Fairly difficult, suitable for competent DIY mechanic | Difficult, suitable for experienced DIY mechanic | Very difficult, suitable for expert DIY or professional |

Servicing specifications

Lubricants and fluids .... Refer to end of *"Weekly checks"*

Capacities .... Refer to end of *"Weekly checks"*

Engine
Oil filter .... Champion F111
Valve clearances:
  Cold engine:
    Inlet .... 0.07 mm
    Exhaust .... 0.17 mm
  Hot engine:
    Inlet .... 0.15 mm
    Exhaust .... 0.25 mm
Drivebelt deflection (Under 10 kg load):
  Alternator drivebelt:
    New belt .... 5.5 to 7.0 mm
    Used belt .... 7.0 to 9.0 mm
  Power steering pump drivebelt .... 6.0 to 9.0 mm

Cooling system
Antifreeze mixture:
  50% antifreeze .... Protection down to -37°C (5°F)
  55% antifreeze .... Protection down to -45°C (-22°F)
Note: *Refer to antifreeze manufacturer for latest recommendations.*

Fuel system
Air filter element:
  Carburettor models .... Champion W143
  Fuel-injected models .... Champion type not available
Fuel filter:
  Carburettor models .... Champion L119
  Fuel-injected models .... Champion type not available

Ignition system
Ignition timing .... Refer to Chapter 5
Spark plugs: **Type**   **Gap**
  All models .... Champion RN9YCC   0.8 mm

*The spark plug gap quoted is that recommended by Champion for their specified plug listed above. If spark plugs of any other type are to be fitted, refer to their manufacturer's recommendations.

Brakes
Brake pad friction material thickness:
  8 valve and MPi models 1.0mm
  12 valve models 2.0mm
Brake shoe lining thickness, minimum 1.0mm

Torque wrench settings

	Nm	lbf ft
Alternator mounting bolts:		
Lower bolt	22	16
Upper bolt	15	11
Automatic transmission:		
Drain plug	35	25
Sump bolts	10	7
Oil filter bolts	7	5
Engine sump drain plug	40	30
Engine rocker arm adjusting screw locknut	15	11
Fuel filter union bolts	30	22
Manual transmission filler/level and drain plug	35	25
Power steering pump mounting bolts	30	22
Roadwheel nuts	100	74
Spark plugs	20	15

Maintenance schedule

The maintenance intervals in this manual are provided with the assumption that you, not the dealer, will be carrying out the work. These are the minimum maintenance intervals recommended by us for vehicles driven daily. If you wish to keep your vehicle in peak condition at all times, you may wish to perform some of these procedures more often. We encourage frequent maintenance, because it enhances the efficiency, performance and resale value of your vehicle.

When the vehicle is new, it should be serviced by a factory-authorised dealer service department, in order to preserve the factory warranty.

Every 6000 miles (7500 km) or 6 months, whichever comes first

- ☐ Renew the engine oil and filter (Section 3)
- ☐ Renew the engine coolant - (anti-rust coolant) (Section 4)
- ☐ Check the condition of the spark plugs (Section 5)
- ☐ Check the tension of auxiliary drivebelt(s) (Section 6)
- ☐ Check the level of refrigerant in the air conditioning system (Section 7)
- ☐ Check the brake and clutch pedal freeplay (Section 8)
- ☐ Check the operation of the handbrake. (Section 9)
- ☐ Check the front brake pads and discs for wear (Section 10)
- ☐ Carry out a road test (Section 11)

Every 12 000 miles (15 000 km) or 12 months, whichever comes first

- ☐ Renew the spark plugs (Section 12)
- ☐ Check the condition of the air filter element (Section 13)
- ☐ Check condition of the ignition system components (Section 14)
- ☐ Check the tension and condition of the timing belt (Section 15)
- ☐ Check and, if necessary, adjust the valve clearances (Section 16)
- ☐ Check the condition and operation of the crankcase emission control system components (Section 17)
- ☐ Check the idle speed and mixture settings (Section 18)
- ☐ Check the manual transmission oil level (Section 19)
- ☐ Check the automatic transmission fluid level (Section 20)
- ☐ Check the condition of the exhaust system and its mountings (Section 21)
- ☐ Check all components, pipes and hoses for fluid leaks (Section 22)
- ☐ Check the rear brake shoes and drums for wear (Section 23)
- ☐ Check the steering and suspension components for condition and security (Section 24)
- ☐ Check the condition of the driveshaft gaiters (Section 25)
- ☐ Check the underbody and sealant for damage (Section 26)
- ☐ Check the front wheel alignment (Section 27)

Every 24 000 miles (30 000 km) or 24 months, whichever comes first

- ☐ Renew the engine coolant - (long-life coolant) (Section 4)
- ☐ Renew air filter element (Section 28)
- ☐ Renew the fuel filter (Section 29)
- ☐ Renew the manual transmission oil (Section 30)
- ☐ Renew the automatic transmission fluid (Section 31)
- ☐ Check the ignition timing (Section 32)
- ☐ Check the headlight beam adjustment (Section 33)
- ☐ Lubricate all hinges and locks (Section 34)

Every 36 000 miles (45 000 km) or 36 months, whichever comes first

- ☐ Re-pack the rear wheel bearings with grease (Section 35)

Every 60 000 miles (75 000 km) or 60 months, whichever comes first

- ☐ Renew the timing belt (Section 36)

Every 2 years, regardless of mileage

- ☐ Renew the brake fluid (Section 37)

Maintenance - component location

Underbonnet view of an 8-valve carburettor model

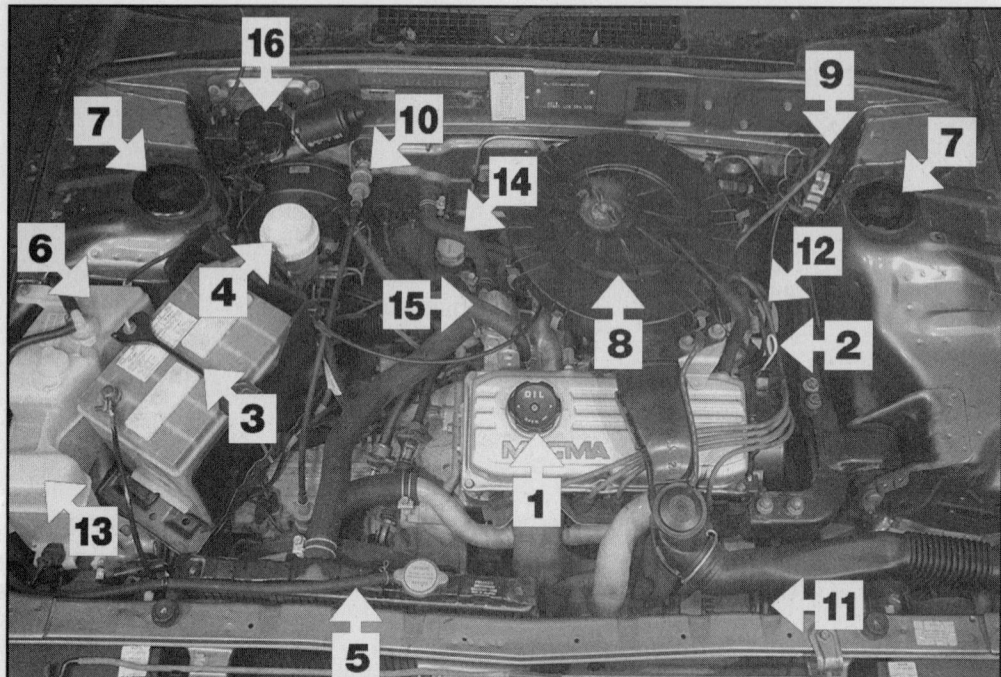

1. Engine oil filler cap
2. Engine oil level dipstick
3. Battery
4. Brake fluid reservoir
5. Radiator
6. Coolant expansion tank
7. Suspension strut upper mounting
8. Air filter housing
9. Ignition HT coil
10. Clutch cable adjuster
11. Alternator
12. Distributor
13. Washer fluid reservoir
14. Fuel filter
15. Thermostat housing
16. Windscreen wiper motor

Underbonnet view of a 12-valve carburettor model

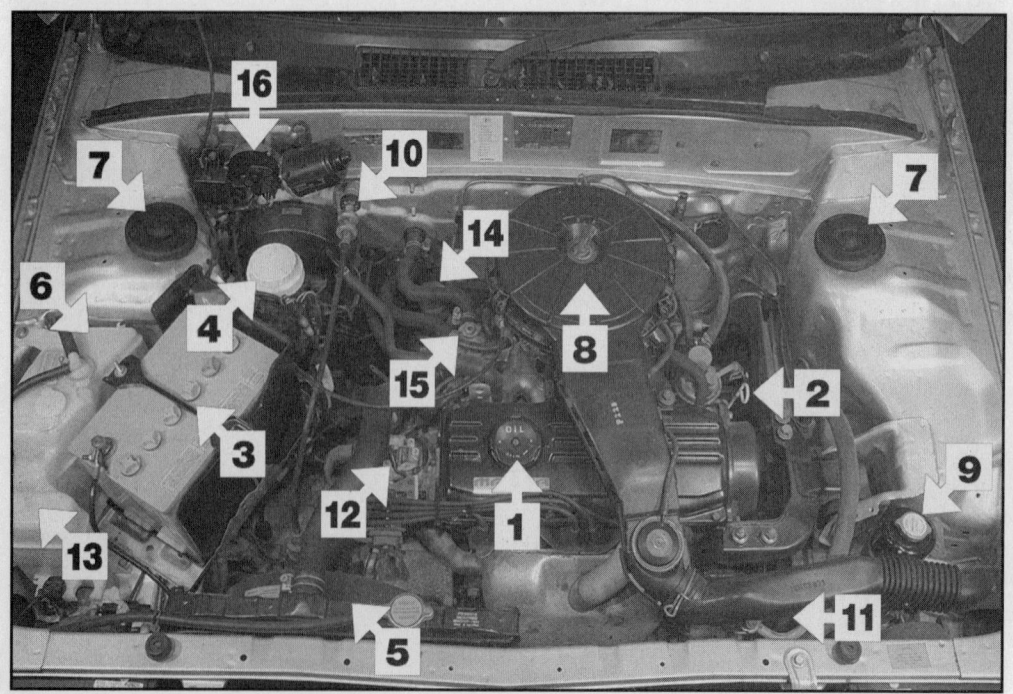

1. Engine oil filler cap
2. Engine oil level dipstick
3. Battery
4. Brake fluid reservoir
5. Radiator
6. Coolant expansion tank
7. Suspension strut upper mounting
8. Air filter housing
9. Power steering fluid reservoir
10. Clutch cable adjuster
11. Power steering pump
12. Distributor
13. Washer fluid reservoir
14. Fuel filter
15. Thermostat housing
16. Windscreen wiper motor

Maintenance - component location

Underbonnet view of a fuel-injected model

1. Engine oil filler cap
2. Engine oil level dipstick
3. Battery
4. Brake fluid reservoir
5. Radiator
6. Coolant expansion tank
7. Suspension strut upper mounting
8. Air filter housing
9. Power steering pump
10. Power steering fluid reservoir
11. Alternator
12. Distributor
13. Washer fluid reservoir
14. Throttle housing
15. MAP sensor
16. Windscreen wiper motor

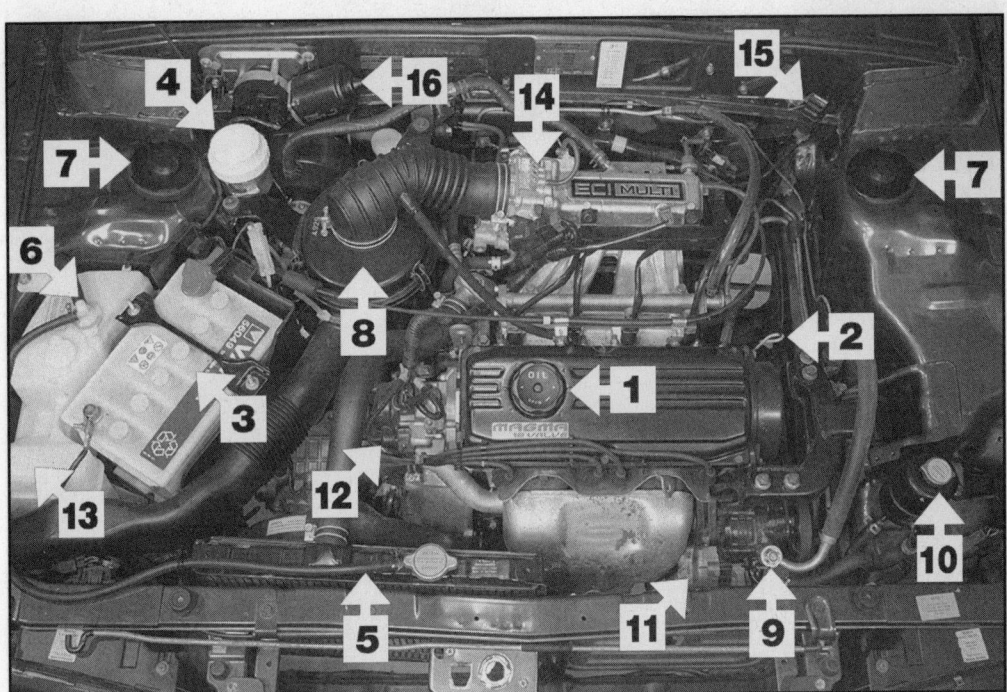

Typical front underbody view

1. Engine oil drain plug
2. Manual transmission filler/level plug
3. Manual transmission drain plug
4. Alternator
5. Front suspension lower arm
6. Track rod
7. Brake caliper
8. Driveshaft
9. Exhaust system front pipe

1•6 Maintenance - component location

Rear underbody view

1 Fuel tank
2 Rear suspension trailing arm
3 Handbrake cable
4 Rear axle mounting bush
5 Rear suspension damper lower mounting
6 Rear suspension anti-roll bar
7 Exhaust system tailpipe

Introduction

1 General information

This Chapter is designed to help the home mechanic maintain his/her vehicle for safety, economy, long life and peak performance.

The Chapter contains a master maintenance schedule, followed by Sections dealing specifically with each task in the schedule. Visual checks, adjustments, component renewal and other helpful items are included. Refer to the accompanying illustrations of the engine compartment and the underside of the vehicle for the locations of the various components.

Servicing your vehicle in accordance with the mileage/time maintenance schedule and the following Sections will provide a planned maintenance programme, which should result in a long and reliable service life. This is a comprehensive plan, so maintaining some items but not others at the specified service intervals, will not produce the same results.

As you service your vehicle, you will discover that many of the procedures can - and should - be grouped together, because of the particular procedure being performed, or because of the proximity of two otherwise-unrelated components to one another. For example, if the vehicle is raised for any reason, the exhaust can be inspected at the same time as the suspension and steering components.

The first step in this maintenance programme is to prepare yourself before the actual work begins. Read through all the Sections relevant to the work to be carried out, then make a list and gather all the parts and tools required. If a problem is encountered, seek advice from a parts specialist, or a dealer service department.

2 Intensive maintenance

If, from the time the vehicle is new, the routine maintenance schedule is followed closely, and frequent checks are made of fluid levels and high-wear items, as suggested throughout this manual, the engine will be kept in relatively good running condition, and the need for additional work will be minimised.

It is possible that there will be times when the engine is running poorly due to the lack of regular maintenance. This is even more likely if a used vehicle, which has not received regular and frequent maintenance checks, is purchased. In such cases, additional work may need to be carried out, outside of the regular maintenance intervals.

If engine wear is suspected, a compression test (refer to Chapter 2A) will provide valuable information regarding the overall performance of the main internal components. Such a test can be used as a basis to decide on the extent of the work to be carried out. If, for example, a compression test indicates serious internal engine wear, conventional maintenance as described in this Chapter will not greatly improve the performance of the engine, and may prove a waste of time and money, unless extensive overhaul work is carried out first.

Maintenance procedures 1•7

The following series of operations are those most often required to improve the performance of a generally poor-running engine:

Primary operations

a) Clean, inspect and test the battery (refer to "Weekly checks").
b) Check all the engine-related fluids (refer to "Weekly checks").
c) Check the condition and tension of the auxiliary drivebelt (Section 6).
d) Renew the spark plugs (Section 5).
e) Inspect the distributor cap and rotor arm (refer to Chapter 5).
f) Check the condition of the air filter, and renew if necessary (Section 13).
g) Renew the fuel filter (Section 29).
h) Check the condition of all hoses, and check for fluid leaks (Section 22).
i) Check the exhaust gas emissions (Section 18).

If the above operations do not prove fully effective, carry out the following secondary operations:

Secondary operations

All items listed under "Primary operations", plus the following:

a) Check the charging system (refer to Chapter 5).
b) Check the ignition system (refer to Chapter 5).
c) Check the fuel system (refer to Chapter 4).
d) Renew the distributor cap and rotor arm (Section 14).
e) Renew the ignition HT leads (Section 14).

Every 6000 miles (10 000 km) or 6 months

3 Engine oil and filter renewal

1 Frequent oil and filter changes are the most important preventative maintenance procedures which can be undertaken by the DIY owner. As engine oil ages, it becomes diluted and contaminated, which leads to premature engine wear.
2 Before starting this procedure, gather together all the necessary tools and materials. Also make sure that you have plenty of clean rags and newspapers handy, to mop up any spills. Ideally, the engine oil should be warm, as it will drain more easily, and more built-up sludge will be removed with it. Take care not to touch the exhaust or any other hot parts of the engine when working under the vehicle. To avoid any possibility of scalding, and to protect yourself from possible skin irritants and other harmful contaminants in used engine oils, it is advisable to wear gloves when carrying out this work.
3 Firmly apply the handbrake then jack up the front of the vehicle and support it on axle stands (see "Jacking and vehicle support").
4 Remove the oil filler cap.
5 Using a spanner, or preferably a suitable socket and bar, slacken the drain plug about half a turn (see illustration). Position the draining container under the drain plug, then remove the plug completely.

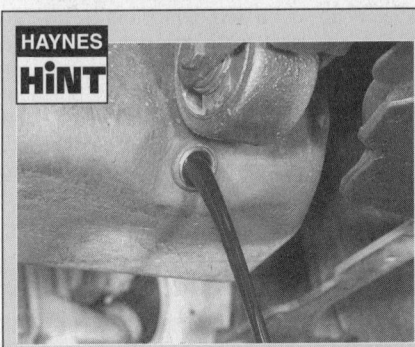

As the drain plug threads release, move it sharply away so the stream of oil issuing from the sump runs into the container, not up your sleeve!

6 Allow some time for the oil to drain, noting that it may be necessary to reposition the container as the oil flow slows to a trickle.
7 After all the oil has drained, wipe the drain plug and the sealing washer with a clean rag. Examine the condition of the sealing washer, and renew it if it shows signs of scoring or other damage which may prevent an oil-tight seal. Clean the area around the drain plug opening, and refit the plug complete with the washer and tighten it to the specified torque.
8 Move the container into position under the oil filter which is located on the front of the cylinder block.
9 Use an oil filter removal tool to slacken the filter initially, then unscrew it by hand the rest of the way (see illustration). Empty the oil from the old filter into the container.
10 Use a clean rag to remove all oil, dirt and sludge from the filter sealing area on the engine. Check the old filter to make sure that the rubber sealing ring has not stuck to the engine. If it has, carefully remove it.
11 Apply a light coating of clean engine oil to the sealing ring on the new filter, then screw the filter into position on the engine. Tighten the filter firmly by hand only - **do not** use any tools.
12 Remove the old oil and all tools from under the vehicle then lower the vehicle to the ground.

3.5 Slackening the sump drain plug

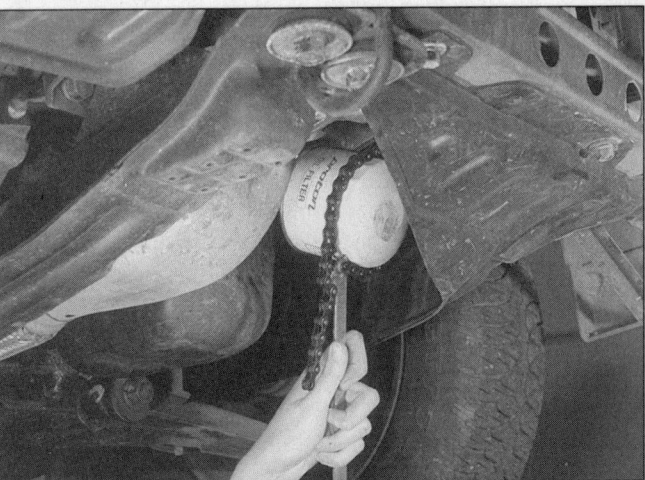
3.9 Using an oil filter removal tool to slacken the oil filter

Every 6000 miles or 6 months

4.2 Unscrew and release the radiator drain plug

4.14 Remove the radiator filler cap and slowly pour the coolant into the filler neck

13 Fill the engine through the filler hole, using the correct grade and type of oil (refer to "*Weekly Checks*" for details of topping-up). Pour in half the specified quantity of oil first, then wait a few minutes for the oil to drain into the sump. Continue to add oil, a small quantity at a time, until the level is up to the lower mark on the dipstick. Adding approximately a further 1.0 litre will bring the level up to the upper mark on the dipstick.

14 Start the engine and run it for a few minutes, while checking for leaks around the oil filter seal and the sump drain plug. Note that there may be a delay of a few seconds before the low oil pressure warning light goes out when the engine is first started, as the oil circulates through the new oil filter and the engine oil galleries before the pressure builds up.

15 Stop the engine, and wait a few minutes for the oil to settle in the sump once more. With the new oil circulated and the filter now completely full, recheck the level on the dipstick, and add more oil as necessary.

4 Coolant renewal

Cooling system draining

⚠ **Warning:** *Wait until the engine is cold before starting this procedure. Do not allow antifreeze to come in contact with your skin, or with the painted surfaces of the vehicle. Rinse off spills immediately with plenty of water. Never leave antifreeze lying around in an open container, or in a puddle in the driveway or on the garage floor. Children and pets are attracted by its sweet smell, but antifreeze can be fatal if ingested.*

1 With the engine completely cold, cover the radiator cap with a wad of rag, and slowly turn the cap anti-clockwise to relieve the pressure in the cooling system (a hissing sound will normally be heard). Wait until any pressure remaining in the system is released, then continue to turn the cap until it can be removed.

2 Position a suitable container beneath the radiator, then unscrew and release the drain plug **(see illustration)**. Allow the coolant to drain into the container.

3 If the coolant has been drained for a reason other than renewal, then it can be re-used, provided it is clean and less than two years old. If the coolant contains corrosion deposits or has been allowed to overheat, it should be renewed.

4 Once all the coolant has drained, refit and tighten the drain plug.

Cooling system flushing

5 If coolant renewal has been neglected, or if the antifreeze mixture has become diluted, then in time, the cooling system may gradually lose efficiency, as the coolant passages become restricted due to rust, scale deposits, and other sediment. The cooling system efficiency can be restored by flushing the system clean.

6 The radiator should be flushed independently of the engine, to avoid unnecessary contamination.

Radiator flushing

7 To flush the radiator disconnect the top and bottom hoses and any other relevant hoses from the radiator, with reference to Chapter 3.

8 Insert a garden hose into the radiator top inlet. Direct a flow of clean water through the radiator, and continue flushing until clean water emerges from the radiator bottom outlet.

9 If after a reasonable period, the water still does not run clear, the radiator can be flushed with a good proprietary cooling system cleaning agent, but note that the manufacturer's instructions must be adhered to. If the contamination is particularly bad, insert the hose in the radiator bottom outlet, and reverse-flush the radiator. If possible, connect a length of old hose to the top of the radiator, to allow the flushed water to be directed into a suitable container.

Engine flushing

10 To flush the engine, remove the thermostat as described in Chapter 3, then temporarily refit the thermostat cover.

11 With the top and bottom hoses disconnected from the radiator, insert a garden hose into the radiator top hose. Direct a clean flow of water through the engine, and continue flushing until clean water emerges from the radiator bottom hose.

12 On completion of flushing, refit the thermostat and reconnect the hoses with reference to Chapter 3.

Cooling system filling

13 Before attempting to fill the cooling system, make sure that all hoses and clips are in good condition, and that the clips are tight. Note that an antifreeze mixture must be used all year round, to inhibit the corrosion of the engine components (see following sub-Section).

14 Remove the radiator filler cap **(see illustration)** and fill the system by slowly pouring the coolant into the filler neck, to prevent airlocks from forming.

15 If the coolant is being renewed, begin by pouring in a couple of litres of water, followed by the correct quantity of antifreeze, then top-up with more water.

16 When the level in radiator reaches the bottom of the filler neck, squeeze the radiator top and bottom hoses to help expel any trapped air in the system and top-up again to the bottom of the filler neck. Refit the radiator cap.

17 On models fitted with a bleed screw on the top of the thermostat housing, slacken the screw until coolant begins to flow out, then re-tighten the screw.

18 Once all the air is expelled from the hoses, prise out the cap and top-up the coolant in the expansion tank to a point midway between the "MAX" and "MIN" marks on the side of the tank **(see illustrations)**.

4.18a Prise out the expansion tank cap . . .

4.18b . . . and top-up the coolant in to a point midway between the "MAX" and "MIN" marks on the side of the tank

Every 6000 miles or 6 months

19 Start the engine and run it until warm coolant can be felt flowing through the radiator top hose (meaning that the thermostat has opened). Stop the engine and allow it to cool.
20 Check for leaks, particularly around disturbed components. Check the coolant level in the radiator and expansion tank, and top-up if necessary.
Caution: If the radiator cap is removed while the engine is still warm, cover the cap with a thick cloth, and unscrew the cap slowly to gradually relieve the system pressure (a hissing sound will normally be heard). Wait until any pressure remaining in the system is released, then continue to turn the cap until it can be removed.

Antifreeze mixture

21 The antifreeze should always be renewed at the specified intervals. This is necessary not only to maintain the antifreeze properties, but also to prevent corrosion which would otherwise occur as the corrosion inhibitors become progressively less effective.
22 Always use an ethylene-glycol based antifreeze which is suitable for use in mixed-metal cooling systems. The quantity of antifreeze and levels of protection are indicated in the *Specifications*.
23 Before adding antifreeze, the cooling system should be completely drained, preferably flushed, and all hoses checked for condition and security.
24 After filling with antifreeze, a label should be attached to the expansion tank, stating the type and concentration of antifreeze used, and the date installed. Any subsequent topping-up should be made with the same type and concentration of antifreeze.
25 Do not use engine antifreeze in the windscreen/tailgate washer system, as it will cause damage to the vehicle paintwork. A screenwash additive should be added to the washer system in the quantities stated on the bottle.

5 Spark plug check

1 The correct functioning of the spark plugs is vital for the correct running and efficiency of the engine. It is essential that the plugs fitted are appropriate for the engine (a suitable type is specified at the beginning of this Chapter). If this type is used and the engine is in good condition, the spark plugs should not need attention between scheduled replacement intervals. Spark plug cleaning is rarely necessary, and should not be attempted unless specialised equipment is available, as damage can easily be caused to the firing ends.
2 If the marks on the original-equipment spark plug (HT) leads cannot be seen, mark the leads to correspond to the cylinder the lead serves. Pull the leads from the plugs by gripping the end fitting, not the lead, otherwise the lead connection may be fractured.
3 It is advisable to remove the dirt from the spark plug recesses using a clean brush, vacuum cleaner or compressed air before removing the plugs, to prevent dirt dropping into the cylinders.
4 Unscrew the plugs using a spark plug spanner, suitable box spanner or a deep socket and extension bar **(see illustration)**. Keep the socket aligned with the spark plug - if it is forcibly moved to one side, the ceramic insulator may be broken off. As each plug is removed, examine it as follows.
5 Examination of the spark plugs will give a good indication of the condition of the engine. If the insulator nose of the spark plug is clean and white, with no deposits, this is indicative of a weak mixture or too hot a plug (a hot plug transfers heat away from the electrode slowly, a cold plug transfers heat away quickly).
6 If the tip and insulator nose are covered with hard black-looking deposits, then this is indicative that the mixture is too rich. Should the plug be black and oily, then it is likely that the engine is fairly worn, as well as the mixture being too rich.
7 If the insulator nose is covered with light tan to greyish-brown deposits, then the mixture is correct and it is likely that the engine is in good condition.
8 The spark plug electrode gap is of considerable importance as, if it is too large or too small, the size of the spark and its efficiency will be seriously impaired. The gap should be set to the value given in the *Specifications* at the beginning of this Chapter.
9 To set the gap, measure it with a feeler blade and then bend open, or closed, the outer plug electrode until the correct gap is achieved. The centre electrode should never be bent, as this may crack the insulator and cause plug failure, if nothing worse. If using feeler blades, the gap is correct when the appropriate-size blade is a firm sliding fit **(see illustrations)**.
10 Special spark plug electrode gap adjusting tools are available from most motor accessory shops, or from some spark plug manufacturers.

5.4 Removing a spark plug

11 Before fitting the spark plugs, check that the threaded connector sleeves are tight, and that the plug exterior surfaces and threads are clean.

It is very often difficult to insert spark plugs into their holes without cross-threading them. To avoid this possibility, fit a short length of 5/16 inch internal diameter rubber hose over the end of the spark plug. The flexible hose acts as a universal joint to help align the plug with the plug hole. Should the plug begin to cross-thread, the hose will slip on the spark plug, preventing thread damage to the aluminium cylinder head

12 Remove the rubber hose (if used), and tighten the plug to the specified torque using the spark plug socket and a torque wrench. Refit the remaining spark plugs in the same manner.
13 Connect the HT leads in their correct order.

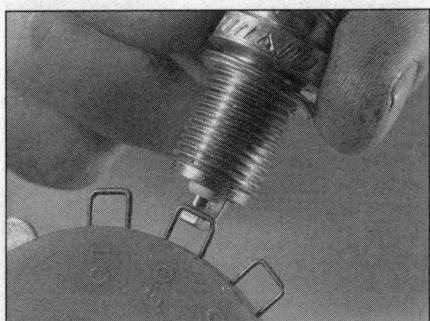

5.9a Measuring the spark plug gap with a wire gauge

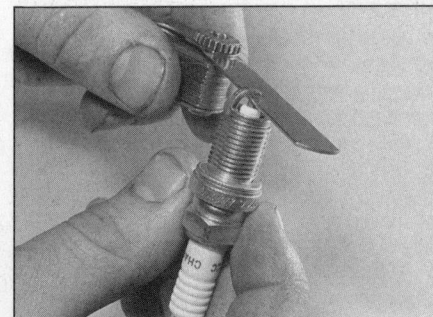

5.9b Measuring the spark plug gap with a feeler blade

1•10 Every 6000 miles or 6 months

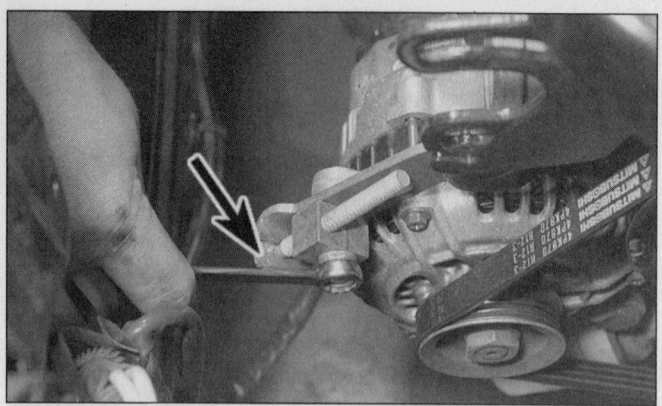

6.7 Slacken the alternator mounting bolts and back off the adjuster bolt (arrowed) to relieve the drivebelt tension

6.16a Slacken the power steering pump front mounting bolts (arrowed) . . .

6 Auxiliary drivebelt check and renewal

1 Depending on specification, either one, two or three auxiliary drivebelts are fitted.

Checking the auxiliary drivebelt condition

2 Apply the handbrake, then jack up the front of the car and support it on axle stands (see "*Jacking and vehicle support*"). Remove the left-hand front roadwheel. Access to the crankshaft pulley bolt can be gained by removing the rubber plug from underneath the left-hand wheelarch. If greater access is required, undo the retaining bolts and remove the plastic undercover.

3 Using a suitable socket and extension bar fitted to the crankshaft pulley bolt, rotate the crankshaft so that the entire length of the drivebelt(s) can be examined. Examine the drivebelt(s) for cracks, splitting, fraying or damage. Check also for signs of glazing (shiny patches) and for separation of the belt plies. Renew the belt if worn or damaged.

4 If the condition of the each belt is satisfactory, check the drivebelt tension as described below.

Alternator drivebelt - removal, refitting and tensioning

Removal

5 Apply the handbrake, then jack up the front of the car and support it on axle stands (see "*Jacking and vehicle support*"). Remove the left-hand front roadwheel and disconnect the battery negative lead.

6 Where necessary remove the power steering pump belt and/or air conditioning compressor belt(s) as described below (as applicable).

7 Slacken both the alternator upper and lower mounting bolts **(see illustration)**.

8 Back off the adjuster bolt to relieve the tension in the drivebelt, then slip the drivebelt from the pulleys.

Refitting

9 If the belt is being renewed, ensure that the correct type is used. Fit the belt around the pulleys, ensuring that it is correctly seated, and take up the slack in the belt by tightening the adjuster bolt.

10 Tension the drivebelt as described in the following paragraphs.

Tensioning

11 Correct tensioning of the drivebelt will ensure that it has a long life. A belt which is too slack will slip and perhaps squeal. Beware, however, of overtightening, as this can cause wear in the alternator/coolant pump bearings.

12 The belt tension is checked at the mid-point between the alternator and coolant pump pulleys. Apply a force of approximately 10 kg to the belt at the specified point and check that the belt deflection is within the limits given in the *Specifications*.

13 To adjust, with the alternator mounting bolts loosened, turn the adjuster bolt until the correct tension is achieved. Rotate the crankshaft a couple of times, recheck the tension, then tighten both the alternator mounting bolts to their specified torque settings.

14 Refit the roadwheel and reconnect the battery negative lead (where necessary). Lower the vehicle to the ground and tighten the roadwheel nuts to the specified torque.

Power steering pump drivebelt - removal, refitting and tensioning

Removal

15 Disconnect the battery negative terminal.
16 Slacken the power steering pump front and rear mounting bolts then slip the belt **off** its pulleys and remove it from the engine **(see illustrations)**.

Refitting

17 If the belt is being renewed, ensure that the correct type is used. Fit the belt around the pulleys, ensuring that it is correctly seated, and take up the slack in the belt by pivoting the pump away from the engine.
18 Tension the drivebelt as described in the following paragraphs.

Tensioning

19 Correct tensioning of the drivebelt will ensure that it has a long life. A belt which is too slack will slip and perhaps squeal. Beware, however, of overtightening, as this can cause wear in the steering/coolant pump bearings.
20 The belt tension is checked at the mid-point between the pulleys. Apply a force of approximately 10 kg to the belt at the specified point and check that the belt deflection is within the limits given in the *Specifications*.
21 To adjust, with the pump mounting bolts loosened, pivot the power steering pump away from the engine until the correct tension is achieved **(see illustration)**. Hold the pump

6.16b . . . and the rear mounting bolt (arrowed) and slip the drivebelt off its pulleys

6.21 Tension the power steering pump drivebelt by carefully levering the pump away from the engine

Every 6000 miles or 6 months

in position and securely tighten its mounting bolts. Rotate the crankshaft a couple of times, recheck the tension, then tighten the pump mounting bolts to the specified torque setting.

Air conditioning compressor drivebelt - removal, refitting and tensioning

Removal

22 Apply the handbrake, then jack up the front of the car and support it on axle stands (see "*Jacking and vehicle support*"). Remove the left-hand front roadwheel and disconnect the battery negative lead.
23 Slacken both the idler pulley retaining bolts to relieve the tension in the drivebelt, then slip the drivebelt from the pulleys.

Refitting

24 If the belt is being renewed, ensure that the correct type is used. Fit the belt around the pulleys, ensuring that it is correctly seated, and take up the slack in the belt using the idler pulley.
25 Tension the drivebelt as described in the following paragraphs.

Tensioning

26 Correct tensioning of the drivebelt will ensure that it has a long life. A belt which is too slack will slip and perhaps squeal. Beware, however, of overtightening, as this can cause wear in the compressor bearings.
27 The belt tension is checked at the mid-point of the lower run of the belt. Apply a force of approximately 10 kg to the belt at the specified point and check that the belt deflection is approximately 6 to 7 mm.
28 To adjust, slacken the retaining bolts and reposition the idler pulley until the correct tension is achieved. Rotate the crankshaft a couple of times, recheck the tension, then securely tighten the idler pulley bolts.
29 Refit the roadwheel and reconnect the battery negative lead (where necessary). Lower the vehicle to the ground and tighten the roadwheel nuts to the specified torque.

7 Air conditioning system check
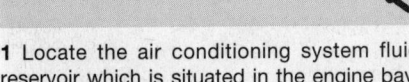

1 Locate the air conditioning system fluid reservoir which is situated in the engine bay, on the left hand side.
2 Carefully wipe clean the inspection window on the side of the fluid reservoir.
3 Start the engine and allow it to idle. Have an assistant turn on the air conditioning at the control panel, whilst observing the inspection window. The refrigerant fluid level should rise into view. Continue watching the fluid level, which should rise beyond the top of the inspection window, until only bubble-free fluid can be seen flowing.
4 If the fluid level appears to be too low, or if there are a lot of bubbles visible, the vehicle should be taken to a Proton dealer or air conditioning specialist for diagnosis and/or re-charging.

8 Brake and clutch pedal freeplay check

Refer to Chapter 6 for details of the clutch pedal check, and to Chapter 9 for details of the brake pedal check.

9 Handbrake check

Checking

1 Apply the handbrake by pulling it through three to four 'clicks' of the ratchet mechanism and check that this locks the rear wheels, holding the vehicle stationary on an incline. In this position, there should be sufficient reserve travel in the handbrake lever to allow for brake shoe wear and cable stretching. If not, the handbrake mechanism is need of adjustment.

Adjustment

2 Park the vehicle on a level surface, select first gear (or 'Park' on models with manual transmission) and chock the roadwheels.
3 Remove the securing screws and lift off the handbrake lever trim cover (see Chapter 11).
4 If new brake shoes or handbrake cables have been fitted, check that with the handbrake lever in the fully-off position, all tension is removed from the handbrake cables - slacken the adjustment nut if necessary. This ensures that the brake shoe self-adjustment mechanism has enough freeplay to operate correctly (see Chapter 9 for details).
5 Pull the handbrake lever through three 'clicks' of the ratchet mechanism and leave it in this position.
6 The adjustment mechanism is to the rear of the handbrake lever. Rotate the adjustment nut with a spanner through one turn clockwise, so that the adjustment mechanism tensions the handbrake cable drawbar **(see illustration)**.

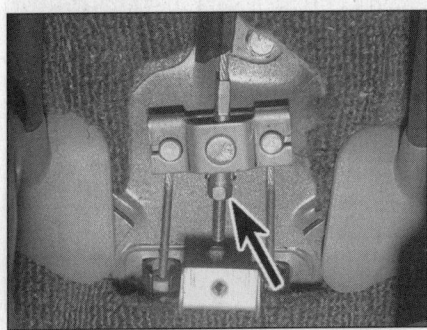

9.6 Handbrake cable adjustment nut (arrowed)

7 Release the handbrake lever, then re-apply it and check the operation of the handbrake as described above. Repeat the adjustment procedure as necessary.
8 Chock the front wheels, select reverse gear and raise the rear of the car on axle stands (see "*Jacking and vehicle support*"). Release the handbrake lever and check that the rear wheels are free to rotate without binding. Re-adjust the cable if the brakes appear to be binding.
9 On completion, tighten the cable locknut and refit the handbrake lever trim cover.
10 Satisfy yourself that the handbrake is operating correctly, by testing it exhaustively, before bringing the vehicle back into service on the public highway.

10 Front brake pad and disc check

1 Firmly apply the handbrake, then jack up the front of the car and support it securely on axle stands. Remove the front roadwheels.
2 For a quick check, the pad thickness can be carried out via the inspection hole on the front of the caliper **(see illustration)**. Using a steel rule, measure the combined thickness of the lining and backing plate on the visible brake pad. This must not be less than that indicated in the *Specifications*.
3 The view through the caliper inspection hole gives a rough indication of the state of the brake pads but only the inboard pad will be fully visible. For a comprehensive check, the brake pads should be removed and cleaned. The operation of the caliper can then also be checked, and the condition of the brake disc itself can be fully examined on both sides. Chapter 9 contains a detailed description of how the brake disc should be checked for wear and/or damage.
4 If any pad's friction material is worn to the specified thickness or less, *all four pads must be renewed as a set*. Refer to Chapter 9 for details.
5 On completion, refit the roadwheels and lower the car to the ground.

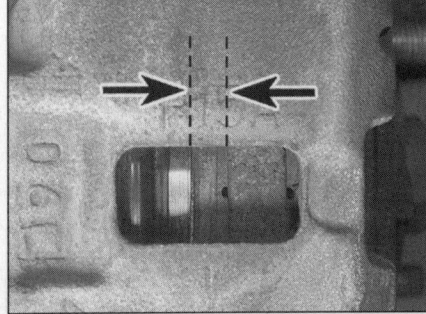

10.2 For a quick check, the brake pad friction material thickness (arrowed) can be carried out via the inspection hole on the front of the caliper

1•12 Every 6000 miles or 6 months

11 Road test

Instruments and electrical equipment

1 Check the operation of all instruments and electrical equipment.
2 Make sure that all instruments read correctly, and switch on all electrical equipment in turn, to check that it functions properly.

Steering and suspension

3 Check for any abnormalities in the steering, suspension, handling or road "feel".
4 Drive the vehicle, and check that there are no unusual vibrations or noises.
5 Check that the steering feels positive, with no excessive "sloppiness", or roughness, and check for any suspension noises when cornering and driving over bumps.

Drivetrain

6 Check the performance of the engine, clutch (where applicable), gearbox/transmission and driveshafts.
7 Listen for any unusual noises from the engine, clutch and gearbox/transmission.
8 Make sure that the engine runs smoothly when idling, and that there is no hesitation when accelerating.
9 Check that, where applicable, the clutch action is smooth and progressive, that the drive is taken up smoothly, and that the pedal travel is not excessive. Also listen for any noises when the clutch pedal is depressed.
10 On manual gearbox models, check that all gears can be engaged smoothly without noise, and that the gear lever action is not abnormally vague or "notchy".
11 Listen for a metallic clicking sound from the front of the vehicle, as the vehicle is driven slowly in a circle with the steering on full-lock. Carry out this check in both directions. If a clicking noise is heard, this indicates wear in a driveshaft joint, in which case renew the joint if necessary.

Check the operation and performance of the braking system

12 Make sure that the vehicle does not pull to one side when braking, and that the wheels do not lock prematurely when braking hard.
13 Check that there is no vibration through the steering when braking.
14 Check that the handbrake operates correctly without excessive movement of the lever, and that it holds the vehicle stationary on a slope.
15 Test the operation of the brake servo unit as follows. With the engine off, depress the footbrake four or five times to exhaust the vacuum. Hold the pedal depressed, then start the engine. As the engine starts, there should be a noticeable "give" in the pedal as vacuum builds up. Allow the engine to run for at least two minutes, and then switch it off. If the pedal is depressed now, it should be possible to detect a hiss from the servo as the pedal is depressed. After about four or five depressions, no further hissing should be heard, and the pedal should feel considerably harder.

Every 12 000 miles (15 000 km) or 12 months

12 Spark plug renewal

Refer to Section 5, renewing the spark plugs regardless of their apparent condition.

13 Air filter element check

8-valve carburettor models

1 Disconnect the breather hose from the top of the air cleaner housing.
2 Unscrew the wing nut then release the retaining clips and remove the air cleaner housing cover. Lift out the air cleaner filter element (see illustrations).

3 Inspect the filter element. If the filter element is excessively dirty or is damaged in anyway, it must be renewed.
4 Wipe clean the filter housing and cover and seat the filter element in position.
5 Refit the housing cover, securing it in position with the wing nut and retaining clips, and reconnect the breather hose.

12-valve carburettor models

6 Release the retaining clip and detach the inlet duct from the end of the air cleaner housing.
7 Unscrew the housing wing nut and lift off the washer and sealing grommet from the mounting stud.
8 Release the retaining clips and remove the air cleaner housing from the top of the carburettor, taking care not to lose the duct connecting the air cleaner to the exhaust manifold. The filter element can then be lifted out of position (see illustration).

9 Inspect the filter element. If the filter element is excessively dirty or is damaged in anyway, it must be renewed.
10 Wipe clean the filter housing and mounting plate and seat the filter element in position.
11 Refit the housing, ensuring it is correctly engaged with the duct connecting it to the exhaust manifold, and secure it in position with the retaining clips.
12 Refit the seal and washer to the mounting stud and securely tighten the wing nut.
13 Reconnect the inlet to the housing and secure it in position with the retaining clip.

Fuel-injected models

14 Disconnect the breather hose from the duct connecting the air cleaner housing to the manifold then slacken the retaining clip and detach the duct from the throttle housing.
15 Release the retaining clips and remove the air cleaner housing lid and duct assembly.

13.2a On 8-valve carburettor models, release the retaining clips then unscrew the wing nut (arrowed) . . .

13.2b . . . then lift off the cover and remove the element from the housing

13.8 Removing the air cleaner element - 12-valve carburettor models

Every 12 000 miles or 12 months

13.15a On fuel-injected models, disconnect the duct from the throttle housing then release the retaining clips . . .

13.15b . . . and lift the off the housing cover and withdraw the filter element

The filter element can then be lifted out of position **(see illustrations)**.

16 Inspect the filter element. If the filter element is excessively dirty or is damaged in anyway, it must be renewed.

17 Wipe clean the filter housing and lid and seat the filter element in position.

18 Refit the lid, securing it in position with the retaining clips, and reconnect the duct to the throttle housing. Securely tighten the duct retaining clip and reconnect the breather hose.

14 Ignition system check

⚠ *Warning: Voltages produced by an electronic ignition system are considerably higher than those produced by conventional ignition systems. Extreme care must be taken when working on the system with the ignition switched on. Persons with surgically-implanted cardiac pacemaker devices should keep well clear of the ignition circuits, components and test equipment.*

1 Pull the leads from the plugs by gripping the end fitting, not the lead, otherwise the lead connection may be fractured.

 *Ensure that the leads are numbered before removing them, to avoid confusion when refitting.*

2 Check inside the end fitting for signs of corrosion, which will look like a white crusty powder. Push the end fitting back onto the spark plug, ensuring that it is a tight fit on the plug. If not, remove the lead again and use pliers to carefully crimp the metal connector inside the end fitting until it fits securely on the end of the spark plug.

3 Using a clean rag, wipe the entire length of the lead to remove any built-up dirt and grease. Once the lead is clean, check for burns, cracks and other damage. Do not bend the lead excessively, nor pull the lead lengthways - the conductor inside might break.

4 Disconnect the other end of the lead from the distributor cap. Again, pull only on the end fitting. Check for corrosion and a tight fit in the same manner as the spark plug end. If an ohmmeter is available, check the resistance of the lead by connecting the meter between the spark plug end of the lead and the segment inside the distributor cap. Refit the lead securely on completion.

5 Check the remaining leads one at a time, in the same way.

6 If new spark plug (HT) leads are required, purchase a set for your specific car and engine.

7 Release the retaining clips (8-valve models) or unscrew the retaining screws (12-valve models) and remove the distributor cap. Wipe it clean, and carefully inspect it inside and out for signs of cracks, black carbon tracks (tracking) and worn, burned or loose contacts; check that the cap's carbon brush is unworn, free to move against spring pressure, and making good contact with the rotor arm. Also inspect the cap seal for signs of wear or damage, and renew if necessary. Remove the rotor arm from the end

14.7 Removing the rotor arm (12-valve model shown)

of the camshaft and inspect it **(see illustration)**. It is common practice to renew the cap and rotor arm whenever new spark plug (HT) leads are fitted. When fitting a new cap, remove the leads from the old cap one at a time, and fit them to the new cap in the exact same location - do not simultaneously remove all the leads from the old cap, or firing order confusion may occur. When refitting, ensure that the rotor arm is securely pressed onto the camshaft. Fit the distributor cap and secure it in position with the retaining clips/screws (as applicable).

8 Even with the ignition system in first-class condition, some engines may still occasionally experience poor starting attributable to damp ignition components. To disperse moisture, a water-dispersant aerosol can be very effective.

15 Timing belt check

Remove the timing belt cover upper cover and check the timing belt for signs of wear or damage whilst turning the engine over using a socket on the crankshaft pulley bolt (see Chapter 2A). If damage, such as damaged or missing teeth, or signs of oil contamination are found, then the belt must be renewed.

16 Valve clearance check and adjustment

Note: *The valve clearances should be checked and adjusted with the engine hot to ensure a greater degree of accuracy. If the clearances are being adjusted with the engine cold, it is recommended that they are rechecked once the engine has been warmed up to normal operating temperature.*

1 The importance of having the valve clearances correctly adjusted cannot be

Every 12 000 miles or 12 months

16.4 Adjusting a valve clearance

18.4 Adjusting the idle speed screw - 8-valve carburettor models (air cleaner housing removed for clarity)

overstressed, as they vitally affect the performance of the engine. If the clearances are too big, the engine will be noisy (characteristic rattling or tapping noises) and engine efficiency will be reduced, as the valves open too late and close too early. A more serious problem arises if the clearances are too small, however. If this is the case, the valves may not close fully when the engine is hot, resulting in serious damage to the engine (eg. burnt valve seats and/or cylinder head warping/cracking). The clearances are checked and adjusted as follows.

2 Warm the engine up to normal operating temperature then, working as described in Chapter 2A, remove the cylinder head cover and position number 1 cylinder at TDC on its compression stroke.

3 With number 1 cylinder at TDC on its compression stroke, check and if necessary adjust the following valve clearances, noting that number 1 cylinder is at the timing belt end of the engine. The valve locations can be determined from the position of the manifolds.

Note: Remember on 12-valve engines that there are two inlet valves for each cylinder.

Number 1 cylinder inlet valve(s)
Number 2 cylinder inlet valve(s)
Number 1 cylinder exhaust valve
Number 3 cylinder exhaust valve

4 Clearances are checked by inserting a feeler blade of the correct thickness between the valve stem and the rocker arm adjusting screw. The feeler blade should be a light, sliding fit. If adjustment is necessary, slacken the adjusting screw locknut, and turn the screw as necessary. Once the correct clearance is obtained, hold the adjusting screw and tighten the locknut to the specified torque **(see illustration)**. Recheck the valve clearance, and adjust again if necessary.

Caution: Take great care not to burn your hands on the hot engine.

5 Once all the relevant valves have been checked, rotate the crankshaft through one complete turn (360°) in a clockwise direction to bring No1 cylinder back to TDC. Ensure that the crankshaft pulley mark is correctly aligned with the 0° mark on the timing belt cover scale then check and, if necessary, adjust the following valve clearances as described in paragraph 4.

Number 3 cylinder inlet valve(s)
Number 4 cylinder inlet valve(s)
Number 2 cylinder exhaust valve
Number 4 cylinder exhaust valve

6 Once all the valve clearances are correctly adjusted, refit the cylinder head cover as described in Chapter 2A.

17 Crankcase emission control system check

Check on the crankcase emission control (PCV) valve and hose as described in Chapter 4C.

18 Idle speed and mixture check and adjustment

1 Before checking the idle speed and mixture setting, always check the following first:
a) Check the ignition timing (Chapter 5).
b) Check that the spark plugs are in good condition and correctly gapped (Section 5).
c) Check that the accelerator cable is correctly adjusted (see Chapter 4).
d) Check that the crankcase breather hoses are secure, with no leaks or kinks (Section 17).
e) Check that the air cleaner filter element is clean (Section 13).
f) Check that the exhaust system is in good condition (Section 21).
g) If the engine is running very roughly, check the compression pressures and valve clearances (see Chapter 2A and Section 16).
h) On fuel-injected models, check that the fuel injection/ignition system warning light is not illuminated (see Chapter 4B).

2 Take the car on a journey of sufficient length to warm it up to normal operating temperature. Proceed as described under the relevant sub-heading.

Note: Adjustment should be completed within two minutes of return, without stopping the engine. If this cannot be achieved, or if the radiator electric cooling fan operates, first wait for the cooling fan to stop. Clear any excess fuel from the inlet manifold by racing the engine two or three times to between 2000 and 3000 rpm, then allow it to idle again.

8-valve carburettor models

3 Ensure that all electrical loads are switched off. If the car does not have a tachometer (rev counter), connect one to the engine following its manufacturer's instructions. Note the idle speed, and compare it with that specified.

4 The idle speed adjusting screw is on the throttle linkage on the rear of the carburettor, on the right-hand side, and access is a little awkward. Turn the idle screw in or out as necessary to obtain the specified speed **(see illustration)**.

5 The idle mixture (exhaust gas CO level) is set at the factory, and should require no further adjustment. If, due to a change in engine characteristics (carbon build-up, bore wear etc) or after a major carburettor overhaul, the mixture setting is lost, it can be reset. Note, however, that an exhaust gas analyser (CO meter) will be required to check the mixture, in order to set it with the necessary standard of accuracy; if this is not available, the car must be taken to a Proton dealer for the work to be carried out. Also note that a special tool will be required to rotate the mixture adjusting screw. Refer to your Proton dealer for further information.

Every 12 000 miles or 12 months

18.6 Idle mixture adjustment screw location - 8-valve carburettor models

6 If the necessary equipment is available, connect the analyser to the vehicle in accordance with the manufacturer's instructions and check the exhaust gas CO level. If adjustment is required, it is made by mixture adjustment screw. The screw is located at the rear of the carburettor base and is covered with a tamperproof plug to prevent unnecessary adjustment (see illustration).

7 Remove the tamperproof cap and using the special tool, turn the mixture adjustment screw (in very small increments) until the CO level is correct. Turning the screw in (clockwise) weakens the mixture and reduces the CO level, turning it out will richen the mixture and increase the CO level.

8 When adjustments are complete, disconnect any test equipment and fit the tamperproof plug to the mixture adjustment screw. Recheck the idle speed and, if necessary, readjust.

12-valve carburettor models

9 Adjust the idle speed and mixture setting using the information given for 8-valve models noting that the idle speed adjusting screw is on the left-hand side of the carburettor and the mixture adjusting screw is on the rear of the carburettor at the top (see illustrations).

Fuel-injected models

10 Experienced home mechanics with a considerable amount of skill and equipment (including a good-quality tachometer and a good-quality, carefully-calibrated exhaust gas analyser) may be able to *check* the exhaust CO level and the idle speed. However, if these are found to be in need of *adjustment*, the car **must** be taken to a suitably-equipped Proton dealer.

11 Both the idle speed and mixture setting (exhaust gas CO level) are under full control of the engine management ECU and are not adjustable; the basic idle speed (throttle linkage stop screw) is adjustable but access to special electronic equipment is required to accurately set the screw. If the idle speed and/or exhaust gas CO level is incorrect, there must be a fault in the engine management system, and the vehicle should be taken to a Proton dealer for testing (see Chapter 4B).

19 Manual transmission oil level check

1 Park the car on a level surface. The oil level must be checked before the car is driven, or at least 5 minutes after the engine has been switched off. If the oil is checked immediately after driving the car, some of the oil will remain distributed around the transmission components, resulting in an inaccurate level reading.

2 Wipe clean the area around the filler/level plug, which is situated on the front of the transmission. Unscrew the plug and clean it; discard the sealing washer (see illustration).

3 The oil level should reach the lower edge of the filler/level hole. A certain amount of oil may have gathered behind the filler/level plug, and will trickle out when it is removed; this does **not** necessarily indicate that the level is correct. To ensure that a true level is established, wait until the initial trickle has stopped, then add oil as necessary until a trickle of new oil can be seen emerging (see illustrations). The level will be correct when the flow ceases; use only good-quality oil of the specified type.

18.9a Idle speed adjusting screw location (arrowed) - 12-valve carburettor models

18.9b Using the special tool to adjust the idle mixture screw - 12-valve carburettor models (air cleaner housing removed for clarity)

19.2 Slackening the manual transmission filler/level plug

19.3a If necessary, top up the oil level via the filler/level plug hole . . .

19.3b . . . and allow excess oil to drain off to ensure the oil level is correct

1•16 Every 12 000 miles or 12 months

4 Filling the transmission with oil is an extremely awkward operation; above all, allow plenty of time for the oil level to settle properly before checking it. If a large amount is added to the transmission, and a large amount flows out on checking the level, refit the filler/level plug and take the vehicle on a short journey so that the new oil is distributed fully around the transmission components, then recheck the level when it has settled again.
5 If the transmission has been overfilled so that oil flows out as soon as the filler/level plug is removed, check that the car is completely level (front-to-rear and side-to-side), and allow the surplus to drain off into a suitable container.
6 When the level is correct, fit a new sealing washer to the filler/level plug. Refit the plug, tightening it to the specified torque wrench setting and wash off any spilt oil.

20 Automatic transmission fluid level check

1 Take the vehicle on a short journey, to warm the transmission up to normal operating temperature, then park the vehicle on level ground and firmly apply the handbrake. The fluid level is checked using the dipstick which is situated on the top of the transmission where it is located beside the battery tray.
2 With the engine idling, apply the brakes then move the selector lever from the "P" (Park) position, to the "L" (low) position and then to the "N" (neutral) position. Withdraw the dipstick from the tube, and wipe all the fluid from its end with a clean rag or paper towel. Insert the clean dipstick back into the tube as far as it will go, then withdraw it once more. Note the fluid level on the end of the dipstick; it should be between the upper and lower marks **(see illustration)**.
3 If topping-up is necessary, add the required quantity of the specified fluid to the transmission via the dipstick tube. Use a funnel with a fine mesh gauze, to avoid spillage, and to ensure that no foreign matter enters the transmission. **Note:** *Never overfill the transmission so that the fluid level is above the upper mark.*

4 After topping-up, take the vehicle on a short run to distribute the fresh fluid, then recheck the level again, topping-up if necessary.
5 Always maintain the level between the two dipstick marks. If the level is allowed to fall below the lower mark, fluid starvation may result, which could lead to severe transmission damage.
6 Frequent need for topping-up indicates that there is a leak, which should be found and corrected before it becomes serious.

21 Exhaust system check

1 Park the vehicle on a level surface and switch off the engine. Chock the front wheels and select first gear, then raise the rear of the vehicle and rest it securely on axle stands (see "*Jacking and vehicle support*").
2 With the engine cold (wait at least an hour after switching off the engine), check the complete exhaust system from the engine to the end of the tailpipe.
3 Check the exhaust pipes and connections for evidence of leaks, severe corrosion and damage. Make sure that all brackets and mountings are in good condition, and that all relevant nuts and bolts are tight. Leakage at any of the joints or in other parts of the system will usually show up as a black sooty stain in the vicinity of the leak.
4 Rattles and other noises can often be traced to the exhaust system, especially the brackets and mountings. Try to move the pipes and silencers. If the components are able to come into contact with the body or suspension parts, secure the system with new mountings. Otherwise, with reference to the relevant part of Chapter 4, loosen the joints between adjacent sections of the exhaust pipe by slackening the joints (where possible) and twist the pipes as necessary to provide additional clearance. Re-tighten the exhaust pipe fasteners on completion.

22 Hose and fluid leak check

1 Visually inspect the engine joint faces, gaskets and seals for any signs of water or oil leaks. Pay particular attention to the areas around the camshaft cover, cylinder head, oil filter and sump joint faces. Bear in mind that, over a period of time, some very slight seepage from these areas is to be expected - what you are really looking for is any indication of a serious leak **(see Haynes Hint)**. Should a leak be found, renew the offending gasket or oil seal by referring to the appropriate Chapters in this manual.
2 Also check the security and condition of all the engine-related pipes and hoses. Ensure that all cable-ties or securing clips are in place and in good condition. Clips which are broken or missing can lead to chafing of the hoses, pipes or wiring, which could cause more serious problems in the future.
3 Carefully check the radiator hoses and heater hoses along their entire length. Renew any hose which is cracked, swollen or deteriorated. Cracks will show up better if the hose is squeezed. Pay close attention to the hose clips that secure the hoses to the cooling system components. Hose clips can pinch and puncture hoses, resulting in cooling system leaks.
4 Inspect all the cooling system components (hoses, joint faces etc.) for leaks. A leak in the cooling system will usually show up as white- or rust-coloured deposits on the area adjoining the leak. Where any problems of this nature are found on system components, renew the component or gasket with reference to Chapter 3.
5 From within the engine compartment, check the security of all fuel hose attachments and pipe unions, and inspect the fuel hoses and vacuum hoses for kinks, chafing and deterioration.
6 Where applicable, check the condition of the power steering fluid hoses and pipes.

23 Rear brake shoe and drum check

Refer to the detailed description given in Chapter 9.

24 Suspension and steering check

Front suspension and steering check

1 Raise the front of the vehicle, and securely support it on axle stands.
2 Visually inspect the balljoint dust covers and the steering rack-and-pinion gaiters for

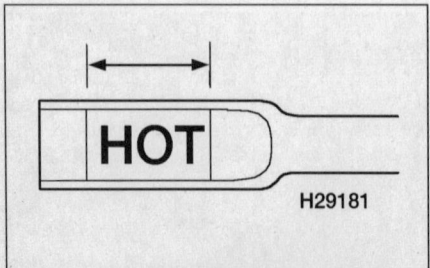

20.2 Check the automatic transmission fluid level as described in text. The level should be between the upper and lower marks on the dipstick

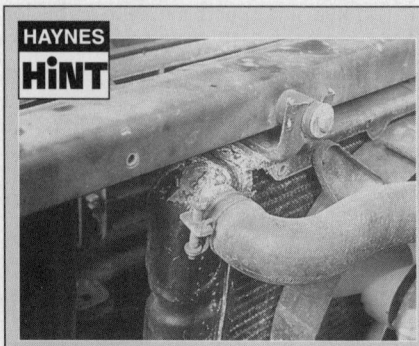

A leak in the cooling system will usually show up as white- or rust-coloured deposits on the area adjoining the leak

Every 12 000 miles or 12 months

splits, chafing or deterioration. Any wear of these components will cause loss of lubricant, together with dirt and water entry, resulting in rapid deterioration of the balljoints or steering gear.

3 On vehicles with power steering, check the fluid hoses for chafing or deterioration, and the pipe and hose unions for fluid leaks. Also check for signs of fluid leakage under pressure from the steering gear rubber gaiters, which would indicate failed fluid seals within the steering gear.

4 Grasp the roadwheel at the 12 o'clock and 6 o'clock positions, and try to rock it **(see illustration)**. Very slight free play may be felt, but if the movement is appreciable, further investigation is necessary to determine the source. Continue rocking the wheel while an assistant depresses the footbrake. If the movement is now eliminated or significantly reduced, it is likely that the hub bearings are at fault. If the free play is still evident with the footbrake depressed, then there is wear in the suspension joints or mountings.

5 Now grasp the wheel at the 9 o'clock and 3 o'clock positions, and try to rock it as before. Any movement felt now may again be caused by wear in the hub bearings or the steering track-rod balljoints. If the inner or outer balljoint is worn, the visual movement will be obvious.

6 Using a large screwdriver or flat bar, check for wear in the suspension mounting bushes by levering between the relevant suspension component and its attachment point. Some movement is to be expected as the mountings are made of rubber, but excessive wear should be obvious. Also check the condition of any visible rubber bushes, looking for splits, cracks or contamination of the rubber.

7 With the car standing on its wheels, have an assistant turn the steering wheel back and forth about an eighth of a turn each way. There should be very little, if any, lost movement between the steering wheel and roadwheels. If this is not the case, closely observe the joints and mountings previously described, but in addition, check the steering column universal joints for wear, and the rack-and-pinion steering gear itself.

Suspension strut/shock absorber check

8 Check for any signs of fluid leakage around the suspension strut/shock absorber body, or from the rubber gaiter around the piston rod. Should any fluid be noticed, the suspension strut/shock absorber is defective internally, and should be renewed. **Note:** *Suspension struts/shock absorbers should always be renewed in pairs on the same axle.*

24.4 Grasp the roadwheel at the 12 o'clock and 6 o'clock positions, and try to rock it

9 The efficiency of the suspension strut/shock absorber may be checked by bouncing the vehicle at each corner. Generally speaking, the body will return to its normal position and stop after being depressed. If it rises and returns on a rebound, the suspension strut/shock absorber is probably suspect. Examine also the suspension strut/shock absorber upper and lower mountings for any signs of wear.

25 Driveshaft gaiter check

With the vehicle raised and securely supported on stands, turn the steering onto full lock, then slowly rotate the roadwheel. Inspect the condition of the outer constant velocity (CV) joint rubber gaiters, squeezing the gaiters to open out the folds. Check for signs of cracking, splits or deterioration of the rubber, which may allow the grease to escape, and lead to water and grit entry into the joint. Also check the security and condition of the retaining clips. Repeat these checks on the inner CV joints **(see illustration)**. If any damage or deterioration is found, the gaiters should be renewed (see Chapter 8).

At the same time, check the general condition of the CV joints themselves by first holding the driveshaft and attempting to rotate the wheel. Repeat this check by holding the inner joint and attempting to rotate the driveshaft. Any appreciable movement indicates wear in the joints, wear in the driveshaft splines, or a loose driveshaft retaining nut.

26 Underbody check

1 Jack up the front and rear of the car and support on axle stands. Alternatively position the car over an inspection pit.

2 Check the complete underbody, wheel housings and side sills for corrosion and/or damage to the underbody sealant. If evident, repair as necessary.

3 Inspect the petrol tank and filler neck for punctures, cracks and other damage. The connection between the filler neck and tank is especially critical. Sometimes a rubber filler neck or connecting hose will leak due to loose retaining clamps or deteriorated rubber.

4 Carefully check all rubber fuel hoses and metal fuel lines leading to and from the fuel tank, fuel filter and fuel pump. Check for loose connections, deteriorated hoses, crimped lines, and other damage. Pay particular attention to the fuel filler vent pipes and hoses, which often loop up around the filler neck and can become blocked or crimped. Follow the lines to the front of the vehicle, carefully inspecting them all the way. Renew damaged sections as necessary.

5 Check along the length of the underside for leaks from the metal brake lines, caused by damage or corrosion.

6 At each front brake caliper, check the area around the brake hoses, brake hose unions and the bleed nipples for hydraulic fluid leakage.

7 Remove the front roadwheels and check for fluid leakage from the area around the caliper piston seal. Check that the lip of the piston dust seal is correctly located in its groove. If it has been displaced, the brake caliper should be removed and overhauled as described in Chapter 9, to check for internal dirt ingress or corrosion.

27 Front wheel alignment check

Accurate wheel alignment requires access to specialised test equipment and as such should be entrusted to a suitably equipped Proton dealer or a tyre specialist

25.1 Check the driveshaft rubber gaiters for signs of cracking or splitting

1•18 Routine maintenance and servicing

Every 24 000 miles (30 000 km) or 24 months

28 Air filter element renewal

Refer to Section 13, renewing the element regardless of its apparent condition.

29 Fuel filter renewal

 Warning: *Before carrying out the following operation, refer to the precautions given in "Safety first!" at the beginning of this manual, and follow them implicitly. Petrol is a highly-dangerous and volatile liquid, and the precautions necessary when handling it cannot be overstressed.*

Carburettor models

1 The fuel filter is situated in the engine compartment where it is clipped onto the bulkhead, just to the right-hand side of the inlet manifold **(see illustration)**.
2 Unclip the filter from its retaining clip on the bulkhead.
3 Release the retaining clips then detach the inlet and outlet hoses, noting each hoses correct fitted position, and remove the filter from the vehicle.

 Warning: *Dispose safely of the old filter; it will be highly inflammable, and may explode if thrown on a fire.*

4 Connect the hoses to the new filter making sure that the inlet hose (from the fuel tank) is connected to the lower filter union, and the outlet hose (to the carburettor) is connected to the upper filter union. Secure both hoses in position with their retaining clips and clip the filter back into position on the bulkhead.
5 Start the engine, check the filter hose connections for leaks.

Fuel-injected models

Note: *New union bolt sealing washers will be required.*

6 Working as described in Chapter 4B, depressurise the fuel system then remove the air cleaner housing. The fuel filter is mounted onto the engine compartment bulkhead.
7 Slacken the inlet and outlet hose union bolts whilst retaining the filter using an open-ended spanner on the flats provided **(see illustration)**. Remove the union bolts and detach the hoses from the filter. Discard the sealing washers these should be renewed whenever they are disturbed.
8 Slacken the filter clamp bolt and slide the filter out of the bottom of the mounting clamp, noting which way around it is fitted.

 Warning: *Dispose safely of the old filter; it will be highly inflammable, and may explode if thrown on a fire.*

9 Slide the new filter into position, ensuring that it is fitted the correct way around with the "OUT" marking uppermost. Align the filter locating lug with the clamp lug and securely tighten the clamp bolt **(see illustration)**.
10 Position the outlet hose between the locating lugs on the top of the fuel filter then position a new sealing washer on each side of the hose union. Refit the union bolt and tighten it to the specified torque setting whilst retaining the filter with an open-ended spanner.
11 Connect the inlet hose to the base of the filter as described above.
12 Start the engine and check the filter hose connections for leaks, prior to refitting the air cleaner housing as described in Chapter 4B.

30 Manual transmission oil renewal

1 This operation is much quicker and more efficient if the car is first taken on a journey of sufficient length to warm the engine/transmission up to normal operating temperature.
2 Park the car on level ground, switch off the ignition and apply the handbrake firmly. For improved access, jack up the front of the car and support it securely on axle stands (see "*Jacking and vehicle support*"). Note that the car must be lowered to the ground and level, to ensure accuracy, when refilling and checking the oil level.
3 Wipe clean the area around the filler/level plug, which is situated on the front of the transmission then unscrew the plug and remove it.
4 Position a suitable container under the drain plug situated on the right-hand side of the transmission housing, directly below the driveshaft.
5 Unscrew the drain plug and allow the oil to drain completely into the container **(see illustration)**. If the oil is hot, take precautions against scalding. Clean both the filler/level and the drain plugs, being especially careful to wipe any metallic particles off the magnetic inserts. Discard the original sealing washers; they should be renewed whenever they are disturbed.
6 When the oil has finished draining, clean the drain plug threads and those of the transmission casing, fit a new sealing washer and refit the drain plug, tightening it to the

29.1 On carburettor models the fuel filter (arrowed) is clipped onto the engine compartment bulkhead

29.7 Fuel filter upper and lower union bolts (arrowed) - fuel-injected models

29.9 On refitting ensure the fuel filter lug (arrowed) is correctly aligned with the mounting bracket and securely tighten the clamp bolt

30.5 Slackening the manual transmission drain plug

Every 24 000 miles or 24 months

specified torque setting. It the car was raised for the draining operation, now lower it to the ground.

7 Refilling the transmission is an extremely awkward operation. Above all, allow plenty of time for the oil level to settle properly before checking it. Note that the car must be parked on flat level ground when checking the oil level.

8 Refill the transmission via the filler/level plug hole with the exact amount of the specified type of oil then check the oil level as described in Section 19. When the level is correct, refit filler/level plug with a new sealing washer and tighten it to the specified torque.
Note: *If the correct amount was poured into the transmission and a large amount flows out on checking the level, refit the filler or filler/level plug and take the car on a short journey so that the new oil is distributed fully around the transmission components, then check the level again on your return.*

31 Automatic transmission fluid renewal

Note: *On early models with no transmission sump drain plug, a new sump gasket will be required.*

1 Take the vehicle on a short run, to warm the transmission up to normal operating temperature.
2 Park the car on level ground, then switch off the ignition and apply the handbrake firmly. For improved access, jack up the front of the car and support it securely on axle stands. Note that, when refilling and checking the fluid level, the car must be lowered to the ground, and level, to ensure accuracy.
3 Remove the dipstick, then position a suitable container under the transmission drain plug which is situated on the right-hand side of the transmission housing, directly below the driveshaft. On later models there is also a second drain plug on the transmission sump **(see illustration)**.
4 Unscrew the drain plug(s), and allow the fluid to drain completely into the container. Clean the drain plug(s), being especially careful to wipe any metallic particles off the magnetic insert. Discard the original sealing washer(s); they should be renewed whenever they are disturbed.

 Warning: *If the fluid is hot, take precautions against scalding.*

5 When the fluid has finished draining, clean the drain plug threads and those of the transmission casing. Fit new sealing washer(s) to the drain plug(s), and refit the plug(s) to the transmission, tightening it/them to the specified torque setting (as applicable).
6 On early models with no drain plug on the sump, in order to fully drain the transmission fluid, slacken and remove the retaining bolts

and remove the sump from the base of the automatic transmission. Recover the sump gasket and discard it. Check the transmission filter gauze for signs of debris or damage and clean the magnet(s) fitted to the base of the sump. If the filter is dirty, unbolt it from the base of the valve block and wash it in solvent to clean the gauze. Renew the filter if it is badly clogged or damaged in anyway. Fit the filter to the base of the valve block and tighten its retaining bolts to the specified torque. Ensure that the sump and transmission mating surfaces are clean and dry and position the new gasket on top of the sump. Refit the sump to the vehicle and tighten its retaining bolts to the specified torque setting.
7 On all models, if the car was raised for the draining operation, now lower it to the ground. Make sure that the car is level (front-to-rear and side-to-side).
8 Refilling the transmission is an awkward operation, adding the specified type and amount of fluid to the transmission a little at a time via the dipstick tube. Use a funnel with a fine mesh gauze, to avoid spillage, and to ensure that no foreign matter enters the transmission. Allow plenty of time for the fluid level to settle properly.
9 Start the engine, and allow it to idle for a few minutes whilst moving the selector lever through its various positions. Position the selector lever in the "N" (neutral) position and, with the engine idling, add sufficient fluid to bring the level up to the lower mark on the dipstick. Take the car on a short run to fully distribute the new fluid around the transmission, then recheck the fluid level as described in Section 20 with the transmission at normal operating temperature.

32 Ignition timing check

Carburettor models
Refer to Chapter 5

Fuel-injected models
On fuel-injected models, the timing is constantly being monitored and adjusted by the engine management ECU and special engine management diagnostic equipment is required for the check. It can therefore be safely assumed that the ignition timing is correct unless the engine management system warning light is illuminated (see Chapters 4 and 5).

33 Headlight beam alignment check

1 Accurate adjustment of the headlight beam is only possible using optical beam-setting equipment, and this work should therefore be carried out by a Proton dealer or service station with the necessary facilities. In an emergency, however, the following procedure will provide an acceptable light pattern.
2 Position the car on a level surface with tyres correctly inflated, approximately 10 metres in front of, and at right-angles to, a wall or garage door.
3 Draw a horizontal line on the wall or door at headlamp centre height. Draw a vertical line corresponding to the centre line of the car, then measure off a point either side of this, on the horizontal line, corresponding with the headlamp centres.

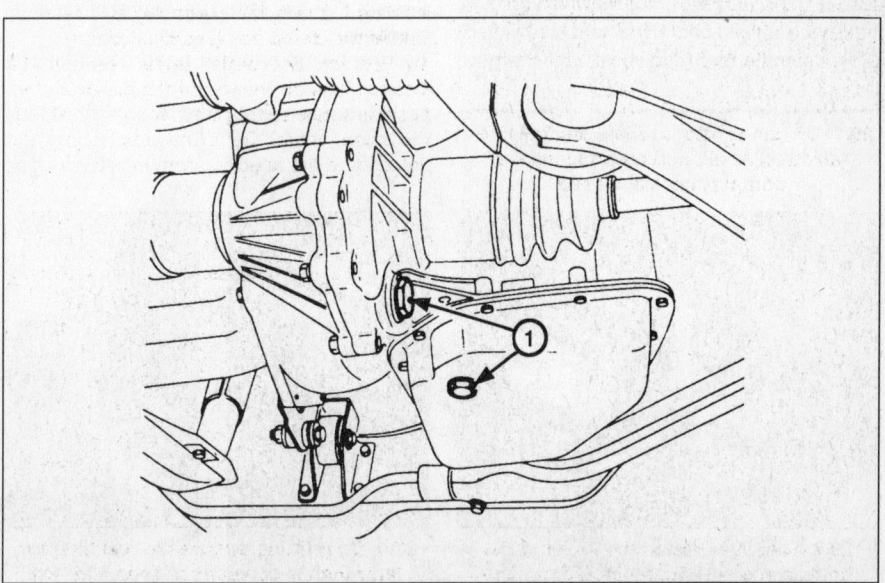

31.3 Automatic transmission drain plugs (1) - later model shown (early models may not have a drain plug on the sump)

1•20 Every 24 000 miles or 24 months

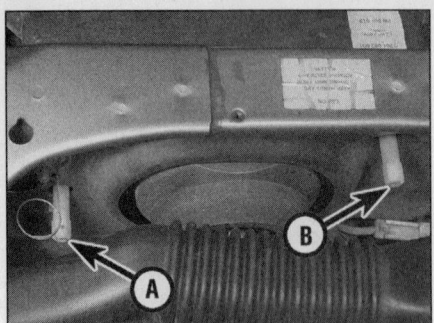

33.4a Headlamp aim adjustment screws (early 8V model, left hand headlamp shown)

A Horizontal adjustment screw
B Vertical adjustment screw

33.4b Headlamp vertical aim adjustment screw (later MPi model, left hand headlamp shown)

33.4c Headlamp horizontal aim adjustment screw (later MPi model, left hand headlamp shown)

4 Switch on the main beam and check that the areas of maximum illumination coincide with the headlamp centre marks on the wall. If not, turn the adjustment screws located on the rear and upper surfaces of the headlight unit (depending on model) to adjust the beam horizontally, and vertically **(see illustrations)**. On models with electric headlight adjustment, make sure that it is set at its basic setting before making the adjustment.

34 Hinge and lock lubrication

Lubricate the hinges of the bonnet, doors and tailgate with a light general-purpose oil. Similarly, lubricate all latches, locks and lock strikers. At the same time, check the security and operation of all the locks, adjusting them if necessary (see Chapter 11).

Lightly lubricate the bonnet release mechanism and cable with a suitable grease.

Every 36 000 miles (45 000 km) or 36 months

35 Rear wheel bearing lubrication

1 Park the vehicle on a level surface, select first gear (or 'Park' on models with automatic transmission) and chock the front roadwheels.
2 Remove the rear roadwheels, then remove the brake drums and wheel bearings, with reference to Chapter 9.
3 Prise the grease seal from the inboard side of the hub, using a large flat bladed screwdriver **(see illustration)**.
4 Wipe all traces of the old grease from the bearing races. Take this opportunity to inspect the bearings for signs of wear or damage.
5 If the bearings are in good condition, re-pack them with grease of the specified grade (this can be obtained as part of a service kit from a Proton dealer) **(see illustration)**.
6 Press a new grease seal into position over the bearing races, with reference to Chapter 10.
7 Refer to Chapter 9 and refit the brake drum/bearing assembly to the stub axle.
8 Refit the roadwheel and lower the vehicle to the ground.

35.3 Prise the grease seal from the inboard side of the hub, using a large flat bladed screwdriver

35.5 If the bearings are in good condition, re-pack them with grease of the specified grade

Routine maintenance and servicing

Every 60 000 miles (75 000 km) or 60 months

36 Timing belt renewal

Refer to Chapter 2A.

Every 2 years, regardless of mileage

37 Brake fluid renewal

Warning: Brake hydraulic fluid can harm your eyes and damage painted surfaces, so use extreme caution when handling and pouring it. Do not use fluid that has been standing open for some time, as it absorbs moisture from the air. Excess moisture can cause a dangerous loss of braking effectiveness.

1 The procedure is similar to that for the bleeding of the hydraulic system as described in Chapter 9, except that the brake fluid reservoir should be emptied by siphoning, using a clean poultry baster or similar before starting, and allowance should be made for the old fluid to be expelled when bleeding a section of the circuit.
2 Working as described in Chapter 9, open the first bleed screw in the sequence, and pump the brake pedal gently until nearly all the old fluid has been emptied from the master cylinder reservoir.

HAYNES HiNT *Old hydraulic fluid is invariably much darker in colour than new fluid, making it easy to distinguish between the two.*

3 Top-up to the "MAX" level with new fluid, and continue pumping until only the new fluid remains in the reservoir, and new fluid can be seen emerging from the bleed screw. Tighten the screw, and top the reservoir level up to the "MAX" level line.
4 Work through all the remaining bleed screws in the sequence until new fluid can be seen at all of them. Be careful to keep the master cylinder reservoir topped-up to above the "MIN" level at all times, or air may enter the system and greatly increase the length of the task.
5 When the operation is complete, check that all bleed screws are securely tightened, and that their dust caps are refitted. Wash off all traces of spilt fluid, and recheck the master cylinder reservoir fluid level.
6 Check the operation of the braking system exhaustively, before brining the vehicle back into service on the public highway.

Notes

Chapter 2 Part A:
In-car repair procedures

Contents

Camshaft - removal, inspection and refitting 9
Camshaft oil seals - renewal 7
Compression test - description and interpretation 2
Crankshaft oil seals - renewal 13
Cylinder head - removal, inspection and refitting 10
Cylinder head cover - removal and refitting 4
Engine mountings - inspection and renewal 15
Engine oil and filter renewal ....See Chapter 1
Engine oil level check ....See "Weekly checks"
Flywheel/driveplate - removal, inspection and refitting 14

General information 1
Oil pump - removal, inspection and refitting 12
Rocker shafts and arms - removal, inspection and refitting 8
Sump - removal and refitting 11
Timing belt - removal and refitting 5
Timing belt sprockets and tensioners - removal, inspection and
   refitting 6
Top dead centre (TDC) for No 1 piston - locating 3
Valve clearances - adjustment ....See Chapter 1

Degrees of difficulty

| **Easy,** suitable for novice with little experience | **Fairly easy,** suitable for beginner with some experience | **Fairly difficult,** suitable for competent DIY mechanic | **Difficult,** suitable for experienced DIY mechanic | **Very difficult,** suitable for expert DIY or professional |

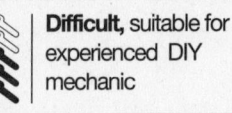

Specifications

General
Type .... Four-cylinder, in-line, single overhead camshaft
Designation:
  1.3 litre models 4G13
  1.5 litre models 4G15
Bore:
  1.3 litre models .... 71.0 mm
  1.5 litre models .... 75.5 mm
Stroke .... 82.0 mm
Firing order .... 1-3-4-2 (No 1 cylinder at timing belt end of engine)
Direction of crankshaft rotation .... Clockwise, viewed from timing belt end

Camshaft
Drive .... Toothed belt
Number of bearings:
  8-valve models 3
  12-valve models 5
Lobe height:
  8-valve models:
    Inlet:
      Standard .... 38.08 mm
      Service limit .... 37.58 mm
    Exhaust:
      Standard .... 39.15 mm
      Service limit .... 38.65 mm
  12-valve models:
    Inlet:
      Standard .... 38.75 mm
      Service limit .... 38.25 mm
    Exhaust:
      Standard .... 39.10 mm
      Service limit .... 38.60 mm

Camshaft (continued)

Fuel pump driving cam diameter - carburettor models:
  8-valve models:
    Standard .... 38.1 mm
    Service limit .... 37.6 mm
  12-valve models:
    Standard .... 38.0 mm
    Service limit .... 37.5 mm
Camshaft bearing running clearance:
  8-valve models .... 0.04 to 0.08 mm
  12-valve models .... 0.06 to 0.10 mm
Camshaft endfloat - 8-valve models .... 0.05 to 0.20 mm

Rocker arms and shafts

Rocker arm bore diameter .... 18.910 to 18.928 mm
Rocker shaft diameter .... 18.885 to 18.898 mm
Rocker arm to shaft running clearance .... 0.01 to 0.04 mm
Rocker shaft length:
  8-valve models:
    Inlet shaft .... 340 mm
    Exhaust shaft .... 327 mm
  12-valve models:
    Inlet shaft .... 365 mm
    Exhaust shaft .... 346 mm

Lubrication system

Minimum oil pressure at specified idle speed (engine hot) .... 1.5 bar (21 psi)
Oil pump clearances - 12-valve models:
  Outer rotor-to-body:
    Standard .... 0.10 to 0.18 mm
    Service limit .... 0.35 mm
  Inner rotor tip-to-outer rotor:
    Standard .... 0.06 to 0.18 mm
    Service limit .... 0.35 mm
  Rotor endfloat:
    Standard .... 0.04 to 0.10 mm
    Service limit .... 0.20 mm

Torque wrench settings

	Nm	lbf ft
Camshaft sprocket	70	52
Connecting rod (big-end) cap nuts:		
8-valve models	35	25
12-valve models:		
Stage 1	22	16
Fully slacken the nuts then tighten to:		
Stage 2	22	16
Stage 3	Angle-tighten a further 90°	
Coolant pump pulley bolts	10	7
Crankshaft pulley bolts:		
Large (centre) bolt	100	74
Smaller (outer) bolts	15	11
Cylinder head bolts - all models (cold engine)	75	54
Engine-to-transmission bolts (manual transmission)	53	39
Engine-to-transmission bolts (automatic transmission):		
Bolts marked 7 on their heads:		
M10 bolts	50	37
M8 bolts:		
14 mm long bolts	12	9
20 mm long bolts	20	15
Bolts marked 10 on their heads	35	25
Engine/transmission mountings:		
Left-hand mounting:		
Through-bolt nut	100	74
Through-bolt retaining nut	55	40
Mounting bracket nuts and bolt	55	40
Right-hand mounting:		
Through-bolt nut	100	74
Mounting to body bolts	40	29
Mounting bracket to transmission nut/bolt	60	43

Torque wrench settings (continued)

	Nm	lbf ft
Front mounting:		
Through-bolt nut	50	37
Mounting to crossmember bolts	40	29
Mounting bracket to cylinder block bolts	75	54
Rear mounting:		
Through-bolt nut	50	37
Mounting to crossmember bolts	50	37
Mounting bracket to cylinder block bolts	75	54
Stabilising rod - manual transmission models:		
Rod to transmission bolt	65	46
Rod to body bolt	50	37
Flywheel/driveplate cover plate bolts	12	9
Flywheel/driveplate bolts	140	103
Main bearing cap bolts	55	40
Oil pump:		
Pick-up/strainer bolts	20	15
Housing bolts	14	10
Cover screws	10	7
Relief valve bolt	45	33
Power steering pump pulley bolts	10	7
Roadwheel nuts	100	74
Rocker arm shaft bolts:		
8-valve models	25	18
12-valve models	35	25
Sump bolts	8	5
Timing belt tensioner pulley bolts	25	18

1 General information

How to use this Chapter

This Part of Chapter 2 is devoted to in-car repair procedures for the engine. All procedures concerning engine removal and refitting, and engine block/cylinder head overhaul for all engine types can be found in Chapter 2B.

Most of the operations included in Chapter 2A are based on the assumption that the engine is still installed in the car. Therefore, if this information is being used during a complete engine overhaul, with the engine already removed, many of the steps included here will not apply.

Engine description

The engine is of four-cylinder, in-line, single overhead camshaft type, mounted transversely at the front of the vehicle. Two versions of the engine are available, early (pre-1991) models are fitted with an 8-valve version of the engine and later (1991-on) models are fitted with a 12-valve version.

The crankshaft is supported in five shell-type main bearings. The centre main bearing incorporates thrustwashers to control crankshaft endfloat.

The connecting rods are attached to the crankshaft by horizontally-split shell-type big-end bearings, and to the pistons by gudgeon pins which are a press fit in the connecting rods. The aluminium alloy pistons are of the slipper type, and are fitted with three piston rings - two compression rings and a scraper-type oil control ring.

The single overhead camshaft is mounted directly in the cylinder head, and is driven by the crankshaft via a toothed timing belt. The camshaft has three bearings on 8-valve engines and five bearings on 12-valve engines.

The camshaft operates the valves via rocker arms which pivot on shafts which are bolted to the cylinder head. Valve clearance adjustment is via a screw-and-locknut arrangement which is incorporated into each rocker arm. The inlet and exhaust valves are mounted in the cylinder head, and are each closed by a single valve spring. On 12-valve models each cylinder has two inlet valves and one exhaust valve to improve the efficiency of the engine.

A semi-closed crankcase ventilation system is employed; crankcase fumes are drawn from the cylinder head cover, through the PCV valve, and passed via a hose to the inlet manifold.

Engine lubrication is by pressure feed from a gear-type oil pump which is driven off the end of the crankshaft. Engine oil is fed through an externally-mounted oil filter to the main oil gallery feeding the crankshaft and camshaft.

Repair operations possible with the engine in the vehicle

The following operations can be carried out without having to remove the engine from the vehicle:

a) Removal and refitting of the cylinder head.
b) Removal and refitting of the timing belt and sprockets.
c) Renewal of the camshaft oil seal.
d) Removal and refitting of the camshaft.
e) Removal and refitting of the sump.
f) Removal and refitting of the connecting rods and pistons*.
g) Removal and refitting of the oil pump.
h) Renewal of the crankshaft oil seals.
i) Renewal of the engine mountings.
j) Removal and refitting of the flywheel/driveplate.

* Although this operation can be carried out with the engine in the car after removal of the sump, it is better for the engine to be removed, in the interests of cleanliness and improved access. For this reason, the procedure is described in Chapter 2B.

2 Compression test - description and interpretation

1 When engine performance is down, or if misfiring occurs which cannot be attributed to the ignition or fuel systems, a compression test can provide diagnostic clues as to the engine's condition. If the test is performed regularly, it can give warning of trouble before any other symptoms become apparent.

2 The engine must be warmed-up to normal operating temperature, the battery must be fully charged, and all the spark plugs must be removed (Chapter 1). The aid of an assistant will also be required.

3 On 8-valve models, disable the ignition system by disconnecting the ignition HT coil lead from the distributor cap and earthing it on the cylinder block. Use a jumper lead or similar wire to make a good connection.

4 On 12-valve models, disable the ignition system by disconnecting the wiring connector(s) from the distributor (see Chapter 5).

2A•4 In-car repair procedures

5 Fit a compression tester to the No 1 cylinder spark plug hole - the type of tester which screws into the plug thread is to be preferred.

6 Have your assistant hold the throttle wide open, and crank the engine on the starter motor; after one or two revolutions, the compression pressure should build up to a maximum figure, and then stabilise. Record the highest reading obtained.

7 Repeat the test on the remaining cylinders, recording the pressure in each.

8 All cylinders should produce very similar pressures; a difference of more than 2 bar (29 psi) between any two cylinders indicates a fault. Note that the compression should build up quickly in a healthy engine; low compression on the first stroke, followed by gradually-increasing pressure on successive strokes, indicates worn piston rings. A low compression reading on the first stroke, which does not build up during successive strokes, indicates leaking valves or a blown head gasket (a cracked head could also be the cause). Deposits on the undersides of the valve heads can also cause low compression.

9 If the pressure in any cylinder is markedly lower than the others, carry out the following test to isolate the cause. Introduce a teaspoonful of clean oil into that cylinder through its spark plug hole and repeat the test.

10 If the addition of oil temporarily improves the compression pressure, this indicates that bore or piston wear is responsible for the pressure loss. No improvement suggests that leaking or burnt valves, or a blown head gasket, may be to blame.

11 A low reading from two adjacent cylinders is almost certainly due to the head gasket having blown between them; the presence of coolant in the engine oil will confirm this.

12 If one cylinder is about 20 percent lower than the others and the engine has a slightly rough idle, a worn camshaft lobe could be the cause.

3.4 Remove the timing belt upper cover to gain access to the camshaft sprocket timing marks

13 If the compression reading is unusually high, the combustion chambers are probably coated with carbon deposits. If this is the case, the cylinder head should be removed and decarbonised.

14 On completion of the test, refit the spark plugs and reconnect the ignition system.

3 Top dead centre (TDC) for No 1 piston - locating

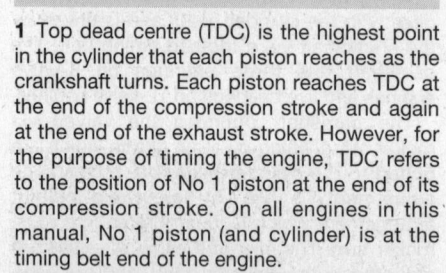

1 Top dead centre (TDC) is the highest point in the cylinder that each piston reaches as the crankshaft turns. Each piston reaches TDC at the end of the compression stroke and again at the end of the exhaust stroke. However, for the purpose of timing the engine, TDC refers to the position of No 1 piston at the end of its compression stroke. On all engines in this manual, No 1 piston (and cylinder) is at the timing belt end of the engine.

2 Disconnect both battery leads and firmly apply the handbrake, then jack up the front of the vehicle and support it securely on axle stands. Remove the left-hand roadwheel.

3 Access to the crankshaft pulley bolt can be gained by removing the rubber grommet from underneath the left-hand wheelarch. To improve access further, undo the retaining bolts and remove the plastic undercover.

4 To view the camshaft sprocket timing marks, undo the retaining bolts and remove the timing belt upper cover along with its sealing strips **(see illustration)**.

5 The crankshaft can be turned by using a spanner or socket on the pulley bolt. Note that the crankshaft must always be turned in a clockwise direction (viewed from the left-hand side of vehicle).

6 Turn the crankshaft whilst keeping an eye on the camshaft sprocket. When the sprocket timing mark is correctly aligned with the raised pointer on the cylinder head, check the that the crankshaft pulley notch is correctly aligned with the TDC (0°) mark on the timing belt cover **(see illustration)**. The engine is now positioned with No1 piston at TDC on its compression stroke.

4 Cylinder head cover - removal and refitting

Removal

1 Disconnect the battery negative lead.

2 On carburettor models, remove the air cleaner housing as described in Chapter 4A.

3 Release the retaining clip(s) (where fitted) and disconnect the breather hose and PCV valve hose from the rear of the cylinder head cover. Where necessary, release the HT leads from their retaining clips and position them clear of the cover.

4 Slacken and remove the retaining bolts then lift off the cylinder head cover, and remove it along with its gasket. Discard the gasket, a new one should be used on refitting.

Refitting

5 Carefully clean the cylinder head and cover mating surfaces, and remove all traces of oil.

3.6a Align the camshaft sprocket timing mark with the mark cast on the cylinder head (arrowed) . . .

3.6b . . . and align the crankshaft pulley notch (arrowed) with the TDC (0°) mark on the timing belt cover to position No1 piston at TDC on its compression stroke

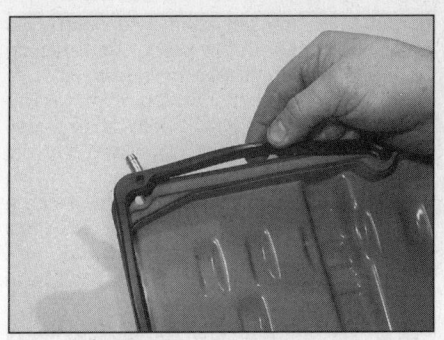

In-car repair procedures 2A•5

4.6 Ensure the seal is correctly located in the cylinder head cover groove

6 Fit the new gasket over the edge of the cylinder head cover, ensuring that it is correctly located along its entire length **(see illustration)**.
7 Carefully refit the cylinder head cover to the engine, taking great care not to displace the gasket.
8 Ensure that the gasket is correctly located, then refit the cover retaining bolts and tighten them securely.
9 Refit the HT lead clips to the head cover and reconnect the breather hose and PCV valve hoses. Refit the air cleaner housing (carburettor models) and reconnect the battery negative lead.

5 Timing belt - removal and refitting

Removal

1 Disconnect both battery leads.
2 Firmly apply the handbrake then jack up the front of the vehicle and support it on axle stands. Remove the left-hand front roadwheel.
3 Undo the retaining screws and remove the protective cover from the underneath the left-hand wheelarch.
4 Slacken the coolant pump pulley and (where fitted) the power steering pump pulley retaining bolts then remove the auxiliary drivebelt as described in Chapter 1. With the belt removed, unscrew the retaining bolts and remove the pulley(s), noting which way around each is fitted (as applicable) **(see illustration)**.
5 Position number 1 cylinder at TDC on its compression stroke as described in Section 3.
6 Slacken and remove the crankshaft pulley retaining bolts (both the large centre bolt and the smaller outer bolts). On manual transmission models, to prevent crankshaft rotation whilst the retaining bolt is slackened, have an assistant select top gear and apply the brakes firmly; if the engine is removed from the vehicle it will be necessary to lock the flywheel (see Section 14). On automatic transmission models, unbolt the lower cover plate from the base of the transmission then remove one of the torque converter retaining bolts and bolt the driveplate to the transmission housing using a metal bar and suitable bolts (see Chapter 7B). Remove the crankshaft pulley(s) and the retaining plate then refit the pulley bolt to the end of the crankshaft **(see illustrations)**.
7 Place a jack beneath the engine, with a block of wood on the jack head. Raise the jack until it is supporting the weight of the engine. Alternatively, attach a support bar to the engine and use the bar to support the weight of the engine/transmission unit.
8 Slacken and remove the nut from the left-hand engine/transmission mounting through-bolt then undo the retaining nut and withdraw the through-bolt. Undo the mounting nuts and bolt and remove the left-hand mounting bracket assembly from the engine **(see illustration)**.
9 Undo the timing belt lower cover retaining bolts then carefully withdraw the dipstick tube from the cylinder block, along with its sealing ring. Remove the timing belt cover along with its sealing strips **(see illustrations)**.
10 Slacken the tensioner pulley retaining bolts and pivot the pulley assembly away from the timing belt to relieve the belt tension. Hold the pulley fully away from the belt and securely tighten its retaining bolts to hold it in position **(see illustration)**.

5.4 Unscrew the retaining bolts and remove the pulley(s) from the coolant pump

5.6a Slacken and remove the large centre bolt and the smaller outer bolts (arrowed) . . .

5.6b . . . and remove the retaining plate and crankshaft pulley(s) from the engine

5.8 Removing the left-hand engine mounting bracket

5.9a Undo the retaining bolts then withdraw the dipstick tube . . .

5.9b . . . and remove the timing belt lower cover from the engine

2A

2A•6 In-car repair procedures

5.10 Slacken the retaining bolts then pivot the tensioner away from the belt, holding it in position by retightening the bolts . . .

5.11 . . . and remove the timing belt from the engine

11 If the timing belt is to be re-used, use white paint or similar to mark the direction of rotation on the belt (if markings do not already exist). Slip the belt off the sprockets and remove it from the engine (see illustration). **Do not** rotate the crankshaft or camshaft whilst the timing belt is removed.

12 Check the timing belt carefully for any signs of uneven wear, splitting, or oil contamination. Pay particular attention to the roots of the teeth. Renew the belt if there is the slightest doubt about its condition. If the engine is undergoing an overhaul, and has covered more than 30 000 miles with the existing belt fitted, renew the belt as a matter of course, regardless of its apparent condition. The cost of a new belt is nothing when compared to the cost of repairs, should the belt break in service. If signs of oil contamination are found, trace the source of the oil leak, and rectify it. Wash down the engine timing belt area and all related components, to remove all traces of oil.

Refitting

13 Check that the timing marks on the camshaft and crankshaft sprockets are still correctly aligned with the timing marks on the cylinder head and oil pump housing (see illustrations).

14 Manoeuvre the timing belt into position; if the original belt is being refitted, use the mark made prior to removal to ensure that it is fitted the same way around.

15 Do not twist the timing belt sharply while refitting it. Fit the belt over the crankshaft and camshaft sprockets. Make sure that the "rear run" of the belt is taut - ie, ensure that any slack is on the tensioner pulley side of the belt, and ensure that the belt teeth are seated centrally in the sprockets.

16 Check that all the timing marks are still aligned then slacken the tensioner pulley bolts to allow the pulley assembly to be forced into contact with the belt by its tensioner spring (see illustration).

17 Check that the sprocket timing marks are correctly aligned then rotate the crankshaft through two complete rotations in a clockwise direction (viewed from the left-hand end of the engine). Do not at any time rotate the crankshaft anti-clockwise. Securely tighten the tensioner pulley retaining bolts, tightening the backplate bolt first followed by the tensioner spring pivot bolt.

18 Check that the sprocket timing marks are correctly positioned then rotate the crankshaft sprocket slightly (approximately 3 teeth further) in a clockwise direction. Check the timing belt tension by pressing the rear run of the belt towards the tensioner pulley at the point where the belt passes in front of the tensioner backplate bolt. Apply firm thumb pressure to the belt and check the belt deflection; if the belt is correctly tensioned the inner edge of the belt teeth should align with a point approximately one quarter of the width across the tensioner pulley backplate retaining bolt head (see illustrations). If

5.13a Prior to fitting the timing belt, ensure the camshaft sprocket mark is correctly aligned with the cylinder head mark (arrowed) . . .

5.13b . . . and the crankshaft sprocket mark (either the locating pin or hole) is aligned with the mark on the oil pump housing (arrows)

In-car repair procedures 2A•7

5.16 Ensure all the timing marks are correctly positioned then slacken the tensioner bolts to tension the belt

5.18a Apply firm thumb pressure to the timing belt at the point where it passes the tensioner backplate bolt (arrowed) ...

adjustment is necessary, slacken the tensioner pulley bolts and move the tensioner as required. Hold the tensioner pulley in the required position and tighten its retaining bolts to the specified torque setting, tightening the backplate bolt first followed by the tensioner spring pivot bolt.

19 Rotate the crankshaft through a further two turns in a clockwise direction and recheck the belt tension as described earlier.
20 Once the belt is correctly tensioned, refit the timing belt lower cover ensuring its sealing strips are correctly positioned and securely tighten its retaining bolts.
21 Refit the left-hand engine/transmission mounting assembly and tighten its nuts and bolts to their specified torque setting. Remove the jack/engine support bar.
22 Refit the crankshaft pulley(s) and retaining plate, making sure it/they are correctly located with the sprocket pin and tighten the retaining bolts to their specified torque settings, using the method employed on removal to prevent rotation. Where necessary, refit the driveplate lower cover plate and tighten its retaining bolts to the specified torque.

23 Refit the timing belt upper cover, ensuring its sealing strips are correctly positioned. Ensure the sealing ring is in position and ease the dipstick into position then securely tighten the timing belt cover retaining bolts.
24 Refit the pulley(s) to the coolant pump and power steering pump (as applicable), making sure each is fitted the correct way around. Refit the auxiliary drivebelt as described in Chapter 1 and tighten the pulley retaining bolts to the specified torque setting.
25 Refit the undercover and wheelarch covers and fit the roadwheel.
26 Lower the vehicle to the ground and tighten the wheel nuts to the specified torque. Reconnect the battery.

6 Timing belt sprockets and tensioners - removal, inspection and refitting

Removal

1 Carry out the operations described in paragraphs 1 to 6 of Section 5 noting there is no need to refit the crankshaft pulley bolt.
2 Undo the timing belt lower cover retaining bolts then carefully withdraw the dipstick tube from the cylinder block, along with its sealing ring. Remove the timing belt cover along with its sealing strips.
3 Slacken the tensioner pulley retaining bolts and pivot the pulley assembly away from the timing belt to relieve the belt tension. Hold the pulley fully away from the belt and securely tighten its retaining bolts to hold it in position. Proceed as described under the relevant heading noting that the crankshaft or camshaft must not be rotated until the timing belt is correctly refitted and tensioned.

Camshaft sprocket

4 Free the timing belt from the sprocket then slacken and remove the sprocket retaining bolt and washer. To prevent rotation as the bolt is slackened, a sprocket-holding tool will be required. In the absence of the special Proton tool, an acceptable substitute can be fabricated as follows. Use two lengths of steel strip (one long, the other short), and three nuts and bolts; one nut and bolt forms the pivot of a forked tool, with the remaining two nuts and bolts at the tips of the "forks" to engage with the sprocket spokes as shown (see illustrations).

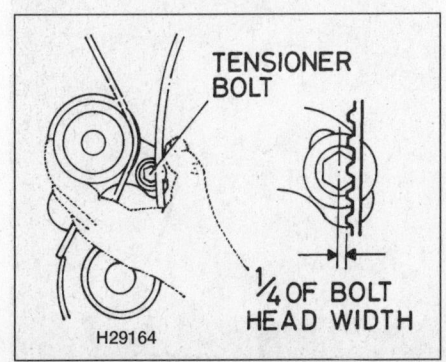

5.18b ... and check that the inner edge of the belt teeth align with a point approximately ¼ of the width across the tensioner backplate bolt head (see text)

6.4a Using a home-made holding tool to prevent rotation as the camshaft sprocket bolt is slackened

6.4b Remove the retaining bolt and washer ...

2A•8 In-car repair procedures

6.5 ... and lift off the camshaft sprocket

6.6 Remove the crankshaft sprocket ...

6.7 ... and slide off the spacer, noting which way around it is fitted

5 With the retaining bolt removed, slide off the sprocket and recover the sprocket locating pin from the end of the camshaft **(see illustration)**. Examine the oil seal for signs of oil leakage and, if necessary, renew it as described in Section 7.

Crankshaft sprocket

6 Position the timing belt clear of the sprocket then slide the sprocket off the end of the crankshaft **(see illustration)**.

7 Slide off the spacer from behind the sprocket, noting which way around it is fitted **(see illustration)**. Examine the oil seal for signs of oil leakage and, if necessary renew as described in Section 13.

Tensioner pulley

8 Using a large screwdriver, carefully unhook the tensioner spring from behind the pulley backplate lug to relieve the spring tension **(see illustration)**.

9 Unscrew the tensioner pulley spring pivot bolt and remove it along with the spacer and spring, noting each components correct fitted location **(see illustration)**.

10 Slacken and remove the pulley backplate bolt and remove the pulley assembly from the cylinder block **(see illustration)**.

Inspection

11 Inspect the teeth of the sprockets for signs of nicks and damage. The teeth are not prone to wear, and should normally last the life of the engine.

12 Spin the tensioner pulley by hand, and check for any roughness or tightness. Do not attempt to clean the pulley with solvent, as this may enter the bearings. If wear is evident, renew the tensioner pulley assembly. The tensioner spring should also be renewed if there is any doubt about its condition.

Refitting

Camshaft sprocket

13 Refit the locating pin to the end of the camshaft and refit the sprocket, making sure its locating hole engages correctly with the pin.

14 Refit the sprocket retaining bolt and washer, ensuring that the washer hole is correctly located with the sprocket pin. Tighten the bolt to the specified torque setting, using the holding tool to prevent rotation.

15 Ensure all timing marks are correctly positioned then refit and tension the timing belt as described in Section 5.

6.8 Carefully unhook the spring from behind the tensioner ...

Crankshaft sprocket

16 Slide the spacer onto the crankshaft end ensuring it is fitted with its chamfered face facing outwards (away from the cylinder block).

17 Fit the sprocket to the crankshaft making sure the pulley locating pin is facing outwards.

18 Ensure all timing marks are correctly positioned then refit and tension the timing belt as described in Section 5.

Tensioner pulley

19 Manoeuvre the tensioner pulley into position and refit the tensioner backplate bolt.

6.9 ... then unscrew the tensioner bolts, noting the correct fitted position of the spring (1) and spacer (2) ...

6.10 ... and remove the tensioner pulley

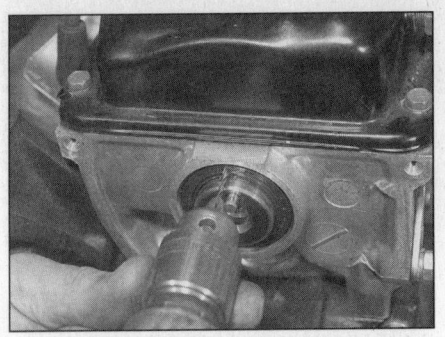

In-car repair procedures 2A•9

7.2a Carefully drill or punch a hole in the seal and screw in a self-tapping screw . . .

7.2b . . . and pull out the oil seal with a pair of pliers

7.4 Tap the new seal into position using a hammer and suitable socket

20 Slide the spacer onto the spring pivot bolt, making sure its collar is against the bolt head, then fit the spring making sure it is fitted the correct way around. Manoeuvre the assembly into position and tighten it lightly. Hook the tensioner spring into position behind the cylinder block and backplate lugs then pivot the tensioner fully away from the belt and securely tighten its retaining bolts to hold it in position.
21 Ensure all timing marks are correctly positioned then refit and tension the timing belt as described in Section 5.

7 Camshaft oil seal - renewal

1 Remove the camshaft sprocket as described in Section 6.
2 Make a note of the correct fitted depth of the seal then punch or drill two small holes opposite each other in the oil seal. Screw a self-tapping screw into each hole and pull on the screws with pliers to extract the seal **(see illustrations)**.
3 Clean the seal housing and polish off any burrs or raised edges which may have caused the seal to fail in the first place.
4 Lubricate the lips of the new seal with clean engine oil and ease it into position on the end of the shaft. Press the seal into its housing until it is positioned at the same depth as the original was prior to removal. If necessary, a tubular drift, such as a socket, which bears only on the hard outer edge of the seal can be used to tap the seal into position **(see illustration)**. Take great care not to damage

the seal lips during fitting and ensure that the seal lips face inwards. If the surface of the shaft was noticed to be badly scored, press the new seal slightly less into its housing so that its lip is running on an unmarked area of the shaft.
5 Refit the camshaft sprocket as described in Section 6 and refit and tension the timing belt as described in Section 5.

8 Rocker shafts and arms - removal, inspection and refitting

Removal

1 The rocker arm assemblies can be removed individually as follows.
2 Remove the cylinder head cover as described in Section 4.
3 Evenly and progressively slacken the rocker

shaft retaining bolts by half-a-turn at a time until the valve spring pressure is relieved from the rocker arms, then unscrew the retaining bolts fully from the cylinder head; **do not** withdraw the bolts from the shaft as they will retain the rocker arms in position as the shaft assembly is removed **(see illustration)**.
4 Lift the rocker shaft and arm assembly away from the top of the cylinder head complete with its retaining bolts and washers **(see illustration)**. If necessary, repeat the operation and remove the remaining shaft assembly.
5 To dismantle each rocker arm assembly, carefully withdraw one of the end rocker shaft bolts and carefully slide the various components off the end of the shaft, keeping all components in their correct fitted order **(see illustrations)**. Make a note of each component's correct fitted position and orientation as it is removed, to ensure it is fitted correctly on reassembly.

8.3 Unscrew the retaining bolts (arrowed) . . .

8.4 . . . and lift off the rocker arm assembly (12-valve engine shown)

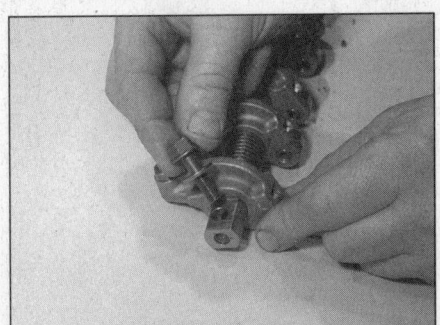

8.5a Withdraw the end retaining bolt and washer . . .

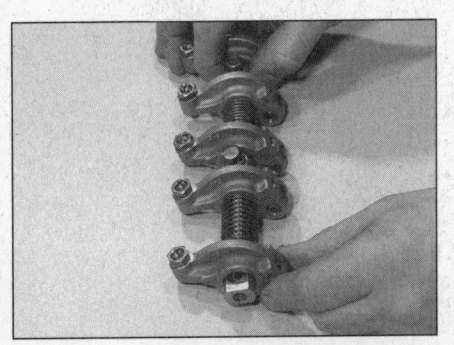

8.5b . . . and slide the rocker arms . . .

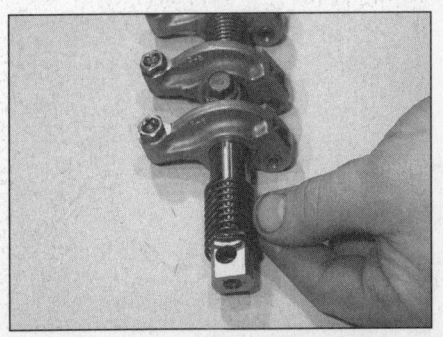

8.5c . . . and springs off of the shaft (12-valve inlet valve shaft shown)

2A•10 In-car repair procedures

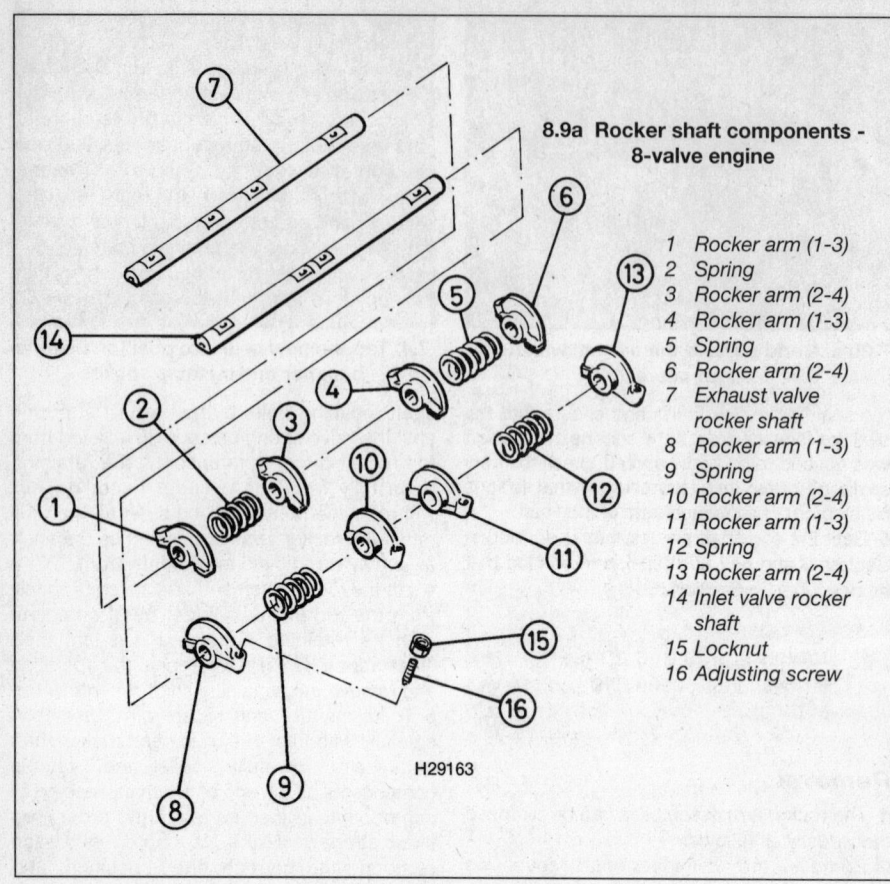

8.9a Rocker shaft components - 8-valve engine

1. Rocker arm (1-3)
2. Spring
3. Rocker arm (2-4)
4. Rocker arm (1-3)
5. Spring
6. Rocker arm (2-4)
7. Exhaust valve rocker shaft
8. Rocker arm (1-3)
9. Spring
10. Rocker arm (2-4)
11. Rocker arm (1-3)
12. Spring
13. Rocker arm (2-4)
14. Inlet valve rocker shaft
15. Locknut
16. Adjusting screw

Inspection

6 Examine the rocker arm bearing surfaces which contact the camshaft lobes for wear ridges and scoring. Renew any rocker arms on which these conditions are apparent. If a rocker arm bearing surface is badly scored, also examine the corresponding lobe on the camshaft for wear, as it is likely that both will be worn. Renew worn components as necessary. The rocker arm assembly can be dismantled as described in paragraph 5.

7 Inspect the ends of the (valve clearance) adjusting screws for signs of wear or damage, and renew as required.

8 If the rocker arm assembly has been dismantled, examine the rocker arm and shaft bearing surfaces for wear ridges and scoring. If there are obvious signs of wear, the relevant rocker arm(s) and/or the shaft must be renewed. Also ensure that the oilways in the base of the rocker shaft are clear and unblocked.

Refitting

9 If the rocker arm assembly was dismantled, refit one of the end retaining bolts and washers then apply a smear of clean engine oil to the shaft, and slide on all removed components, ensuring each is correctly fitted in its original position. If confusion arises, the rocker arms are marked for identification. On 8-valve models, the rocker arms for cylinders No 1 and 3 are marked "1-3" and those for cylinders No 2 and 4 are marked "2-4". On

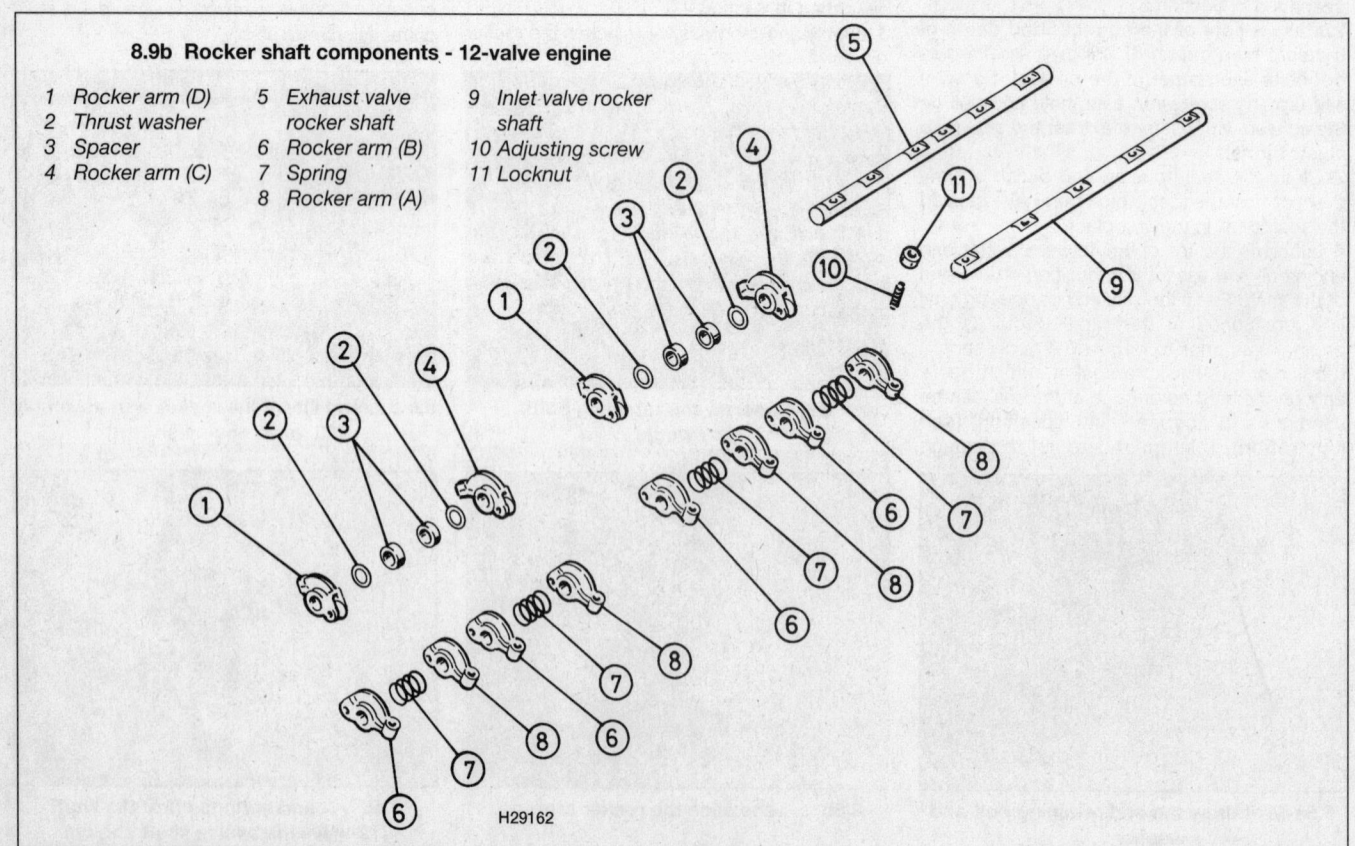

8.9b Rocker shaft components - 12-valve engine

1. Rocker arm (D)
2. Thrust washer
3. Spacer
4. Rocker arm (C)
5. Exhaust valve rocker shaft
6. Rocker arm (B)
7. Spring
8. Rocker arm (A)
9. Inlet valve rocker shaft
10. Adjusting screw
11. Locknut

12-valve models the rocker arms are marked with a letter between A and D; the correct fitted location of each arm can be determined using the key to the accompanying illustrations (see illustrations).

10 Manoeuvre the rocker arm assembly into position on the cylinder head and screw in each of its retaining bolts by a couple of turns.
11 Evenly and progressively tighten the rocker shaft retaining bolts by half-a-turn at a time to pull the shaft assembly squarely down onto the cylinder head.
Caution: As the rocker shaft bolts are tightened, take great care not to trap any of the rocker arms/spacers (as applicable) between the shaft and the top of the cylinder head. As the shaft is pulled down onto the cylinder head ensure that each rocker arm/spacer is correctly positioned so that it bears against the side of the cylinder head casting.
12 Once the rocker shaft is in contact with the cylinder head, tighten its retaining bolts to the specified torque setting.
13 Check and, if necessary, adjust the valve clearances as described in Chapter 1 then refit the cylinder head cover as described in Section 4. Warm the engine up to normal operating temperature and recheck the valve clearances with the engine hot.

9 Camshaft - removal, inspection and refitting

Removal

1 Remove the battery and distributor as described in Chapter 5.
2 Remove the camshaft sprocket as described in Section 6.
3 Remove the rocker arm assemblies as described in Section 8.
4 On carburettor models, remove the fuel pump as described in Chapter 4A.
5 On 8-valve models, undo the retaining screws and remove the cover from the right-hand end of the cylinder head. Recover the gasket and discard it, a new one will be needed on refitting. Slacken and remove the

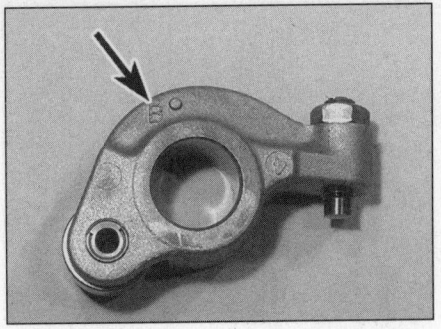

8.9c On 12-valve engines, each rocker arm is stamped with an identification letter (arrowed) to aid installation

camshaft thrust case retaining bolt from the top of the cylinder head then slide the camshaft out of position and remove it from the cylinder head (see illustration).
6 On 12-valve models, carefully slide the camshaft out of the right-hand end of the cylinder head (see illustration).

Inspection

7 Examine the camshaft bearing surfaces and lobes for wear ridges, pitting or scoring (see illustration). Renew the camshaft if evident. The camshaft oil seal should be renewed as a matter of course.
8 Examine the camshaft bearing surfaces in the cylinder head. Deep scoring or other damage means that the cylinder head must be renewed.
9 Inspect the rocker arms as described in Section 8.
10 On 8-valve models, using feeler blades, measure the clearance between the end of the camshaft and the camshaft thrust case on the camshafts right-hand end. If the measurement is not within the specified endfloat range given in the Specifications, the thrust case and its retaining washer must be renewed. To do this, firmly grip the camshaft then slacken and remove the thrust case retaining bolt and washer. Fit the new thrust case and washer and securely tighten the retaining bolt.

Refitting

11 Lubricate the camshaft bearings with clean engine oil.

12 On 12-valve models, slide the camshaft into position in the cylinder head.
13 On 8-valve models, slide the camshaft into position in the cylinder head, aligning the thrust case threaded hole with the cylinder head hole. Refit the thrust case retaining bolt and tighten it securely. Ensure the mating surfaces are clean and dry then refit the cylinder head end cover, using a new gasket, and securely tighten its retaining bolts.
14 On all models rotate the camshaft so that the camshaft sprocket locating pin hole is uppermost; this will position the camshaft correctly in the No1 cylinder at TDC on its compression stroke position.
15 Refit the distributor as described in Chapter 5.
16 Refit the rocker arm assemblies to the cylinder head then install a new camshaft oil seal and refit the camshaft sprocket (see Sections 6, 7 and 8).
17 On carburettor models refit the fuel pump as described in Chapter 4A.
18 Check and, if necessary, adjust the valve clearances as described in Chapter 1 then refit the cylinder head cover and battery. Warm the engine up to normal operating temperature and recheck the valve clearances with the engine hot.

10 Cylinder head - removal, inspection and refitting

Removal

1 Disconnect both battery leads.
2 Drain the cooling system with reference to Chapter 1.
3 Remove the timing belt with reference to Section 5 noting that it will be necessary to support the engine weight with a jack rather than the support bar.
4 On carburettor models, remove the air cleaner housing and intake duct then disconnect the fuel hoses from the pump. If the cylinder head is to be overhauled, remove the pump completely (refer to Chapter 4A).
5 Remove the inlet and exhaust manifolds as described in Chapter 4.

9.5 On 8-valve engines unscrew the thrust case retaining bolt and withdraw the camshaft from the head

9.6 Removing the camshaft - 12-valve engine

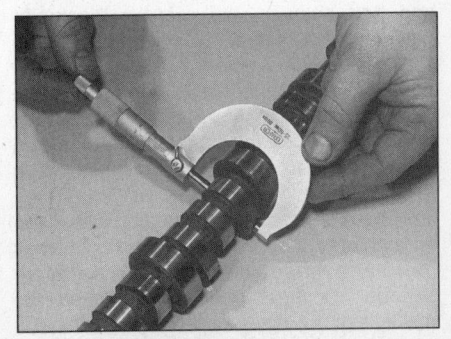

9.7 Using a micrometer to measure camshaft lobe height

10.18 Ensure the gasket is fitted the right way up and locate it on the dowels (arrowed)

10.19 Lower the cylinder carefully into position...

10.21 ...then insert the cylinder head bolts and washers

6 Disconnect the wiring connector(s) from the distributor. If the cylinder head is to be overhauled, remove the distributor (refer to Chapter 5).
7 Remove the cylinder head cover as described in Section 4.
8 Working in the **reverse** of the sequence shown in **illustration 10.22a**, progressively slacken the cylinder head bolts by half a turn at a time until all nuts and bolts can be unscrewed by hand and removed along with their washers.
9 Lift the cylinder head upwards and off the cylinder block. If it is stuck, tap it upwards using a hammer and block of wood. *Do not* try to turn it (it is located by two dowels), nor attempt to prise it free using a screwdriver inserted between the block and head faces. If the locating dowels are a loose fit, remove them and store them with the head for safe-keeping.

Inspection

10 The mating faces of the cylinder head and block must be perfectly clean before refitting the head. Use a scraper to remove all traces of gasket and carbon, and also clean the tops of the pistons. Take particular care with the aluminium cylinder head, as the soft metal is damaged easily. Also, make sure that debris is not allowed to enter the oil and water channels - this is particularly important for the oil circuit, as carbon could block the oil supply to the camshaft or crankshaft bearings. Using adhesive tape and paper, seal the water, oil and bolt holes in the cylinder block. To prevent carbon entering the gap between the pistons and bores, smear a little grease in the gap. After cleaning the piston, rotate the crankshaft so that the piston moves down the bore, then wipe out the grease and carbon with a cloth rag. Clean the piston crowns in the same way.
11 Check the block and head for nicks, deep scratches and other damage. If slight, they may be removed carefully with a file. More serious damage may be repaired by machining, but this is a specialist job.
12 If warpage of the cylinder head is suspected, use a straight-edge to check it for distortion. Refer to Chapter 2B if necessary.

13 Ensure that the cylinder head bolt holes in the crankcase are clean and free of oil. Syringe or soak up any oil left in the bolt holes. This is most important in order that the correct bolt tightening torque can be applied and to prevent the possibility of the block being cracked by hydraulic pressure when the bolts are tightened.
14 Examine the cylinder head bolt threads in the cylinder block for damage. If necessary, use the correct-size tap to chase out the threads in the block, and use a die to clean the threads on the bolts.
15 Although Proton do not actually specify that the cylinder head bolts must be renewed, it is highly recommended that new bolts are used on refitting.

Refitting

16 Ensure that the mating faces of the cylinder block and head are spotlessly clean, that the retaining bolt threads are also clean and dry, and that they screw easily in and out of their locations.
17 Check that No 1 piston is still at TDC, and that the camshaft sprocket timing mark is correctly aligned with the mark on the cylinder head (see Section 5)
Caution: If the camshaft/crankshaft is positioned wrongly, there is a risk of valves hitting pistons as the head is refitted.
18 Ensure the locating dowels are correctly fitted to the block and fit a new cylinder head gasket, making sure it is the right way up **(see illustration)**.
19 Carefully lower the cylinder head onto the

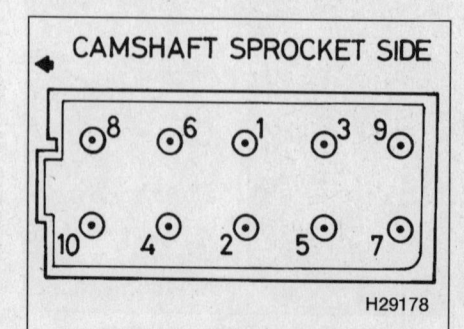

10.22a Cylinder head bolt tightening sequence

block, engaging it over the dowels **(see illustration)**.
20 Lightly oil the new cylinder head bolts, both on their threads and under their heads and allow excess oil to drain off.
21 Fit the washers to the cylinder head bolts and carefully insert the bolts into the cylinder head tightening them all by hand only **(see illustration)**.
22 Working progressively and in the sequence shown, tighten the cylinder head bolts to the specified torque setting, using a torque wrench and socket **(see illustrations)**. It is recommended that the bolts are tightened in several stages, ie. tighten all bolts in sequence first to approximately a third of the specified torque, then go around and tighten all bolts to approximately two thirds of the specified torque before finally tightening them to the full specified torque setting.
23 Refit the timing belt as described in Section 5
24 Refit the inlet and exhaust manifolds as described in Chapter 4.
25 On carburettor models, refit the fuel pump and/or reconnect the fuel hoses as described in Chapter 4A (as applicable).
26 Refit the distributor and/or reconnect its wiring (see Chapter 5).
27 Refit the cylinder head cover as described in Section 4. If the cylinder head has been overhauled, adjust the valve clearances as described in Chapter 1 prior to refitting the cover.
28 Reconnect the battery and refill the cooling system as described in Chapter 1.

10.22b Tighten the cylinder head bolts to the specified torque in sequence

In-car repair procedures 2A•13

29 Before starting the engine, check the oil level (see "Weekly checks").
30 On completion, warm the engine up to normal operating temperature and recheck the valve clearances with the engine hot (see Chapter 1).

11 Sump - removal and refitting

Removal

1 Firmly apply the handbrake, then jack up the front of the vehicle and support it securely on axle stands.
2 Drain the engine oil as described in Chapter 1, then fit a new sealing washer and refit the drain plug, tightening it securely.
3 Unscrew and remove the bolts securing the sump to the crankcase. Tap the sump with a hide or plastic mallet to break the seal, then remove the sump.
4 While the sump is removed, take the opportunity to check the oil pump pick-up/strainer for signs of clogging or splitting. If necessary, unbolt the pick-up/strainer and remove it from the base of the oil pump

11.6a Refit the pick-up/strainer using a new gasket . . .

housing along with its gasket. The strainer can then be cleaned easily in solvent or renewed.

Refitting

5 Remove all traces of dirt and oil from the mating surfaces of the sump and cylinder block and (where removed) the pick-up/strainer and oil pump housing.
6 Where necessary, position a new gasket on top of the oil pump pick-up/strainer and fit the strainer, tightening its retaining bolts to the specified torque (see illustrations).
7 Using a good quality sealant, apply a bead of sealant approximately 4 mm in diameter to

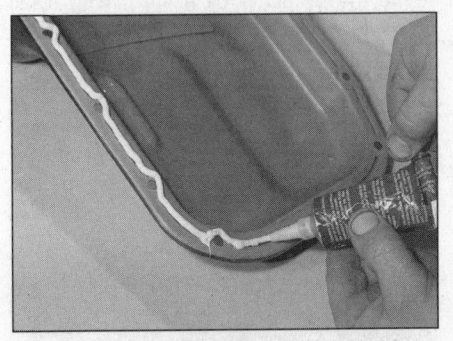

11.7a Apply sealant to the sump mating surface . . .

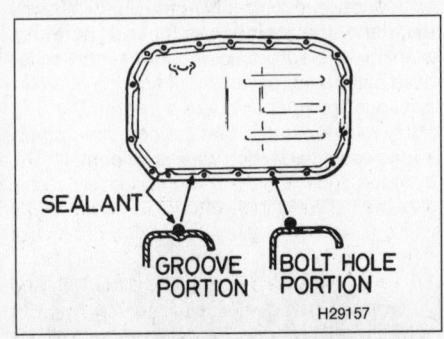

11.7b . . . making sure it goes around the inside of every retaining bolt hole and in the groove inbetween the bolt holes

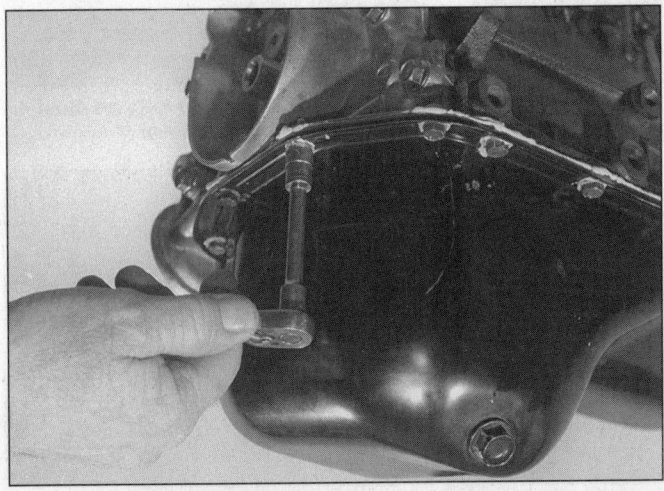

11.8 Refit the sump and tighten its retaining bolts to the specified torque

11.6b . . . and tighten its retaining bolts to the specified torque

the sump mating surface. Ensure the bead is located in the sump groove, inbetween the retaining bolts holes, and around the inside of each hole (see illustrations).
8 Lift the sump into position, then insert the bolts and tighten them progressively to the specified torque (see illustration).
9 Lower the vehicle to the ground and tighten the wheel nuts to the specified torque.
10 Fill the engine with fresh oil, with reference to Chapter 1.

12 Oil pump - removal, inspection and refitting

Removal

1 Remove the sump and oil pump pick-up strainer as described in Section 11.
2 Remove the oil filter as described in Chapter 1. If the filter is damaged or disfigured on removal, a new one will have to be used on refitting.
3 Remove the crankshaft sprocket and spacer as described in Section 6.
4 Slacken and remove the oil pump housing retaining bolts, noting each bolts correct fitted location since the bolts are all different lengths (see illustration).

12.4 Oil pump retaining bolt locations
1 Short (20 mm long) bolts
2 Medium (30 mm long) bolts
3 Long (60 mm long) bolts

2A•14 In-car repair procedures

12.8a Remove the cover and lift the inner rotor . . .

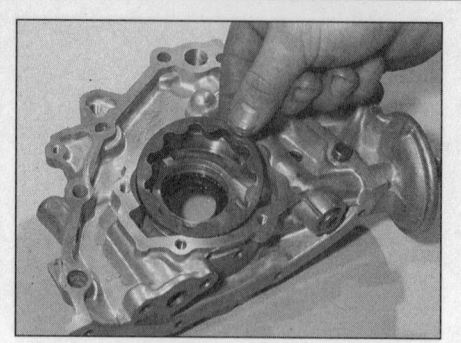

12.8b . . . and outer rotor out from the pump housing

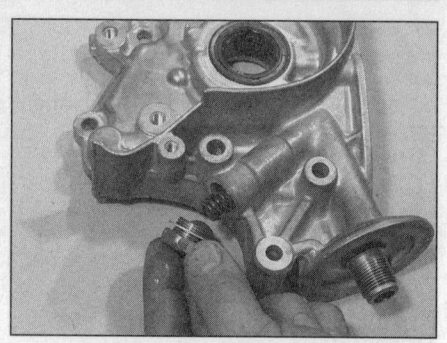

12.9a Slacken and remove the oil pressure relief valve bolt and washer . . .

5 Slide the oil pump housing assembly off of the end of the crankshaft, taking great care not to lose the locating dowels. Remove the housing gasket and discard it.

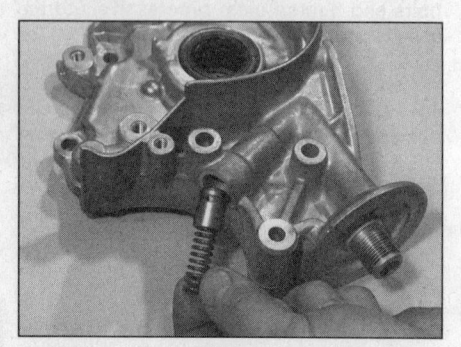

Inspection

6 Undo the retaining screws and lift off the pump cover from the rear of the housing.
7 Using a marker pen, mark the surface of both the pump inner and outer rotors; the marks can then be used to ensure the rotors are refitted the correct way around.
8 Lift out the inner and outer rotors from the pump housing (see illustrations).
9 Unscrew the oil pressure relief valve bolt from the top of the housing and recover its sealing washer. Withdraw the spring and plunger from the housing noting which way around the plunger is fitted (see illustrations).
10 Clean the components, and carefully examine the rotors, pump body and relief valve plunger for any signs of scoring or wear. Individual components are available but it is highly recommended that the complete pump is renewed if excessive wear is evident.

11 On 12-valve models, if the components appear serviceable, measure the clearance between the pump body and the outer rotor, and the inner rotor tip to outer rotor clearance using feeler blades. Also measure the rotor endfloat, and check the flatness of the end cover (see illustrations). If the clearances exceed the specified tolerances, the pump must be renewed.
12 If the pump is satisfactory, reassemble the components in the reverse order of removal, tightening the cover screws and relief valve bolt to the specified torque (see illustrations). Prime the oil pump by filling it with clean engine oil whilst rotating the inner rotor.

Refitting

13 Prior to refitting, note the correct fitted depth of the crankshaft oil seal then carefully lever out the seal using a flat-bladed

12.9b . . . and withdraw the spring and plunger

12.11a Measuring outer rotor to pump body clearance - 12-valve engine

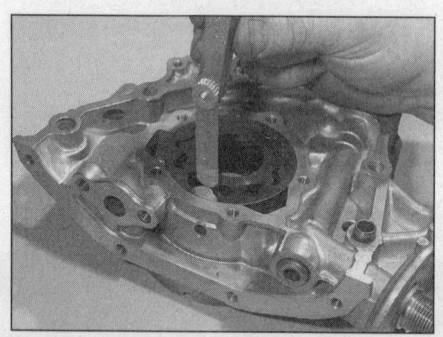

12.11b Measuring inner rotor tip to outer rotor clearance - 12-valve engine

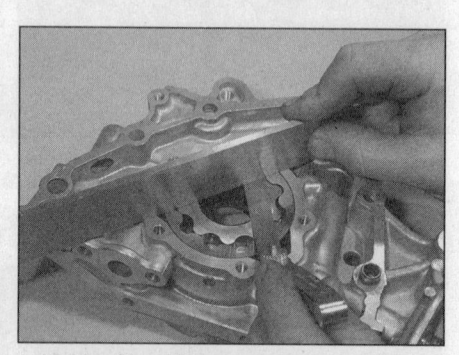

12.11c Checking pump rotor endfloat - 12-valve engine

12.12a Tighten the cover screws to the specified torque

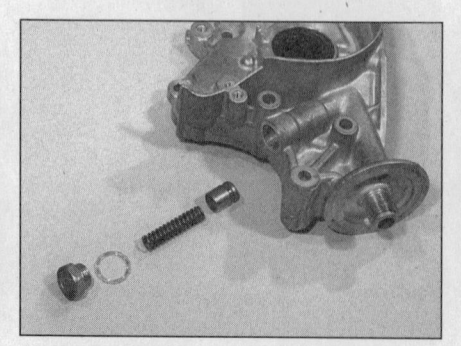

12.12b Ensure the relief valve components are fitted in the correct order . . .

12.12c . . . and tighten the bolt to the specified torque

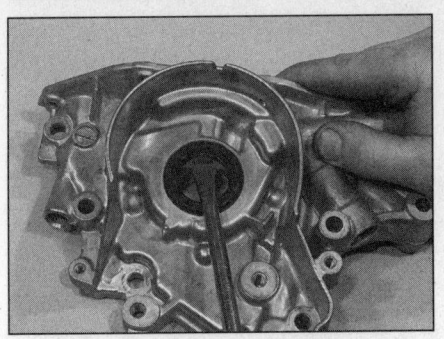

In-car repair procedures 2A•15

12.13a Prior to refitting, carefully lever out the oil seal . . .

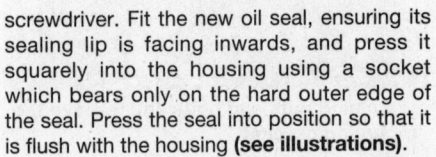

12.13b . . . and fit a new one using a socket as a drift

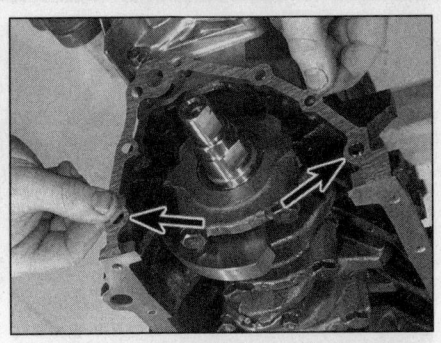

12.14 Fit a new gasket over the locating dowels (arrowed) . . .

screwdriver. Fit the new oil seal, ensuring its sealing lip is facing inwards, and press it squarely into the housing using a socket which bears only on the hard outer edge of the seal. Press the seal into position so that it is flush with the housing **(see illustrations)**.

14 Ensure the locating dowels are in position, then wipe clean the mating faces of the oil pump and cylinder block and position the new gasket on the cylinder block face **(see illustration)**.

15 Carefully manoeuvre the oil pump into position, engaging the inner rotor with the crankshaft, taking great care not damage the oil seal lip.

16 Refit the pump housing retaining bolts in their original locations and tighten them to the specified torque **(see illustration)**.

17 Refit the pick-up/strainer and sump as described in Section 11.

18 Refit the crankshaft sprocket and timing belt as described in Sections 5 and 6.

19 Fit the oil filter and refill the engine with clean oil as described in Chapter 1.

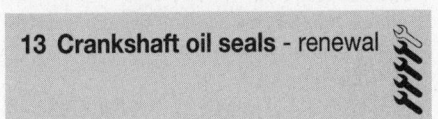

13 Crankshaft oil seals - renewal

Front (timing belt end) oil seal

1 Remove the crankshaft sprocket as described in Section 6.

2 Carefully punch or drill two small holes opposite each other in the oil seal. Screw a self-tapping screw into each and pull on the screws with pliers to extract the seal.

Caution: Great care must be taken to avoid damage to the oil pump

3 Clean the seal housing and polish off any burrs or raised edges which may have caused the seal to fail in the first place.

4 Lubricate the lips of the new seal with clean engine oil and ease it into position on the end of the shaft. Press the seal squarely into position until it is flush with the oil pump housing. If necessary, a tubular drift, such as a socket, which bears only on the hard outer edge of the seal can be used to tap the seal into position. Take great care not to damage the seal lips during fitting and ensure that the seal lips face inwards.

5 Where necessary, refit the crankshaft sprocket and timing belt as described in Sections 5 and 6.

Rear (flywheel/driveplate end) oil seal

6 Remove the flywheel/driveplate as described in Section 14.

7 Prise out the old oil seal using a small screwdriver, taking care not to damage the surface of the crankshaft. Alternatively, the oil seal can be removed as described in paragraph 2.

8 Clean the seal housing and polish off any burrs or raised edges which may have caused the seal to fail in the first place.

9 Wipe clean the oil seal seating, then dip the

12.15 . . . then ease the pump into position and tighten its retaining bolts to the specified torque

new seal in fresh engine oil. Locate it over the crankshaft, making sure its sealing lip is facing inwards. Make sure that the oil seal lip is not damaged as it is located on the crankshaft.

10 Using a tubular drift, such as a socket, drive the oil seal squarely into position until it is in firm contact with the housing. A block of wood cut to pass over the end of the crankshaft may be used instead.

11 Refit the flywheel/driveplate with reference to Section 14.

14 Flywheel/driveplate - removal, inspection and refitting

Removal

Manual transmission models

1 Remove the transmission as described in Chapter 7A then remove the clutch assembly as described in Chapter 6.

2 Prevent the flywheel from turning by locking the ring gear teeth with a similar arrangement to that shown **(see illustration)**. Alternatively, bolt a strap between the flywheel and cylinder block/crankcase. Make alignment marks between the flywheel and crankshaft using paint or a marker pen.

3 Slacken and remove the flywheel retaining bolts and remove the flywheel **(see illustration)**. Do not drop it, as it is very heavy.

14.2 Home-made flywheel holding tool which is used to lock the ring gear teeth and prevent crankshaft rotation

14.3 Slacken and remove the retaining bolts and remove the flywheel from the engine (holding tool arrowed)

2A•16 In-car repair procedures

15.7a Unscrew the retaining nut and withdraw the through-bolt from the left-hand mounting . . .

15.7b . . . then undo the retaining nuts and bolts and remove the mounting bracket

Automatic transmission models

4 Remove the transmission as described in Chapter 7B.
5 Prevent the driveplate from turning by bolting it to the cylinder block/crankcase with a metal strap. Make alignment marks between the driveplate and crankshaft using paint or a marker pen.
6 Slacken and remove the retaining bolts and remove the driveplate, noting which way around it is fitted, along with the spacers which are fitted on each side of the plate.

Inspection

7 On models with manual transmission, examine the flywheel for scoring of the clutch face, and for wear or chipping of the ring gear teeth. If the clutch face is scored, the flywheel may be surface-ground, but renewal is preferable. Seek the advice of a Proton dealer or engine reconditioning specialist to see if machining is possible. It is possible to renew the ring gear separately, but this task should be entrusted to a suitably equipped workshop as the temperature to which the ring gear needs to be heated is critical; if the gear is overheated the hardness of the teeth will be affected.
8 On models with automatic transmission, check the torque converter driveplate carefully for signs of distortion. Look for any hairline cracks around the bolt holes or radiating outwards from the centre. If any sign of wear or damage is found, the driveplate must be renewed.

Refitting

Manual transmission models

9 Clean the mating surfaces of the flywheel and crankshaft.
10 Offer up the flywheel and refit the retaining bolts. If the original is being refitted align the marks made prior to removal.
11 Lock the flywheel using the method employed on dismantling, and tighten the retaining bolts to the specified torque.
12 Refit the clutch as described in Chapter 6 then remove the locking tool, and refit the transmission as described in Chapter 7A.

Automatic transmission models

13 Clean the mating surfaces of the driveplate, spacers and crankshaft.
14 Offer up the driveplate, ensuring it is the correct way around. Align the marks made on removal (if the original is being refitted) then position a spacer on each side of the plate and refit the retaining bolts.
15 Lock the driveplate using the method employed on dismantling and tighten the retaining bolts to the specified torque.
16 Refit the transmission as described in Chapter 7B.

15 Engine mountings - inspection and renewal

Inspection

1 If improved access is required, raise the front of the car and support it securely on axle stands.
2 Check the mounting rubber to see if it is cracked, hardened or separated from the metal at any point; renew the mounting if any such damage or deterioration is evident.
3 Check that all the mounting's fasteners are securely tightened; use a torque wrench to check if possible.
4 Using a large screwdriver or a crowbar, check for wear in the mounting by carefully levering against it to check for free play. Where this is not possible, enlist the aid of an assistant to move the engine/transmission unit back and forth, or from side to side, while you watch the mounting. While some free play is to be expected even from new components, excessive wear should be obvious. If excessive free play is found, check first that the fasteners are correctly secured, then renew any worn components as described below.

Renewal

Left-hand mounting

5 Disconnect the battery negative lead.
6 Place a jack beneath the engine, with a block of wood on the jack head (if necessary, remove the undercover to improve access to the sump). Raise the jack until it is supporting the weight of the engine. Alternately, attach an engine support bar to the lifting brackets and support the weight of the engine with the bar.
7 Slacken and remove the nut from the left-hand engine/transmission mounting through-bolt then undo the retaining nut and withdraw the through-bolt. Undo the mounting nuts and bolt and remove the left-hand mounting bracket assembly from the engine **(see illustrations)**.
8 Check carefully for signs of wear or damage on all components, and renew them where necessary.
9 Manoeuvre the mounting bracket assembly into position and tighten its retaining nuts and bolt to their specified torque settings. Insert the through-bolt then refit its retaining nut and main nut and tighten them to their specified torque settings.
10 Remove the jack from underneath the engine or the engine support bar (as applicable), and reconnect the battery negative lead.

Right-hand mounting

11 Firmly apply the handbrake then jack up the front of the vehicle and support it on axle stands. Remove the right-hand front roadwheel then undo the retaining screws and remove the undercover to improve access to the mounting assembly. On fuel-injected models, to further improve access, remove the air cleaner housing (see Chapter 4B).
12 Place a jack beneath the transmission, with a block of wood on the jack head. Raise the jack until it is supporting the weight of the transmission.

In-car repair procedures 2A•17

13 Slacken and remove the through-bolt and nut then prise out the trim caps from underneath the right-hand wheelarch to reveal the mounting retaining bolts. Undo the bolts securing the mounting to the body and remove the mounting from the engine compartment. If necessary, undo the retaining nuts/bolts and remove the mounting bracket from the transmission housing.

14 Check carefully for signs of wear or damage on all components, and renew them where necessary.

15 Where removed, refit the mounting bracket to the transmission unit and tighten its retaining bolts to the specified torque.

16 Manoeuvre the mounting into position then tighten its retaining bolts to the specified torque and refit the trim caps. Insert the through-bolt and tighten its nut to the specified torque.

17 Remove the jack from below the transmission then refit the undercover and roadwheel. Lower the vehicle to the ground and tighten the roadwheel nuts to the specified torque. Where necessary, refit the air cleaner housing.

Front mounting

18 Firmly apply the handbrake then jack up the front of the vehicle and support it on axle stands. If necessary, undo the retaining screws and remove the undercover to improve access to the mounting assembly.

19 Slacken and remove the mounting through-bolt and nut then undo the retaining bolts and remove the mounting from the crossmember, noting which way around it is fitted (see illustration). If necessary, the mounting bracket can then be unbolted and remove from the engine.

20 Check carefully for signs of wear or damage on all components, and renew them where necessary.

21 Where removed, refit the mounting bracket to the engine and tighten its retaining bolts to the specified torque.

22 Manoeuvre the mounting into position, making sure the hole on the mounting base is at the front, and tighten its retaining bolts to the specified torque. Insert the through-bolt and tighten its nut to the specified torque. Refit the undercover (where removed) and lower the vehicle to the ground.

Rear mounting

23 Firmly apply the handbrake then jack up the front of the vehicle and support it on axle stands.

24 Slacken and remove the mounting through-bolt and nut then undo the retaining bolts and remove the mounting from the crossmember, noting which way around it is fitted (see illustration). If necessary, the mounting bracket can then be unbolted and remove from the engine.

25 Check carefully for signs of wear or damage on all components, and renew them where necessary.

26 Where removed, refit the mounting bracket to the engine and tighten its retaining bolts to the specified torque.

27 Manoeuvre the mounting into position and tighten its retaining bolts to the specified torque. Insert the through-bolt and tighten its nut to the specified torque then lower the vehicle to the ground.

Stabilising rod - manual transmission models only

28 Firmly apply the handbrake then jack up the front of the vehicle and support it on axle stands.

29 Slacken and remove the bolt and washers securing the stabilising rod to the rear of the transmission unit then remove the nut and bolt securing the rod to the body then remove the stabilising rod from underneath the vehicle, noting which way around it is fitted.

30 Check the rod for signs of wear or damage and renew if necessary.

31 Offer up the rod, making sure it is fitted the correct way around, and insert the bolt securing it to the body bracket. Position a washer on each side of the transmission end of the rod then screw in the mounting bolt. Tighten both bolts to their specified torque settings then lower the vehicle to the ground.

15.19 Slackening the front mounting through-bolt (mounting base hole location arrowed)

15.24 Rear mounting through-bolt (arrowed)

Notes

Chapter 2 Part B:
General engine overhaul procedures

Contents

Crankshaft - inspection 14
Crankshaft - refitting and main bearing running clearance check ... 18
Crankshaft - removal 11
Cylinder block - cleaning and inspection 12
Cylinder head - dismantling 7
Cylinder head - reassembly 9
Cylinder head and valves - cleaning and inspection 8
Engine - initial start up after overhaul 20
Engine and automatic transmission - removal, separation and refitting 5
Engine and manual transmission - removal, separation and refitting .. 4

Engine overhaul - dismantling sequence 6
Engine overhaul - general information 2
Engine overhaul - reassembly sequence 16
Engine removal - methods and precautions 3
General information 1
Main and big-end bearings - inspection 15
Piston rings - refitting 17
Piston/connecting rod assembly - inspection 13
Piston/connecting rod assembly - refitting and big-end running clearance check 19
Piston/connecting rod assembly - removal 10

Degrees of difficulty

Easy, suitable for novice with little experience | **Fairly easy,** suitable for beginner with some experience | **Fairly difficult,** suitable for competent DIY mechanic | **Difficult,** suitable for experienced DIY mechanic | **Very difficult,** suitable for expert DIY or professional

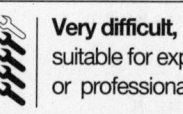

Specifications

Cylinder head

Gasket face distortion:
   Standard .... 0.05 mm
   Service limit .... 0.20 mm
Cylinder head height .... 106.9 to 107.1 mm
Valve guide bore diameter - for use when renewing the valve guides:
   1st (0.05 mm) oversize .... 12.050 to 12.068 mm
   2nd (0.25 mm) oversize .... 12.250 to 12.268 mm
   3rd (0.50 mm) oversize .... 12.500 to 12.518 mm
Valve seat bore diameter - for use when renewing the valve seats:
   8-valve engine:
     Inlet:
       1st (0.3 mm) oversize .... 36.300 to 36.325 mm
       2nd (0.6 mm) oversize .... 36.600 to 36.625 mm
     Exhaust:
       1st (0.3 mm) oversize .... 32.300 to 32.325 mm
       2nd (0.6 mm) oversize .... 32.600 to 32.625 mm
   12-valve engine:
     Primary inlet:
       1st (0.3 mm) oversize .... 27.421 to 27.441 mm
       2nd (0.6 mm) oversize .... 27.721 to 27.741 mm
     Secondary inlet:
       1st (0.3 mm) oversize .... 32.425 to 32.445 mm
       2nd (0.6 mm) oversize .... 32.725 to 32.745 mm
     Exhaust:
       1st (0.3 mm) oversize .... 35.425 to 35.445 mm
       2nd (0.6 mm) oversize .... 35.725 to 35.745 mm

Valves, valve springs and guides

Valve stem diameter:
- Inlet .... 6.565 to 6.580 mm
- Exhaust .... 6.530 to 6.550 mm

Valve length:
- 8-valve engine:
  - Inlet .... 102.1 mm
  - Exhaust .... 100.9 mm
- 12-valve engine:
  - Inlet .... 100.8 mm
  - Exhaust .... 101.1 mm

Valve seat angle .... 45.0 to 45.5°

Valve seat width:
- Inlet valve:
  - Standard .... 1.0 mm
  - Service limit .... 0.5 mm
- Exhaust valve:
  - Standard .... 1.5 mm
  - Service limit .... 1.0 mm
- Cylinder head .... 0.9 to 1.3 mm

Valve guide internal diameter .... 6.600 to 6.615 mm

Valve guide external diameter:
- Standard .... 12.055 to 12.065 mm
- Oversizes available .... 0.05, 0.25 and 0.50 mm

Valve guide length:
- Inlet .... 44.1 mm
- Exhaust .... 49.5 mm

Valve stem to guide clearance:
- Inlet:
  - Standard .... 0.02 to 0.05 mm
  - Maximum .... 0.1 mm
- Exhaust:
  - Standard .... 0.05 to 0.09 mm
  - Maximum .... 0.15 mm

Valve spring free length:
- Standard .... 44.6 mm
- Minimum .... 43.6 mm

Cylinder block

Cylinder bore diameter (standard):
- 1.3 litre engine .... 71.00 to 71.03 mm
- 1.5 litre engine .... 75.50 to 75.53 mm

Cylinder block height .... 255.9 to 256.1 mm

Pistons

Piston diameter (standard):
- 1.3 litre engine .... 70.97 to 71.00 mm
- 1.5 litre engine .... 75.47 to 75.50 mm
- Oversizes available .... 0.25, 0.50, 0.75 and 1.00 mm

Piston-to-bore clearance (all engines) .... 0.02 to 0.04 mm

Connecting rod

Big-end side clearance:
- Standard .... 0.10 to 0.25 mm
- Service limit .... 0.40 mm

Crankshaft

Endfloat:
- Standard .... 0.05 to 0.18 mm
- Service limit .... 0.25 mm

Main bearing journal diameter:
- Standard .... 48.000 mm
- 1st (0.25 mm) undersize* .... 47.725 to 47.740 mm
- 2nd (0.50 mm) undersize* .... 47.475 to 47.490 mm
- 3rd (0.75 mm) undersize* .... 47.225 to 47.240 mm

Big-end bearing journal diameter:
- Standard .... 42.000 mm
- 1st (0.25 mm) undersize* .... 41.725 to 41.740 mm
- 2nd (0.50 mm) undersize* .... 41.475 to 41.490 mm
- 3rd (0.75 mm) undersize* .... 41.225 to 41.240 mm

*Undersize measurements are only relevant for 8-valve engines. On 12-valve engines, regrinding of the crankshaft journals is not permitted - see text

General engine overhaul procedures 2B•3

Crankshaft (continued)

Maximum bearing journal out-of-round	0.05 mm
Maximum bearing journal taper	0.05 mm
Main bearing running clearance:	
Standard	0.02 to 0.07 mm
Service limit	0.15 mm
Big-end bearing running clearance:	
Standard	0.02 to 0.06 mm
Service limit	0.15 mm

Piston rings

Ring end gap:	
Compression ring:	
Standard	0.20 to 0.35 mm
Service limit	0.80 mm
Oil control ring:	
Standard	0.20 to 0.70 mm
Service limit	1.00 mm

Torque wrench settings
Refer to Chapter 2A Specifications

1 General information

Included in this Part of Chapter 2 are details of removing the engine/transmission from the car and general overhaul procedures for the cylinder head, cylinder block and all other engine internal components.

The information given ranges from advice concerning preparation for an overhaul and the purchase of replacement parts, to detailed step-by-step procedures covering removal, inspection, renovation and refitting of engine internal components.

After Section 6, all instructions are based on the assumption that the engine has been removed from the car. For information concerning in-car engine repair, as well as the removal and refitting of those external components necessary for full overhaul, refer to Part A of this Chapter and to Section 6. Ignore any preliminary dismantling operations described in Part A that are no longer relevant once the engine has been removed from the car.

Apart from torque wrench settings, which are given at the beginning of Part A, all specifications relating to engine overhaul are at the beginning of this Part of Chapter 2.

2 Engine overhaul - general information

1 It is not always easy to determine when, or if, an engine should be completely overhauled, as a number of factors must be considered.
2 High mileage is not necessarily an indication that an overhaul is needed, while low mileage does not preclude the need for an overhaul. Frequency of servicing is probably the most important consideration. An engine which has had regular and frequent oil and filter changes, as well as other required maintenance, should give many thousands of miles of reliable service. Conversely, a neglected engine may require an overhaul very early in its life.
3 Excessive oil consumption is an indication that piston rings, valve seals and/or valve guides are in need of attention. Make sure that oil leaks are not responsible before deciding that the rings and/or guides are worn. Perform a compression test, as described in Part A of this Chapter, to determine the likely cause of the problem.
4 Check the oil pressure with a gauge fitted in place of the oil pressure switch, and compare it with that specified (see Chapter 2A Specifications). If it is extremely low, the main and big-end bearings, and/or the oil pump, are probably worn out.
5 Loss of power, rough running, knocking or metallic engine noises, excessive valve gear noise, and high fuel consumption may also point to the need for an overhaul, especially if they are all present at the same time. If a complete service does not remedy the situation, major mechanical work is the only solution.
6 An engine overhaul involves restoring all internal parts to the specification of a new engine. During an overhaul, the pistons and the piston rings are renewed. New main and big-end bearings are generally fitted; if necessary, the crankshaft may be renewed, to restore the journals. The valves are also serviced as well, since they are usually in less-than-perfect condition at this point. While the engine is being overhauled, other components, such as the starter and alternator, can be overhauled as well. The end result should be an as-new engine that will give many trouble-free miles. **Note:** *Critical cooling system components such as the hoses, thermostat and water pump should be renewed when an engine is overhauled. The radiator should be checked carefully, to ensure that it is not clogged or leaking. Also, it is a good idea to renew the oil pump whenever the engine is overhauled.*
7 Before beginning the engine overhaul, read through the entire procedure, to familiarise yourself with the scope and requirements of the job. Overhauling an engine is not difficult if you follow carefully all of the instructions, have the necessary tools and equipment, and pay close attention to all specifications. It can, however, be time-consuming. Plan on the car being off the road for a minimum of two weeks, especially if parts must be taken to an engineering works for repair or reconditioning. Check on the availability of parts and make sure that any necessary special tools and equipment are obtained in advance. Most work can be done with typical hand tools, although a number of precision measuring tools are required for inspecting parts to determine if they must be renewed. Often the engineering works will handle the inspection of parts and offer advice concerning reconditioning and renewal. **Note:** *Always wait until the engine has been completely dismantled, and until all components (especially the cylinder block and the crankshaft) have been inspected, before deciding what service and repair operations must be performed by an engineering works. The condition of these components will be the major factor to consider when determining whether to overhaul the original engine, or to buy a reconditioned unit. Do not, therefore, purchase parts or have overhaul work done on other components until they have been thoroughly inspected. As a general rule, time is the primary cost of an overhaul, so it does not pay to fit worn or sub-standard parts.*
8 As a final note, to ensure maximum life and minimum trouble from a reconditioned engine, everything must be assembled with care, in a spotlessly-clean environment.

2B•4 General engine overhaul procedures

3 Engine removal - methods and precautions

1 If you have decided that the engine must be removed for overhaul or major repair work, several preliminary steps should be taken.
2 Locating a suitable place to work is extremely important. Adequate work space, along with storage space for the car, will be needed. If a workshop or garage is not available, at the very least, a flat, level, clean work surface is required.
3 Cleaning the engine compartment and engine/transmission before beginning the removal procedure will help keep tools clean and organised.
4 An engine hoist or A-frame will also be necessary. Make sure the equipment is rated in excess of the combined weight of the engine and transmission. Safety is of primary importance, considering the potential hazards involved in lifting the engine/transmission out of the car.
5 If this is the first time you have removed an engine, an assistant should ideally be available. Advice and aid from someone more experienced would also be helpful. There are many instances when one person cannot simultaneously perform all of the operations required when lifting the engine out of the vehicle.
6 Plan the operation ahead of time. Before starting work, arrange for the hire of or obtain all of the tools and equipment you will need. Some of the equipment necessary to perform engine/transmission removal and installation safely and with relative ease (in addition to an engine hoist) is as follows: a heavy duty trolley jack, complete sets of spanners and sockets as described in the Reference section of this manual, wooden blocks, and plenty of rags and cleaning solvent for mopping up spilled oil, coolant and fuel. If the hoist must be hired, make sure that you arrange for it in advance, and perform all of the operations possible without it beforehand. This will save you money and time.
7 Plan for the car to be out of use for quite a while. An engineering works will be required to perform some of the work which the do-it-yourselfer cannot accomplish without special equipment. These places often have a busy schedule, so it would be a good idea to consult them before removing the engine, in order to accurately estimate the amount of time required to rebuild or repair components that may need work.
8 Always be extremely careful when removing and refitting the engine/transmission. Serious injury can result from careless actions. Plan ahead and take your time, and a job of this nature, although major, can be accomplished successfully.

4 Engine and manual transmission - removal, separation and refitting

Removal

Note: *The engine can be removed from the car only as a complete unit with the transmission; the two are then separated for overhaul.*

1 Park the vehicle on firm, level ground. Chock the rear wheels, then firmly apply the handbrake. Jack up the front of the vehicle, and securely support it on axle stands. Remove both front roadwheels.
2 Remove the bonnet as described in Chapter 11.
3 Undo the retaining screws and remove the plastic undercovers from beneath the engine/transmission unit.
4 If the engine is to be dismantled, working as described in Chapter 1, first drain the oil and remove the oil filter. Clean and refit the drain plug, tightening it to the specified torque.
5 Drain the transmission oil as described in Chapter 1. Refit the drain and filler plugs, and tighten them securely.
6 On models with power steering, referring to Chapter 10, unbolt the power steering pump and position it clear of the engine unit noting there is no need to disconnect the fluid hoses from the pump.
7 Remove the alternator, battery and mounting bracket as described in Chapter 5. Also disconnect the wiring from the starter motor and the oil pressure warning light switch.
8 Remove the air cleaner housing and associated components as described in Chapter 4.
9 Remove the radiator as described in Chapter 3. Slacken the retaining clips and disconnect the heater hoses from the right-hand side of the engine **(see illustration)**.
10 On models equipped with air conditioning, remove the auxiliary drivebelt (see Chapter 1) then unbolt the compressor, and position it clear of the engine unit. Support the weight of the compressor by tying it to the vehicle body, to prevent any excess strain being placed on the compressor lines whilst the engine is removed. **Do not** disconnect the refrigerant lines from the compressor (refer to the warnings given in Chapter 3).
11 On carburettor models, referring to Chapter 4A, carry out the following operations.
  a) Disconnect the fuel hoses from the fuel pump.
  b) Disconnect the accelerator cable from the carburettor.
  c) Remove the exhaust system front pipe.
  d) Disconnect the relevant vacuum and coolant hoses from the inlet manifold. Where necessary also disconnect the wiring connector(s) from the manifold sensor(s).

12 On fuel injection models, referring to Chapter 4B, carry out the following operations.
  a) Disconnect the fuel hoses from the fuel rail.
  b) Disconnect the accelerator cable from the throttle housing.
  c) Remove the exhaust system front pipe.
  d) Noting the correct routing, disconnect the wiring connectors from the fuel injectors, the distributor, the throttle position sensor, the idle control valve motor, the coolant temperature sensor(s) and the intake air temperature sensor then undo the retaining bolts and position the wiring harness tray clear of the engine unit so that it will not hinder engine removal.
  e) Disconnect the relevant vacuum and coolant hoses from the inlet manifold and unbolt the earth lead from the rear of the manifold.

13 Working as described in Chapter 8, remove both driveshafts.
14 Disconnect the wiring connector from the reversing light switch then unscrew the retaining ring and detach the speedometer cable from the transmission. Undo the retaining bolt(s) and disconnect the earth lead(s) from the engine and transmission unit (see Chapter 7A).
15 On carburettor models, slacken the clutch cable adjuster to obtain maximum free play in the cable then remove the split pin securing the lower end of the cable to the clutch release lever. Free the clutch cable from the release lever and mounting bracket and position it clear of the transmission (see Chapter 6).
16 On fuel-injected models, slacken and remove the bolt securing the clutch hydraulic hose/pipe bracket to the top of the transmission and release the hose/pipe from all the necessary clips. Remove the retaining clip and clevis pin connecting the slave cylinder pushrod to the release arm then undo the retaining bolts and free the cylinder. Fully retract the pushrod into the slave cylinder and secure it in position with a stout elastic band or cable tie (to prevent the piston being accidentally expelled) then position the cylinder clear of the engine/transmission unit.

4.9 Slacken the retaining clips and disconnect the heater hoses from the engine

General engine overhaul procedures 2B•5

4.19 Slacken and remove the bolt and washers and pivot the stabilising rod away from the transmission unit

4.20a Remove the through-bolt from the right-hand mounting ...

17 Remove the split pins and washers securing the gearchange cables to the transmission levers (see Chapter 7A) then undo the retaining bolts and free the cable mounting bracket from the top of the transmission.

18 Manoeuvre the engine hoist into position, and attach it to the lifting brackets bolted onto the cylinder head. Raise the hoist until it is supporting the weight of the engine.

19 From underneath the vehicle, slacken and remove the bolt and washers securing the stabilising rod to the rear of the transmission unit then loosen the nut and bolt securing the rod to the body and pivot the rod downwards and clear of the transmission **(see illustration)**.

20 From underneath the right-hand wheelarch, remove the trim caps to gain access to the engine/transmission mounting retaining bolts. Slacken and remove the through-bolt and nut then undo the retaining bolts and remove the mounting bracket from the top of the transmission **(see illustrations)**. Slacken and remove the bolts securing the mounting to the body and remove the mounting from the engine compartment.

21 Slacken and remove the nut from the engine/transmission left-hand mounting through-bolt then undo the retaining nut and withdraw the through-bolt. Undo the mounting nuts and bolt and remove the left-hand mounting bracket assembly from the engine **(see illustration)**.

22 Slacken and remove the nut and through-bolts from the engine/transmission front and rear mountings.

23 Make a final check that any components which would prevent the removal of the engine/transmission from the car have been removed or disconnected. Ensure that components such as the driveshafts are secured so that they cannot be damaged on removal.

24 Lift the engine/transmission out of the car, ensuring that nothing is trapped or damaged **(see illustration)**. Enlist the help of an assistant during this procedure, as it will be necessary to tilt the assembly slightly to clear the body panels.

25 Once the engine is high enough, lift it out over the front of the body, and lower the unit to the ground.

Separation

26 With the engine/transmission assembly removed, support the assembly on blocks of wood, on a workbench (or failing that, on a clean area of the workshop floor).

27 Undo the retaining bolts, and remove the flywheel lower cover plate from the transmission.

28 Undo the retaining bolts and remove the starter motor from the transmission (see Chapter 5).

29 Ensure that both engine and transmission are adequately supported, then slacken and remove the remaining bolts securing the transmission housing to the engine. Note the correct fitted positions of each bolt (and the relevant brackets) as they are removed, to use as a reference on refitting.

30 Carefully withdraw the transmission from the engine, ensuring that the weight of the transmission is not allowed to hang on the input shaft while it is engaged with the clutch friction disc.

31 If they are loose, remove the locating dowels from the engine or transmission, and keep them in a safe place.

4.20b ... then undo the mounting bolts and remove the bracket from the top of the transmission

4.21 Removing the left-hand engine/transmission mounting bracket

4.24 Lifting out the engine/transmission unit

General engine overhaul procedures

Refitting

32 If the engine and transmission have been separated, perform the operations described below in paragraphs 33 to 38. If not, proceed as described from paragraph 39 onwards.

33 Ensure the clutch plate and transmission input shaft splines are clean and dry. Apply a little high-melting-point grease to the splines of the transmission input shaft. Do not apply too much, otherwise there is a possibility of the grease contaminating the clutch friction plate.

34 Ensure the locating dowels are correctly positioned prior to installation and make sure the clutch release mechanism components are correctly fitted (see Chapter 6).

35 Carefully offer the transmission to the engine, until the locating dowels are engaged. Ensure that the weight of the transmission is not allowed to hang on the input shaft as it is engaged with the clutch friction disc.

36 Refit the transmission housing-to-engine bolts, ensuring that all the necessary brackets are correctly positioned, and tighten them to the specified torque setting.

37 Refit the starter motor and tighten its mounting bolts to the specified torque (see Chapter 5).

38 Refit the flywheel lower cover plate to the transmission, and tighten its retaining bolts to the specified torque.

39 Reconnect the hoist and lifting tackle to the engine lifting brackets. With the aid of an assistant, lift the assembly over the engine compartment.

40 The assembly should be tilted as necessary to clear the surrounding components, as during removal; lower the assembly into position in the engine compartment, manipulating the hoist and lifting tackle as necessary.

41 Lower the engine/transmission assembly into position, aligning it with the front and rear mountings. Insert the mounting through-bolts and refit their nuts, tightening by hand only at this stage.

42 Refit the left-hand mounting bracket assembly to the engine and tighten its retaining nuts and bolts to the specified torque. Insert the through-bolt, tightening its retaining nut to the specified torque, and fit the nut tightening lightly only at this stage.

43 Refit the right-hand mounting bracket to the transmission unit and tighten its retaining bolts to the specified torque. Manoeuvre the mounting into position then tighten its retaining bolts to the specified torque and refit the trim caps. Insert the through-bolt and refit its nut, tightening it lightly only.

44 Align the stabilising rod with the transmission, ensuring the washers are correctly positioned, and refit its retaining bolt.

45 Rock the engine to settle it on its mountings then go around and tighten all the mounting through-bolt nuts and the stabilising rod bolts to their specified torque settings then detach the hoist from the engine.

46 The remainder of the refitting procedure is a direct reversal of the removal sequence, noting the following points:
a) Ensure that all wiring is correctly routed and retained by all the relevant retaining clips and that all connectors are correctly and securely reconnected.
b) Prior to refitting the driveshafts to the transmission, renew the driveshaft oil seals as described in Chapter 7.
c) Ensure that all disturbed hoses are correctly reconnected, and securely retained by their clips.
d) On carburettor models reconnect and adjust the clutch cable as described in Chapter 6.
e) On fuel injected models, refit the slave cylinder and ensure the hydraulic pipe/hose is securely retained by all the necessary clips. On completion, check the operation of the clutch as described in Chapter 6.
f) Adjust the accelerator cable as described in Chapter 4 part A or B as applicable.
g) Refill the engine and transmission with the correct quantity and type of oil, as described in Chapter 1.
h) Refill the cooling system as described in Chapter 1.

5 Engine and automatic transmission - removal, separation and refitting

Removal

Note: *The engine can be removed from the car only as a complete unit with the transmission; the two are then separated for overhaul.*

1 Carry out the operations described in paragraphs 1 to 13 of Section 4.

2 Referring to Chapter 7B, disconnect the selector cable from the transmission and position it clear.

3 Disconnect the wiring connector from the starter inhibitor/reversing light switch then unscrew the retaining ring and detach the speedometer cable from the transmission. Undo the retaining bolt(s) and detach the earth lead(s) from the engine and transmission unit.

4 Manoeuvre the engine hoist into position, and attach it to the lifting brackets bolted onto the cylinder head. Raise the hoist until it is supporting the weight of the engine then remove the engine as described in paragraphs 20 to 25 of Section 4.

Separation

5 With the engine/transmission assembly removed, support the assembly on blocks of wood, on a workbench (or failing that, on a clean area of the workshop floor).

6 Undo the retaining bolts and remove the driveplate lower cover plate from the base of the transmission housing.

7 Undo the retaining bolts and remove the starter motor from the transmission (see Chapter 5).

8 Slacken and remove the three bolts securing the torque converter to the engine driveplate. The bolts are accessible through the cover plate aperture. Unscrew the visible bolt then, using a socket and extension bar to rotate the crankshaft pulley, undo the remaining bolts securing the torque converter to the driveplate as they become accessible.

9 Ensure that both the engine and transmission are adequately supported, then slacken and remove the remaining bolts securing the transmission housing to the engine. Note the correct fitted positions of each bolt (and any relevant brackets) as they are removed, to use as a reference on refitting.

10 With the bolts removed, make sure the torque converter is pushed fully onto the transmission unit shaft, then carefully withdraw the transmission from the engine. If the locating dowels are a loose fit in the engine/transmission, remove them and keep them in a safe place. Secure the torque converter in position by bolting a length of metal bar to one of the housing holes.

Refitting

11 If the engine and transmission have been separated, perform the operations described below in paragraphs 12 to 19. If not, proceed as described from paragraph 20 onwards.

12 Ensure that the torque converter centering ring is in good condition and apply a smear of high-melting point grease to its contact surface. Do not apply too much, otherwise there is a possibility of the grease contaminating the torque converter.

13 Ensure that the locating dowels are correctly positioned in the engine or transmission.

14 Remove the retaining strap (where fitted) and make sure the torque converter is pushed fully into position.

15 Carefully offer the transmission to the engine, aligning the torque converter with the driveplate holes, until the locating dowels are correctly engaged.

16 Refit the transmission housing-to-engine bolts, ensuring that all the necessary brackets are correctly positioned, and tighten them to the specified torque setting.

17 Refit the torque converter retaining bolts and tighten them to the specified torque (see Chapter 7B).

18 Refit the driveplate lower cover plate and tighten its retaining bolts to the specified torque.

19 Refit the starter motor and tighten its mounting bolts to the specified torque setting (see Chapter 5).

20 Refit the engine unit to the vehicle as described in paragraphs 39 to 45 of Section 4, ignoring the information about the transmission stabilising rod.

General engine overhaul procedures 2B•7

21 The remainder of the refitting procedure is a reversal of the removal sequence, noting the following points:
a) Ensure that all wiring is correctly routed and retained by all the relevant retaining clips and that all connectors are correctly and securely reconnected.
b) Prior to refitting the driveshafts to the transmission, renew the driveshaft oil seals as described in Chapter 7.
c) Ensure that all disturbed hoses are correctly reconnected, and securely retained by their retaining clips.
d) Adjust the selector cable as described in Chapter 7B.
e) Adjust the accelerator cable as described in Chapter 4 then adjust the kickdown cable as described in Chapter 7B.
f) Refill the engine and transmission with the correct quantity and type of oil, and refill the cooling system as described in Chapter 1.

6 Engine overhaul - dismantling sequence

1 It is much easier to dismantle and work on the engine if it is mounted on a portable engine stand. These stands can often be hired from a tool hire shop. Before the engine is mounted on a stand, the flywheel/driveplate should be removed, so that the stand bolts can be tightened into the end of the cylinder block.
2 If a stand is not available, it is possible to dismantle the engine with it blocked up on a sturdy workbench, or on the floor. Be extra-careful not to tip or drop the engine when working without a stand.
3 If you are going to obtain a reconditioned engine, all the external components must be removed first, to be transferred to the replacement engine (just as they will if you are doing a complete engine overhaul yourself). These components include the following:
a) Inlet and exhaust manifolds (Chapter 4).
b) Alternator/power steering pump/air conditioning compressor bracket(s) (as applicable).
c) Coolant pump (Chapter 3).
d) Fuel system components (Chapter 4).
e) Wiring harness and all electrical switches and sensors.
f) Oil filter (Chapter 1).
g) Flywheel/driveplate (Part A of this Chapter).
Note: *When removing the external components from the engine, pay close attention to details that may be helpful or important during refitting. Note the fitted position of gaskets, seals, spacers, pins, washers, bolts, and other small items.*
4 If you are obtaining a "short" engine (the engine cylinder block, crankshaft, pistons and connecting rods all assembled), then the cylinder head, sump, oil pump, and timing belt will have to be removed also.

5 If you are planning a complete overhaul, the engine can be dismantled, and the internal components removed, in the order given below, referring to Part A of this Chapter unless otherwise stated.
a) Inlet and exhaust manifolds (Chapter 4).
b) Timing belt, sprockets and tensioner.
c) Cylinder head.
d) Flywheel/driveplate.
e) Sump.
f) Oil pump.
g) Piston/connecting rod assemblies.
h) Crankshaft.
6 Before beginning the dismantling and overhaul procedures, make sure that you have all of the correct tools necessary. Refer to *"Tools and working facilities"* in the Reference section of this manual for further information.

7 Cylinder head - dismantling

Note: *New and reconditioned cylinder heads are available from the manufacturer, and from engine overhaul specialists. Be aware that some specialist tools are required for the dismantling and inspection procedures, and new components may not be readily available. It may therefore be more practical and economical for the home mechanic to purchase a reconditioned head, rather than dismantle, inspect and recondition the original head.*
1 Remove the cylinder head as described in Part A of this Chapter.
2 Remove the rocker shafts and camshaft as described in Part A of this Chapter.
3 Using a valve spring compressor, compress each valve spring in turn until the split collets can be removed. Release the compressor, and lift off the spring retainer, spring and spring seat. Using a pair of pliers, carefully extract the valve stem seal from the top of the guide **(see illustration)**. On 12-valve models note which way up the valve spring is fitted as it is taken off; the spring should be fitted with its paint marking uppermost. If the marking is no longer visible mark the spring with a marker pen prior to removal.
4 If, when the valve spring compressor is screwed down, the spring retainer refuses to free and expose the split collets, gently tap the top of the tool, directly over the retainer, with a light hammer. This will free the retainer.
5 Withdraw the valve through the combustion chamber.
6 It is essential that each valve is stored together with its collets, retainer, spring, and spring seat. The valves should also be kept in their correct sequence, unless they are so badly worn that they are to be renewed. If they are going to be kept and used again, place each valve assembly in a labelled polythene bag or similar small container **(see illustration)**. Note that No 1 valve is nearest to the timing belt end of the engine.

8 Cylinder head and valves - cleaning and inspection

1 Thorough cleaning of the cylinder head and valve components, followed by a detailed inspection, will enable you to decide how much valve service work must be carried out during the engine overhaul. **Note:** *If the engine has been severely overheated, it is best to assume that the cylinder head is warped - check carefully for signs of this.*

Cleaning

2 Scrape away all traces of old gasket material from the cylinder head.
3 Scrape away the carbon from the combustion chambers and ports, then wash the cylinder head thoroughly with paraffin or a suitable solvent.
4 Scrape off any heavy carbon deposits that may have formed on the valves, then use a power-operated wire brush to remove deposits from the valve heads and stems.

Inspection

Note: *Be sure to perform all the following inspection procedures before concluding that the services of a machine shop or engine overhaul specialist are required. Make a list of all items that require attention.*

Cylinder head

5 Inspect the head very carefully for cracks, evidence of coolant leakage, and other damage. If cracks are found, a new cylinder head should be obtained.

7.3 Pull off the valve guide oil seal using a pair of pliers

7.6 Place each valve and its associated components in a labelled polythene bag

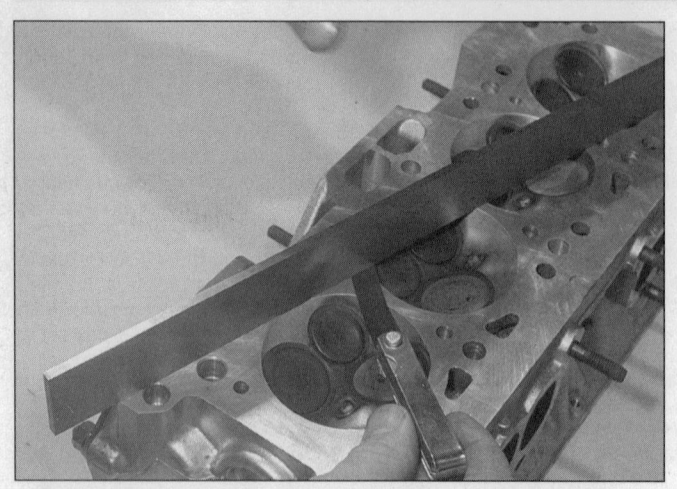

8.6a Measuring the cylinder head gasket face distortion

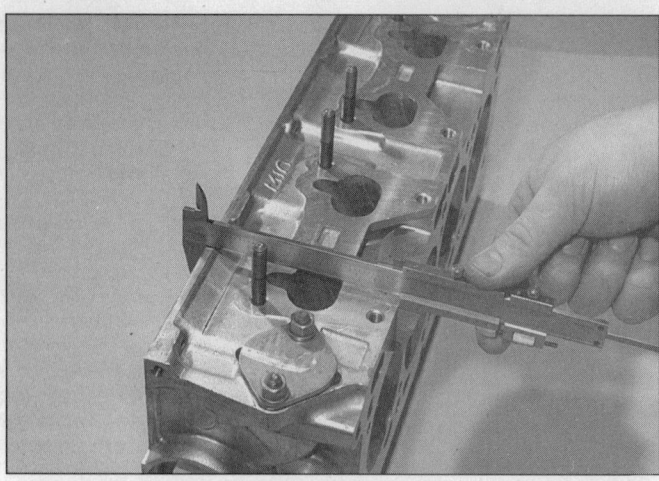

8.6b If the gasket face is distorted, measure the cylinder head height to see if it is possible to have the head resurfaced (see text)

6 Use a straight-edge and feeler blade to check that the cylinder head surface is not distorted. If the head surface is distorted, the gasket face can be resurfaced so long as the overall height of the cylinder head is not reduced beyond the specified minimum **(see illustrations)**.
Caution: Proton state that a maximum of 0.2 mm may be removed from the cylinder head/block mating surface; this figure takes into account both the cylinder head and cylinder block surfaces and must not be exceeded. For example if 0.1 mm has already been removed from the cylinder block surface then a maximum of 0.1 mm can be removed from the cylinder head. Should the grinding limit be exceeded then engine damage is likely.

7 Examine the valve seats in each of the combustion chambers. If they are severely pitted, cracked, or burned, they will need to be re-cut by an engine overhaul specialist or in extreme cases renewed. If they are only slightly pitted, this can be removed by grinding-in the valve heads and seats with fine valve-grinding compound, as described below.

8 Check the valve guides for wear by inserting the relevant valve, and checking for side-to-side motion of the valve. A very small amount of movement is acceptable. If the movement seems excessive, remove the valve. Measure the valve stem diameter (see below), and renew the valve if it is worn. If the valve stem is not worn, the wear must be in the valve guide, and the guide must be renewed (if the necessary measuring equipment is available this can be checked). The renewal of valve guides is best carried out by a Proton dealer or engine overhaul specialist, who will have the necessary tools available. Where no valve stem diameter is specified, seek the advice of a Proton dealer on the best course of action.

9 If renewing the valve guides, the valve seats should be re-ground only *after* the guides have been fitted.

Valves

10 Examine the head of each valve for pitting, burning, cracks, and general wear. Check the valve stem for scoring and wear ridges. Rotate the valve, and check for any obvious indication that it is bent. Look for pits or excessive wear on the tip of each valve stem. Renew any valve that shows any such signs of wear or damage.

11 If the valve appears satisfactory at this stage, measure the valve stem diameter at several points using a micrometer **(see illustration)**. Any significant difference in the readings obtained indicates wear of the valve stem. Should any of these conditions be apparent, the valve(s) must be renewed.

12 If the valves are in satisfactory condition, they should be ground (lapped) into their respective seats, to ensure a smooth, gas-tight seal. If the seat is only lightly pitted, or if it has been re-cut, fine grinding compound *only* should be used to produce the required finish. Coarse valve-grinding compound should *not* be used, unless a seat is badly burned or deeply pitted. If this is the case, the cylinder head and valves should be inspected by an expert, to decide whether seat re-cutting, or even the renewal of the valve or seat insert (where possible) is required.

13 Valve grinding is carried out as follows. Place the cylinder head upside-down on a bench.

14 Smear a trace of (the appropriate grade of) valve-grinding compound on the seat face, and press a suction grinding tool onto the valve head. With a semi-rotary action, grind the valve head to its seat, lifting and turning the valve occasionally to redistribute the grinding compound. A light spring placed under the valve head will greatly ease this operation.

15 If coarse grinding compound is being used, work only until a dull, matt even surface is produced on both the valve seat and the valve, then wipe off the used compound, and repeat the process with fine compound. When a smooth unbroken ring of light grey matt finish is produced on both the valve and seat, the grinding operation is complete. *Do not* grind-in the valves any further than absolutely necessary, or the seat will be prematurely sunk into the cylinder head.

16 When all the valves have been ground-in, carefully wash off *all* traces of grinding compound using paraffin or a suitable solvent, before reassembling the cylinder head.

Valve components

17 Examine the valve springs for signs of damage and discoloration. Measure the free length of each spring and compare it to the measurements given in the Specifications **(see illustration)**.

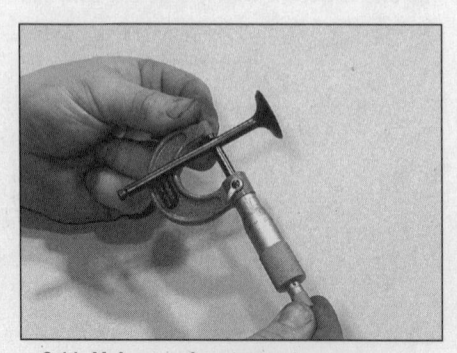

8.11 Using a micrometer to measure a valve stem diameter

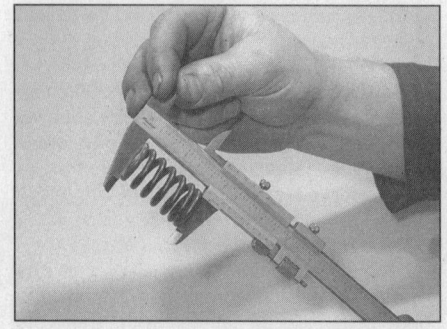

8.17 Measuring valve spring free length

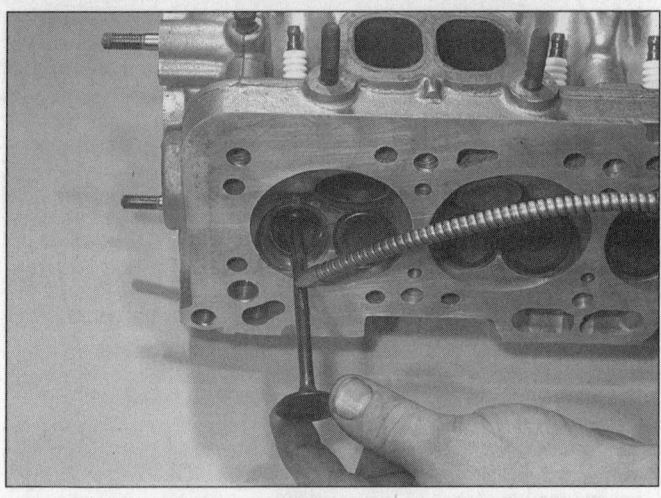

General engine overhaul procedures 2B•9

9.1 Lubricate the valve stem and insert the valve into its respective guide

9.2 Press the new oil seal onto the valve guide using a socket

18 Stand each spring on a flat surface, and check it for squareness. If any of the springs are damaged, distorted or have lost their tension, obtain a complete new set of springs. It is normal to renew the valve springs as a matter of course if a major overhaul is being carried out.

19 Renew the valve stem oil seals regardless of their apparent condition.

9 Cylinder head - reassembly

1 Lubricate the stems of the valves, and insert the valves into their original guides **(see illustration)**. If new valves are being fitted, insert them into the locations to which they have been ground.

2 Refit the spring seat then, working on the first valve, dip the new valve stem seal in fresh engine oil. Carefully locate it over the valve and onto the guide. Take care not to damage the seal as it is passed over the valve stem. Use a socket or metal tube to press the seal firmly onto the guide **(see illustration)**.

3 Locate the valve spring on top of its seat, then refit the spring retainer **(see illustrations)**. On 12-valve models ensure that the valve spring is installed with its paint marking uppermost.

4 Compress the valve spring, and locate the split collets in the recess in the valve stem **(see illustration)**. Release the compressor, then repeat the procedure on the remaining valves.

HAYNES HiNT

Use a little dab of grease to hold the collets in position on the valve stem while the spring compressor is released.

5 With all the valves installed, place the cylinder head flat on the bench and, using a hammer and interposed block of wood, tap the end of each valve stem to settle the components.

6 Refit the camshaft and rocker shafts as described in Part A of this Chapter.

7 The cylinder head can then be refitted as described in Part A of this Chapter.

10 Piston/connecting rod assembly - removal

1 Remove the cylinder head and sump as described in Part A of this Chapter.

2 If there is a pronounced wear ridge at the top of any bore, it may be necessary to remove it with a scraper or ridge reamer, to avoid piston damage during removal. Such a ridge indicates excessive wear of the cylinder bore.

3 Prior to removal, using feeler blades, measuring the connecting rod big-end side clearance of each rod **(see illustration)**. If any rod exceeds the specified clearance, it must be renewed.

4 Using a hammer and centre-punch, paint or similar, mark each connecting rod and its bearing cap with its respective cylinder number on the flat machined surface provided; if the engine has been dismantled

9.3a Refit the valve spring (note the paint marking - 12-valve models only) . . .

9.3b . . . then fit the spring retainer

9.4 Compress the valve spring and fit the collets, using grease to hold them in position

2B•10 General engine overhaul procedures

before, note carefully any identifying marks made previously **(see illustration)**. Note that No 1 cylinder is at the timing belt end of the engine.

5 Turn the crankshaft to bring pistons 1 and 4 to BDC (bottom dead centre).

6 Unscrew the nuts from No 1 piston big-end bearing cap. Take off the cap and recover the bottom half bearing shell. If the bearing shells are to be re-used, tape the cap and the shell together.

7 Using a hammer handle, push the piston up through the bore, and remove it from the top of the cylinder block. Recover the bearing shell, and tape it to the connecting rod for safe-keeping.

8 Loosely refit the big-end cap to the connecting rod, and secure with the nuts - this will help to keep the components in their correct order.

9 Remove No 4 piston assembly in the same way.

10 Turn the crankshaft through 180° to bring pistons 2 and 3 to BDC (bottom dead centre), and remove them in the same way.

11 Crankshaft - removal

1 Remove the oil pump and the flywheel/driveplate as described in Part A of this Chapter. If the piston and connecting rod assemblies are also to be removed, remove the cylinder head.

2 Check the crankshaft endfloat as described in Section 14, then proceed as follows.

3 Remove the piston and connecting rod assemblies as described in Section 10. If no work is to be done on the pistons and connecting rods, unbolt the caps and push the pistons far enough up the bores that the connecting rods are positioned clear of the crankshaft journals.

10.3 Measuring connecting rod big-end side clearance

4 Slacken and remove the retaining bolts securing the crankshaft rear oil seal housing to the cylinder block and remove the housing from the crankshaft end along with its gasket. If the cover locating dowels are a loose fit, remove and store them with the cover for safe-keeping.

5 The main bearing caps should be numbered 1 to 5 from the timing belt end of the engine and have an arrow stamped on them indicating their correct fitted direction **(see illustration)**. If not, mark them accordingly using a centre-punch or paint in the same way as the connecting rods.

6 Unscrew and remove the main bearing cap retaining bolts, and withdraw the caps. Recover the lower main bearing shells, and tape them to their respective caps for safe-keeping.

7 Carefully lift out the crankshaft, taking care not to displace the upper main bearing shells **(see illustration)**.

8 Recover the upper bearing shells from the cylinder block, and tape them to their respective caps for safe-keeping.

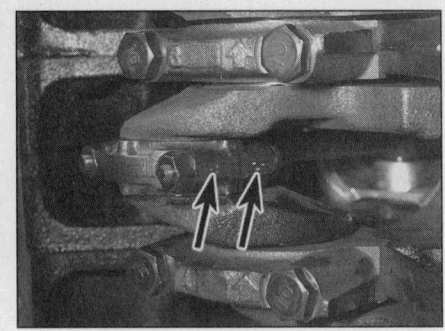

10.4 Make identification marks on the connecting rod and cap prior to removal (cylinder No 3 shown)

12 Cylinder block - cleaning and inspection

Cleaning

1 Remove all external components and electrical switches/sensors from the block. For complete cleaning, the core plugs should ideally be removed. Drill a small hole in the plugs, then insert a self-tapping screw into the hole. Pull out the plugs by pulling on the screw with a pair of grips, or by using a slide hammer.

2 Scrape all traces of gasket from the cylinder block, and from the main bearing casting (where fitted), taking care not to damage the gasket/sealing surfaces.

3 Remove all oil gallery plugs (where fitted). The plugs are usually very tight - they may have to be drilled out, and the holes re-tapped. Use new plugs when the engine is reassembled.

4 If any of the castings are extremely dirty, all should be steam-cleaned.

5 After the castings are returned, clean all oil holes and oil galleries one more time. Flush all

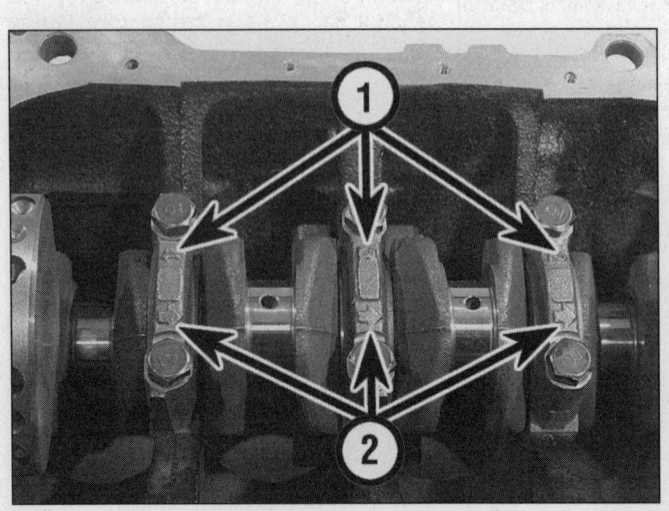

11.5 Main bearing cap location (1) and direction (2) identification markings

11.7 Removing the crankshaft

General engine overhaul procedures 2B•11

internal passages with warm water until the water runs clear. Dry thoroughly, and apply a light film of oil to all mating surfaces, to prevent rusting. Also oil the cylinder bores. If you have access to compressed air, use it to speed up the drying process, and to blow out all the oil holes and galleries **(see illustration)**.

⚠️ **Warning: Wear eye protection when using compressed air!**

6 If the castings are not very dirty, you can do an adequate cleaning job with hot (as hot as you can stand!), soapy water and a stiff brush. Take plenty of time, and do a thorough job. Regardless of the cleaning method used, be sure to clean all oil holes and galleries very thoroughly, and to dry all components well. Protect the cylinder bores as described above, to prevent rusting.

7 All threaded holes must be clean, to ensure accurate torque readings during reassembly. To clean the threads, run the correct-size tap into each of the holes to remove rust, corrosion, thread sealant or sludge, and to restore damaged threads. If possible, use compressed air to clear the holes of debris produced by this operation. An alternative is to inject aerosol-applied water-dispersant lubricant into each hole, using the long spout usually supplied, but be sure to soak up all traces of the lubricant prior to reassembly.

⚠️ **Warning: Wear eye protection when cleaning out these holes in this way!**

8 Apply suitable sealant to the new oil gallery plugs, and insert them into the holes in the block. Tighten them securely.

9 If the engine is not going to be reassembled right away, cover it with a large plastic bag to keep it clean; protect all mating surfaces and the cylinder bores as described above, to prevent rusting.

Inspection

10 Visually check the castings for cracks and corrosion. Look for stripped threads in the threaded holes. If there has been any history of internal water leakage, it may be worthwhile having an engine overhaul specialist check the cylinder block with special equipment. If defects are found, have them repaired if possible, or renew the assembly.

11 Check each cylinder bore for scuffing and scoring. Check for signs of a wear ridge at the top of the cylinder, indicating that the bore is excessively worn.

12 If the necessary measuring equipment is available, measure the bore diameter of each cylinder liner at the top (just under the wear ridge), centre, and bottom of the cylinder bore, parallel to the crankshaft axis.

13 Next, measure the bore diameter at the same three locations, at right-angles to the crankshaft axis. Compare the results with the figures given in the Specifications. Where no figures are stated by Proton, if there is any doubt about the condition of the cylinder

12.5 Clean out all the cylinder block oilways using compressed air

bores seek the advice of a Proton dealer or engine reconditioning specialist.

14 If the cylinder bores are worn, it is possible to have them rebored and fit oversize pistons. Proton produce oversize pistons in the following sizes; 0.25 mm, 0.50 mm, 0.75 mm and 1.00 mm oversize. Seek the advice of a Proton dealer or engine overhaul specialist for further information.

13 Piston/connecting rod assembly - inspection

1 Before the inspection process can begin, the piston/connecting rod assemblies must be cleaned, and the original piston rings removed from the pistons.

2 Carefully expand the old rings over the top of the pistons. The use of two or three old feeler blades will be helpful in preventing the rings dropping into empty grooves **(see illustration)**. Be careful not to scratch the piston with the ends of the ring. The rings are brittle, and will snap if they are spread too far. They're also very sharp - protect your hands and fingers. Note that the third (oil control) ring consists of a spacer and two side rails. Always remove the rings from the top of the piston. Keep each set of rings with its piston if the old rings are to be re-used.

3 Scrape away all traces of carbon from the top of the piston. A hand-held wire brush (or a piece of fine emery cloth) can be used, once the majority of the deposits have been scraped away. The piston identification markings should now be visible.

4 Remove the carbon from the ring grooves in the piston, using an old ring. Break the ring in half to do this (be careful not to cut your fingers). Be careful to remove only the carbon deposits - do not remove any metal, and do not nick or scratch the sides of the ring grooves.

5 Once the deposits have been removed, clean the piston/connecting rod assembly with paraffin or a suitable solvent, and dry thoroughly. Make sure that the oil return holes in the ring grooves are clear.

6 If the pistons and cylinder bores are not damaged or worn excessively, and if the cylinder block does not need to be rebored, the original pistons can be refitted. Normal piston wear shows up as even vertical wear on the piston thrust surfaces, and slight looseness of the top ring in its groove. New piston rings should always be used when the engine is reassembled.

7 Carefully inspect each piston for cracks around the skirt, around the gudgeon pin holes, and at the piston ring "lands" (between the ring grooves).

8 Look for scoring and scuffing on the piston skirt, holes in the piston crown, and burned areas at the edge of the crown. If the skirt is scored or scuffed, the engine may have been suffering from overheating, and/or abnormal combustion which caused excessively high operating temperatures. The cooling and lubrication systems should be checked thoroughly. Scorch marks on the sides of the pistons show that blow-by has occurred. A hole in the piston crown, or burned areas at the edge of the piston crown, indicates that abnormal combustion (pre-ignition, knocking, or detonation) has been occurring. If any of the above problems exist, the causes must be investigated and corrected, or the damage will occur again. The causes may include incorrect ignition timing, or a faulty carburettor/injector (as applicable).

9 Corrosion of the piston, in the form of pitting, indicates that coolant has been leaking into the combustion chamber and/or the crankcase. Again, the cause must be corrected, or the problem may persist in the rebuilt engine.

10 Examine each connecting rod carefully for signs of damage, such as cracks around the big-end and small-end bearings. Check that the rod is not bent or distorted. Damage is highly unlikely, unless the engine has been seized or badly overheated. Detailed checking of the connecting rod assembly can only be carried out by a Proton dealer or engine repair specialist with the necessary equipment.

11 The gudgeon pins are an interference fit in the connecting rod small-end bearing. Therefore, piston and/or connecting rod renewal should be entrusted to a Proton dealer or engine repair specialist, who will have the necessary tooling to remove and install the gudgeon pins. If new pistons are to be fitted, ensure that the correct size pistons are fitted to each bore (see Section 12).

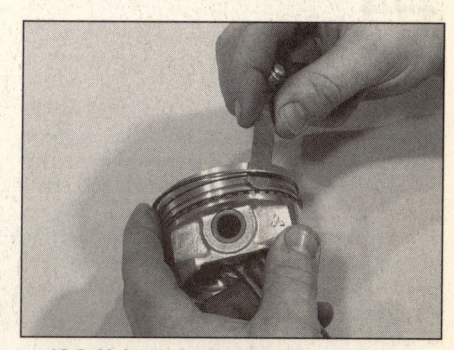

13.2 Using a feeler blade to remove a piston ring

2B•12 General engine overhaul procedures

14.2 Using a dial gauge to measure crankshaft endfloat

14.3 Using feeler blades to check crankshaft endfloat

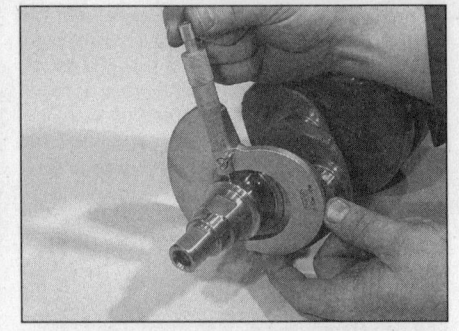

14.10 Using a micrometer to measure a crankshaft journal

14 Crankshaft - inspection

Checking crankshaft endfloat

1 If the crankshaft endfloat is to be checked, this must be done when the crankshaft is still installed in the cylinder block, but is free to move (see Section 11).
2 Check the endfloat using a dial gauge in contact with the end of the crankshaft. Push the crankshaft fully one way, and then zero the gauge. Push the crankshaft fully the other way, and check the endfloat **(see illustration)**. The result can be compared with the specified amount, and will give an indication as to whether new main bearing shells are required.
3 If a dial gauge is not available, feeler gauges can be used. First push the crankshaft fully towards the flywheel end of the engine, then use feeler gauges to measure the gap between the web of the crankpin and the timing belt side of the centre main bearing shell **(see illustration)**.

Inspection

4 Clean the crankshaft using paraffin or a suitable solvent, and dry it, preferably with compressed air if available. Be sure to clean the oil holes with a pipe cleaner or similar probe, to ensure that they are not obstructed.

⚠ *Warning: Wear eye protection when using compressed air.*

5 Check the main and big-end bearing journals for uneven wear, scoring, pitting and cracking.
6 Big-end bearing wear is accompanied by distinct metallic knocking when the engine is running (particularly noticeable when the engine is pulling from low speed) and some loss of oil pressure.
7 Main bearing wear is accompanied by severe engine vibration and rumble - getting progressively worse as engine speed increases - and again by loss of oil pressure.
8 Check the bearing journal for roughness by running a finger lightly over the bearing surface. Any roughness (which will be accompanied by obvious bearing wear) indicates that the crankshaft requires regrinding (where possible) or renewal.
9 If the crankshaft has been reground, check for burrs around the crankshaft oil holes (the holes are usually chamfered, so burrs should not be a problem unless regrinding has been carried out carelessly). Remove any burrs with a fine file or scraper, and thoroughly clean the oil holes as described previously.
10 Using a micrometer, measure the diameter of the main and big-end bearing journals, and compare the results with the Specifications **(see illustration)**. By measuring the diameter at a number of points around each journal's circumference, you will be able to determine whether or not the journal is out-of-round. Take the measurement at each end of the journal, near the webs, to determine if the journal is tapered. Compare the results obtained with those given in the Specifications.
11 Check the oil seal contact surfaces at each end of the crankshaft for wear and damage. If the seal has worn a deep groove in the surface of the crankshaft, consult an engine overhaul specialist; repair may be possible, but otherwise a new crankshaft will be required.
12 At the time of writing, oversize bearing shells were available only for the 8-valve engine. On 8-valve engines, if the crankshaft journals have not already been reground, it may be possible to have the crankshaft reconditioned, and to fit oversize shells; Proton produce both big-end and main bearing shells in the following sizes; 0.25 mm, 0.50 mm and 0.75 mm oversize. On 12-valve engines, due to the design of the crankshaft, no oversize shells are produced by Proton and if the crankshaft has worn beyond the specified limits, it will have to be renewed. Seek the advice of a Proton dealer or engine overhaul specialist for further information.

15 Main and big-end bearings - inspection

1 Even though the main and big-end bearings should be renewed during the engine overhaul, the old bearings should be retained for close examination, as they may reveal valuable information about the condition of the engine.
2 Bearing failure can occur due to lack of lubrication, the presence of dirt or other foreign particles, overloading the engine, or corrosion **(see illustration)**. Regardless of the cause of bearing failure, the cause must be corrected (where applicable) before the engine is reassembled, to prevent it from happening again.

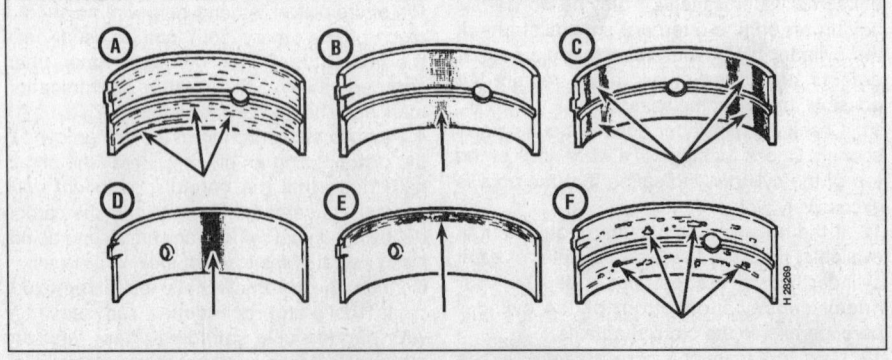

15.2 Typical bearing failures

A Scratched by dirt; dirt embedded in bearing material
B Lack of oil; overlay wiped out
C Improper seating; bright (polished) sections
D Tapered journal; overlay gone from entire surface
E Radius ride
F Fatigue failure; craters or pockets

General engine overhaul procedures 2B•13

3 When examining the bearing shells, remove them from the cylinder block, the main bearing caps, the connecting rods and the connecting rod big-end bearing caps. Lay them out on a clean surface in the same general position as their location in the engine. This will enable you to match any bearing problems with the corresponding crankshaft journal.
4 Dirt and other foreign matter gets into the engine in a variety of ways. It may be left in the engine during assembly, or it may pass through filters or the crankcase ventilation system. It may get into the oil, and from there into the bearings. Metal chips from machining operations and normal engine wear are often present. Abrasives are sometimes left in engine components after reconditioning, especially when parts are not thoroughly cleaned using the proper cleaning methods. Whatever the source, these foreign objects often end up embedded in the soft bearing material, and are easily recognised. Large particles will not embed in the bearing, and will score or gouge the bearing and journal. The best prevention for this cause of bearing failure is to clean all parts thoroughly, and keep everything spotlessly-clean during engine assembly. Frequent and regular engine oil and filter changes are also recommended.
5 Lack of lubrication (or lubrication breakdown) has a number of interrelated causes. Excessive heat (which thins the oil), overloading (which squeezes the oil from the bearing face) and oil leakage (from excessive bearing clearances, worn oil pump or high engine speeds) all contribute to lubrication breakdown. Blocked oil passages, which usually are the result of misaligned oil holes in a bearing shell, will also oil-starve a bearing, and destroy it. When lack of lubrication is the cause of bearing failure, the bearing material is wiped or extruded from the steel backing of the bearing. Temperatures may increase to the point where the steel backing turns blue from overheating.
6 Driving habits can have a definite effect on bearing life. Full-throttle, low-speed operation (labouring the engine) puts very high loads on bearings, tending to squeeze out the oil film. These loads cause the bearings to flex, which produces fine cracks in the bearing face (fatigue failure). Eventually, the bearing material will loosen in pieces, and tear away from the steel backing.
7 Short-distance driving leads to corrosion of bearings, because insufficient engine heat is produced to drive off the condensed water and corrosive gases. These products collect in the engine oil, forming acid and sludge. As the oil is carried to the engine bearings, the acid attacks and corrodes the bearing material.
8 Incorrect bearing installation during engine assembly will lead to bearing failure as well. Tight-fitting bearings leave insufficient bearing running clearance, and will result in oil starvation. Dirt or foreign particles trapped behind a bearing shell result in high spots on the bearing, which lead to failure.
9 As mentioned at the beginning of this Section, the bearing shells should be renewed as a matter of course during engine overhaul; to do otherwise is false economy.

16 Engine overhaul - reassembly sequence

1 Before reassembly begins, ensure that all new parts have been obtained, and that all necessary tools are available. Read through the entire procedure to familiarise yourself with the work involved, and to ensure that all items necessary for reassembly of the engine are at hand. In addition to all normal tools and materials, thread-locking compound will be needed. A good quality tube of liquid sealant will also be required for the joint faces that are fitted without gaskets.
2 In order to save time and avoid problems, engine reassembly can be carried out in the following order:
  a) Crankshaft.
  b) Piston/connecting rod assemblies.
  c) Oil pump.
  d) Sump.
  e) Flywheel/driveplate.
  f) Cylinder head.
  g) Timing belt tensioner and sprockets, and timing belt.
  h) Engine external components.
3 At this stage, all engine components should be absolutely clean and dry, with all faults repaired. The components should be laid out (or in individual containers) on a completely clean work surface.

17 Piston rings - refitting

1 Before fitting new piston rings, the ring end gaps must be checked as follows.
2 Lay out the piston/connecting rod assemblies and the new piston ring sets, so that the ring sets will be matched with the same piston and cylinder during the end gap measurement and subsequent engine reassembly.
3 Insert the top ring into the first cylinder, and push it down the bore using the top of the piston. This will ensure that the ring remains square with the cylinder walls. Push the ring down into the bore until the piston skirt is level with the block mating surface, then withdraw the piston.
4 Measure the end gap using feeler gauges, and compare the measurements with the figures given in the Specifications (see illustration).
5 If the gap is too small (unlikely if genuine Proton parts are used), it must be enlarged, or the ring ends may contact each other during engine operation, causing serious damage. Ideally, new piston rings providing the correct end gap should be fitted. As a last resort, the end gap can be increased by filing the ring ends very carefully with a fine file. Mount the file in a vice with soft jaws, slip the ring over the file with the ends contacting the file face, and slowly move the ring to remove material from the ends. Take care, as piston rings are sharp, and are easily broken.
6 With new piston rings, it is unlikely that the end gap will be too large. If the gaps are too large, check that you have the correct rings for your engine and for the particular cylinder bore size.
7 Repeat the checking procedure for each ring in the first cylinder, and then for the rings in the remaining cylinders. Remember to keep rings, pistons and cylinders matched up.
8 Once the ring end gaps have been checked and if necessary corrected, the rings can be fitted to the pistons.
9 Fit the piston rings using the same technique as for removal. Fit the bottom (oil control) spacer first then install both the side rails, noting that both the spacer and side rails can be installed either way up. Fit the second and top compression rings ensuring that each ring is fitted the correct way up with its identification mark uppermost (see illustrations). Note: *Always follow any instructions supplied with the new piston ring sets - different manufacturers may specify different procedures. Do not mix up the top and second compression rings, as they have different cross-sections.*

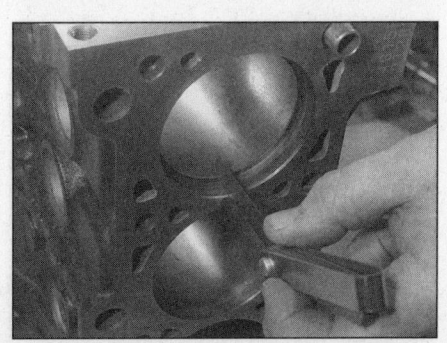

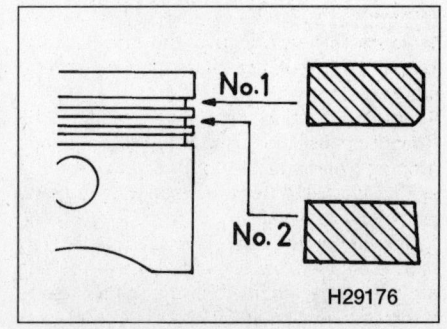

17.4 Checking a piston ring end gap

17.9a Ensure the top and second compression rings are fitted in the correct locations . . .

2B•14 General engine overhaul procedures

10 With the piston rings correctly installed, check that each ring is free to rotate easily in its groove. Position the ring end gaps as shown (see illustration).

18 Crankshaft - refitting and main bearing running clearance check

Note: *It is recommended that new main bearing shells are fitted regardless of the condition of the original ones.*

Selection of bearing shells

8-valve engine

1 There are four different sizes of bearing shell available; the standard size shell for use with an original crankshaft and three different sizes of oversize for use once the crankshaft has been reground.

2 The relevant set of bearing shells required can be obtained by measuring the diameter of the crankshaft main bearing journals (see Section 14). This will show if the crankshaft is original or whether its journals have been reground, identifying if either standard or oversize bearing shells are required. If the access to the necessary measuring equipment cannot be gained, the size of the bearing shells can be identified by the markings stamped on the rear of each shell **(see illustration)**. Details of these markings should be supplied to your Proton dealer who will then be able to identify the size of shell fitted.

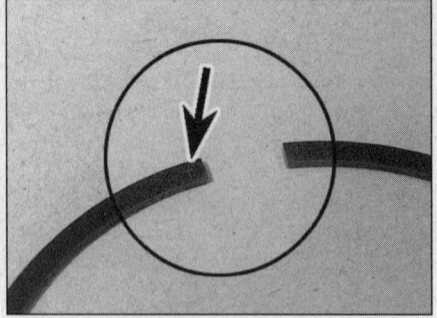

17.9b ... with their identification markings (arrowed) uppermost

3 Whether the original shells or new shells are being fitted, it is recommended that the running clearance is checked as follows prior to installation.

12-valve engine

4 On the 12-valve engine, at the time of writing, only standard size bearing shells were available. Proton do not produce oversize bearing shells. Whether the original shells or new shells are being fitted, it is recommended that the running clearance is checked as follows prior to installation.

Main bearing running clearance check

5 Clean the backs of the bearing shells and the bearing locations in both the cylinder block and the main bearing caps.

6 Press the bearing shells into their locations, ensuring that the tab on each shell engages in the notch in the cylinder block or main bearing cap. Ensure the flanged bearing shells are fitted to the centre (No 3) main bearing (both upper and lower bearings) and that four grooved bearing shells are fitted in the upper (No 1, 2, 4 and 5) locations in the block and the plain bearing shells to the (No 1, 2, 4 and 5) bearing caps **(see illustrations)**. If the original bearing shells are being used for the check ensure they are refitted in their original locations. The clearance can be checked in either of two ways.

7 One method (which will be difficult to achieve without a range of internal

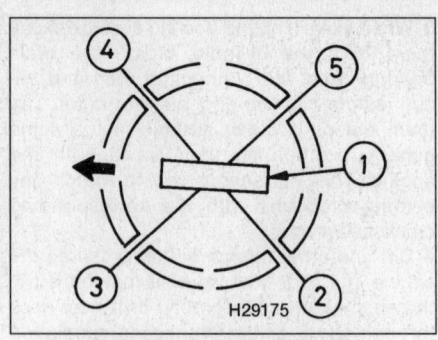

17.10 Ring end gap positions - arrow points towards the timing belt end of the engine

1. *Gudgeon pin*
2. *Oil control (bottom) ring lower side rail gap*
3. *Second compression ring and oil control (bottom) ring spacer gap*
4. *Oil control (bottom) ring upper side rail gap*
5. *Top compression ring gap*

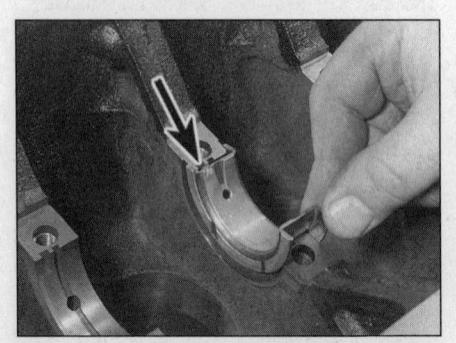

micrometers or internal/external expanding calipers) is to refit the main bearing caps to the cylinder block, with bearing shells in place. With the cap retaining bolts correctly tightened, measure the internal diameter of each assembled pair of bearing shells. If the diameter of each corresponding crankshaft journal is measured and then subtracted from the bearing internal diameter, the result will be the main bearing running clearance.

8 The second (and more accurate) method is to use a product known as Plastigauge. This consists of a fine thread of perfectly round plastic which is compressed between the bearing shell and the journal. When the shell is removed, the plastic is deformed and can be measured with a special card gauge supplied with the kit. The running clearance is determined from this gauge. Plastigauge is sometimes difficult to obtain but enquiries at one of the larger specialist quality motor factors should produce the name of a stockist in your area. The procedure for using Plastigauge is as follows.

18.2 Typical marking on the back of a bearing shell

18.6a Fit the bearing shells ensuring their tabs are correctly aligned with the notches in the cylinder block/caps

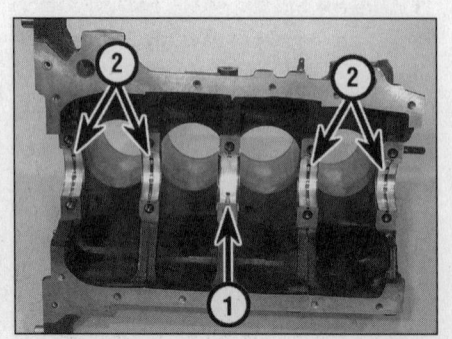

18.6b The centre main bearing shells (1) are flanged whilst the other upper bearing shells (2) are grooved ...

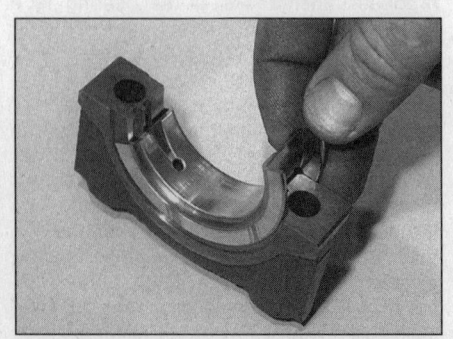

18.6c ... all the lower bearing shells are plain with the flanged bearing (shown) being fitted to the centre cap

General engine overhaul procedures 2B•15

18.10 Lay a strip of Plastigauge on the clean journal then refit the bearing cap and tighten its bolts to the specified torque

18.11 Remove the bearing cap carefully to reveal the crushed Plastigauge . . .

9 With the main bearing upper shells in place, carefully lay the crankshaft in position. Do not use any lubricant; the crankshaft journals and bearing shells must be perfectly clean and dry.

10 Cut several lengths of the appropriate size Plastigauge (they should be slightly shorter than the width of the main bearings) and place one length carefully on each crankshaft journal axis **(see illustration)**.

11 With the main bearing lower shells in position, refit the main bearing caps, tightening their retaining bolts to the specified torque. Take care not to disturb the Plastigauge and **do not** rotate the crankshaft at any time during this operation. Remove the main bearing caps again taking great care not to disturb the Plastigauge or rotate the crankshaft **(see illustration)**.

12 Compare the width of the crushed Plastigauge on each journal to the scale printed on the Plastigauge envelope to obtain the main bearing running clearance **(see illustration)**. Compare the clearance measured with that given in the Specifications at the start of this Chapter.

13 If the clearance is significantly different from that expected, the bearing shells may be the wrong size (or excessively worn if the original shells are being re-used). Before deciding that the crankshaft is worn, make sure that no dirt or oil was trapped between the bearing shells and the caps or block when the clearance was measured. If the Plastigauge was wider at one end than at the other, the crankshaft journal may be tapered.

14 Before condemning the components concerned, seek the advice of your Proton dealer or engine repair specialist. They will be able to inform as to the best course of action and whether it is possible to have the crankshaft journals reground (where possible) or whether renewal will be necessary.

15 Where necessary, obtain the correct size of bearing shell and repeat the running clearance checking procedure as described above.

16 On completion, carefully scrape away all traces of the Plastigauge material from the crankshaft and bearing shells using a fingernail or other object which is unlikely to score the bearing surfaces.

Final crankshaft refitting

17 Carefully lift the crankshaft out of the cylinder block once more.

18 Place the bearing shells in their locations as described above in paragraphs 5 and 6. If new shells are being fitted, ensure that all traces of the protective grease are cleaned off using paraffin. Wipe dry the shells and caps with a lint-free cloth.

19 Liberally lubricate each bearing shell in the cylinder block with clean engine oil then lower the crankshaft into position ensuring that the bearing shells remain correctly seated **(see illustration)**.

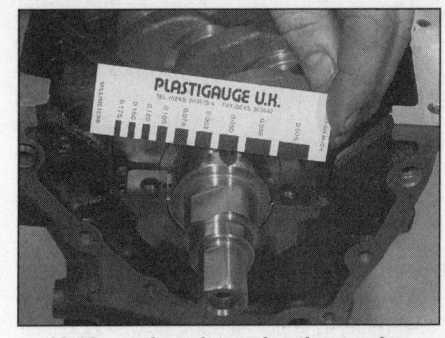

20 Check the crankshaft endfloat as described in Section 14.

21 Ensure the bearing shells are correctly located in the caps and refit the caps to the cylinder block. Ensure the caps are fitted in their correct locations, with No 1 cap at the timing belt end, and are fitted the correct way around so that all the arrows point towards the timing belt end of the engine. Insert the bearing cap bolts and tighten them to the specified torque setting **(see illustrations)**.

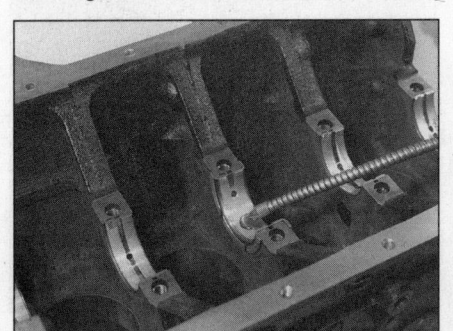

18.12 . . . then determine the running clearance by measuring the Plastigauge using the scale provided

18.19 Lubricate the bearing shells with clean engine oil before fitting the crankshaft

18.21a Refit the bearing caps . . .

18.21b . . . and tighten the main bearing bolts to the specified torque setting

2B•16 General engine overhaul procedures

18.22 Support the housing and tap out the rear oil seal using a hammer and punch

18.23a Ensure the locating pins (arrowed) are in position and fit the new gasket

22 Securely support the outer face of the rear oil seal housing and carefully tap out the crankshaft oil seal from behind using a hammer and punch **(see illustration)**. Fit the new oil seal, ensuring its sealing lip is facing inwards, and press it squarely into the housing using a tubular drift which bears only on the hard outer edge of the seal.
23 Ensure the locating dowels are in position, then wipe clean the mating faces of the oil seal housing and cylinder block and position the new gasket on the cylinder block face. Carefully ease the seal housing into position, taking great care not to damage the oil seal lip as it passes over the end of the crankshaft, and securely tighten its retaining bolts **(see illustrations)**.
24 Refit/reconnect the piston connecting rod assemblies to the crankshaft as described in Section 19.
25 Refit the oil pump, flywheel/driveplate, cylinder head, timing belt sprockets (as applicable) and fit a new timing belt as described in Part A.

19 Piston/connecting rod assembly - refitting and big-end running clearance check

Note: *It is recommended that new piston rings and big-end bearing shells are fitted regardless of the condition of the original ones.*

Selection of bearing shells

1 See Section 18.

Big-end bearing running clearance check

2 Clean the backs of the bearing shells and the bearing locations in both the connecting rod and bearing cap.
3 Press the bearing shells into their locations, ensuring that the tab on each shell engages in the notch in the connecting rod and cap **(see illustration)**. If the original bearing shells are being used for the check ensure they are refitted in their original locations. The clearance can be checked in either of two ways.
4 One method is to refit the big-end bearing cap to the connecting rod, with bearing shells in place. With the cap retaining nuts correctly tightened, use an internal micrometer or vernier caliper to measure the internal diameter of each assembled pair of bearing shells. If the diameter of each corresponding crankshaft journal is measured and then subtracted from the bearing internal diameter, the result will be the big-end bearing running clearance.
5 The second method is to use Plastigauge as described in Section 18, paragraphs 8 to 16. Place a strand of Plastigauge on each (cleaned) crankpin journal and refit the (clean) piston/connecting rod assemblies, shells and big-end bearing caps. On 8-valve engines, tighten the nuts to the specified torque wrench setting and on 12-valve engines tighten the nuts as described in paragraph 12. Take care not to disturb the Plastigauge. Dismantle the assemblies without rotating the crankshaft and use the scale printed on the Plastigauge envelope to obtain the big-end bearing running clearance. On completion of the measurement, carefully scrape off all traces of Plastigauge from the journal and shells using a fingernail or other object which will not score the components.

18.23b Carefully ease the housing into position, taking care not to damage the oil seal lip ...

18.23c ... and securely tighten its retaining bolts

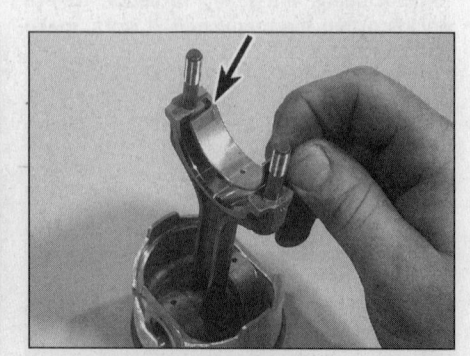

19.3 Fit the bearing shells making sure their tabs are correctly engaged with the rod/cap notch (arrowed)

General engine overhaul procedures 2B•17

19.9a Insert the piston/connecting rod assembly, ensuring the piston marking (arrowed) is pointing towards the timing belt end of the engine . . .

19.9b . . . and carefully tap the assembly into the cylinder using a hammer handle

Final piston/connecting rod assembly refitting

6 Ensure the bearing shells are correctly refitted as described above in paragraphs 2 and 3. If new shells are being fitted, ensure that all traces of the protective grease are cleaned off using paraffin. Wipe dry the shells and connecting rods with a lint-free cloth.

7 Lubricate the bores, the pistons and piston rings then lay out each piston/connecting rod assembly in its respective position.

8 Starting with assembly number 1, make sure that the piston rings are still spaced as described in Section 17, then clamp them in position with a piston ring compressor.

9 Insert the piston/connecting rod assembly into the top of cylinder No 1, ensuring that the arrow marking on the piston crown is pointing towards the timing belt end of the engine. Using a block of wood or hammer handle against the piston crown, tap the assembly into the cylinder until the piston crown is flush with the top of the cylinder **(see illustrations)**.

10 Taking care not to mark the cylinder bore, liberally lubricate the crankpin and both bearing shells, then pull the piston/connecting rod assembly down the bore and onto the crankpin and refit the big-end bearing cap using the markings to ensure it is fitted the correct way around (the upper and lower bearing shells locating tabs should be on the same side) **(see illustration)**.

11 On 8-valve engines, refit the bearing cap nuts and tighten them evenly and progressively to the specified torque setting.

12 On 12-valve engines, fit the bearing cap nuts and tighten them evenly and progressively to the Stage 1 torque setting. Fully slacken both nuts then tighten both nuts to the specified Stage 2 torque setting and then angle-tighten them through the specified Stage 3 angle, using a socket and extension bar **(see illustrations)**. It is recommended that an angle-measuring gauge is used during this stage of the tightening, to ensure accuracy.

19.10 Pull the connecting rod down onto the crankshaft and refit the bearing cap

13 Refit the remaining three piston and connecting rod assemblies in the same way.

14 Rotate the crankshaft, and check that it turns freely, with no signs of binding or tight spots.

15 Refit oil pump, sump and the cylinder head as described in Part A of this Chapter.

19.12a On 12-valve models, tighten the bearing cap nuts to the Stage 1 torque setting, then slacken them and tighten them to the Stage 2 torque . . .

19.12b . . . before tightening them through the specified Stage 3 angle

20 Engine - initial start up after overhaul

1 With the engine refitted in the vehicle, double-check the engine oil and coolant levels. Make a final check that everything has been reconnected, and that there are no tools or rags left in the engine compartment.
2 Remove the spark plugs. On 8-valve models, disable the ignition system by disconnecting the ignition HT coil lead from the distributor cap and earthing it on the cylinder block. Use a jumper lead or similar wire to make a good connection. On 12-valve models, disable the ignition system by disconnecting the wiring connector(s) from the distributor (see Chapter 5).
3 Turn the engine on the starter until the oil pressure warning light goes out. Refit the spark plugs, and reconnect the spark plug (HT) leads, referring to Chapter 1 for further information. Reconnect any HT leads or wiring which was disconnected in paragraph 2.
4 Start the engine, noting that this may take a little longer than usual, due to the fuel system components having been disturbed.
5 While the engine is idling, check for fuel, water and oil leaks. Don't be alarmed if there are some odd smells and smoke from parts getting hot and burning off oil deposits.
6 Assuming all is well, keep the engine idling until hot water is felt circulating through the top hose, then switch off the engine.
7 Check the ignition timing, and the idle speed settings (as appropriate), then switch the engine off. If necessary, remove the cylinder head cover and recheck the valve clearances with the engine "hot".
8 After a few minutes, recheck the oil and coolant levels as described in *"Weekly checks"*, and top-up as necessary.
9 If new pistons, rings or crankshaft bearings have been fitted, the engine must be treated as new, and run-in for the first 500 miles (800 km). *Do not* operate the engine at full-throttle, or allow it to labour at low engine speeds in any gear. It is recommended that the oil and filter be changed at the end of this period.

Chapter 3
Cooling, heating and ventilation systems

Contents

Air conditioning system - general information and precautions 10	Cooling fan switch - testing, removal and refitting 6
Air conditioning system components - removal and refitting 11	Cooling system hoses - disconnection and renewal 2
Air conditioning system - refrigerant level check .... see Chapter 1	General information and precautions 1
Auxiliary cooling fan - testing, removal and refitting 5	Heater/ventilation components - removal and refitting 9
Coolant level check .... see 'Weekly Checks'	Radiator - removal, inspection and refitting 3
Coolant pump - removal, inspection and refitting 7	Temperature gauge coolant sensor - testing, removal and refitting . 8
Coolant renewal .... see Chapter 1	Thermostat - removal, testing and refitting 4

Degrees of difficulty

Easy, suitable for novice with little experience	Fairly easy, suitable for beginner with some experience	Fairly difficult, suitable for competent DIY mechanic	Difficult, suitable for experienced DIY mechanic	Very difficult, suitable for expert DIY or professional

Specifications

General
Radiator cap relief valve opening pressure	0.75 - 1.05 bar
Radiator cap vacuum valve opening depression	< 0.05 Bar
Coolant pump/alternator drivebelt deflection (tension):	
New belt	5.5 - 7.0 mm
Used belt	7.0 - 9.0 mm

Thermostat
Opening temperature:	
Starts to open at	88 °C
Fully open at	100 °C
Valve lift when fully open (approx.)	8 mm

Electric cooling fan
Cut-in temperature	90 to 94 °C
Cut-out temperature	85 to 89 °C

Temperature gauge coolant sensor
Electrical resistance:	
At 70°C	104 W
At 100°C	38 W

Torque wrench settings
	Nm	lbf ft
Coolant pump pulley securing bolts	10	7
Coolant pump to cylinder block bolts	15	11
Alternator bracing bracket (through coolant pump) to cylinder block ..	25	18
Thermostat housing cover bolts	15	11
Alternator lower mounting bolt	20	15
Alternator tensioning bolt lockbolt	10	7
Coolant temperature gauge sensor	30	22

3•2 Cooling, heating and ventilation systems

1 General information and precautions

General information

The engine cooling/cabin heating system is of the pressurised type, comprising a centrifugal coolant pump driven by the auxiliary belt, a crossflow radiator, a coolant expansion tank, an electric cooling fan, a thermostat, heater matrix, and all associated hoses and switches.

The system functions as follows: the coolant pump circulates cold water around the engine block cylinder and head passages, and through the inlet manifold, heater matrix and throttle body to the thermostat housing.

When the engine is cold, the thermostat remains closed and prevents coolant from circulating through the radiator. When the coolant reaches a predetermined temperature, the thermostat opens, and the coolant passes through the top hose to the radiator. As the coolant circulates through the radiator, it is cooled by the in-rush of air when the car is in forward motion. The airflow is supplemented by the action of the electric cooling fan, when necessary. As the temperature of the coolant in the radiator drops, it flows to the bottom of the radiator by convection, and passes out through the bottom hose to the coolant pump - the cycle is then repeated.

When the engine is at normal operating temperature, the coolant expands, and some of it is displaced into the expansion tank. Coolant collects in the tank, and is returned to the radiator when the system cools. The tank is a separate unit to the radiator, mounted on the right hand side of the engine compartment.

The electric cooling fan, which is mounted on the engine side of the radiator, is controlled by a thermostatic switch. At a predetermined coolant temperature, the switch/sensor actuates the fan to provide additional airflow through the radiator. The switch cuts the electrical supply to the fan when the coolant temperature has dropped below a preset threshold (see *Specifications*).

Precautions

Warning: Do not attempt to remove the radiator pressure cap, or to disturb any part of the cooling system, while the engine is hot, as there is a high risk of scalding. If the radiator pressure cap must be removed before the engine and radiator have fully cooled (even though this is not recommended), the pressure in the cooling system must first be relieved. Cover the cap with a thick layer of cloth, to avoid scalding, and slowly unscrew the pressure cap until a hissing sound is heard. When the hissing stops, indicating that the pressure has reduced, slowly unscrew the pressure cap until it can be removed; if more hissing sounds are heard, wait until they have stopped before unscrewing the cap completely. At all times, keep your face well away from the pressure cap opening, and protect your hands.

Warning: Do not allow antifreeze to come into contact with your skin, or with the painted surfaces of the vehicle. Rinse off spills immediately, with plenty of water. Never leave antifreeze lying around in an open container, or in a puddle in the driveway or on the garage floor. Children and pets are attracted by its sweet smell, but antifreeze can be fatal if ingested.

Warning: If the engine is hot, the electric cooling fan may start rotating, even if the engine and ignition are switched off. Be careful to keep your hands, hair, and any loose clothing well clear when working in the engine compartment.

2 Cooling system hoses - disconnection and renewal

1 The number, routing and pattern of hoses will vary slightly according to model, but the same basic procedure applies. Before commencing work, make sure that the new hoses are to hand, along with new hose clips if needed. It is good practice to renew the hose clips at the same time as the hoses.

2 Drain the cooling system, as described in Chapter 1, saving the coolant if it is fit for re-use. Squirt a little penetrating oil onto the hose clips if they are corroded.

3 Release the hose clips from the hose concerned. Three types of clip are used; worm-drive, spring and "sardine-can". The worm-drive clip is released by turning its screw anti-clockwise. The spring clip is released by squeezing its tags together with pliers, at the same time working the clip away from the hose stub. The "sardine-can" clips are not re-usable, and are best cut off with snips or side cutters.

4 Unclip any wires, cables or other hoses which may be attached to the hose being removed. Make notes for reference when reassembling if necessary.

5 Release the hose from its stubs with a twisting motion. Be careful not to damage the stubs on delicate components such as the radiator, or thermostat housings. If the hose is stuck fast, the best course is often to cut it off using a sharp knife, but again be careful not to damage the stubs.

6 Before fitting the new hose, smear the stubs with washing-up liquid or a suitable rubber lubricant to aid fitting. Do not use oil or grease, which may attack the rubber.

7 Fit the hose clips over the ends of the hose, then fit the hose over its stubs. Work the hose into position. When satisfied, locate and tighten the hose clips.

8 Refill the cooling system as described in Chapter 1. Run the engine, and check that there are no leaks.

9 Recheck the tightness of the hose clips on any new hoses after a few hundred miles.

10 Top-up the coolant level, if necessary.

3 Radiator - removal, inspection and refitting

Removal

Note: *If the radiator, bear in mind that minor leaks can often be cured using proprietary radiator sealing compound, with the radiator in situ.*

1 Disconnect the battery negative cable and position it away from the terminal. Unplug the electrical wiring from the auxiliary cooling fan at the connector - see Section 6 for details.

2 At the heater control panel, set the temperature control lever the 'HOT' position, then drain the cooling system as described in Chapter 1.

3 Slacken the clips and disconnect the top, bottom and overflow coolant hoses from the radiator **(see illustrations)**.

4 Slacken and remove the radiator upper mounting bolts. Support the radiator, then remove the lower mounting bolts **(see illustration)**.

3.3a Slacken the clips and disconnect the top . . .

3.3b . . . and bottom hoses from the radiator

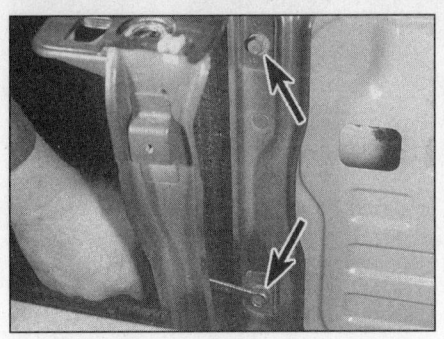

Cooling, heating and ventilation systems 3•3

3.4 Removing a radiator lower mounting bolt

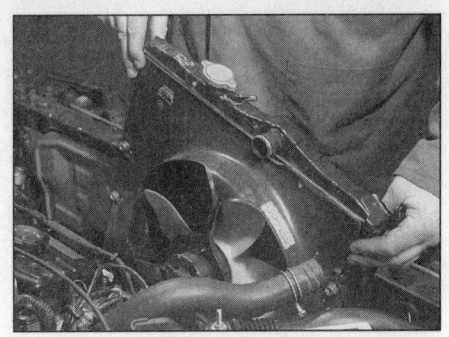

3.5 Carefully lift the radiator from the engine compartment

5 Carefully tilt the radiator back towards the engine, then lift it from the engine compartment, complete with the auxiliary cooling fan and motor **(see illustration)**.

Inspection

6 If the radiator has been removed due to suspected blockage, it may be flushed out as described in the coolant renewal procedure (see Chapter 1).

7 Foreign bodies (such as leaves, dust or insects) lodged between the cooling fins will impede the air flow through the radiator and reduce its cooling efficiency. Clean out all traces of dirt and debris using a soft brush or a compressed air supply, if one is available. Note that the cooling fins are quite fragile and can easily be damaged by rough treatment.

⚠ *Warning: Eye protection should be worn, if compressed air is used to clean the radiator. Be careful,* *as the edges of the cooling fins are sharp enough to cause injury.*

8 If necessary, a radiator specialist can perform a "flow test" on the radiator, to establish whether an internal blockage exists.

9 A leaking radiator must be referred to a specialist for permanent repair. Do not attempt to weld or solder a leaking radiator, as damage to the plastic components may result. **Note:** *In an emergency, minor leaks from the radiator can often be cured by using a suitable radiator sealing compound, in accordance with its manufacturer's instructions, with the radiator in situ.*

10 Inspect the radiator mounting bolts. Renew them if they are badly corroded.

Refitting

11 Refitting is a reversal of removal. On completion, refill the cooling system as described in Chapter 1.

4 Thermostat - removal, testing and refitting

General

1 On 8-valve and 12-valve carburettor models, the thermostat housing is integral with the inlet manifold and is located at the right hand end of the manifold casting. On MPi models, the thermostat is mounted in a separate housing, which is bolted to the right hand side of the cylinder head, adjacent to the inlet manifold.

Removal

2 Refer to Chapter 1 and drain approximately one third of the coolant from the cooling system. Provided that the coolant is in good condition (free from corrosion deposits) it can be retained and reused later.

3 Slacken the clip and detach the coolant hose from the thermostat housing cover **(see illustrations)**.

4 Unscrew the securing bolts, and remove the cover from the thermostat housing **(see illustration)**. If it sticks, tap it *gently* with a soft-faced mallet, first on one side and then the other to free it - **do not** lever between the mating faces. Recover the remains of the old gasket.

5 Remove the gasket, then lift the thermostat from its housing **(see illustrations)**.

Testing

6 A rough test of the thermostat may be made by suspending it with a piece of string in a container full of water. Heat the water to bring it to the boil and observe the movement of the thermostat valve.

7 As a rough guide, the thermostat valve must be fully open by the time the water boils. If a thermometer is available, the opening temperature of the thermostat may be determined more precisely. With the valve fully open, measure the valve lift with a ruler. Compare the opening temperature and valve lift figures with those given in the *Specifications*. Renew the thermostat if its operation is suspect.

4.3a Slacken the clip . . .

4.3b . . . and detach the coolant hose from the thermostat housing cover (MPi shown)

4.4 Remove the cover from the thermostat housing (8V/12V model shown)

4.5a Remove the gasket . . .

4.5b . . . then lift the thermostat from its housing (MPi model shown)

3•4 Cooling, heating and ventilation systems

4.10 Fit the new thermostat squarely into its housing (8V/12V model shown)

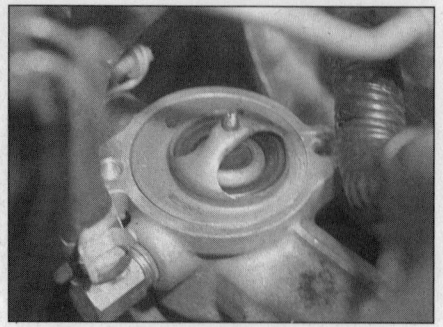

4.11 Correctly fitted thermostat (MPi model shown)

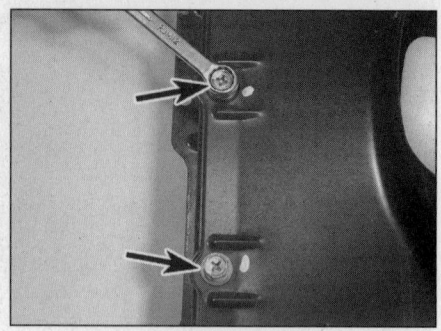

5.3 Radiator auxiliary cooling fan securing bolts (arrowed)

8 Remove the thermostat from the water, allow it to cool and check that the valve closes. Renew the thermostat if the valve fails to close completely.

Refitting

9 Ensure that the thermostat housing and cover mating surfaces are completely clean and free from all traces of the old gasket material.
10 Fit the thermostat squarely into its housing, observing the correct orientation - the compression spring side of the thermostat must face downwards **(see illustration)**.
11 Lay a new gasket in position over the thermostat **(see illustration)**. Fit the thermostat housing cover in position, then insert the retaining bolts, and tighten to the specified torque.
Caution: Take care to avoid over-tightening the retaining bolts, as the alloy casting could easily be damaged.
12 Refit the coolant hose to the port on the thermostat housing cover and tighten the hose clip securely.
13 Refill the cooling system as described in Chapter 1.

5 Auxiliary cooling fan - removal and refitting

Removal

1 Drain the cooling system, with reference to Chapter 1.
2 Refer to Section 3 and remove the radiator / cooling fan assembly from the engine bay.
3 Remove the securing bolts, then lift the cooling fan and shroud assembly away from the radiator **(see illustration)**.
4 Slacken and withdraw the nut from the end of the motor shaft, to release the fan blades.
5 Unscrew the mounting bolts, then remove the fan motor from the shroud. Remove the screws and detach the wiring clips from the shroud support struts.

Refitting

6 Refitting is reversal of removal. On completion, refill the cooling system, as described in Chapter 1.

6 Cooling fan switch - testing, removal and refitting

Testing

1 The switch is threaded into the lower left hand corner of the radiator **(see illustration)**.
2 To test the switch, remove it from the radiator and check that the switching action occurs at the correct temperature, as follows. Connect a continuity tester, or resistance meter, across the switch connector terminals. Heat the sensor probe in a container of water, whilst monitoring the temperature of the water with a thermometer.
3 There should only be continuity (short circuit) between the switch connector terminals when the cooling fan cut-in temperature is reached (see *Specifications*). If the switch operates at a much lower temperature, or fails to operate at all, it must be renewed.

Removal

4 Disconnect the battery negative cable and position it away from the terminal.
5 Ensure that the engine has cooled completely, then drain the cooling system, with reference to Chapter 1.
6 Disconnect the wiring plug from the cooling fan switch **(see illustration)**.
7 Carefully unscrew the switch from the radiator using a ring spanner. Where applicable, recover the sealing ring.

6.1 The cooling fan switch (arrowed) is threaded into the lower left hand corner of the radiator

Refitting

8 Refitting is a reversal of removal, noting the following points:
a) If the switch was originally fitted using sealing compound (visible as coloured deposits on the switch threads), clean the switch threads thoroughly, and coat them with fresh sealing compound.
b) Where applicable, use a new sealing ring.
c) Refill the cooling system, as described in Chapter 1.

9 On completion, start the engine and run it until it reaches normal operating temperature. Allow the engine to idle and verify that the cooling fan cuts in and out correctly, as the coolant temperature rises and falls.

7 Coolant pump - removal, inspection and refitting

Removal

1 Disconnect the battery negative cable and position it away from the terminal.
2 Drain the cooling system as described in Chapter 1.
3 On models with power steering, refer to Chapter 10 and remove the power steering pump drivebelt.
4 Relieve the tension on the coolant pump/alternator drivebelt as follows: Slacken the alternator lower mounting bolt, then slacken the alternator tensioning bolt lockbolt (refer to Chapter 5A for details). Turn the

6.6 Disconnect the wiring plug from the cooling fan switch

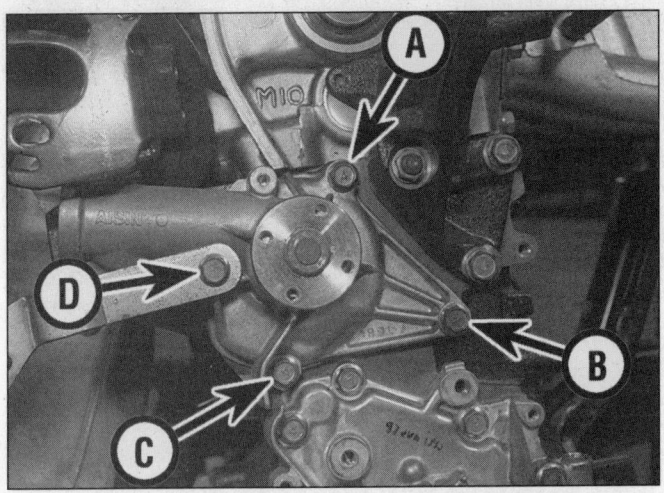

Cooling, heating and ventilation systems 3•5

7.6 Unscrew the coolant pump securing bolts (arrowed) - note the fitted position of each bolt, as they are of different lengths

A 28mm   B 28mm   C 28mm   D 65mm

7.13 Fit a new O-ring seal to the end of the water inlet pipe

tensioning bolt anticlockwise until the belt becomes loose, then remove the belt from the coolant pump pulley.

5 Counterhold the coolant pump pulley, then unscrew the securing bolts, and remove the pulley from the pump shaft. **Note:** *This is most easily achieved by wrapping an old drivebelt (or a length of old rubber hose) tightly around the pulley, to act as a strap wrench. Alternatively, a stout screwdriver can be braced between two of the pulley bolts, whilst the others are slackened.*

6 Unscrew the coolant pump securing bolts - note the fitted position of each bolt, as some are of different lengths **(see illustration)**.

7 Withdraw the coolant pump from the cylinder block and remove the remains of the gasket. If the pump sticks to the block, tap on the upper and lower surfaces of the pump casting *gently*, using a soft-faced mallet, to free it. **Do not** lever between the pump and cylinder block mating faces.

8 As the pump is withdrawn, release the water inlet pipe from the rear of the of the pump inlet port and recover the O-ring seal. Note that a new O-ring must be used on refitting.

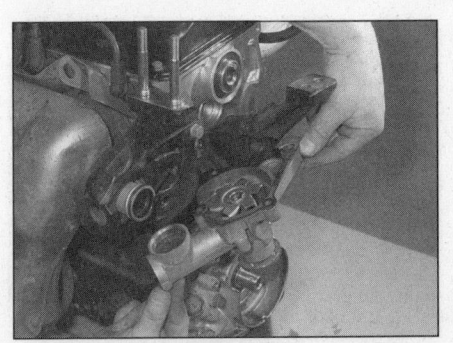

Inspection

9 Examine the pump body and impeller for signs of excessive corrosion, or damage. Turn the impeller and check its rotation. Note that a certain amount of stiffness is to be expected, as the pump shaft runs in plain bearings. However, if the shaft is difficult to turn, or feels rough in rotation, it should be renewed.

10 Grasp the impeller and attempt to slide the pump shaft backwards and forwards in its bushing. If excessive end play is evident, the pump must be renewed. Similarly, if the shaft spins easily, with little or no resistance, this indicates that the bearings and seal are worn. If this is case, then the pump must be renewed.

11 No spare components are available; the coolant pump can only be renewed as a complete assembly.

Refitting

12 Commence refitting by thoroughly cleaning the mating faces of the pump and cylinder block, to remove all traces of old gasket material.

13 Fit a new O-ring seal to the end of the water inlet pipe and lubricate it with clean water **(see illustration)**. Push the water pipe firmly into the rear of the of the pump inlet port, taking care to avoid displacing the O-ring seal. **Note:** *Do not lubricate the O-ring seal with oil or grease, as these will attack the rubber and may contaminate the cooling system.*

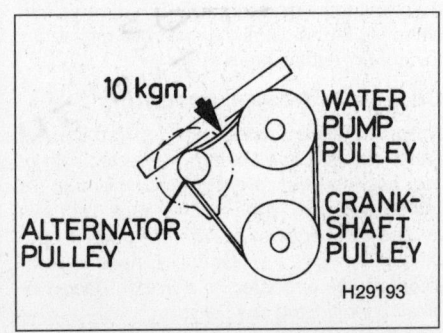

14 Place a new pump gasket in position on the cylinder block. Fit the coolant pump into position over the gasket, then loosely insert and hand tighten the securing bolts **(see illustration)**. **Note:** *The bolts are of different lengths - ensure that they are fitted in the correct positions (refer to 'Removal').*

15 Refit the pump pulley, then insert the pulley securing bolts and tighten them to the specified torque. Counterhold the pulley using one of the methods described in 'Removal'.

16 Pass the coolant pump/alternator drivebelt over the coolant pump pulley. Ensure that the ribs on the drive surface of the belt engage correctly with those on the surface of the pulley.

17 Tension the belt to the correct setting (see *Specifications*) by turning the alternator tensioning bolt clockwise (refer to Chapter 5A for details). Check the belt tension, as described in the following paragraphs.

18 Lay a piece of wood on top of the drivebelt, so that it rests on the coolant pump and alternator pulleys.

19 Apply a weight of 10 kg (with, for example, a spring balance) to the belt at a point midway between the two pulleys **(see illustration)**. Using the edge of the piece of wood as a guide, measure the amount by which the belt deflects.

20 Compare this measurement with the data given in the *Specifications*. If required, adjust the tension by turning the alternator tensioning bolt and re-check the setting **(see illustration)**. On completion, tighten the tensioning bolt lockbolt and the alternator lower mounting bolt to the specified torque.

7.14 Fit the coolant pump into position over the gasket, then insert the securing bolts

7.19 Measuring the tension of the coolant pump/alternator drivebelt

3•6 Cooling, heating and ventilation systems

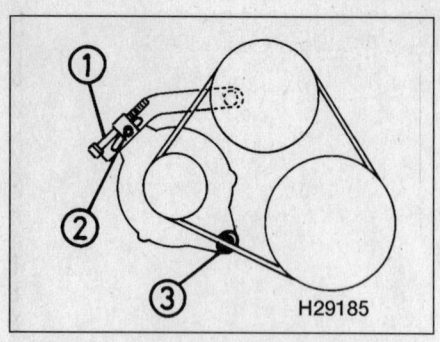

7.20 Coolant pump/alternator drivebelt tensioning mechanism

1 Adjuster bolt
2 Lockbolt
3 Alternator lower mounting bolt

21 On models with power steering, refit and tension the power steering pump drivebelt, with reference to Chapter 10.
22 Refill the cooling system, as described in Chapter 1.
23 Reconnect the battery negative lead.

8 Temperature gauge coolant sensor - testing, removal and refitting

Testing

1 On 12-valve and 8-valve models, the sensor is threaded into the underside of the inlet manifold casting. On MPI models, the sensor is threaded into the thermostat housing, adjacent to the fuel injection system coolant temperature sensor.
2 Run the engine until it reaches normal operating temperature. Switch off the engine and turn the ignition switch to the 'Off' position.
3 Unplug the wiring from the sensor terminal, and connect the probes of a resistance meter across the sensor connector terminal and a good earth point on the engine.
4 The resistance of the sensor should be between 30 and 60 W (approximately), with the engine at normal operating temperature. If the tester indicates a much different figure, then the sensor is faulty and must be renewed. Note that a sensor which reads open circuit or short circuit will manifest itself on the temperature gauge as a permanent 'fully hot' or 'fully cold' reading, with the ignition switched on.

Removal

5 Disconnect the battery negative cable and position it away from the terminal.
6 Ensure that the engine has cooled completely, then drain the cooling system, with reference to Chapter 1.
7 Disconnect the wiring plug from the coolant sensor.
8 Carefully unscrew the sensor from the manifold/thermostat housing using a ring spanner. Where applicable, recover the sealing ring.

Refitting

9 Refitting is a reversal of removal, noting the following points:
a) If the sensor was originally fitted using sealing compound (visible as coloured deposits on the switch threads), clean the switch threads thoroughly, and coat them with fresh sealing compound.
b) Where applicable, use a new sealing ring.
c) Refill the cooling system, as described in Chapter 1.

9 Heater/ventilation components - removal and refitting

Heater control unit

Removal

1 Refer to Chapter 11 and remove the glovebox assembly from the facia.
2 At the recirculation/fresh air changeover valve, mark the position of the control cable within its securing clip(s), then unhook the cable from the actuating lever.
3 Release the water valve control cable from its securing clips, after marking its position in relation to the clips, to allow correct refitting later. Disconnect the end of the control cable from the water valve actuating lever.
4 At the air outlet changeover valve, mark the position of the control cable within its securing clip(s), then unhook the cable from the actuating lever.
5 Carefully prise the knobs from heater control levers. Using a flat bladed instrument, ease the trim panel away from the front of the heater control unit.
6 Slacken and remove the securing screws, then withdraw the heater control panel from the facia, until the wiring connectors become accessible. Unplug the connectors from the rear of the control unit, making a careful note of their positions to aid refitting later.
7 Remove the heater unit from the facia completely, guiding the control cable out through the facia aperture.

Refitting

8 Refitting is a reversal of removal. Lubricate the moving parts of each of the heater unit actuating levers with multi-purpose grease, as the control cables are refitted.

Complete heater assembly

Note: *This Section does not apply to models fitted with air conditioning, where removal of the cooling unit entails disconnection of refrigerant fluid pipes. This task requires access to specialist equipment (refer to the precautions given in Section 11) and should, therefore, be entrusted to a Proton dealer, or an air conditioning specialist.*

Removal

Note: *This is an involved procedure, and it is recommended that the following Section is read through thoroughly before commencing work. Plenty of time should be allowed to complete the operation. During dismantling, make notes on the routing of all wiring and cables, and the locations of all fixings, to aid correct reassembly.*
9 Disconnect the battery negative cable and position it away from the terminal.
10 Set the heater control to 'HOT', then drain the cooling system as described in Chapter 1.
11 Refer to Chapter 11 and remove the entire facia assembly from the vehicle bulkhead. Rest the assembly on the front seats.
12 Working in the engine bay, slacken the clips and detach the heater unit coolant hoses from the ports at the bulkhead (see illustration). Recover the rubber grommets.
13 Disconnect the control cables from the heater unit, as described in the previous sub-section.
14 Detach the blower motor air ducting from the side of the heater unit (see illustration).
15 Slacken the hose clip and disconnect the heater supply hose from the pipe that protrudes from the right hand side of the heater unit. Be prepared for an amount of coolant spillage - position a container under the end of the hose and pad the surrounding area with absorbent rags.
16 Label the electrical connections to the heater assembly, to aid correct refitting later and then unplug them at the connectors.
17 Slacken and remove the securing nuts, then lift the heater assembly off its mounting studs (see illustration).
18 To remove the heater matrix core, refer to the information given in the next sub-section.

Refitting

19 Refit the heater assembly by following the removal procedure in reverse, noting the following points:
a) Make sure that all wiring and cables are routed as noted during dismantling.
b) Make sure that the air ducting is securely reconnected.
c) Reconnect the heater panel control cables, with reference to the previous sub-section.
d) Refit the facia components with reference to Chapter 11.

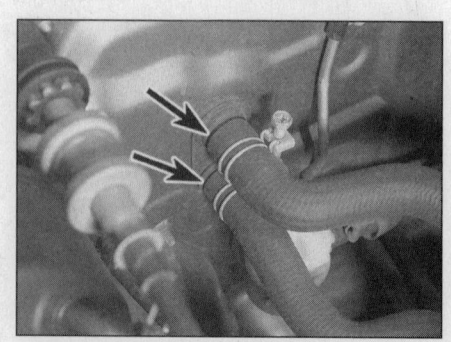

9.12 Slacken the clips and detach the heater unit coolant hoses (arrowed) from the ports at the bulkhead

Cooling, heating and ventilation systems 3•7

9.14 Heater/ventilation system assembly

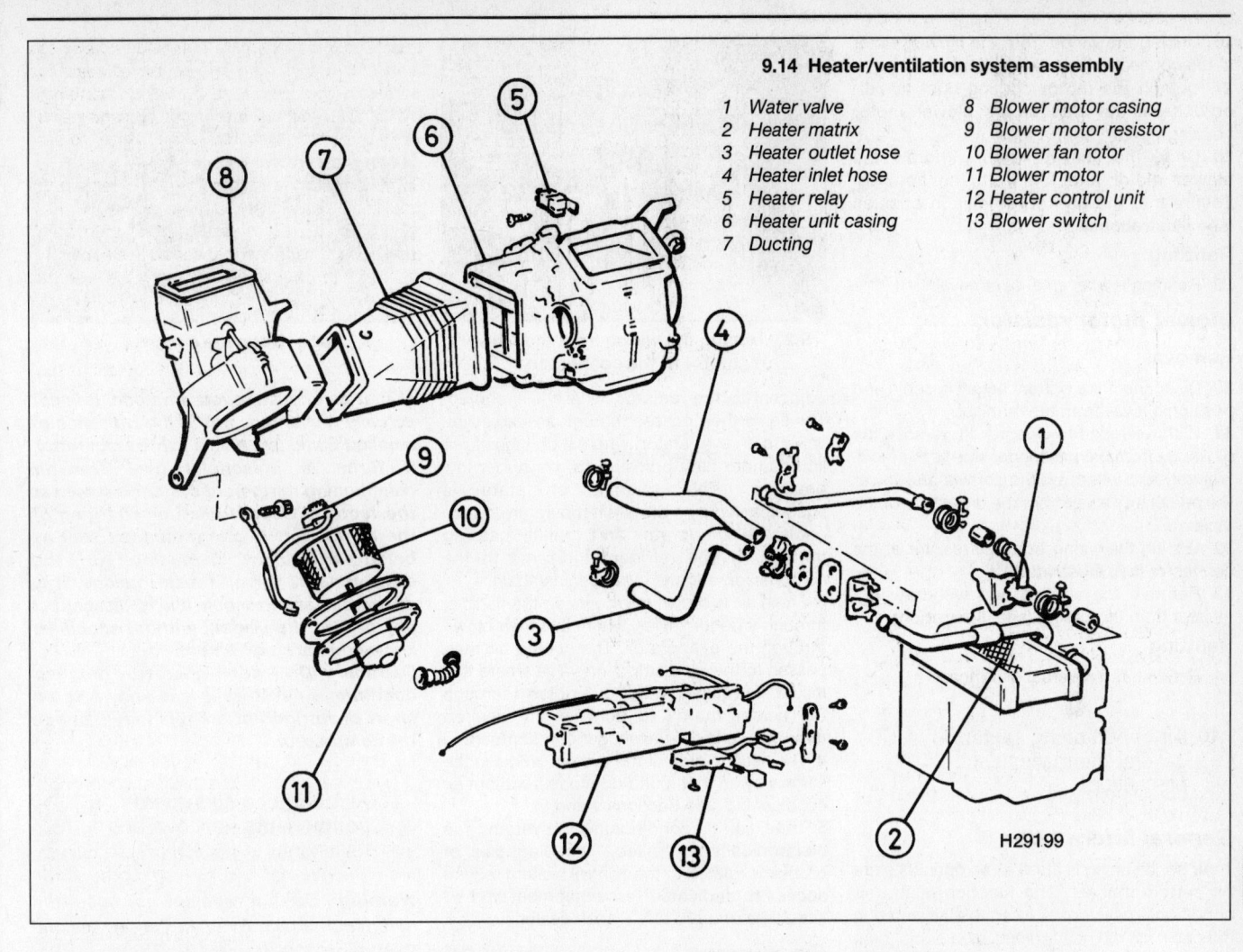

1. Water valve
2. Heater matrix
3. Heater outlet hose
4. Heater inlet hose
5. Heater relay
6. Heater unit casing
7. Ducting
8. Blower motor casing
9. Blower motor resistor
10. Blower fan rotor
11. Blower motor
12. Heater control unit
13. Blower switch

e) On completion, refill the cooling system as described in Chapter 1.

Heater matrix

Removal

20 Remove the complete heater assembly, as described in the previous sub-section.

21 Slacken the hose and pipe clamps, then remove the water valve assembly from the from the side of the heater unit.

22 Slacken and remove the securing screws, then withdraw the matrix core from the heater assembly casing **(see illustration)**. Exercise caution, as the edges of the matrix core cooling fins are sharp enough to cause injury.

Refitting

23 Refitting is a reversal of removal; refit the heater assembly as described previously in this Section.

Heater blower motor

Removal

24 Disconnect the battery negative cable and position it away from the terminal.

25 With reference to Chapter 11, remove the glovebox from the passenger side of the facia. Slacken and withdraw the screws, then lower the parcel tray away from the underside of the facia **(see illustration)**.

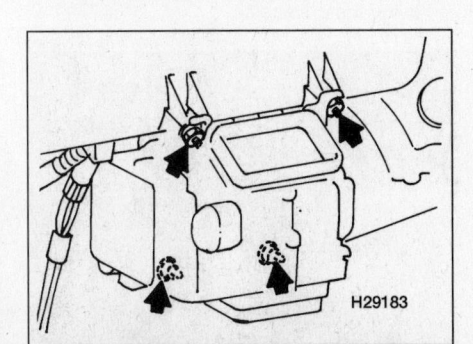

9.17 Slacken and remove the securing nuts (arrowed), then lift the heater assembly off its mounting studs

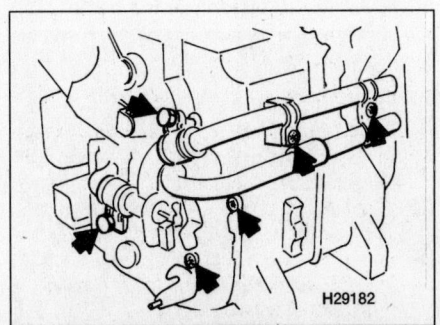

9.22 Remove the securing screws (arrowed), then withdraw the matrix core from the heater assembly casing

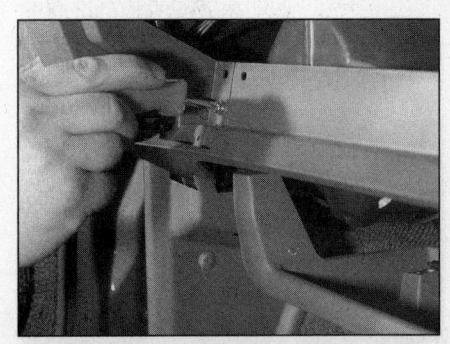

9.25 Slacken and withdraw the screws, then lower the parcel tray away from the underside of the facia

3•8 Cooling, heating and ventilation systems

26 Unplug the wiring from the blower motor at the connector **(see illustration)**.
27 Detach the motor cooling duct (small-bore) from the side of the blower motor housing.
28 Undo the screws, then withdraw the blower motor and fan from the housing. Ensure that the gasket remains in position **(see illustrations)**.

Refitting
29 Refitting is a reversal of removal.

Blower motor resistor

Removal
30 Disconnect the battery negative cable and position it away from the terminal.
31 With reference to Chapter 11, remove the glovebox from the passenger side of the facia. Slacken and withdraw the screws and lower the parcel tray away from the underside of the facia.
32 Unplug the wiring from the resistor at the connector **(see illustration)**.
33 Remove the screws and withdraw the resistor from the casing **(see illustration)**.

Refitting
34 Refitting is a reversal of removal.

10 Air conditioning system - general information and precautions

General information
1 Air conditioning is fitted as an optional extra on certain models. The function of the air conditioning system is to enable air entering the cabin via the heater/ventilation ducts to be cooled and dehumidified. This allows the cabin temperature to be controlled at a comfortable level, whilst driving in high ambient temperatures. In addition, the dehumidified air aids rapid windscreen demisting.
2 The cooling side of the system works in the same way as a domestic refrigerator. Refrigerant gas is drawn into a belt-driven compressor where the increase in pressure causes the refrigerant gas to turn to liquid. It then passes through a condenser, mounted adjacent to the radiator, where it is cooled. The liquid then passes through an expansion valve to an evaporator, where it changes from liquid under high pressure to gas under low pressure. This change of state is accompanied by a drop in temperature, which cools the evaporator and the air passing through it. The refrigerant returns to the compressor, and the cycle begins again.
3 Fresh air is drawn from outside the vehicle, through a dehumidifier, where it is then blown through the evaporator. The cooled air then passes to the air distribution valve where it is mixed, if required, with hot air blown through the heater matrix to achieve the desired temperature in the passenger compartment.
4 The heating side of the system works in the same way as that found on models without air conditioning (see Sections 1 and 9).
5 The air conditioning system is electronically-controlled. The diagnosis of problems related to the control system require access to dedicated test equipment and so should be referred to a Proton dealer.

Precautions
6 Special precautions must be observed, when working on any part of the air conditioning system and its associated components, as described in the following warning:

Warning: *The refrigeration circuit contains a Freon-based liquid refrigerant. The refrigerant is potentially very dangerous, and should only be handled by qualified persons. If it is splashed onto the skin, it can cause severe frostbite. It is not actually poisonous, but in the presence of a naked flame (such as a lighted cigarette), it forms a poisonous gas. The air conditioning refrigerant system is sealed at the factory. Uncontrolled discharging of the refrigerant is dangerous, as well as being extremely damaging to the environment. For all these reasons, it is dangerous and irresponsible to disconnect any part of the system without specialist knowledge and equipment.*

Caution: *Do not operate the air conditioning system if it is known to be short of refrigerant, as this may damage the compressor.*

11 Air conditioning system components - removal and refitting

Warning: *Do not attempt to open the refrigerant circuit. Refer to the precautions given in Section 10.*

The only operation which can be carried out easily without discharging the refrigerant is renewal of the compressor drivebelt - this procedure is described in Chapter 1. All other operations must be referred to a Proton dealer or an air conditioning specialist.

If necessary for access to other components, the compressor can easily be unbolted and moved aside, without disconnecting its flexible hoses, after removing the drivebelt.

9.26 Unplug the wiring from the blower motor at the connector

9.28a Undo the screws . . .

9.28b . . . then withdraw the blower motor and fan from the housing

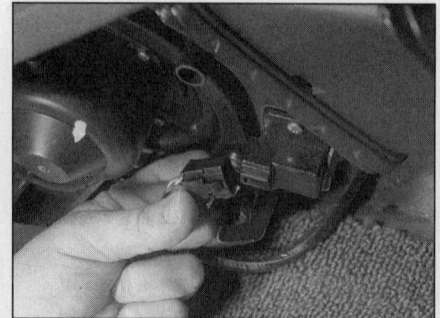

9.32 Unplug the wiring from the resistor at the connector

9.33 Remove the screws and withdraw the resistor from the casing

Chapter 4 Part A:
Fuel and exhaust systems - carburettor engines

Contents

Accelerator cable - removal, refitting and adjustment 7
Accelerator pedal - removal and refitting 8
Air cleaner air temperature control system - general information ... 3
Air cleaner assembly - removal and refitting 2
Air cleaner filter element renewal .... See Chapter 1
Carburettor (12-valve models) - fault diagnosis, overhaul and
    adjustments 13
Carburettor (8-valve models) - fault diagnosis, overhaul and
    adjustments 12
Carburettor - general information 10
Carburettor - removal and refitting 11
Exhaust manifold - removal and refitting 15
Exhaust system - general information, removal and refitting 16
Exhaust system check .... See Chapter 1
Fuel filter - renewal .... See Chapter 1
Fuel gauge sender unit - removal and refitting 5
Fuel pump - testing, removal and refitting 4
Fuel tank - removal and refitting 6
General fuel system checks .... See Chapter 1
General information and precautions 1
Idle speed and mixture adjustment .... See Chapter 1
Inlet manifold - removal and refitting 14
Unleaded petrol - general information and usage 9

Degrees of difficulty

| Easy, suitable for novice with little experience | Fairly easy, suitable for beginner with some experience | Fairly difficult, suitable for competent DIY mechanic | Difficult, suitable for experienced DIY mechanic | Very difficult, suitable for expert DIY or professional |

Specifications

Fuel pump
Type .... Mechanical, driven by eccentric on camshaft

Carburettor
Type:
    8-valve models .... Aisan 28/32
    12-valve models .... Aisan VV (variable venturi)
Choke type .... Automatic

Carburettor data - 8-valve models

	Primary	Secondary
Throttle valve diameter	28 mm	32 mm
Main jet:		
1.3 litre engine	94	150
1.5 litre engine	93	150
Idle jet	51	
Enrichment jet	50	
Float height setting (see text):		
Float tang to needle valve clearance	1.5 to 1.7 mm	
Float upper edge to body clearance	7.0 mm	
Throttle valve fast idle setting	0.9 mm	
Choke pull-down setting	1.5 mm	
Idle speed	850 ± 50 rpm	
Idle mixture CO content	1.0 ± 0.5%	

Carburettor data - 12-valve models

Float height setting (see text):
- Float tang to needle valve clearance .... 1.0 mm
- Float upper edge to body clearance .... 4.3 mm

Main jet adjustment data (see text):
- Adjustment screw to plug measurement:
  - 1.3 litre models .... 4.1 mm
  - 1.5 litre models .... 4.0 mm
- Idle mixture adjustment screw protrusion from body:
  - 1.3 litre models .... 8.7 mm
  - 1.5 litre models .... 8.6 mm

Idle speed:
- Manual transmission models .... 800 ± 50 rpm
- Automatic transmission models .... 850 ± 50 rpm

Idle mixture CO content .... 1.0 ± 0.5%

Recommended fuel

Minimum octane rating .... 95 RON unleaded (UK unleaded premium) or 97 RON leaded (UK 4-star)

Torque wrench settings

	Nm	lbf ft
Carburettor mounting nuts	12	9
Fuel pump retaining nuts/bolts	12	9
Exhaust manifold retaining nuts	20	15
Exhaust system fasteners:		
Front pipe to manifold nuts	35	25
Front pipe mounting bolt	25	18
Front pipe to tailpipe bolts	10	7
Tailpipe mounting bolt	10	7
Mounting rubber fixing nuts/bolts	15	11
Inlet manifold:		
Manifold retaining nuts/bolts	20	15
Support bracket bolts	30	22

1 General information and precautions

The fuel system consists of a fuel tank mounted under the rear of the car, a mechanical fuel pump, and a carburettor. The fuel pump is operated by an eccentric on the camshaft, and is mounted on the rear of the cylinder head. The air cleaner contains a disposable paper filter element, and incorporates a flap valve air temperature control system; this allows cold air from the outside of the car, and warm air from the exhaust manifold, to enter the air cleaner in the correct proportions.

The fuel pump lifts fuel from the fuel tank via a filter, which is mounted on the engine compartment bulkhead, and supplies it to the carburettor. Excess fuel is returned from the pump to the fuel tank.

Two different carburettors are used; on 8-valve models a fixed twin-venturi Aisan carburettor is fitted and on 12-valve models variable venturi Aisan carburettor is fitted. On both carburettors, mixture enrichment for cold starting (choke) is of the automatic type.

The exhaust system consists of two sections; the front pipe section, incorporating the front silencer box, and the tailpipe section which incorporates the main silencer box. The system is suspended throughout its entire length by rubber mountings.

⚠️ **Warning: Many of the procedures in this Chapter require the removal of fuel lines and connections, which may result in some fuel spillage. Before carrying out any operation on the fuel system, refer to the precautions given in "Safety first!" at the beginning of this manual, and follow them implicitly. Petrol is a highly-dangerous and volatile liquid, and the precautions necessary when handling it cannot be overstressed.**

2 Air cleaner assembly - removal and refitting

Removal

8-valve models

1 Disconnect the breather hose from the top of the air cleaner housing (see illustration).

2 Unscrew the wing nut then release the retaining clips and remove the air cleaner housing cover and filter element.

3 Release the retaining clip and detach the inlet duct from the end of the air cleaner housing body (see illustration).

4 Slacken and remove the mounting nuts and washers and lift the air cleaner housing body away from the carburettor, disconnecting the vacuum hose(s) as they become accessible (see illustrations). Recover the duct connecting the air cleaner to the exhaust manifold.

2.1 Disconnect the breather hose from the air cleaner housing lid

2.3 Release the retaining clip and disconnect the inlet duct from the air cleaner

2.4a Undo the retaining nuts and washers (arrowed) ...

2.4b ... then lift off the air cleaner housing body and disconnect the vacuum hose

5 Recover the spacers from the housing mounting rubbers and remove the sealing ring from the top of the carburettor. Inspect the mounting rubbers and sealing ring for signs of damage or deterioration and renew as necessary.

12-valve models

6 Release the retaining clip and detach the inlet duct from the end of the air cleaner housing.

7 Unscrew the housing wing nut and lift off the washer and sealing grommet from the mounting stud.

8 Release the retaining clips and remove the air cleaner housing from the top of the carburettor and lift off the filter element. Recover the duct connecting the air cleaner to the exhaust manifold.

9 Slacken and remove the mounting nut and washer and lift the air cleaner housing mounting plate away from the carburettor, disconnecting and relevant vacuum/breather hoses as they become accessible. Recover the spacer from the plate mounting rubber and remove the sealing ring/gasket from the top of the carburettor **(see illustrations)**. Inspect the mounting rubbers and sealing ring/gasket for signs of damage or deterioration and renew as necessary.

Refitting

10 Refitting is a reversal of the removal procedure, ensuring that all the air cleaner housing seals are air tight and that all hoses are correctly and securely reconnected.

3 Air cleaner air temperature control system - general information

The system is controlled by a heat-sensitive vacuum switch in the air cleaner housing. When the engine is started from cold, the switch is open, allowing inlet manifold depression to act on the air temperature control valve diaphragm in the inlet duct. This vacuum causes the diaphragm to rise, drawing a flap valve across the cold-air inlet, thus allowing only (warmed) air from the exhaust manifold to enter the air cleaner.

As the temperature of the exhaust-warmed air in the air cleaner rises, the wax capsule in the vacuum switch deforms and closes the switch, cutting off the vacuum supply to the air temperature control valve assembly. As the vacuum supply is cut, the flap is gradually lowered across the hot-air inlet until, when the engine is fully warmed-up air cleaner temperature above 45°C) to normal operating temperature, only cold air from the front of the car is entering the air cleaner.

To check the system, allow the engine to cool down completely, then slacken the retaining clip and disconnect the inlet duct from the air cleaner assembly; the flap valve in the duct should be securely seated across the hot-air inlet. Start the engine; the flap should immediately rise to close off the cold-air inlet, and should then lower steadily as the engine warms up, until it is eventually seated across the hot-air inlet again.

To check the vacuum switch, disconnect the vacuum pipe from the control valve when the engine is running, and place a finger over the pipe end. When the engine is cold (air cleaner temperature below 30°C), full inlet manifold vacuum should be present in the pipe, and when the engine is at normal operating temperature (air cleaner temperature above 45°C), there should be no vacuum in the pipe.

To check the air temperature control valve assembly, slacken the retaining clip and disconnect the inlet duct from the front of the valve assembly; the flap valve should be securely seated across the hot-air inlet. Disconnect the vacuum pipe, and suck hard at the control valve stub; the flap should rise to shut off the cold-air inlet.

If either component is faulty, it must be renewed. At the time of writing it appeared that the components were not available individually and if faulty the complete air cleaner housing had to be renewed. Refer to your Proton dealer for the latest parts information.

4 Fuel pump - testing, removal and refitting

Note: *Refer to the warning note in Section 1 before proceeding.*

Testing

1 To test the fuel pump on the engine, disconnect the outlet pipe which leads to the carburettor. Hold a wad of rag by the pump outlet while an assistant spins the engine on the starter. *Keep your hands away from the electric cooling fan.* Regular spurts of fuel should be ejected as the engine turns. Be careful not to spill fuel onto hot engine components.

2 The pump can also be tested by removing it. With the pump outlet pipe disconnected but the inlet pipe still connected, hold the wad of rag by the outlet. Operate the pump lever by hand, moving it in and out; if the pump is in a satisfactory condition, the lever should move and return smoothly, and a strong jet of fuel should be ejected.

2.9a On 12-valve models, remove the mounting nut and washer ...

2.9b ... lift off the housing mounting plate, disconnecting the vacuum hose ...

2.9c ... and recover the gasket from the top of the carburettor

4A•4 Fuel and exhaust systems - carburettor engines

Removal

8-valve models

3 Remove the air cleaner housing as described in Section 2. To gain access to the pump from underneath, firmly apply the handbrake then jack up the front of the vehicle and support it on axle stands (see "Jacking and vehicle support").

4 Identify the pump inlet, outlet and return hoses then slacken the retaining clips. Place wads of rag beneath the hose unions to catch any spilled fuel, then disconnect the hoses from the pump; plug the hose ends to minimise fuel loss.

5 Slacken and remove the bolts securing the pump to the rear of the cylinder head (see illustration). Remove the pump, along with its insulating spacer and gaskets, and withdraw the pump pushrod from the cylinder head. Discard the gaskets, new one must be used on refitting.

12-valve models

6 Identify the pump inlet, outlet and return hoses then slacken the retaining clips (see illustration). Place wads of rag beneath the hose unions to catch any spilled fuel, then disconnect the hoses from the pump; plug the hose ends to minimise fuel loss.

7 Slacken and remove the bolts securing the pump to the rear of the cylinder head. Remove the pump along with its insulating spacer and gaskets. Discard the gaskets, new one must be used on refitting.

Refitting

8-valve models

8 Ensure that the pump, cylinder head and insulating spacer mating surfaces are clean and dry.

9 Insert the pushrod into the cylinder then position a new gasket on each side of the spacer refit the pump to the cylinder head. Refit the pump mounting bolts and tighten them to the specified torque setting.

10 Reconnect the inlet, outlet and return hoses to the relevant pump unions, and securely tighten their retaining clips. Refit the air cleaner housing (Section 2) and lower the vehicle to the ground.

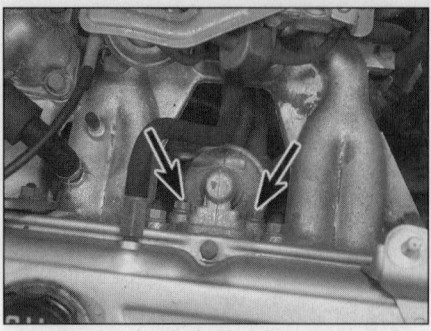

4.5 Fuel pump mounting bolts (arrowed) - 8-valve models (viewed from above)

12-valve models

11 Ensure that the pump, cylinder head and insulating spacer mating surfaces are clean and dry.

12 Position a new gasket on each side of the spacer refit the pump to the cylinder head, tightening the bolts to the specified torque.

13 Reconnect the inlet, outlet and return hoses to the relevant pump unions, and securely tighten their retaining clips.

5 Fuel gauge sender unit - removal and refitting

Note: *Refer to the warning note in Section 1 before proceeding.*

Removal

1 Disconnect the battery negative lead.

2 For access to the sender unit, lift out the luggage compartment carpet and (where necessary) remove the spare wheel.

3 Using a screwdriver, carefully prise the plastic access cover from the floor to expose the sender unit.

4 Disconnect the wiring connector(s) from the sender unit, and tape the connector(s) to the vehicle body to prevent it disappearing behind the tank (see illustration).

5 Make alignment marks between the sender unit and tank then slacken and remove the retaining nuts and washers securing the sender unit in position (see illustration).

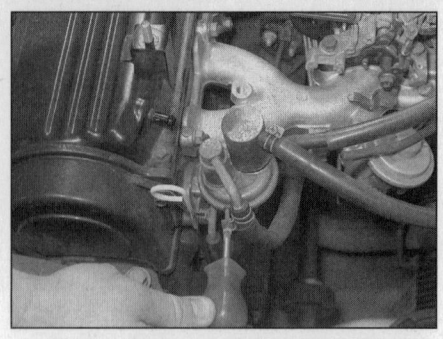

4.6 On 12-valve models, slacken the retaining clips and disconnect the fuel hoses from the pump

6 Carefully lift the sender unit from the top of the fuel tank, taking great care not to bend the sender unit float arm, or to spill fuel onto the interior of the vehicle (see illustration). Recover the sender unit gasket and discard it - a new one must be used on refitting.

Refitting

7 Ensure that the sender unit and tank mating surfaces are clean and dry and fit a new gasket to the tank.

8 Manoeuvre the sender unit into position, taking great care not to damage the float arm, then refit the washers and retaining nuts tightening them securely.

9 Reconnect the wiring connector to the sender unit then apply a smear of sealant to the edge of the access cover then refit the cover to the floor.

10 Install the spare wheel and/or carpet (as necessary) and reconnect the battery.

6 Fuel tank - removal and refitting

Note: *Refer to the warning note in Section 1 before proceeding.*

Removal

1 Before removing the fuel tank, all fuel must be drained from the tank. A drain plug is provided on the base of the tank for this operation. **Note:** *It is best that the tank should be nearly empty before it is drained.*

5.4 Remove the access cover and disconnect the wiring connector from the fuel gauge sender unit

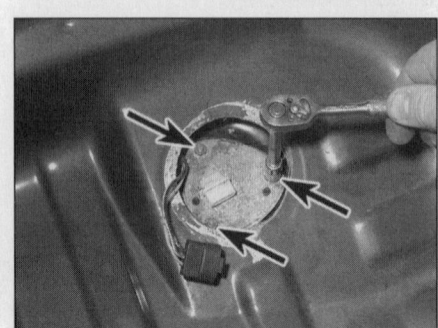

5.5 Undo the retaining nuts (arrowed) . . .

5.6 . . . then carefully manoeuvre the sender unit out of position (gasket arrowed)

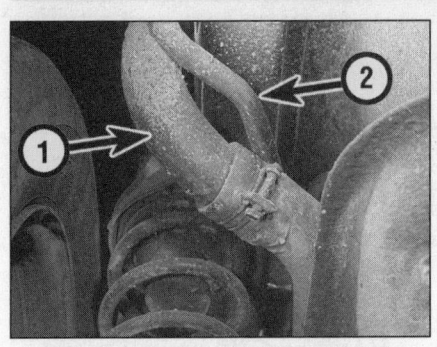

Fuel and exhaust systems - carburettor engines 4A•5

6.6 Slacken the retaining clips and disconnect the filler neck (1) and vent pipe (2) from the left-hand side of the tank

2 Disconnect the battery negative terminal then remove the fuel tank cap and position a suitable container underneath the fuel tank. Slacken and remove the drain plug and sealing washer and allow the tank contents to drain. Once the fuel tank is drained fit a new sealing washer to the drain plug then refit the plug and tighten it securely. Store the drained fuel safely in suitable containers.

3 Disconnect the wiring connector from the fuel gauge sender unit as described in paragraphs 2 to 4 of Section 5.

4 Chock the front wheels then jack up the rear of the vehicle and support it on axle stands (see *"Jacking and vehicle support"*). Remove the left-hand rear roadwheel.

5 Trace the fuel feed and return hoses back from the left-hand side of the tank to their union with the fuel pipes. Mark the hoses for identification purposes, then release the feed and return hose retaining clips. Plug the hose and pipe ends, to prevent the entry of dirt into the system.

6 Working at the left-hand side of the fuel tank, release the retaining clips then disconnect the filler neck vent pipe and main filler neck hose from the fuel tank/filler neck **(see illustration)**. Where necessary also disconnect the breather hose(s).

7 Place a trolley jack with an interposed block of wood beneath the tank, then raise the jack until it is supporting the weight of the tank.

8 Slacken and remove the retaining nuts/bolts, then remove the two support bars from the underside of the tank **(see illustration)**.

9 Slowly lower the fuel tank out of position, disconnecting any other relevant vent pipes as they become accessible (where necessary), and remove the tank from underneath the vehicle.

10 If the tank is contaminated with sediment or water, remove the drain plug and swill the tank out with clean fuel. The tank is injection-moulded from a synthetic material - if seriously damaged, it should be renewed. However, in certain cases, it may be possible to have small leaks or minor damage repaired. Seek the advice of a specialist before attempting to repair the fuel tank.

Refitting

11 Refitting is the reverse of the removal procedure, noting the following points:
a) When lifting the tank back into position, take care to ensure that none of the hoses become trapped between the tank and vehicle body.
b) Ensure that all pipes and hoses are correctly routed, and securely held in position with their retaining clips.
c) On completion, refill the tank with a small amount of fuel, and check for signs of leakage prior to taking the vehicle out on the road.

7 Accelerator cable - removal, refitting and adjustment

Removal

1 Working in the engine compartment, free the accelerator inner cable from the carburettor throttle cam.

2 Slacken the outer cable locknut and adjuster nut then release the outer cable from its mounting bracket **(see illustration)**.

3 Working back along the length of the cable, free it from any retaining clips or ties, noting its correct routing and slacken and remove the cable clip retaining bolt.

4 From inside the vehicle, reach up behind the facia and unhook the inner cable from the top of the accelerator pedal. Tie a length of string to the end of the inner cable then depress the retaining clips and free the outer cable from the bulkhead.

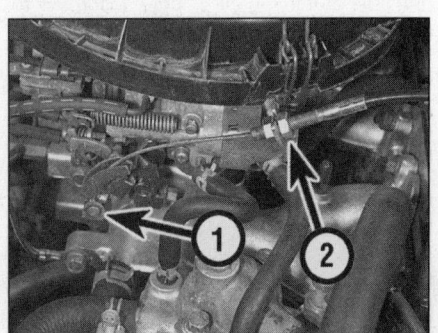

5 Return to the engine compartment and remove the cable from the vehicle. When the end of the cable appears, untie the string and leave it in position - it can then be used to draw the cable back into position on refitting.

Refitting

6 Tie the string to the end of the cable, then use the string to draw the cable into position through the bulkhead. Once the cable end is visible, untie the string, and connect the inner cable to the upper end of the accelerator pedal.

7 From within the engine compartment, clip the outer cable end fitting securely into the bulkhead.

8 Work along the cable, ensuring it is correctly routed, securing it in position with the retaining clips and ties. Securely tighten the cable clip retaining bolt.

9 Connect the inner cable to the carburettor throttle cam and locate the outer cable in its mounting bracket. Adjust the cable as described below and securely tighten the cable locknut.

Adjustment

10 The accelerator cable should be adjusted so that there is a small amount of freeplay in the cable. Ensuring that the throttle cam is fully against its stop, check the exposed length of inner cable for signs of freeplay. If adjustment is necessary, slacken the outer cable locknut then rotate the adjuster nut until only a small amount of freeplay is present in the inner cable. Once the cable is correctly adjusted, hold the adjuster nut stationary and securely tighten the locknut.

11 Have an assistant depress the accelerator pedal, and check that the throttle cam opens fully and returns smoothly to its stop then recheck the cable adjustment. On models with automatic transmission, once the accelerator cable is correctly adjusted, check the kickdown cable adjustment as described in Chapter 7B.

8 Accelerator pedal - removal and refitting

Removal

1 Reach up behind the facia and unhook the accelerator inner cable from the top of the pedal.

2 Using pliers unhook and remove the return spring from the upper end of the pedal.

3 Remove the split pin and outer washer then slide the pedal off from its mounting and remove the inner washer.

Refitting

4 Refitting is a reversal of the removal procedure, applying a little multi-purpose grease to the pedal pivot point. On completion, adjust the accelerator cable as described in Section 7.

6.8 Fuel tank retaining nut (arrowed)

7.2 Free the inner cable from the throttle cam (1), slacken the locknut and adjuster nut (2) and free the cable

4A•6 Fuel and exhaust systems - carburettor engines

9 Unleaded petrol - general information and usage

Note: *The information given in this Chapter is correct at the time of writing. If updated information is thought to be required, check with a Proton dealer. If travelling abroad, consult one of the motoring organisations (or a similar authority) for advice on the fuel available.*

The fuel recommended by Proton is given in the Specifications of this Chapter, followed by the equivalent petrol currently on sale in the UK.

All Proton carburettor models are designed to run on 95 octane petrol. Both leaded and unleaded petrol can be used without modification. Super leaded (97 octane, UK "4-star") and super unleaded (98 octane) petrol can also be used if wished, though there is no advantage in doing so.

10 Carburettor - general information

8-valve models

1 The Aisan carburettor fitted to 8-valve models is a downdraught progressive twin venturi instrument, with a vacuum-controlled secondary throttle **(see illustration)**. The choke control is automatic in operation, and is controlled by a coolant-heated wax capsule.

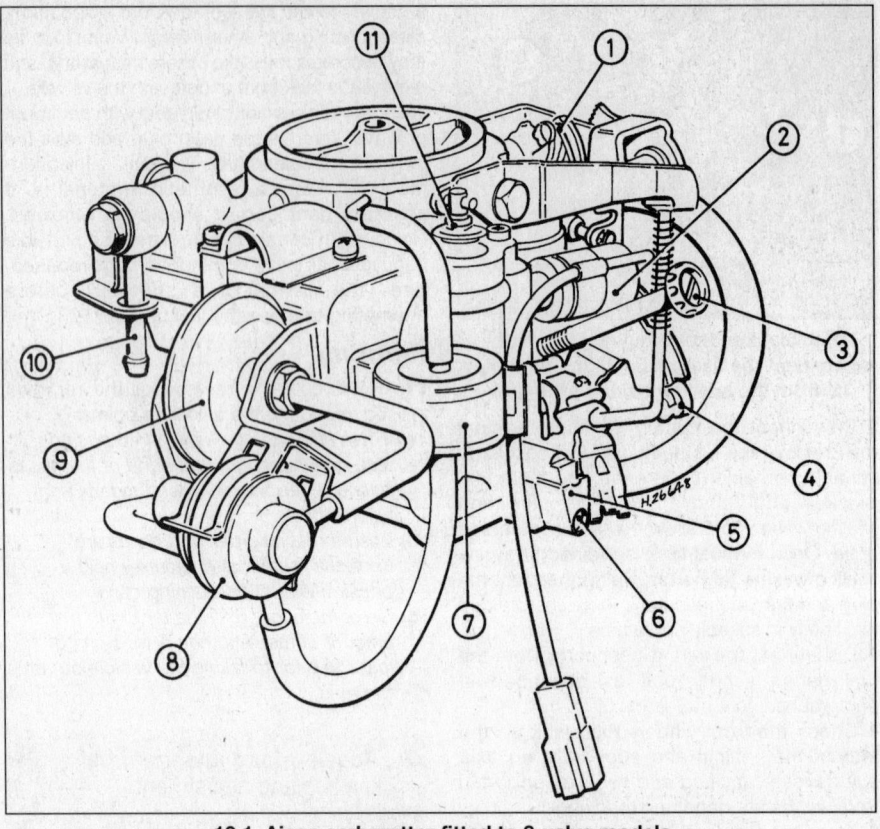

2 During slow running and at idle, fuel from the float chamber passes into the idle channel through a metered idle jet. Here it is mixed with a small amount of air from a calibrated air bleed. The resulting mixture is drawn through a channel, to be discharged from the idle orifice under the primary throttle plate. A tapered mixture screw is used to vary the outlet, and this ensures fine control of the idle mixture.

3 An idle cut-off valve is used to prevent run-on when the engine is switched off. The valve uses a solenoid plunger to block the idle jet when the ignition is switched off.

4 A progression slot provides extra enrichment as it is uncovered by the opening of the throttle valve during initial acceleration.

5 Under normal operating conditions, the amount of fuel discharged into the airstream is controlled by a calibrated main jet. Fuel is drawn through the main jet. The fuel is then mixed with air, drawn in through the air correction jet and through the holes in the emulsion tube. The resulting mixture is discharged from the main orifice through an auxiliary vent.

6 The carburettor also has an accelerator pump to provide an initial spurt of extra fuel during sudden acceleration. During acceleration, fuel is pumped through a ball valve located in the pump injector, and is discharged into both the primary and secondary venturis.

7 The idle speed is set by an adjustable screw. The adjustable mixture screw is sealed during production with a tamperproof plug, to prevent unnecessary or inexpert adjustment.

12-valve models

8 The Aisan carburettor fitted to 12-valve models is a downdraught variable venturi instrument, with an automatic choke. The variable venturi carburettor relies on the principle of varying air volume according to the engine's demand; air velocity will therefore remain high - no matter what the engine speed or load the piston will automatically adjust the venturi to give the exact volume of air required, and the venturi will thus move to its proper position for any given airflow.

9 A tapered metering needle is attached to the air valve, and locates into the main jet. This needle almost blocks the main jet at idle and low engine loads. As engine load increases, and the piston moves in response to an increased secondary air requirement, the needle is withdrawn from the jet to maintain the AFR and allow more fuel to be drawn into the engine. The needle is very accurately machined so that the correct amount of fuel is delivered at all speeds and loads.

10 This system does not require a separate progression system, and transition from idle to higher speeds is much smoother than with a fixed type venturi. The carburettor also has an accelerator pump to provide an initial spurt of extra fuel during sudden acceleration. During acceleration, fuel is pumped through a valve located in the carburettor and is discharged into the venturi.

11 At idle, fuel from the float chamber passes into the idle channel through a metered idle jet. Here it is mixed with a small amount of air from a calibrated air bleed. The resulting mixture is drawn through a channel, to be discharged from the idle orifice above the primary throttle plate. A tapered mixture screw is used to vary the outlet, and this ensures fine control of the idle mixture.

12 The idle speed is set by an adjustable screw. The adjustable mixture screw is tamper-proofed at production level, in accordance with emission regulations.

13 An idle cut-off valve is used to prevent run-on when the engine is shut down. It utilises a 12-volt solenoid plunger to block the idle channel when the ignition is switched off.

10.1 Aisan carburettor fitted to 8-valve models

1 Automatic choke
2 Idle fuel cut-off solenoid valve
3 Idle speed adjusting screw
4 Throttle cam
5 Limiter cap
6 Idle mixture adjustment screw
7 Delay valve
8 Servo valve
9 Dashpot
10 Fuel inlet union
11 Accelerator pump

Fuel and exhaust systems - carburettor engines 4A•7

11.3 Slacken the locknut and adjuster nut and detach the accelerator cable from the carburettor

11.5 Release the retaining clips and disconnect the fuel hose . . .

11 Carburettor - removal and refitting

Note: *Refer to the warning note in Section 1 before proceeding.*

Removal

1 Disconnect the battery negative terminal.
2 Remove the air cleaner housing as described in Section 2.
3 Free the accelerator inner cable from the carburettor throttle cam then slacken the outer cable locknut and adjuster nut then release the outer cable from its mounting bracket **(see illustration)**.
4 Disconnect the wiring connector from the carburettor idle cut-off solenoid.
5 Release the retaining clip, and disconnect the fuel feed hose from the carburettor **(see illustration)**. Place wads of rag around the union to catch any spilled fuel, and plug the hose as soon as it is disconnected, to minimise fuel loss.
6 Make a note of the correct fitted positions of all the coolant hoses and the relevant vacuum pipes and breather hoses, to ensure that they are correctly positioned on refitting, then release the retaining clips (where fitted)

and disconnect them from the carburettor **(see illustration)**. Plug the coolant hose ends to minimise coolant loss.
7 Unscrew the four bolts securing the carburettor to the inlet manifold **(see illustration)**. Remove the carburettor assembly from the car. Remove the insulating spacer and gaskets. Discard the gaskets; new ones must be used on refitting. Plug the inlet manifold port with a wad of clean cloth, to prevent the possible entry of foreign matter.

Refitting

8 Refitting is the reverse of the removal procedure, noting the following points:
 a) Ensure that the carburettor, inlet manifold and insulating spacer sealing faces are clean and flat.
 b) On 8-valve models, position a gasket on each side of the insulating spacer then refit the carburettor and tighten its mounting bolts to the specified torque.
 c) On 12-valve models, ensure that the insulating spacer is fitted the correct way up with the embossed triangle on its side pointing upwards, and ensure that the upper and lower gaskets are correctly fitted **(see illustration)**. Refit the carburettor mounting bolts and tighten them to the specified torque.

 d) Use the notes made on dismantling to ensure that all hoses are refitted to their original positions and, where necessary, are securely held by their retaining clips.
 e) Refit and adjust the accelerator cables as described in Section 7.
 f) Refit the air cleaner as described in Section 2.
 g) On completion, check and, if necessary, adjust the idle speed and mixture settings as described in Chapter 1.

12 Carburettor (8-valve models) - fault diagnosis, overhaul and adjustments

Fault diagnosis

1 If a carburettor fault is suspected, always check first that the ignition timing is correctly set, that the spark plugs are in good condition and correctly gapped, that the accelerator cable is correctly adjusted, and that the air cleaner filter element is clean; refer to the relevant Sections of Chapter 1, Chapter 5 or this Chapter. If the engine is running very

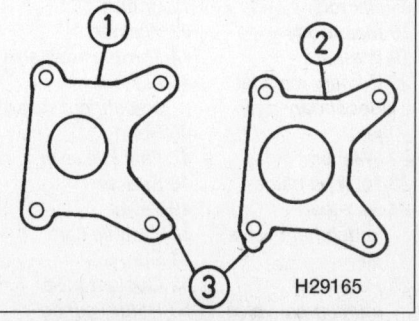

11.6 . . . and coolant hoses (arrowed) from the carburettor (8-valve model shown)

11.7 Carburettor mounting bolts (arrowed) - 12-valve model

11.8 On 12-valve models ensure upper gasket (1) and lower gasket (2) are correctly positioned on fitting. Each gasket can be identified by the location of the protrusion (3)

4A•8 Fuel and exhaust systems - carburettor engines

roughly, first check the valve clearances as described in Chapter 1, then check the compression pressures as described in Chapter 2.

2 If careful checking of all the above produces no improvement, the carburettor must be removed for cleaning and overhaul.

3 Prior to overhaul, check the availability of component parts before starting work; note that most sealing washers, screws and gaskets are available in kits, as are some of the major sub-assemblies. In most cases, it will be sufficient to dismantle the carburettor and to clean the jets and passages.

Overhaul

Note: *Refer to the warning note in Section 1 before proceeding.*

4 Remove the carburettor from the engine as described in Section 11.

5 Make a note of the correct fitted locations of all the relevant hoses still attached to the carburettor then disconnect and remove them.

6 Unscrew the idle cut-off solenoid from the carburettor body, and remove it along with its plunger and spring (where loose) **(see illustration)**. To test the solenoid, connect a 12-volt battery to it (positive terminal to the solenoid terminal, negative to the solenoid body), and check that the plunger is retracted fully into the body. Disconnect the battery, and check that the plunger is pushed out by spring pressure. If the valve does not perform as expected, and cleaning does not improve the situation, the solenoid valve must be renewed.

7 Remove the throttle return spring, fast idle cam follower and the damper spring.

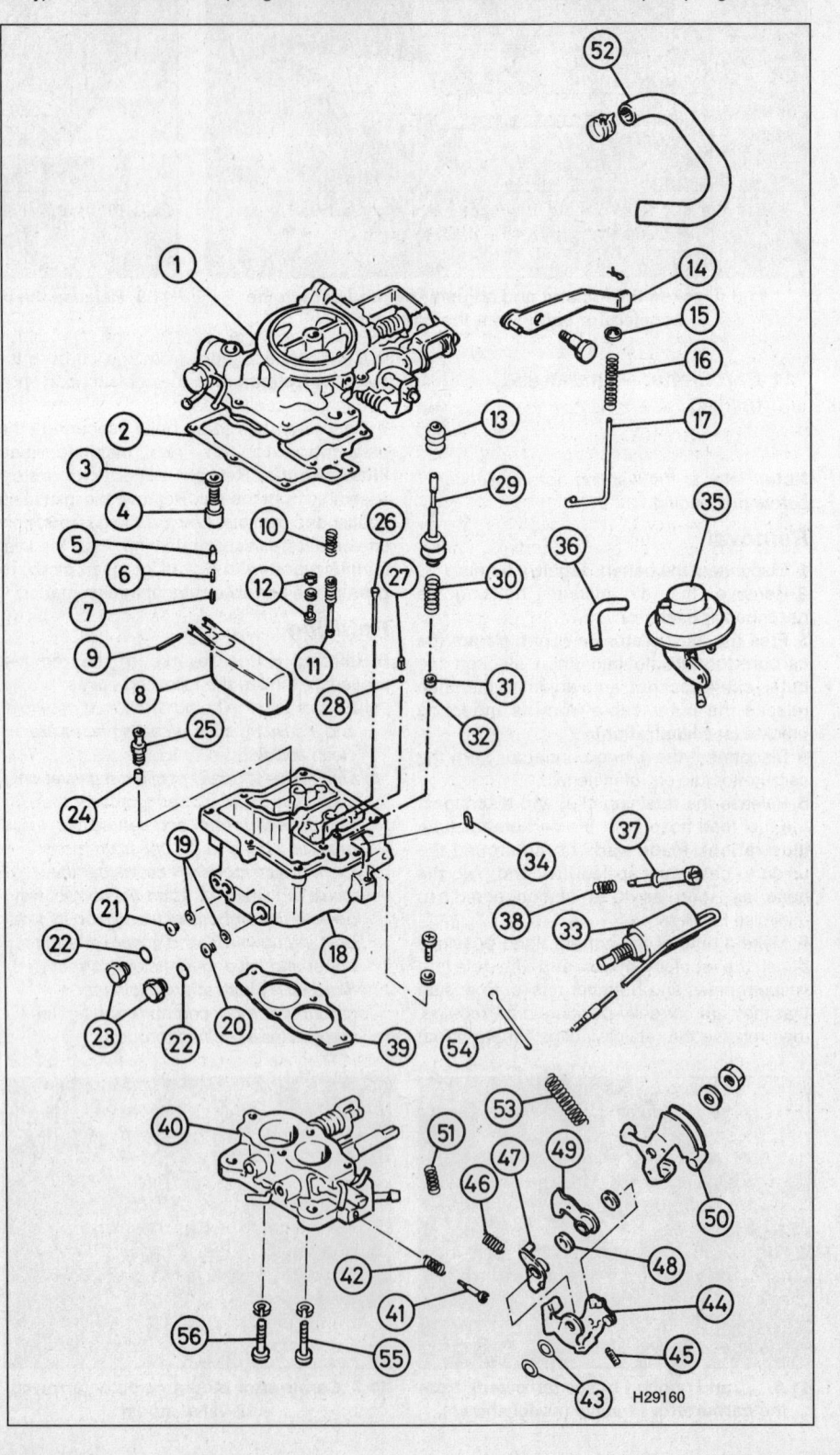

12.6 Exploded view of the carburettor - 8-valve model

1 Upper body	29 Accelerator pump plunger
2 Gasket	30 Spring
3 Washer	31 Accelerator pump clip
4 Needle valve seat	32 Accelerator pump ball weight
5 Needle valve	33 Idle cut-off solenoid
6 Spring	34 Washer
7 Needle valve pin	35 Secondary throttle valve diaphragm
8 Float	36 Hose
9 Pivot pin	37 Idle speed adjusting screw
10 Spring	38 Spring
11 Accelerator pump piston	39 Gasket
12 Accelerator pump piston stopper components	40 Lower body
13 Gaiter	41 Idle mixture adjusting screw
14 Pump arm	42 Spring
15 Bush	43 Washer
16 Spring	44 Throttle shaft arm
17 Accelerator pump link rod	45 Fast idle adjustment screw
18 Main body	46 Spring
19 Washers	47 Fast idle lever
20 Primary main jet	48 Spacer
21 Secondary main jet	49 Lever
22 Washers	50 Throttle cam
23 Main jet plugs	51 Spring
24 Part-load enrichment valve jet	52 Coolant hose
25 Part-load enrichment valve	53 Return spring
26 Idle jet	54 Damper spring
27 Accelerator pump discharge weight	55 Screw
28 Accelerator pump ball weight	56 Screw with hole

Fuel and exhaust systems - carburettor engines

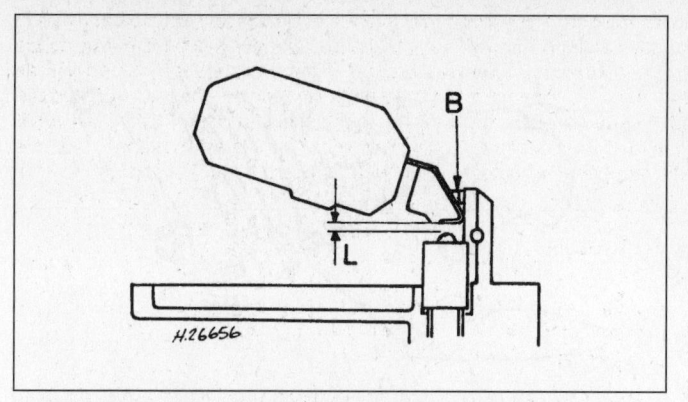

12.27 Float tang to needle valve clearance measurement (L). Bend the stopper tang (B) to adjust

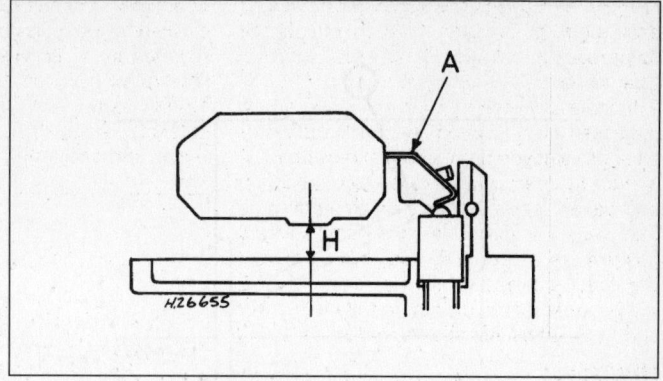

12.28 Float upper edge to body clearance measurement (H). Bend the float arm (A) to adjust

8 Remove the clip and detach the fast idle link rod.
9 Remove the clip and disconnect the accelerator pump rod.
10 Detach the dashpot assembly (where fitted); this may be retained by an upper body fixing screw.
11 Remove the retaining screws and lift off the carburettor upper body.
Caution: If the top is tight, a gentle tap with a plastic hammer is usually sufficient to free it. Do not lever the assemblies apart, as there is a risk of damaging the mating surfaces.
12 Tap out the float pin, and remove the float, needle valve and seat components, fuel filter and float chamber gasket.
13 Remove the idle mixture adjustment screw tamperproof cap. Screw the screw in until it seats lightly, counting the *exact* number of turns required to do this, then unscrew it and remove along with its spring. **Note:** *A special tool will be required to remove the mixture screw - refer to your Proton dealer for further information.*
14 Remove the accelerator pump gaiter and piston assembly and recover the accelerator pump inlet spring, retaining clip and ball from the carburettor followed by the pump outlet spring, weight and ball (where possible).
15 Note the sizes and locations of the primary and secondary jets, for correct installation during assembly. It is possible to accidentally transpose the jets between the primary and secondary sides.
16 Remove the primary idle jet, then unscrew the primary and secondary main jets. The main jets are accessed after removing the plugs located under the float chamber. **Note:** *Use a close-fitting screwdriver to prevent damage to the jets.*
17 Unscrew and remove the part-load enrichment valve from the float chamber. Check the action of the enrichment valve plunger in the upper body, then release the retaining screw and detach the enrichment valve plunger from the upper body.
18 Remove the retaining screws, and detach the primary and secondary auxiliary venturis and the emulsion tube assemblies from the main venturis.
19 Disconnect the secondary throttle control rod, after removing the retaining clip. Remove the retaining screws and detach the diaphragm assembly from the body.
20 If necessary, remove the fixing bolts (upper and lower), and separate the carburettor main body and throttle body assemblies; note the position of the insulation block for reference when reassembling. **Note:** *On some versions, one bolt may be hollow (it doubles as a vacuum passage); if so, note its location for reference when reassembling.*
21 Clean the jets, carburettor body assemblies, float chamber and internal drillings. An air line may be used to clear the internal passages once the carburettor is fully dismantled.

Warning: If high pressure air is directed into drillings and passages were a diaphragm is fitted, the diaphragm is likely to be damaged. Aerosol cans of carburettor cleaner are widely available and can prove very useful in helping to clear internal passages of stubborn obstructions.

22 Use a straight edge to check all carburettor body assembly mating surfaces for distortion.
23 To check the secondary throttle valve diaphragm, push the control rod fully into the housing and seal the vacuum passage with a finger. Release the rod and check that the rod remains retracted for at least 10 seconds. If not, renew the diaphragm assembly.
24 On reassembly renew any worn components and fit a complete set of new gaskets and seals. Spare parts are available from your Proton dealer.
25 Reassembly is a reversal of the dismantling procedure, noting the following.
a) *Ensure that all jets are securely locked in position, but take great care not to overtighten them.*
b) *Ensure that all mating surfaces are clean and dry, and that all body sections are correctly assembled with their fuel and air passages correctly aligned.*
c) *On refitting the idle mixture adjustment screw, screw the screw in until it seats lightly, then back the screw off by the number of turns noted on removal, to return the screw to its original position.*
d) *During reassembly/prior to refitting the carburettor to the vehicle, set the float height, throttle valve fast idle and choke pull-down settings as described below. Also ensure that the pump throttle and accelerator pump linkages work smoothly and easily.*

Adjustments

Idle speed and mixture

26 Refer to Chapter 1.

Float height setting

27 Invert the carburettor body, so the float is at the top then lift up the float so that it contacts its stop. Hold the float in this position and check that the clearance between the end of the needle valve and the float tang is as given in the *Specifications* **(see illustration)**. If adjustment is necessary, alter the clearance by carefully bending the float stopper tang until the clearance is as specified.
28 With the carburettor body still inverted, slowly release the float and allow it to hang down under its own weight and depress the needle valve. Measure the distance between the upper edge of the float and the sealing face of the upper body **(see illustration)**. This measurement should be as given in the *Specifications* at the start of this Chapter. If necessary, the float height can be adjusted by *carefully* bending the float arm at the point where it joins the floats. **Note:** *It will be a lot easier to bend the float arm if the float is removed from the carburettor.*

Throttle valve fast idle setting

29 To ensure accuracy, the carburettor must be at room temperature (20°C) or colder.
30 Use the shank of a twist drill to measure the clearance between the wall of the throttle bore and the primary throttle valve **(see illustration)**. Refer to the *Specifications* at the start of this Chapter for the required drill size.

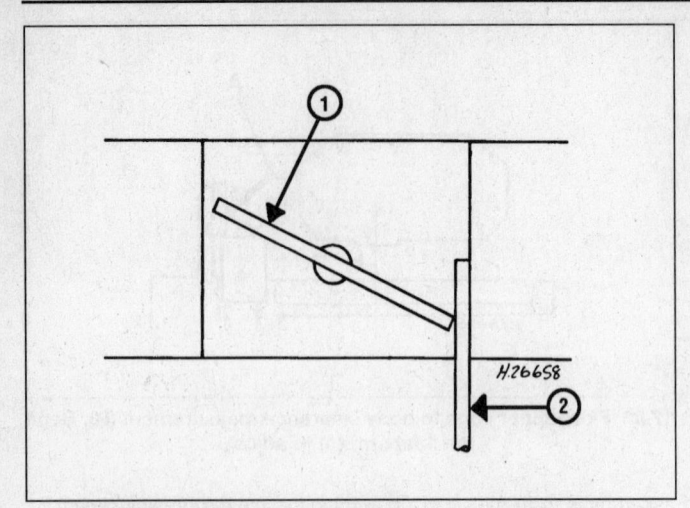

4A•10 Fuel and exhaust systems - carburettor engines

12.30 Measuring the primary throttle valve (1) to throttle bore clearance using a twist drill (2)

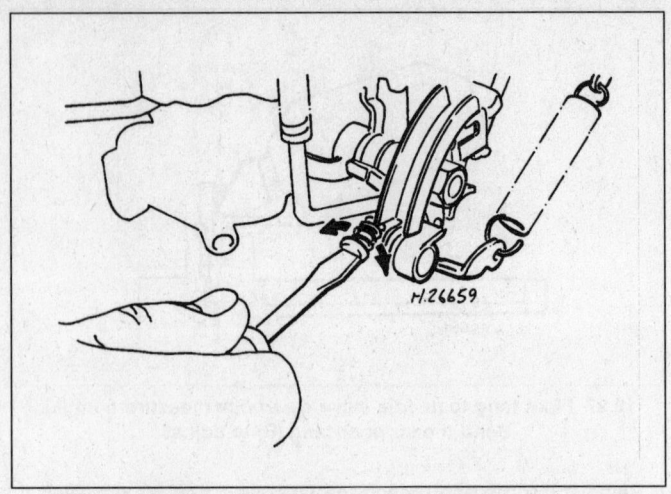

12.31 Adjust the fast idle setting by rotating the adjustment screw on the throttle mechanism

31 If necessary, adjust the clearance by turning the fast idle adjustment screw in the appropriate direction **(see illustration)**. Once the clearance is correctly set, remove the twist drill.

Choke pull-down setting

32 To ensure accuracy, the carburettor must be at room temperature (20°C) or colder.
33 Attach a vacuum pump to the choke pull-down connector. Operate the pump and check that the diaphragm pullrod retracts fully and that the vacuum is maintained for at least 30 seconds. Renew the diaphragm assembly if it fails these tests.
34 With the pullrod fully retracted, use the shank of a twist drill to measure the gap between the upper edge of the choke flap and the air inlet, as shown **(see illustration)**. Refer to the *Specifications* at the start of this Chapter for the required drill size.
35 If necessary, adjust the clearance by carefully bending the end of the choke pull-down diaphragm pullrod **(see illustration)**.

Once the clearance is correctly set, remove the twist drill.

13 Carburettor (12-valve models) - fault diagnosis, overhaul and adjustments

Fault diagnosis

1 Refer to Section 12.

Overhaul

Note: *Refer to the warning note in Section 1 before proceeding.*

2 Remove the carburettor from the engine as described in Section 11.
3 Make a note of the correct fitted locations of all the relevant hoses still attached to the carburettor then disconnect and remove them.
4 Unscrew the idle cut-off solenoid from the carburettor body, and remove it along with its plunger and spring **(see illustration)**. To test

the solenoid, connect a 12-volt battery to it (positive terminal to the solenoid terminal, negative terminal to the solenoid body), and check that the plunger is retracted fully into the body. Disconnect the battery, and check that the plunger is pushed out by spring pressure. If the valve does not perform as expected, and cleaning does not improve the situation, the solenoid valve must be renewed.
5 Detach the dashpot assembly (where fitted); this may be retained by an upper body fixing screw.
6 Undo the retaining screws and remove the air filter mounting bracket.
7 Unhook the spring(s), noting their correct fitted locations, then undo the retaining screws and remove the compensator assembly.
8 Remove the pin then unscrew the accelerator pump lever retaining bolt and detach the pump lever and spring.
9 Remove the retaining screws and lift off the float chamber.

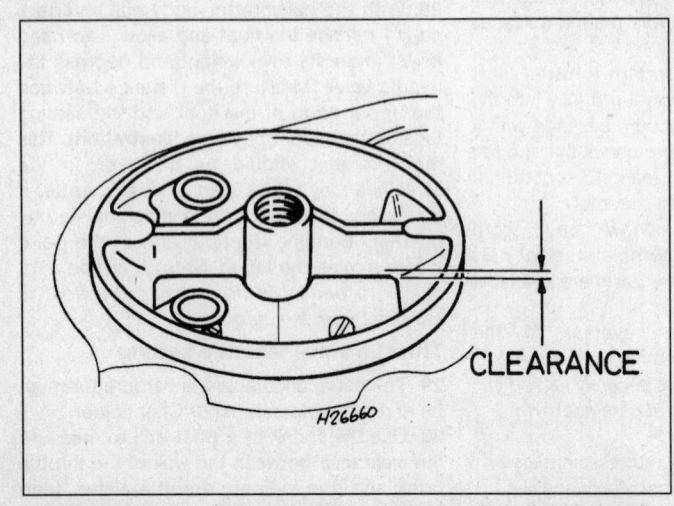

12.34 Check the choke pull-down setting as described in text by measuring the gap between the choke flap and inlet as shown

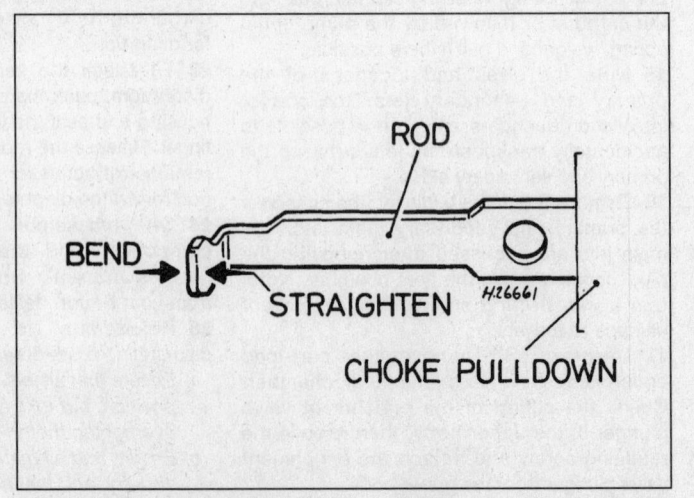

12.35 Adjust the choke pull-down setting by carefully bending the end of the diaphragm pullrod

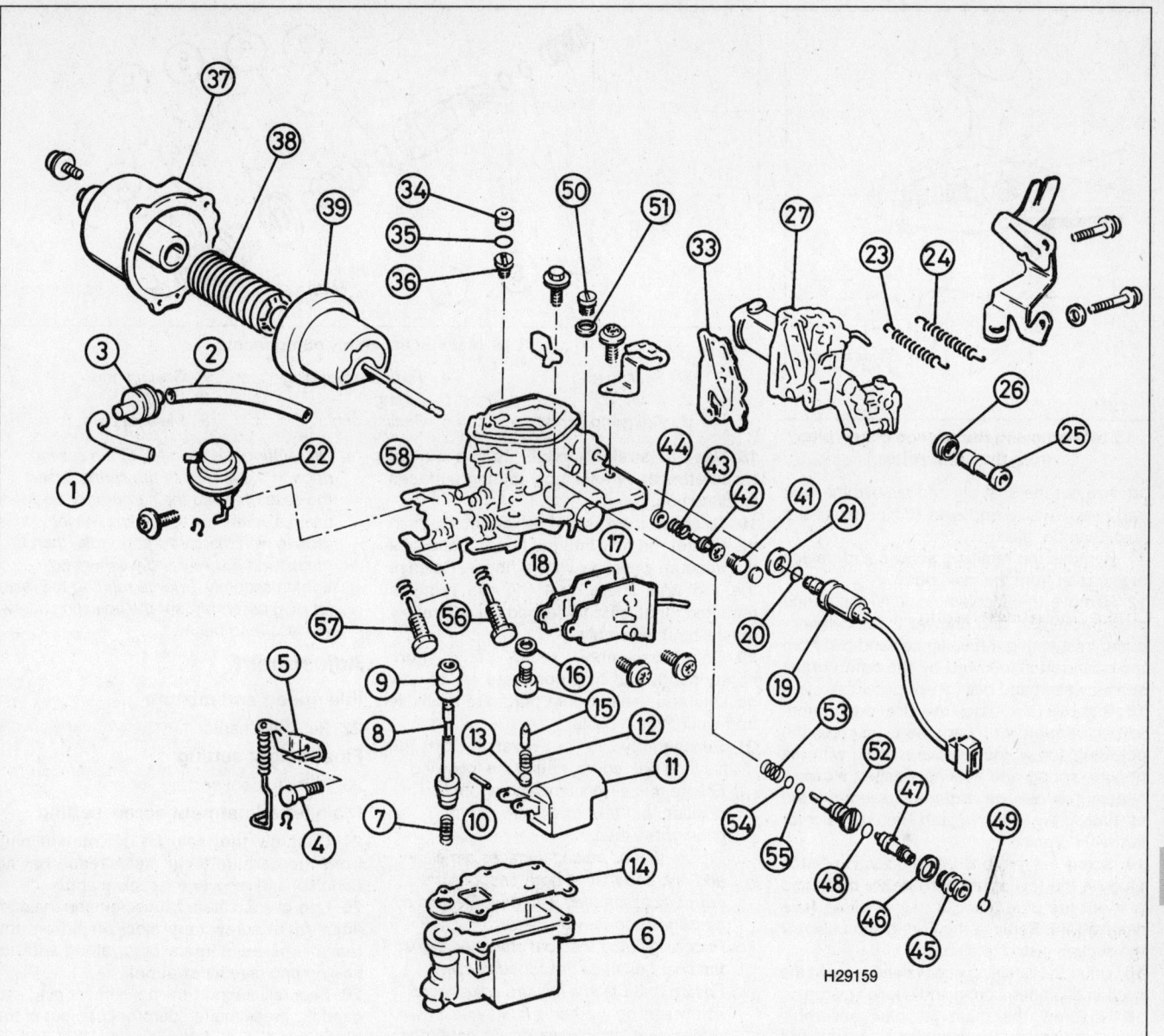

Fuel and exhaust systems - carburettor engines 4A•11

13.4 Exploded view of the carburettor - 12-valve models

1 Hose*	18 Gasket	42 Needle
2 Hose*	19 Idle cut-off solenoid	43 Spring
3 Delay valve*	20 Sealing ring	44 Washer
4 Pivot screw	21 Washer	45 Main jet plug
5 Accelerator pump lever	22 Dashpot	46 Washer
6 Float bowl	23 Spring	47 Main jet adjusting screw
7 Spring	24 Spring	48 Sealing ring
8 Accelerator pump plunger	25 Cold enrichment rod	49 Tamperproof plug
9 Gaiter	26 Gaiter	50 Main jet retaining screw
10 Pivot pin	27 Compensator	51 Washer
11 Float	33 Gasket	52 Main jet
12 Spring	34 Suction piston plug	53 Spring
13 Pin	35 Sealing ring	54 Sealing ring
14 Gasket	36 Suction piston retainer pin	55 Sealing ring
15 Needle valve and seat	37 Suction chamber	56 Idle speed adjusting screw
16 Washer	38 Spring	57 Dashpot adjusting screw*
17 Adapter	39 Suction piston	58 Main body
	41 Idle mixture adjusting screw	*Not fitted to all models

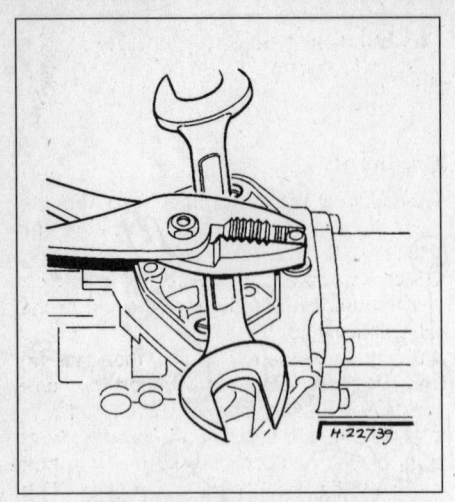

4A•12 Fuel and exhaust systems - carburettor engines

13.14 Removing the suction piston plug from the carburettor

10 Tap out the float pin and remove the float and needle valve and seat components and float chamber gasket.
11 Remove the retaining screws and detach the adapter from the main body.
12 Remove the accelerator pump gaiter and piston assembly and recover the accelerator pump inlet spring, retaining clip and ball from the carburettor followed by the pump outlet spring, weight and ball (where possible).
13 Remove the idle mixture adjustment screw tamperproof cap then unscrew the adjusting screw and remove it along with the needle, spring and sealing washer. **Note:** *A special tool will be required to remove the mixture screw - refer to your Proton dealer for further information.*
14 Screw a 4 mm bolt into the suction piston plug on the top of the carburettor body and pull out the plug using a pair of pliers **(see illustration)**. Remove the O-ring and unscrew the suction piston retainer pin.
15 Undo the retaining screws and remove the suction chamber, spring and suction piston.
16 Unscrew the main jet plug assembly (which contains the adjusting screw) and remove it from the carburettor body along with its sealing ring. Unscrew the main jet retaining screw and washer then recover the main jet, sealing rings and spring **(see illustration)**. **Note:** *Take care not to allow the jet to fly out of the carburettor as the retaining screw is removed.*
17 Clean the jets, carburettor body assemblies, float chamber and internal drillings. An air line may be used to clear the internal passages once the carburettor is fully dismantled.

⚠ **Warning:** *If high pressure air is directed into drillings and passages were a diaphragm is fitted, the diaphragm is likely to be damaged. Aerosol cans of carburettor cleaner are widely available and can prove very useful in helping to clear internal passages of stubborn obstructions.*

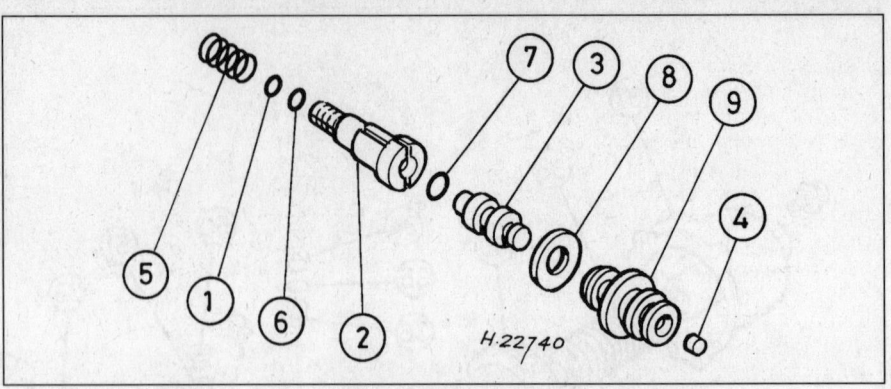

13.16 Main jet assembly components

1 Sealing ring
2 Main jet
3 Adjusting screw
4 Tamperproof plug
5 Spring
6 Sealing ring
7 Sealing ring
8 Washer
9 Main jet plug

18 Use a straight edge to check all carburettor body assembly mating surfaces for distortion.
19 To check the dashpot (where fitted), push the control rod fully into the housing and seal the vacuum passage with a finger. Release the rod and check that the rod remains retracted for at least 10 seconds. If not, renew the dashpot assembly.
20 On reassembly renew any worn components and fit a complete set of new gaskets and seals. Spare parts are available from your Proton dealer.
21 Reassembly is a reversal of the dismantling procedure, noting the following.
 a) *Ensure that all jets are securely locked in position, but take great care not to overtighten them.*
 b) *Ensure that all mating surfaces are clean and dry, and that all body sections are correctly assembled with their fuel and air passages correctly aligned.*
 c) *Prior to refitting the float chamber, adjust the float height as described below.*
 d) *Ensure that the idle mixture adjustment screw sealing washer is fitted with its rubber seal facing inwards. Do not fit the tamperproof cap until the screw is correctly adjusted.*
 e) *On refitting the main jet, fit the sealing rings to the jet and fit the spring. Insert the assembly into the carburettor body using a screwdriver, aligning the jet groove with the carburettor hole, then fit the retaining screw and washer and tighten securely. Prior to refitting the main jet plug assembly, set the adjusting screw as described below.*

Adjustment

Idle speed and mixture
22 Refer to Chapter 1.

Float height setting
23 Refer to Section 12.

Main jet adjustment screw setting
24 Unscrew the main jet adjustment plug from the carburettor (if not already having done so) and recover the sealing ring.
25 Use pliers, carefully unscrew the main jet adjustment screw (anti-clockwise) from the rear of the adjustment plug, along with its sealing ring **(see illustration)**.
26 Securely support the adjustment plug and carefully press the tamperproof cap out of the plug using a suitable punch; the cap is pushed out from inside the plug **(see illustration)**.

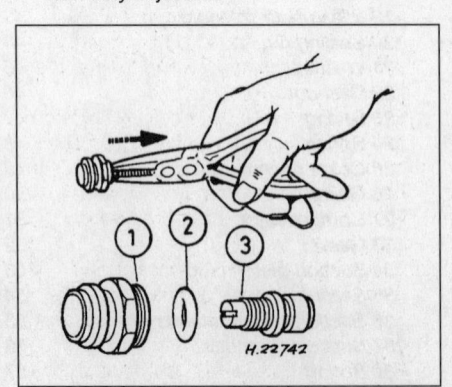

13.25 Removing the adjusting screw (3) and sealing ring (2) from the rear of the main jet plug (1)

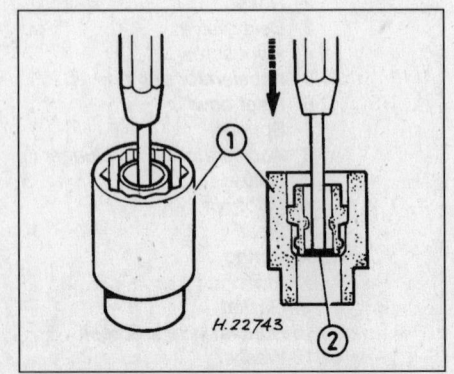

13.26 Support the main jet plug in a suitable socket (1) and press out the tamperproof plug (2)

27 Refit the main jet adjustment screw and sealing ring to the plug then refit the plug assembly and sealing washer to the carburettor, tightening it securely.
28 Rotate the adjustment screw until its outer face is positioned at the specified distance bin from the outer edge of the plug (see *Specifications*) **(see illustration)**. Do not refit the tamperproof cap yet as further adjustment will be required when the carburettor is refitted to the engine.
29 Remove the tamperproof cap from the idle mixture adjustment screw (if not already having done so) and position the screw so that it protrudes from the carburettor body by the specified distance (see *Specifications*). **Note:** *A special tool will be required to remove the mixture screw - refer to your Proton dealer for further information.*
30 If the adjustment is being carried out with the carburettor removed from the vehicle, it will now be necessary to refit it to the vehicle (see Section 11).
31 Referring to Chapter 1, ensure that all the requirements needed to ensure that the idle speed and mixture check are accurate are met. Connect a tachometer and exhaust gas analyser (CO meter) to the vehicle.
32 Allow the engine to idle then hold the engine speed at 3000 rpm and let the CO level stabilise.
33 With the engine at 3000 rpm, the exhaust gas CO level should be approximately 0.5%. If necessary, adjust the level by altering the position of the main jet adjustment screw; turning the screw clockwise will reduce the CO level, and turning the screw anti-clockwise will increase the CO level.
34 Turn the main jet adjusting screw another half of a turn clockwise; the reading at 3000 rpm should decrease to 0.125%. If the CO level is incorrect, repeat the operations described in paragraphs 32 and 33.
35 Once the CO level is correctly set, allow the engine to for a few minutes then adjust the idle speed and mixture settings as described in Chapter 1. Once they are correctly set, disconnect the tachometer and gas analyser and fit the tamperproof caps to the main jet adjustment plug and idle mixture adjusting screw.

14 Inlet manifold - removal and refitting

Note: *Refer to the warning note in Section 1 before proceeding.*

Removal

1 Remove the carburettor as described in Section 12.
2 Drain the cooling system as described in Chapter 1.
3 Noting the correct fitted location of each hose, release the retaining clips and disconnect the vacuum servo unit hose, the coolant hoses and the vacuum/breather hoses from the manifold.
4 Unscrew the retaining bolts and remove the support bracket from underneath the manifold.
5 Make a final check that all the necessary vacuum/breather hoses have been disconnected from the manifold.
6 Slacken and remove the manifold retaining nuts and bolts, noting the correct fitted location of the engine lifting bracket, then manoeuvre the manifold away from the head and out of the engine compartment. Recover the gasket(s) from the manifold studs and discard.

Refitting

7 Refitting is the reverse of the removal procedure, noting the following points:
a) *Prior to refitting, examine all the manifold studs for signs of damage and corrosion; remove all traces of corrosion, and repair or renew any damaged studs.*
b) *Ensure that the manifold and cylinder head mating surfaces are clean and dry, and fit the new gasket(s) (as applicable). Install the manifold, ensuring that the lifting bracket is correctly positioned, and tighten its retaining nuts and bolts to the specified torque setting.*
c) *Ensure that the support bracket is fitted the correct way up with the "UP" marking at the top. Tighten by the bracket bolts by hand to settle the bracket in position then tighten them to the specified torque setting.*
d) *Ensure that all relevant hoses are reconnected to their original positions, and are securely held (where necessary) by their retaining clips.*
e) *Refit the carburettor as described in Section 11.*
f) *On completion, refill the cooling system as described in Chapter 1.*

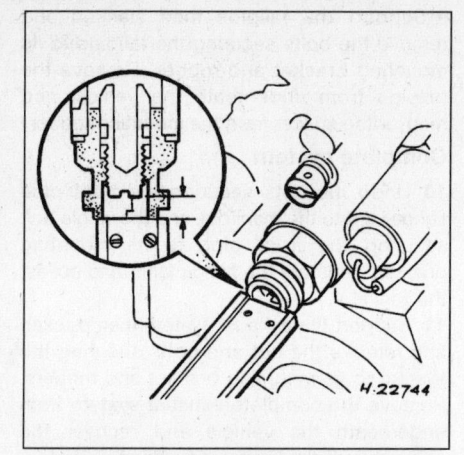

13.28 Set the adjustment screw to main jet plug distance to the measurement given in the Specifications (see text)

15 Exhaust manifold - removal and refitting

Removal

1 Disconnect the hot-air inlet hose from the manifold shroud, and remove it from the vehicle.
2 Slacken and remove the retaining screws, and remove the shroud from the top of the exhaust manifold.
3 Firmly apply the handbrake, then jack up the front of the vehicle and support it on axle stands (see "*Jacking and vehicle support*").
4 Undo the nuts securing the exhaust front pipe to the manifold, then remove the bolt securing the front pipe to its mounting bracket. Disconnect the front pipe from the manifold, and recover the gasket.
5 Slacken and remove the retaining nuts securing the manifold to the head, noting the correct fitted location of the engine lifting bracket. Manoeuvre the manifold out of the engine compartment, and discard the manifold gasket.

Refitting

6 Refitting is the reverse of the removal procedure, noting the following points:
a) *Examine all the exhaust manifold studs for signs of damage and corrosion; remove all traces of corrosion, and repair or renew any damaged studs.*
b) *Ensure that the manifold and cylinder head sealing faces are clean and flat, and fit the new manifold gasket. Refit the manifold retaining nuts, ensuring that the lifting bracket is correctly positioned, and tighten them to the specified torque.*
c) *Reconnect the front pipe to the manifold using the information given in Section 16.*

16 Exhaust system - general information, removal and refitting

General information

1 The exhaust system consists of two sections; the front pipe section, incorporating the front silencer box, and the tailpipe section which incorporates the main silencer box. The sections are joined by flanged joints which are secured by nuts or bolts.
2 The system is suspended throughout its entire length by rubber mountings.

Removal

3 The exhaust sections can be removed individually, or alternatively, the complete system can be removed as a unit.
4 To remove the system or part of the system, first jack up the front or rear of the car, and support it on axle stands (see

"*Jacking and vehicle support*"). Alternatively, position the car over an inspection pit, or on car ramps.

Front pipe

5 Undo the nuts securing the front pipe flange joint to the manifold, and the single bolt securing the front pipe to its mounting bracket. Separate the flange joint, and collect the gasket.

6 Slacken and remove the bolts securing the front pipe flange joint to the tailpipe and recover the gasket.

7 Support the front pipe then slacken and remove the retaining nut securing the pipe to the rubber mounting. Remove the front pipe from underneath the vehicle and recover the spacer from the mounting rubber.

Tailpipe

8 Slacken and remove the bolts securing the tailpipe flange joint to the front pipe and recover the gasket.

9 Support the tailpipe then slacken and remove the bolts securing the tailpipe to its mounting bracket and rubber. Remove the tailpipe from underneath the vehicle and recover the spacer from the mounting rubber.

Complete system

10 Undo the nuts securing the front pipe flange joint to the manifold, and the single bolt securing the front pipe to its mounting bracket. Separate the flange joint, and collect the gasket.

11 Support the exhaust system then slacken and remove the nut and bolts securing the system to its mounting bracket and rubbers. Remove the complete exhaust system from underneath the vehicle and recover the spacers from the rubber mountings.

Refitting

12 Each section is refitted by reversing the removal sequence, noting the following points:

a) *Ensure that all traces of corrosion have been removed from the flanges, and renew all necessary gaskets.*
b) *Inspect the rubber mountings for signs of damage or deterioration, and renew as necessary.*
c) *Prior to tightening the exhaust system fasteners, ensure that all rubber mountings are correctly located, and that there is adequate clearance between the exhaust system and vehicle underbody. Ensure that all fasteners are tightened to their specified torque settings.*

Chapter 4 Part B:
Fuel and exhaust systems - multi-point fuel injection models

Contents

Accelerator cable - removal, refitting and adjustment 3
Accelerator pedal - removal and refitting 4
Air cleaner assembly and inlet ducts - removal and refitting 2
Air cleaner filter element renewal .... See Chapter 1
Exhaust manifold - removal and refitting 16
Exhaust system - general information, removal and refitting 16
Exhaust system check .... See Chapter 1
Fuel filter - renewal .... See Chapter 1
Fuel gauge sender unit - removal and refitting 9
Fuel injection system - depressurisation 7
Fuel injection system - general information 6

Fuel injection system - testing and adjustment 11
Fuel injection system components - removal and refitting 13
Fuel pump - removal and refitting 8
Fuel tank - removal and refitting 10
General fuel system checks .... See Chapter 1
General information and precautions 1
Idle speed and mixture adjustment .... See Chapter 1
Inlet manifold - removal and refitting 14
Throttle housing - removal and refitting 12
Unleaded petrol - general information and usage 5

Degrees of difficulty

| Easy, suitable for novice with little experience | Fairly easy, suitable for beginner with some experience | Fairly difficult, suitable for competent DIY mechanic | Difficult, suitable for experienced DIY mechanic | Very difficult, suitable for expert DIY or professional |

Specifications

Fuel system data
Fuel pump type .... Electric, immersed in tank
Fuel system pressure (at specified idle speed):
  With pressure regulator vacuum hose connected .... 2.7 bar
  With pressure regulator vacuum hose disconnected .... 3.3 to 3.5 bar
Specified idle speed .... 750 ± 50 rpm
Idle mixture CO content .... Less than 1.0 % (not adjustable - controlled by ECU)

Recommended fuel
Minimum octane rating .... 95 RON unleaded (UK unleaded premium). Leaded fuel must **not** be used

Torque wrench settings

	Nm	lbf ft
Exhaust manifold nuts	20	15
Exhaust system fasteners:		
Front pipe to manifold nuts	40	29
Front pipe mounting bolt	35	25
Front pipe to catalytic converter bolts	15	11
Tailpipe to catalytic converter nuts	25	18
Tailpipe mounting bolt	10	7
Mounting rubber fixing nuts/bolts	15	11
Fuel feed hose union bolts	9	7
Fuel rail mounting bolts	12	9
Fuel pressure regulator retaining bolts	9	7
Inlet manifold:		
Manifold retaining nuts/bolts	18	13
Support bracket bolts	30	22
Throttle housing retaining bolts	19	14

4B•2 Fuel and exhaust systems - multi-point fuel injection models

2.1a Disconnect the breather hose . . .

2.1b . . . then slacken the retaining clips (arrowed) and remove the duct

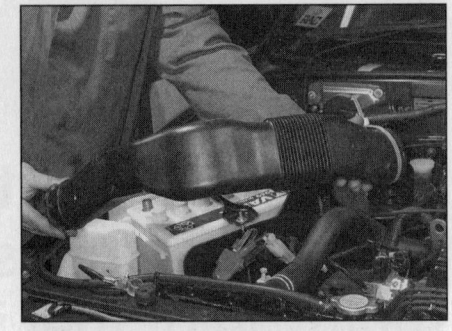

2.2 Removing the air cleaner housing inlet duct

2.3 Slacken and remove the retaining nuts and washers (locations arrowed) and lift out the air cleaner housing

3.1 Detach the accelerator cable from the throttle cam then undo the retaining bolts (arrowed) . . .

3.3 . . . and release the cable from all the relevant retaining clips

1 General information and precautions

The fuel supply system consists of a fuel tank (which is mounted under the rear of the car, with an electric fuel pump immersed in it), a fuel filter, fuel feed and return lines. The fuel pump supplies fuel to the fuel rail, which acts as a reservoir for the four fuel injectors which inject fuel into the inlet tracts. The fuel filter incorporated in the feed line from the pump to the fuel rail ensures that the fuel supplied to the injectors is clean.

Refer to Section 6 for further information on the operation of the fuel injection system, and to Section 16 for information on the exhaust system.

Warning: *Many of the procedures in this Chapter require the removal of fuel lines and connections, which may result in some fuel spillage. Before carrying out any operation on the fuel system, refer to the precautions given in "Safety first!" at the beginning of this manual, and follow them implicitly. Petrol is a highly-dangerous and volatile liquid, and the precautions necessary when handling it cannot be overstressed.*

Note: *Residual pressure will remain in the fuel lines long after the vehicle was last used. When disconnecting any fuel line, first depressurise the fuel system as described in Section 7.*

2 Air cleaner assembly and inlet ducts - removal and refitting

Removal

1 Disconnect the breather hose then release the retaining clips and remove the duct connecting the air cleaner housing to the throttle housing (see illustration).
2 Release the retaining clips and remove the inlet duct connecting the air cleaner housing to the wing valance (see illustration).
3 Slacken and remove the retaining nuts and washers and lift the housing out of the engine compartment (see illustration). Recover the spacer and mounting rubbers (where fitted) from the housing mounting. If necessary, the mounting bracket can be removed once its retaining nuts have been undone.

Refitting

4 Refitting is a reversal of the removal procedure, ensuring that the ducts are correctly seated and securely held by their retaining clips.

3 Accelerator cable - removal, refitting and adjustment

Removal

1 Working in the engine compartment, free the accelerator inner cable from the throttle cam (see illustration).
2 Slacken and remove the outer cable retaining bolts and free the outer cable from the inlet manifold.
3 Working back along the length of the cable, free it from any retaining clips or ties, noting its correct routing (see illustration).
4 From inside the vehicle, reach up behind the facia and unhook the inner cable from the top of the accelerator pedal. Tie a length of string to the end of the inner cable then depress the retaining clips and free the outer cable from the bulkhead.
5 Return to the engine compartment and remove the cable from the vehicle. When the end of the cable appears, untie the string and leave it in position - it can then be used to draw the cable back into position on refitting.

Refitting

6 Tie the string to the end of the cable, then use the string to draw the cable into position through the bulkhead. Once the cable end is visible, untie the string, and connect the inner cable to the upper end of the accelerator pedal.
7 From within the engine compartment, clip the outer cable end fitting securely into the bulkhead.
8 Work along the cable, ensuring it is correctly routed, securing it in position with the retaining clips and ties.
9 Connect the inner cable to the throttle cam then refit the outer cable bolts tightening them lightly. Adjust the cable as described below then securely tighten both bolts.

Adjustment

10 Ensure that all electrical items are switched off then start the engine and warm it up to normal operating temperature.
11 Ensure that the idle speed is correctly set (see Chapter 1) then switch the engine off.
12 Ensure that the cable is correctly routed then check that there is a small amount of freeplay (approximately 1 to 2 mm of slack) in the cable.
13 If adjustment is necessary, turn on the ignition switch (without starting the engine) and leave it switched on for approximately 15 seconds; this will initialise the idle speed control servo. Slacken the bolts securing the accelerator cable to the inlet manifold and adjust the cable so that there is 1 to 2 mm) freeplay in the inner cable before securely retightening the cable retaining bolts **(see illustration)**.
14 Ensure that the throttle cam is fully against its stop then have an assistant depress the accelerator pedal, and check that the throttle cam opens fully and returns smoothly to its stop then recheck the cable adjustment. On models with automatic transmission, once the accelerator cable is correctly adjusted, check the kickdown cable adjustment as described in Chapter 7B.

4 Accelerator pedal - removal and refitting

Refer to Chapter 4A, Section 8.

5 Unleaded petrol - general information and usage

Note: *The information given in this Chapter is correct at the time of writing. If updated information is thought to be required, check with a Proton dealer. If travelling abroad, consult one of the motoring organisations (or a similar authority) for advice on the fuel available.*

1 The fuel recommended by Proton is given in the Specifications Section of this Chapter, followed by the equivalent petrol currently on sale in the UK.
2 All Proton multi-point injection (MPI) models are designed to run on fuel with a minimum octane rating of 95 (RON). All models have a catalytic converter, and so must be run on unleaded fuel only. Under no circumstances should leaded fuel (UK "4-star") be used, as this may damage the converter.
3 Super unleaded petrol (98 octane) can also be used in all models if wished, though there is no advantage in doing so.

3.13 Adjust the accelerator cable by slackening the retaining bolts (arrowed) and repositioning the outer cable

6 Fuel injection systems - general information

The engine management (fuel injection/ignition) system is fitted to all fuel-injected models, incorporates a closed-loop catalytic converter and an evaporative emission control system, and complies with the very latest emission control standards. Refer to Chapter 5 for information on the ignition side of the system; the fuel side of the system operates as follows.

The fuel pump (which is immersed in the fuel tank) supplies fuel from the tank to the fuel rail, via a filter located in the engine compartment. Fuel supply pressure is controlled by the pressure regulator on the end of the fuel rail. When the optimum operating pressure of the fuel system is exceeded, the regulator allows excess fuel to return to the tank.

The electrical control system consists of the ECU, along with the following sensors:
a) *Throttle position sensor (also contains the idle position switch) - informs the ECU of the throttle position, and the rate of throttle opening/closing.*
b) *Coolant temperature sensor - informs the ECU of engine temperature.*
c) *Inlet air temperature sensor - informs the ECU of the temperature of the air passing through the inlet manifold.*
d) *Lambda sensor - informs the ECU of the oxygen content of the exhaust gases (explained in greater detail in Part C of this Chapter).*
e) *Manifold Absolute Pressure (MAP) sensor - informs the ECU of the load on the engine (expressed in terms of inlet manifold vacuum).*
f) *Crank angle sensor and TDC sensor (contained in the distributor assembly) - informs the ECU of the crankshaft position and speed of rotation and the position of No1 cylinder piston (see Chapter 5).*
g) *Vehicle speed sensor (contained in the speedometer assembly) - informs the ECU of the vehicle speed.*
h) *Power steering pressure switch (contained in the power steering pump) - informs the ECU when the power steering pump is under load.*

All the above signals are analysed by the ECU, and it selects the fuelling response appropriate to those values. The ECU controls the fuel injectors (varying the pulse width - the length of time the injectors are held open - to provide a richer or weaker mixture, as appropriate). The mixture is constantly varied by the ECU, to provide the best setting for cranking, starting (with either a hot or cold engine), warm-up, idle, cruising, and acceleration.

The ECU also has full control over the engine idle speed, via the idle speed control servo which bypasses the throttle valve. When the throttle valve is closed, the ECU controls the opening of the servo, which in turn regulates the amount of air entering the manifold, and so controls the idle speed.

The ECU also controls the exhaust and evaporative emission control systems, which are described in detail in Part C of this Chapter.

If there is an abnormality in any of the readings obtained from either the coolant temperature sensor, the inlet air temperature sensor or the lambda sensor, the ECU enters its back-up mode. In this event, it ignores the abnormal sensor signal, and assumes a pre-programmed value which will allow the engine to continue running (albeit at reduced efficiency). If the ECU enters this back-up mode, the warning light on the instrument panel will come on, and the relevant fault code will be stored in the ECU memory.

If the warning light comes on, the vehicle should be taken to a Proton dealer at the earliest opportunity where a complete test of the engine management system can then be carried out.

7 Fuel system - depressurisation

Note: *Refer to the warning note in Section 1 before proceeding.*

Warning: The following procedure will merely relieve the pressure in the fuel system - remember that fuel will still be present in the system components and take precautions accordingly before disconnecting any of them.

1 The fuel system referred to in this Section is defined as the tank-mounted fuel pump, the fuel filter, the fuel injectors, the fuel rail and the pressure regulator, and the metal pipes and flexible hoses of the fuel lines between these components. All these contain fuel which will be under pressure while the engine is running, and/or while the ignition is switched on. The pressure will remain for some time after the ignition has been

4B•4 Fuel and exhaust systems - multi-point fuel injection models

switched off, and it must be relieved in a controlled fashion when any of these components are disturbed for servicing work.

2 Remove the rear seat cushion (see Chapter 11) and disconnect the fuel pump wiring connector which is located underneath the seat on the left-hand side **(see illustration)**. This will disable the fuel pump.

3 Start the engine and allow it to run until it stalls, indicating that the fuel pressure present in the fuel lines/rail assembly has been released, then switch off the engine.

4 Reconnect the fuel pump wiring connector and refit the seat cushion.

8 Fuel pump - removal and refitting

Note: *Refer to the warning note in Section 1 before proceeding.*

Removal

1 Remove the fuel tank as described in Section 10.

2 Mark the hoses for identification purposes, then slacken the retaining clips and disconnect the fuel hoses from the top of the pump, and plug the hose ends.

3 Make alignment marks between the fuel pump and tank then slacken and remove the pump retaining nuts.

4 Carefully unclip the fuel pump assembly and lift it out of the fuel tank, taking great care not to damage the filter, or to spill fuel onto the interior of the vehicle. Recover the pump gasket and discard it - a new one must be used on refitting.

5 Note that the fuel pump is only available as a complete assembly, the only component being available separately is the fuel pick-up filter which should be renewed if it shows signs of damage or clogging.

Refitting

6 Ensure that the fuel pump pick-up filter is clean and free of debris and that the tank and pump mating surfaces are clean and dry.

7 Fit the new gasket to the top of the fuel tank and carefully manoeuvre the pump assembly into the fuel tank, and clip it into position in the base of the tank.

8 Refit the pump retaining nuts and tighten them securely.

9 Reconnect the hoses to the top of the fuel pump, using the marks made on removal to ensure that they are correctly reconnected, and securely tighten their retaining clips.

10 Refit the fuel tank to the vehicle (see Section 10).

9 Fuel gauge sender unit - removal and refitting

Refer to Chapter 4A, Section 5.

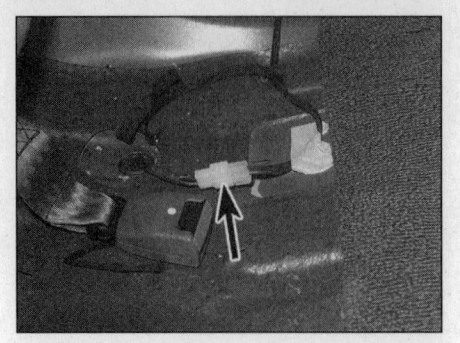

7.2 Fuel pump wiring connector (arrowed) for use when depressurising the fuel system

10 Fuel tank - removal and refitting

Refer to Chapter 4A, Section 6, bearing in mind the following.

a) Depressurise the fuel system as described in Section 7 of this Chapter before disconnecting the battery negative terminal. Once the fuel system has been depressurised, free the fuel pump wiring grommet from the floor so the wiring connector is free to move as the fuel tank is lowered out of position.

b) The high pressure fuel supply line hose union on the left-hand side of the tank is disconnected by unscrewing the union nut **(see illustration)**.

c) On refitting, ensure that the pump wiring is routed up through the floor as the tank is raised into position. Start the engine and check carefully for fuel leaks before taking the vehicle on the road.

11 Fuel injection system - testing and adjustment

Testing

1 If a fault appears in the fuel injection system, first ensure that all the system wiring connectors are securely connected and free

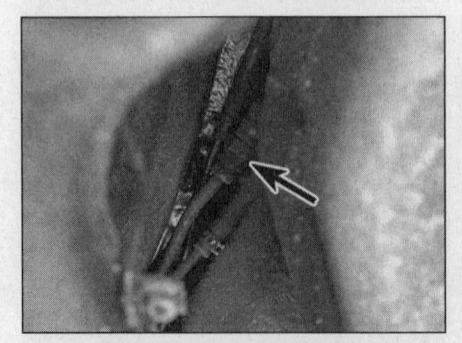

10.1 The high pressure fuel supply line (arrowed) is disconnected from the tank by unscrewing the union nut

of corrosion. Ensure that the fault is not due to poor maintenance; ie, check that the air cleaner filter element is clean, the spark plugs are in good condition and correctly gapped, the cylinder compression pressures are correct, the ignition timing is correct, and that the engine breather hoses are clear and undamaged, referring to Chapters 1, 2 and 5 for further information.

2 If these checks fail to reveal the cause of the problem, the vehicle should be taken to a suitably-equipped Proton dealer for testing. A wiring block connector is incorporated in the engine management circuit, into which a special electronic diagnostic tester can be plugged. The connector is coloured white and is located in the left-hand rear corner of the engine compartment; the brown coloured connector is the ignition timing adjustment connector **(see illustration)**. The tester will locate the fault quickly and simply, alleviating the need to test all the system components individually, which is a time-consuming operation that also carries a risk of damaging the ECU.

Adjustment

3 Experienced home mechanics with a considerable amount of skill and equipment (including a tachometer and an accurately calibrated exhaust gas analyser) may be able to check the exhaust CO level and the idle speed. However, if these are found to be in need of adjustment, the car *must* be taken to an equipped Proton dealer for further testing.

4 It is possible to adjust the idle speed and ignition timing. However, adjustments can be made only by re-programming the ECU, using special diagnostic equipment connected to the system via the diagnostic connector.

12 Throttle housing - removal and refitting

Removal

1 Disconnect the battery negative terminal.

2 Slacken the retaining clip then disconnect the inlet duct from the throttle housing and recover the sealing ring.

11.2 Engine management system diagnostic wiring connector location (arrowed)

Fuel and exhaust systems - multi-point fuel injection models 4B•5

13.2a Slacken and remove the retaining bolts . . .

13.2b . . . then detach the fuel feed hose union from the fuel rail noting its sealing ring (arrowed)

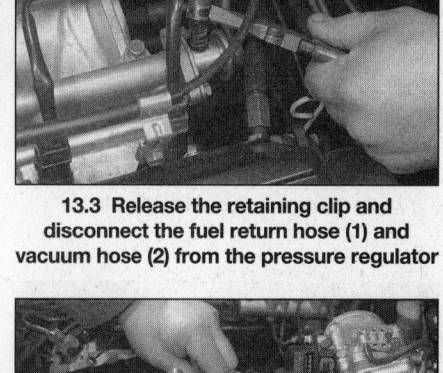

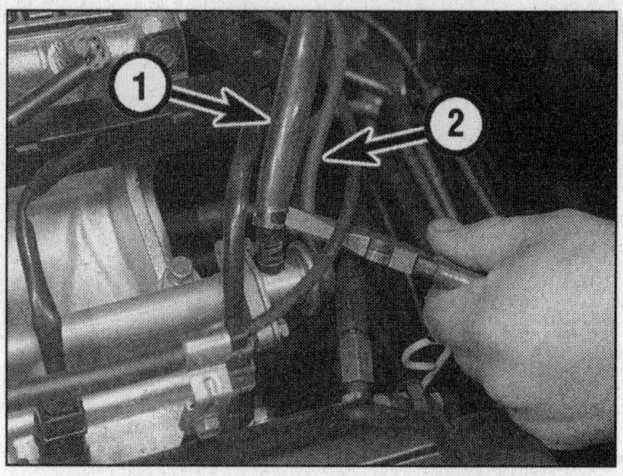

13.3 Release the retaining clip and disconnect the fuel return hose (1) and vacuum hose (2) from the pressure regulator

3 Disconnect the accelerator inner cable from the throttle cam. On automatic transmission models, also disconnect the kickdown cable.
4 Clamp the coolant hoses connecting the throttle housing to the thermostat housing then release the retaining clips and disconnect both hoses. Mop up any spilt coolant.
5 Depress the retaining clip and disconnect the wiring connectors from the throttle position sensor and the idle speed control servo assembly.
6 Slacken and remove the retaining screws and remove the throttle housing from the inlet manifold. Recover the housing gasket and discard it; a new one must be used on refitting.

Refitting

7 Ensure that the mating surfaces are clean and dry then offer up the new gasket and refit the throttle housing, tightening its retaining bolts to the specified torque.
8 Reconnect the wiring connectors to the throttle housing and connect the accelerator cable to the throttle cam.
9 Reconnect the coolant hoses to the housing, securing them in position with the retaining clips, and remove the hose clamps.
10 Reconnect the inlet duct securely to the throttle housing and reconnect the battery.
11 On completion, adjust the accelerator cable as described in Section 3 and, where necessary, the kickdown cable as described in Chapter 7B.

13 Fuel injection system components - removal and refitting

Fuel rail and injectors

Note: *Refer to the warning note in Section 1 before proceeding.*

> **HAYNES HINT** *If a faulty injector is suspected, before condemning the injector, it is worth trying the effect of one of the proprietary injector-cleaning treatments.*

Removal

1 Depressurise the fuel system as described in Section 7 then disconnect the battery negative terminal.
2 Unscrew the retaining bolts and disconnect the fuel feed hose union from the end of the fuel rail. Recover the sealing ring from the union and discard it; a new one must be used on refitting **(see illustrations)**.
3 Release the retaining clip and disconnect the fuel return hose and the vacuum pipe from the fuel pressure regulator **(see illustration)**.
4 Release the retaining clips and disconnect the wiring connectors from the four injectors **(see illustration)**.
5 Slacken and remove the fuel rail retaining bolts then carefully ease the fuel rail and injector assembly out from the inlet manifold

13.4 Release the retaining clips and disconnect the wiring connectors from the injectors

and remove it from the vehicle. Recover the spacers which are fitted between the fuel rail and inlet manifold. Recover the injector seals from the inlet manifold and discard them; they must be renewed whenever they are disturbed **(see illustrations)**.
6 Slide out the retaining clip(s) and remove the relevant injector(s) from the fuel rail. Remove the upper O-ring and rubber seal from each disturbed injector and discard; all disturbed O-rings and seals must be renewed **(see illustrations)**.

Refitting

7 Refitting is a reversal of the removal procedure, noting the following points.
 a) Fit new O-rings and seals to all disturbed injector unions **(see illustration)**.

13.5a Undo the retaining bolts (arrowed) . .

13.5b . . . then ease the fuel rail assembly out from the manifold . . .

13.5c . . . and recover the spacers (arrowed)

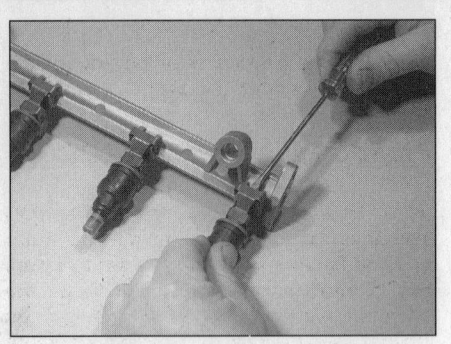

4B•6 Fuel and exhaust systems - multi-point fuel injection models

13.6a Slide out the retaining clip . . .

13.6b . . . then ease the injector out from the fuel rail and recover its upper O-ring and seal

13.7 On refitting, renew all the injector seals and O-rings

13.9a Disconnect the vacuum pipe . . .

13.9b . . . and the fuel return hose then undo the retaining bolts (arrowed) . . .

13.10 . . . and ease the pressure regulator out from the end of the fuel rail (sealing ring arrowed)

b) Apply a smear of engine oil to the O-ring and seal to aid installation then ease the injectors and fuel rail into position ensuring that the O-ring is not displaced.
c) Ensure that the spacers are correctly positioned between the fuel rail and manifold before tightening the retaining bolts to the specified torque.
d) Fit a new sealing ring to the feed hose union groove and tighten the union retaining bolts to the specified torque.
e) On completion start the engine and check for fuel leaks.

Fuel pressure regulator

Note: *Refer to the warning note in Section 1 before proceeding.*

Removal

8 Depressurise the fuel system as described in Section 7 then disconnect the battery negative terminal.
9 Release the retaining clip and disconnect the fuel return hose and the vacuum pipe from the fuel pressure regulator **(see illustrations)**.
10 Unscrew the retaining bolts and remove the pressure regulator from the end of the fuel rail. Recover the sealing ring from the regulator and discard it; a new one must be used on refitting **(see illustration)**.

Refitting

11 Refitting is the reverse of removal, noting the following.
a) Fit the new sealing ring to the regulator groove and smear it with engine oil to ease installation.
b) Tighten the regulator bolts to the specified torque and securely reconnect the fuel return hose and vacuum hose.

Throttle position sensor

Removal

12 Disconnect the battery negative terminal.
13 Release the retaining clip and disconnect the wiring connector from the throttle position sensor **(see illustration)**.
14 Slacken and remove the two retaining screws then disengage the sensor from the throttle valve spindle and remove it from the vehicle.

Refitting

15 Engage the sensor with the throttle valve spindle and lightly tighten its retaining screws.
16 Connect a multimeter, set to the resistance (ohmmeter) function, to the terminals of the sensor as shown **(see illustration)**.

13.13 Disconnecting the throttle position sensor wiring connector

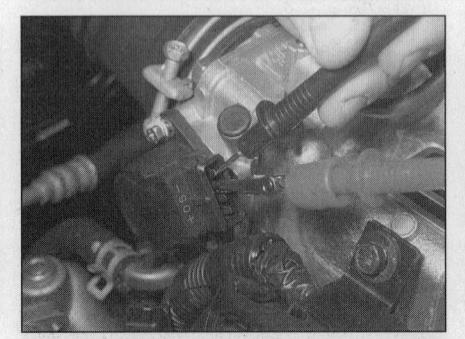

13.16 Connect a multimeter to the throttle position sensor as shown . . .

13.17 . . . then insert a 0.45 mm feeler blade in-between the throttle cam and fixed idle speed screw

Fuel and exhaust systems - multi-point fuel injection models 4B•7

13.30 Disconnect the wiring connector and vacuum hose from the MAP sensor

17 Insert a 0.45 mm feeler blade in between the throttle cam and the end of the fixed idle speed (SAS) adjustment screw **(see illustration)**. **Note:** *The fixed idle screw should not be moved.*
18 Slacken the retaining screws and rotate the sensor fully anti-clockwise. In this position there should be continuity between the sensor terminals. Slowly rotate the sensor in a clockwise direction until the point is found where an open circuit is present between the sensor terminals. Hold the sensor in this position and securely tighten its retaining screws.
19 Remove the feeler blade and reconnect the sensor wiring connector and battery negative terminal.

Electronic Control Unit (ECU)

Removal

20 The ECU is located under the front of the centre console assembly.
21 To remove the ECU first disconnect the battery.
22 Undo the retaining screws and remove the protective covers from the each side ECU.
23 Disconnect the wiring connector then undo the retaining screws and remove the ECU from the vehicle.

Refitting

24 Refitting is a reverse of the removal procedure ensuring that the wiring connector is securely reconnected.

Idle speed control servo assembly

Removal

25 Remove the throttle housing as described in Section 12.
26 Undo the retaining screws and remove the idle speed control servo assembly and seal from the base of the throttle housing. Discard the seal; a new one should be used on refitting.

Refitting

27 Ensure that the new seal is correctly located in its groove then fit the servo assembly to the base of the throttle housing and securely tighten its retaining screws.
28 Refit the throttle housing as described in Section 12.

13.33 The coolant temperature sensor (1) is screwed into the side of the thermostat housing. The rear sender (2) operates the coolant temperature gauge

Manifold absolute pressure (MAP) sensor

Removal

29 The MAP sensor is situated in the rear, left-hand corner of the engine compartment where it is mounted onto the bulkhead. To remove it, first disconnect the battery negative terminal.
30 Disconnect the wiring connector and vacuum hose from the MAP sensor **(see illustration)**.
31 Free the MAP sensor from the bracket and remove it from the engine compartment.

Refitting

32 Refitting is the reverse of the removal procedure.

Coolant temperature sensor

33 The coolant temperature sensor is screwed into the right-hand end of the thermostat housing **(see illustration)**. Refer to Chapter 3 for removal and refitting details.

Inlet air temperature sensor

Removal

34 The **inlet** air temperature sensor is screwed into the top of the inlet manifold. To remove the sensor first disconnect the battery negative terminal.
35 Disconnect the wiring connector then unscrew the sensor and remove it from the manifold along with its sealing washer **(see illustration)**.

13.35 Disconnecting the inlet air temperature sensor wiring connector

Refitting

36 Refitting is the reverse of removal using a new sealing washer if the original shows signs of damage.

Crank angle sensor and TDC sensor

37 Both the crank angle sensor and the TDC sensor are incorporated in the distributor body. At the time of writing, the sensors were not available separately and if faulty the complete distributor body will have to be renewed (see Chapter 5). Refer to your Proton dealer for the latest information.

Engine management system relay unit

Removal

38 The relay unit is located underneath the driver's side of the facia. To remove the relay unit, first disconnect the battery.
39 Reach up behind the facia and disconnect the wiring connector from the relay then undo the retaining screw(s) and remove the relay unit from underneath the facia.

Refitting

40 Refitting is the reverse of removal.

Vehicle speed sensor

41 The vehicle speed sensor is incorporated in the speedometer unit in the instrument panel. Refer to Chapter 12 for details.

14 Inlet manifold - removal and refitting

Note: *Refer to the warning note in Section 1 before proceeding.*

Removal

1 Carry out the operations described in paragraphs 1 to 4 of Section 13.
2 Slacken the retaining clip then disconnect the inlet duct from the throttle housing.
3 Disconnect the wiring connectors from the inlet air temperature sensor, the throttle housing, the distributor and the coolant temperature sensor(s) then undo the retaining bolts and free the wiring harness tray from the inlet manifold. Also slacken and remove the bolt securing the earth lead to the rear of the manifold **(see illustrations)**.
4 Drain the cooling system as described in Chapter 1. Slacken and remove the retaining nut and bolt, noting the correct fitted location of the engine lifting bracket, and free the thermostat housing assembly from the right-hand end of the cylinder head.
5 Disconnect the accelerator inner cable from the throttle cam, then undo the outer cable retaining bolts and free the cable from the manifold. On automatic transmission models also disconnect the kickdown cable (see Chapter 7B).

4B

Fuel and exhaust systems - multi-point fuel injection models 4B•9

16 Exhaust system - general information, removal and refitting

General information

1 On all fuel-injected models, the exhaust system consists of three sections; the front pipe, the catalytic converter, and the tailpipe and main silencer box. All exhaust sections are joined by flanged joints which are secured by nuts and/or bolts.
2 The system is suspended throughout its entire length by rubber mountings.

Removal

3 The exhaust sections can be removed individually, or alternatively, the complete system can be removed as a unit.
4 To remove the system or part of the system, first jack up the front or rear of the car, and support it on axle stands (see "*Jacking and vehicle support*"). Alternatively, position the car over an inspection pit, or on car ramps.

Front pipe

5 Trace the wiring back from the lambda sensor and disconnect it at the wiring connector.
6 Undo the nuts securing the front pipe flange joint to the manifold, and the single bolt securing the front pipe to its mounting bracket **(see illustration)**. Separate the flange joint, and collect the gasket. Discard the nuts; they should be renewed whenever they are disturbed.
7 Slacken and remove the bolts securing the front pipe flange joint to the catalytic converter and recover the gasket **(see illustration)**.
8 Support the front pipe then slacken and remove the retaining nut securing the pipe to the rubber mounting. Remove the front pipe from underneath the vehicle and recover the spacer from the mounting rubber.

Catalytic converter

9 Slacken and remove the bolts securing the front pipe flange joint to the catalytic converter and recover the gasket.
10 Slacken and remove the nuts securing the catalytic converter to the tailpipe then manoeuvre the converter out from underneath the vehicle and recover its rear gasket.

Tailpipe

11 Slacken and remove the nuts securing the tailpipe flange joint to the catalytic converter.
12 Support the tailpipe then slacken and remove the bolts securing the tailpipe to its mounting bracket and rubber. Remove the tailpipe from underneath the vehicle and recover the spacer from the mounting rubber and the gasket from its flange joint.

Complete system

13 Trace the wiring back from the lambda sensor and disconnect it at the wiring connector.
14 Undo the nuts securing the front pipe flange joint to the manifold, and the single bolt securing the front pipe to its mounting bracket. Separate the flange joint, and collect the gasket. Discard the nuts, they should be renewed whenever they are disturbed.
15 Support the exhaust system then slacken and remove the nut and bolts securing the system to its mounting bracket and rubbers. Remove the complete exhaust system from underneath the vehicle and recover the spacers from the rubber mountings.

Refitting

16 Each section is refitted by reversing the removal sequence, noting the following points:
  a) Ensure that all traces of corrosion have been removed from the flanges, and renew all necessary gaskets.
  b) Inspect the rubber mountings for signs of damage or deterioration, and renew as necessary.
  c) Ensure that the front pipe to manifold nuts are renewed whenever they are disturbed.
  d) Prior to tightening the exhaust system fasteners, ensure that all rubber mountings are correctly located, and that there is adequate clearance between the exhaust system and vehicle underbody. Ensure that all fasteners are tightened to their specified torque settings.
  e) Ensure that the lambda sensor wiring is correctly routed and in no danger of touching the hot exhaust/engine.

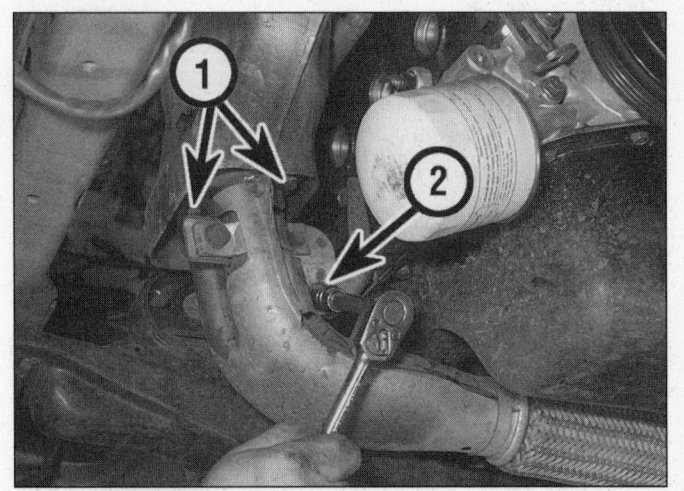

16.6 Slacken and remove the nuts (1) securing the front pipe to the manifold and the front pipe mounting bolt (2)

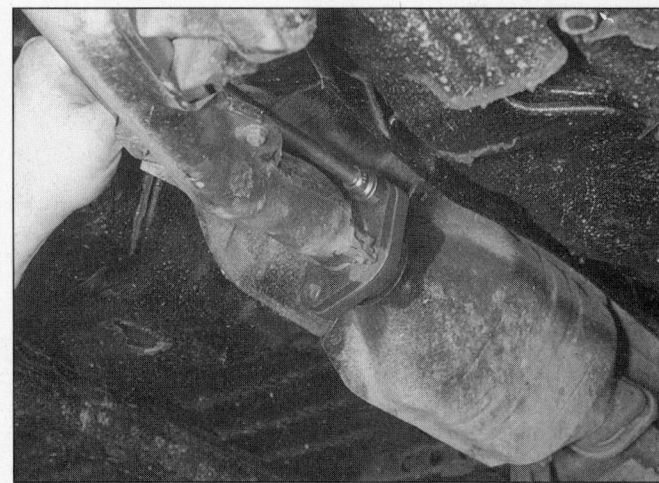

16.7 Removing the front pipe to catalytic converter bolts

Notes

Chapter 4 Part C:
Emissions control systems

Contents

Catalytic converter - general information and precautions 3
Emissions control systems - testing and component renewal 2
General information 1

Degrees of difficulty

| Easy, suitable for novice with little experience | Fairly easy, suitable for beginner with some experience | Fairly difficult, suitable for competent DIY mechanic | Difficult, suitable for experienced DIY mechanic | Very difficult, suitable for expert DIY or professional |

Specifications

Adjustment data - carburettor models

8-valve models:
Dashpot contact speed:
  1.3 litre models .... 1300 to 1700 rpm
  1.5 litre models:
    Manual transmission models .... 1200 to 2100 rpm
    Automatic transmission models .... 1300 to 1700 rpm
Deceleration time to drop back to 1000 rpm (see text):
  1.3 litre models .... 1.5 to 4.5 seconds
  1.5 litre models:
    Manual transmission models .... 3.5 to 6.5 seconds
    Automatic transmission models .... 1.5 to 4.5 seconds

12-valve models:
Dashpot speed:
  1.3 litre models .... 1500 ± 200 rpm
  1.5 litre models .... 1200 ± 200 rpm
Deceleration time from 3500 rpm (see text):
  1.3 litre models (drop to 900 rpm) .... 2.0 to 4.0 seconds
  1.5 litre models (drop to 1000 rpm) .... 2.2 to 4.2 seconds

Torque wrench settings

	Nm	lbf ft
Exhaust gas recirculation (EGR) system:		
Valve mounting bolts:		
M6 bolts	10	7
M8 bolts	24	17
Thermo valve	30	22
Lambda sensor	45	33
PCV valve	10	7

1 General information

All Proton models covered in this manual are capable of using unleaded petrol, and also have various other features built into the fuel system to help minimise harmful emissions as follows.

Carburettor models

Crankcase emissions control

To reduce the emission of unburned hydrocarbons from the crankcase into the atmosphere, the engine is sealed, and the blow-by gases and oil vapour are drawn from inside the crankcase, through the PCV valve, into the inlet tract, to be burned by the engine during normal combustion.

Under conditions of high manifold vacuum, the gases will be sucked positively out of the crankcase. Under conditions of low manifold vacuum, the gases are forced out of the crankcase by the (relatively) higher crankcase pressure; if the engine is worn, the raised crankcase pressure (due to increased blow-by) will cause some of the flow to return under all manifold conditions.

Dashpot - all models except 12-valve manual transmission models

The dashpot is fitted to reduce the amount of unburnt hydrocarbons in the exhaust gases on the overrun. It does this by preventing the throttle valve from being snapped shut, such as when the driver lifts off suddenly at high engine speeds. The dashpot acts as a damper, and slowly closes throttle valve during its final stages. This reduces the amount of unburnt hydrocarbons in the exhaust gases by preventing the excessively-high inlet manifold vacuum which would otherwise draw unburnt fuel into the exhaust.

4C•2 Emissions control systems

Exhaust gas recirculation (EGR) system - 1.3 litre models and 1.5 litre automatic transmission models

This system reduces the amount of unburnt hydrocarbons in the exhaust gases. This is achieved by taking some of the exhaust gases from the cylinder head exhaust ports and recirculating them back into the inlet manifold, where they are burned again during normal combustion. The exhaust gas recirculation (EGR) valve is fitted to the top of the inlet manifold with the gas being drawn back from the cylinder head, through a drilling in the inlet manifold and into the main inlet.

The system is controlled by the thermo valve (on 12-valve models there are two valves) which is screwed into the top of the inlet manifold, on the right-hand side. When the engine is cold, the thermo valve cuts off the vacuum supply to the EGR valve, and the valve remains closed. When the engine reaches operating temperature (approximately 80°C), the thermo valve opens, allowing the vacuum supply to act on the EGR valve; this opens the EGR valve and allows some of the exhaust gases to be recirculated back into the inlet manifold under certain operating conditions.

Fuel-injected models

Crankcase emissions control

Refer to paragraphs 2 and 3.

Catalytic converter

To minimise the amount of pollutants which escape into the atmosphere, all models are fitted with a catalytic converter in the exhaust system. The system is of the "closed-loop" type, in which an exhaust gas sensor provides the engine management control unit constant feedback, enabling the unit to adjust the mixture to provide the best possible conditions for the converter to operate.

The sensor's tip is sensitive to oxygen, and sends the control unit a varying voltage depending on the amount of oxygen in the exhaust gases; if the inlet air/fuel mixture is too rich, the sensor sends a high-voltage signal. The voltage falls as the mixture weakens. Peak conversion efficiency of all major pollutants occurs if the inlet air/fuel mixture is maintained at the chemically-correct ratio for the complete combustion of petrol - 14.7 parts (by weight) of air to 1 part of fuel (the "stoichiometric" ratio). The sensor output voltage alters in a large step at this point, the control unit using the signal change as a reference point, and correcting the inlet air/fuel mixture accordingly by altering the fuel injector pulse width (injector opening time). The sensor has a built-in heating element (controlled by the control unit), to quickly bring the sensor's tip to an efficient operating temperature.

Evaporative emissions control system

To minimise the escape of unburned hydrocarbons into the atmosphere, an evaporative emissions control system is fitted to models with a catalytic converter. The fuel tank filler cap is sealed, and a carbon canister collects the petrol vapours generated in the tank (fuel-injected models) or tank and carburettor float chamber (carburettor models) when the car is parked. It stores them until the vapours can be cleared into the inlet tract when the engine is running.

The system is controlled by the engine management control unit via a solenoid valve. To ensure that the engine runs correctly when it is cold and/or idling, and to protect the catalytic converter from the effects of an over-rich mixture, the solenoid valve is not opened by the control unit until the engine has warmed up and is under load. Once these conditions are met, the valve solenoid is modulated on and off to allow the stored vapour to pass into the inlet tract.

2 Emissions control systems - testing and component renewal

Crankcase emissions control

Testing

1 Inspect the breather hose for signs of damage or deterioration and renew if necessary.
2 If the hose is in good condition, remove the PCV valve from the cylinder head cover (see below) and reconnect it to the breather hose. Start the engine, allowing it to idle, and place a finger over the end of the PCV valve; if the valve is functioning correctly vacuum should be present in the hose. If not, the PCV valve is faulty and must be renewed. **Note:** *Prior to renewing the valve, trying cleaning the valve in solvent and see if this frees the valve internals.*

PCV valve - renewal

3 Disconnect the breather hose from the PCV valve then unscrew the valve from the cylinder head cover **(see illustration)**.
4 Fit the new valve to the cylinder head cover, tightening it to the specified torque, and reconnect the breather hose.

2.3 Removing the PCV valve from cylinder head cover

Dashpot - 8-valve carburettor models

Testing

5 Push the dashpot rod into the dashpot, making sure that the rod enters the dashpot slowly, then release the rod and check that it returns quickly. If not, the dashpot must be renewed.

Dashpot - renewal

6 Unscrew the retaining nut and washer and remove the dashpot from the side of the carburettor. If necessary, remove the air cleaner housing to improve access to the dashpot (see Chapter 4A).
7 Refitting is the reverse of removal. On completion, check and adjust the carburettor idle speed as described in Chapter 1. With the engine idling at the specified speed, carefully close the carburettor throttle lever until it just contacts the dashpot rod. Hold the throttle lever in this position and note the engine speed, then release the lever whilst noting the time it takes for the engine to return to 1000 rpm. Compare the results to the specified limits given in the Specifications. If adjustment is necessary, rotate the adjusting screw as required then recheck both the contact speed and return time **(see illustration)**. Once both values are within the specified limits, stop the engine and disconnect the tachometer.

Dashpot - 12-valve carburettor models

Testing

8 Disconnect the vacuum hose from the carburettor dashpot and connect a length of hose to the dashpot union. Suck on the hose and check that the dashpot rod retracts fully and that the vacuum is maintained for at least 10 seconds. If not the dashpot assembly should be renewed. Remove the hose used for the check and reconnect the vacuum hose.

Dashpot - renewal

9 If necessary, remove the air cleaner housing to improve access to the dashpot.
10 Disconnect the vacuum hose then remove the retaining clip securing the dashpot rod to the linkage.

2.7 Dashpot adjusting screw (arrowed) - 8-valve carburettor models

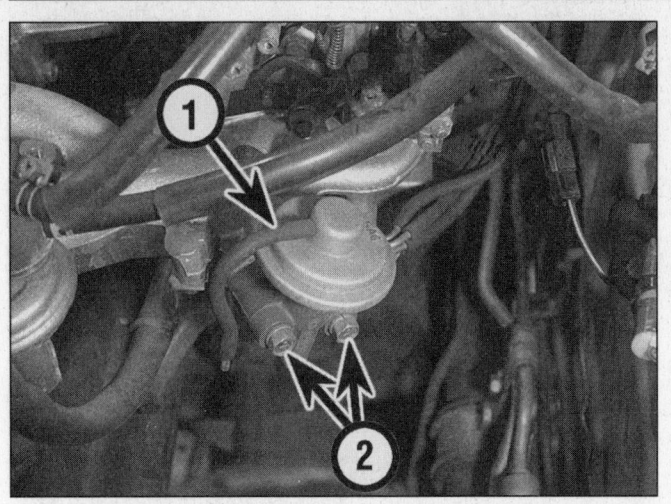

Emissions control systems 4C•3

2.17 Exhaust gas recirculation (EGR) valve vacuum hose (1) and retaining bolts (2) - 12-valve carburettor models

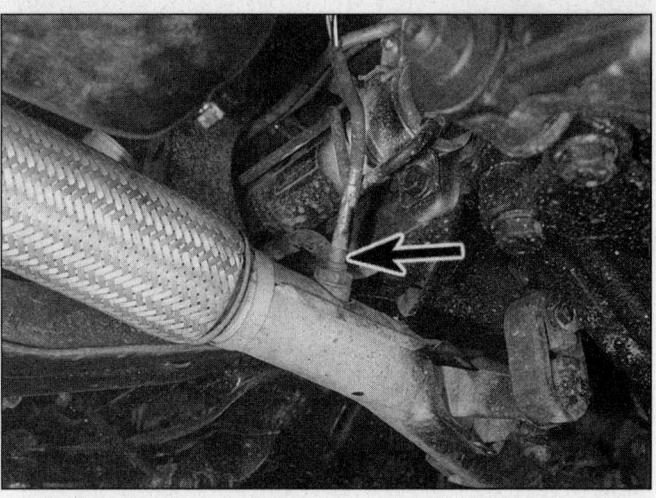

2.26 On fuel-injected models the Lambda sensor (arrowed) is screwed into the top of the exhaust front pipe

11 Undo the retaining screw and remove the dashpot from the carburettor.
12 Refitting is the reverse of removal. On completion, check and adjust the carburettor idle speed and mixture settings as described in Chapter 1. With the engine idling, disconnect the vacuum hose from the dashpot and plug the hose end. Move the throttle lever and increase the engine speed to 3500 rpm then slowly decrease the engine speed until the throttle lever is fully released. Check that the engine is idling at the specified dashpot speed (see Specifications), if necessary, adjustments can be made using the screw on the dashpot linkage. Once the speed is correctly set, reconnect the hose to the dashpot and increase the engine speed to 3500 rpm again. Release the throttle lever, noting the time taken for the engine to return to the specified speed (see Specifications) and compare this to the time given. If adjustment is necessary, rotate the adjusting screw as required then stop the engine and disconnect the tachometer.

Exhaust gas recirculation (EGR) system - carburettor 1.3 litre and 1.5 litre automatic transmission models

Testing

13 If the system is thought to be faulty, first check that the hose(s) linking the thermo valve(s) and the exhaust gas recirculation (EGR) valve are in good condition and unblocked.
14 To check the thermo valve, which is screwed into the right-hand end of the inlet manifold, with the engine cold, disconnect the EGR valve hose from the valve. Start the engine and allow it to idle; with the engine cold no vacuum should be present at the valve union. Warm the engine up to normal operating temperature (coolant temperature approximately 80°C) and check that vacuum is now present at the valve union. If the valve(s) do not perform as expected, it is faulty and must be renewed.
15 To check the operation of the EGR valve, disconnect the vacuum hose from the top of the valve, and fit a length of hose to the valve union. Suck on the hose end; check that the valve diaphragm is pulled up, and returns quickly when the vacuum is released. If the valve operation is sticky or does not move at all, the EGR valve must be renewed.

Exhaust gas recirculation (EGR) valve - renewal

16 Disconnect the vacuum hose from the EGR valve, which is mounted on the left-hand end of the inlet manifold.
17 Unscrew the two retaining bolts and remove the valve from the manifold **(see illustration)**. Remove the gasket and discard it.
18 Refitting is the reverse of removal, using a new gasket and tightening the mounting bolts to the specified torque.

Thermo valve - renewal

19 The thermo valve(s) is/are screwed into the right-hand side of the inlet manifold. The engine and manifold should be cold before removing the valve.
20 Have ready a suitable plug which can be used to plug the valve aperture in the manifold whilst it is removed. Ensure that the plug used, will not damage the manifold, and do not use anything which will allow foreign matter to enter the cooling system.
21 Disconnect both the vacuum hose(s) from the valve then carefully unscrew the valve from the manifold. Plug the valve aperture and wash off any spilt coolant (where applicable).
22 Refitting is the reverse of removal, applying a smear of sealing compound to the valve threads prior to refitting and tighten the valve to the specified torque.

Exhaust emissions control system - fuel-injected models

Testing

23 If the CO level at the tailpipe is too high, then a fault is present in the fuel injection/ignition system. Detailed testing of the sensor and catalytic converter must be left to a Proton dealer who has access to the necessary test equipment required (see Part B of this Chapter).

Catalytic converter - renewal

24 Refer to Part B of this Chapter.

Lambda (oxygen) sensor - renewal

Note: *The Lambda sensor is delicate, and it will not work if it is dropped or knocked, if its power supply is disrupted, or if any cleaning materials are used on it.*

25 Firmly apply the handbrake, then jack up the front of the vehicle and support it on axle stands (see "Jacking and vehicle support"). Trace the wiring back from the sensor (which is screwed into the front pipe), freeing it from any relevant retaining clips. Disconnect the wiring at the connector.
26 Unscrew the sensor, and remove it from underneath the vehicle **(see illustration)**.
27 Refitting is a reverse of the removal procedure. Prior to installing the sensor, apply a smear of high-temperature grease to the sensor threads. Tighten the sensor to the specified torque and ensure that the wiring is correctly routed, and in no danger of contacting either the exhaust system or the engine.

Evaporative emissions control system - fuel-injected models

Testing - all other fuel-injected models

28 If the system is thought to be faulty, disconnect the hoses from the carbon

4C•4 Emissions control systems

2.32 Release the retaining clip then free the carbon canister from its mounting bracket ...

2.33 ... and disconnect its hoses, noting each ones correct fitted location

canister and solenoid control valve, and check that they are clear by blowing through them. The canister is located on the right-hand side of the engine compartment, and the solenoid valve is located to the rear of the inlet manifold.

29 Detailed checking of the operation of the solenoid valve should be entrusted to a Proton dealer who will have the necessary equipment to check not only the valve but also the ECU which controls it. If the solenoid valve is faulty it must be renewed.

Carbon canister - renewal

30 The carbon canister is located on the right-hand rear corner of the engine compartment. To gain access to the canister, remove the air cleaner housing as described in Chapter 4B.

31 Make a note of the correct fitted location of each hose on the canister. To avoid the possibility of connecting the hoses incorrectly on refitting, make identification marks between each hose and its canister union (the canister unions are marked for identification).

32 Release the retaining clips and free the canister from its mounting bracket **(see illustration)**.

33 Disconnect the hoses from the top of the canister and remove it from the engine compartment **(see illustration)**.

34 Refitting is a reverse of the removal procedure, ensuring that the hoses are correctly reconnected.

Solenoid control valve - renewal

35 The solenoid control valve is located at the rear of the inlet manifold where it is mounted onto the engine compartment bulkhead **(see illustration)**.

36 To renew the solenoid valve, disconnect the battery negative terminal, then depress the retaining clip and disconnect the wiring connector from the valve.

37 Release the retaining clips (where fitted) then disconnect the hoses from the valve, and free the valve from its mounting bracket.

38 Refitting is a reverse of the removal procedure, ensuring that the hoses are correctly reconnected.

3 Catalytic converter - general information and precautions

The catalytic converter is a reliable and simple device which needs no maintenance in itself, but there are some facts of which an owner should be aware if the converter is to function properly for its full service life.

a) DO NOT use leaded petrol in a car with a catalytic converter - the lead will coat the precious metals, reducing their converting efficiency, and will eventually destroy the converter.
b) Always keep the ignition and fuel systems well-maintained in accordance with the manufacturer's schedule.
c) If the engine develops a misfire, do not drive the car at all (or at least as little as possible) until the fault is cured.
d) DO NOT push- or tow-start the car - this will soak the catalytic converter in unburned fuel, causing it to overheat when the engine does start.
e) DO NOT switch off the ignition at high engine speeds.
f) DO NOT use fuel or engine oil additives - these may contain substances harmful to the catalytic converter.
g) DO NOT continue to use the car if the engine burns oil to the extent of leaving a visible trail of blue smoke.
h) Remember that the catalytic converter operates at very high temperatures. DO NOT, therefore, park the car in dry undergrowth, over long grass, or over piles of dead leaves, after a long run.
i) Remember that the catalytic converter is FRAGILE - do not strike it with tools during servicing work.
j) In some cases, a sulphurous smell (like that of rotten eggs) may be noticed from the exhaust. This is common to many catalytic converter-equipped cars when new - once the car has covered a few thousand miles, the problem should disappear.
k) The catalytic converter, used on a well-maintained and well-driven car, should last for between 50 000 and 100 000 miles, but if the converter is no longer effective, it must be renewed.

2.35 Purge valve location - fuel-injected models

Chapter 5
Engine electrical systems

Contents

Alternator drivebelt - removal, refitting and tensioning 11
Alternator - removal and refitting 12
Alternator - testing and overhaul 13
Battery check .... See Chapter 1
Battery - removal and refitting 4
Battery - testing and charging 3
Charging system - testing 10
Distributor - removal and refitting 8
Electrical fault-finding - general information 2
Electrical system check .... See Chapter 1
General information and precautions 1
Ignition switch - removal and refitting 17
Ignition system - general information 5
Ignition system - testing 6
Ignition timing - checking and adjustment 9
Ignition system check .... See Chapter 1
Ignition HT coil - removal, testing and refitting 7
Oil pressure warning light switch - removal and refitting 18
Spark plug renewal .... See Chapter 1
Starter motor - removal and refitting 15
Starter motor - testing and overhaul 16
Starting system - testing 14

Degrees of difficulty

| **Easy,** suitable for novice with little experience | **Fairly easy,** suitable for beginner with some experience | **Fairly difficult,** suitable for competent DIY mechanic | **Difficult,** suitable for experienced DIY mechanic | **Very difficult,** suitable for expert DIY or professional |

Specifications

System type .... 12-volt, negative earth

Battery
Type .... Low-maintenance or maintenance-free, depending on model
Charge condition:
  Poor .... 12.5 volts
  Normal .... 12.6 volts
  Good .... 12.7 volts

Ignition system
System type:*
  Carburettor models .... Breakerless electronic ignition
  Fuel-injected models .... Breakerless electronic ignition controlled by fuel injection ECU
Refer to text for further information on each relevant system
Firing order .... 1-3-4-2 (No 1 cylinder at timing belt end)
Ignition timing (at specified idle speed):
  Carburettor models:
    8-valve models .... 4° ± 2° BTDC
  12-valve models:
    1.3 litre .... 3° ± 2° BTDC
    1.5 litre .... 2° ± 2° BTDC
  Fuel-injected models* .... 5° ± 2° BTDC
Special diagnostic equipment is needed to check the ignition timing on fuel-injected models - see text
Ignition HT coil resistances:*
  8-valve models:
    Primary windings .... 1.2 ohms
    Secondary windings .... 13.7 kilohms
  12-valve models:
    Primary windings .... 0.9 to 1.2 ohm
    Secondary windings .... 20 to 29 kilohms
The above results are approximate values, and are accurate only when the coil is at 20°C. See text for further information.

Torque wrench settings

	Nm	lbf ft
Alternator mounting bolts:		
Lower bolt	22	16
Upper bolt	15	11
Starter motor mounting bolts	30	22

1 General information and precautions

General information

1 The "engine" electrical system includes all charging, starting and ignition system components. Because of their engine-related functions, these components are covered separately from the "body" electrical devices such as the lights, instruments, etc (which are covered in Chapter 12).
2 The electrical system is of the 12-volt negative earth type.
3 The battery is of the low-maintenance or "maintenance-free" (sealed for life) type, and is charged by the alternator, which is belt-driven from the crankshaft pulley.
4 The starter motor is of the pre-engaged type, incorporating an integral solenoid. On starting, the solenoid moves the drive pinion into engagement with the flywheel ring gear before the starter motor is energised. Once the engine has started, a one-way clutch prevents the motor armature being driven by the engine until the pinion disengages from the flywheel.
5 Refer to Section 5 for further information on the ignition system.

Precautions

6 Further details of the various systems are given in the relevant Sections of this Chapter. While some repair procedures are given, the usual course of action is to renew the component concerned.
7 It is necessary to take extra care when working on the electrical system, to avoid damage to semi-conductor devices (diodes and transistors), and to avoid the risk of personal injury. In addition to the precautions given in *"Safety first!"* at the beginning of this manual, observe the following when working on the system:
8 *Always remove rings, watches, etc before working on the electrical system.* Even with the battery disconnected, capacitive discharge could occur if a component's live terminal is earthed through a metal object. This could cause a shock or nasty burn.
9 *Do not reverse the battery connections.* Components such as the alternator, or any other components having semi-conductor circuitry, could be irreparably damaged.
10 If the engine is being started using jump leads and a slave battery, connect the batteries *positive-to-positive* and *negative-to-negative* (see *" Jump starting"*). This also applies when connecting a battery charger.
11 Never disconnect the battery terminals, the alternator, any electrical wiring, or any test instruments, when the engine is running.
12 Do not allow the engine to turn the alternator when the alternator is not connected.
13 Never "test" for alternator output by "flashing" the output lead to earth.
14 Never use an ohmmeter of the type incorporating a hand-cranked generator for circuit or continuity testing.
15 Always ensure that the battery negative lead is disconnected when working on the electrical system.
16 Before using electric-arc welding equipment on the car, disconnect the battery, alternator and components such as electronic control units, to protect them from the risk of damage.
17 Most of the radio/cassette units fitted as standard equipment by Proton have a built-in security code, to deter thieves. If the power source to the unit is cut, the anti-theft system will activate. Even if the power source is immediately reconnected, the radio/cassette unit will not function until the correct security code has been entered. Therefore, if you do not know the correct security code for the radio/cassette unit, **do not** disconnect the battery negative terminal, or remove the radio/cassette unit from the vehicle. Refer to *"Radio/cassette unit anti-theft system - precaution"* in the *Reference Section* of this manual.

2 Electrical fault-finding - general information

Refer to Chapter 12.

3 Battery - testing and charging

Standard and low-maintenance battery - testing

1 If the vehicle covers a small annual mileage, it is worthwhile checking the specific gravity of the electrolyte every three months, to determine the state of charge of the battery. Use a hydrometer to make the check, and compare the results with the following table. Note that the specific gravity readings assume an electrolyte temperature of 15°C (60°F); for every 10°C (18°F) below 15°C (60°F), subtract 0.007. For every 10°C (18°F) above 15°C (60°F), add 0.007. However, for convenience, the temperatures quoted in the following table are ambient (outdoor air) temperatures, above or below 25°C (77°F):

	Above 25°C	Below 25°C
Fully-charged	1.210 to 1.230	1.270 to 1.290
70% charged	1.170 to 1.190	1.230 to 1.250
Fully-discharged	1.050 to 1.070	1.110 to 1.130

2 If the battery condition is suspect, first check the specific gravity of electrolyte in each cell. A variation of 0.040 or more between any cells indicates loss of electrolyte, or deterioration of the internal plates.
3 If the specific gravity variation is 0.040 or more, a new battery should be fitted. If the cell variation is satisfactory but the battery is discharged, it should be charged as described later in this Section.

Maintenance-free battery - testing

4 In cases where a "sealed for life" maintenance-free battery is fitted, topping-up and testing of the electrolyte in each cell is not possible. The condition of the battery can therefore only be tested using a battery condition indicator or a voltmeter.
5 One type of maintenance-free battery which may be fitted is the "Delco" type maintenance-free battery, with a built-in charge condition indicator. The indicator is located in the top of the battery casing, and indicates the condition of the battery from its colour. If the indicator shows green, then the battery is in a good state of charge. If the indicator turns darker, eventually to black, then the battery requires charging, as described later in this Section. If the indicator shows clear/yellow, then the electrolyte level in the battery is too low to allow further use, and the battery should be renewed. **Do not** attempt to charge, load or jump start a battery when the indicator shows clear/yellow.
6 If testing the battery using a voltmeter, connect the voltmeter across the battery, and compare the result with those given in the *Specifications* under "charge condition". The test is only accurate if the battery has not been subjected to any kind of charge for the previous six hours. If this is not the case, switch on the headlights for 30 seconds, then wait four to five minutes before testing the battery after switching off the headlights. All other electrical circuits must be switched off, so check that the doors and tailgate are fully shut when making the test.
7 If the voltage reading is less than 12.2 volts, then the battery is discharged, whilst a reading of 12.2 to 12.4 volts indicates a partially-discharged condition.
8 If the battery is to be charged, remove it from the vehicle (Section 4) and charge it as described later in this Section.

Standard and low-maintenance battery - charging

Note: *The following is intended as a guide only. Always refer to the manufacturer's recommendations (often printed on a label attached to the battery) before charging a battery.*

9 Charge the battery at a rate of 3.5 to 4 amps, and continue to charge the battery at this rate until no further rise in specific gravity is noted over a four-hour period.
10 Alternatively, a trickle charger charging at the rate of 1.5 amps can safely be used overnight.
11 Specially rapid "boost" charges which are claimed to restore the power of the battery in 1 to 2 hours are not recommended, as they can cause serious damage to the battery plates through overheating.

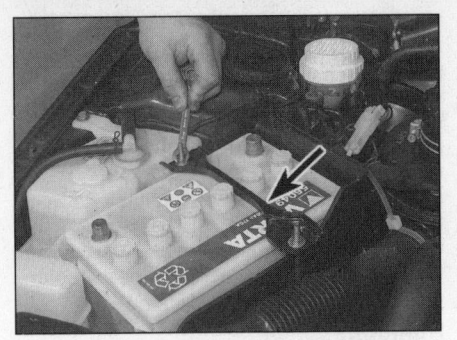

Engine electrical systems 5•3

4.4 Unscrew the retaining nuts and remove the battery clamp (arrowed)

4.5a Lift out the plastic battery tray ...

4.5b ... and, if necessary, unbolt and remove the battery mounting bracket

12 While charging the battery, note that the temperature of the electrolyte should never exceed 37.8°C (100°F).

Maintenance-free battery - charging

Note: *The following is intended as a guide only. Always refer to the manufacturer's recommendations (often printed on a label attached to the battery) before charging a battery.*

13 This battery type takes considerably longer to fully recharge than the standard type, the time taken being dependent on the extent of discharge, but it can take anything up to three days.

14 A constant-voltage type charger is required, to be set, when connected, to 13.9 to 14.9 volts, with a charger current below 25 amps. Using this method, the battery should be usable within three hours, giving a voltage reading of 12.5 volts, but this is for a partially-discharged battery and, as mentioned, full charging can take considerably longer.

15 If the battery is to be charged from a fully-discharged state (condition reading less than 12.2 volts), have it recharged by your Proton dealer or local automotive electrician, as the charge rate is higher, and constant supervision during charging is necessary.

4 Battery - removal and refitting

Removal

1 The battery is located on the right-hand side of the engine compartment.
2 Slacken the nut/bolt, and disconnect the clamp from the battery negative terminal.
3 Remove the insulation cover (where fitted) and disconnect the positive clamp in the same way.
4 Unscrew the nuts and washers and remove the battery retaining clamp **(see illustration)**.
5 Lift the battery out of the engine compartment and, where necessary, remove the plastic battery tray. If necessary, the battery mounting bracket can also be unbolted and removed from the engine compartment, once the wiring has been freed from its retaining clips **(see illustrations)**.

Refitting

6 Refitting is a reversal of removal, but smear petroleum jelly on the terminals when reconnecting the leads, and always reconnect the positive lead first, and the negative lead last.

5 Ignition system - general information

8-valve models

1 On 8-valve models, a breakerless electronic ignition system is used. The system comprises solely of the HT ignition coil and the distributor, the distributor being driven off the camshaft.
2 The distributor contains a toothed rotor mounted onto its shaft, and the igniter unit which is fixed to its body. The system operates as follows.
3 When the ignition is switched on but the engine is stationary, the igniter unit prevents current flowing through the ignition system primary (LT) circuit.
4 As the crankshaft rotates, the rotor moves through the magnetic field created by the igniter unit. When the rotor teeth are correctly positioned, a small AC voltage is created. The igniter unit uses this voltage to switch and complete the ignition system primary (LT) circuit.
5 As the rotor teeth move out of alignment, the AC voltage changes, and the igniter unit switches again to interrupt the primary (LT) circuit. This causes a high voltage to be induced in the coil secondary (HT) windings, which then travels down the HT lead to the distributor and onto the relevant spark plug.

12-valve carburettor models

6 On 12-valve models, the ignition system is very similar to that described above for the 8-valve model, the main difference being that the ignition HT coil is incorporated into the distributor main body. Another minor difference is that a separate pick-up coil is fitted (instead of the unit being integrated into the igniter unit).

12-valve fuel-injected models

7 On these models, the ignition system is integrated with the fuel system, to form a combined fuel/ignition system which is controlled by the fuel injection ECU (see Chapter 4 for further information on the fuelling side of the system).
8 The distributor contains a crank angle sensor, which informs the ECU of engine speed and crankshaft position, and a TDC sensor which informs the ECU of the position of No1 cylinder piston; the ignition HT coil is also contained in the distributor housing. Based on this information, and the information received from its other sensors, the ECU then calculates the correct ignition timing setting, and switches the power transistor unit on and off accordingly. This causes a high voltage to be induced in the coil secondary (HT) windings, which then travels onto the relevant spark plug.

6 Ignition system - testing

> **Warning:** *Voltages produced by an electronic ignition system are considerably higher than those produced by conventional ignition systems. Extreme care must be taken when working on the system with the ignition switched on. Persons with surgically-implanted cardiac pacemaker devices should keep well clear of the ignition circuits, components and test equipment*

Note: *Refer to the warning given in Section 1 before starting work. Always switch off the ignition before disconnecting or connecting any component, and when using a multi-meter to check resistances.*

1 The components of electronic ignition systems are normally very reliable; most faults are far more likely to be due to loose or dirty connections, or to "tracking" of HT voltage due to dirt, dampness or damaged insulation, than to the failure of any of the system's components. **Always** check all wiring thoroughly before condemning an electrical component, and work methodically to eliminate all other possibilities before deciding that a particular component is faulty.

5•4 Engine electrical systems

2 The old practice of checking for a spark by holding the live end of an HT lead a short distance away from the engine is **not** recommended; not only is there a high risk of a powerful electric shock, but the HT coil or power transistor unit will very likely be damaged. Similarly, **never** try to "diagnose" misfires by pulling off one HT lead at a time.

Engine will not start

3 If the engine either will not turn over at all, or only turns very slowly, check the battery and starter motor. Connect a voltmeter across the battery terminals (meter positive probe to battery positive terminal), then disconnect the ignition coil HT lead from the distributor cap and earth it. Note the voltage reading obtained while turning over the engine on the starter for (no more than) ten seconds. If the reading obtained is less than approximately 9.5 volts, first check the battery, starter motor and charging system as described in the relevant Sections of this Chapter.

4 If the engine turns over at normal speed but will not start, check the HT circuit by connecting a timing light (following the equipment manufacturer's instructions) and turning the engine over on the starter motor; if the light flashes, voltage is reaching the spark plugs, so these should be checked first. If the light does not flash, check the HT leads themselves, followed by the distributor cap, carbon brush and rotor arm using the information given in Chapter 1.

5 If there is a spark, check the carburettor/fuel injection system (as applicable) referring to Chapter 4 for further information.

6 If there is still no spark, check the voltage at the ignition HT coil "+" terminal; it should be the same as the battery voltage (ie, at least 11.7 volts). If the voltage at the coil is more than 1 volt less than that at the battery, check the feed back through the fusebox and ignition switch to the battery and its earth until the fault is found.

7 If the feed to the HT coil is sound, check the coil's primary and secondary winding resistance as described later in this Section; renew the coil if faulty, but be careful to check carefully the condition of the wiring (LT)

connections themselves before doing so, to ensure that the fault is not due to dirty or poorly-fastened connectors.

8 If the HT coil is in good condition, the fault is probably within the distributor assembly (ie. the igniter unit and/or pick-up coil/crank angle sensor/No1 cylinder TDC sensor - as applicable). Testing of the distributor assembly should be entrusted to a Proton dealer.

Engine misfires

9 An irregular misfire suggests either a loose connection or intermittent fault on the primary circuit, or an HT fault on the coil side of the rotor arm.

10 With the ignition switched off, check carefully through the system, ensuring that all connections are clean and securely fastened. If the equipment is available, check the LT circuit as described above.

11 Check that the HT coil, the distributor cap and the HT leads are clean and dry. Check the leads themselves and the spark plugs (by substitution, if necessary), then check the distributor cap, carbon brush and rotor arm as described in Chapter 1.

12 Regular misfiring is almost certainly due to a fault in the distributor cap, HT leads or spark plugs. Use a timing light (paragraph 4 above) to check whether HT voltage is present at all leads.

13 If HT voltage is not present on any particular lead, the fault will be in that lead, or in the distributor cap. If HT is present on all leads, the fault will be in the spark plugs; check and renew them if there is any doubt about their condition.

14 If no HT is present, check the HT coil; its secondary windings may be breaking down under load.

7 Ignition HT coil - removal, testing and refitting

8-valve models

Removal

1 The ignition coil is situated in the left-hand rear corner of the engine compartment. Prior to removal, disconnect the battery negative terminal.

2 Note the correct fitted locations of the coil LT wiring then unscrew the retaining nuts and disconnect the wiring from the coil. Also disconnect the HT lead from the coil **(see illustration)**.

3 Slacken the coil clamp bolt then slide the coil out of position and remove it from the engine compartment.

Testing

4 Testing of the coil consists of using a multimeter set to its resistance function, to check the primary (LT "+" to "-" terminals) and secondary (LT "+" to HT lead terminal)

windings for continuity. Compare the results obtained to those given in the *Specifications* at the start of this Chapter. Note that the resistance of the coil windings will vary slightly according to the coil temperature - the results in the *Specifications* are approximate values for when the coil is at 20°C.

5 Check that there is no continuity between the HT lead terminal and the coil body.

6 If the coil is thought to be faulty, have your findings confirmed by a Proton dealer before renewing the coil.

Refitting

7 Refitting is a reversal of the removal procedure, ensuring that the wiring connector and HT lead are securely reconnected.

12-valve models

8 On these models the ignition HT coil is an integral part of the distributor body and can not be renewed individually. Refer to Section 8 for distributor removal and refitting details. The coil can be checked as described in paragraphs 4 to 6, measuring the coil resistance at the distributor wiring connector.

8 Distributor - removal and refitting

Removal

1 Disconnect the battery negative terminal.
2 Position number 1 cylinder at TDC on its compression stroke as described in Chapter 2A and continue as described under the relevant sub-heading.

8-valve models

3 Release the retaining clips then remove the distributor cap, positioning it clear of the distributor body **(see illustration)**. Recover the cap seal from the distributor and mark the position of the rotor arm end on the distributor body using a scriber or a marker pen.

4 Trace the distributor wiring back to the ignition coil then, noting the wiring correct fitted locations, unscrew the retaining nuts and disconnect the wiring from the coil terminals.

7.2 On 8-valve models the ignition HT coil is located in the left-hand rear corner of the engine compartment

8.3 On 8-valve models release the retaining clips and remove the cap from the distributor

Engine electrical systems 5•5

8.8 Disconnecting the distributor wiring connectors (fuel-injected model shown)

8.9a Slacken the retaining screws (arrowed) . . .

8.9b . . . and remove the cap from the distributor

5 Disconnect the hose from the vacuum diaphragm unit.

6 Check the distributor flange for signs of an alignment mark; there should be a line cast onto the flange which aligns with one of the mounting studs. If no marks are visible, using a scriber or suitable marker pen, mark the relationship of the distributor body to the cylinder head. Slacken and remove the mounting nuts and washers, and withdraw the distributor from the cylinder head. Remove the O-ring from the end of the distributor body and discard it; a new one must be used on refitting.

7 If necessary, pull off the rotor arm then undo the igniter unit retaining screws and disconnect the wiring connectors, noting their correct fitted locations, and remove the igniter unit from the distributor. The vacuum diaphragm unit can also be removed by unscrewing its retaining screws and detaching it from the base unit.

12-valve models

8 Disconnect the wiring connector(s) from the distributor and (where necessary) disconnect the vacuum hose from the diaphragm unit **(see illustration)**.

9 Undo the retaining screws then remove the distributor cap, positioning it clear of the distributor body. Recover the cap seal from the distributor and mark the position of the rotor arm end on the distributor body using a scriber or a marker pen **(see illustrations)**.

10 Remove the distributor as described in paragraph 5 **(see illustration)**.

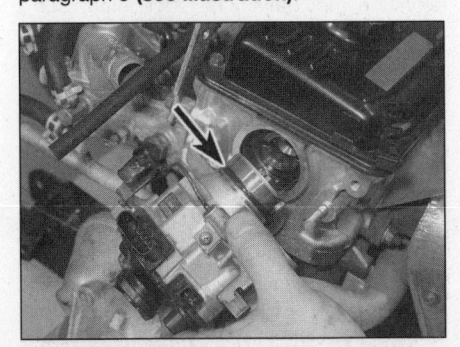

11 On carburettor models, if necessary, remove the rotor arm then undo the pick-up coil retaining screws and, noting the wiring correct fitted locations, wiring screws and remove the coil from the distributor. The igniter unit can then be removed once its screws have been undone.

12 On fuel-injected models, at the time of writing no individual components were available for the distributor assembly. Therefore if any of the distributor components are faulty the complete assembly must be renewed. Refer to your Proton dealer for the latest parts information.

Refitting

8-valve models

13 Where necessary, fit the vacuum diaphragm unit, making sure its pushrod is correctly engaged with the base pin, and securely tighten its retaining screws. Fit the igniter unit, ensuring its wiring is correctly reconnected, and lightly tighten its retaining screws. Align one of the rotor teeth with the igniter pick-up lug and set the air gap between two components to approximately 0.4 mm before securely tightening the igniter retaining screws **(see illustration)**. Refit the rotor arm.

14 Lubricate the new O-ring with a smear of engine oil, and fit it to the groove in the distributor body. Examine the distributor cap seal for wear or damage, and renew if necessary.

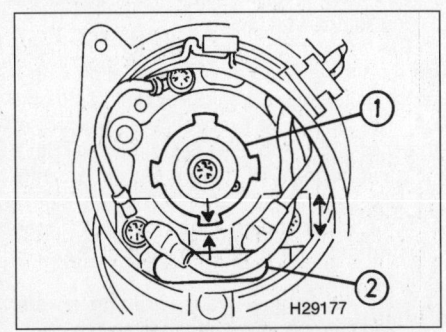

8.9c If no marks are visible, make alignment marks between the distributor and cylinder head prior to removal

15 Position the rotor arm slightly to the side of the mark made on the distributor prior to removal, in this position the punch mark on the side of the distributor drive gear will align with the cutout on the base of the distributor housing **(see illustration)**.

16 Align the distributor rotor shaft drive gear with the camshaft end and carefully insert the distributor into the cylinder head, whilst rotating the rotor arm slightly to ensure that the camshaft and drive gear engage correctly.

17 Align the mark cast onto the distributor flange with the centre of the mounting stud (where present) or alternately align the marks made prior to removal. Refit the washers and mounting nuts, tightening them lightly only.

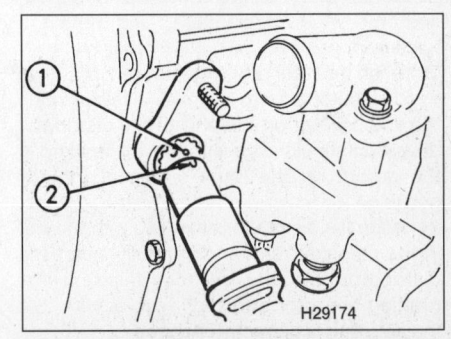

8.10 Remove the distributor from the cylinder head (sealing ring arrowed)

8.13 On refitting ensure the air gap between the rotor (1) and igniter pick-up (2) is correctly set

8.15 On 8-valve models, align the mark on the drive gear (1) with the cutout (2) to correctly position the rotor arm when installing the distributor

5•6 Engine electrical systems

9.2 Crankshaft pulley notch (1) and timing belt cover scale (2)

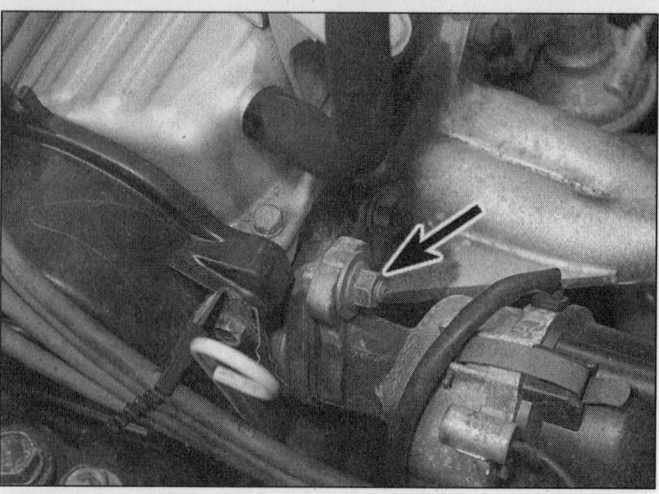

9.6 On carburettor models, slacken the mounting nuts (upper nut arrowed) and rotate the distributor to adjust the ignition timing

18 Ensure that the seal is correctly located in its groove, then refit the cap assembly to the distributor and secure it in position with the retaining clips.

19 Reconnect the distributor wiring to the ignition HT coil terminals, ensuring each wire is correctly connected, and securely tighten the retaining nuts. Reconnect the vacuum hose to the diaphragm unit.

20 Check and, if necessary, adjust the ignition timing as described in Section 9, then securely tighten the distributor mounting nuts.

12-valve models

21 On carburettor models, where necessary, fit the igniter unit, ensuring its wiring is correctly reconnected, and securely tighten its retaining screws. Refit the pick-up coil and securely tighten its wiring retaining screws, ensuring that the wiring is correctly positioned. Align one of the rotor teeth with the pick-up coil contact lug and set the air gap between two components to 0.4 mm before securely tightening the coil retaining screws. Refit the rotor arm.

22 Lubricate the new O-ring with a smear of engine oil, and fit it to the groove in the distributor body. Examine the distributor cap seal for wear or damage, and renew if necessary.

23 Align the rotor arm with the mark made on the distributor prior to removal, in this position the line scribed on the end of the distributor drive dog should align with the line marked in the cutout on the base of the distributor housing.

24 Align the distributor drive dog with the slot in the camshaft end and carefully insert the distributor into the cylinder head, whilst rotating the rotor arm slightly to ensure that the coupling is correctly engaged.

25 Align the mark cast onto the distributor flange with the centre of the mounting stud (where present) or alternately align the marks made prior to removal. Refit the washers and mounting nuts, tightening them lightly only.

26 Ensure that the seal is correctly located in its groove, then refit the cap assembly to the distributor and securely tighten its retaining screws.

27 Reconnect the distributor wiring connector and (carburettor models only) connect the vacuum hose to the diaphragm unit.

28 Check and, if necessary, adjust the ignition timing as described in Section 9, then securely tighten the distributor mounting nuts. On fuel-injected models, if necessary equipment for checking the timing is not available align the distributor mark with the stud or the marks made prior to removal and securely tighten the nuts, noting that it is recommended that the timing be checked at the earliest possible opportunity.

9 Ignition timing - checking and adjustment

Carburettor models

1 To check the ignition timing, a stroboscopic timing light will be required.

2 The timing marks are in the form of marks on the timing belt cover, which align with a notch on the crankshaft pulley rim. The marks on the timing belt cover are spaced at intervals of 5°, with TDC being marked with a "T", and go from 15° before top dead centre (BTDC) to 5 or 10° after top dead centre (ATDC) (depending on model) **(see illustration)**. The ignition timing is checked as follows.

3 Start the engine, warm it up to normal operating temperature, and then switch off.

4 Connect the timing light to No 1 cylinder (nearest the timing belt) plug lead as described in the timing light manufacturer's instructions.

5 Start the engine, allowing it to idle at the specified speed, and point the timing light at the crankshaft pulley. The pulley notch should be aligned with the relevant point on the timing belt cover scale (see Specifications for the correct timing setting).

6 If adjustment is necessary, slacken the distributor mounting nuts, then slowly rotate the distributor body as required until the crankshaft pulley notch is correctly positioned **(see illustration)**.

⚠ **Warning: At all times, avoid touching the HT leads, and keep loose clothing, long hair, etc, well away from the moving parts of the engine. Once the marks are correctly aligned, hold the distributor stationary, and tighten its mounting nuts securely. Recheck that the timing marks are still correctly aligned and, if necessary, repeat the adjustment procedure.**

7 When the timing is correctly set, increase the engine speed, and check that the pulley mark advances to beyond the beginning of the timing plate reference marks, returning to close to the specified mark when the engine is allowed to idle; this shows that the distributor advance mechanism is functioning, but a detailed check must be left to a Proton dealer.

8 When the ignition timing is correct, stop the engine and disconnect the timing light.

Fuel-injected models

9 On all fuel-injected models, the timing is constantly being monitored and adjusted by the engine management ECU. Therefore, it is not possible for the home mechanic to check the ignition timing without access to the special engine management diagnostic equipment. Adjustment of the ignition timing is possible, however, adjustments can only be made using the special test equipment (see Chapter 4). The figure given in the Specifications is the nominal ignition timing value for use with the special diagnostic equipment.

Engine electrical systems

10 Charging system - testing

Note: *Refer to the warnings given in "Safety first!" and in Section 1 of this Chapter before starting work.*

1 If the ignition/no-charge warning light fails to come on when the ignition is switched on, first check the alternator wiring connections for security. If satisfactory, check that the warning light bulb has not blown, and that the bulbholder is secure in its location in the instrument panel. If the light still fails to come on, check the continuity of the warning light feed wire from the alternator to the bulbholder. If all is satisfactory, the alternator is at fault, and should be taken to an auto-electrician for testing and repair.

2 If the ignition warning light comes on when the engine is running, stop the engine as soon as possible. Check that the drivebelt is correctly tensioned (see Chapter 1), that the drivebelt is not contaminated (with oil or water, for example), and that the alternator connections are secure. If all is so far satisfactory, the alternator should be taken to an auto-electrician for testing and repair.

3 If the alternator output is suspect, even though the warning light functions correctly, the regulated voltage may be checked as follows.

4 Connect a voltmeter across the battery terminals, and start the engine.

5 Increase the engine speed until the voltmeter reading remains steady; the reading should be approximately 12 to 13 volts, and no more than 14 volts.

6 Switch on as many electrical accessories (eg, the headlights, heated rear window and heater blower) as possible, and check that the alternator maintains the regulated voltage at around 13 to 14 volts.

7 If the regulated voltage is not as stated, the fault may be due to worn brushes, weak brush springs, a faulty voltage regulator, a faulty diode, a severed phase winding, or worn or damaged slip-rings. If this is the case then the alternator should taken to an auto-electrician for testing and repair.

11 Alternator drivebelt - removal, refitting and tensioning

Refer to the procedure given for the auxiliary drivebelt in Chapter 1.

12 Alternator - removal and refitting

Removal

1 Disconnect the battery negative lead. To improve access, firmly apply the handbrake then jack up the front of the vehicle and support it on axle stands (see *"Jacking and vehicle support"*). Undo the retaining bolts and remove the undercover from the left-hand wheelarch.

2 Slacken the auxiliary drivebelt as described in Chapter 1, and disengage it from the alternator pulley.

3 Remove the rubber covers (where fitted) from the alternator terminals, then unscrew the retaining nut(s) and disconnect the wiring from the rear of the alternator. Where necessary, also undo the retaining screw and disconnect the earth lead **(see illustration)**.

4 Unscrew the alternator upper and lower mounting bolts and washers, then manoeuvre the alternator away from its mounting brackets and out of position.

Refitting

5 Refitting is a reversal of removal. Prior to tightening the lower mounting bolt, push the alternator fully towards the timing belt end of the engine and check that the clearance between the alternator end cover and mounting bracket is less than 0.2 mm **(see illustration)**. If not, withdraw the bolt and insert a washer of suitable thickness in-between the alternator and bracket; failure to ensure that the clearance is correct could lead to the alternator casing breaking as the lower mounting bolt is tightened. Tension the auxiliary drivebelt as described in Chapter 1 then tighten the alternator mounting bolts to the specified torque settings.

13 Alternator - testing and overhaul

If the alternator is thought to be suspect, it should be removed from the vehicle and taken to an auto-electrician for testing. Most auto-electricians will be able to supply and fit brushes at a reasonable cost. However, check on the cost of repairs before proceeding as it may prove more economical to obtain a new or exchange alternator.

14 Starting system - testing

Note: *Refer to the precautions given in "Safety first!" and in Section 1 of this Chapter before starting work.*

1 If the starter motor fails to operate when the ignition key is turned to the appropriate position, the following may be to blame:
   a) The battery is faulty.

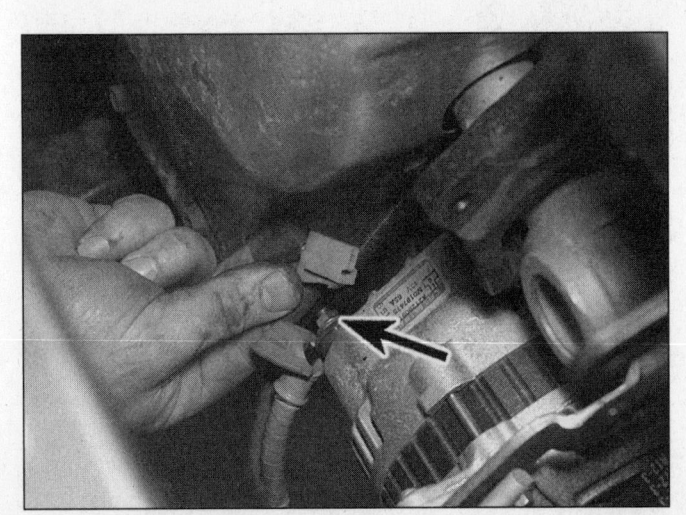

12.3 Disconnect the wiring connector then unscrew the retaining nut (arrowed) and disconnect the main lead from the rear of the alternator

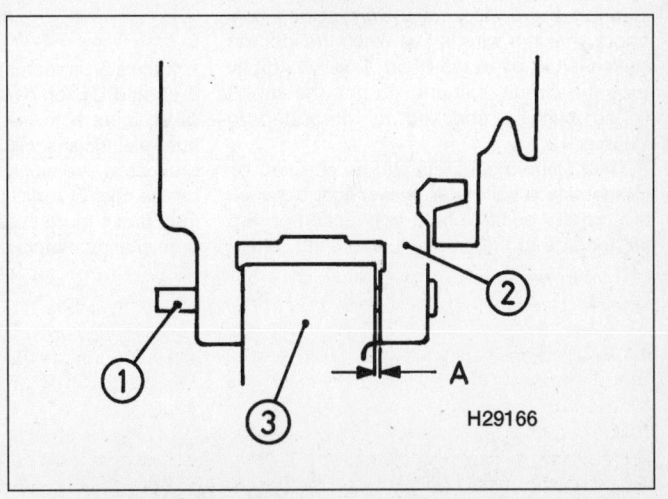

12.5 Prior to tightening the lower mounting bolt (1), check that the clearance (A) between the alternator lug (2) and the mounting bracket (3) is correct - see text

b) The electrical connections between the switch, solenoid, battery and starter motor are somewhere failing to pass the necessary current from the battery through the starter to earth.
c) The solenoid is faulty.
d) The starter motor is mechanically or electrically defective.

2 To check the battery, switch on the headlights. If they dim after a few seconds, this indicates that the battery is discharged - recharge (see Section 3) or renew the battery. If the headlights glow brightly, operate the ignition switch and observe the lights. If they dim, then this indicates that current is reaching the starter motor, therefore the fault must lie in the starter motor. If the lights continue to glow brightly (and no clicking sound can be heard from the starter motor solenoid), this indicates that there is a fault in the circuit or solenoid - see following paragraphs. If the starter motor turns slowly when operated, but the battery is in good condition, then this indicates that either the starter motor is faulty, or there is considerable resistance somewhere in the circuit.

3 If a fault in the circuit is suspected, disconnect the battery leads (including the earth connection to the body), the starter/solenoid wiring and the engine/transmission earth strap. Thoroughly clean the connections, reconnect the leads and wiring, then use a voltmeter or test light to check that full battery voltage is available at the battery positive lead connection to the solenoid, and that the earth is sound. Smear petroleum jelly around the battery terminals to prevent corrosion - corroded connections are amongst the most frequent causes of electrical system faults.

4 If the battery and all connections are in good condition, check the circuit by disconnecting the wire from the solenoid blade terminal. Connect a voltmeter or test light between the wire end and a good earth (such as the battery negative terminal), and check that the wire is live when the ignition switch is turned to the "start" position. If it is, then the circuit is sound - if not, the circuit wiring can be checked as described in Chapter 12.

5 The solenoid contacts can be checked by connecting a voltmeter or test light between the battery positive feed connection on the starter side of the solenoid, and earth. When the ignition switch is turned to the "start" position, there should be a reading or lighted bulb, as applicable. If there is no reading or lighted bulb, the solenoid is faulty and should be renewed.

6 If the circuit and solenoid are proved sound, the fault must lie in the starter motor. In this event, it may be possible to have the starter motor overhauled by a specialist, but check on the availability and cost of spares before proceeding, as it may prove more economical to obtain a new or exchange motor.

15 Starter motor - removal and refitting

Removal

1 Disconnect the battery negative lead. On fuel-injected models remove the air cleaner housing as described in Chapter 4.
2 So that access to the motor can be gained both from above and below, firmly apply the handbrake, then jack up the front of the vehicle and support it on axle stands (see "*Jacking and vehicle support*").
3 Slacken and remove the retaining nut, and disconnect the main battery cable from the starter motor solenoid. Also disconnect the wiring connector from the solenoid.
4 Unscrew the starter motor mounting bolts, supporting the motor as the bolts are withdrawn, and manoeuvre the starter motor out from underneath the engine.

Refitting

5 Refitting is a reversal of removal tightening the mounting bolts to the specified torque setting.

16 Starter motor - testing and overhaul

If the starter motor is thought to be suspect, it should be removed from the vehicle and taken to an auto-electrician for testing. Most auto-electricians will be able to supply and fit brushes at a reasonable cost. However, check on the cost of repairs before proceeding as it may prove more economical to obtain a new or exchange motor.

17 Ignition switch - removal and refitting

The ignition switch is integral with the steering column lock, and can be removed as described in Chapter 10.

18 Oil pressure warning light switch - removal and refitting

Removal

1 The switch is located on the front of the cylinder block, on the left-hand side of the exhaust manifold. To gain access to the switch, firmly apply the handbrake then jack up the front of the vehicle and support it on axle stands (see "*Jacking and vehicle support*").
2 Disconnect the battery negative lead.
3 Disconnect the wiring connector then unscrew the switch and recover the sealing washer (where fitted). Be prepared for oil spillage. If the switch is to be left removed from the engine for any length of time, plug the hole to prevent excessive oil loss.

Refitting

4 Where the switch was fitted with a sealing washer, examine the sealing washer for signs of damage or deterioration, and if necessary renew it. Where no sealing washer was fitted, clean the switch and apply a smear of sealant to its threads.
5 Refit the switch, tightening it securely, and reconnect the wiring connector.
6 Lower the vehicle to the ground then check and if necessary, top-up the engine oil as described in Chapter 1.

Chapter 6
Clutch

Contents

Clutch - check and adjustment 2
Clutch assembly - removal, inspection and refitting 8
Clutch cable - removal and refitting 3
Clutch hydraulic system - bleeding 6
Clutch master cylinder - removal, overhaul and refitting 4
Clutch pedal - removal and refitting 7
Clutch release mechanism - removal, inspection and refitting 9
Clutch slave cylinder - removal, overhaul and refitting 5
General check .... See Chapter 1
General information 1

Degrees of difficulty

| Easy, suitable for novice with little experience | Fairly easy, suitable for beginner with some experience | Fairly difficult, suitable for competent DIY mechanic | Difficult, suitable for experienced DIY mechanic | Very difficult, suitable for expert DIY or professional |

Specifications

Type .... Single dry plate with diaphragm spring, cable operated on carburettor models and hydraulically operated on fuel-injected models

Clutch adjustment data
Carburettor models:
  Clutch pedal height .... 167 to 172 mm
  Clutch pedal free play .... 20 to 30 mm
Fuel-injected models:
  Clutch pedal height .... 165 to 171 mm
  Clutch pedal pushrod linkage freeplay .... 1 to 3 mm
  Clutch pedal free play .... 6 to 13 mm

Friction plate
Diameter .... 184 mm
Minimum friction material-to-rivet head depth .... 0.3 mm

Torque wrench settings
	Nm	lbf ft
Hydraulic hose union nut	15	11
Hydraulic pipe union bolt	25	18
Master cylinder:		
Retaining nuts	15	11
Reservoir retaining clamp bolt	7	5
Pedal pivot bolt nut	20	15
Pressure plate retaining bolts	20	15

1 General information

The clutch consists of a friction plate, a pressure plate assembly, a release bearing and the release mechanism; all of these components are contained in the large cast-aluminium alloy bellhousing, sandwiched between the engine and the transmission.

The friction plate is fitted between the engine flywheel and the clutch pressure plate, and is allowed to slide on the transmission input shaft splines.

The pressure plate assembly is bolted to the engine flywheel. When the engine is running, drive is transmitted from the crankshaft, via the flywheel, to the friction plate (these components being clamped securely together by the pressure plate assembly) and from the friction plate to the transmission input shaft.

To interrupt the drive, the spring pressure must be relaxed. On the models covered in this manual, two different types of clutch release mechanism are used.

On carburettor models a cable-operated release mechanism is used. Depressing the clutch pedal pulls the control cable inner wire, and this rotates the release fork by acting on the lever at the fork's upper end. The release fork then presses the release bearing against the pressure plate spring fingers. This causes the springs to deform and releases the clamping force on the pressure plate. To ensure correct operation, the clutch must be regularly adjusted.

On fuel-injected models the clutch release mechanism is operated hydraulically. Depressing the pedal pushes on the master cylinder pushrod. This hydraulically forces the slave cylinder piston which is connected to the end of the clutch release fork lever. The release fork acts on its pivot and presses the release bearing against the pressure plate spring fingers. This causes the springs to deform and releases the clamping force on the pressure plate. The hydraulic clutch is self-adjusting and requires no manual adjustment.

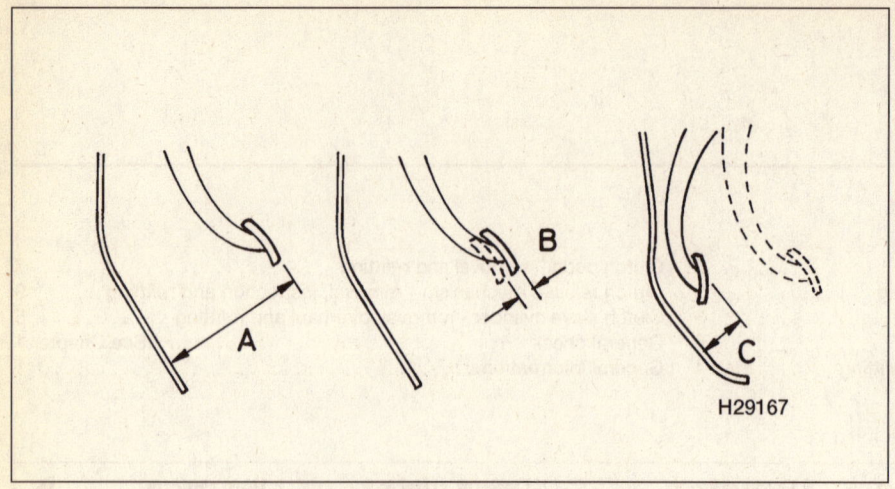

2.2 Clutch pedal measurement details

A Pedal height measurement   B Freeplay measurement   C Minimum height measurement

2.6a On carburettor models, the clutch pedal is adjusted using the cable adjuster...

2 Clutch - check and adjustment

Carburettor models

1 The clutch adjustment is checked by first by setting the clutch pedal height, and then by adjusting the pedal free play.

2 Peel back the carpet from underneath the clutch pedal, and ensure that there are no obstructions between the pedal and floor panel. Measure the distance from the centre of the clutch pedal pad to the floor **(see illustration)**. *Note: This measurement can be taken with the carpet in position, so long as the thickness of the carpet is added onto the pedal height measurement.* The pedal height should be within the range given in the *Specifications* at the start of this Chapter.

3 If the pedal height is not within the specified range, then the pedal and/or mounting bracket must be damaged, no adjustment of the height is possible. Examine the clutch pedal components as described in Section 7.

4 If the pedal height is within the specified limits, check the pedal free play as follows.

5 Slowly depress the clutch pedal, and measure the distance that the clutch pedal pad travels from the at-rest position to the point where resistance is felt **(see illustration 2.2)**. This is the pedal free play, and should be within the range given in this Chapter's *Specifications*.

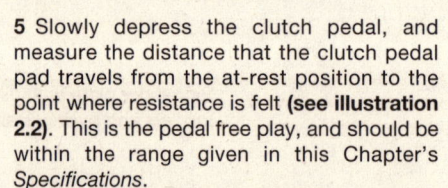

6 If freeplay adjustment is necessary, working within the engine compartment, locate the clutch cable adjuster nut, which is situated at the bulkhead end of the clutch cable. Remove all freeplay from the cable by gently pulling the outer cable out from the bulkhead, then rotate the knurled adjusting ring until the clearance between the ring and cable sealing grommet is approximately 5 to 6 mm **(see illustrations)**. Recheck the clutch pedal free play as described in paragraph 5, and readjust if necessary.

7 With the pedal height and free play within the specified limits, depress the clutch pedal and check that the distance from the centre of the clutch pedal pad to floor is 80 mm or greater with the clutch fully disengaged. If the distance is less than 80 mm, this indicates that the clutch assembly is in a less than perfect condition and may soon require renewal. Seek the advice of your Proton dealer.

Fuel-injected models

8 The clutch hydraulic system is self-adjusting and therefore requires no checking or manual adjustment other than ensuring the fluid level remains correct. The following is a check of the pedal and pushrod adjustments which should only be necessary should the pedal/master cylinder be disturbed.

9 Measure the clutch pedal height as described in paragraph 2. With the clutch pedal in the at-rest position check the freeplay in the pedal pushrod linkage by gently rocking the pedal whilst measuring the distance that the clutch pedal pad travels. *Note: This check is measuring the slack in the pushrod/clevis pin only and should not be confused with the pedal freeplay check (paragraph 11) which also measures the initial movement of the master cylinder piston.*

10 If the pedal height and/or linkage freeplay are not within the specified limits, slacken the locknut and unscrew the pedal stop bolt from the mounting bracket so that it is positioned clear of the pedal. Slacken the pushrod linkage locknut and adjust the pedal height by rotating the pushrod with a pair of pliers **(see illustrations)**. Once the pedal height is

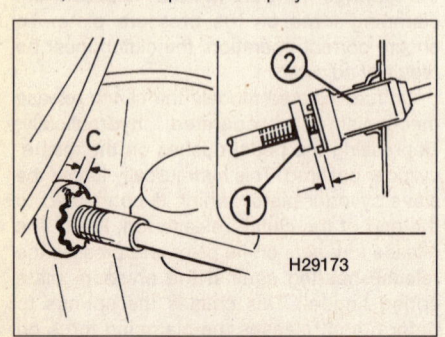

2.6b ...rotate the adjuster nut (1) so that the clearance (C) between it and the sealing grommet (2) is approximately 5 to 6 mm

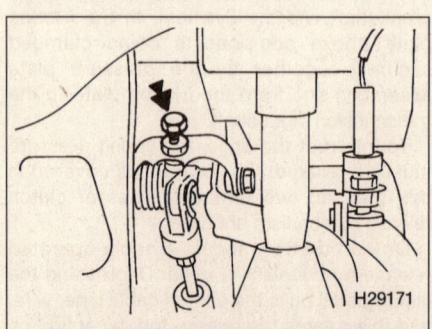

2.10a On fuel-injected models, adjust the pedal height and freeplay using the stop bolt (arrowed)...

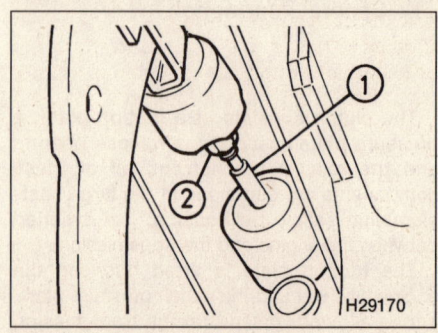

2.10b ...and the master cylinder pushrod (1) and locknut (2)

correctly set, carefully screw in the stop bolt until it just contacts the pedal then securely tighten its locknut. Check that the pedal height is correctly set then adjust the pushrod freeplay to within the specified limits and securely tighten the pushrod locknut.

11 With the pedal height and pushrod free play within the specified limits, depress the clutch pedal a few times to settle it in position then fully depress it and check that the distance from the centre of the clutch pedal pad to floor is 35 mm or greater. Release the pedal and check the pedal freeplay as described in paragraph 5, measuring the pedal travel from the at-rest position to the point where resistance in the hydraulic circuit is felt. If the pedal clearance or freeplay are not within the specified limits, then it is likely that there is air in the hydraulic system and the system should be bled as described in Section 6. If this fails to solve the problem then it is likely that the clutch or master/slave cylinder are faulty. Seek the advice of your Proton dealer on the best course of action.

3 Clutch cable - removal and refitting

Note: *A new cable split pin will be required on refitting.*

Removal

1 If necessary, to improve access to the transmission end of the cable, firmly apply the handbrake then jack up the front of the vehicle and support it on axle stands (see "*Jacking and vehicle support*").

2 Working in the engine compartment, locate the clutch cable adjuster nut, which is situated at the bulkhead end of the clutch cable, and fully slacken the adjuster knurled ring to obtain maximum freeplay in the cable.

3 From inside the vehicle, reach up behind the facia and unhook the cable from the upper end of the clutch pedal.

4 Return to the engine compartment and remove the split pin securing the inner cable to the clutch release lever. Detach the inner cable from the lever then free the outer cable from the transmission bracket.

5 Release the cable grommet from the bulkhead and withdraw the cable forwards, releasing it from any relevant retaining clips and guides. Note its correct routing, and remove it from the vehicle.

6 Examine the cable, looking for worn end fittings or a damaged outer casing, and for signs of fraying of the inner wire. Check the cable's operation; the inner wire should move smoothly and easily through the outer casing. Remember that a cable that appears serviceable when tested off the car may well be much heavier in operation when in its working position. Renew the cable if it shows signs of excessive wear or any damage.

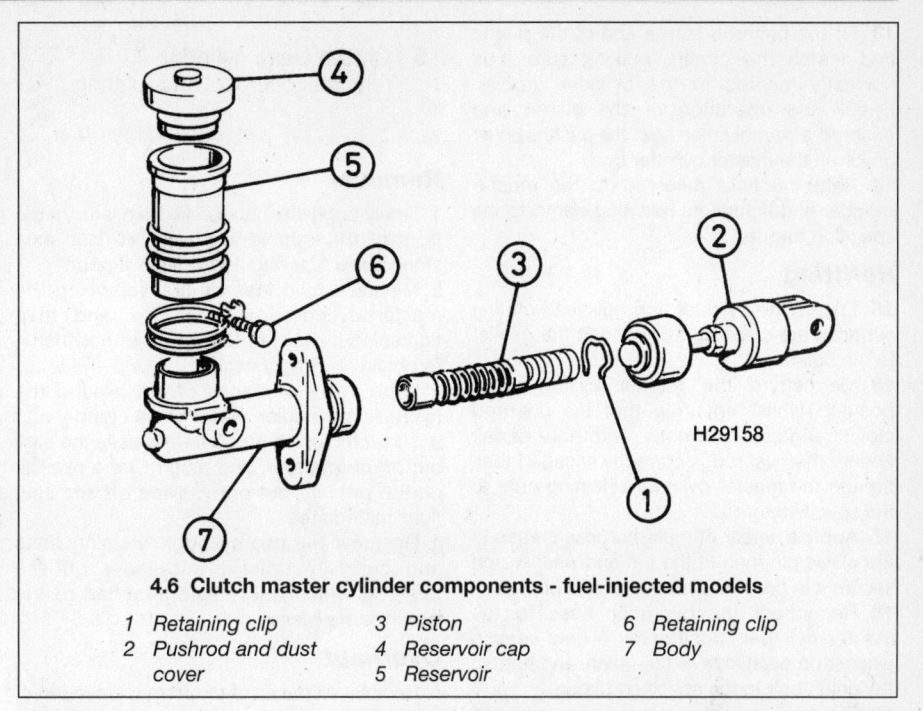

4.6 Clutch master cylinder components - fuel-injected models

1 Retaining clip
2 Pushrod and dust cover
3 Piston
4 Reservoir cap
5 Reservoir
6 Retaining clip
7 Body

Refitting

7 Apply a thin smear of multi-purpose grease to the cable end fittings, then pass the cable through the engine compartment bulkhead and locate the cable grommet securely in its guide.

8 From inside the vehicle, hook the inner cable onto the clutch pedal, and check that it is correctly located.

9 Ensuring that the cable is correctly routed and retained by all the relevant retaining clips and guides, pass the lower end of the cable through the mounting bracket. Engage the inner cable with the release lever and secure it in position with a new split pin.

10 Adjust the clutch as described in Section 2 then refit any components removed for access.

4 Clutch master cylinder - removal, overhaul and refitting

Note: *New union bolt sealing washers and a clevis pin split pin will be required on refitting.*

Removal

1 Remove the master cylinder reservoir cap, and syphon the hydraulic fluid from the reservoir. Alternatively, open the slave cylinder bleed screw, and gently pump the clutch pedal to expel the fluid through a plastic tube connected to the screw (see Section 6).

⚠ **Warning:** *Do not syphon the fluid by mouth, as it is poisonous; use a syringe or an old poultry baster*

2 Remove all traces of dirt from the master cylinder. Slacken and remove the union bolt and sealing washers and disconnect the hydraulic hose from the master cylinder. Catch any fluid in a suitable container and plug the hose end and master cylinder ports to minimise fluid loss and prevent the entry of dirt into the system.

3 From inside the vehicle, reach up behind the facia and withdraw the split pin from the clutch pedal pushrod clevis pin. Remove the washer and withdraw the clevis pin from the pushrod end.

4 Return to the engine compartment then slacken and remove the retaining nuts and remove the master cylinder from the vehicle, along with its gasket.

Overhaul

5 Remove all traces of dirt from the outside of the cylinder and carefully clamp the cylinder in a vice equipped with soft jaws.

6 Slacken the retaining clip and remove the fluid reservoir from the master cylinder body **(see illustration)**.

7 Release the dust cover from the rear of the master cylinder to gain access to the piston retaining clip.

8 Compress the retaining clip then remove it from the end of the cylinder and withdraw the pushrod, piston assembly and spring.

9 Examine the surfaces of the piston and cylinder. If they are scored or corroded, renew the master cylinder complete.

10 If the cylinder is in good condition, obtain a piston repair kit which will contain all the necessary renewable items.

11 Ensure all components are clean and dry and lubricate the piston assembly with fresh hydraulic fluid.

12 Fit the spring to the piston then carefully enter the assembly into the cylinder. Ease the piston into position with a twisting motion, taking great care not to trap the seal lips.

13 Fit the pushrod to the end of the piston and install the circlip, making sure it is correctly located in the cylinder groove. Check the operation of the piston and pushrod assembly then seat the pushrod dust cover on the master cylinder body.
14 Refit the fluid reservoir to the master cylinder and tighten its retaining clamp to the specified torque.

Refitting

15 Ensure the cylinder and bulkhead mating surfaces are clean and dry and fit the gasket to the bulkhead.
16 Manoeuvre the master cylinder into position whilst ensuring that the pushrod clevis engages correctly with the pedal. Ensure the pushrod is correctly engaged then tighten the master cylinder retaining nuts to the specified torque.
17 Apply a smear of multi-purpose grease to the clevis pin then fit the pin and washer and secure it in position with a new split pin.
18 Reconnect the hydraulic hose to the master cylinder, positioning a new sealing washer on each side of the union, and tighten the union bolt to the specified torque.
19 Refill the master cylinder reservoir with the correct type of fluid and bleed the hydraulic system as described in Section 6.
20 On completion check the clutch pedal settings as described in Section 2.

5 Clutch slave cylinder - removal, overhaul and refitting

Removal

1 Firmly apply the handbrake then jack up the front of the vehicle and support it on axle stands (see "*Jacking and vehicle support*").
2 Minimise fluid loss by first removing the master cylinder reservoir cap, and then tightening it down onto a piece of polythene, to obtain an airtight seal.
3 Wipe away all traces of dirt around the hydraulic pipe union on the slave cylinder and unscrew the union nut. Carefully ease the pipe out of the cylinder, and plug or tape over its end to prevent dirt entry. Wipe off any spilt fluid immediately.
4 Unscrew the two cylinder retaining bolts and carefully draw the cylinder off the pushrod which will remain attached to the clutch release lever.

Overhaul

5 Remove all traces of dirt from the outside of the cylinder.
6 Remove the dust cover from the cylinder and withdraw the piston assembly and spring, noting which way around the spring is fitted **(see illustration)**.

7 If necessary, slacken and remove the union bolt and washers securing the fluid union piece to the side of the cylinder and withdraw the restrictor valve and spring from the cylinder body. New sealing washers will be needed.
8 Examine the surfaces of the piston and cylinder. If they are scored or corroded, renew the slave cylinder complete.
9 If the cylinder is in good condition, obtain a piston repair kit which will contain all the necessary renewable items.
10 Ensure all components are clean and dry and lubricate the piston assembly with fresh hydraulic fluid.
11 Fit the spring to the piston, with its tapered end facing the piston, then carefully enter the assembly into the cylinder. Ease the piston into position with a twisting motion, taking great care not to trap the seal lips.
12 Depress the piston and fit the dust cover, making sure it is correctly located on the cylinder body.
13 Where removed, refit the spring and restrictor valve to the slave cylinder. Position a new sealing washer on each side of the fluid union then fit the union bolt and tighten it to the specified torque.

Refitting

14 Apply a smear of grease to the release fork pushrod and ease the slave cylinder onto the rod. Fit the cylinder retaining bolts and tighten them securely.
15 Reconnect the hydraulic pipe to the slave cylinder and tighten its union nut to the specified torque. Remove the polythene from the master cylinder.
16 Bleed the hydraulic system as described in Section 6.
17 On completion check the clutch pedal settings as described in Section 2.

6 Clutch hydraulic system - bleeding

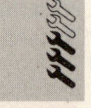

Warning: Hydraulic fluid is poisonous; wash off immediately and thoroughly in the case of skin contact, and seek immediate medical advice if any fluid is swallowed or gets into the eyes. Certain types of hydraulic fluid are flammable, and may ignite when allowed into contact with hot components; when servicing any hydraulic system, it is safest to assume that the fluid is flammable, and to take precautions against the risk of fire as though it is petrol that is being handled. Hydraulic fluid is also an effective paint stripper, and will attack plastics; if any is spilt, it should be washed off immediately, using copious quantities of fresh water. Finally, it is hygroscopic (it absorbs moisture from the air) - old fluid may be contaminated and unfit for further use.

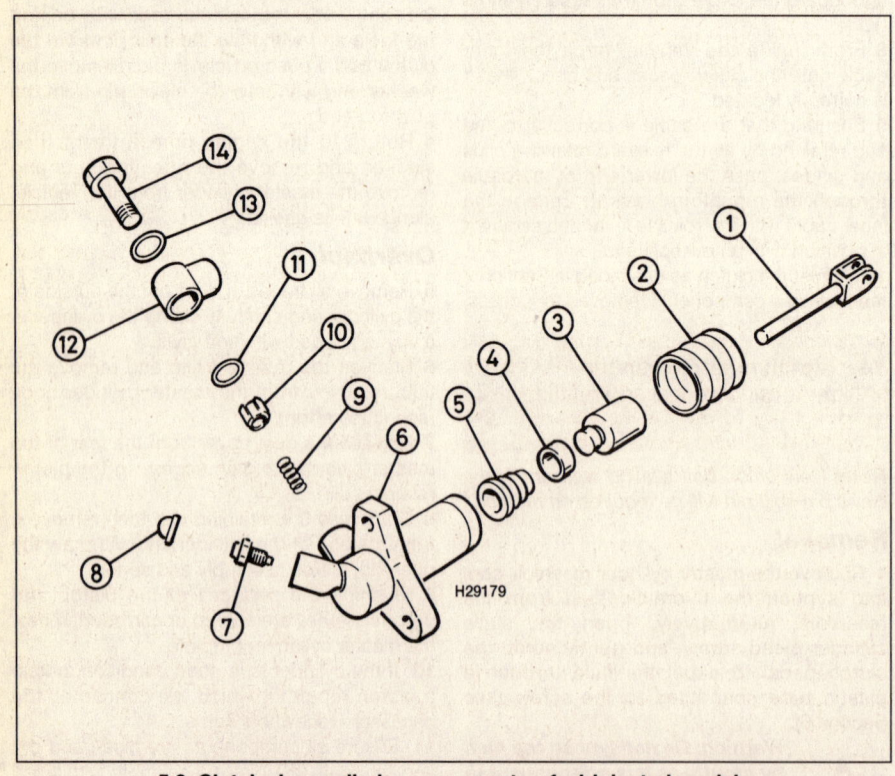

5.6 Clutch slave cylinder components - fuel-injected models

1 Pushrod	4 Seal	8 Dust cap	12 Fluid union
2 Dust cover	5 Spring	9 Spring	13 Sealing washer
3 Piston	6 Body	10 Restrictor valve	14 Union bolt
	7 Bleed screw	11 Sealing washer	

When topping-up or renewing the fluid, always use the recommended type, and ensure that it comes from a freshly opened sealed container.

1 The correct operation of any hydraulic system is only possible after removing all air from the components and circuit; this is achieved by bleeding the system.
2 During the bleeding procedure, add only clean, unused hydraulic fluid of the recommended type; never re-use fluid that has already been bled from the system. Ensure that sufficient fluid is available before starting work.
3 If there is any possibility of incorrect fluid being already in the system, the hydraulic circuit must be flushed completely with uncontaminated, correct fluid.
4 If hydraulic fluid has been lost from the system, or air has entered because of a leak, ensure that the fault is cured before continuing further.
5 The bleed screw is screwed directly into the top of the slave cylinder body; to gain access firmly apply the handbrake then jack up the front of the vehicle and support it on axle stands (see "*Jacking and vehicle support*").
6 Check that all pipes and hoses are secure, unions tight and the bleed screw is closed. Clean any dirt from around the bleed screw.
7 Unscrew the master cylinder fluid reservoir cap, and top the master cylinder reservoir up to the upper (MAX) level line; refit the cap loosely, and remember to maintain the fluid level at least above the lower (MIN or A) level line throughout the procedure, or there is a risk of further air entering the system.
8 There are a number of one-man, do-it-yourself bleeding kits currently available from motor accessory shops. It is recommended that one of these kits is used whenever possible, as they greatly simplify the bleeding operation, and reduce the risk of expelled air and fluid being drawn back into the system. If such a kit is not available, the basic (two-man) method must be used, which is described in detail below.
9 If a kit is to be used, prepare the vehicle as described previously, and follow the kit manufacturer's instructions, as the procedure may vary slightly according to the type being used; generally, they are as outlined below in the relevant sub-section.

Bleeding - basic (two-man) method

10 Collect a clean glass jar, a suitable length of plastic or rubber tubing which is a tight fit over the bleed screw, and a ring spanner to fit the screw. The help of an assistant will also be required.
11 Remove the dust cap from the slave cylinder bleed screw. Fit the spanner and tube to the screw, place the other end of the tube in the jar, and pour in sufficient fluid to cover the end of the tube.
12 Ensure that the fluid level is maintained at least above the lower level line in the reservoir throughout the procedure.
13 Have the assistant fully depress the clutch pedal several times to build up pressure, then maintain it on the final downstroke.
14 While pedal pressure is maintained, unscrew the bleed screw (approximately one turn) and allow the compressed fluid and air to flow into the jar. The assistant should maintain pedal pressure and should not release it until instructed to do so. When the flow stops, tighten the bleed screw again, have the assistant release the pedal slowly, and recheck the reservoir fluid level.
15 Repeat the steps given in paragraphs 13 and 14 until the fluid emerging from the bleed screw is free from air bubbles. If the master cylinder has been drained and refilled allow approximately five seconds between cycles for the master cylinder passages to refill.
16 When no more air bubbles appear, tighten the bleed screw securely, remove the tube and spanner, and refit the dust cap. Do not overtighten the bleed screw.

Bleeding - using a one-way valve kit

17 As their name implies, these kits consist of a length of tubing with a one-way valve fitted, to prevent expelled air and fluid being drawn back into the system; some kits include a translucent container, which can be positioned so that the air bubbles can be more easily seen flowing from the end of the tube.
18 The kit is connected to the bleed screw, which is then opened. The user returns to the driver's seat, depresses the clutch pedal with a smooth, steady stroke, and slowly releases it; this is repeated until the expelled fluid is clear of air bubbles.
19 Note that these kits simplify work so much that it is easy to forget the clutch fluid reservoir level; ensure that this is maintained at least above the lower level line at all times.

Bleeding - using a pressure-bleeding kit

20 These kits are usually operated by the reservoir of pressurised air contained in the spare tyre. However, note that it will probably be necessary to reduce the pressure to a lower level than normal; refer to the instructions supplied with the kit.
21 By connecting a pressurised, fluid-filled container to the clutch fluid reservoir, bleeding can be carried out simply by opening the bleed screw and allowing the fluid to flow out until no more air bubbles can be seen in the expelled fluid.
22 This method has the advantage that the large reservoir of fluid provides an additional safeguard against air being drawn into the system during bleeding.

All methods

23 When bleeding is complete, and correct pedal feel is restored, tighten the bleed screw securely and wash off any spilt fluid. Refit the dust cap to the bleed screw then lower the vehicle to the ground.
24 Check the hydraulic fluid level in the master cylinder reservoir, and top-up if necessary (see "*Weekly Checks*" and Chapter 1).
25 Discard any hydraulic fluid that has been bled from the system; it will not be fit for re-use.
26 Check the operation of the clutch pedal as described in Section 2. If the clutch is still not operating correctly, air must still be present in the system, and further bleeding is required. Failure to bleed satisfactorily after a reasonable repetition of the bleeding procedure may be due to worn master cylinder/slave cylinder seals.

7 Clutch pedal - removal and refitting

Removal

Carburettor models

1 Detach the clutch cable from the upper end of the pedal as described in paragraphs 2 and 3 of Section 3.
2 Using circlip pliers, remove the circlip from the end of the pedal pivot shaft and slide off the washer.
3 Slide the pedal out of position and recover the wave washer from the pedal pivot shaft. Remove the pedal pivot bushes from the mounting bracket. Examine all components for signs of wear or damage and renew as necessary.

Fuel-injected models

4 Carefully unhook the return spring end from the pedal to relieve the spring tension.
5 Remove the split pin and washers and withdraw the clevis pin securing the clutch pedal to the master cylinder pushrod.
6 Slacken and remove the pivot nut and bolt then remove the pedal and spring assembly from the vehicle, noting which way around the spring is fitted.
7 Inspect the pivot bushes and springs for signs of wear of damage and renew as necessary.

Refitting

Carburettor models

8 Prior to refitting, apply a smear of multi-purpose grease to the pedal pivot shaft and the pedal end.
9 Ensure the pivot bushes are pressed securely into position then fit the wave washer to the pedal shaft. Slide the pedal into position then fit the second washer and circlip, making sure it is correctly located in the pivot shaft groove.
10 Reconnect the cable to the top of the pedal and adjust the clutch as described in Section 2.

Fuel-injected models

11 Prior to refitting, apply a smear of multi-purpose grease to the pedal pivot bolt, the pivot bushes and the pushrod clevis and pin.

8.7 Measuring friction plate to rivet head depth

8.14 Fit the friction plate with its spring hub facing away from the flywheel . . .

8.15 . . . and install the pressure plate

12 Fit the return spring to the pedal and manoeuvre the pedal into position, engaging it with the pushrod clevis. Insert the pivot bolt then fit the retaining nut and tighten it to the specified torque.
13 Insert the clevis pin and washer and secure it in position with a new split pin.
14 Ensure the inner end of the return spring is correctly located and hook it back over the clutch pedal.
15 Check the operation of the clutch pedal as described in Section 2.

8 Clutch assembly - removal, inspection and refitting

Warning: Dust created by clutch wear and deposited on the clutch components may contain asbestos, which is a health hazard. DO NOT blow it out with compressed air, or inhale any of it. DO NOT use petrol or petroleum-based solvents to clean off the dust. Brake system cleaner or methylated spirit should be used to flush the dust into a suitable receptacle. After the clutch components are wiped clean with rags, dispose of the contaminated rags and cleaner in a sealed, marked container.
Note: *Although some friction materials may no longer contain asbestos, it is safest to assume that they do, and to take precautions accordingly.*

Removal

1 Unless the complete engine/transmission unit is to be removed from the car and separated for major overhaul (see Chapter 2), the clutch can be reached by removing the transmission as described in Chapter 7.
2 Before disturbing the clutch, use chalk or a marker pen to mark the relationship of the pressure plate assembly to the flywheel.
3 Working in a diagonal sequence, slacken the pressure plate bolts by half a turn at a time, until spring pressure is released and the bolts can be unscrewed by hand.
4 Prise the pressure plate assembly off its locating dowels, and collect the friction plate, noting which way round the friction plate is fitted.

Inspection

Note: *Due to the amount of work necessary to remove and refit clutch components, it is usually considered good practice to renew the clutch friction plate, pressure plate assembly and release bearing as a matched set, even if only one of these is actually worn enough to require renewal. It is also worth considering the renewal of the clutch components on a preventive basis if the engine and/or transmission have been removed for some other reason.*

5 Remove the clutch assembly.
6 When cleaning clutch components, read first the warning at the beginning of this Section; remove dust using a clean, dry cloth, and working in a well-ventilated atmosphere.
7 Check the friction plate facings for signs of wear, damage or oil contamination. If the friction material is cracked, burnt, scored or damaged, or if it is contaminated with oil or grease (shown by shiny black patches), the friction plate must be renewed. Measure the depth of the rivets below the friction material surface **(see illustration)**. If depth of any rivet is equal to, or less than, the service limit given in the *Specifications*, then the friction plate must be renewed.
8 If the friction material is still serviceable, check that the centre boss splines are unworn, that the torsion springs are in good condition and securely fastened, and that all the rivets are tight. If any wear or damage is found, the friction plate must be renewed.
9 If the friction material is fouled with oil, this must be due to an oil leak from the crankshaft left-hand oil seal, from the sump-to-cylinder block joint, or from the transmission input shaft. Renew the seal or repair the joint, as appropriate, as described in Chapter 2 or 7, before installing the new friction plate.
10 Check the pressure plate assembly for obvious signs of wear or damage; shake it to check for loose rivets or worn or damaged fulcrum rings, and check that the drive straps securing the pressure plate to the cover do not show signs (such as a deep yellow or blue discoloration) of overheating. If the diaphragm spring is worn or damaged, or if its pressure is in any way suspect, the pressure plate assembly should be renewed.
11 Examine the machined bearing surfaces of the pressure plate and of the flywheel; they should be clean, completely flat, and free from scratches or scoring. If either is discoloured from excessive heat, or shows signs of cracks, it should be renewed - although minor damage of this nature can sometimes be polished away using emery paper.
12 Check that the release bearing contact surface rotates smoothly and easily, with no sign of noise or roughness. Also check that the surface itself is smooth and unworn, with no signs of cracks, pitting or scoring. If there is any doubt about its condition, the bearing must be renewed.

Refitting

13 On reassembly, ensure that the bearing surfaces of the flywheel and pressure plate are completely clean, smooth, and free from oil or grease. Use solvent to remove any protective grease from new components.
14 Fit the friction plate so that its spring hub assembly faces away from the flywheel; there may also be a marking showing which way round the plate is to be refitted **(see illustration)**.
15 Refit the pressure plate assembly, aligning the marks made on dismantling (if the original pressure plate is re-used), and locating the pressure plate on its three locating dowels **(see illustration)**. Fit the pressure plate bolts, but tighten them only finger-tight, so that the friction plate can still be moved.
16 The friction plate must now be centralised, so that when the transmission is refitted, its input shaft will pass through the splines at the centre of the friction plate.
17 Centralisation can be achieved by passing a screwdriver or other long bar through the friction plate and into the hole in the crankshaft; the friction plate can then be moved around until it is centred on the crankshaft hole. Alternatively, a clutch-aligning -tool can be used to eliminate the guesswork; these can be obtained from most accessory shops. A home-made aligning tool can be fabricated from a length of metal rod or wooden dowel which fits closely inside the crankshaft hole, and has insulating tape wound around it to match the diameter of the friction plate splined hole.

Clutch 6•7

8.18 Centralise the friction plate with an alignment tool (arrowed) and tighten the pressure plate bolts to the specified torque setting

9.2 Disengage the retaining clip ends (arrowed) and slide the release bearing off of the fork

18 When the friction plate is centralised, tighten the pressure plate bolts evenly and in a diagonal sequence to the specified torque setting **(see illustration)**.
19 Apply a smear of molybdenum disulphide grease to the splines of the friction plate and the transmission input shaft, and also to the release bearing bore and release fork shaft.
Caution: Do not apply too much grease as there is a risk that it will contaminate the friction plate material.
20 Refit the transmission (see Chapter 7).

9 Clutch release mechanism - removal, inspection and refitting

Note: Refer to the warning concerning the dangers of asbestos dust at the beginning of Section 8.

Removal

1 Unless the complete engine/transmission unit is to be removed from the car and separated for major overhaul (see Chapter 2), the clutch release mechanism can be reached by removing the transmission only (Chapter 7).

2 Using pliers, unhook the bearing retaining clip from the release fork and slide the bearing and clip off from the input shaft **(see illustration)**.
3 To remove the release lever and fork, drill out or extract the roll pins securing the fork to the shaft **(see illustration)**. Noting the correct fitted location of the lever return spring (carburettor models only), withdraw the release lever from the transmission housing then remove the release fork, spring (if fitted) and foam seals from the bellhousing. Renew the foam seals if they show signs of damage or deterioration.

Inspection

4 Check the release mechanism, renewing any component which is worn or damaged. Carefully check all bearing surfaces and points of contact.
5 When checking the release bearing itself, note that it is often considered worthwhile to renew it as a matter of course. Check that the contact surface rotates smoothly and easily, with no sign of noise or roughness, and that the surface itself is smooth and unworn, with no signs of cracks, pitting or scoring. If there is any doubt about its condition, the bearing must be renewed.

Refitting

6 Apply a smear of molybdenum disulphide grease to the release lever shaft pivot bushes and the contact surfaces of the release fork and bearing.
7 Engage the return spring (where fitted) with the release fork and fit the assembly to the bellhousing.
8 Position the foam seals on either side of the fork and spring assembly ensuring the return spring is correctly located in the transmission housing. Slide the release lever into the housing, engaging it with the seals, spring and fork. Align the shaft holes with those of the release fork and secure the fork to the shaft by tapping in the new roll pins.
9 Ensure the retaining clip is correctly engaged in the release bearing groove then slide the release bearing and spring clip into position **(see illustration)**. Engage the bearing with the release fork and secure it in position by locating the ends of the retaining clip in the fork holes.
10 Check the operation of the release mechanism then refit the transmission as described in Chapter 7.

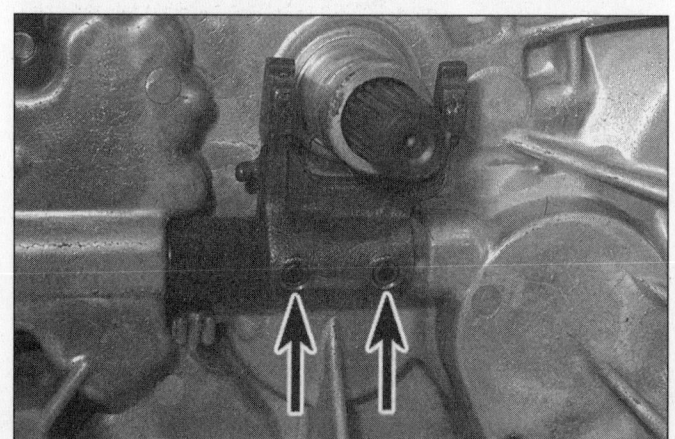

9.3 To remove the release lever and fork it will be necessary to dill out/extract the roll pins (arrowed)

9.9 Ensure the retaining clip is correctly located in the bearing groove then engage the spring ends in the release fork holes

Chapter 7 Part A:
Manual transmission

Contents

Gearchange cables - removal and refitting 3
Gearchange lever - removal and refitting 4
Gearchange mechanism - adjustment 2
General information 1
Oil seals - renewal 5
Reversing light switch - testing, removal and refitting 6
Speedometer drive - removal and refitting 7
Transmission - removal and refitting 8
Transmission oil level check .... See Chapter 1
Transmission oil renewal .... See Chapter 1
Transmission overhaul - general information 9

Degrees of difficulty

| **Easy,** suitable for novice with little experience | **Fairly easy,** suitable for beginner with some experience | **Fairly difficult,** suitable for competent DIY mechanic | **Difficult,** suitable for experienced DIY mechanic | **Very difficult,** suitable for expert DIY or professional |

Specifications

General
Type .... Manual, five forward speeds and reverse. Synchromesh on all forward speeds

Torque wrench settings

	Nm	lbf ft
Engine/transmission right-hand mounting:		
Mounting to body bolts	40	29
Mounting through bolt	100	74
Mounting bracket to transmission nut/bolt	60	43
Engine/transmission stabilising rod:		
Rod to transmission bolt	65	46
Rod to body bolt	50	37
Engine to transmission unit bolts	53	39
Flywheel lower cover plate bolts	12	9
Gearchange cable grommet retaining nuts	14	10
Gearchange lever mounting bolts	14	10
Roadwheel nuts	100	74
Reversing light switch	35	25

1 General information

The transmission is contained in a cast-aluminium alloy casing bolted to the engine's right-hand end, and consists of the gearbox and final drive differential - often called a transaxle.

Drive is transmitted from the crankshaft via the clutch to the input shaft, which has a splined extension to accept the clutch friction plate, and rotates in sealed ball-bearings. From the input shaft, drive is transmitted to the output shaft, which rotates in a roller bearing at its right-hand end, and a sealed ball-bearing at its left-hand end. From the output shaft, the drive is transmitted to the differential crownwheel, which rotates with the differential case and planetary gears, thus driving the sun gears and driveshafts. The rotation of the planetary gears on their shaft allows the inner roadwheel to rotate at a slower speed than the outer roadwheel when the car is cornering.

The input and output shafts are arranged side by side, parallel to the crankshaft and driveshafts, so that their gear pinion teeth are in constant mesh. In the neutral position, the output shaft gear pinions rotate freely, so that drive cannot be transmitted to the crownwheel.

Gear selection is via a floor-mounted lever and selector cable mechanism. The selector cables cause the appropriate selector fork to move its respective synchro-sleeve along the shaft, to lock the gear pinion to the synchro-hub. Since the synchro-hubs are splined to the output shaft, this locks the pinion to the shaft, so that drive can be transmitted. To ensure that gear-changing can be made quickly and quietly, a synchro-mesh system is fitted to all forward gears, consisting of baulk rings and spring-loaded fingers, as well as the gear pinions and synchro-hubs. The synchro-mesh cones are formed on the mating faces of the baulk rings and gear pinions.

7A•2 Manual transmission

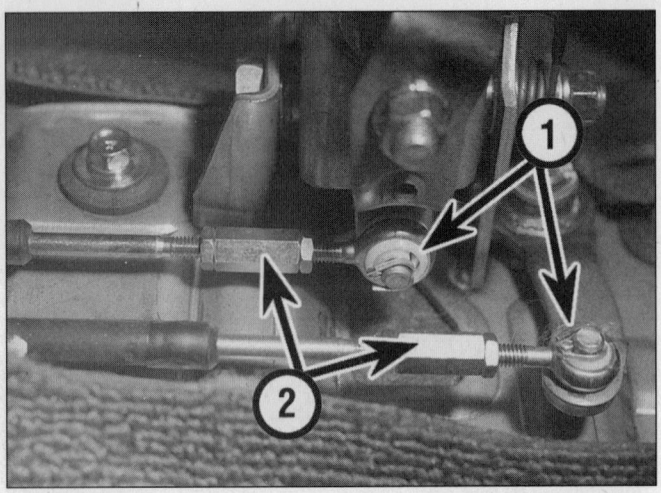

2.3 Remove the split pins (1) and detach the gearchange cables from the lever. The cable lengths are altered using the adjusters (2)

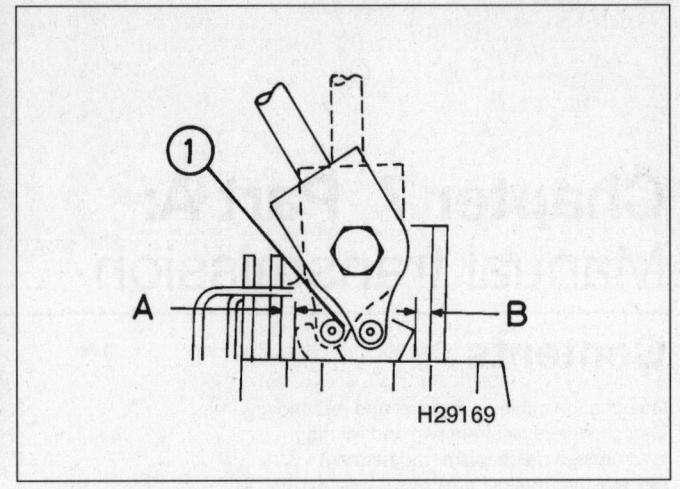

2.5 Adjust the gearchange upper (shift) cable - distance between the lever stopper (1) and mounting is equal (dimensions A and B) when 3rd and 4th gear are selected - see text

2 Gearchange mechanism - adjustment

1 If a stiff, sloppy or imprecise gearchange leads you to suspect that a fault exists within the linkage, adjust the cables as follows.
2 Remove the centre console as described in Chapter 11.
3 Set the gearchange lever to the neutral position then remove the split pins and detach both the gearchange cables from the base of the lever (see illustration).
4 Working in the engine compartment, move the transmission shift lever forwards to select 4th gear on the transmission.
5 Return to the inside of the vehicle and move the gearchange lever backwards into the 4th gear position so that the lever contacts the stopper. With the lever and transmission position as described, the upper (shift) cable end fitting should be correctly aligned with its pin on the gearchange lever. If adjustment is necessary, slacken the locknut and alter the length of the cable using the adjuster. Reconnect the cable to the lever then move the gearchange lever from 4th to 3rd and check that the clearance between the shift lever stopper and mounting plate is equal on both sides, adjusting if necessary (see illustration). Once the cable length is correctly set securely tighten the locknut and connect the cable to the gearchange lever, securing it in position with a new split pin.
6 Return to the engine compartment and move the transmission shift lever back to the neutral position. Ensure both the transmission shift and selector levers are in the neutral position.
7 Return to the inside of the vehicle again and position the gearchange lever in the neutral position. The lower (select) cable end fitting should be correctly aligned with its pin on the gearchange lever. If adjustment is necessary, slacken the locknuts and alter the length of the cable using the adjuster. Securely tighten the locknuts then reconnect the cable to the lever and secure it in position with a new split pin.
8 Check the operation of the gearchange linkage then refit the centre console as described in Chapter 11.

3 Gearchange cables - removal and refitting

Removal

1 Remove the centre console assembly as described in Chapter 11. On fuel-injected models, remove the air cleaner housing as described in Chapter 4 to gain access to the transmission end of the cables.
2 Prior to removal make alignment marks between the cables and gearchange/transmission levers to avoid confusion on refitting.
3 Position the gearchange lever in the neutral position then remove the split pins and detach the cables from the base of the lever. Take care not to disturb the position of the transmission shift and select levers whilst the cables are disconnected.
4 Slide out the retaining clips and free the cables from their brackets.
5 Work back along the cables, freeing them from any relevant retaining clips, and undo the two nuts securing the cable grommet to the bulkhead.
6 From inside the engine compartment, remove the split pins and washers and free the cables from the transmission levers (see illustrations).
7 Slide out the retaining clips securing the cables to the transmission bracket then, noting the cable assembly correct routing, free the cable grommet from the bulkhead and remove the assembly from the engine compartment (see illustration).
8 Examine each cable, looking for worn end fittings or a damaged outer casing, and for signs of fraying of the inner wire. Check the cable's operation; the inner wire should move smoothly and easily through the outer casing. Remember that a cable that appears serviceable when tested off the car may well be much heavier in operation when in its working position. Renew the cable if it shows signs of excessive wear or any damage.

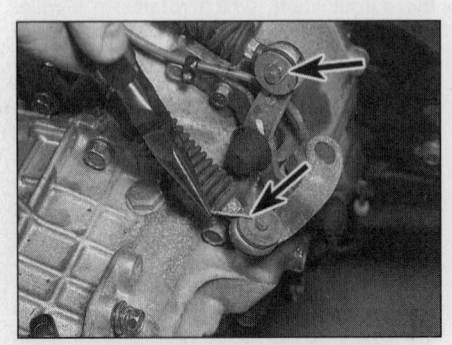

3.6a Remove the split pins (arrowed) ...

3.6b ... and washers and disconnect the cables from the transmission levers

Manual transmission 7A•3

Refitting

9 Apply a smear of multi-purpose grease to the cable end fittings and the lever pivots. If new cables are being fitted, transfer the marks made prior to removal to aid refitting.
10 Manoeuvre the cables into position, ensuring they are correctly routed, and locate the cable grommet in the bulkhead.
11 Engage the lower end of each outer cable with its relevant transmission bracket and secure the cables in position with the retaining clips. Connect the inner cables to the transmission levers then refit the washers and secure them in position with new split pins.
12 From inside the vehicle, refit the cable grommet retaining nuts and tighten them to the specified torque.
13 Ensure the cables are correctly routed then engage the cables with their respective locations in the lever base and secure then in position with the retaining clips.
14 Ensure both the transmission shift and select levers are still in the neutral position then adjust the cables as described in paragraph 4 onwards of Section 2.

4 Gearchange lever - removal and refitting

Removal

1 Carry out the operations described in paragraphs 1 to 4 of Section 3.
2 Slacken and remove the bolts securing the lever assembly to the body and remove it from the vehicle, along with its mounting rubbers and spacers. Renew the mounting rubbers if they show signs of damage or deterioration.

Refitting

3 Ensure the mounting rubbers are correctly fitted to the lever mounting plate and insert the spacers.
4 Refit the gearchange lever assembly to the vehicle and tighten its retaining bolts to the specified torque.
5 Ensure the cables are correctly routed then engage the cables with their respective locations in the lever base and secure then in position with the retaining clips.
6 Ensure both the transmission shift and select levers are still in the neutral position then adjust the cables as described in paragraph 4 onwards of Section 2.

5 Oil seals - renewal

Driveshaft oil seals

1 Chock the rear wheels, apply the handbrake, then jack up the front of the car and support it on axle stands. Remove the appropriate front roadwheel.
2 Drain the transmission oil as described in Chapter 1.
3 Working as described in Chapter 8, free the inner end of the driveshaft from the transmission, and place it clear of the seal, noting that there is no need to unscrew the driveshaft retaining nut; the driveshaft can be left secured to the hub. Support the driveshaft, to avoid placing any strain on the driveshaft joints or gaiters.
4 Carefully prise the oil seal out of the transmission using a large flat-bladed screwdriver.
5 Remove all traces of dirt from the area around the oil seal aperture, then apply a smear of grease to the outer lip of the new oil seal. Ensure the seal is correctly positioned, with its sealing lip facing inwards, and drive it squarely into position, using a tubular drift (such as a socket) which bears only on the hard outer edge of the seal.
6 Refit the driveshaft (Chapter 8).
7 Refill the transmission with the specified type and amount of oil, (see Chapter 1).

Input shaft and gearchange lever shaft oil seals

8 To renew these oil seals, the transmission must be dismantled. This task should therefore be entrusted to a Proton dealer or transmission specialist.

6 Reversing light switch - testing, removal and refitting

Testing

1 The reversing light circuit is controlled by a plunger-type switch that is screwed into the top of the transmission casing. If a fault develops in the circuit, first ensure that the circuit fuse has not blown.
2 To test the switch, disconnect the wiring connector, and use a multimeter (set to the resistance function) or a battery-and-bulb test circuit to check that there is continuity between the switch terminals only when reverse gear is selected. If this is not the case, and there are no obvious breaks or other damage to the wires, the switch is faulty, and must be renewed.

Removal

3 To improve access to the switch, remove the air intake duct as described in Chapter 4. If necessary, also remove the battery mounting tray (see Chapter 5).
4 Disconnect the wiring connector, then unscrew it from the transmission casing along with its sealing washer **(see illustration)**.

Refitting

5 Fit a new sealing washer to the switch, then screw it back into position in the top of the transmission housing and tighten it to the specified torque. Reconnect the wiring connector, and test the operation of the circuit. Refit any components removed for access.

3.7 Slide out the retaining clips (arrowed) and free the outer cables from the mounting bracket

6.4 Disconnecting the reversing light switch wiring connector (battery tray removed for clarity)

7A•4 Manual transmission

7 Speedometer drive - removal and refitting

Removal

1 The speedometer drive is situated on the rear of the transmission housing, next to the inner end of the right-hand driveshaft. Access to the drive can be gained from above noting that it will be necessary to remove the air cleaner housing on fuel-injected models. If necessary to further improve access, chock the rear wheels, firmly apply the handbrake, then jack up the front of the car and support it on axle stands.
2 Unscrew the knurled retaining ring and disconnect the speedometer cable from the drive **(see illustration)**.
3 Slacken and remove the retaining bolt and withdraw the speedometer drive and driven pinion assembly from the transmission housing, along with its sealing ring.
4 If necessary, carefully tap out the roll pin and slide the driven pinion out of the housing. The oil seal can then be levered out from the top housing.

Refitting

5 Where necessary, press the new seal into position in the top of the housing making sure its sealing lip is facing inwards. Lubricate the pinion shaft with a smear of oil and slide the pinion into position. Align the pinion groove with the housing hole and secure the pinion in position with the roll pin.
6 Fit a new sealing ring to the speedometer housing and lubricate it with a smear of oil of oil to ease installation.
7 Ease the speedometer drive into position in the transmission, ensuring that the drive and driven pinions are correctly engaged, and securely tighten the retaining bolt.
8 Reconnect the cable to the drive and securely tighten its retaining ring. Lower the

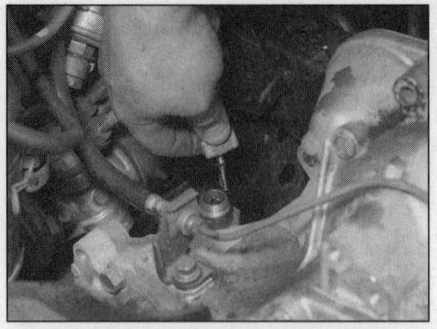

7.2 Unscrew the knurled ring and disconnect the speedometer cable from the drive

vehicle to the ground.

8 Transmission - removal and refitting

Removal

1 Chock the rear wheels, then firmly apply the handbrake. Jack up the front of the vehicle, and securely support it on axle stands. Remove both front roadwheels then undo the retaining screws and remove the undercover from inside the right-hand wheel arch.
2 Drain the transmission oil as described in Chapter 1, then refit the drain and filler plugs, and tighten them to their specified torque settings.
3 Remove the battery, battery tray and mounting plate as described in Chapter 5.
4 On fuel injected models remove the air cleaner housing and/or intake duct as described in Chapter 4.
5 Remove the starter motor as described in Chapter 5.
6 On carburettor models, slacken the clutch cable adjuster to obtain maximum free play in the cable then remove the split pin securing the lower end of the cable to the clutch release lever. Free the clutch cable from the release lever and mounting bracket and position it clear of the transmission (see Chapter 6).
7 On fuel-injected models, slacken and remove the bolt securing the clutch hydraulic hose/pipe bracket to the top of the transmission and release the hose/pipe from all the necessary clips. Remove the retaining clip and clevis pin connecting the slave cylinder pushrod to the release arm then undo the retaining bolts and free the cylinder. Fully retract the pushrod into the slave cylinder and secure it in position with a stout elastic band or cable tie (to prevent the piston being accidentally expelled) and position the cylinder clear of the transmission unit.
8 Disconnect the wiring connector from the reversing light switch. Undo the retaining bolt and disconnect the earth strap from the transmission housing **(see illustration)**.
9 Remove the split pins and washers securing the gearchange cables to the transmission levers (see Section 3) then undo the retaining bolts and free the cable mounting bracket from the top of the transmission **(see illustrations)**.
10 Undo the retaining bolts and remove the flywheel lower cover plate from the transmission **(see illustration)**.
11 Unscrew the retaining ring and disconnect the speedometer cable from the drive housing.
12 Referring to Chapter 8, remove the right-hand driveshaft and disconnect the left-hand driveshaft from the transmission. Note that it is not necessary to remove the left-hand driveshaft completely, it can be left attached to the hub assembly and released from the transmission as the hub is pulled outwards. **Note:** *Do not allow the shaft to hang down under its own weight as this could damage the constant velocity joints/gaiters.*
13 Place a jack and block of wood beneath the transmission, and raise the jack to take the weight of the transmission.

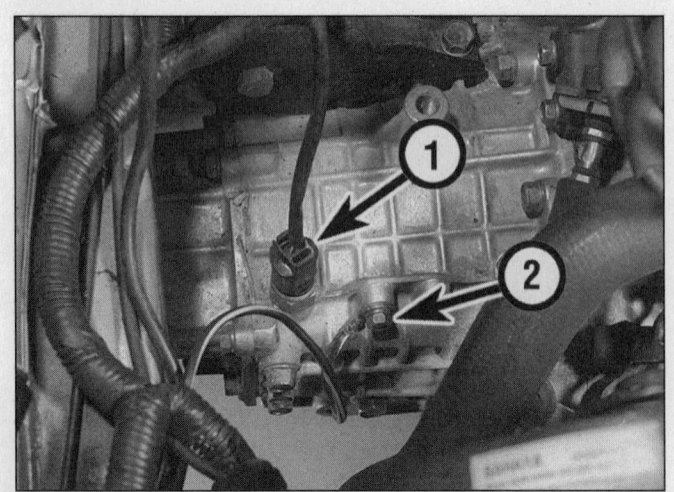

8.8 Disconnect the reversing light switch wiring connector (1) then undo the bolt (2) and free the earth lead from the transmission

8.9a Remove the split pins and washers (arrowed) . . .

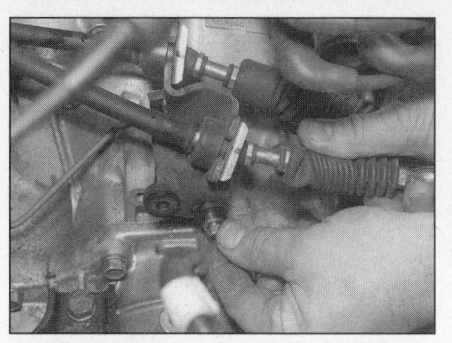

Manual transmission 7A•5

8.9b ... then slacken and remove the bolts and position the cable mounting bracket clear of the transmission

8.10 Removing the flywheel lower cover plate

Refitting

18 The transmission is refitted by a reversal of the removal procedure, bearing in mind the following points:

a) Apply a little high-melting-point grease to the splines of the transmission input shaft. Do not apply too much, otherwise there is a possibility of the grease contaminating the clutch friction plate.
b) Ensure the locating dowels are correctly positioned prior to installation.
c) Tighten all nuts and bolts to the specified torque (where given).
d) Renew the driveshaft oil seals (see Section 5) then refit the driveshafts as described in Chapter 8.
e) Reconnect the gearchange cables to the transmission and secure them in position with new split pins. If necessary adjust the cables as described in Section 2.
f) On carburettor models, reconnect the clutch cable and secure it in position with a new split pin. Adjust the clutch as described in Chapter 6.
g) On fuel injected models, refit the slave cylinder and ensure the hydraulic pipe/hose is securely retained by all the necessary clips. On completion, check the operation of the clutch as described in Chapter 6.
h) On completion, refill the transmission with the specified type and quantity of lubricant, as described in Chapter 1.

14 Slacken and remove the bolt and washers securing the engine/transmission stabilising rod to the rear of the transmission unit then slacken the nut and bolt securing the rod to the body and pivot the stabilising rod clear of the transmission unit **(see illustration)**.

15 Slacken and remove the through-bolt and nut from the right-hand engine/transmission mounting then undo the bolts and remove the mounting bracket from the top of the transmission unit **(see illustration)**.

16 With the jack positioned beneath the transmission taking the weight, slacken and remove the remaining bolts securing the transmission housing to the engine. Note the correct fitted positions of each bolt, and the necessary brackets, as they are removed, to use as a reference on refitting. Make a final check that all components have been disconnected, and are positioned clear of the transmission so that they will not hinder the removal procedure.

17 With the bolts removed, move the trolley jack and transmission to the right, to free it from its locating dowels. Once the transmission is free, lower the jack and manoeuvre the unit out from under the car. Remove the locating dowels from the transmission or engine if they are loose, and keep them in a safe place.

9 Transmission overhaul - general information

1 Overhauling a manual transmission unit is a difficult and involved job for the DIY home mechanic. In addition to dismantling and reassembling many small parts, clearances must be precisely measured and, if necessary, changed by selecting shims and spacers. Internal transmission components are also often difficult to obtain, and in many instances, extremely expensive. Because of this, if the transmission develops a fault or becomes noisy, the best course of action is to have the unit overhauled by a specialist repairer, or to obtain an exchange reconditioned unit.

2 Nevertheless, it is not impossible for the more experienced mechanic to overhaul the transmission, provided the special tools are available, and the job is done in a deliberate step-by-step manner, so that nothing is overlooked.

3 The tools necessary for an overhaul include internal and external circlip pliers, bearing pullers, a slide hammer, a set of pin punches, a dial test indicator, and possibly a hydraulic press. In addition, a large, sturdy workbench and a vice will be required.

4 During dismantling of the transmission, make careful notes of how each component is fitted, to make reassembly easier and more accurate.

5 Before dismantling the transmission, it will help if you have some idea what area is malfunctioning. Certain problems can be closely related to specific areas in the transmission, which can make component examination and replacement easier. Refer to the Fault diagnosis Section of this manual for more information.

8.14 Slacken and remove the bolt securing the stabilising rod to the rear of the transmission and pivot the rod clear

8.15 Slacken and remove the right-hand engine/transmission through-bolt (1) then undo the retaining bolts (2) and remove the mounting bracket from the top of the transmission

Notes

Chapter 7 Part B:
Automatic transmission

Contents

Automatic transmission - removal and refitting 11
Automatic transmission fluid level check .... See Chapter 1
Automatic transmission fluid renewal .... See Chapter 1
Automatic transmission overhaul - general information 12
Fluid cooler - general information 9
General information 1
Kickdown cable - adjustment 5
Kickdown cable - removal and refitting 6
Oil seals - renewal 8
Selector cable - adjustment 2
Selector cable - removal and refitting 3
Selector lever assembly - removal and refitting 4
Speedometer drive - removal and refitting 7
Starter inhibitor/reversing light switch - general information, removal,
  refitting and adjustment 10

Degrees of difficulty

| Easy, suitable for novice with little experience | Fairly easy, suitable for beginner with some experience | Fairly difficult, suitable for competent DIY mechanic | Difficult, suitable for experienced DIY mechanic | Very difficult, suitable for expert DIY or professional |

Specifications

General

Type .... Automatic, three forward speeds and reverse
Designation:
  Carburettor models .... KM 170
  Fuel-injected models F3A21

Torque wrench settings | Nm | lbf ft

Engine/transmission right-hand mounting:
  Mounting to body bolts .... 40 | 29
  Mounting to bracket bolt .... 100 | 74
  Mounting bracket to transmission nut/bolt ...... 60 | 43
Engine-to-transmission unit securing bolts:
  Bolts marked 7 on their heads:
    M10 bolts .... 50 | 37
  M8 bolts:
    14 mm long bolts .... 12 | 9
    20 mm long bolts .... 20 | 15
  Bolts marked 10 on their heads .... 35 | 25
Starter inhibitor/reversing light switch bolts ... 12 | 8
Sump retaining bolts .... 10 | 7
Torque converter-to-driveplate bolts .... 50 | 37
Transmission oil filter retaining bolts .... 7 | 5
Transmission selector lever retaining nut .... 20 | 15

1 General information

Most 1.5 litre models covered in this manual were offered with the option of a three-speed fully-automatic transmission, consisting of a torque converter, an epicyclic geartrain, and hydraulically-operated clutches and brakes.

The torque converter provides a fluid coupling between engine and transmission, which acts as an automatic clutch, and also provides a degree of torque multiplication when accelerating.

The epicyclic geartrain provides either of the four forward or one reverse gear ratios, according to which of its component parts are held stationary or allowed to turn. The components of the geartrain are held or released by brakes and clutches which are activated by a hydraulic control unit. A fluid pump within the transmission provides the necessary hydraulic pressure to operate the brakes and clutches.

Driver control of the transmission is by a seven-position selector lever. The transmission has a "drive" position, and a "hold" facility on the first two gear ratios. The "drive" position "D" provides automatic changing throughout the range of all four gear ratios, and is the one to select for normal driving. An automatic kickdown facility shifts the transmission down a gear if the accelerator pedal is fully depressed. The "hold" facility is very similar, but limits the number of gear ratios available - ie when the selector lever is in the "2" position, only the first two ratios can be selected; in the "L" (Low) position, only the first ratio can be selected, and so on. The lower ratio "hold" is useful for providing engine braking when travelling down steep gradients, or for preventing unwanted selection of top gear on twisty roads. Note, however, that the transmission should *never* be shifted down a position at high engine speeds.

7B•2 Automatic transmission

Due to the complexity of the automatic transmission, any repair or overhaul work must be left to a Proton dealer with the necessary special equipment for fault diagnosis and repair. The contents of the following Sections are therefore confined to supplying general information, and any service information and instructions that can be used by the owner.

2 Selector cable - adjustment

1 Position the selector lever firmly against its detent in the "N" position.
2 To improve access to the transmission end of the selector cable, remove the battery, battery tray and mounting plate as described in Chapter 5. On fuel-injected models it may also be necessary to remove the air cleaner housing (see Chapter 4).
3 Ensure the transmission selector lever hole is correctly aligned with the hole in the housing (and the inhibitor switch) and lock it in position with a twist drill of the correct diameter (see illustration). This will ensure the lever is in the "N" position.
4 On early models, with both the selector and transmission levers correctly positioned, slacken the locknut and rotate the adjuster nut to remove all freeplay from the selector cable without placing the cable under any tension. Once the cable is correctly adjusted, securely tighten the locknut.
5 On later models, remove the split pin and washer and detach the cable from the transmission selector lever. With both the selector and transmission levers correctly positioned, the cable end fitting should by correctly aligned with the transmission selector lever pin. If adjustment is necessary, slacken the locknut and alter the length of the cable using the adjuster. Securely tighten the locknut then reconnect the cable to the lever and secure it in position with a washer and new split pin.
6 Remove the twist drill from the selector lever then check the operation of the starter inhibitor/reversing light switch (Section 10). Refit any components removed to improve access.

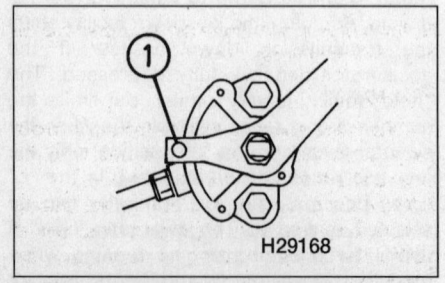

2.3 Ensure the transmission selector lever is in the neutral (N) position by aligning the selector lever hole (1) with the transmission housing hole

3 Selector cable - removal and refitting

Removal

1 Firmly apply the handbrake, then jack up the front of the vehicle and support it on axle stands. Position the selector lever in the "N" position.
2 To improve access, remove the battery, battery tray and mounting plate as described in Chapter 5. On fuel-injected models it may also be necessary to remove the air cleaner housing (see Chapter 4).
3 If necessary, remove the exhaust system heatshield(s) to gain access to the base of the selector lever assembly (see Chapter 4).
4 Undo the retaining screw and remove the handle from the top of the lever (see illustration).
5 Remove the centre console (see Chapter 11).
6 Undo the retaining screws and remove the indicator panel from the selector lever, disconnecting the wiring connector from the illumination light.

Early models

7 Remove the split pin then withdraw the clevis pin and detach the selector cable from the lever.
8 From underneath the vehicle, unscrew the retaining nuts securing the lever end of the cable to the floor and withdraw the cable.
9 Work back along the cable, releasing it from any relevant retaining clips, and slacken and remove the bolt securing the cable clip to the floor.
10 Remove the split pin and detach the cable from the transmission lever, noting the correct fitted location of the cable fitting washers. Slacken the outer cable retaining nut(s) then free the cable from its mounting bracket and remove it from the vehicle.
11 Examine the cable, looking for worn end fittings or a damaged outer casing, and for signs of fraying of the inner cable. Check the cable's operation; the inner cable should move smoothly and easily through the outer casing. Remember that a cable that appears serviceable when tested off the car may well be much heavier in operation when compressed into its working position. Renew the cable if it shows any signs of excessive wear or any damage.

Later models

12 Remove the split pin and detach the inner cable then slide out the retaining clip and free the outer cable from the lever bracket.
13 From underneath the vehicle, unscrew the retaining bolts securing the lever end of the cable to the floor and withdraw the cable.
14 Work back along the cable, releasing it from any relevant retaining clips, and slacken and remove the bolt securing the cable clip to the floor.
15 Remove the split pin and washer and detach the cable from the transmission lever then slide out the outer cable retaining clip and remove the cable from the vehicle.

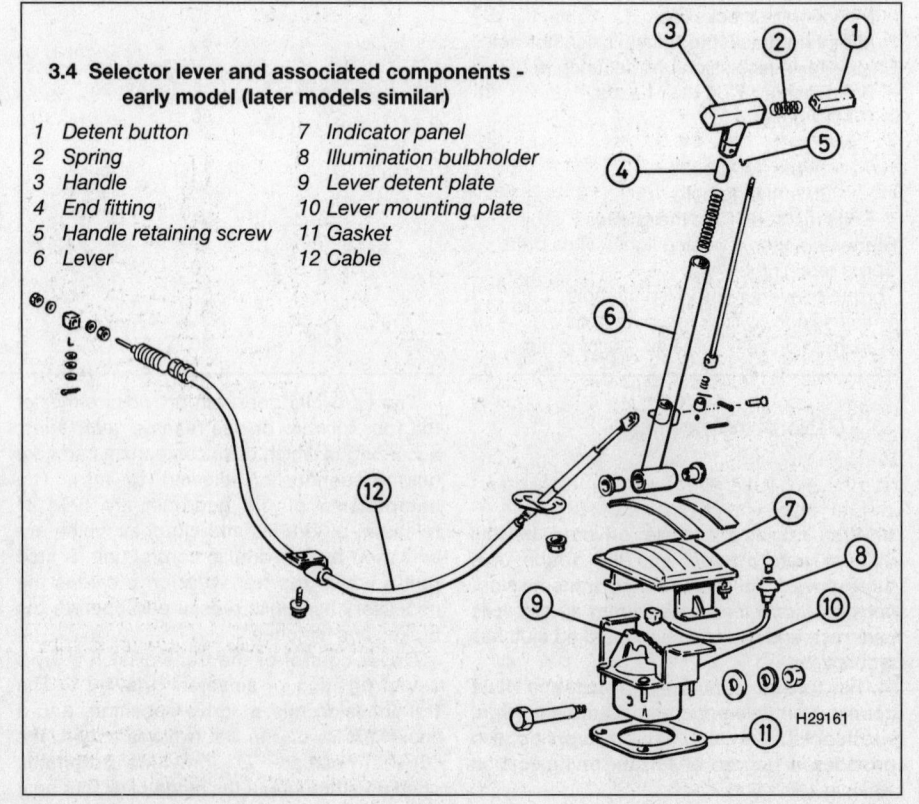

3.4 Selector lever and associated components - early model (later models similar)

1 Detent button
2 Spring
3 Handle
4 End fitting
5 Handle retaining screw
6 Lever
7 Indicator panel
8 Illumination bulbholder
9 Lever detent plate
10 Lever mounting plate
11 Gasket
12 Cable

Automatic transmission 7B•3

16 Inspect the cable as described in paragraph 11 and renew if necessary.

Refitting

Early models

17 Apply a smear of molybdenum disulphide grease to the cable end fittings and to the pivots of the selector lever.
18 Ensuring the cable is correctly routed, locate the transmission end of the outer cable in its mounting bracket and securely tighten its retaining nuts.
19 Connect the inner cable to the transmission lever, ensuring the washers are correctly positioned, and secure it in position with a new split pin.
20 Work along the length of the selector cable, ensuring that it is retained by all the relevant clips, and pass the cable up through the floor. Refit the cable retaining clip bolt and outer cable nuts and tighten them securely.
21 From inside the vehicle, align the cable end fitting with the selector lever and slide in the clevis pin. Secure the clevis pin in position with a new split pin.
22 Reconnect the wiring connector to the illumination bulb and refit the indicator panel to the lever. Ensure the lever is still in the neutral position then align the panel "N" with the lever and securely tighten the retaining screws.
23 Refit the centre console as described in Chapter 11.
24 Refit the handle to the top of the selector lever and securely tighten its retaining screw. Check the operation of the handle detent button ensuring that there is a small amount of freeplay in the button. If necessary adjustments can be made by removing the handle and screwing the end fitting into/out of the selector lever.
25 Check and, if necessary, adjust the selector cable as described in Section 2.
26 Refit all components removed for access and lower the vehicle to the ground.

Later models

27 Apply a smear of molybdenum disulphide grease to the cable end fittings and to the pivots of the selector lever.
28 Ensuring the cable is correctly routed, locate the transmission end of the outer cable in its mounting bracket and secure in it position with the retaining clip.
29 Connect the inner cable to the transmission lever then refit the washer and secure it in position with a new split pin.
30 Work along the length of the selector cable, ensuring that it is retained by all the relevant clips, and pass the cable up through the floor. Refit the cable retaining clip and outer cable retaining bolts and tighten them securely.
31 From inside the vehicle, engage the outer cable with the selector lever and secure it in position with the retaining clip. Connect the inner cable to the lever and secure it in position with a new split pin.

32 Carry out the operations described in paragraphs 22 to 26.

4 Selector lever assembly - removal and refitting

Removal

Early models

1 Undo the retaining screw and remove the handle from the top of the lever.
2 Remove the centre console as described in Chapter 11.
3 Undo the retaining screws and remove the indicator panel from the selector lever, disconnecting the wiring connector from the illumination light.
4 Remove the split pin then withdraw the clevis pin and detach the selector cable from the lever.
5 Firmly apply the handbrake, then jack up the front of the vehicle and support it on axle stands. Position the selector lever in the "N" position.
6 Remove the exhaust system heat shield(s) to gain access to the base of the selector lever assembly (see Chapter 4).
7 Unscrew the retaining nuts securing the lever assembly to the body then lift the lever assembly out of position. Recover the gasket which is fitted between the lever and body and renew it if it shows signs of damage.

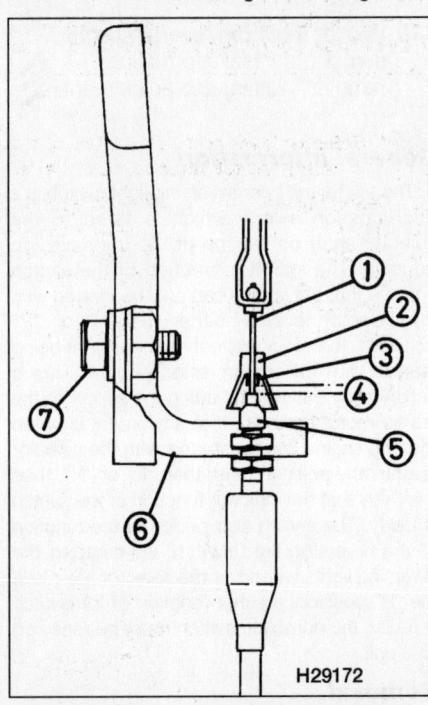

5.1 Kickdown cable adjustment details

1 Cable
2 Dust cover
3 Stopper
4 Adjustment measuring point
5 Outer cable end cover
6 Mounting bracket
7 Mounting bracket bolt

Later models

8 Carry out the operations described in paragraphs 1 to 3.
9 Remove the split pin and detach the inner cable from the selector lever then slide out the retaining clip and free the outer cable from the lever bracket.
10 Slacken and remove the retaining bolts and remove the lever assembly from the vehicle.

Refitting

11 Refitting is the reverse of removal, noting the following points.
a) Check the operation of the handle detent button ensuring that there is a small amount of freeplay in the button. If necessary adjustments can be made by removing the handle and screwing the end fitting into/out of the selector lever.
b) On completion, check and, if necessary, adjust the selector cable as described in Section 2.

5 Kickdown cable - adjustment

1 Locate the kickdown cable attachment on the carburettor/throttle housing and slide the rubber dust cover along the inner cable to reveal the inner cable stopper (see illustration).
2 Measure the distance between the end of the stopper and the outer cable end cover; this should be 1 ± 0.5 mm. If adjustment is necessary, slacken the cable mounting bracket retaining bolt and move the bracket to set the correct clearance then securely tighten the bracket bolt.
3 Slide the dust cover back into position then have an assistant fully depress the accelerator pedal whilst you check the operation of the cable. Ensure the cable moves smoothly and easily and returns quickly, if not renew the cable as described in Section 6.

6 Kickdown cable - removal and refitting

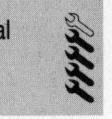

Note: *A new transmission sump gasket will be required on refitting.*

Removal

1 Detach the upper end of the kickdown inner cable from the throttle linkage and free the outer cable from its mounting bracket.
2 Work along the length of the cable, freeing it from any retaining clips and ties, whilst noting its correct routing. If necessary, on fuel-injected models remove the air cleaner housing to improve access to the transmission end of the cable (see Chapter 4).
3 Drain the transmission fluid as described in Chapter 1.

> **HAYNES HINT**: Whilst the sump is removed, check the transmission filter gauze for signs of debris or damage. If the filter is dirty, unbolt it from the base of the valve block and wash it in solvent to clean the gauze. Renew the filter if it is badly clogged or damaged in anyway. Fit the filter to the base of the valve block and tighten its retaining bolts to the specified torque.

4 Slacken and remove the retaining bolts and remove the sump from the base of the automatic transmission unit. Recover the gasket and discard it.
5 Free the lower end of the kickdown cable from the cam on the valve block then unscrew the outer cable from the top of the transmission and remove the cable from the vehicle. Recover the sealing ring which is fitted to the cable end fitting.

Refitting

6 Fit a new sealing ring to the kickdown cable lower end fitting and lubricate it with a smear of oil to ease installation.
7 Manoeuvre the cable into position, ensuring it is correctly routed, and screw the cable end fitting into position in the transmission unit, tightening it securely.
8 Connect the lower end of the cable to the valve block cam.
9 Ensure the cable is securely held in position then connect the upper end of the cable to the throttle linkage and secure the outer cable to its mounting bracket.
10 Check the operation of the kickdown cable and adjust it as described in Section 5.
11 Ensure the sump and transmission mating surfaces are clean and dry and position the new gasket on top of the sump. Refit the sump to the vehicle and tighten its retaining bolts to the specified torque setting.
12 Refill the transmission (Chapter 1), and refit any components removed for access.

7 Speedometer drive - removal and refitting

Refer to Chapter 7A noting that the pinion oil seal is replaced with a sealing ring which is seated in a groove in the housing.

8 Oil seals - renewal

Differential oil seals
1 Refer to Chapter 7A.

Torque converter oil seal
2 Remove the transmission as described in Section 11.

3 Carefully slide the torque converter off of the transmission shaft whilst being prepared for fluid spillage.
4 Note the correct fitted depth of the seal in the transmission casing then carefully lever the seal out of position using a flat-bladed screwdriver.
5 Remove all traces of dirt from the area around the oil seal aperture, then apply a smear of grease to the outer lip of the new oil seal, and locate it in its aperture ensuring its sealing lip is facing inwards. Drive the seal squarely into position, using a tubular drift (such as a socket) which bears only on the hard outer edge of the seal, until it is positioned at the same depth the original was prior to removal.
6 Lubricate the seal lip with clean transmission fluid then carefully ease the torque converter into position.
7 Refit the transmission as described in Section 11.

9 Fluid cooler - general information

The transmission fluid cooler is an integral part of the radiator assembly. Refer to Chapter 3 for removal and refitting details, if the cooler is damaged the complete radiator assembly must be renewed.

10 Starter inhibitor/reversing light switch - general information, removal, refitting and adjustment

General information
1 The starter inhibitor/reversing light switch is a dual-function switch which is fitted to the selector shaft on the top of the transmission housing. The inhibitor function of the switch ensures that the engine can only be started with the selector lever in either the "N" or "P" positions, therefore preventing the engine being started with the transmission in gear. This is achieved by the switch cutting the supply to the starter motor solenoid. If at any time it is noted that the engine can be started with the selector lever in any position other than "P" or "N", then it is likely that the inhibitor function of the switch is faulty. The switch also performs the function of the reversing light switch, illuminating the reversing lights whenever the selector lever is in the "R" position. If either function of the switch is faulty, the complete switch must be renewed as a unit.

Removal
2 To improve access to the switch, remove the battery, battery tray and mounting plate as described in Chapter 5.
3 Slacken and remove the retaining nut and washer free the selector lever from the transmission shaft.
4 Trace the wiring back from the switch, and disconnect it at the wiring connector.
5 Slacken and remove the retaining bolts and remove the switch from the top of the transmission housing.

Refitting and adjustment
6 Slide the switch into position and refit its retaining bolts, tighten them lightly only at this stage.
7 Ensure the switch wiring is correctly routed and reconnect the wiring connector.
8 Engage the selector lever with the transmission shaft then refit the washer and retaining nut, tightening it to the specified torque.
9 Ensure the selector lever is in the "N" (neutral) position then align the (12 mm wide) tab on the switch body with the tab on the inner end of the selector lever **(see illustration 2.3)**. Ensure both tabs are correctly aligned then tighten the switch retaining bolts to the specified torque.
10 Where necessary, refit the battery as described in Chapter 5, and test the operation of the switch.

11 Automatic transmission - removal and refitting

Removal
1 Chock the rear wheels, apply the handbrake, and place the selector lever in the "N" (neutral) position. Jack up the front of the vehicle, and securely support it on axle stands. Remove both front roadwheels then undo the retaining bolts and remove the undercover from beneath the right-hand wheelarch.
2 Drain the transmission fluid as described in Chapter 1, then refit the drain plugs, tightening them securely.
3 Remove the battery, battery tray and mounting plate as described in Chapter 5.
4 Remove the starter motor as described in Chapter 5.
5 Make identification marks between the oil cooler hoses and their unions on the top of the transmission housing. Clamp the hoses to minimise fluid loss then slacken the hose clamps and disconnect the hoses from the transmission. Plug the hose and transmission union ends to prevent the entry of dirt into the hydraulic system.
6 Disconnect the kickdown cable from the throttle linkage and release it from its retaining clips so the cable is free to be removed with the transmission (see Section 6).
7 Position the selector lever in the "N" (neutral) position then disconnect the selector cable from the transmission unit (see Section 3).
8 Trace the wiring back from the starter inhibitor/reversing light switch on the top of the transmission unit and disconnect it at the wiring connector. Undo the retaining nut/bolt

Automatic transmission 7B•5

and disconnect the earth strap from the transmission housing (where necessary).
9 Unscrew the retaining ring and disconnect the speedometer cable from the transmission unit.
10 Referring to Chapter 8, remove the right-hand driveshaft and disconnect the left-hand driveshaft from the transmission. Note that it is not necessary to remove the left-hand driveshaft completely, it can be left attached to the hub assembly and released from the transmission as the hub is pulled outwards.
Note: *Do not allow the shaft to hang down under its own weight as this could damage the constant velocity joints/gaiters.*
11 Undo the retaining bolts and remove the lower driveplate cover plate from the transmission, to gain access to the torque converter retaining bolts. Slacken and remove the visible bolt then, using a socket and extension bar to rotate the crankshaft pulley, undo the remaining bolts securing the torque converter to the driveplate as they become accessible. There are three bolts in total.
12 To ensure that the torque converter does not fall out as the transmission is removed, slide the converter along the shaft and fully into the transmission housing. If necessary, secure it in position using a length of metal strip bolted to one of the starter motor bolt holes.
13 Place a jack and block of wood beneath the transmission, and raise the jack to take the weight of the transmission.
14 Slacken and remove the through-bolt and nut from the right-hand engine/transmission mounting then undo the retaining bolts and remove the mounting bracket from the top of the transmission housing.
15 With the jack positioned beneath the transmission taking the weight, slacken and remove the remaining bolts securing the transmission housing to the engine. Note the correct fitted positions of each bolt, and the necessary brackets, as they are removed, to use as a reference on refitting. Make a final check that all components have been disconnected, and are positioned clear of the transmission so that they will not hinder the removal procedure.
16 With the bolts removed, move the trolley jack and transmission to the right, to free it from its locating dowels, ensuring the torque converter moves with the transmission housing. Once the transmission is free, lower the jack and manoeuvre the unit out from under the car. Remove the locating dowels from the transmission or engine if they are loose, and keep them in a safe place.

Refitting
17 The transmission is refitted by a reversal of the removal procedure, bearing in mind the following points.
  a) *Ensure the engine/transmission locating dowels are correctly positioned prior to installation.*
  b) *Once the transmission and engine are correctly joined, refit the securing bolts, tightening them to the specified torque setting noting that the torque setting for each bolt varies according to its size and grade (number stamped onto the bolt head) and sometimes the bolt length.*
  c) *Tighten all nuts and bolts to the specified torque (where given).*
  d) *Renew the driveshaft oil seals (see Chapter 7A) and refit the driveshafts to the transmission as described in Chapter 8.*
  e) *Adjust the selector cable, kickdown cable and starter inhibitor/reversing light switch as described in Sections 2, 5 and 10 of this Chapter.*
  f) *On completion, refill the transmission with the specified type and quantity of fluid as described in Chapter 1.*

12 Automatic transmission overhaul - general information

1 In the event of a fault occurring with the transmission, it is first necessary to determine whether it is of a mechanical or hydraulic nature, and to do this, special test equipment is required. It is therefore essential to have the work carried out by a Proton dealer if a transmission fault is suspected.
2 Do not remove the transmission from the car for possible repair before professional fault diagnosis has been carried out, since most tests require the transmission to be in the vehicle.

Chapter 8
Driveshafts

Contents

Driveshaft rubber gaiter check .... See Chapter 1
Driveshaft - overhaul and rubber gaiter renewal 3
Driveshafts - removal and refitting 2
General information 1

Degrees of difficulty

| Easy, suitable for novice with little experience | Fairly easy, suitable for beginner with some experience | Fairly difficult, suitable for competent DIY mechanic | Difficult, suitable for experienced DIY mechanic | Very difficult, suitable for expert DIY or professional |

Specifications

General
Type .... Unequal-length, solid steel shafts, splined to tripod-type inner and Rzeppa-type outer constant velocity joints.

Lubrication
Lubricant type .... Proton specification grease, supplied with gaiter repair kit

Torque wrench settings
	Nm	lbf ft
Driveshaft nut:		
Minimum	195	144
Maximum	255	188
Roadwheel nuts	100	74

1 General information

Power is transmitted from the gearbox output shafts to the roadwheels by unequal length, solid steel driveshafts, via inboard and outboard constant velocity (CV) joints.

The outer Rzeppa type CV joints allow smooth transmission of drive to the wheels at all steering and suspension angles. Drive is transmitted by means of a number of radially static steel balls that run in grooves between the two halves of the joint.

The inboard CV joints are of the tripod (or plunge cup) type; drive is transmitted across the joint by means of three rollers, mounted on the driveshaft in a tripod arrangement, that are radially static but are free to slide in the grooved plunge cup.

The right and left hand driveshafts are of different lengths, due to the transverse mounting arrangement of the engine and transmission. The left-hand driveshaft is the longer of the two and has a damping weight bolted midway along its length, to reduce rotational vibration.

The joints are protected by rubber gaiters that are sealed with metal clips and packed with grease, to provide permanent lubrication. If wear is detected in the inboard CV joint, it can be detached from the driveshaft and renewed. The outboard CV joint and driveshaft cannot be separated and must be renewed as a complete assembly.

Normally, the CV joints do not require additional lubrication, unless they have been overhauled or the rubber gaiters have been damaged, allowing the grease to become contaminated.

Both driveshafts are splined at their outboard ends, to accept the wheel hubs, and are threaded so that the hubs can be fastened to the driveshafts by means of a large castellated nut and split pin.

2 Driveshafts - removal and refitting

Note: *A balljoint separator tool will be required for this operation. A new driveshaft nut and track-rod end nut should be used on refitting. In addition, new lower arm balljoint nuts should be used.*

Removal

1 Chock the rear wheels, apply the handbrake, then jack up the front of the vehicle and support on axle stands (see *"Jacking and vehicle support"*). Remove the appropriate roadwheel(s).

2 The front hub must be held stationary in order to loosen the driveshaft nut. Ideally, the hub should be held by a suitable tool bolted into place using two of the roadwheel nuts. Alternatively, have an assistant firmly apply the brake pedal to prevent the hub from rotating. Using a socket and extension bar, slacken and remove the driveshaft nut.

8•2 Driveshafts

2.5 Extracting the outboard end of the driveshaft from the hub

2.8 Prising the inboard end of the driveshaft from the transmission differential casing using a prybar (arrowed)

⚠️ *Warning: The nut is extremely tight! Discard the nut - a new one must be used on refitting. Recover the washer (where fitted).*

3 Remove the locking clip and extract the brake caliper hydraulic hose (and where applicable, the brake pad wear indicator cable) from the bracket on the base of the suspension strut.

4 Refer to Chapter 10 and unbolt the lower end of the suspension strut from the top of the hub carrier. To gain extra clearance, refer again to Chapter 10 and unbolt the anti-roll bar from the suspension lower arm. This operation is not essential to allow the removal the driveshaft but does prevent the anti-roll bar drop link components from being strained.

5 Temporarily refit the driveshaft nut to the end of the driveshaft, to prevent damage to the driveshaft threads, then using a soft-faced mallet, carefully tap the driveshaft from the hub carrier **(see illustration)**. If the shaft is a tight fit, a suitable hub puller can be used to force the end of the shaft from the hub. Support the end of the driveshaft - do not allow the end of the driveshaft to hang down as this will strain the joint components and gaiters.

6 On models with manual transmission, refer to Chapter 7A and drain the oil from the transmission. On models with automatic transmission, refer to Chapter 7B and drain the oil from the differential casing.

7 Wedge two flat bladed screwdrivers or prybars between the transmission casing and the rear surface of the plunge-cup section of the inner CV joint. Do not force the blades of the screwdrivers in too far, as the driveshaft oil seal may be damaged Likewise, do not lever against the gaiter sealing lip, as this may damage the surface and could cause leakage during operation.

8 Carefully lever the plunge-cup stub out of the transmission, using just enough force to overcome the tension of the snap-ring **(see illustration)**. Be prepared for a small amount of transmission oil loss as you do this.

9 Remove the driveshaft assembly from under the vehicle. Cover the transmission driveshaft aperture(s) to prevent the ingress of dirt.

Caution: At this stage, do not refit the roadwheel and allow the weight of the vehicle to rest on the hub. With the driveshaft removed, the wheel bearing inner race has no internal support and may be dislodged from the hub and hub carrier, if loaded. If the vehicle must be moved before the driveshaft is refitted, retain the hub and wheel bearing in the hub carrier by passing a large bolt through the driveshaft hole and securing it with large flat washers and a nut.

Inspection

10 Grasp the middle of the driveshaft and assess the lateral wear by attempting to pull the outer CV joint away from the end of the shaft. If any freeplay is detected, overhaul of the driveshaft and outer CV joint must be considered.

11 Hold the driveshaft still and rotate the outer CV joint through its full range of motion. If there is any sign of stiffness, sticking, freeplay or roughness in its movement, the joint may be worn and again, overhaul should be considered.

12 Repeat the operation described in the previous paragraph at the inner CV joint. Grasp the splined section of the joint and check that the tripod joint can slide freely inside plunge cup. **Note:** *Be careful to avoid pulling the tripod joint right out of the plunge-cup, or straining the rubber gaiter.*

13 Inspect the splined sections at either end of the driveshaft for signs of wear or damage.

14 Check the condition of the rubber gaiters - open out each of the folds, as small splits may be concealed when the gaiter is fully compressed.

15 If, following inspection, the condition of the driveshaft assembly is in doubt, refer to Section 3 and carry out an overhaul.

Refitting

16 At the inner CV joint, remove the snap ring using circlip pliers and fit a new item - the existing snap ring is not reusable.

17 Refer to the relevant part of Chapter 7 and renew the driveshaft oil seals at the transmission.

18 Ensure that the splines at the inboard end of the driveshaft are clean, then offer up the driveshaft to the transmission casing. Slide the splined section of the inner CV joint into the transmission casing until resistance is felt.

19 Bear on the lugs on the outer surface of the plunge cup and push the inner CV joint fully into the transmission, applying just enough force to overcome the tension of the snap-ring.

20 Ensure that the splines at the outboard end of the driveshaft are clean, then pivot the hub carrier away from the vehicle and push the splined section of the outer CV joint into the hub. Thread the washer and the new driveshaft nut onto the end of the driveshaft, but only partially tighten the nut at this stage **(see illustrations)**

2.20a Refit the driveshaft washer . . .

Driveshafts 8•3

2.20b ... and castellated nut

2.23 Tighten the driveshaft nut to the specified torque

2.25a Fit the split pin through the holes/recesses in the driveshaft and nut

21 With reference to Chapter 10, refit the suspension strut the hub carrier, then where applicable bolt the anti-roll bar to the suspension lower arm. **Note:** *Observe the anti-roll bar fixing dimensions give in Chapter 10.*
22 Refit the brake caliper hydraulic hose (and where applicable, the brake pad wear indicator cable) to the bracket on the base of the suspension strut.
23 Tighten the driveshaft nut to the specified torque **(see illustration)**. Check that the split pin holes and recesses on the nut and driveshaft shaft are aligned. If this is not the case, the driveshaft nut may be further tightened (up to the *maximum* torque quoted in the *Specifications*), until the holes/recesses are aligned.
Caution: *If the driveshaft slips due to the effort exerted on the torque wrench, get an assistant to depress the brake pedal whilst the driveshaft nut is tightened. Do not use the transmission to prevent the wheel from rotating, by selecting first gear (or 'Park' on automatic transmissions) as driveshaft or transmission damage may result.*
24 Refit the roadwheel(s), then insert and hand tighten the nuts, rocking the roadwheel on the hub as you do this to ensure that it seats correctly. Lower the vehicle to the ground and then tighten the roadwheel nuts to the specified torque.
25 Fit the split pin through the holes/recesses in the driveshaft and nut. Splay out the ends of the split pin and bend them back around the top of the nut, to lock it in position **(see illustrations)**.
26 Refit the wheel trim/centre cap, as applicable.

3 Driveshaft - overhaul and rubber gaiter renewal

Dismantling

1 Obtain a driveshaft service kit. These can normally be purchased from a Proton dealer and contain all components required for a complete driveshaft overhaul **(see illustration)**.
2 Remove the driveshaft from the vehicle, as described in Section 2. Unfasten the clips securing rubber gaiters to the driveshaft and the inner and outer CV joints.
3 Slide both gaiters towards the centre of the shaft, away from the CV joints. The grease inside the joints will have turned to liquid with use, so be prepared for some spillage. Wipe off the majority of the remaining grease with a rag. **Note:** *At the inboard CV joint, do not allow the tripod joint to slide out of the plunge cup at this point.*

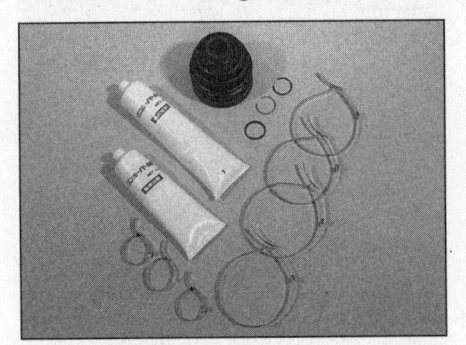

2.25b Splay out the ends of the split pin (arrowed) and bend them back around the top of the nut, to lock it in position

Outboard CV joint - removal

4 The outer CV joint cannot be separated from the driveshaft; the two components can only be renewed as a complete assembly.

Inboard CV joint removal

5 At the inboard end of the driveshaft, use a hammer and centre punch, or paint, to mark the relationship between the driveshaft, tripod joint and plunge cup **(see illustrations)**. This will allow correct reassembly later, if the original components are fit for re-use.
6 Remove the circlip from the end of the driveshaft with a pair of circlip pliers **(see illustration)**.

3.1 Driveshaft overhaul kit

3.5a At the inboard end of the driveshaft, use paint to mark the relationship between the tripod joint and plunge cup ...

3.5b .... and the driveshaft and the tripod joint

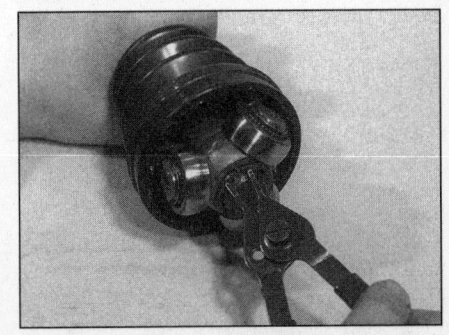

3.6 Remove the circlip from the end of the driveshaft with a pair of circlip pliers

8•4 Driveshafts

3.14 Wrap PVC tape around the splines at the inboard end of the driveshaft, to protect the inner surface of the rubber gaiter

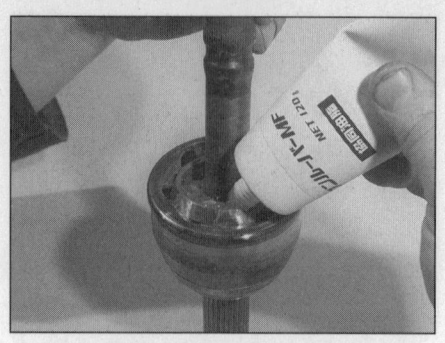

3.16 Pack the outboard joint with grease from the service kit

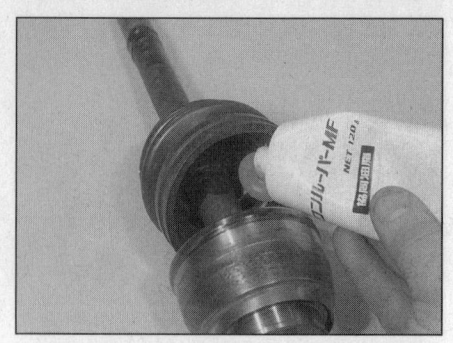

3.17 Fold the gaiter back, then pack the void with grease from the service kit

7 Using a three-legged puller if required, draw the tripod joint off the end of the driveshaft. Ensure that the legs of the puller bear upon the cast centre section of the joint, not the roller bearings.

Inspection

8 Slide both rubber gaiters off the driveshaft and discard them; it is recommended that new ones are fitted on reassembly as a matter of course.
9 Thoroughly clean the driveshaft splines, and CV joint components with paraffin or a suitable solvent, taking care not to destroy any alignment marks made during removal.
10 Examine the CV joint components for wear and damage; in particular, check the balls and corresponding grooves for pitting and corrosion. If evidence of wear is visible, then the joint must be renewed.
11 Examine the tripod joint components for wear. Check that the three rollers are free to rotate without resistance and are not worn, damaged or corroded. The rollers are supported by arrays of needle bearings; wear or damage will show up as play in the rollers and/or roughness in rotation. If wear is discovered, the tripod joint must be renewed.
12 Examine the inside of the plunge cup section of the inner CV joint. If the three grooves show signs of excessive scoring, cracking or corrosion, it should be renewed. If this is case, the tripod joint must also be renewed - assembling new and part-worn components will lead to accelerated wear and early failure.
13 Prior to reassembly, ensure that all traces of cleaning solvent have been removed from all components. Use compressed air, if possible, but ensure that eye protection is worn. Pay particular attention to the insides of the CV joints - any solvent left in here will dilute the grease packed into the joint later.

Reassembly

14 Temporarily wrap PVC tape around the splines at the inboard end of the driveshaft, to protect the inner surface of the rubber gaiter **(see illustration)**.
15 Fit the new outboard CV joint rubber gaiter (and its associated clip) to the inboard end of the driveshaft, then slide it along the driveshaft to the outboard end.
16 Pack the outboard joint with grease from the service kit **(see illustration)**.
17 Fold the gaiter back, then pack the void with grease from the service kit **(see illustration)**. Note: *Do not allow grease to come into contact with vehicles paintwork, as discolouring may result.*
18 Slide the gaiter over the outboard joint, then briefly lift the lip of the gaiter to expel all the air from the joint **(see illustration)**.
19 Secure the gaiter in place over the driveshaft and the joint with a pair of new clips. **(see illustrations)**.
20 Pass the inner clip for the inboard joint over the end of the driveshaft, then slide a new rubber gaiter over the inboard end of the driveshaft **(see illustration)**. Remove the protective PVC tape from the driveshaft splines.

3.18 Slide the gaiter over the outboard joint

3.19a Secure the gaiter in place over the driveshaft and the joint with new inner . . .

3.19b . . . and outer clips

3.19c To secure a clip, fold the locking strip over . . .

3.19d . . . and press the tabs over the locking strip

3.19e Fully assembled outboard joint

3.20 Slide a new rubber gaiter over the inboard end of the driveshaft

3.23 Slide the gaiter over the tripod joint, then pack the void with grease from the service kit

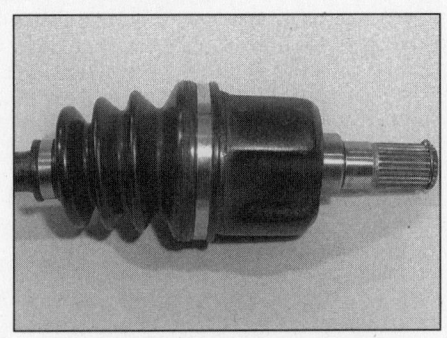

3.27a Fully assembled inboard joint

3.27b Complete driveshaft assembly

21 Using the alignment marks made during removal, fit the tripod joint onto the splines of the driveshaft. Tap it into position using a soft faced mallet. To ensure that the tripod joint rollers and driveshaft splines are not damaged, use a socket - with an internal diameter slightly larger than that of the driveshaft - as a drift.
22 Secure the tripod joint in position with a new circlip.
23 Slide the gaiter over the tripod joint, then pack the void with grease from the service kit

(see illustration). *Note: Do not allow grease to come into contact with vehicles paintwork, as discolouring may result.*
24 Take the plunge cup section of the inboard CV joint and lubricate the three inner grooves with grease from the service kit.
25 Using the alignment marks made during dismantling, push the tripod joint into plunge cup.
26 Pack additional grease into the joint to displace any air pockets, then slide the rubber gaiter over the joint. Secure the gaiter to the

driveshaft using a new clip.
27 Briefly lift the lip of the gaiter to expel all the air from the CV joint, then secure it in place over the joint with a new clip **(see illustrations)**.
28 Hold the driveshaft still and rotate the outboard CV joint through its full range of motion to distribute the grease around the inside of the joint. Repeat this operation at the inboard CV joint.
29 Refit the driveshaft the vehicle, as described in Section 2.

Notes

Chapter 9
Braking system

Contents

Brake disc - inspection, removal and refitting	7
Brake fluid level check	See Weekly Checks
Brake fluid renewal	See Chapter 1
Brake pedal - adjustment	5
Front brake caliper - removal, overhaul and refitting	9
Front brake pad condition check	See Chapter 1
Front brake pads - renewal	4
General information	1
Handbrake "on" warning light switch - removal and refitting	17
Handbrake cables - removal and refitting	14
Handbrake check and adjustment	See Chapter 1
Hydraulic pipes and hoses - renewal	3
Hydraulic system - bleeding	2
Master cylinder - removal and refitting	11
Rear brake drum and hub assembly - removal, inspection and refitting	8
Rear brake pressure proportioning valve - removal and refitting	16
Rear brake shoes - renewal	6
Rear wheel cylinder - removal, overhaul and refitting	10
Stop-light switch - adjustment, removal and refitting	15
Vacuum servo unit - removal and refitting	12
Vacuum servo unit check	See Chapter 1
Vacuum servo unit check valve - removal, testing and refitting	13

Degrees of difficulty

Easy, suitable for novice with little experience	Fairly easy, suitable for beginner with some experience	Fairly difficult, suitable for competent DIY mechanic	Difficult, suitable for experienced DIY mechanic	Very difficult, suitable for expert DIY or professional

Specifications

General
Brake system type and layout:
- Footbrake: Diagonally split dual hydraulic circuits; front right/rear left (primary) and front left/rear right (secondary), vacuum servo assisted. Pressure regulating valves operate on rear wheel hydraulic circuits. Outboard disc fitted at the front, leading/trailing shoe drum brakes at the rear.
- Handbrake: Floor-mounted lever operating dual cables, acting on trailing shoe of rear drums.

Front brakes
Discs:
- Outside diameter:
  - 8-valve models: 243 mm, type PFS15
  - 12-valve models: 234 mm, type M-R315
  - MPi models: 243 mm, type M-R315
- Thickness (new disc): 13.0 mm
- Minimum thickness: 11.4 mm
- Maximum runout: 0.15 mm

Calipers:
- Type: Single piston, sliding caliper body.
- Cylinder internal diameter: 51.1 mm

Pads, friction material thickness:
- New pad: 10.0 mm
- Minimum thickness (wear limit):
  - 8-valve and MPi models: 1.0 mm
  - 12-valve models: 2.0 mm

Rear drum brakes
Drum inner diameter:
- New drum: 180.0 mm
- Maximum diameter (wear limit): 182.0 mm
- Minimum shoe lining thickness: 1.0 mm
- Wheel cylinder internal diameter: 0.15 mm

Master cylinder
Type .... Tandem
Bore internal diameter:
   8-valve and MPi models .... 22.22 mm
   12-valve models .... 20.40 mm

Vacuum servo unit cylinder diameter
8-valve and MPi models .... 180.0 mm
12-valve models .... 155.0 mm

Miscellaneous
Brake pedal height, at rest .... 167 to 172 mm
Brake pedal freeplay .... 10 to 15 mm
Brake pedal height, pedal applied .... 80.0 mm (minimum)
Stop lamp switch casing to brake pedal clearance .... 0.5 to 1.0 mm
Vacuum servo unit pushrod to master cylinder primary piston
   clearance .... 0.1 to 0.5 mm
Number of ratchet 'clicks' to full application of handbrake .... 5 to 7

Torque wrench settings

	Nm	lbf ft
Front caliper bracket to hub carrier bolts	90	66
Front caliper to carrier bracket guide bolts:		
8-valve models	30	22
12-valve and MPi models:		
Upper guide bolt (M10)	50	37
Lower guide bolt (M14)	90	66
Brake pipe union	15	11
Front brake disc to hub bolts	55	41
Bleed screw to caliper/wheel cylinder	8	6
Roadwheel bolts	see Chapter 10	
Rear hub nut	see Chapter 10	
Rear brake backplate to suspension member	55	41
Rear wheel cylinder mounting bolts	10	7
Master cylinder securing nuts	10	7
Brake pedal pushrod adjustment locknut	20	15
Fluid reservoir through-bolt (early 8-valve and 12-valve models)	2	1
Vacuum servo unit to bulkhead nuts	10	7

1 General information

The braking system is of the vacuum servo-assisted, dual-circuit hydraulic type. The arrangement of the hydraulic system is such that each circuit operates one front and one rear brake from a tandem master cylinder. Under normal circumstances, both circuits operate in unison. In the event of hydraulic failure in one circuit, full braking force will still be available at two diagonally-opposite wheels.

All models covered in this manual are fitted with front disc brakes and rear drum brakes.

The front disc brakes are actuated by single-piston sliding type calipers, which ensure equal pressure is applied to each disc pad.

The rear drum brakes incorporate leading and trailing shoes, which are actuated by twin-piston wheel cylinders. A self-adjust mechanism is incorporated, to automatically compensate for brake shoe wear. As the brake shoe linings wear, the footbrake operation automatically operates the adjuster mechanism, which effectively lengthens the shoe strut and repositions the brake shoes, to remove the lining-to-drum clearance.

The mechanical handbrake linkage operates the brake shoes via a lever attached to the trailing brake shoe.

Load sensitive proportioning valves operate on the rear brake hydraulic circuits, to prevent the possibility of the rear wheels locking before the front wheels, under heavy braking. **Note:** *When servicing any part of the system, work carefully and methodically; also observe scrupulous cleanliness when overhauling any part of the hydraulic system. Always renew components (in axle sets, where applicable) if in doubt about their condition, and use only genuine Proton replacement parts, or at least those of known good quality. Note the Warnings given in "Safety first" and at relevant points in this Chapter concerning the dangers of asbestos dust and hydraulic fluid.*

2 Hydraulic system - bleeding

Warning: Hydraulic brake fluid is poisonous; wash off immediately and thoroughly in the case of skin contact, and seek medical advice if any fluid is swallowed, or gets into the eyes. Certain types of hydraulic fluid are inflammable, and may ignite when allowed into contact with hot components. When servicing any hydraulic system, it is safest to assume that the fluid is inflammable, and to take precautions against the risk of fire as though it were petrol that were being handled. Hydraulic fluid is also an effective paint stripper, and will attack plastics; if any is spilt, it should be washed off immediately using copious quantities of fresh water. Finally, it is hygroscopic (it absorbs moisture from the air) - old fluid may be contaminated and unfit for further use. When topping-up or renewing the fluid, always use the recommended type, and ensure it comes from a newly-opened, sealed container.

General

1 The correct operation of any hydraulic system is only possible after removing all air from the components and circuit; and this is achieved by bleeding the system.

2 During the bleeding procedure, add only clean, unused hydraulic fluid of the recommended type; never re-use fluid that has already been bled from the system. Ensure that sufficient fluid is available before starting work.

Braking system 9•3

3 If there is any possibility of incorrect fluid being already in the system, the brake components and circuit must be flushed completely with uncontaminated, correct fluid, and new seals should be fitted throughout the system.

4 If hydraulic fluid has been lost from the system, or air has entered because of a leak, ensure that the fault is cured before proceeding further.

5 Park the vehicle on level ground, switch off the engine and select first or reverse gear (or "PARK"), then chock the wheels and release the handbrake.

6 Check that all pipes and hoses are secure, unions tight and bleed screws closed. Remove the dust caps (where applicable), and clean any dirt from around the bleed screws.

7 Unscrew the master cylinder reservoir cap, and top the master cylinder reservoir up to the "MAX" level line; refit the cap loosely. Remember to maintain the fluid level at least above the "MIN" level marking throughout the procedure, otherwise there is the risk that air may enter the system, if the fluid level is allowed to drop too low.

8 There are a number of one-man, do-it-yourself brake bleeding kits currently available from motor accessory shops. It is recommended that one of these kits is used whenever possible, as they greatly simplify the bleeding operation, and also reduce the risk of expelled air and fluid being drawn back into the system via the open bleed screw. If such a kit is not available, the basic (two-man) method should be used - this is described in below.

9 If a bleeding kit is to be used, prepare the vehicle as described previously. The general procedures are as outlined in the following sub-sections, but adhere to the kit manufacturer's instructions, as the details of the procedure may vary slightly, according to the type of kit being used.

10 Whichever method is used, the same sequence must be followed (paragraphs 11 and 12) to ensure that the removal of all air from the system.

Bleeding sequence

11 If the hydraulic system has only been partially disconnected, and suitable precautions were taken to minimise fluid loss/air ingress , it should only be necessary to bleed that particular part of the system (ie just the primary, or the secondary circuit).

12 If the entire hydraulic system is to be bled, then it should be carried out in the following sequence:
  1) Left-hand rear wheel.
  2) Right-hand front wheel.
  3) Right-hand rear wheel.
  4) Left-hand front wheel.

Note: *Bleeding the rear brakes on a vehicle fitted with load proportioning valves: If the rear of the vehicle has been raised to allow access to the wheel cylinder bleed screws, the rear suspension must be compressed to its normal ride height (e.g. by raising the beam axle with a trolley jack) to ensure that the load proportioning valves remain open throughout the bleeding process..*

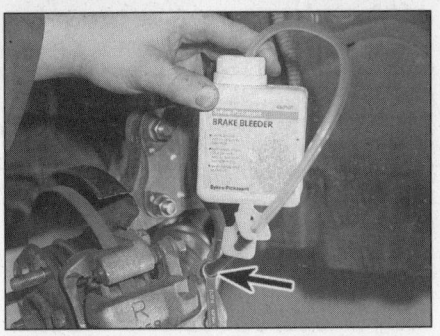

2.14 Fit a ring spanner (arrowed) over the bleed screw and connect the tubing to the bleed nipple

Bleeding - basic (two-man) method

13 Collect a clean container, a suitable length of plastic or rubber tubing which is a tight fit over the bleed screw and a ring spanner to fit the screw. The help of an assistant will also be required.

14 Remove the dust cap from the first screw in the sequence if not already done. Fit a suitable ring spanner to the screw. Press one end of the tubing over the bleed nipple and pass the other end into the container. Pour in sufficient fluid to cover the end of the tube **(see illustration)**.

15 Ensure that the master cylinder reservoir fluid level is maintained at least above the "MIN" level line throughout the bleeding procedure.

16 Have the assistant fully depress the brake pedal several times to build up pressure, then maintain the pressure on the final downstroke.

17 While pedal pressure is maintained, slacken the bleed screw (approximately one turn) and allow the compressed fluid and air to flow into the jar. The assistant should maintain pedal pressure, following the pedal down to the floor if necessary, and should not release the pedal until instructed to do so. When the flow stops, immediately tighten the bleed screw again, have the assistant release the pedal slowly - ensure that the expelled fluid and/or air is not sucked from the jar back into the hydraulic system. Recheck the reservoir fluid level and top-up if required.

18 Repeat the steps given in paragraphs 16 and 17 until the fluid emerging from the bleed screw is free from air bubbles. If the master cylinder has been drained and refilled, and air is being bled from the first screw in the sequence, allow approximately 5-10 seconds to elapse between cycles for the master cylinder passages to refill.

19 When no more air bubbles appear, tighten the bleed screw, remove the tube and spanner and refit the dust cap (where applicable). Do not overtighten the bleed screw - observe the correct torque wrench setting (where specified).

20 Repeat the procedure on the remaining bleed screws in the sequence, until all air is removed from the system and the brake pedal feels firm when depressed.

Bleeding - using a one-way valve kit

21 As the name implies, these kits consist of a length of tubing with an integral one-way valve, to prevent expelled air and fluid being drawn back into the system between each stroke of the brake pedal. Some kits include a translucent container, which can be positioned so that the air bubbles can be more easily seen flowing from the end of the tube.

22 The kit is connected to the bleed screw, which is then opened. The user returns to the driver's seat, depresses the brake pedal with a smooth, steady stroke, and slowly releases it; this is repeated until the expelled fluid is clear of air bubbles.

23 Note that these kits simplify the bleeding operation to such an extent, that it is very easy to forget about the level of fluid in the master cylinder reservoir; ensure that this is maintained at least above the "MIN" level line at all times.

Bleeding - using a pressure-bleeding kit

24 These kits are generally operated by the reservoir of pressurised air contained in the vehicles spare tyre. It is important to note that it will be necessary to reduce the air pressure in the spare tyre, before it can be connected to the bleeding kit - refer to the instructions supplied with the kit for details.

25 By connecting the pressurised, fluid-filled container supplied with the kit to the master cylinder reservoir bleeding can be carried out by simply opening each bleed screw in turn (in the specified sequence), and allowing the fluid to flow out until no more air bubbles can be seen in the expelled fluid.

26 This method has the advantage that the large reservoir of fluid provides an additional safeguard against air being drawn into the system during bleeding. Note however that the level of fluid in the pressurised container must still be checked frequently, to prevent it from falling too low.

27 Pressure-bleeding is particularly effective when bleeding "difficult" systems, or when bleeding the complete system at the time of routine fluid renewal. It also reduces the risk of master cylinder seal failure, which can sometimes be caused by the extended travel of the piston during "manual" bleeding.

All methods

28 When bleeding is complete, and firm pedal feel is restored, wash off any spilt fluid, tighten the bleed screws to the specified torque setting (where specified) and refit the dust caps.

29 Re-check the feel of the brake pedal. If there is no firm resistance, or the pedal has a "spongy" feel to it, air may still be present in the system, and further bleeding will be

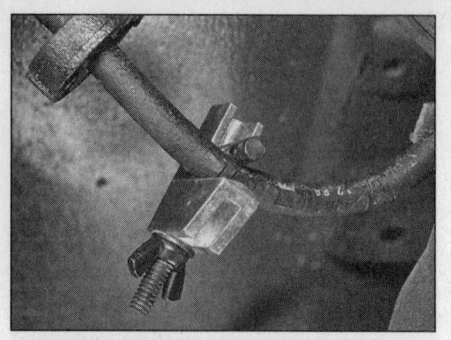

9•4 Braking system

3.1 Flexible hoses can be sealed off using a proprietary brake hose clamp

required. Note that failure to restore satisfactory brake pedal feel after a reasonable repetition of the bleeding procedure may be due to worn master cylinder seals.

30 Check the hydraulic fluid level in the master cylinder reservoir, and top-up if necessary (see *Weekly Checks*).

31 Safely dispose of the fluid that was bled from the system; it will not be fit for re-use.

3 Hydraulic pipes and hoses - renewal

Note: *Before starting work, refer to the note at the beginning of Section 11 concerning the dangers of hydraulic fluid.*

1 If any pipe or hose is to be renewed, minimise fluid loss by first removing the master cylinder reservoir cap, then tighten the cap down onto a piece of polythene to obtain an airtight seal. Alternatively, flexible hoses can be sealed, if required, using a proprietary brake hose clamp **(see illustration)**. Metal brake pipe unions can be plugged (if care is taken not to allow dirt into the system) or capped immediately they are disconnected. Place a small container and/or a wad of absorbent rag under any union that is to be disconnected, to catch any spilt fluid.

2 If a flexible hose is to be disconnected, unscrew the brake pipe union nut before removing the spring clip which secures the hose to its mounting bracket.

3 To unscrew the union nuts, it is preferable to obtain a brake pipe spanner of the correct size; these are available from most large motor accessory shops. Failing this, a close-fitting open-ended spanner will be required, though if the nuts are tight or corroded, their flats may be rounded-off if the spanner slips. In such a case, a self-locking wrench is often the only way to unscrew a stubborn union, but this means that the pipe and the damaged nuts must be renewed on reassembly.

4 To prevent contamination of the brake fluid, always clean the union and the area surrounding it before disconnecting a brake pipe. If disconnecting a component with more than one union, make a careful note of the connections before disturbing any of them.

5 If a brake pipe is to be renewed, replacement pipes can be obtained cut to the correct length, with the union nuts and end flares in place, from Proton dealers. All that is then necessary is to bend it to shape, following the line of the original pipe, before fitting it to the vehicle. Alternatively, most motor accessory shops can make up brake pipes from kits, but this requires very careful measurement of the original, to ensure that the replacement is cut to the correct length. The safest method is to take the original pipe to the shop as a pattern.

6 On refitting, do not overtighten the union nuts. Observe the correct torque setting, where given. A sound, leakproof joint can be achieved without exerting excessive force.

7 Ensure that the pipes and hoses are correctly routed, with no kinks, and that they are secured in the clips or brackets provided. Move the steering and suspension through the full extent of their travel, to ensure that no chaffing or straining occurs.

8 Finally, remove the polythene from the reservoir, and bleed the hydraulic system as described in Section 2. Wash off any spilt fluid, and check carefully for brake fluid leaks.

4 Front brake pads - renewal

> **Warning:** *Renew BOTH sets of front brake pads at the same time - NEVER renew the pads on only one wheel, as uneven braking may result. Note that the dust created by*

HAYNES HiNT

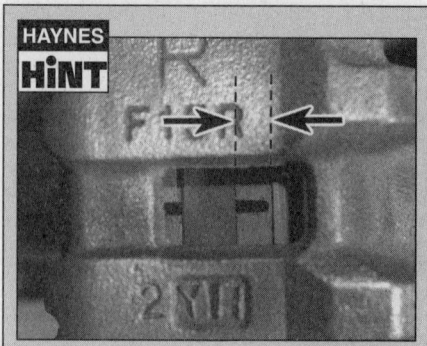

For a quick check, the thickness of the brake pad friction material can be carried out via the inspection hole on the front of the caliper. The view through the caliper inspection hole gives a rough indication of the state of the brake pads but only the inboard pad will be fully visible. For a comprehensive check, the brake pads should be removed and cleaned.

wear of the pads may contain asbestos, which is a health hazard. Never blow it out with compressed air, and don't inhale any of it. An approved filtering mask should be worn when working on the brakes. DO NOT use petrol or petroleum-based solvents to clean brake parts; use proprietary brake cleaner or methylated spirit only.

1 Chock the rear wheels, apply the handbrake, then jack up the front of the vehicle and support it on axle stands (see "*Jacking and vehicle support*"). Remove the front roadwheels.

2 Working on one side of the vehicle, push the caliper piston into its bore as far as possible, by sliding the caliper body away from the hub. The level of brake fluid in the reservoir will rise slightly as you do this - ensure that it does not exceed the 'MAX' marking.

3 Where applicable, release the locking clip and remove the pad wear indicator wiring and brake fluid line from the bracket at the base of the suspension strut.

4 Slacken and withdraw the lower of the two caliper guide bolts **(see illustrations)**.

5 Pivot the caliper body upwards, away from the brake pads **(see illustration)**. Support it in

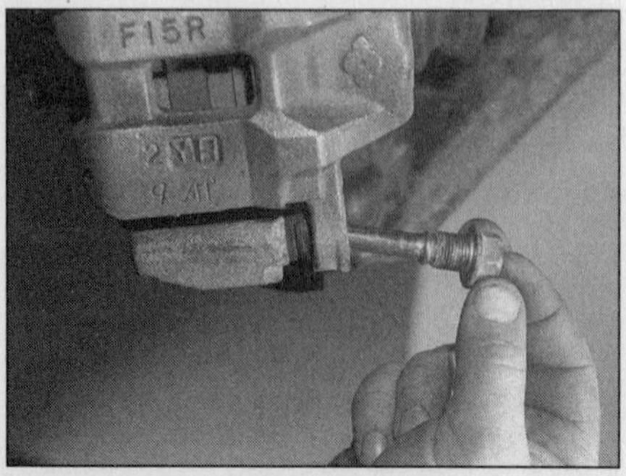

4.4a Slacken and withdraw lower caliper guide bolt - MPi and 12-valve models

4.4b Slacken and withdraw the lower caliper guide bolt (arrowed) - 8-valve model

4.5 Pivot the caliper body upwards, away from the brake pads

Braking system 9•5

4.6 Withdraw the shim(s) from the outboard brake pad...

4.7 ...then retrieve the outboard brake pad from the carrier bracket

4.8a Withdraw the shim(s) from the outboard brake pad...

4.8b ...then retrieve the outboard brake pad from the carrier bracket

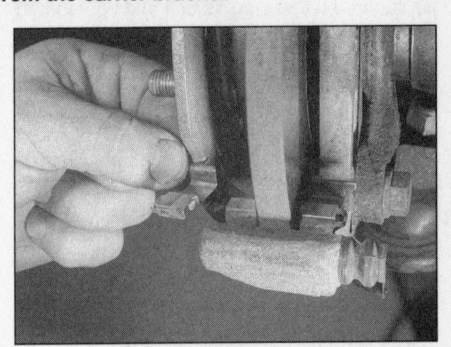

4.8c Remove both spring clips from the carrier bracket

this position with a length of wire or a cable-tie, to avoid straining the hydraulic hose.

Caution: Do not depress the brake pedal until the caliper is reassembled, or the piston will be pushed out of its bore.

6 Withdraw the shim(s) from the outboard brake pad, and mark them to indicate the side to which they were fitted **(see illustration)**.
7 Retrieve the outboard brake pad from the carrier bracket. **(see illustration)**.
8 Repeat the above operations at the inboard pad. Remove the spring clips from the carrier bracket **(see illustrations)**.
9 Measure the thickness of each brake pad's friction material. If either pad is worn at any point to the specified minimum thickness or less, all four pads must be renewed. If either of the brake pads is worn unevenly, trace and rectify the cause before reassembling the caliper.

Warning: Do not be tempted to swap brake pads over to compensate for uneven wear.

10 The pads should also be renewed if any are fouled with oil or grease; there is no satisfactory way of degreasing friction material, once contaminated. Trace and rectify the cause of the contamination before reassembling the caliper.

11 Inspect the brake pad metal backing plates. If they show signs of wear or excessive corrosion, or if the friction material has separated from the backing plates, then the pads must be renewed.
12 If the brake pads are still serviceable, carefully clean them using a clean, fine wire brush dampened with brake cleaning fluid. Pay particular attention to the sides and back of the metal backing plate. Where applicable, clean out the grooves in the friction material.
13 Clean the surfaces of the brake pad contact points in the caliper body and carrier bracket.
14 Using an old paint brush or similar, remove the dust and dirt from the caliper and piston, but take care to avoid damaging the piston dust seal. During cleaning, douse the area with brake cleaning fluid, to prevent the dust particles from becoming airborne - observe the Warning at the beginning of this section.
15 Inspect the dust seal and the area around the piston for signs of damage, corrosion or brake fluid leaks. Check that the dust seal has not popped out of its retaining groove. If this has happened, it will be necessary to refer to Section 9 and overhaul the caliper assembly, as the internal piston seal may well be contaminated with dirt.

16 If new brake pads are to be fitted, the caliper piston must be pushed back into the cylinder, to accommodate the extra depth of friction material. If a proprietary piston retraction tool is not available, use a G-clamp, or suitable pieces of wood as levers. Monitor the brake fluid level in the reservoir whilst the piston is retracted. If the level rises above the "MAX" marking, the surplus fluid should be siphoned off or ejected via a plastic tube connected to the bleed screw (see Section 2)

Warning: Do not syphon the fluid by mouth, as it is highly poisonous - use a syringe or a clean poultry baster.

17 Apply a little high temperature brake grease to the contact surfaces of the pad backing plates; take great care not to allow any grease onto the pad friction linings. Similarly, apply brake grease to the pad contact points on the caliper bracket - again take care not to apply excess grease, which may contaminate the pads.
18 Fit the spring clips in position on the carrier bracket. Place the brake pads in position on the caliper bracket, with the friction material facing the surfaces of the brake disc. Fit the shims according to the markings made during removal. Where

9•6 Braking system

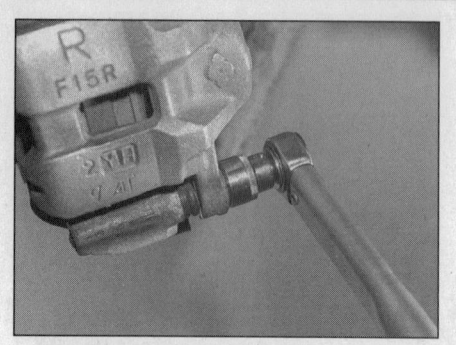

4.20 Insert the lower guide bolt and tighten it to the specified torque

applicable, feed the pad wear indicator cable through the caliper body aperture.
19 Pivot the caliper body down over the brake pads, taking care to avoid dislodging the pads, shims and spring clips
20 Insert the lower guide bolt and tighten it to the specified torque **(see illustration)**
21 Check that the caliper body is free to slide on the guide bolts. Ensure that the flexible hydraulic hose is not twisted or kinked in any way. Turn the steering from lock to lock and check that the hose does not chafe against the suspension or steering gear.
22 Where applicable, reconnect the pad wear indicator wiring and press it into the retaining clips at the base of the suspension strut.
23 Repeat the pad renewal procedure on the opposite front caliper.
24 With both sets of front brake pads fitted, depress the brake pedal repeatedly until the pads are pressed into firm contact with the brake disc, and normal pedal pressure is restored. Any 'sponginess' felt when pressing the pedal is most probably due to air trapped inside the hydraulic system - bleed the braking system before progressing any further.
25 Refit the roadwheels, lower the vehicle to the ground and tighten the roadwheel nuts to the specified torque.
26 Check the level of brake fluid in the reservoir and top-up if required.
27 Check the operation of the braking system exhaustively before bringing the vehicle back into service on public roads.

5 Brake pedal - adjustment

1 With the engine off and the brake pedal in the rest position, measure the distance between the floor and the top of the brake pedal rubber foot pad. Compare the measurement with the figure given in the *Specifications*.
2 If the pedal height is incorrect, adjust it as follows. Slacken the pushrod locknut, then turn the adjusting collar until the correct pedal height is achieved **(see illustration)**. Tighten the locknut securely.
3 Depress the brake pedal several times, to

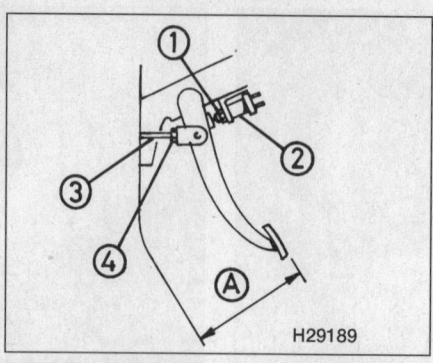

5.2 Brake pedal free height adjustment

  A Brake pedal height
  1 Stop light switch locknut
  2 Stop light switch
  3 Operating rod
  4 Operating rod locknut

discharge the vacuum servo - the pedal resistance will increase sharply when the servo has been discharged.
4 Allow the brake pedal to return to its rest position, then depress the pedal by hand until firm resistance is felt. Measure the distance that the pedal travels through (i.e. the pedal freeplay) as you do this and compare the measurement with the figure given in the *Specifications* **(see illustration)**.
5 Excessive pedal freeplay is probably due to a worn clevis pin. To renew this component, extract the split pin then remove the washer and withdraw the clevis pin from the brake pedal and pushrod.
6 Lubricate the new clevis pin with multi-purpose grease, then engage it with the brake pedal and pushrod. Lubricate and fit the new washer, then pass the new split pin through the hole in the end of the clevis pin. Secure the split pin in position by bending the legs over.
7 Start the engine, then depress the brake pedal as if normal braking were being carried out. Measure the distance between the floor and the top of the pedal rubber foot pad and compare the measurement with that given in the *Specifications* **(see illustration)**. Too little clearance may be an indication of air trapped in the hydraulic system - refer to Section 2 and bleed the hydraulic system. If the condition persists after bleeding, a fault exists in the

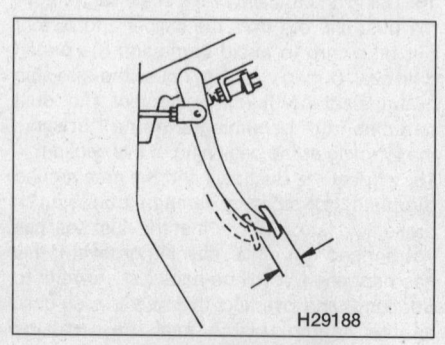

5.4 Brake pedal freeplay

braking system - refer to the appropriate Sections and examine each of the system components in turn.
8 On completion, check and if necessary adjust the operation of the stop light switch.

6 Rear brake shoes - renewal

⚠ **Warning:** *Renew BOTH sets of rear brake shoes at the same time - NEVER renew the shoes on only one wheel, as uneven braking may result.*

⚠ **Warning:** *Note that the dust created by brake shoes may contain asbestos, which is a health hazard. Never blow it out with compressed air, and do not inhale any of it - ideally, a filtering mask should be worn. Dampen the brake components with plenty of brake cleaning fluid during the dismantling process, to prevent the dust from becoming airborne. DO NOT use petrol or petroleum-based solvents to clean brake parts; only use proprietary brake cleaning fluid or methylated spirits.*

Removal - all models

1 Park the vehicle on a level surface and chock the front wheels. Select first gear (manual transmission) or 'Park' (automatic transmission) and release the handbrake, then raise the rear of the vehicle and rest it securely on axle stands (see *"Jacking and vehicle support"*).
2 Remove both rear brake drum and hub assemblies, as described in Section 8.
3 Dampen the brake components with brake cleaning fluid, then brush off the majority of the dirt and dust. Avoid inhaling airborne brake dust - refer to the *Warning* at the beginning of this section.

Removal - 8-valve models

4 With reference to Section 14 and Chapter 1, remove the rear section of the centre console to expose the base handbrake lever. Slacken off the handbrake adjustment mechanism.
5 Note the position of each shoe, and the location of each of the springs. Also make a

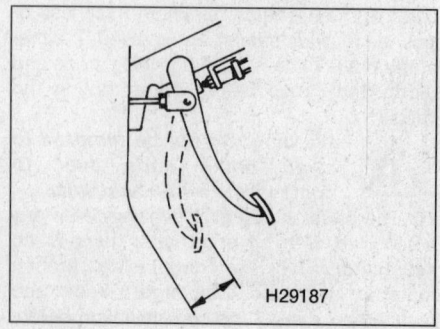

5.7 Brake pedal depressed height

Braking system 9•7

6.6 Release the metal retaining clip from the base of the large shoe return spring

6.8 Disengage the large return spring from both brake shoes

note of the self-adjuster component locations, to aid refitting later.

6 Release the metal retaining clip from the base of the large shoe return spring **(see illustration)**.

7 Release the lower return coil spring from the base of both brake shoes.

8 Disengage the large return spring and remove it from the brake shoes **(see illustration)**.

9 Remove the hold-down cup and spring from the leading shoe. The spring cups are a bayonet-style fit - use a large pair of pliers to depress and then turn them through 90°. Repeat this operation at the trailing shoe.

10 Unhook the self-adjuster return spring from the leading brake shoe. Disengage the self-adjuster mechanism and remove the shoe.

11 Disengage the self-adjuster mechanism from the trailing brake shoe. Tilt the shoe away from the backplate then disconnect the handbrake cable from the lever at the rear of the shoe.

12 Remove the trailing brake shoe from the backplate.

13 Remove any traces of old sealant from the rear of the brake backplate, then extract both shoe hold-down pins.

14 If the new shoes are not going to be fitted immediately, wrap a stout rubber band, or a nylon cable-tie over the wheel cylinder, to prevent the pistons from being accidentally ejected **(see illustration)**.

15 If there is any evidence of fluid leakage from the wheel cylinder seal, it should be renewed.

16 Using a pair of pliers, or a stout screwdriver, prise the metal clip from the handbrake lever retainer at the trailing shoe. Lift off the washer and remove the handbrake lever from the trailing brake shoe. Unhook the return spring.

17 Thoroughly clean the surface of the backplate, using plenty of brake cleaning fluid, to remove all traces of dust and old lubricant. Examine all components for signs of corrosion or wear.

18 Apply high temperature brake grease sparingly to the shoe contact surfaces of the brake backplate **(see illustration)**.

19 Similarly, apply high temperature brake grease sparingly to the shoe contact surfaces of the wheel cylinder pistons and the lower anchor points.

20 Fit the handbrake lever to the new trailing brake shoe, using a new washer and metal clip. Where applicable, ensure the concave surface of the washer faces away from the handbrake lever. When the components are correctly

6.14 Wrap a stout rubber band (arrowed) over the wheel cylinder, to prevent the pistons from being accidentally ejected

6.18 Apply high temperature brake grease to the shoe contact surfaces of the backplate

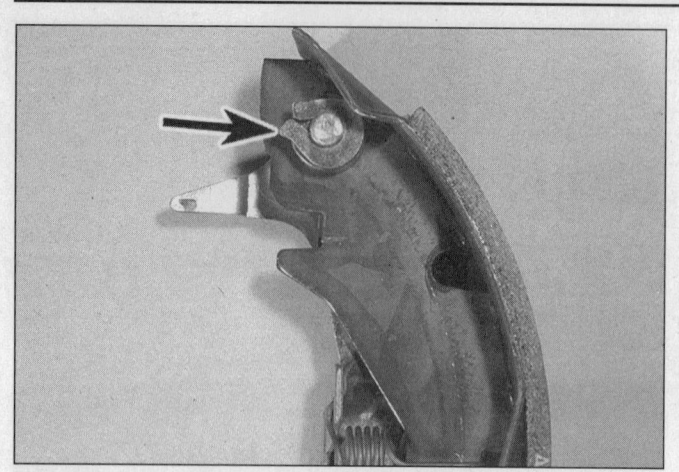

6.20 Fit the handbrake lever to the new trailing brake shoe, using a new washer and metal clip (arrowed)

6.35 Reconnect the handbrake cable to the trailing shoe handbrake lever

assembled, bend the ends of the metal clip around the retainer using pliers, then hook the return spring into position **(see illustration)**.

Removal - 12-valve and MPi models

21 With reference to Section 14 and Chapter 1, remove the rear section of the centre console to expose the base handbrake lever. Slacken off the handbrake adjustment mechanism.
22 Note the position of each shoe, and the location of all springs. Also make a note of the adjuster component locations, to aid refitting.
23 Remove the hold-down cups and springs from both brake shoes. The spring cups are a bayonet-style fit - use a large pair of pliers to depress and then turn them through 90°.
24 Carefully tilt the brake shoes away from the backplate, then unhook the handbrake cable from the base of the lever attached to the rear of the trailing shoe.
25 Remove both brake shoes, the return springs and the self-adjuster mechanism from the backplate as a complete assembly.
26 Remove any traces of sealant from the rear of the backplate, then extract both shoe hold-down pins from the rear of the backplate.
27 If the new shoes are not going to be fitted immediately, wrap a stout rubber band, or a nylon cable-tie over the wheel cylinder, to prevent the pistons from being accidentally ejected **(refer to illustration 6.14)**.
28 If there is any evidence of fluid leakage from the wheel cylinder seal, it should be renewed.
29 Dismantle the brake shoe assembly on the bench, as follows. Unhook the shoe upper return spring from the upper rear surface of both brake shoes.
30 Unhook the self-adjuster return spring from the leading shoe and self-adjuster mechanism lever.
31 Disengage the self-adjuster mechanism from both brake shoes, then remove the self-adjuster lever from the trailing brake shoe.
32 Remove the lower return spring from the base of both brake shoes.

33 Using a pair of pliers, or a stout screwdriver, prise the metal clip from the handbrake lever retainer, on the rear of the trailing shoe. Lift off the washer and remove the handbrake lever from the trailing brake shoe.
34 Thoroughly clean the surface of the backplate, using plenty of brake cleaning fluid, to remove all traces of dust and old lubricant. Examine all components for signs of corrosion or wear.

Refitting - 8-valve models

35 Offer up the trailing shoe to the backplate, then reconnect the handbrake cable to the trailing shoe handbrake lever **(see illustration)**.
36 Apply a suitable dry cure sealant to the heads of the shoe hold-down pins, then insert them through the rear surface of the backplate **(see illustration)**.
37 Hold the trailing brake shoe in position on the backplate, over the hold-down pin. Secure the shoe in position with the hold down spring and cups. Using pliers, press the cup against the pressure of the hold down spring, then turn it through 90° and release it, to lock it in position **(see illustrations)**.
38 Ensure that the upper edges of the brake

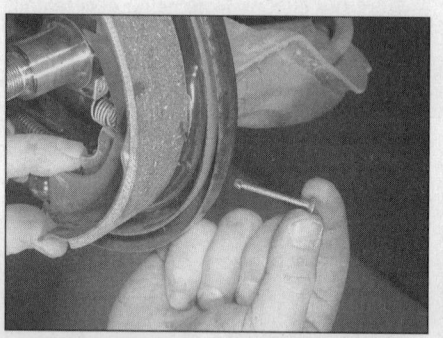

6.36 Insert the shoe hold-down pins through the rear surface of the backplate

6.37a Fit the lower cup in position...

6.37b ...then secure the shoe in position with the hold down spring and cup

6.37c Press the cup against the pressure of the hold down spring, then turn it through 90° and release it, to lock it in position

Braking system 9•9

6.40a Engage the self-adjuster mechanism with the recesses in the trailing ...

6.40b ... and leading brake shoes

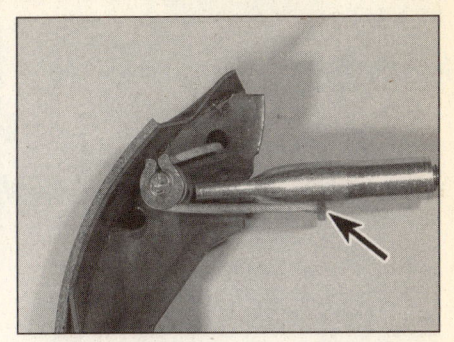

6.40c Push the arm of the return spring under the adjuster mechanism body, so that it is held securely in position

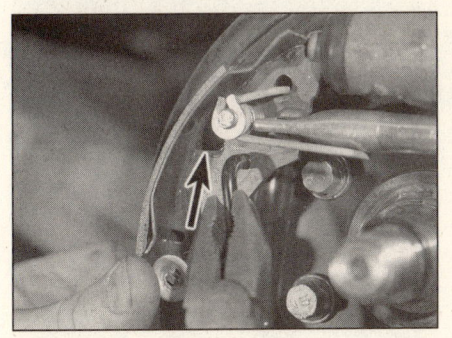

6.41 Fit the ends of the large return spring into the locating hole (arrowed) in the brake shoe (leading shoe shown)

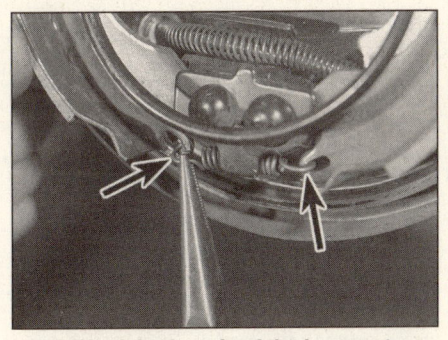

6.42 Hook both ends of the lower return spring into the holes in the base of both brake shoes

6.43 Press the metal retaining clip into position over the base of the large shoe return spring

shoes engage correctly with the recesses in the wheel cylinder piston. Similarly, ensure that the lower edges are securely inserted into their anchor points.
39 Repeat the above operations to secure the leading brake shoe in position.
40 Engage the self-adjuster mechanism with the recesses provided in both brake shoes. Push the arm of the return spring under the adjuster mechanism body, so that it is held securely in position **(see illustrations)**.
41 Expand the large shoe return spring by hand, then fit the ends into the locating holes in the brake shoes **(see illustration)**.
42 Hook both ends of the lower return spring into the holes in the base of both brake shoes **(see illustration)**.
43 Press the metal retaining clip into position over the base of the large shoe return spring **(see illustration)**.
44 Apply a smear of brake grease to the moving parts of the self-adjuster mechanism.
45 Using a ruler, set the overall diameter of the shoe linings to between 179.3 and 179.6 mm, by turning the serrated wheel at the end of the self-adjuster mechanism. This will give the correct clearance to allow the drum to pass over the shoes during refitting.
46 Repeat the brake shoe renewal procedure at the opposite rear wheel **(see illustration)**.

Refitting - 12-valve and MPi models

47 Apply high temperature brake grease sparingly to the shoe contact surfaces of the brake backplate **(see illustration)**. Similarly,

6.46 Rear brake components correctly refitted

6.47 Apply high temperature brake grease sparingly to the shoe contact surfaces (arrowed) of the backplate

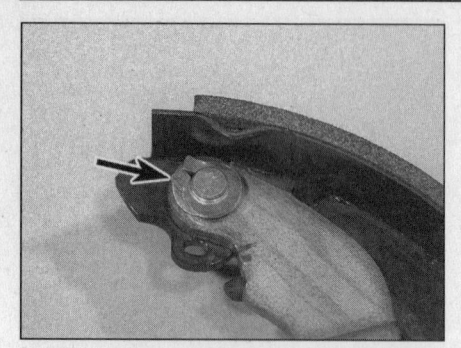

6.48 Fit the handbrake lever to the new trailing brake shoe, using a new washer and metal clip (arrowed)

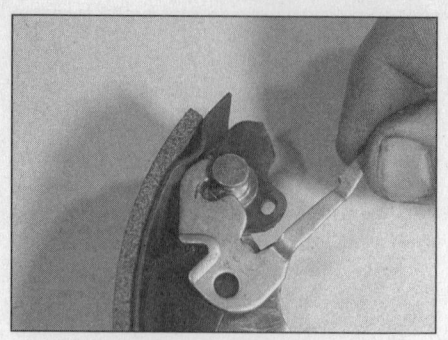

6.49 Refit the self-adjuster mechanism lever to the spigot on the trailing brake shoe

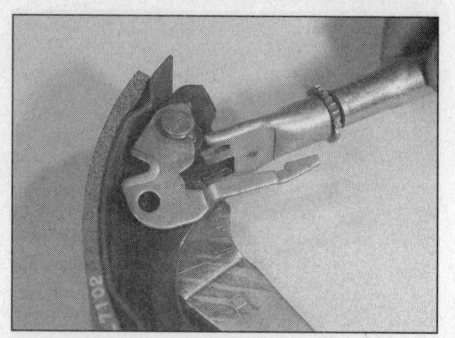

6.50 Engage the self adjuster mechanism with the recesses provided in the trailing shoe

6.51a Hook the end of the self adjuster mechanism return spring over the adjuster mechanism lever

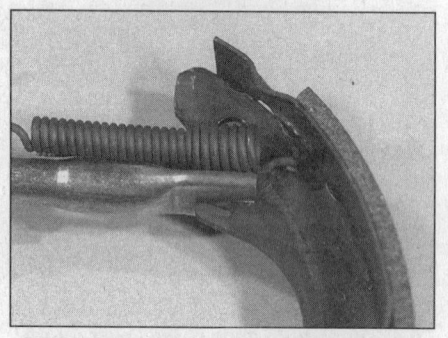

6.51b Anchor the other end of the spring in the leading brake shoe, so that the self adjuster mechanism is held in the recess

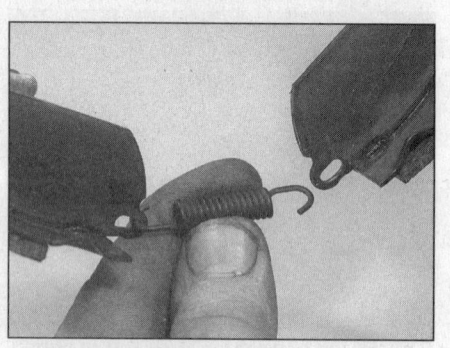

6.52 Hook both ends of the lower return spring into the holes in the base of both brake shoes

apply grease sparingly to the shoe contact surfaces of the wheel cylinder piston and the lower shoe anchor points.

48 Fit the handbrake lever to the new trailing brake shoe, using a new washer and metal clip **(see illustration)**. Ensure that the concave surface of the washer faces away from the handbrake lever. When the components are correctly assembled, bend the ends of the metal clip around the retainer, using pliers, to lock it in position.

49 Reassemble the shoes, return springs and self-adjuster mechanism on the bench as follows. Refit the self-adjuster mechanism lever to the spigot on the trailing brake shoe **(see illustration)**.

50 Engage the self adjuster mechanism with the recesses provided in the trailing shoe **(see illustration)**.

51 Hook the end of the self adjuster mechanism return spring over the adjuster mechanism lever. Anchor the other end of the spring in the slot provided in the leading brake shoe, so that it holds the self adjuster mechanism in recess in the leading shoe **(see illustration)**.

52 Hook both ends of the lower return spring into the holes in the base of both brake shoes **(see illustration)**.

53 Turn the assembly over and hook the upper return spring into the holes at the top of both brake shoes **(see illustrations)**.

54 Apply a suitable dry curing sealant to the

6.53a Hook the upper return spring into the holes at the top of both brake shoes

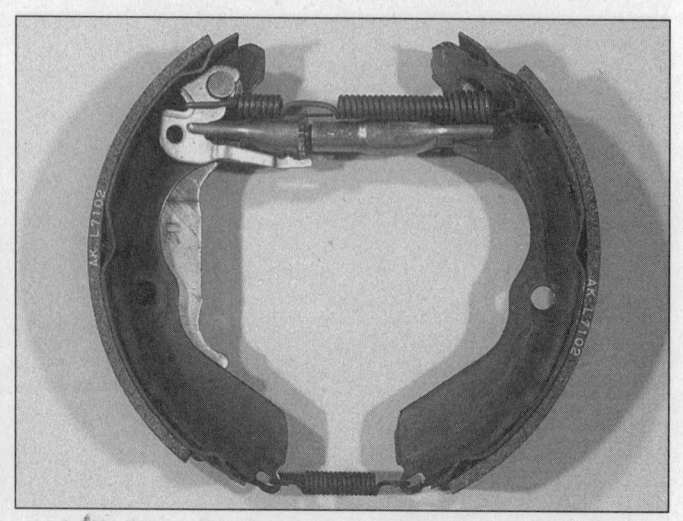

6.53b Rear brake shoe components correctly assembled

Braking system 9•11

6.55 Engage the end of the handbrake cable with the lever at the rear of the trailing shoe

6.56a Ensure that the upper edges of the shoes engage with the recesses in the wheel cylinder pistons (arrowed)

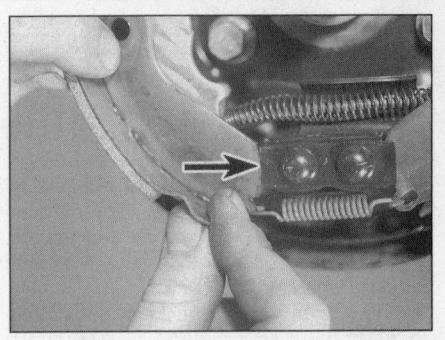

6.56b Ensure that the lower edges of the shoes fit securely into their anchor points (arrowed)

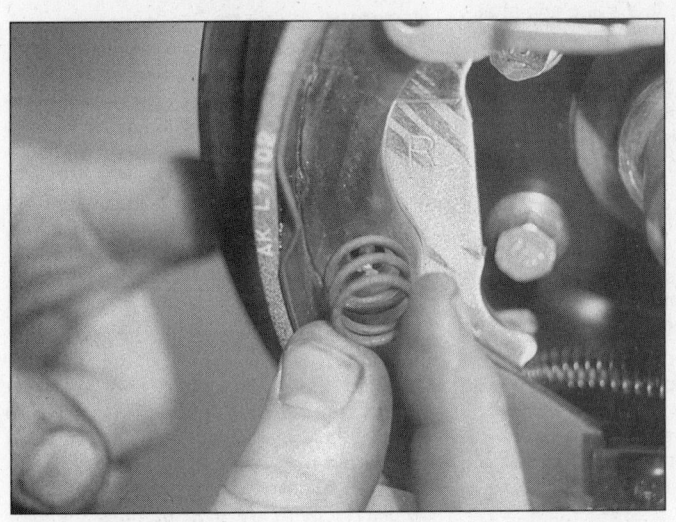

6.57a Secure the shoes in position with the hold down springs . . .

6.57b . . . and cups. Press the cups against the pressure of the hold springs, then turn them through 90° and release them, to lock them in position as shown

heads of the shoe hold-down pins, then insert them through the rear surface of the backplate.
55 Offer up the whole assembly to the backplate, then engage the end of the handbrake cable with the lever at the rear of the trailing shoe **(see illustration)**.
56 Fit the assembly over the shoe-hold pins, ensuring that the upper edges of the shoes engage with the recesses in the wheel cylinder pistons. Similarly, ensure that the lower edges of the shoes fit securely into their anchor points **(see illustrations)**.
57 Secure the shoes in position with the hold down springs and cups. Using pliers, press the cups against the pressure of the hold springs, then turn them through 90° and release them, to lock them in position **(see illustrations)**.
58 Apply a smear of brake grease to the moving parts of the self-adjuster mechanism.
59 Using a ruler, set the overall diameter of the shoe linings to between 203.0 and 203.3 mm, by turning the serrated wheel at the end of the self-adjuster mechanism. This will give the correct clearance to allow the drum to pass over the shoes during refitting.
60 Repeat the brake shoe renewal procedure at the opposite rear wheel **(see illustration)**.

Refitting - all models

61 Refit the brake drum and hub assemblies, as described in Section 8. If the drum proves difficult to fit, try tapping both brake shoes lightly with a soft faced mallet, to centre them on the backplate. Once the drum is fitted, refit the roadwheels.
62 Adjust the operation of the handbrake, as described in Chapter 1. **Note:** *It is important that this procedure is carried out accurately, as incorrect handbrake cable adjustment will*

6.60 Rear brake shoe components correctly fitted to the backplate

affect the operation of the brake shoe self-adjustment mechanism.
63 Apply and release the brake pedal and handbrake lever several times, to set the self-adjusting mechanism. With both rear wheels refitted and the rear of the vehicle still raised, turn the wheels by hand to check that the brake shoes are not binding on the drums.
64 Lower the vehicle to the ground and test the operation of the braking system exhaustively, before using the car on the road.

7 Brake disc - inspection, removal and refitting

Inspection

1 Park the vehicle on a firm, level surface, then chock the rear wheels and apply the handbrake. Raise the front of the vehicle, rest it securely on axle stands and remove the front roadwheels (see *"Jacking and vehicle support"*).
2 Rotate the brake disc by hand and examine the whole of the surface area swept by the

brake pads, on both sides of the disc. **Note:** *It will be necessary to remove the brake pads, to allow an adequate inspection the disc rear surface; refer to Section 4 for details.* Typically, the surface will have a polished appearance and should be free from heavy scoring. Smooth rippling is produced by normal operation and does not indicate excessive wear. Deep scoring and cracks, however, are indications of more serious in need of correction.

3 If deep scoring revealed, it may be possible to have the disc reground to restore the surface, depending on the extent of the damage. To determine whether this is a feasible course of action, it will be necessary to measure the thickness of the disc, as described later in this section.

4 Check the whole surface of the disc for cracks, particularly around the roadwheel stud holes. A cracked disc must be renewed.

5 Where vented discs are fitted, inspect the cooling vents between the two friction surfaces of the disc and clear out any accumulation of dirt and brake dust; blocked air ways will impair the cooling efficiency. Use a piece of rag wrapped around a length of wire, soaked in brake cleaning fluid to clear the air ways. Do not use compressed air as this will propel the potentially harmful brake dust into the air.

6 A ridge of rust and brake dust at the inner and outer edges of the disc, beyond the pad contact area is normal. This can be removed quite easily by rotating the disc by hand whilst bracing a stout screwdriver against the pad carrier bracket, using the screwdriver tip as a scraper. Be careful to avoid scoring the pad contact surface though.

7 Deep, raised ridges caused by the brake pads eroding the disc material, however, are an indication of excessive wear. If close examination reveals such ridges, the thickness of the disc must be measured, to assess whether it is still fit for use.

8 To measure the thickness of the disc, take readings at several points on the surface using a micrometer, in the area swept by the brake pads. Include any points where the disc has been scored; align the jaws of the micrometer with the deepest area of scoring, to get a true indication of the extent of the wear. Compare these measurements with the limits listed in *Specifications*. If the disc has worn below its minimum thickness, at any point, it must be renewed.

9 If the discs are the suspected cause of brake judder, check the disc runout, using one of the following methods.

Runout measurement - DTI gauge method

10 Clamp a DTI gauge to a stand and attach the stand, preferably via a magnetic base, to the hub carrier. Align the gauge so that its pointer rests upon the area of the disc swept by the brake pads, on an arc 2 or 3 mm from the outer edge of the disc

11 Zero the gauge and slowly rotate the disc through one revolution, observing the pointer movement. Note the maximum deflection recorded and compare the figure with that listed in *Specifications*.

Runout measurement - Feeler blade method

12 Use the gauges to measure the clearance between the disc and a convenient fixed point, such as the disc backplate. Rotate the disc and measure the variation in clearance at several points around the disc. Compare the maximum figure with that listed in *Specifications*.

13 If the disc runout is outside of its specified tolerance, first check that the hub is not worn - refer to Chapter 10 for guidance.

14 If the runout is due to distortion of the disc, then it may be possible to restore the disc by regrinding. Consult your Proton dealer or a machine shop for a professional opinion first, as it may prove more economical to purchase a new disc. If the disc cannot be reground, then it must be renewed.

Removal and refitting

15 The entire hub assembly must be removed and dismantled, before the brake disc can be unbolted. This procedure is described in Chapter 10.

8 Rear brake drum and hub assembly - removal, inspection and refitting

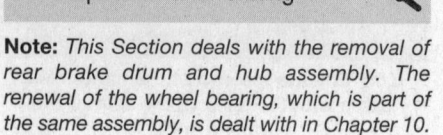

Note: *This Section deals with the removal of rear brake drum and hub assembly. The renewal of the wheel bearing, which is part of the same assembly, is dealt with in Chapter 10.*

Removal

1 Park the vehicle on a level surface and chock the front wheels. Select first gear (manual transmission) or 'Park' (automatic transmission) and apply the handbrake, then raise the rear of the vehicle and rest it securely on axle stands. (see "*Jacking and vehicle support*")

2 Using a large flat bladed screwdriver and mallet, carefully tap the dust cap off the brake drum **(see illustration)**.

3 With the handbrake firmly applied, slacken and remove the hub centre nut. Discard the hub nut, as a new one must be used on refitting.

Caution: *The nut is tighten to a very high torque. Use a long extension bar to remove the nut and ensure that you have access to torque wrench capable of tightening the new nut to the specified torque setting, before removing the existing nut.*

4 Release the handbrake fully, then pull the drum and hub assembly off the stub axle. Be ready to catch the wheel bearing outer race, as it will probably fall out as the drum is removed.

5 If the drum is binding on the brake shoes, refer to Section 14 and Chapter 1 and slacken off the handbrake cable adjustment mechanism. If the drums are badly lipped, the shoes can be retracted via the bunged access hole in the brake backplate **(see illustration)**

8.2 Carefully tap the dust cap off the brake drum

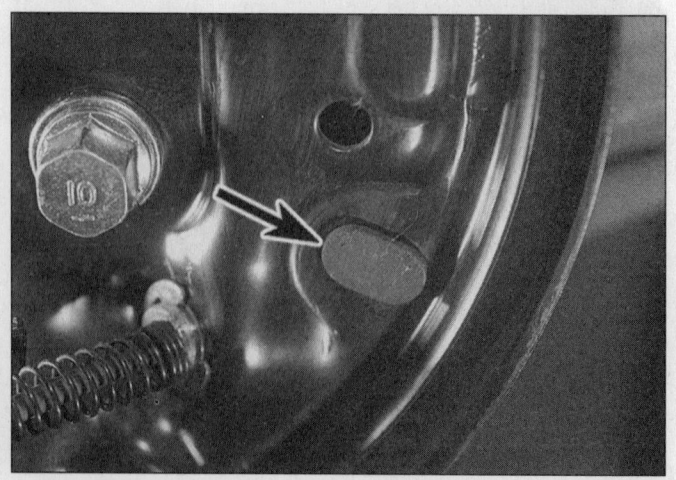

8.5 Access hole bung (arrowed) in the brake backplate - viewed from the front with drum and shoes removed for clarity

Braking system 9•13

8.13 Clean all traces of the old grease from the stub axle

8.15 Fit the drum/hub assembly over the brake shoes

Inspection

Note: *If either drum requires renewal, BOTH should be renewed at the same time, to ensure even and consistent braking. New brake shoes should also be fitted.*

6 If the hub/brake drum assembly has been removed to allow renewal of the wheel bearing, details of this procedure are given in Chapter 10.

7 Remove all traces of brake dust from the drum, but avoid inhaling the dust, as it is a health hazard.

Caution: *If the wheel bearings are not being renewed, take great care to avoid contaminating the wheel bearing inner race with debris or solvents when cleaning the brake drum.*

8 Check the inner and outer surfaces of the drum for obvious signs of wear or damage, such as cracks around the roadwheel stud holes.

9 Carefully examine the friction surface on the inside of the drum. Light scoring of the friction surface is normal, but if heavy scoring is found, the drum must be renewed.

10 It is usual to find a lip on the drum's inboard edge which consists of a mixture of rust and brake dust; this should be carefully scraped away, to leave a smooth surface which can be polished with fine (120 to 150-grade) emery paper. If, however, the lip is due to the friction surface being recessed by excessive wear, then the drum must be renewed.

11 If the drum is thought to be excessively worn, or oval, its internal diameter must be measured at several points using an internal micrometer. Take measurements in pairs, the second at right-angles to the first, and compare the two, to check for ovality. Provided that it does not enlarge the drum to beyond the specified maximum diameter, it may be possible to have the drum refinished by skimming or grinding; if this is not possible, the drums on **both** sides must be renewed. Note that if the drum is to be skimmed, **both** drums must be refinished, to maintain a consistent internal diameter on both sides.

Refitting

12 If a new brake drum/hub assembly is to be installed, use a suitable solvent to remove any preservative coating that may have been applied to its internal friction surfaces.

13 Clean all traces of the old grease from the stub axle **(see illustration)**. With reference to Chapter 1, re-pack the wheel bearings with new grease, then fit the outer race back into the hub at the centre of the drum.

14 With reference to Section 6, alter the length of the brake shoe self-adjuster, to set the brake shoes the correct external diameter. This allow the drum to pass over the brake shoes.

15 Fit the drum/hub assembly over the brake shoes **(see illustration)**. If the drum proves difficult to fit, tap the brake shoes up or down slightly to centralise them on the backplate.

16 Check that the wheel bearing outer race is correctly located, then thread the hub nut onto the end of the stub axle and tighten it to the specified torque Check that the hub spins smoothly and freely, with no freeplay. Carefully tap the dust cap into position over the nut **(see illustrations)**.

17 Refit the roadwheel, then lower the vehicle to the ground and tighten the roadwheel bolts to the specified torque.

9 Front brake caliper - removal, overhaul and refitting

Removal

1 Chock the rear wheels, apply the handbrake, then jack up the front of the vehicle and support it on axle. (see *"Jacking*

8.16a Thread the hub nut onto the end of the stub axle ...

8.16b ... and tighten it to the specified torque

8.16c Tap the dust cap into position over the nut

9•14 Braking system

9.7a Slacken and withdraw the caliper upper guide bolt...

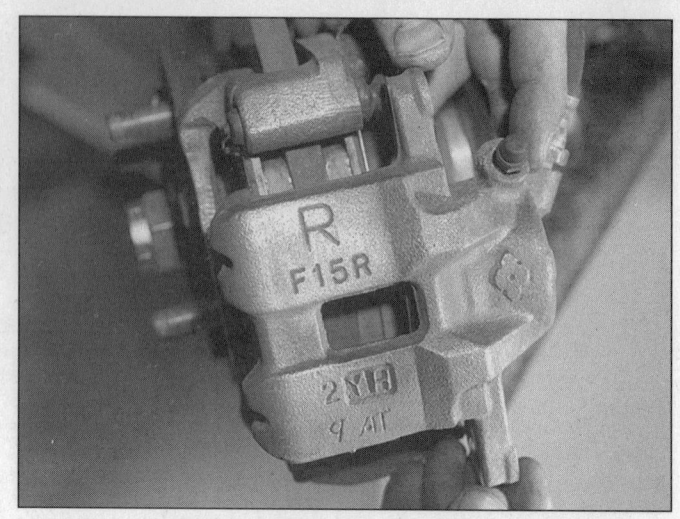

9.7b ...then remove the caliper from the carrier bracket

and vehicle support") Remove the appropriate front roadwheel.

2 Remove the brake pads from the caliper, as described in Section 2.

3 To minimise brake fluid loss during the following operations, remove the master cylinder reservoir filler cap, then tighten it down onto a piece of polythene, to obtain an airtight seal.

4 Working in the wheelarch, slide back the coiled protective sleeving, then using a proprietary brake hose clamp, seal off the flexible brake hose close to the union mounting bracket (see Section 2).

⚠️ **Warning: Do not clamp off the hose using an ordinary G-clamp or mole grips, as these can easily damage the hydraulic hose internally, possibly leading to failure.**

5 Clean the area surrounding the brake hose to brake pipe union. Using two close-fitting, open ended spanners, slacken the flare nut and separate the caliper brake hose from the rigid brake pipe. Be prepared for an amount of brake fluid loss - if the flow of fluid does not cease after a few seconds, check the security of the brake hose clamp.

6 Unbolt the brake line support bracket from the rear of the suspension strut.

7 Unscrew and withdraw the caliper upper guide bolt, then remove the caliper body from the carrier bracket **(see illustrations)**.

8 If desired, the caliper carrier bracket can be detached from the hub carrier, after removing the two securing bolts, but note that locking compound should be applied to the bolt threads on refitting **(see illustrations)**.

Overhaul

Note: Before commencing work, ensure the appropriate caliper overhaul kit is obtained.

9 With the caliper on the bench, brush off all traces of dust and dirt. Avoid inhaling the brake dust, as it is a health hazard (refer to *Warning* given at the beginning if Section 4).

10 On 8-valve models, slide the sleeves from the upper and lower guide bolt bores. Clean off all traces of the old grease.

11 Extract the rubber gaiters from the upper and lower guide bolt bores.

12 Place a small block of softwood between the caliper body and the piston, to act as padding. Drive the piston out of its bore, by applying compressed air (such as that produced by a tyre foot pump) to the fluid inlet port.

⚠️ **Warning: Protect your hands and eyes when using compressed air in this manner - brake fluid may be ejected under pressure when the piston pops out of its bore. Note that the piston may leave the bore quite suddenly and with considerable force - keep your hands well away from the end of the piston to avoid injury.**

13 Peel the dust seal from the piston, then use a soft, blunt instrument (ie **not** a screwdriver) to extract the piston seal from the caliper bore.

14 Thoroughly clean all components, using only methylated spirit or clean hydraulic fluid. Never use mineral-based solvents such as

9.8a Slacken the withdraw the bolts...

9.8b ...and remove the carrier bracket

petrol or paraffin, as these will attack the hydraulic system rubber components.

15 The caliper piston seal, the dust seal and the bleed nipple dust cap, are only available as part of a seal kit. All of these components should be discarded on disassembly and new ones fitted on reassembly.

16 Carefully examine all parts of the caliper assembly, looking for signs of wear or damage. In particular, the cylinder bore and piston must be free from any signs of scratches, corrosion or wear. If there is any doubt about the condition of any part of the caliper, the relevant part should be renewed.

17 Note that the piston surface is plated, and **must not** be polished with emery or similar abrasives to remove corrosion or scratches. In addition, the piston is matched to the caliper bore and can only be renewed as a part of a complete caliper assembly.

18 Check that the threads in the caliper body and the carrier bracket are in good condition. Check that both guide bolts are undamaged, and are (when cleaned) a good sliding fit in the guide bolt sleeves. Corroded or worn components must be renewed.

19 Direct compressed air through the caliper fluid inlet passage, to clear it out.

> **Warning: Wear eye protection when using compressed air.**

20 Before commencing reassembly, ensure that all components are spotlessly-clean and dry.

21 Coat the new piston seal with the rubber grease supplied with the service kit. Fit the seal into the groove in the cylinder bore by hand. Do not use tools or implements to manipulate it into place, as these may damage the seal and lead to early failure.

22 Smear clean hydraulic fluid over the piston and cylinder bore, then push the piston squarely into the cylinder bore, ensuring that the seal is not twisted or pinched.

23 Coat the new dust seal with grease from the service kit, then press the outer lip of the dust seal into the recess at the outer edge of the cylinder bore. Press the inner lip of the dust seal into the recess at the outer edge of the piston.

8-valve models

24 Take the single-piece guide bolt rubber gaiter and coat its outer surface with clean brake fluid. Press it into the guide bolt bore in the caliper body.

25 Apply a coat of grease from the service kit to the outer surface of the guide sleeve, then insert it through the rubber gaiter.

26 Take the two-piece guide bolt rubber gaiter and press the two pieces into either end of the second guide bolt bore.

27 Apply a smear of grease from the service kit to the inner lips of both rubber gaiters.

28 Coat the outer surface of the guide sleeve with grease from the service kit, then insert it through the rubber gaiter.

9.31 Tighten the carrier bracket bolts to the specified torque

12-valve and MPi models

29 Apply a coat of grease from the service kit to the inner surface of the lower of the guide bolt bores, in the carrier bracket.

30 Coat the internal surfaces of the new guide bolt rubber gaiters with grease from the service kit, then press them into their respective guide bolt bores in the carrier bracket.

Refitting

31 Where applicable, refit the carrier bracket to the hub carrier. Coat the threads of the mounting bolts with locking compound, then tighten them to the specified torque **(see illustration)**.

32 Place the caliper in position on the carrier bracket, then insert and tighten the upper guide bolt to the specified torque.

33 Refit the brake pads as described in Section 4, noting the following:
a) Lubricate the threads if the lower guide bolt with clean brake fluid.
b) Tighten the lower guide bolt to the specified torque.

34 Check that the caliper slides smoothly on the guide bolts.

35 Check that the brake fluid hose is correctly routed, without being twisted or kinked, then reconnect the union at the mounting bracket, using new sealing washer(s). Tighten the union to the specified torque and reinsert the metal locking clip.

36 Where applicable, remove the polythene from the master cylinder reservoir cap, or remove the clamp from the fluid hose, as applicable.

37 Bleed the hydraulic fluid circuit as described in Section 2. Note that if no other part of the system has been disturbed, it should only be necessary to bleed the relevant front circuit.

38 Depress the brake pedal repeatedly to bring the pads into contact with the brake disc, and ensure that normal pedal pressure is restored.

39 Refit the roadwheel, and lower the vehicle to the ground.

10 Rear wheel cylinder - removal, overhaul and refitting

> **Warning: Before starting work, refer to the 'Warnings' at the beginning of Sections 1 and 2 concerning the dangers of asbestos dust and hydraulic fluid.**

Removal

1 Park the vehicle on a level surface and chock the front wheels. Select first gear (manual transmission) or 'Park' (automatic transmission) and release the handbrake, then raise the rear of the vehicle and rest it securely on axle stands.

2 Remove the brake drum and hub assembly, as described in Section 8.

3 On 8-valve models, with reference to Section 6, unhook and remove the large return spring from the brake shoes. Prise the upper ends of the brake shoes apart, to disengage them from the wheel cylinder pistons.

4 On 12-valve and MPi models, refer to Section 6 and remove the brake shoes from the backplate.

5 To minimise fluid loss during the following operations, remove the master cylinder reservoir cap, then tighten it down onto a piece of polythene, to obtain an airtight seal.

6 Trace the relevant brake pipe back to the flexible hose, which allows it to pivot with the rear axle. Clamp off the hose at this point, using a proprietary hose clamp.

> **Warning: Do not clamp off the hose using an ordinary G-clamp or mole grips, as these can easily damage the hydraulic hose internally, possibly leading to failure.**

7 Clean the brake backplate around the wheel cylinder mounting bolts and the brake pipe union, then unscrew the union nut and disconnect the brake pipe. Cover the open ends of the pipe and the master cylinder to prevent dirt ingress.

8 Remove the securing bolts then withdraw the wheel cylinder from the backplate **(see illustration)**. Recover the gasket

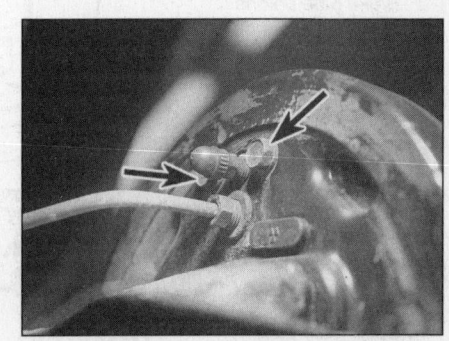

10.8 Remove the wheel cylinder securing bolts (arrowed) from the rear of the backplate

9•16 Braking system

9 Unscrew and remove the bleed nipple from the wheel cylinder.

Overhaul

Note: *Before commencing work, ensure that the appropriate wheel cylinder overhaul kit is obtained.*

10 Clean the assembly thoroughly, using only methylated spirit or clean brake fluid.

11 Peel off both rubber dust covers, then use paint or similar to mark one of the pistons so that they are not interchanged on reassembly.

12 Withdraw both pistons from the wheel cylinder

13 Using a blunt, soft instrument (i.e. not a screwdriver) prise the rubber piston cups from the pistons. The piston cups and dust covers should be renewed as a matter of course. They are available as part of an overhaul kit, which also includes a new bleed nipple dust cap.

14 Check the condition of the cylinder bore and the piston - the surfaces must be perfect and free from scratches, scoring and corrosion. It is advisable to renew the complete wheel cylinder if there is any doubt as to the condition of the cylinder bore or piston.

15 Ensure that all components are clean and dry. The pistons and cups should be fitted wet, using hydraulic fluid as a lubricant - soak them in clean fluid before installation.

16 Fit the cups to the pistons, ensuring that they are the correct way round. Use only your fingers (no tools) to manipulate the cups into position.

17 Fit the first piston to the cylinder, taking care not to distort the cup. If the original pistons are being re-used, the marks made on dismantling should be used to ensure that the pistons are refitted to their original bores.

18 Fit the second piston to the wheel cylinder in the same manner.

19 Apply grease from the overhaul kit to the gap between the piston and the cylinder bore. Fit the dust covers to each end of the wheel cylinder

20 Thread the bleed screw into the wheel cylinder and tighten it to the specified torque. Fit the new rubber dust cap

Refitting

21 Refitting is a reversal of removal, bearing in mind the following points:
a) Remember to fit the gasket between the wheel cylinder and the backplate.
b) Tighten the wheel cylinder mounting bolts to the specified torque.
c) On 12-valve and MPi models, refit the brake shoes as described in Section 6.
d) On 8-valve models, refit the large return spring to the brake shoes as described in Section 6.
e) Refit the brake drum and hub assembly, as described in Section 8
f) Remove the polythene from the brake fluid reservoir (where applicable), and the clamp from the brake hose.
g) Bleed the air from wheel cylinder and brake pipes and hoses leading to it, via the bleed nipple, as described in Section 2. Note that providing the necessary precautions were taken to minimise brake fluid loss, it should not be necessary to bleed any other part of the braking system.

11 Master cylinder - removal and refitting

Note: *Before starting work, refer to the warning at the beginning of Section 11 concerning the dangers of hydraulic fluid.*

Removal

1 Remove the master cylinder fluid reservoir cap, and syphon the hydraulic fluid from the reservoir. **Note:** *Do not syphon the fluid by mouth, as it is poisonous; use a syringe or an old poultry baster.* Alternatively, open any convenient bleed screw in the system, and gently pump the brake pedal to expel the fluid through a tube connected to the screw (see Section 11). Disconnect the wiring connector from the brake fluid level sender unit.

2 On earlier 8-valve and 12-valve models, remove the through-bolt, carefully prise the fluid reservoir from the seals and release it from the top of the master cylinder **(see illustration)**.

3 On MPi and later 8-valve and 12-valve models, remove the screws and prise the inlet elbows from the seals at the top of the master cylinder.

4 Wipe clean the area around the brake pipe unions on the upper surface of the master cylinder, and place absorbent rags beneath the unions to catch any surplus fluid. Make a note of the correct fitted positions of each union, then unscrew the union nuts and carefully withdraw the brake pipes **(see illustration)**. Plug or tape over the pipe ends and master cylinder orifices, to minimise the loss of brake fluid, and to prevent the entry of dirt into the hydraulic system. If brake fluid is spilt, wash it off immediately with plenty of cold water.

> **TOOL TIP** *Cut the finger tips from an old rubber glove and secure them over the open ends of the brake pipes with elastic bands - this will help to minimise fluid loss and prevent the ingress of contaminants.*

5 Slacken and remove the nuts and washers securing the master cylinder to the vacuum servo unit, then withdraw the unit from the engine compartment.

6 Where applicable, recover the seals from the rear of the master cylinder, and discard them; new items must be used on refitting.

Refitting

7 To ensure correct operation, there must be a clearance between the end of the servo unit

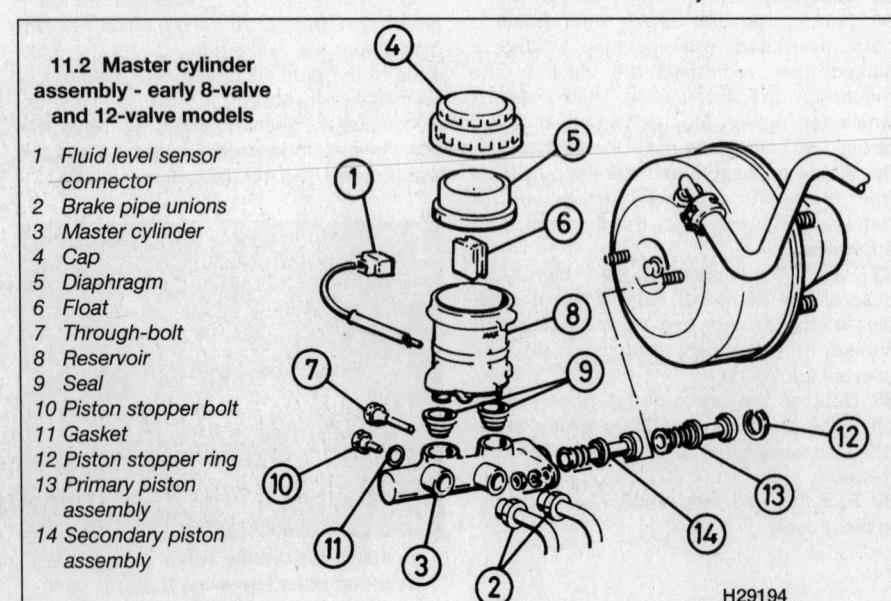

11.2 Master cylinder assembly - early 8-valve and 12-valve models

1. Fluid level sensor connector
2. Brake pipe unions
3. Master cylinder
4. Cap
5. Diaphragm
6. Float
7. Through-bolt
8. Reservoir
9. Seal
10. Piston stopper bolt
11. Gasket
12. Piston stopper ring
13. Primary piston assembly
14. Secondary piston assembly

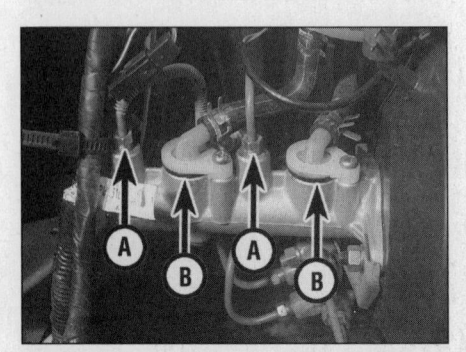

11.4 Master cylinder - MPi and later 8-valve and 12-valve models

A Brake line unions
B Fluid reservoir inlet elbow seals

Braking system 9•17

pushrod and the corresponding mating socket in the master cylinder primary piston. Check that this clearance is within the limit given in the *Specifications*, as described in the following paragraph.

8 First measure the distance between the deepest part of the primary piston mating socket and the end of the cylinder bore. Use a length of welding rod a depth gauge.
9 Now measure the distance between the end of the cylinder bore and the mating surface.
10 Finally, measure the distance between the servo unit mating surface and the tip of the pushrod.
11 Subtract the second and third measurements from the first, then compare this result with the figure given in the *Specifications*. If the clearance is incorrect, it can be adjusted by gripping the servo pushrod and turning the locknut as required, to alter its length.
12 Fit new rubber seals into the ports at the top of the master cylinder.
13 On earlier 8-valve and 12-valve models, press the ports on the base of the fluid reservoir firmly into the new seals at the top of the master cylinder.
14 On MPi and later 8-valve and 12-valve models, press the inlet elbows into the new seals on the top of master cylinder. Refit the elbow securing screws and tighten them securely.
15 Remove all traces of dirt from the master cylinder and servo unit mating surfaces, and where applicable, fit a new seal between the master cylinder body and the servo.
16 Fit the master cylinder to the servo unit, ensuring that the servo unit pushrod enters the master cylinder bore centrally. Refit the master cylinder mounting washers and nuts, then tighten them to the specified torque.
17 Wipe clean the brake pipe unions, then refit them to the correct master cylinder ports, as noted during removal, and tighten the union nuts securely.
18 Refill the master cylinder reservoir with new brake fluid, and bleed the entire braking system as described in Section 2.
19 Check the operation of the braking system thoroughly before bringing the vehicle back into service on the public highway

12 Vacuum servo unit - removal and refitting

Removal

1 Ensure that the vehicle is parked on a level surface, with the handbrake firmly applied.
2 Disconnect the battery negative cable and position it away from the terminal.
3 Remove the master cylinder from the vacuum servo unit, with reference to Section 11.
4 Disconnect the vacuum hose from the servo.

5 With reference to the relevant paragraphs of Section 5, remove the clevis pin and disconnect the servo pushrod from the brake pedal.
6 Unscrew the four nuts securing the servo mounting studs to the bulkhead.
7 Working in the engine compartment, withdraw the servo from the bulkhead.
Caution: Take care to avoid damaging the threads of the vacuum unit studs.
8 Recover the spacer block and the two seals from the bulkhead.

Refitting

9 Refitting is a reversal of removal, bearing in mind the following points:
 a) *Before refitting the servo, check that the clearance between the end of the servo unit pushrod and the master cylinder primary piston is as specified - refer to Section 11 for details.*
 b) *Refit the master cylinder as described in Section 11.*
 c) *Tighten all fixings to the specified torque.*
 d) *Bleed the entire braking system as described in Section 2.*
 e) *On completion, check the brake pedal height as described in Section 5.*

13 Vacuum servo unit check valve - removal, testing and refitting

Removal

1 The valve is located in the vacuum hose leading to the servo, and is threaded into a tapping at the inlet manifold.
2 Unscrew the valve from the manifold. Take note of the direction of the arrow on the valve body, which points in the direction of flow towards the engine.
3 Release the retaining clips (where fitted), and disconnect the vacuum hose from the valve.

Testing

4 Examine the check valve for signs of damage, and renew if necessary. The valve may be tested by blowing through it in both directions. Air should flow through the valve in one direction only - when blown through from the servo unit end of the valve. Renew the valve if this is not the case.

Refitting

5 Refitting is a reversal of removal. Apply suitable sealant to the threaded section of the valve.
6 On completion, start the engine and check the hose connections to the valve for air leaks.

14 Handbrake cables - removal and refitting

Removal

1 There are two rear handbrake cables, one serving each rear wheel drum brake. The description in the following paragraphs is applicable to either rear cable.
2 Park the vehicle on a level surface and chock the front wheels. Select first gear (manual transmission) or 'Park' (automatic transmission) and apply the handbrake, then raise the rear of the vehicle and rest it securely on axle stands. (see "*Jacking and vehicle support*")
3 Refer to Sections 8 and 6 and remove the relevant brake drum and shoes.
4 Extract the circlip using a pair of long-nosed pliers, to detach the handbrake cable outer from the brake backplate. Withdraw the handbrake cable from the brake backplate **(see illustrations)**.
5 Unscrew the bolts securing the handbrake cable clips to the suspension arms and floorpan.
6 Working inside the vehicle, remove the screws and lift off the handbrake lever trim panel (refer to Chapter 11 for more detail).
7 At the base of the handbrake lever, fully slacken off the handbrake adjusting screw and locknut, to remove all tension from the cable drawbar, then disconnect the relevant handbrake cable inner from the cable drawbar
8 Refer to Chapter 11 and remove the rear seat cushion from the floor mountings.
9 Release the handbrake cable grommets from the floorpan, then withdraw the cable from the vehicle **(see illustration)**.

14.4a Extract the circlip (arrowed) using a pair of long-nosed pliers . . .

14.4b . . . and withdraw the handbrake cable from the brake backplate

9•18 Braking system

14.9 Release the handbrake cable grommet (arrowed) from the floorpan

15.3 Disconnect the wiring plug (arrowed) from the stop light switch

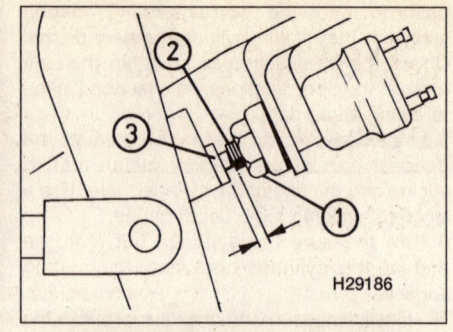

15.8 Stop light switch adjustment
1 Locknut 2 Outer casing 3 Pedal stopper

Refitting

10 Refitting is a reversal of removal, bearing in mind the following points:
a) Ensure that the cables are securely fastened in the clips on the floopan heatshield and lower suspension arm.
b) Ensure that the floorpan cable grommets face towards the inside of the vehicle.
c) On completion, check the handbrake adjustment, as described in Section 9.

15 Stop-light switch - removal, refitting and adjustment

Removal

1 Ensure that the ignition is switched to 'OFF'.
2 For improved access, remove the driver's side lower facia panel, as described in Chapter 11.
3 Disconnect the wiring plug from the switch **(see illustration)**.
4 Unscrew the locknut and collar, then withdraw the switch from its mounting bracket.

Refitting

5 Refitting is a reversal of removal. On completion, adjust the position of the switch as described in the following sub-Section.

Adjustment

6 Disconnect the wiring connector from the rear of the stop light switch.
7 Slacken the locknut, then adjust the protrusion of the switch in its bracket by turning it. With the brake pedal at rest, the switch plunger should be fully depressed.

8 Now turn the switch body through one half-turn anticlockwise, to retract it from the pedal slightly, then secure the switch in this position by tightening the locknut **(see illustration)**.
9 Restore the wiring at the connector, switch on the ignition and test the operation of the brake lights.
10 On completion, refit the facia lower trim panel.

16 Rear brake pressure proportioning valve - removal and refitting

Removal

1 The rear brake pressure proportioning valve is mounted on a bracket, below the master cylinder.
2 Remove the master cylinder fluid reservoir cap, and syphon the hydraulic fluid from the reservoir. **Note:** *Do not syphon the fluid by mouth, as it is poisonous; use a syringe or an old poultry baster.* Alternatively, open any convenient bleed screw in the system, and gently pump the brake pedal to expel the fluid through a tube connected to the screw (see Section 11).
3 Slacken each union in turn and disconnect the brake pipes from the proportioning valve. Be prepared for some brake fluid loss - position a small container underneath the valve and pad the surrounding area with absorbent rags.
4 Remove the securing bolts and lift the valve away from its mounting bracket.
5 Plug or cover all exposed brake pipes and unions, to minimise brake fluid loss and prevent the ingress of dirt into the hydraulic system.

TOOL TIP *Cut the fingers from an old rubber glove and secure them over the brake pipe unions with an elastic band.*

Refitting

6 Refitting is reversal of removal., noting the following points:
a) Refill the brake fluid reservoir with the specified grade of fluid, then bleed the entire braking system as described in Section 2.
b) Check the operation of the braking system thoroughly before bringing the vehicle back into service on the public highway.

17 Handbrake "on" warning light switch - removal and refitting

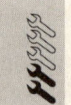

Removal

1 Ensure that the ignition is switched to the 'OFF' position.
2 Remove the centre console, as described in Chapter 11.
3 Disconnect the wiring plug from the switch.
4 Remove the securing screw, and withdraw the switch.

Refitting

5 Refitting is a reversal of removal, but before refitting the centre console, check that the warning light comes on after the specified number of handbrake clicks (refer to the *Specifications*). If necessary, bend the switch bracket to give the correct adjustment.

Chapter 10
Suspension and steering

Contents

Front hub bearings - renewal 2
Front suspension anti-roll bar - removal and refitting 6
Front suspension lower arm - removal, overhaul and refitting 4
Front suspension lower arm balljoint - renewal 5
Front suspension strut - removal, overhaul and refitting 3
General information 1
Ignition switch/steering column lock - removal and refitting 10
Power steering fluid level check .... See Chapter 1
Power steering hydraulic system - bleeding 14
Power steering pump - removal and refitting 15
Power steering pump drivebelt - adjustment 17
Rear hub bearings - renewal 7
Rear suspension components - removal and refitting 8
Steering column - removal and refitting 11
Steering gear assembly - removal and refitting 12
Steering gear rubber gaiters - renewal 13
Steering wheel - removal and refitting 9
Track-rod end - removal and refitting 16
Tyre checks .... See Chapter 1

Degrees of difficulty

| Easy, suitable for novice with little experience | Fairly easy, suitable for beginner with some experience | Fairly difficult, suitable for competent DIY mechanic | Difficult, suitable for experienced DIY mechanic | Very difficult, suitable for expert DIY or professional |

Specifications

Front suspension
Type .... Independent, incorporating transverse lower arms. and coil spring-over-telescopic damper strut units. Anti-roll bar fitted to all models

Coil spring:
  Free height .... 343.1 mm
  Identification colours .... Green and blue
Anti-roll bar diameter .... 14 mm

Rear suspension
Type .... Twist beam rear axle with semi-trailing suspension arms, anti-roll bar, telescopic dampers and coil springs

Coil spring:
  Free height .... 324.5 mm
  Identification colours .... Red and blue
Anti-roll bar diameter .... 16 mm

Steering
Type .... Rack-and-pinion, manual or power assisted, depending on model and specification
Power steering pump drivebelt deflection .... 6 to 9 mm

Roadwheels and tyres
See 'Weekly Checks'

Torque wrench settings

	Nm	lbf ft
Front suspension		
Suspension strut to hub carrier	80	59
Suspension strut to inner wing	50	37
Suspension strut damper nut	45	33
Front hub nut	240	177
Lower arm front bush mounting pin bracket-to-body bolts	175	129
Lower arm front bush mounting pin nut	110	81
Lower arm rear bush securing bolts	70	52
Lower arm ball joint to hub carrier	65	48
Anti-roll bar bush bracket bolts	20	15
Anti-roll bar drop link to lower arm nut	see text	
Brake disc-to-hub nuts	55	41

10•2 Suspension and steering

Torque wrench settings (continued)

	Nm	lbf ft
Rear suspension		
Damper upper securing bolt	65	48
Damper lower securing bolt	75	63
Trailing arm bush mounting pin nuts	90	66
Trailing arm bush mounting brackets-to-body bolts	20	15
Hub nut	120	89
Steering		
Steering wheel nut	40	30
Steering column mounting bolts	10	7
Track rod end to hub carrier	30	22
Track rod end locknuts	40	30
Steering gear mounting bracket bolts	70	52
Universal joint clamp bolts	30	22
Ignition switch/steering column lock securing bolts	see text	
Power steering pump mounting bolts	30	22
Power steering hydraulic fluid union nuts	15	11
Roadwheels		
Roadwheel nuts	100	74

1 General information

Front suspension

1 The front suspension is independent, comprising transverse lower wishbones, coil spring-over-damper strut units and an anti-roll bar. The hub carriers are bolted to the base of the strut units and are linked to the lower arms by means of balljoints.

Rear suspension

2 The rear suspension incorporates a twist beam axle, semi-trailing arms, coil springs and separate telescopic dampers. This arrangement means that the rear dampers can be easily renewed, without having to strip a strut assembly. A rear anti-roll bar, anchored to the twist beam axle, is fitted to all models.

Steering

3 The two-piece steering shaft runs in a tubular column assembly, which is bolted to a bracket, mounted on the vehicles bulkhead. The shaft is articulated at its lower end by means of a universal joint, which is secured to the steering shaft and the steering gear pinion by means of clamp bolts.

4 The steering gear is mounted on the engine compartment bulkhead, and is connected to the steering arms, which project rearwards from the hub carriers. The track-rods are fitted with balljoints at their inner and outer ends, to allow for suspension movement, and are threaded to facilitate adjustment.

5 Hydraulically-assisted power steering is fitted to some models. The hydraulic system is powered by a belt-driven servo pump, which is driven from the crankshaft pulley.

2 Front hub bearings - renewal

General information

1 This section describes the following:
a) The removal (and refitting) of the hub carrier, hub and brake disc assembly.
b) The renewal of the front hub bearings.
c) The renewal of the front brake disc.

Removal

Note: *A balljoint separator tool, and access to a hydraulic press or suitable alternative tools (see text) will be required for this operation. The existing hub bearing will be destroyed during the removal procedure.*

2 Chock the rear wheels, apply the handbrake, then jack up the front of the vehicle and support on axle stands (see *"Jacking and vehicle support"*). Remove the appropriate roadwheel.

3 Remove the brake caliper, with reference to Chapter 9 **(see illustration)**. Note that the caliper body and brake pads can remain bolted to the carrier bracket: there is no need to disconnect the brake fluid hose from the caliper. Support the caliper from a suitable point on the suspension using a length of wire or a nylon cable-tie.

4 With reference to Chapter 8, slacken and remove the driveshaft hub nut.

5 With reference to Section 16, separate the track rod end from the hub carrier, using a suitable ball joint splitter.

6 Remove the two nuts from the bolts that secure the top of the hub carrier to the base of the suspension strut (refer to Section 3). Withdraw the bolts and separate the top of hub carrier from the strut **(see illustrations)**

7 Disconnect the outboard end of the driveshaft from the hub, as described during

2.3 Remove the brake caliper from the hub carrier

2.6a Withdraw the bolts . . .

2.6b . . . then separate top of hub carrier from the base of the suspension strut

Suspension and steering 10•3

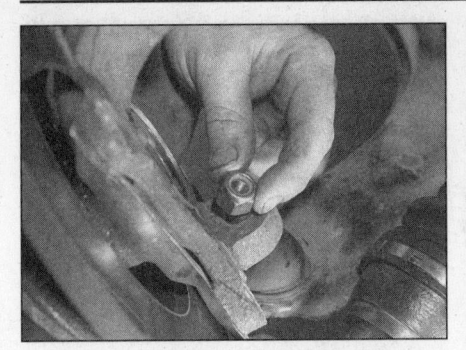

2.8 Once the lower arm balljoint stud is released from hub carrier, remove the nut

2.9a Separate the base of the hub carrier from the lower arm balljoint

2.9b Rest driveshaft on the suspension lower arm to prevent the CV joints from being strained

the driveshaft removal and refitting procedure in Chapter 8. **Note:** *There is no need to disconnect the inboard end of the driveshaft from the transmission.*
Caution: *Do not allow the end of the driveshaft to hang down under its own weight, as this places strain on the CV joints; support the end of the shaft using wire or string.*

8 Slacken (but do not remove) the nut, then press the ball joint stud out of the base of the hub carrier using the ball joint splitter. Once the stud is released from the hub carrier, remove the nut **(see illustration)**.
9 With reference to Section 6, unbolt the anti-roll bar drop link from the suspension lower arm, then press the lower arm down and separate the balljoint from the base of the hub carrier **(see illustrations)**. Temporarily refit the drop link.
10 At this stage, it is recommended that the hub carrier be taken to a engineering workshop, as the hub and bearing should ideally be removed from the hub carrier using a hydraulic press and/or special tools **(see illustration)**. Owners wishing to attempt the work themselves should proceed as follows.
11 Mount the hub carrier firmly in a bench vice. Attach a slide hammer to the hub flange and extract the hub, together with the outer bearing inner race, which will remain on the hub shaft. Recover the inner bearing inner race, which will be driven off the other end of the hub shaft, as the hub is withdrawn.
12 Remove the nuts and spring washers, then withdraw the brake disc from the hub. If the original disc is to be refitted, mark the surface of the disc in relation to the hub, to preserve the alignment on refitting.
13 Mount the hub carrier horizontally in the vice. Using a suitable length of soft metal bar or tubing as a drift, drive the inner and outer bearing outer races from the hub carrier bearing housing. Take great care to avoid damaging the internal surfaces of the bearing housing.
14 Pull the outer bearing inner race from the hub shaft, using a suitable two or three-legged puller. Pad the end of the hub shaft with large steel washers, to prevent the hub puller from damaging the hub shaft.
15 Before installing the new bearing, thoroughly clean the bearing housing in the hub carrier with a suitable solvent. Check that the inside of bearing housing has not been accidentally damaged during the removal process.
16 Mount the hub carrier horizontally in the bench vice, with the inboard side facing upwards. Fit the new inner bearing outer race from the inboard side the hub, with the chamfered surface facing outwards. Press or drive the bearing squarely into position, using a section of soft metal tubing, or an old socket. **Do not** lubricate the bearing or the housing, in an attempt to ease installation.
17 Turn the hub carrier over and re-mount it in the vice, with the outboard side facing upwards. Fit the new outer bearing outer race from the outboard side the hub, with the chamfered surface facing outwards. Press or drive the bearing squarely into position, using a section of soft metal tubing, or an old socket, and a mallet. **Do not** lubricate the bearing or the housing, in an attempt to ease installation.
18 Apply grease from the bearing service kit to the inside surface of the bearing housing and the chamfered surfaces of the newly-installed outer bearing races.
19 Similarly, apply grease from the bearing service kit to the roller bearings of the both inner bearing races. Drive the grease past the rollers, to fill the inside of the bearing race.
20 Push the outer bearing inner race into the hub carrier, so that the roller bearings mate with the chamfered surface of the outer race.
21 Place the outer oil seal in position the outer bearing, then using a socket of suitable diameter as a drift, drive the oil seal into the bearing housing. Stop when the surface of the oil seal is flush with the outer edge of the bearing housing.
22 Apply grease from the bearing service kit to the sealing lips.
23 Push the inner bearing inner race into position, so that the rollers bear against the chamfered surface of the inner bearing outer race.
24 Bolt the brake disc to the hub, using the marks made during removal (where applicable) to achieve the correct alignment. Tighten the securing nuts to the specified torque.
25 Carefully press or draw the hub into the bearing, noting that the inner bearing inner race **must** be supported during this operation, to prevent it from being separated from the outer race. This can be achieved using a

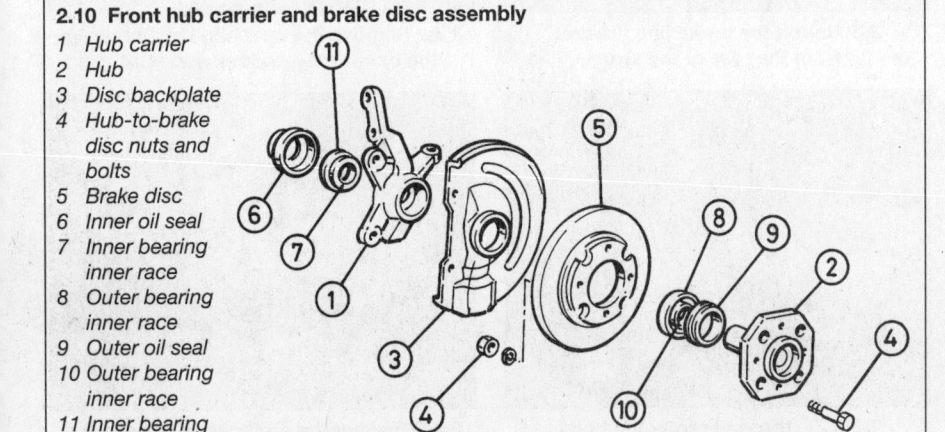

2.10 Front hub carrier and brake disc assembly
1 Hub carrier
2 Hub
3 Disc backplate
4 Hub-to-brake disc nuts and bolts
5 Brake disc
6 Inner oil seal
7 Inner bearing inner race
8 Outer bearing inner race
9 Outer oil seal
10 Outer bearing inner race
11 Inner bearing outer race

10•4 Suspension and steering

2.25 Refitting the hub using improvised tools

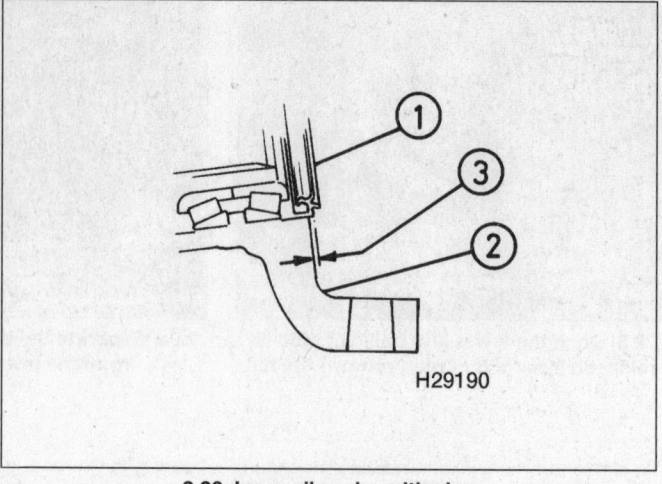

2.26 Inner oil seal positioning
1 Oil seal   2 Hub carrier   3 2.5 mm protrusion

suitable socket, a long bolt and nut, and a number of large flat washers. Mount the components as shown, then tighten the nut to a torque of 250 Nm **(see illustration)**.

26 Drive the inner oil seal into position, using the same method as that described previously for the outer oil seal. Stop when the surface of the oil seal protrudes above the inner edge of the bearing housing by 2.5 mm **(see illustration)**

27 Rotate the hub to seat the bearings and check that are no signs of stiffness or roughness in the movement.

Refitting

28 Engage the hub carrier with the suspension strut, then refit the securing bolts and nuts, tightening them to the specified torque.

29 Reconnect the outboard end of the driveshaft to the hub as described in Chapter 8. Ensure that the driveshaft nut is tightened to the correct torque and that the split pin is fitted securely.

30 Reconnect the hub carrier to the lower arm balljoint, then fit a new clamp bolt nut. Tighten the nut firmly at this stage, but do not tighten it to its final torque until the vehicle has been lowered to the ground.

31 Reconnect the anti-roll bar to the suspension lower arm, as described in Section 6.

32 Reconnect the steering track rod ball joint to the hub carrier steering arm. Use a new nut and tighten it to the specified torque.

33 Refer to Chapter 9 and refit the brake disc and caliper.

34 Refit the roadwheel, and lower the vehicle to the ground.

35 Tighten the suspension lower arm ball joint to the specified torque.

36 Have the front wheel alignment checked by a Proton dealer or a tyre specialist at the earliest opportunity.

3 Front suspension strut - removal, overhaul and refitting

Warning: *If renewing the strut damper during overhaul, both the left and right hand dampers should be renewed as a pair, to preserve the handling characteristics of the vehicle.*

Removal

1 Chock the rear wheels and apply the handbrake. Jack up the front of the vehicle and support it securely on axle stands then, remove the relevant roadwheel (see "*Jacking and vehicle support*").

2 Unbolt the brake line bracket from the rear of the strut **(see illustration)**.

3 Remove the two nuts and washers from the bolts securing the lower end of the strut to the hub carrier, noting that the bolts are withdrawn from the rearward side of the strut. Withdraw the bolts, and support the underside of the hub carrier with trolley jack or blocks of wood **(see illustrations)**

4 At the top of the suspension strut, prise out the dust cap to expose the top mounting nut **(see illustration)**.

3.2 Unbolt the brake line bracket from the rear of the strut

3.3a Remove the nuts and washers from the base of the suspension strut . . .

3.3b . . . then withdraw the bolts

3.4 Prise out the dust cap to expose the top mounting nut

Suspension and steering 10•5

Grind flats (arrowed) onto the sides of an old 19mm socket to make a damper top nut holding tool

3.5 Using the home made tool to hold the damper rod stationary, whilst slackening the top nut

3.6 Removing the strut upper mounting plate

5 The damper rod must be prevented from rotating as the top mounting nut is slackened; this can be achieved by grinding flats onto the sides of an old 19mm socket and inserting a hex Allen bit (or Allen key) through the top of the socket **(see Tool Tip)**. The socket can then be turned with a spanner, whilst the damper rod is held stationary **(see illustration)**.
6 Remove the top mounting nut, the damper rod washer, upper mounting plate and rubber bush. Discard the top mounting nut as a new item must be used on refitting **(see illustration)**.
7 Release the lower end of the strut from the hub carrier, then withdraw the strut assembly from the wheel arch.

Overhaul

Note: *Suitable coil spring compressor tools will be required for this operation.*
8 Clamp the lower end of the strut in a vice fitted with jaw protectors - take care to avoid deforming the mounting bracket at the lower end of the strut.
9 Fit suitable spring compressors to the coil spring, and compress the spring sufficiently to enable the upper spring seat to be turned by hand **(see illustration)**.

⚠ *Warning: Ensure that the coil spring is compressed sufficiently to remove all the tension from the upper spring seat, before attempting to remove the damper rod nut.*

Failing to observe this precaution can easily result in personal injury and component damage.
10 Fully unscrew and remove the damper rod nut. Counterhold the damper rod, using a suitable Allen key or hex bit, as the nut is unscrewed - do not allow the rod to rotate inside the damper, as this may damage the strut internally **(see illustrations)**.
11 Withdraw the rubber insulator, support plate, bearing and upper spring seat - make a careful note of the order of assembly **(see illustrations)**.
12 Withdraw the spring, complete with the compressors, then withdraw the dust cover and bump stop **(see illustrations)**

3.9 Use spring compressors to compress the coil spring

3.10a Counterhold the damper rod, then fully unscrew ...

3.10b ... and remove the damper rod nut

3.11a Withdraw the rubber insulator ...

3.11b ... support plate and bearing ...

3.11c ... and upper spring seat

10

10•6 Suspension and steering

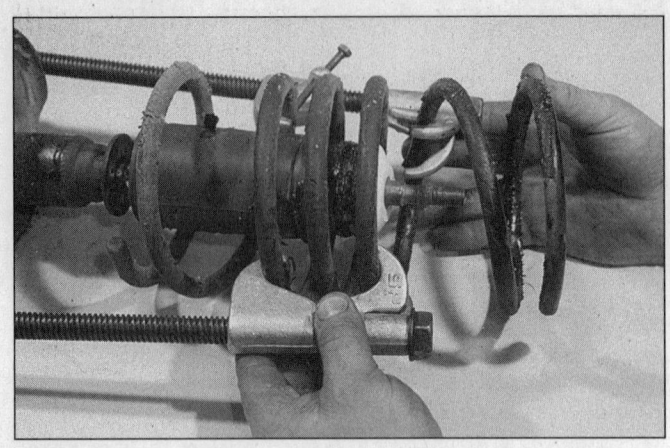

3.12a Withdraw the spring, complete with the compressors ...

3.12b ... then withdraw the dust cover and bump

13 With the strut assembly now dismantled, examine all the components for wear, damage or deformation. Check the rubber components for deterioration. Renew any of the components as necessary.
14 Examine the damper for signs of fluid leakage. Check the damper rod for signs of pitting along its entire length, and check the strut body for signs of damage. While holding it in an upright position, test the operation of the strut by moving the damper rod through a full stroke, and then through short strokes of 50 to 100 mm. In both cases, the resistance felt should be smooth and continuous.
15 If the resistance is jerky, or uneven, or if there is any visible sign of wear, damage or corrosion on the strut, renewal will be necessary.
16 Note that the damper is not an insert and therefore can only be renewed as part of a complete strut/damper assembly (in which case, the spring, upper mountings, bushes, and associated components must be transferred to the new strut assembly).
17 The bearing will have remained pressed into the support plate. Rotate it by hand and check for excessive roughness, sticking or freeplay.
18 To renew the bearing, drive the old unit from the support plate using a soft metal punch and mallet. Support the plate on a flat solid surface, then press the new bearing

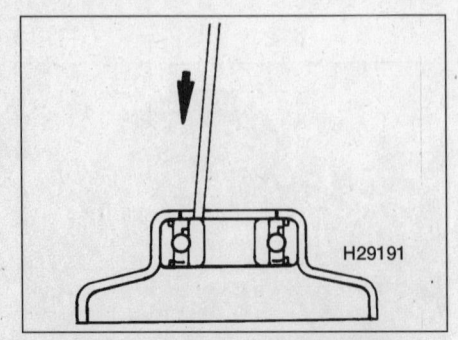

3.18 To renew the bearing, drive the old unit from the support plate using a soft metal punch and mallet

squarely into position, using an old socket of suitable diameter as a drift **(see illustration)**.
19 If any doubt exists about the condition of the coil spring, carefully remove the spring compressors, and check the spring for distortion and signs of cracking. Measure the free height of the spring using a square and ruler - check this measurement against the figure quoted in *Specifications*. Renew the spring if it is damaged, distorted or worn.

> ⚠ **Warning**: *Coil springs are classified by their height when under load - this is indicated by a coloured paint marking on the side of the coil windings (either green or yellow). All coil springs fitted to the vehicle must be of the same classification to ensure that the correct ride height.*

20 Clamp the strut body in a vice, as during dismantling, then refit the dust cover and bump rubber.
21 Ensure that the coil spring is compressed sufficiently to enable the upper mounting components to be fitted, then fit the spring over the damper rod, ensuring that the lower end of the spring is correctly located in the recess on the lower spring seat.
22 Refit the upper spring seat, bearing and support plate ensuring that the top end of the spring is correctly located in the recess in the upper spring seat.
23 Fit the new damper rod top nut together with its washer and bush, then tighten the nut to the specified torque, counterholding the damper rod in a manner similar to that used during dismantling. Note that a suitable crows-foot type adapter will be required to tighten the damper rod top nut to the specified torque.
24 Release the spring compressors gradually, ensuring that the top end of the coil spring remains located in the recess in the upperspring seat.

Refitting

25 Manoeuvre the strut assembly into position under the wheel arch, passing the top of the damper rod through the hole in the suspension turret. Ensure that the rubber

insulator engages correctly with the underside of the suspension turret.
26 Refit the rubber bush and upper mounting plate. Fit a new top mounting nut with its associated washer, then tighten the nut to the specified torque, counterholding the damper rod in a manner similar to that employed during dismantling - note that a suitable crows-foot type adapter will be required for this operation. On completion, press the dust cover into position over the top mounting nut.
27 Engage the lower end of the strut with the hub carrier, then fit the securing bolts and nuts, noting that the nuts fit on the forward side of the strut.
28 Refit the brake hydraulic line to the bracket on the base of the strut.
29 Refit the roadwheel, and lower the vehicle to the ground.
30 Have the front wheel alignment checked by a Proton dealer or a tyre specialist at the earliest opportunity.

4 Front suspension lower arm - removal, overhaul and refitting

Removal

Note: *A balljoint separator tool will be required for this operation. The lower arm balljoint nut and the anti-roll bar drop link nut must be renewed on reassembly.*

1 Disconnect battery negative cable and position it away from the terminal.
2 Chock the rear wheels and apply the handbrake firmly.
3 Jack up the front of the vehicle, then support it securely on axle stands and remove the relevant roadwheel (see "*Jacking and vehicle support*").
4 Remove the screws and lower the undertray away from the engine bay.
5 Unscrew the nut securing the anti-roll bar drop link bolt to the lower arm, and recover the washers and bushes - refer to Section 6 for details. Discard the nut - a new one should be used on refitting.

Suspension and steering 10•7

4.7 Unscrew the two bolts (arrowed) securing the lower arm rear mounting clamp to the underside of the vehicle

4.8 Slacken the nut (arrowed) securing the front of the lower arm to the mounting pin

4.9 Remove the three bolts (arrowed) that secure the front mounting pin bracket to the underside of the vehicle

6 With reference to Section 2, separate the base of the hub carrier from the lower arm using a balljoint separator tool. Remove the nut, and lever the end of the lower arm down to release the balljoint stud from the hub carrier.
7 Unscrew the two bolts securing the lower arm rear mounting clamp to the underside of the vehicle, and remove the clamp **(see illustration)**.
8 Slacken the nut securing the front of the lower arm to the mounting pin **(see illustration)**. Do not remove the nut completely.
Caution: The nut on the left-hand suspension arm has a left-hand thread.
9 Remove the three bolts that secure the front mounting pin bracket to the underside of the vehicle **(see illustration)**. Recover the washers. making a careful note of their order of fitment, to aid correct refitting.
10 Pivot the lower arm down to release it from the anti-roll bar drop link, then recover the remaining bushes and washers and sleeves from the drop link bolt (see Section 6 for details).
11 Remove the suspension lower arm from under the vehicle.

Overhaul

12 With the lower arm removed, check the balljoint for wear, excessive play, or stiffness. Also check the balljoint dust boot for cracks or damage. Note that the balljoint assembly is integral with the lower arm and cannot be renewed independently **(see illustration)**.
13 Examine the lower arm itself, including the mounting bushes, for wear, cracks or damage. Worn bushes can be renewed, as described in the following paragraphs.
14 To renew the rear bushing, soak the rubber bush in soapy water, then prise it off the mounting pin with a flat bladed screwdriver. Apply soapy water to the new rubber bush and slide it onto the mounting pin, noting the following points:
 a) The dimple protruding from the lower surface must be at an angle of 85° to the lower arm **(see illustration)**
 b) There must be a clearance of 6 mm between the bush and the end of the lower arm mounting pin.
15 To renew the front bushing, remove the securing nut and washers (noting their order of fitment), then slide out the mounting pin and bracket. Press the old bush out from its housing in the lower arm, then fit the new bush in its place, using soapy water as a lubricant. Refit the washers in the order noted during removal.

Refitting

Note: *Final tightening of all fixings must be carried out with the vehicle lowered to the ground, resting on its wheels.*

4.12 Front suspension lower arm assembly
1 Front mounting pin bracket
2 Rear bush
3 Ball joint dust boot
4 Front bush

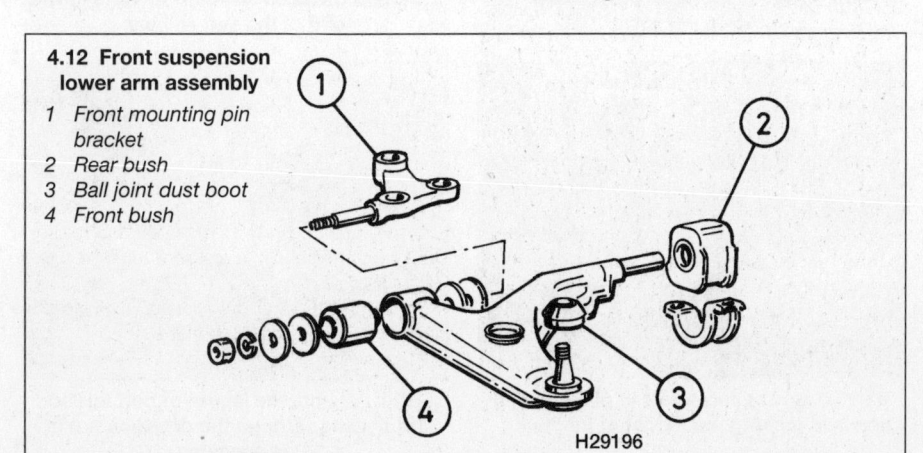

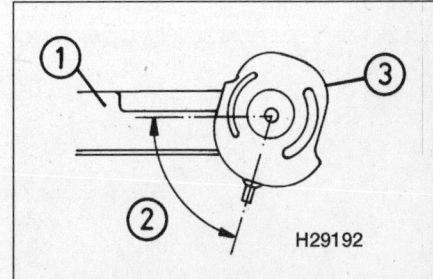

4.14 When fitting a new rear bushing, note that the dimple protruding from the lower surface must be at an angle of 85° to the lower arm
1 Lower arm   2 85° angle   3 Rear bush

10•8 Suspension and steering

16 Refitting is a reversal of removal, noting the following points:
a) Use a new self-locking nut when refitting the suspension lower arm balljoint to the base of the hub carrier.
b) Use a new self-locking nut when refitting the anti-roll bar droplink to the suspension lower arm - see Section 6 for details)
c) The protrusion of the anti-roll bar drop link bolt, below the suspension lower arm must be as specified - see Section 6 for details.
d) Note that on the left hand lower suspension arm, the nut securing the front bushing to the mounting pin bracket has a LEFT-HAND THREAD.
e) When refitting the front bush mounting pin bracket to the body and the suspension lower arm, only partially tighten the mounting bolts to begin with - delay tightening to the final torque setting until the vehicle is lowered to the ground and resting on its roadwheels.
f) Tighten all fixings to the specified torque.

17 On completion, have the front wheel alignment be checked by a Proton dealer, or a tyre fitting specialist, as soon as possible.

5 Front suspension lower arm balljoint - renewal

General information

1 The balljoint is integral with the suspension lower arm and can only be renewed as part of a complete assembly.
2 It is possible to renew the balljoint dust cover, should the existing cover become damaged. Proceed as described in the following paragraphs.
3 Refer to Section 4 and unbolt the suspension lower arm from the base of the hub carrier. A ball joint splitter will be required for this operation.
4 Lever the existing dust cover from the ball joint using a stout screwdriver.
5 Wipe the old grease from the ball joint components. If the old dust cover has split, check the ball joint is not contaminated with dirt or grit.

6 Fill the inside of the new dust cover with multi-purpose grease, then fit it over the ball joint. Using a socket of suitable outside diameter, drive the dust cover squarely into position, until it is properly seated.
7 Wipe off any surplus grease, then refit the suspension lower arm to the base of the hub carrier, as described in Section 4.

6 Front suspension anti-roll bar - removal and refitting

Removal

Note: *New drop link-to-suspension lower arm nuts should be used on refitting.*
1 Chock the rear wheels and apply the handbrake. Jack up the front of the vehicle, then support it securely on axle stands and remove the relevant roadwheel (see *"Jacking and vehicle support"*).
2 Remove the screws and lower the undertray away from the engine bay.
3 Unscrew the bolts and detach the upper section of both anti-roll bar bush mounting brackets
4 Working at one side of the anti-roll bar, counterhold the drop link bolt, then unscrew the nut securing the drop link bolt to the suspension lower arm. Recover the washers and bushes, making a careful note of their order of fitment. Discard the nut - a new one must be used on refitting.
5 Repeat the operation on the remaining side of the anti-roll bar.
6 Manipulate the anti-roll bar out from under the vehicle.

Refitting

7 Inspect the mounting clamps and rubber bushes for cracks or deterioration. If renewal is necessary, slide the old bushes from the bar, and fit the new items - use soapy water as a lubricant to aid fitting. If necessary, obtain a new drop link kit from a motor factor or a Proton dealer **(see illustration)**.
8 Refit the drop link components to both ends of the anti-roll bar, ensuring that the dished washers, rubber bushes and sleeves are fitted in the correct order **(see illustration)**. Note that the concave surfaces of the dished washers must always face the rubber bushes.
9 Offer up the anti-roll bar to its mountings. Pass the drop-link bolts through the suspension lower arms, fit the remaining bushes and washers and secure them in place with new self-locking nuts. Tighten the nuts until the length of bolt thread protruding through the drop link nut is as specified. **(see illustrations)**.
10 Ensure that the rubber bushes are aligned with the lower sections of their respective mounting brackets. Fit the upper sections of the mounting brackets, then insert the securing bolts and tighten them to the specified torque.
11 Refit the roadwheels and lower the vehicle to the ground.

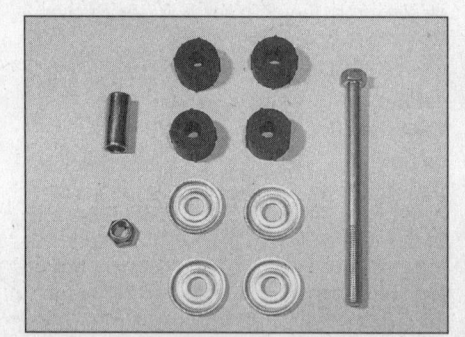

6.7 Front suspension anti-roll bar drop link kit

6.8 Refit the drop link components to the end of the anti-roll bar

6.9a Pass the drop-link bolt through the suspension lower arm, fit the remaining bushes and washers . . .

6.9b . . .and secure them in place with a new self-locking nut. Tighten the nut . . .

6.9c . . . until the length of bolt thread protruding through the drop link nut is as specified

Suspension and steering 10•9

7 Rear hub bearings - renewal

1 Park the car on a level surface and chock the front wheels. Select first gear (or 'PARK' on models with automatic transmission) and release the handbrake. Jack up the rear of the vehicle and support it securely on axle stands.
2 Remove the relevant roadwheel, then refer to Chapter 9 and remove the rear brake drum.
3 Prise the oil seal from the inboard side of the hub, using a large flat bladed screwdriver (see Chapter 1 for details).
4 Mount the drum/hub assembly horizontally on a flat surface, then drive out the outboard and inboard inner races using a soft metal punch and mallet.
5 Before installing the new bearings, thoroughly clean the bearing housing in the hub carrier with a suitable solvent. Check that the inside of bearing housing has not been accidentally damaged during the removal process.
6 Mount the hub/drum assembly horizontally in a bench vice, with the inboard side facing upwards. Fit the new inboard bearing outer race from the inboard side the hub, with the chamfered surface facing outwards. Press or drive the bearing squarely into position, using a section of soft metal tubing, or an old socket. **Do not** lubricate the bearing or the housing, in an attempt to ease installation.
7 Turn the hub carrier over and re-mount it in the vice, with the outboard side facing upwards. Fit the new outboard bearing outer race from the outboard side the hub, with the chamfered surface facing outwards. Press or drive the bearing squarely into position, using a section of soft metal tubing, or an old socket, and a mallet. **Do not** lubricate the bearing or the housing, in an attempt to ease installation.
8 Apply grease from the bearing service kit to the inside surface of the bearing housing and the chamfered surfaces of the newly-installed outer bearing races.
9 Similarly, apply grease from the bearing service kit to the roller bearings of the both inner bearing races. Drive the grease past the rollers, to fill the inside of the bearing race (see Chapter 1 for details).
10 Push the inboard bearing inner race into the hub, so that the roller bearings mate with the chamfered surface of the outer race.
11 Place the oil seal in position over the inboard bearing, then using a socket of suitable diameter as a drift, drive the oil seal squarely into the bearing housing.
12 Push the outboard bearing inner race into position, so that the rollers bear against the chamfered surface of the outer race.
13 Refer to Chapter 9 and refit the brake drum/hub assembly to the rear stub axle.

8 Rear suspension components - removal and refitting

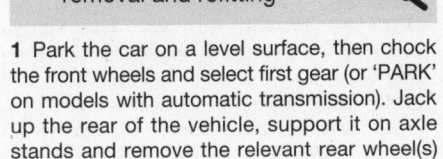

1 Park the car on a level surface, then chock the front wheels and select first gear (or 'PARK' on models with automatic transmission). Jack up the rear of the vehicle, support it on axle stands and remove the relevant rear wheel(s) (see "Jacking and vehicle support").

Damper
Removal

2 Using a trolley jack positioned under the trailing arm, raise the trailing arm to take the strain from the damper.
3 Slacken and withdraw the damper lower retaining bolt **(see illustration)**.
4 Lower the jack and allow the damper to separate from the trailing arm. Take care to avoid displacing the coil spring.
5 Slacken and withdraw the damper upper retaining bolt **(see illustration)**.
6 Lower the damper away from the suspension subframe.

Refitting

7 Refitting is a reversal of removal. Position elongated rubber flanges at the damper upper mounting towards the rear of the vehicle. Tighten the damper upper and lower retaining bolts to the specified torque, but delay this operation until the full weight vehicle is resting on the roadwheels - this prevents the damper bushes from being strained.

Coil spring
Removal

8 With reference to the previous sub-Section, unbolt the lower end of the damper from the trailing arm.
9 Lower the trailing arm gradually using a trolley jack, until the coil spring is released from its lower seat on the trailing arm and its upper seat on the subframe. Make a note of the orientation of the coil spring, to aid correct refitting later. Recover the upper spring seat.

Refitting

10 Refitting is a reversal of removal. Tighten the damper lower retaining bolt to the specified torque.

Rear axle components
Removal

11 With reference to Chapter 9, carry out the following:
 a) Remove the brake drums
 b) Remove the brake shoe assemblies from the backplates
 c) Disconnect the brake fluid pipes from the rear of the wheel cylinders.
 d) Unbolt the brake backplates from the suspension trailing arms.

12 Refer to Chapter 4C and detach the rear section of the exhaust system from the underside of the vehicle.

8.3 Slacken and withdraw the damper lower retaining bolt (arrowed)

8.5 Slacken and withdraw the damper upper retaining bolt (arrowed)

10•10 Suspension and steering

8.16 Rear suspension tube bush bracket bolts (arrowed)

8.24 Rear suspension tube gaiter
1 Gaiter 2 Clip

13 Support the trailing arms, then unbolt both lower damper mountings - refer to the information given earlier in this Section.
14 Remove both coil springs, as described in the previous sub-Section.
15 Remove the screws and disconnect the hydraulic brake lines from the brackets on the trailing arms.
16 Support the weight of the suspension on a trolley jack, then unbolt the bush brackets from the body (see illustration).
17 Lower the rear suspension assembly away from the underside of the vehicle.

Mounting bush renewal

18 Mark the relationship between the cross tube and the bush bracket with a dab of paint, to aid correct reassembly.
19 Remove the retaining nuts from the bush mounting pins, at the ends of the cross tubes.
20 Slide off the rubber bushes, washers and the bush brackets - make a careful note of their order of fitment to aid correct refitting.
21 Fit the new bush components to the ends of the cross tubes, using soapy water to lubricate the rubber bushes. Do not apply grease in an attempt to ease installation. Fit the retaining nuts and partially tighten them - delay tightening the nuts to their final torque until the vehicle is resting on its roadwheels.

Cross tube bush renewal

22 With the rear suspension assembly removed, remove the clip from the gaiter at the centre joint of the cross tube.
23 Mark the relationship between the anti-roll bar and its anchor brackets, using a dab of paint.
24 Pull the two halves of the cross tube apart. The gaiter will remain on the right hand side (see illustration).
25 Extract the plastic stop from the right hand section of the cross tube, then tap off the bush.
26 Using a mallet and soft metal bush, drive out the bush from the opposite section of the cross tube.
27 Apply grease to the new bush components, then drive them into the cross tube sections.
28 Re-assemble the two cross tube sections, making sure that the gaiter is fitted the correct way around and fully packed with grease. Tighten the gaiter clip securely.
29 Ensure that the anti-roll bar is correctly aligned with its anchor brackets, according to the marks made during removal.

Refitting

30 Refitting is a reversal of removal, noting the following points:
a) Refit the bush brackets to the body, using the marks made during removal to achieve the correct alignment.
b) Delay tightening all fixings to their final torque settings until the vehicle is resting on its roadwheels
c) After refitting the rear brake components, bleed the brake hydraulic system, as described in Chapter 9.

9 Steering wheel - removal and refitting

Removal

1 Switch off the ignition, then prise the horn centre pad from the steering wheel hub. Use the blade of a screwdriver, padded with PVC tape to protect the steering wheel.
2 Unplug the horn switch wiring from the contact plate at the connector.
3 Turn the steering wheel to its centre position, so that the roadwheels are pointing straight ahead.
4 Make alignment marks between the steering wheel and the end of the steering column shaft, to aid correct refitting later.
5 Unscrew and remove the steering wheel securing nut. Discard the nut as a new item must used on refitting.
6 Lift the steering wheel off the column splines. If the wheel is particularly tight, a suitable puller should be used. Do not attempt to jar the steering wheel from the shaft by striking it - this may damage the collapsible section of the steering column.

Refitting

7 Before commencing refitting, lightly coat the surfaces of the direction indicator cancelling mechanism with grease.
8 Refitting is a reversal of removal, bearing in mind the following points:
a) Use a new steering wheel securing nut and tighten it to the specified torque.
b) Ensure that the direction indicator switch is in the central (cancelled/off) position, otherwise the switch may be damaged as the wheel is refitted.
c) Align the marks made on the wheel and the steering column shaft during removal.
9 Note that if necessary, the position of the steering wheel on the column shaft can be altered in order to centralise the wheel (ensure that the front roadwheels are pointing in the straight-ahead position), by moving the wheel the required number of splines on the shaft. Fine adjustment can be carried out by adjusting the length of both track rods simultaneously, but this operation is best entrusted to a Proton dealer or tyre specialist.

10 Ignition switch/ steering column lock - removal and refitting

Removal

1 Remove the steering wheel (see Section 9).
2 Remove the securing screws and detach the plastic shroud from the steering column.

Suspension and steering 10•11

10.5 Ignition/steering column lock assembly

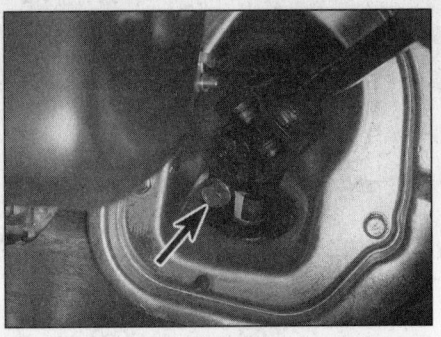

11.7 Fold back the rubber boot, then slacken the nut and clamp bolt (arrowed) on the lower half of the universal joint

3 Shear head bolts are used to secure the lock to the steering column. To remove them, slots must be cut in the bolt shanks that remain, using a small hacksaw.
4 Engage a flat bladed screwdriver with the slots cut in the bolt shanks and unscrew the shear bolts.
5 Withdraw the lock assembly from the steering column **(see illustration)**. The ignition switch can be detached by removing the securing screw.

Refitting

6 Refitting is a reversal of removal. Align the new lock assembly with the boss on the steering column, then insert and partially tighten the new shear bolts. Verify the operation of the new lock mechanism using the ignition key, before shearing the heads off the bolts.

11 Steering column - removal and refitting

Removal

1 Disconnect the battery negative cable and position it away from the terminal.
2 Ensure that the roadwheels are set in the 'dead ahead' position.
3 Remove the steering wheel (see Section 9).
4 With reference to Chapter 11, unscrew the fixings and remove the plastic shroud from the steering column.
5 Working from Chapter 12, remove the column stalk switch assemblies.
6 Unplug the wiring from the rear of the ignition switch/column lock at the multi-way connectors- refer to Section 10 for details.
7 Working in the drivers footwell, peel back the carpet trim to gain access to the base of the steering column. Fold back the rubber boot, then slacken the nut and clamp bolt on the lower half of the universal joint **(see illustration)**.
8 Remove the nuts from the steering column upper and lower mounting bolts and lower the assembly away from the bulkhead bracket **(see illustrations)**.
9 Disconnect the universal joint at the base of the steering column from the steering gear pinion.
10 Remove the steering column from the vehicle **(see illustration)**.

Refitting

11 Refitting the steering column by following the removal procedure in reverse. Tighten all fixings to the specified torque setting.

12 Steering gear assembly - removal and refitting

Manual steering gear

Removal

1 Disconnect the battery cable and position it away from the terminal.
2 To improve access, refer to Chapter 4 and remove the air cleaner assembly.
3 Chock the rear wheels and apply the handbrake. Jack up the front of the vehicle, then support it securely on axle stands and

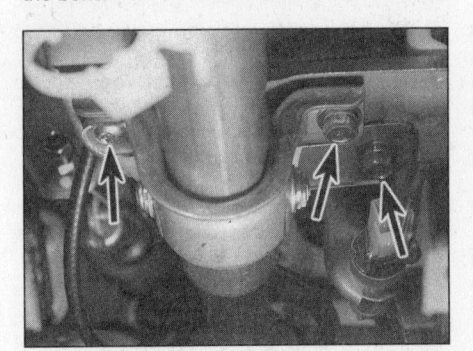

11.8a Remove the nuts from the steering column upper . . .

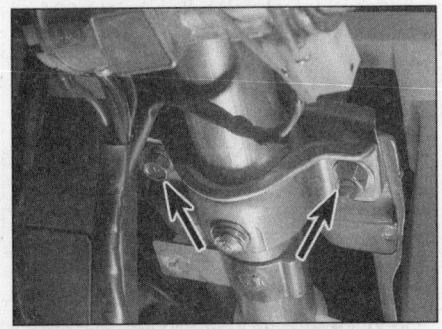

11.8b . . . and lower mounting bolts

11.10 Steering column assembly
1 Dust cover
2 Boot
3 Snap ring
4 Spacer
5 Steering shaft
6 Column tube
7 Lower bearing
8 Lock assembly
9 Mounting screws
10 Mounting bracket

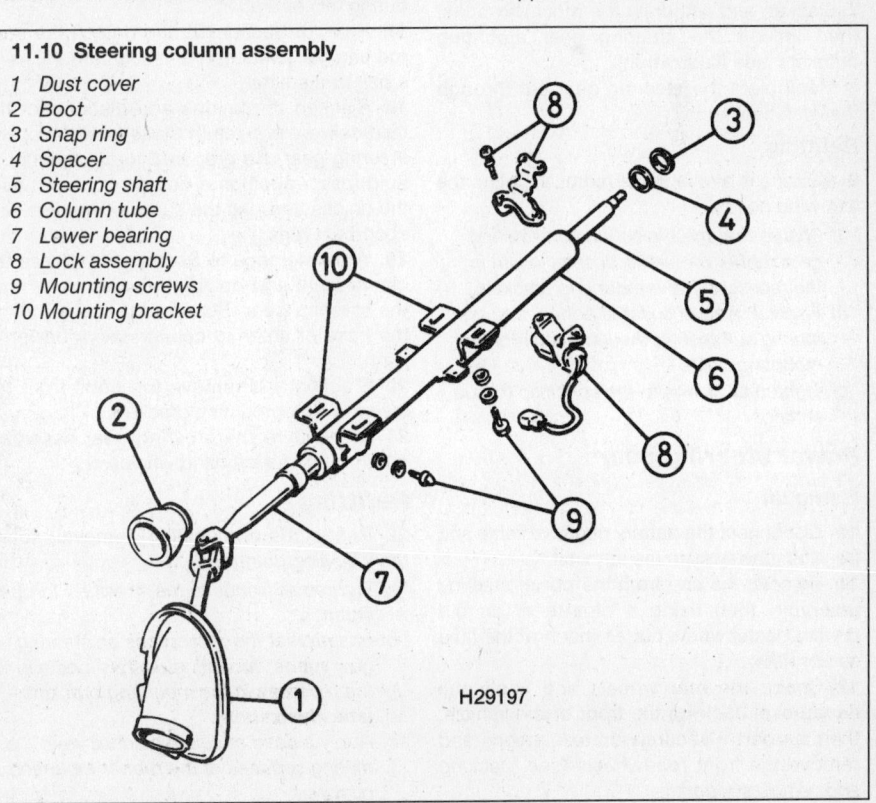

H29197

10•12 Suspension and steering

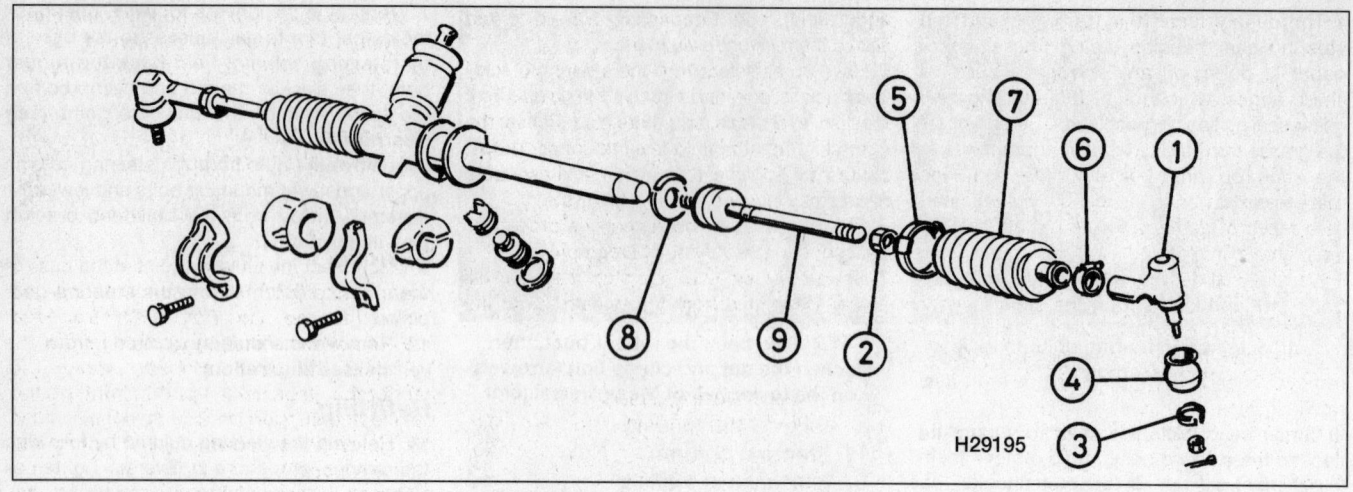

12.7 Manual steering gear assembly

1 Track rod end	3 Snap ring	5 Clip	7 Gaiter	9 Track rod
2 Locknut	4 Duct cover	6 Clip	8 Tab washer	

remove the front roadwheels (see "Jacking and vehicle support").
4 Remove the screws and lower the undertray away from the engine bay.
5 With reference to Section 11, unbolt the universal joint at the base of the steering column from the steering gear pinion. Cut off the clip and detach the dust cover from the steering gear.
6 Disconnect the track rod ends from the hub carrier steering arms, using a ball joint splitter. Refer to Section 16 for details.
7 Slacken and withdraw the mounting bolts, then lift off the steering gear mounting brackets **(see illustration)**.
8 Manipulate the steering gear out through the left wheel arch.

Refitting

9 Refitting is a reversal of removal, noting the following points.
 a) Ensure that the projections on steering gear rubber mounting bushes locate in the recesses in the mounting brackets.
 b) Apply a bead of suitable adhesive to the mating surfaces of the left hand rubber mounting bush.
 c) Tighten all fixings to the specified torque setting.

Power steering gear

Removal

10 Disconnect the battery negative cable and position it away from the terminal.
11 Remove the cap from the power steering reservoir, then using a pipette or an old poultry baster, draw out as much of the fluid as possible.
12 Chock the rear wheels and apply the handbrake. Jack up the front of the vehicle, then support it securely on axle stands and remove the front roadwheels (see "Jacking and vehicle support").
13 Remove the screws and lower the undertray away from the engine bay.
14 To improve access, refer to Chapter 4 and remove the air cleaner assembly and inlet air ducting.
15 With reference to Section 4, unbolt the anti-roll bar from its mountings and remove it from the vehicle.
16 Refer to Chapter 2A and unbolt the rear left hand engine mounting from the crossmember. It will be necessary to support the engine with a lifting beam or similar, during this operation.
17 Refer to Section 16 and detach the track rod end ball joints from the hub carriers, using a ball joint splitter.
18 Slacken the unions and disconnect the fluid delivery and return pipes from the power steering gear. Be prepared for an amount of fluid loss - position a container underneath the unions and pad the surrounding area with absorbent rags.
19 With reference to Section 11, release the clamp band and detach the dust cover from the steering gear. Slacken the clamp bolt at the base of steering column lower universal joint.
20 Slacken and remove the bolts from the steering gear mounting brackets.
21 Manoeuvre the steering gear assembly out through the left hand wheelarch.

Refitting

22 Refitting is a reversal of removal, noting the following points:
 a) Tighten all fixings to the specified torque settings.
 b) Ensure that the projections on steering gear rubber mounting bushes locate in the recesses in the mounting brackets **(see illustration)**.
 c) Apply a bead of suitable adhesive to the mating surfaces of the rubber mounting bushes.
 d) Refill the hydraulic system with the specified grade and quantity of power steering fluid, then thoroughly bleed the system as described in Section 14.
 e) On completion, have the front wheel alignment checked by a Proton dealer or a tyre specialist.

13 Steering gear rubber gaiters - renewal

Note: *New gaiter retaining clips should be used on refitting.*

1 Remove the relevant track-rod end as described in Section 16.
2 If not already done, unscrew the track-rod end locknut from the end of the track-rod.
3 Mark the correct fitted position of the gaiter on the track-rod, then release the gaiter securing clips. Slide the gaiter from the steering gear, and off the end of the track-rod.

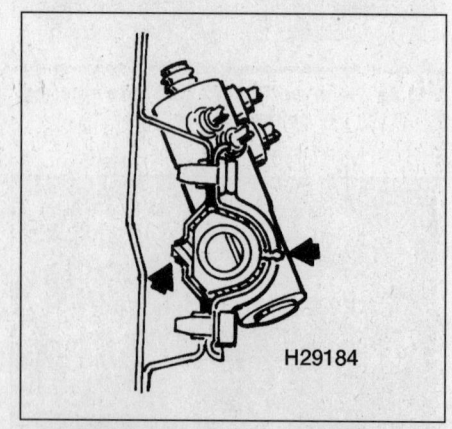

12.22 Ensure that the projections (arrowed) on the steering gear rubber mounting bushes locate in the recesses in the mounting brackets

Suspension and steering 10•13

4 Thoroughly clean the track-rod and the steering gear housing, using fine abrasive paper to polish off any corrosion, burrs or sharp edges, which might damage the new gaiter sealing lips on installation. Scrape off all the grease from the old gaiter, and apply it to the track rod inner balljoint. (This assumes that grease has not been lost or contaminated as a result of damage to the old gaiter. Use fresh grease if in doubt.)

5 Carefully slide the new gaiter onto the track-rod, and locate it on the steering gear housing. Align the outer edge of the gaiter with the mark made on the track-rod prior to removal, then secure it in position with new retaining clips.

6 Screw the track-rod end locknut onto the end of the track-rod.

7 Refit the track rod end (see Section 16).

14 Power steering hydraulic system - bleeding

General

1 The following symptoms indicate that there is air present in the power steering system:
  a) Generation of air bubbles in fluid reservoir.
  b) "Clicking" from the power steering pump.
  c) Excessive "buzzing" or "groaning" from power steering pump.
  d) Increased steering effort.

2 Note that when the vehicle is stationary, or while moving the steering wheel slowly, a "hissing" noise may be produced in the steering gear or the fluid pump. This noise is inherent in the system, and does not indicate any cause for concern.

Bleeding

3 Chock the rear wheels, apply the handbrake, then jack up the front of the vehicle and support securely on axle stands.

4 Check the fluid level in the power steering fluid reservoir (bear in mind that the vehicle will be tilted, so the level cannot be read accurately), and if necessary top-up to just above the relevant level mark.

5 Have an assistant turn the steering quickly from lock to lock, and observe the fluid level. If the fluid level drops, add more fluid. Repeat the operation until the fluid level no longer drops. Failure to achieve this within a reasonable period may indicate a leak in the system.

6 Start the engine and repeat the procedure described in the previous paragraph.

7 Once the fluid level has stabilised, and all air has been bled from the system, lower the vehicle to the ground.

15 Power steering pump - removal and refitting

Removal

1 Drain as much fluid as possible from the power steering reservoir, using a pipette or an old poultry baster.

2 Remove the clip and disconnect the rubber fluid supply hose from the port on the side of the power steering pump. Be prepared for an amount of fluid loss - position a container underneath the port and pad the surrounding area with absorbent rags.

3 Slacken the union and disconnect the fluid delivery hose from the top of the power steering pump. Be prepared for fluid loss.

4 Partially unscrew the upper and lower power steering pump mounting bolts, then rotate the pump towards the engine slightly, to release the tension from the belt. Carefully ease the drivebelt from the pump pulley.

5 Remove the two pump mounting bolts that were slackened earlier, then remove the pump from the engine.

Refitting

6 Refitting is a reversal, noting the following:
  a) On completion, check and if necessary adjust the drivebelt tension (Section 17).
  b) Refill the hydraulic system with the specified grade and quantity of power steering fluid, then thoroughly bleed the system as described in Section 14.
  c) Tighten all fixings to the specified torque.

16 Track-rod end - removal and refitting

Removal

Note: *A balljoint separator tool will be required for this operation. A new track-rod end nut split pin should be used on refitting.*

1 Chock the rear wheels, apply the handbrake, then jack up the front of the vehicle and support on axle stands. Remove the relevant front roadwheel (see "Jacking and vehicle support").

2 Partially unscrew the nut securing the track-rod end to the steering arm. Using a balljoint splitter tool, separate the track-rod end from the steering arm **(see illustration)**.

3 Counterhold the track-rod end using the flats provided, then loosen the track-rod end locknut.

4 Unscrew the track-rod end from the track-rod, counting the exact number of turns required to do so. Alternatively, mark the relationship between the track-rod end and the track-rod using a dab of paint.

Refitting

5 Carefully clean the track-rod end and the track-rod threads.

6 Renew the track-rod end if the rubber dust cover is cracked, split or perished, or if the movement of the balljoint is either excessively slack or stiff. Also check for other signs of damage such as worn threads.

7 Screw the track-rod end onto the track-rod by the number of turns noted before removal. Tighten the locknut temporarily.

8 Ensure that the balljoint taper is clean, then engage the taper with the steering arm on the hub carrier.

9 Refit the balljoint nut, and tighten to the specified torque **(see illustration)**. Check that the split pin holes on the balljoint stud and the

16.2 Using a balljoint splitter tool, separate the track-rod end from the hub carrier steering arm

16.9 Refit the balljoint nut, and tighten to the specified torque

10•14 Suspension and steering

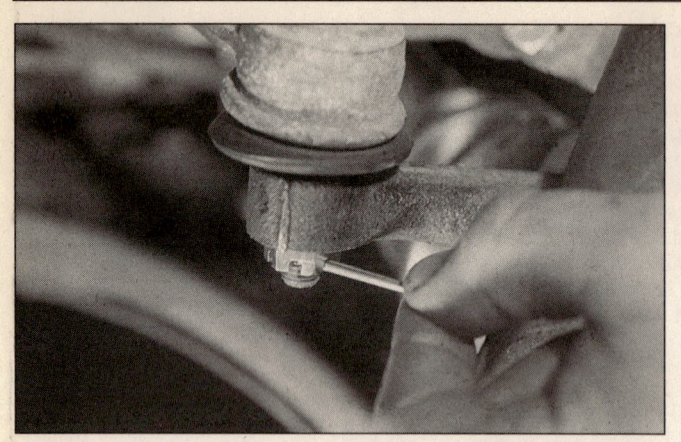

16.10a Fit a new split pin through the end of the ball joint stud

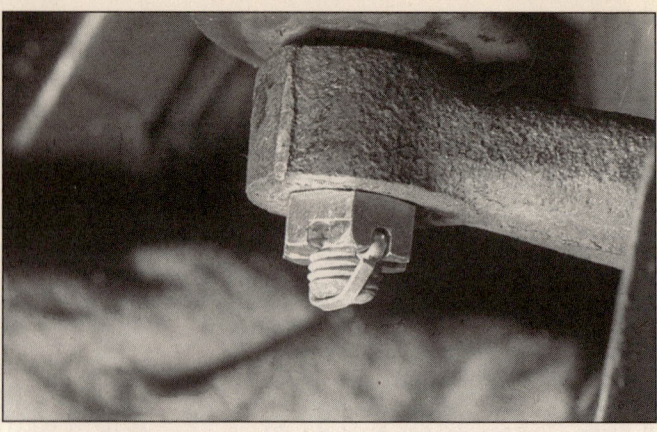

16.10b Splay out the ends of the split pin and bend them back around the top of the nut, to lock it in position

castellations on the nut are aligned. If this is not the case, the nut may be further tightened (up to the *maximum* torque quoted in the *Specifications*), until the holes/castellations are aligned.

10 Fit the split pin through the holes in the balljoint stud. Using a suitable pair of pliers, splay out the ends of the split pin and bend them back around the top of the nut, to lock it in position **(see illustrations)**.

11 Refit the roadwheel, and lower the vehicle to the ground.

12 Have the front wheel alignment checked by a Proton dealer or tyre specialist at the earliest opportunity. **Note:** *If the vehicle has to be driven to have the wheel alignment checked, the track-rod end locknut should be tightened before driving the vehicle.*

17 Power steering pump drivebelt - adjustment

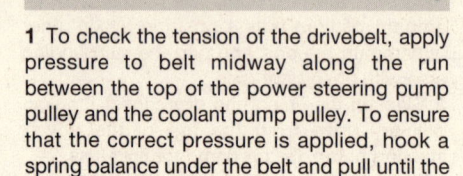

1 To check the tension of the drivebelt, apply pressure to belt midway along the run between the top of the power steering pump pulley and the coolant pump pulley. To ensure that the correct pressure is applied, hook a spring balance under the belt and pull until the gauge reads roughly 10 kg.

2 With the correct pressure applied, check that the deflection of the belt is within the limits given in the *Specifications*.

3 If the deflection is incorrect, due to the belt being either too tight or too loose, adjust the belt tension as follows.

4 Slacken the power steering pump upper and lower mounting bolts by roughly half a turn (see Chapter 1 for details).

5 Pivot the power steering pump body towards or away from the engine, to increase or decrease the tension on the drivebelt, as appropriate.

6 Re-check the belt tension and repeat the above adjustment as required. On completion, tighten the power steering pump mounting bolts to the specified torque wrench setting.

Chapter 11
Bodywork and fittings

Contents

Bonnet - removal, refitting and adjustment 8
Bonnet lock - removal and refitting 10
Bonnet release cable - removal and refitting 9
Boot lid (Saloon models) - removal, refitting and adjustment 16
Boot lid lock components (Saloon models) - removal and refitting 18
Central locking system components - removal and refitting 20
Centre console - removal and refitting 24
Door - removal, refitting and adjustment 12
Door inner trim panel - removal and refitting 13
Door latch, lock cylinder and handle components -
   removal and refitting 14
Door window glass and regulator - removal and refitting 15
Exterior mirror and associated components - removal and refitting .. 21
Facia - removal and refitting 25

Front bumper - removal and refitting 6
General information 1
Maintenance - bodywork and underframe 2
Maintenance - upholstery and carpets 3
Major body damage - repair 5
Minor body damage - repair 4
Radiator grille - removal and refitting 11
Rear bumper - removal and refitting 7
Seats - removal and refitting 23
Sunroof - general information 22
Tailgate and support struts (Aeroback models) -
   removal, refitting and adjustment 17
Tailgate lock and handle components (Aeroback models) -
   removal and refitting 19

Degrees of difficulty

| Easy, suitable for novice with little experience | Fairly easy, suitable for beginner with some experience | Fairly difficult, suitable for competent DIY mechanic | Difficult, suitable for experienced DIY mechanic | Very difficult, suitable for expert DIY or professional |

Specifications

Torque wrench settings	Nm	lbf ft
Door hinge-to-body bolts	25	18
Bonnet hinge-to-body bolts	5	4
Tailgate-to-hinge bolts	15	11
Bootlid-to-hinge bolts	15	11
Seat frame-to-floorpan bolts	20	15

1 General information

The bodyshell is composed of pressed-steel sections which are welded together, although some use of structural adhesives is made. In addition, the front wings are bolted on.

The bonnet, door and some other panels vulnerable to corrosion are fabricated from zinc-coated metal. A coating of anti-chip primer, applied prior to paint spraying provides further protection.

Extensive use is made of plastic materials, mainly in the interior, but also in exterior components. The outer sections of the front and rear bumpers are injection-moulded from a strong, lightweight synthetic material. Plastic components such as wheel arch liners are fitted, to improve the body's resistance to corrosion.

2 Maintenance - bodywork and underframe

1 The general condition of a vehicle's bodywork significantly affects its value. Maintenance is easy, but needs to be regular. Neglect, particularly after minor damage, can lead quickly to further deterioration and costly repair bills. It is important also to keep watch on those parts of the vehicle not immediately visible, for instance the underside, inside all the wheel arches, and the lower part of the engine compartment.

2 The basic maintenance routine for the bodywork is washing - preferably with a lot of water, from a hose. This will remove all the loose solids which may have stuck to the vehicle. It is important to flush these off in such a way as to prevent grit from scratching the finish. The wheel arches and underframe need washing in the same way, to remove any accumulated mud which will retain moisture and tend to encourage rust. Strangely enough, the best time to clean the underframe and wheel arches is in wet weather, when the mud is thoroughly wet and soft. In very wet weather, the underframe is usually cleaned of large accumulations automatically, and this is a good time for inspection.

3 Periodically, except on vehicles with a wax-based underbody protective coating, it is a good idea to have the whole of the underframe of the vehicle steam-cleaned, engine compartment included, so that a thorough inspection can be carried out to see what minor repairs and renovations are necessary. Steam-cleaning is available at many garages, and is necessary for the removal of the accumulation of oily grime, which sometimes is allowed to become thick in certain areas. If steam-cleaning facilities are not available, there are some excellent grease solvents available which can be brush-applied; the dirt can then be simply hosed off.

Note that these methods should not be used on vehicles with wax-based underbody protective coating, or the coating will be removed. Such vehicles should be inspected annually, preferably just prior to Winter, when the underbody should be washed down, and any damage to the wax coating repaired using Undershield. Ideally, a completely fresh coat should be applied. It would also be worth considering the use of such wax-based protection for injection into door panels, sills, box sections, etc, as an additional safeguard against rust damage, where such protection is not provided by the vehicle manufacturer.

4 After washing paintwork, wipe off with a chamois leather to give an unspotted clear finish. A coat of clear protective wax polish will give added protection against chemical pollutants in the air. If the paintwork sheen has dulled or oxidised, use a cleaner/polisher combination to restore the brilliance of the shine. This requires a little effort, but such dulling is usually caused because regular washing has been neglected. Care needs to be taken with metallic paintwork, as special non-abrasive cleaner/polisher is required to avoid damage to the finish. Always check that the door and ventilator opening drain holes and pipes are completely clear, so that water can be drained out. Brightwork should be treated in the same way as paintwork. Windscreens and windows can be kept clear of the smeary film which often appears by the use of a proprietary glass cleaner. Never use any form of wax or other body or chromium polish on glass.

3 Maintenance - upholstery and carpets

Mats and carpets should be brushed or vacuum-cleaned regularly, to keep them free of grit. If they are badly stained, remove them from the vehicle for scrubbing or sponging, and make quite sure they are dry before refitting. Seats and interior trim panels can be kept clean by wiping with a damp cloth and a proprietary cleaner. If they do become stained (which can be more apparent on light-coloured upholstery), use a little liquid detergent and a soft nail brush to scour the grime out of the grain of the material. Do not forget to keep the headlining clean in the same way as the upholstery. When using liquid cleaners inside the vehicle, do not over-wet the surfaces being cleaned. Excessive damp could get into the seams and padded interior, causing stains, offensive odours or even rot. If the inside of the vehicle gets wet accidentally, it is worthwhile taking some trouble to dry it out properly, particularly where carpets are involved. *Do not leave oil or electric heaters inside the vehicle for this purpose.*

4 Minor body damage - repair

Repairs of minor scratches in bodywork

1 If the scratch is very superficial, and does not penetrate to the metal of the bodywork, repair is very simple. Lightly rub the area of the scratch with a paintwork renovator, or a very fine cutting paste to remove loose paint from the scratch, and to clear the surrounding bodywork of wax polish. Rinse the area with clean water.

2 Apply touch-up paint to the scratch using a fine paint brush; continue to apply fine layers of paint until the surface of the paint in the scratch is level with the surrounding paintwork. Allow the new paint at least two weeks to harden, then blend it into the surrounding paintwork by rubbing the scratch area with a paintwork renovator or a very fine cutting paste. Finally, apply a good wax polish.

3 Where the scratch has penetrated right through to the metal of the bodywork, causing the metal to rust, a different repair technique is required. Remove any loose rust from the bottom of the scratch with a penknife, then apply rust-inhibiting paint to prevent the formation of rust in the future. Using a rubber or nylon applicator, fill the scratch with bodystopper paste. If required, this paste can be mixed with cellulose thinners to provide a very thin paste which is ideal for filling narrow scratches. Before the stopper-paste in the scratch hardens, wrap a piece of smooth cotton rag around the top of a finger. Dip the finger in cellulose thinners, and quickly sweep it across the surface of the stopper-paste in the scratch; this will ensure that the surface of the stopper-paste is slightly hollowed. The scratch can now be painted over as described earlier in this Section.

Repairs of dents in bodywork

4 When deep denting of the vehicle's bodywork has taken place, the first task is to pull the dent out, until the affected bodywork almost attains its original shape. There is little point in trying to restore the original shape completely, as the metal in the damaged area will have stretched on impact, and cannot be reshaped fully to its original contour. It is better to bring the level of the dent up to a point which is about 3 mm below the level of the surrounding bodywork. In cases where the dent is very shallow anyway, it is not worth trying to pull it out at all. If the underside of the dent is accessible, it can be hammered out gently from behind, using a mallet with a wooden or plastic head. Whilst doing this, hold a suitable block of wood firmly against the outside of the panel, to absorb the impact from the hammer blows and thus prevent a large area of the bodywork from being "belled-out".

5 Should the dent be in a section of the bodywork which has a double skin, or some other factor making it inaccessible from behind, a different technique is called for. Drill several small holes through the metal inside the area - particularly in the deeper section. Then screw long self-tapping screws into the holes, just sufficiently for them to gain a good purchase in the metal. Now the dent can be pulled out by pulling on the protruding heads of the screws with a pair of pliers.

6 The next stage of the repair is the removal of the paint from the damaged area, and from an inch or so of the surrounding "sound" bodywork. This is accomplished most easily by using a wire brush or abrasive pad on a power drill, although it can be done just as effectively by hand, using sheets of abrasive paper. To complete the preparation for filling, score the surface of the bare metal with a screwdriver or the tang of a file, or alternatively, drill small holes in the affected area. This will provide a really good "key" for the filler paste.

7 To complete the repair, see the Section on filling and respraying.

Repairs of rust holes or gashes in bodywork

8 Remove all paint from the affected area, and from an inch or so of the surrounding "sound" bodywork, using an abrasive pad or a wire brush on a power drill. If these are not available, a few sheets of abrasive paper will do the job most effectively. With the paint removed, you will be able to judge the severity of the corrosion, and therefore decide whether to renew the whole panel (if this is possible) or to repair the affected area. New body panels are not as expensive as most people think, and it is often quicker and more satisfactory to fit a new panel than to attempt to repair large areas of corrosion.

9 Remove all fittings from the affected area, except those which will act as a guide to the original shape of the damaged bodywork (eg headlight shells, etc). Then, using tin snips or a hacksaw blade, remove all loose metal and any other metal badly affected by corrosion. Hammer the edges of the hole inwards, in order to create a slight depression for the filler paste.

10 Wire-brush the affected area to remove the powdery rust from the
surface of the remaining metal. Paint the affected area with rust-inhibiting paint; if the back of the rusted area is accessible, treat this also.

11 Before filling can take place, it will be necessary to block the hole in some way. This can be achieved by the use of aluminium or plastic mesh, or aluminium tape.

12 Aluminium or plastic mesh, or glass-fibre matting, is probably the best material to use for a large hole. Cut a piece to the approximate size and shape of the hole to be filled, then position it in the hole so that its edges are below the level of the surrounding bodywork. It can be retained in position by several blobs of filler paste around its periphery.

13 Aluminium tape should be used for small or very narrow holes. Pull a piece off the roll, trim it to the approximate size and shape required, then pull off the backing paper (if used) and stick the tape over the hole; it can be overlapped if the thickness of one piece is insufficient. Burnish down the edges of the tape with the handle of a screwdriver or similar, to ensure that the tape is securely attached to the metal underneath.

Bodywork repairs - filling and respraying

14 Before using this Section, see the Sections on dents, scratches, rust holes and gash repairs.

15 Many types of bodyfiller are available, but generally speaking, those proprietary kits which contain a tin of filler paste and a tube of resin hardener are best for this type of repair, or a proprietary ready mixed filler, which can be used directly from the tube. A wide, flexible plastic or nylon applicator will be found invaluable for imparting a smooth and well-contoured finish to the surface of the filler.

16 Mix up a little filler on a clean piece of card or board - measure the hardener carefully (follow the maker's instructions on the pack), otherwise the filler will set too rapidly or too slowly. Alternatively, a ready mixed filler can be used straight from the tube without mixing, but daylight is required to cure it. Using the applicator, apply the filler paste to the prepared area; draw the applicator across the surface of the filler to achieve the correct contour and to level the surface. As soon as a contour that approximates to the correct one is achieved, stop working the paste - if you carry on too long, the paste will become sticky and begin to "pick-up" on the applicator. Continue to add thin layers of filler paste at 20-minute intervals, until the level of the filler is just proud of the surrounding bodywork.

17 Once the filler has hardened, the excess can be removed using a metal plane or file. From then on, progressively-finer grades of abrasive paper should be used, starting with a 40-grade production paper, and finishing with a 400-grade wet-and-dry paper. Always wrap the abrasive paper around a flat rubber, cork, or wooden block - otherwise the surface of the filler will not be completely flat. During the smoothing of the filler surface, the wet-and-dry paper should be periodically rinsed in water. This will ensure that a very smooth finish is imparted to the filler at the final stage.

18 At this stage, the "dent" should be surrounded by a ring of bare metal, which in turn should be encircled by the finely "feathered" edge of the good paintwork. Rinse the repair area with clean water, until all of the dust produced by the rubbing-down operation has gone.

19 Spray the whole area with a light coat of primer - this will show up any imperfections in the surface of the filler. Repair these imperfections with fresh filler paste or bodystopper, and once more smooth the surface with abrasive paper. If bodystopper is used, it can be mixed with cellulose thinners, to form a really thin paste which is ideal for filling small holes. Repeat this spray-and-repair procedure until you are satisfied that the surface of the filler, and the feathered edge of the paintwork, are perfect. Clean the repair area with clean water, and allow to dry fully.

20 The repair area is now ready for final spraying. Paint spraying must be carried out in a warm, dry, windless and dust-free atmosphere. This condition can be created artificially if you have access to a large indoor working area, but if you are forced to work in the open, you will have to pick your day very carefully. If you are working indoors, dousing the floor in the work area with water will help to settle the dust which would otherwise be in the atmosphere. If the repair area is confined to one body panel, mask off the surrounding panels; this will help to minimise the effects of a slight mis-match in paint colours. Bodywork fittings (eg chrome strips, door handles etc) will also need to be masked off. Use genuine masking tape, and several thicknesses of newspaper, for the masking operations.

21 Before commencing to spray, agitate the aerosol can thoroughly, then spray a test area (an old tin, or similar) until the technique is mastered. Cover the repair area with a thick coat of primer; the thickness should be built up using several thin layers of paint, rather than one thick one. Using 400-grade wet-and-dry paper, rub down the surface of the primer until it is really smooth. While doing this, the work area should be thoroughly doused with water, and the wet-and-dry paper periodically rinsed in water. Allow to dry before spraying on more paint.

22 Spray on the top coat, again building up the thickness by using several thin layers of paint. Start spraying in the centre of the repair area, and then, using a circular motion, work outwards until the whole repair area and about 2 inches of the surrounding original paintwork is covered. Remove all masking material 10 to 15 minutes after spraying on the final coat of paint.

23 Allow the new paint at least two weeks to harden, then, using a paintwork renovator or a very fine cutting paste, blend the edges of the paint into the existing paintwork. Finally, apply wax polish.

Plastic components

24 With the use of more and more plastic body components by the vehicle manufacturers (eg bumpers, spoilers, and in some cases major body panels), rectification of more serious damage to such items has become a matter of either entrusting repair work to a specialist in this field, or renewing complete components. Repair of such damage by the DIY owner is not really feasible, owing to the cost of the equipment and materials required for effecting such repairs. The basic technique involves making a groove along the line of the crack in the plastic, using a rotary burr in a power drill. The damaged part is then welded back together, using a hot air gun to heat up and fuse a plastic filler rod into the groove. Any excess is then removed, and the area rubbed down to a smooth finish. It is important that a filler rod of the correct plastic is used, as body components can be made of many different types (eg polycarbonate, ABS, polypropylene).

25 Damage of a less serious nature (abrasions, minor cracks etc) can be repaired by the DIY owner using a two-part epoxy filler repair material, or a ready mixed filler which can be used directly from the tube. Once mixed in equal proportions (or applied directly from the tube in the case of the ready mixed filler), this is used in similar fashion to the bodywork filler used on metal panels. The filler is usually cured in twenty to thirty minutes, ready for sanding and painting.

26 If the owner is renewing a complete component himself, or if he has repaired it with epoxy filler, he will be left with the problem of finding a suitable paint for finishing which is compatible with the type of plastic used. At one time, the use of a universal paint was not possible, owing to the complex range of plastics encountered in body component applications. Standard paints, generally speaking, will not bond to plastic or rubber satisfactorily, but a proprietary brand of paint, to match any plastic or rubber finish, can be obtained from dealers. However, it is now possible to obtain a plastic body parts finishing kit which consists of a pre-primer treatment, a primer and coloured top coat. Full instructions are normally supplied with a kit, but basically, the method of use is to first apply the pre-primer to the component concerned, and allow it to dry for up to 30 minutes. Then the primer is applied, and left to dry for about an hour before finally applying the special-coloured top coat. The result is a correctly-coloured component, where the paint will flex with the plastic or rubber; a property that standard paint does not normally posses.

5 Major body damage - repair

Where serious damage has occurred, or large areas need renewal due to neglect, it means that complete new panels will need welding-in, and this is best left to professionals. If the damage is due to impact, it will also be necessary to check completely the alignment of the bodyshell, and this can only be carried out accurately by a Proton dealer using special jigs. If the alignment of the bodyshell is not corrected, the cars handling may be seriously affected. In addition, excessive stress may be imposed on the steering, suspension, tyres transmission, causing abnormal wear or complete failure.

11•4 Bodywork and fittings

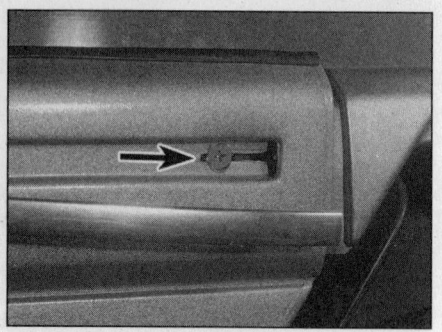

6.1 Release the protective insert from the bumper, then slacken and withdraw the bumper side mounting screw (arrowed) - Mpi model shown

6.3 On later 12-valve and MPi models, work along the lower edge of the bumper and remove the securing screws (arrowed)

6.4 Remove the nut (arrowed) that secures the side stay to the inside of the bumper

6 Front bumper - removal and refitting

Removal

1 On Mpi models, remove the protective insert from the bumper (where applicable), by working along its length and releasing the adhesive backing, using a flat bladed instrument such as a filling knife. Slacken and withdraw the bumper side mounting screws **(see illustration)**.
2 Refer to Chapter 12 and remove the front indicator lamp units (Mpi models) / sidelight units (8-valve and 12-valve models).
3 On later 12-valve and MPi models, work along the lower edge of the bumper and remove the securing screws **(see illustration)**.
4 Working from the underside of the vehicle, remove the nuts that secure the side stays to the inside of the bumper **(see illustration)**.
5 On early 8-valve models, remove the screws and unclip both cover panels from either side of the bumper **(see illustration)**.
6 Working between the front of the bumper and the bodywork, remove the nuts from the bolts that secure the bumper to its mounting brackets **(see illustration)**.
7 Withdraw the bolts from the mounting brackets, then carefully lift the bumper away from the front of the vehicle.

Refitting

8 Refitting is a reversal of removal.

7 Rear bumper - removal and refitting

8-valve models

Removal

1 If required, the protective strip can be removed from the upper edge of the bumper. Work along its length and release the retaining clips one by one, using a flat bladed instrument such as a filling knife.

6.5 On early 8-valve models, remove the screw(s) (arrowed) and unclip both cover panels from either side of the bumper

2 Lift the tailgate/bootlid, unscrew the fixings and remove the plastic moulding from the sill.
3 Similarly, unscrew the fixings and remove the plastic mouldings from either side of the loadspace.
4 Partially fold back the load space carpet trim (where applicable), to expose the rear bumper mounting nuts. Remove the nuts and lift the bumper away from the rear of the vehicle.

Refitting

5 Refitting is a reversal of removal.

12-valve and MPi models

Removal

6 Carefully unclip the protective strip from the

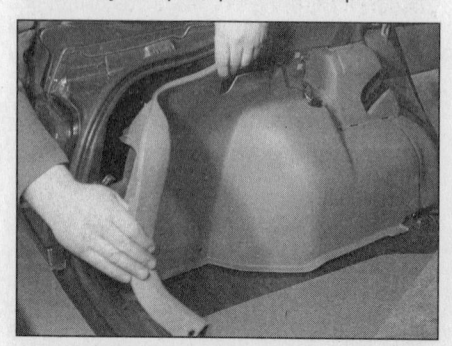

7.7 Extract the fasteners and remove the trim panels from either side of the load space area

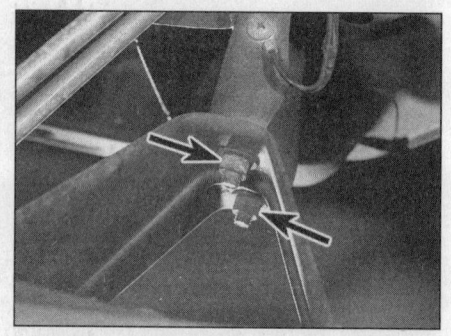

6.6 Remove the nuts (arrowed) from the bolts that secure the bumper to its mounting brackets

upper edge of the bumper, using a suitable tool if necessary. On Aeroback models, prise off the rubber seal.
7 Where applicable, extract the fasteners and remove the trim panels from either side of the load space area **(see illustration)**.
8 Release the press stud fixings and remove the plastic moulding from the sill **(see illustration)**.
9 Remove the nuts from the bumper side securing screws, from within the load space **(see illustration)**.
10 Partially fold back the load space carpet trim (where applicable), to expose the rear bumper mounting nuts
11 Unplug the wiring from the number plate lamp at the connector.

7.8 Release the press stud fixings and remove the plastic moulding from the sill

Bodywork and fittings 11•5

7.9 Remove the nut (arrowed) from the bumper side securing screw, from within the load space

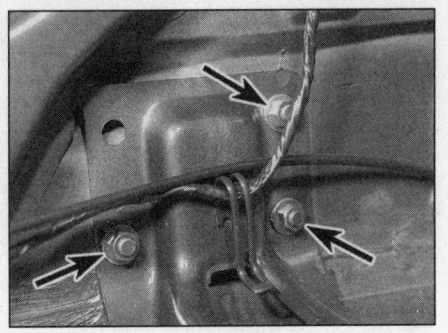

7.12 Bumper-to-bracket mounting nuts (arrowed)

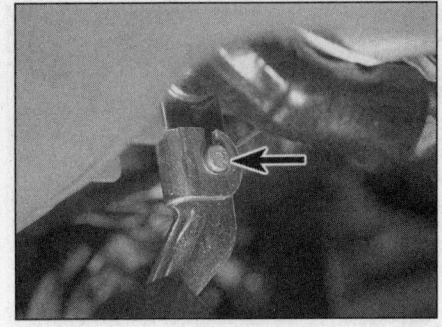

9.4 Unhook the nipple (arrowed) at the end of the inner part of the release cable from the release handle

12 Remove the bumper mounting nuts **(see illustration)** from both brackets, then lift the bumper away from the rear of the vehicle, carefully sliding the leading edges of the bumper off their brackets.

Refitting

13 Refitting is a reversal of removal.

8 Bonnet - removal, refitting and adjustment

⚠ **Warning: It is essential that the help of an assistant is enlisted during this operation.**

Removal

1 Open the bonnet and prop it up with a stout pole.
2 Disconnect the washer jet hoses at the three way joint.
3 Mark the relationship between the hinges and the edge of the bonnet using a soft pencil or a marker pen. Slacken and unscrew the hinge-to-bonnet bolts - have an assistant support the bonnet whilst the last bolts are removed.
4 With the help of your assistant, lift off the bonnet and set it down on its edge, using a dust sheet to protect the paintwork.

Refitting

5 Refit the bonnet by reversing the removal process, using the markings made during removal to achieve the correct alignment. Note that the bolt mounting holes are slotted to allow adjustment if required. On completion, tighten the bolts to the specified torque.
6 Check that the bonnet fastens and releases in a satisfactory manner. If necessary, adjust the bonnet lock components, as described in Section 12.

9 Bonnet release cable - removal and refitting

Removal

1 Secure the bonnet in the fully open position. Detach the bonnet release cable from the striker plate operating lever.
2 Work along the exposed length of the release cable in the engine bay and extract the cable from its securing clips.
3 In the right hand footwell, extract the fixings and lower the sound insulation panel (where fitted) away from the underside of the steering column/facia.
4 Unhook the nipple at the end of the inner part of the release cable **(see illustration)** from the release handle.
5 Release the cable from the remaining clips under the facia, then carefully pull the entire cable, together with the bulkhead grommet, into the footwell.

Refitting

6 Refit the cable by reversing the removal process. Position the cable in the engine bay securing clips, according to the alignment markings on the cables outer sheath.

10 Bonnet lock - removal and refitting

Latch and release lever assembly

Removal

1 Slacken and unscrew the bolts, then lower the latch assembly away from the bonnet.

Refitting

2 Refitting is a reversal of removal. Use the alignment markings made during removal to aid accurate refitting. Note that the mounting holes are slotted to allow adjustment if required. On completion, tighten the bolts securely.

3 The extension of the bonnet pin may be adjusted in necessary, by slackening the locknut and turning the pin with a flat-bladed screwdriver.

Striker plate

Removal

4 Remove the front grille (see Section 11).
5 Mark the relationship between the striker plate and the bodywork using a soft pencil or marker pen. The striker plate can then be removed by slackening and withdrawing the securing bolts and unhooking the release cable from the operating lever **(see illustration)**.

Refitting

6 Refitting is a reversal of removal. Use the alignment markings made during removal to aid accurate refitting. Note that the mounting holes are slotted to allow adjustment if required. On completion, tighten the bolts securely.

Buffers

7 If necessary, adjust the protrusion of the rubber buffers on the front crossmember, (located above each headlamp unit) by slackening the locknut and screwing them in or out, as appropriate. When the rubber buffers are correctly adjusted, there should be just enough free movement to allow the bonnet to be closed and locked easily, without using excessive force, but not enough to allow the bonnet to rattle when secured in the locked position.

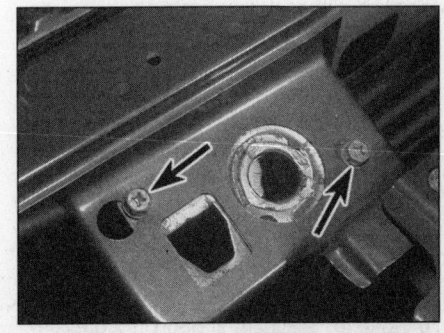

10.5 Bonnet lock striker plate securing bolts (arrowed)

11•6 Bodywork and fittings

11.2 Remove the self-tapping screws (arrowed) from the upper edge of the grille

11.4 Ensure that the lug (arrowed) on the lower edge of the grille engages with the recess in the bumper moulding

12.4 Prise the wiring harness grommet (arrowed) from the leading edge of the door

11 Radiator grille - removal and refitting

Removal

1 Open the bonnet and secure it in the fully open position using the stay.
2 Remove the self-tapping screws from the upper edge of the grille **(see illustration)**.
3 Unclip the lower edge of the grille from the bumper and remove it from the front of the vehicle.

Refitting

4 Refitting is a reversal of removal. Ensure that the lugs on the lower edge of the grille engage with the corresponding recesses in the bumper moulding **(see illustration)**.

12 Door - removal, refitting and adjustment

Note: *This procedure is applicable both to the front and rear doors.*

Removal

Note: *A new door check strut roll-pin will be required on refitting.*

1 Disconnect the battery negative lead and position it away from the terminal.
2 Refer to Section 13 and remove the door inner trim panel.
3 Unplug all electrical wiring from the connectors inside the door space, labelling each one to aid correct refitting later.
4 Prise the wiring harness grommet from the leading edge of the door, then draw the wiring harness out through the exposed hole **(see illustration)**.
5 Extract the roll-pin and separate the door check strut from the door pillar **(see illustration)**.
6 Have an assistant support the door, then unscrew the door hinge bolts, and lift the door from the vehicle **(see illustration)**.

12.5 Extract the roll-pin and separate the door check strut from the door pillar

Refitting

7 Refitting is a reversal of removal. On completion, tighten the hinge bolts securely.

Adjustment

8 Close the door carefully (in case the alignment is incorrect) and check the fit of the door with the surrounding panels.
9 If adjustment is required, loosen the hinge-to-body securing bolts (the bolt holes are elongated to allow for adjustment) and move the hinges as required to achieve satisfactory alignment. Tighten the hinge bolts securely on completion.
10 Check the operation of the door lock. If necessary, slacken the securing bolts, and adjust the position of the lock striker on the body pillar to achieve satisfactory alignment. Tighten the bolts securely on completion.

13.3a Fold back the cap and remove the screw . . .

12.6 Unscrew the door hinge bolts (arrowed) then lift the door from the vehicle

13 Door inner trim panel - removal and refitting

Removal

Note: *This section describes the removal of the front door trim panel; the procedure for removing the rear door trim panel is essentially the same.*

1 Disconnect the battery negative lead and position it away from the terminal.
2 With reference to Section 21, remove the trim panel from the rear of the door mirror fixings.
3 Fold back the cap and remove the screw, then lift off the door grab handle moulding **(see illustrations)**.

13.3b . . . then lift off the door grab handle moulding

Bodywork and fittings 11•7

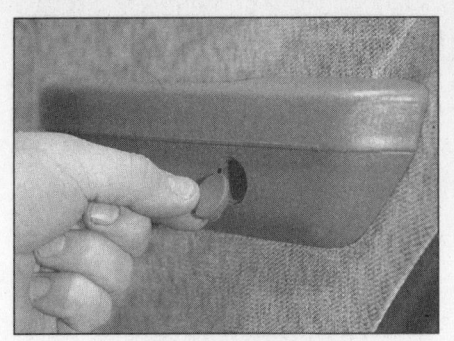

13.4a Lift off the plastic caps (rear door shown) . . .

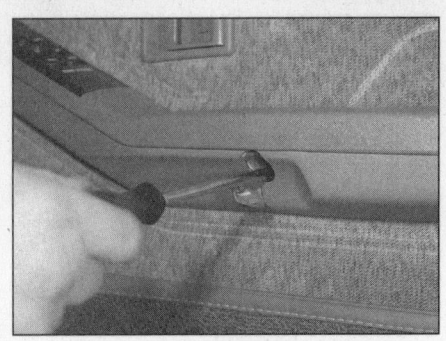

13.4b . . . and remove the screws (front door shown) . . .

13.4c . . . then prise out the door grab handle moulding (front door shown)

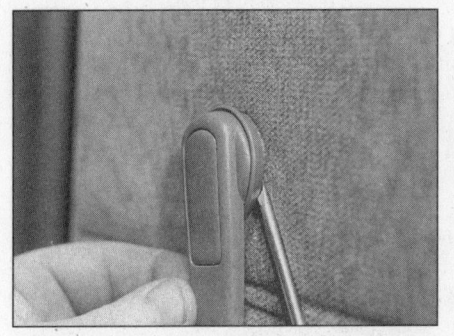

13.5a On models with manual windows, insert a flat-bladed screwdriver between door trim panel and the winder handle. . .

13.5b . . . then release the clip (arrowed) using the tip of the screwdriver and pull the winder handle from its shaft

13.6 Using a forked tool, release the press-stud clips located around the edge of the trim panel

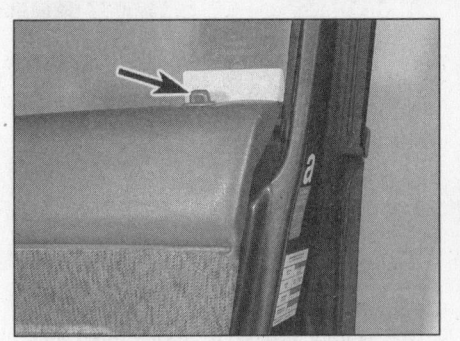

13.7 Lift the trim panel upwards over the locking knob (arrowed) and away from the door

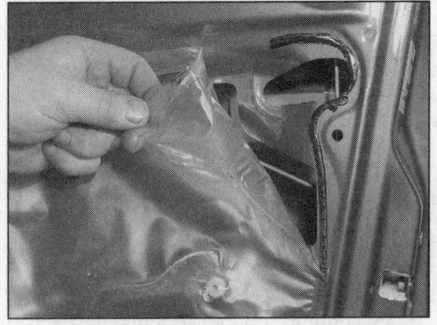

13.8 Peel the plastic sealing sheet away from the door. If necessary, use a sharp blade to split the sealant bead

4 Prise out the plastic caps, then remove the securing screws and lift off the armrest. Unplug the wiring connector for the electric window switch unit from the armrest - label it to aid correct refitting later **(see illustrations)**.
5 On models with manual windows, insert a flat-bladed screwdriver between the door trim panel and the window winder handle. Release the clip using the tip of the screwdriver then pull the winder handle from its shaft **(see illustrations)**.
6 Using a suitable forked tool inserted between the door and the trim panel, release the press-stud clips located around the edge of the panel **(see illustration)**.
7 Lift the trim panel upwards over the locking knob and away from the door **(see illustration)**.
8 If work is to be carried out on the door internal components, it will be necessary to remove the plastic sealing sheet from the inside of the door. Start at one corner of the sheet and carefully peel it away, using a sharp blade to split the sealant bead **(see illustration)**.
9 Store the detached sealing sheet such that it cannot become contaminated with dust; this will allow it to be re-used later.

Refitting
10 Refitting is a reversal of removal, bearing in mind the following points:
a) Ensure that the sealing sheet is correctly refitted, press it on firmly to ensure that it is adequately sealed around its edges. It should be possible to use the original sealant, but if necessary, new sealant can be obtained from a Proton dealer.
b) Before refitting the trim panel, feed the electric window switch wiring through the aperture in the front of the panel (where applicable).
c) Make sure that the weatherstrip engages securely with the edge of the door as the panel is refitted.

14 Door latch, lock cylinder and handle components - removal and refitting

1 Ensure the door window glass is in the fully closed position, then disconnect the battery negative cable and position it away from the terminal. Refer to Section 13 and remove the door inner trim panel and sealing sheet.

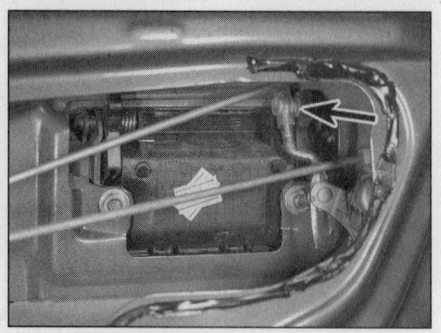

11•8 Bodywork and fittings

14.2a Compress the lugs of plastic clip (arrowed) - rear door shown

14.2b Link rod clip (arrowed) at rear of front door exterior handle (removed for clarity)

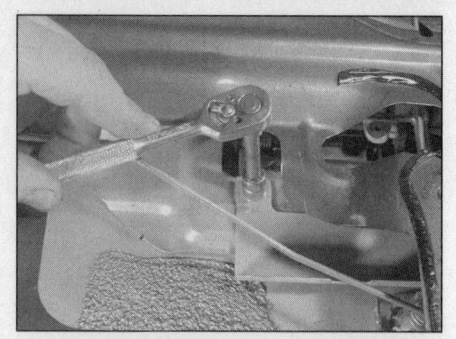

14.3a Slacken and remove the handle retaining nuts (front door shown) . . .

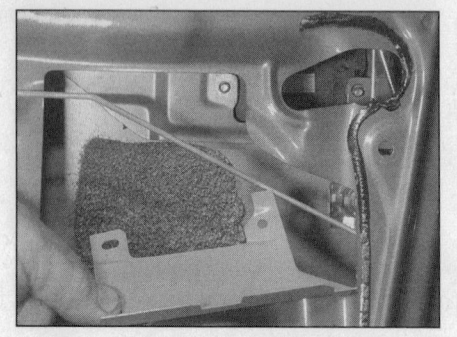

14.3b . . . remove the anti-theft plate . . .

14.3c . . . then lift the handle assembly from the door

14.3d Location of rear door exterior handle mounting nuts (arrowed)

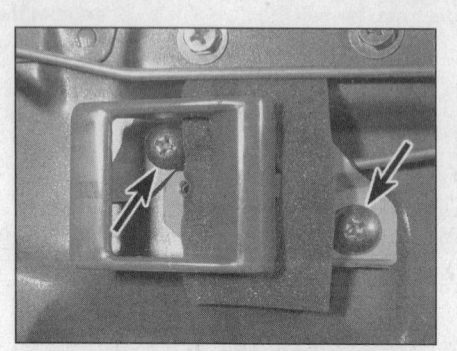

14.5 Interior handle securing screws (arrowed)

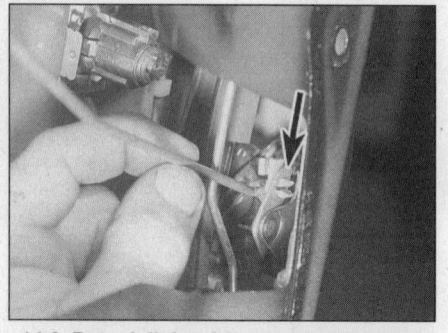

14.6 Detach linkrod from operating lever (arrowed) on the side of lock mechanism

Door exterior handle

Removal

2 At the rear of the door exterior handle mechanism, compress the lugs of the plastic clip and detach the link rod from the lever **(see illustrations)**.

3 Slacken and remove the handle retaining nuts. Where applicable, remove the anti-theft plate, then lift the handle assembly from the door **(see illustrations)**.

Refitting

4 Refit the door handle by following the removal procedure in reverse. Ensure that the link rod engages correctly with the handle mechanism operating lever.

Door interior handle

5 Remove the two screws that secure the handle assembly to the door **(see illustration)**.

6 Detach the linkrod from the operating lever on the side of the lock mechanism **(see illustration)**.

7 Lift the handle and link rod from the door **(see illustration)**.

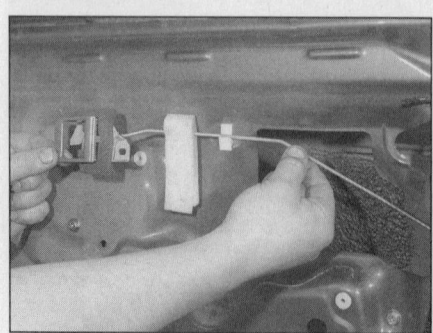

14.7 Lift the handle and link rod from the door

Lock cylinder

8 Slide the metal retaining clip from the rear of the cylinder using a pair of pliers **(see illustration)**.

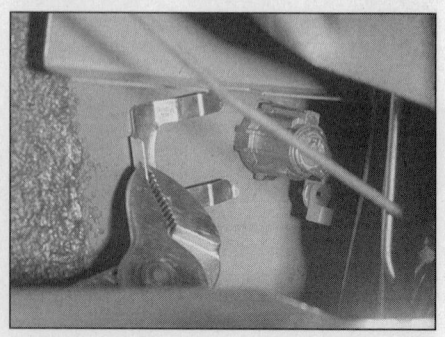

14.8 Slide the metal retaining clip from the rear of the cylinder

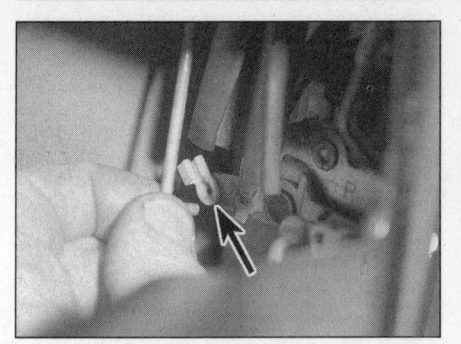

Bodywork and fittings 11•9

14.9 Release link rod from operating lever (arrowed) on side of the lock mechanism

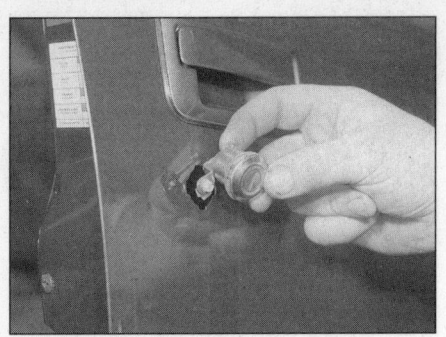

14.10 Extract the lock cylinder from the door

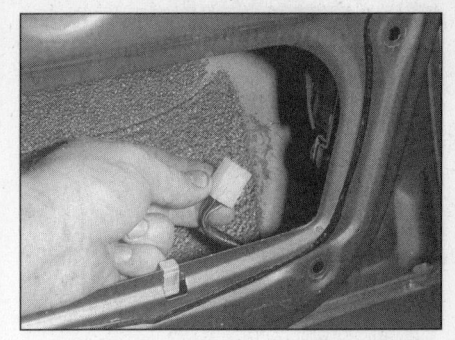

14.12 Unplug the wiring for the central locking motor and switches, at the multiway connector

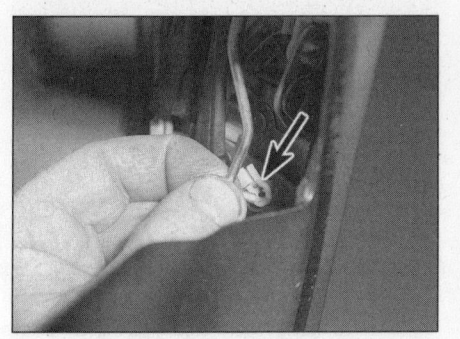

14.13a Disconnect the locking knob link rod from the operating lever (arrowed) on the top of the lock mechanism . . .

14.13b . . . then withdraw the rod from the door

9 Release the link rod from the operating lever on the side of the lock mechanism (see illustration).
10 Extract the lock cylinder from the door, together with the link rod (see illustration).
11 Refitting is a reversal of removal.

Lock mechanism

Removal

12 Working inside the door, unplug the wiring for the central locking motor and switches, at the multiway connector (see illustration).
13 Disconnect the locking knob link rod from the operating lever on the top of the lock mechanism, then withdraw the rod from the door (see illustrations).
14 Detach the exterior door handle link rod from the lock mechanism operating lever - refer to the earlier sub-section.
15 At the trailing edge of the door, remove the three screws that secure the lock mechanism to the door (see illustration).
16 Withdraw the lock mechanism from the door space (see illustration).

17 Note that on the rear door, the arrangement is slightly different, in that the central locking servo motor is mounted separately (see Section 20). In addition, the locking knob link rod operates horizontally, although the method of connection to the lock mechanism is the same.

Refitting

18 Refitting is a reversal of removal. On completion, tighten the lock mechanism retaining screws securely.

15 Door window glass and regulator - removal and refitting

Door window glass

Removal

1 Operate the window regulator mechanism, such that the glass is positioned halfway down the aperture.
2 On models with electric windows, disconnect the battery negative cable and position it away from the terminal.

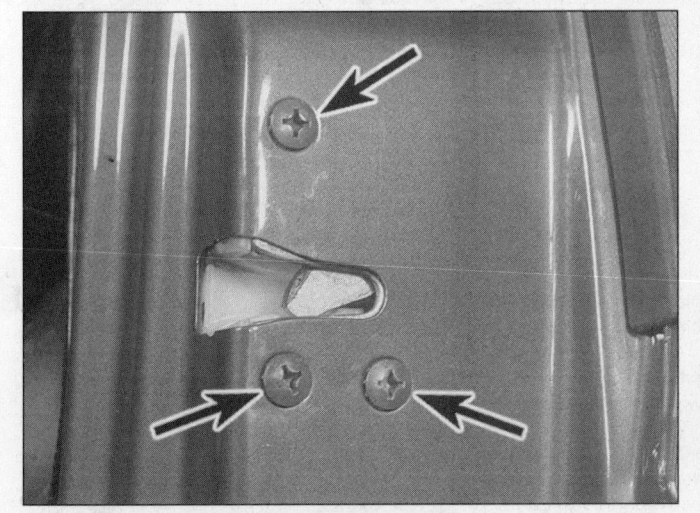

14.15 Remove the three screws (arrowed) that secure the lock mechanism to the door

14.16 Withdraw the lock mechanism from the door space (front door shown)

11•10 Bodywork and fittings

15.4a Remove the window glass holder-to-regulator mechanism screws (front door with electric windows shown)

15.4b Window glass holder to regulator mechanism screws (Rear door with manual windows shown)

15.5 Tilt the glass forward, then lift it out through the door aperture

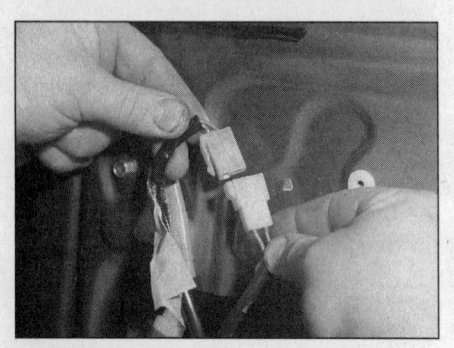

15.8 On models with electric windows, unplug the regulator motor wiring connector

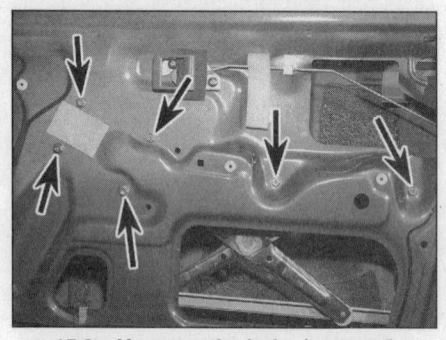

15.9a Unscrew the bolts (arrowed) securing the regulator to the door (front door with electric windows shown)

15.9b Regulator upper securing bolts (rear door with manual windows)

15.9c Regulator lower securing bolt (rear door with manual windows)

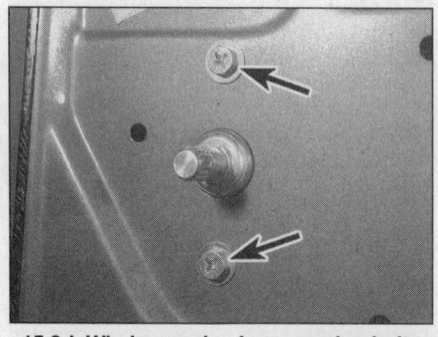

15.9d Winder mechanism securing bolts (rear door with manual windows)

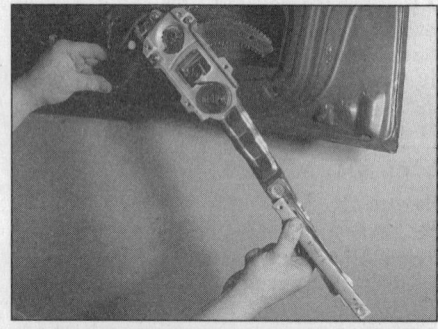

15.10 Manipulate the complete regulator assembly out through aperture in the door (front door with electric windows shown)

3 Remove the door inner trim panel and the plastic sealing sheet (see Section 13).
4 Support the window glass, then slacken and remove the screws that secure the window glass holder to the regulator mechanism **(see illustrations)**.
5 Tilt the glass forward, then lift it out through the door aperture, manipulating it past the weatherstrips **(see illustration)**.

Refitting

6 Refitting is a reversal of removal, bearing in mind the following points:
  a) Ensure all weather strips are seated on the edges of the window aperture.
  b) Check the operation of the window regulator mechanism before refitting the door inner trim panel.

  c) Refit the door inner trim panel with reference to Section 13.

Door window regulator

Removal

7 Detach the window glass from the regulator mechanism, as described earlier in this Section.
8 On models with electric windows, unplug the regulator motor wiring connector **(see illustration)**.
9 Unscrew the bolts securing the regulator to the door **(see illustrations)**. **Note:** *Carefully mark the relationship between the guide rails and the door to ensure correct adjustment on refitting.*

10 Manipulate the complete regulator assembly out through the aperture in the door **(see illustration)**.
11 The winder/motor assembly remains connected to the regulator mechanism.

Refitting

12 Refitting is a reversal of removal, bearing in mind the following points:
  a) Ensure that all weather strips are securely seated on the edges of the window aperture.
  b) Check the operation of the window mechanism before refitting the door inner trim panel.
  c) Refit the door inner trim panel with reference to Section 13.

Bodywork and fittings 11•11

16 Boot lid (Saloon models) - removal, refitting and adjustment

Removal

1 Disconnect the battery negative lead.
2 Open the boot lid, and have an assistant support it in the open position.
3 Release the securing clips, and release the lock release cable from its securing clips.
4 Disconnect the lock release cable from the bootlid lock mechanism.
5 Using a pencil or felt-tipped pen, mark the outline of each boot hinge relative to the boot lid, to use as a guide on refitting.
6 Unscrew the bolts securing the hinges to the boot lid, then lift the boot lid from the vehicle - take care not to scratch the bodywork as the boot lid is removed (see illustration).

Refitting

7 With the aid of an assistant, offer up the boot lid, and loosely fit the retaining bolts. Align the hinges with the marks made on removal, then tighten the retaining bolts securely.
8 Adjust the alignment of the boot lid as follows.

Adjustment

9 Close the boot lid carefully, in case the alignment is incorrect, which may cause scratching on the lid or the body as the boot lid is closed), and check for alignment with the adjacent panels. If necessary, slacken the hinge bolts and re-align the boot lid to suit. Once the boot lid is correctly aligned, tighten the hinge bolts to the specified torque.
10 Once the boot lid is correctly aligned, check that the boot lid fastens and releases in a satisfactory manner. If adjustment is necessary, slacken the boot lid lock retaining bolts, and adjust the position of the lock to suit. Once the lock is operating correctly, securely tighten its retaining bolts.

16.6 Bootlid hinge bolts (arrowed)

17 Tailgate and support struts (Aeroback models) - removal, refitting and adjustment

Support struts

1 Open the tailgate and support it using a suitable prop.
2 At the top of the strut, prise out the locking clip with a screwdriver (see illustration).
3 Compress the strut slightly and detach it from the tailgate.

⚠️ **Warning: The strut may still be under tension and could extend suddenly once it is detached.**

4 Detach the lower end of the strut unit from the bodywork in a similar manner.
5 Refitting is a reversal of removal.

Tailgate

Removal

6 Disconnect the battery negative lead.
7 Extract the press-stud fixings and remove the tailgate interior trim panel (see illustrations).
8 Working inside the tailgate, disconnect all wiring harness connectors and unbolt the earth lead(s). Check for any other wiring connectors which must be disconnected to facilitate tailgate removal. **Note:** *Carefully label each wiring harness connector to aid correct refitting.*
9 Tie a length of string to the wiring harness, then prise the wiring harness grommets from the edge of the tailgate (see illustration), and feed the wiring through the aperture in the tailgate. Untie the string from the wiring connector, and leave the string in place in the tailgate, to aid refitting.
10 Where applicable, remove the fluid hose from the tailgate washer nozzle (see illustration). Tie a length of string to the hose and draw it out of the tailgate using the procedure carried out on the wiring harness.

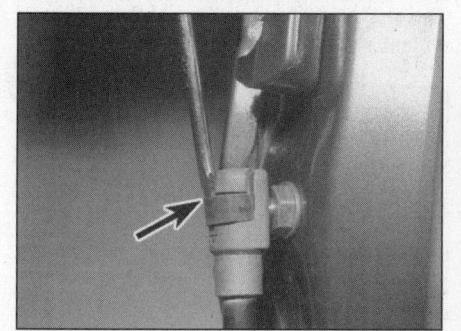

17.2 Prise out the locking clip (arrowed) with a screwdriver

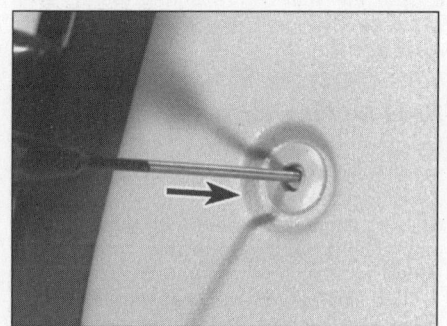

17.7a To remove the press-stud fixings, first press in the centre button with a thin punch...

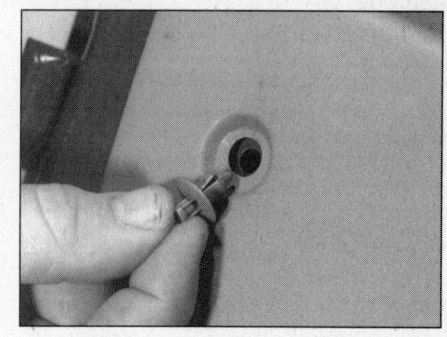

17.7b ...then prise out the clip with a forked tool

17.9 Wiring harness grommets (arrowed) inside tailgate aperture

17.10 Remove the fluid hose from the tailgate washer nozzle

11•12 Bodywork and fittings

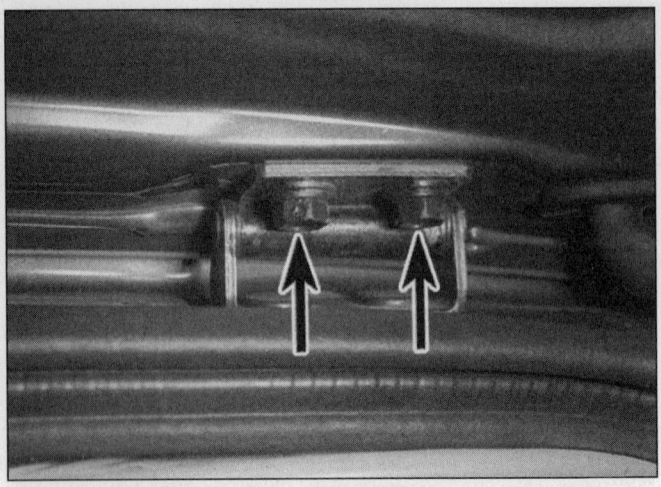

17.14 Unscrew the bolts (arrowed) securing the hinges to the tailgate

18.3 Bootlid lock securing screws (arrowed)

11 Have an assistant support the tailgate in the open position.
12 Using a pencil of felt tip pen, mark the outline of each hinge relative to the tailgate, to use as a guide on refitting.
13 Detach the upper ends of the support struts from the tailgate as described earlier in this Section.
14 Unscrew the bolts securing the hinges to the tailgate (see illustration), then lift the tailgate from the vehicle.

Refitting
15 Refitting is a reversal of removal, bearing in mind the following points.
16 Tie the string to the wiring harness and use it to pull the harness through the aperture and into the tailgate.
17 Do not fully tighten the hinge bolts until the tailgate adjustment has been checked, as described in the following paragraphs.

Adjustment
18 Close the tailgate carefully, in case the alignment is incorrect, which may cause scratching on the tailgate or the body as the tailgate is closed), and check for alignment with the adjacent panels. If necessary, slacken the hinge bolts and re-align the tailgate to suit. Once the tailgate is correctly aligned, tighten the hinge bolts to the specified torque.
19 Once the tailgate is correctly aligned, check that the tailgate fastens and releases in a satisfactory manner. If adjustment is necessary, slacken the tailgate lock retaining bolts, and adjust the position of the lock to suit. Once the lock is operating correctly, securely tighten its retaining bolts.

18 Boot lid lock components (Saloon models) - removal and refitting

Boot lid lock
1 Where applicable, unclip the plastic cover from the lock.
2 Disconnect the lock release cable from the lock mechanism.
3 Unscrew the two securing bolts, and withdraw the lock from the boot lid (see illustration).
4 Refitting is a reversal of removal.

Boot lid lock striker
5 Pull the weatherstrip from the plastic trim panel at the rear of the boot, then pull the trim panel from the body.
6 Using a suitable forked tool, prise out the plastic clips securing the trim panel to the body.
7 Mark the relationship between the lock striker and the bodywork by drawing around the outside of the striker with a marker pen. Unscrew the two securing bolts, then withdraw the lock striker assembly, and disconnect the boot lid release cable from the lever on the striker assembly.
8 Refitting is a reversal of removal, but check the operation of the boot lid release mechanism before refitting the luggage compartment trim panels.

19 Tailgate lock and handle components (Aeroback models) - removal and refitting

Lock mechanism
1 With the tailgate held in the fully open position, slacken and unscrew the bolts securing the lock assembly to the lower edge of the sill (see illustration).
2 Carefully withdraw the lock assembly and disconnect the release cable.

Lock cylinder
3 Release the press stud fixings and remove the tailgate trim panel.
4 Compress the lugs of the plastic clip, then unhook the link rod from the rear of the cylinder (see illustration).
5 Slide out the metal locking plate, then withdraw the cylinder.
6 Refitting is a reversal of removal.

19.1 Tailgate lock securing bolts (arrowed)

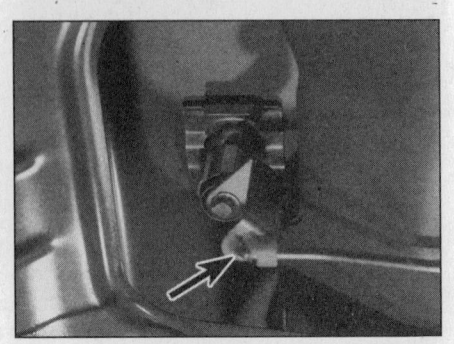

19.4 Tailgate lock cylinder link rod (arrowed)

Bodywork and fittings 11•13

19.8 Tailgate lock striker plate bolts (arrowed)

20.2a Front door servo motor screws (arrowed)

20.2b Front door servo motor link rod (arrowed)

Striker plate

Removal

7 With the tailgate held in the fully open position, mark the position of the striker plate in relation to the tailgate using a pencil or marker pen, to aid accurate refitting.
8 Slacken and unscrew the bolts securing the striker plate to the tailgate (see illustration).
9 Remove the striker plate from its mountings, then disconnect the remote release cable.

Refitting

10 Refitting is a reversal of removal. Use the markings made during removal to give the correct alignment.
11 Check that the tailgate fastens and releases in a satisfactory manner. If adjustment is necessary, slacken the striker plate retaining bolts, and adjust the position of the plate to suit. Once the lock is operating correctly, securely tighten the striker plate retaining bolts.

20 Central locking system components - removal and refitting

Front door servo motor

1 The front door servo motor is part of the lock mechanism - refer to Section 14.
2 The motor is secured to the lock assembly by two screws and a link rod (see illustrations).
3 Refitting is a reversal of removal

Rear door servo motor

4 Disconnect the battery negative cable and position it away from the terminal.
5 Refer to Section 13 and remove the door inner trim panel.
6 Release the clip that connects the servo motor arm to the lock operating rod.
7 Remove the screws and lift the servo motor from the door (see illustration).

21 Exterior mirror and associated components - removal and refitting

Mirror assembly

Removal - electric mirrors

1 Disconnect the battery negative lead and position it away from the terminal.

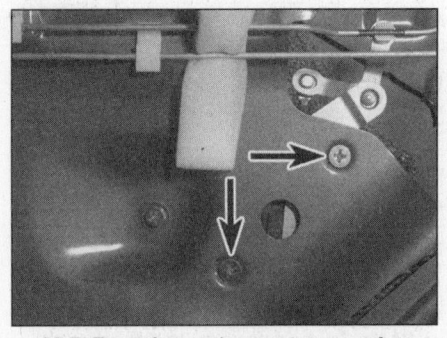

20.7 Rear door servo motor securing screws (arrowed)

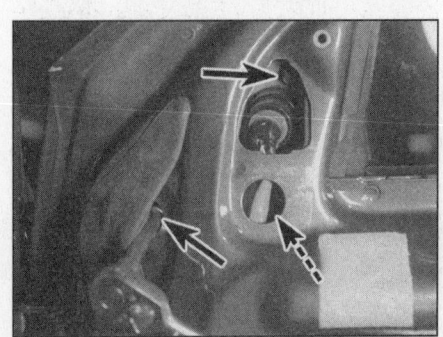

21.3 Prise out the window corner trim piece

21.4a Remove the three securing bolts (arrowed)...

2 Remove the door inner trim panel (see Section 13). Reach inside the door space and unplug the electrical supply to the mirror at the multiway connector (see illustration). Unclip the mirror wiring from the door, noting its routing.
3 Prise out the window corner trim piece (see illustration)
4 Remove the three securing bolts, and detach the mirror assembly from the outer surface of the door (see illustrations).

Removal - manual mirrors

5 Remove the door inner trim panel (see Section 13).
6 Prise out the window corner trim piece.
7 Remove the three securing bolts, and detach the mirror assembly from the outer surface of the door.

Refitting

8 Refitting is a reversal of removal. Tighten

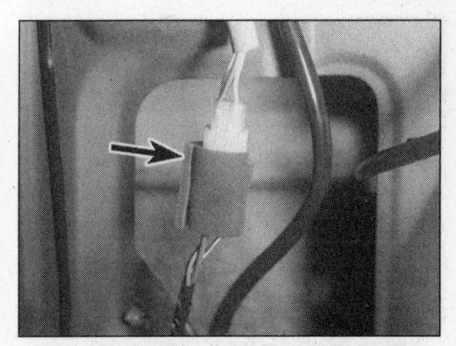

21.2 Unplug the electrical supply to the mirror at the multiway connector

21.4b ... and detach the mirror assembly from the outer surface of the door

11•14 Bodywork and fittings

the mirror securing screws securely. On models with electric mirrors, ensure that the electrical wiring is correctly routed so that it cannot foul the electric window mechanism.

22 Sunroof - general information

Due to the complexity of the sunroof mechanism, considerable expertise is needed to repair, replace or adjust the sunroof components successfully. Removal of the sunroof first requires the headlining to be removed, which is a complex and tedious operation, and not a task to be undertaken lightly. Therefore, any problems with the sunroof should be referred to a Proton dealer.

23 Seats - removal and refitting

Front seats

Removal

1 Remove the securing screws and lift off the door sill scuff plate.
2 Remove the handbrake lever cover from the centre console (see Section 24).
3 Slide the seat towards the rear of the car to gain access to the two bolts at the front of the seat frame. Prise off the plastic covers, then slacken and withdraw the bolts.
4 Slide the seat fully forwards and remove the two bolts from the rear of the seat frame.
5 Lift the seat out of the cabin area.

Refitting

6 Refit the seat by reversing the removal procedure, noting the following points:
 a) Set the seat sliding mechanism to its rearward position, before refitting the seat to the floorpan.
 b) Insert the seat frame securing bolts loosely - check that the sliding mechanism operates correctly before tightening them.
 c) Tighten the seat frame bolts to the specified torque.

Rear seat back rests

Removal

7 Using the hand straps, raise the seat cushion and tilt it fully forward.
8 The rear seat back rests are mounted on hinged brackets which are bolted to the floorpan. To remove both back rests together, first remove the screws and detach the load space carpet panel.
9 Unbolt the back rest panel from the mounting brackets.

Refitting

10 Refit the back rests by reversing the removal procedure.

Rear seat cushion

Removal

11 Using the hand straps, raise the seat cushion and tilt it fully forward.
12 Remove the screws that secure the hinged brackets to the floorpan, then lift out the cushion.

Refitting

13 Refit the seat cushion by reversing the removal procedure.

24 Centre console - removal and refitting

Removal

1 Disconnect the battery negative lead.
2 Prise off the handbrake lever trim panel. On models with electric mirrors, unplug the wiring at the connector (see illustrations)
3 Release the ashtray module from the rear of the console.
4 Slacken and withdraw the console front and rear securing screws (see illustration).
5 Prise the plastic cover plate from the top of the console, and unscrew the console upper securing screws (see illustrations).

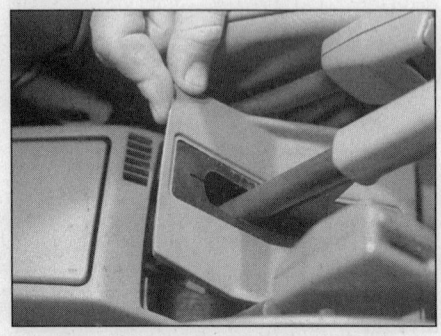

24.2a Prise off the handbrake lever trim panel

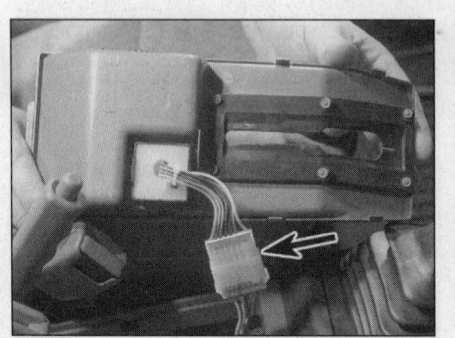

24.2b On models with electric mirrors, unplug the wiring at the connector (arrowed)

24.4a Slacken and withdraw the console front . . .

24.4b . . . and rear securing screws

24.5a Prise the plastic cover plate from the top of the console . . .

24.5b . . . and unscrew the console upper securing screws

Bodywork and fittings 11•15

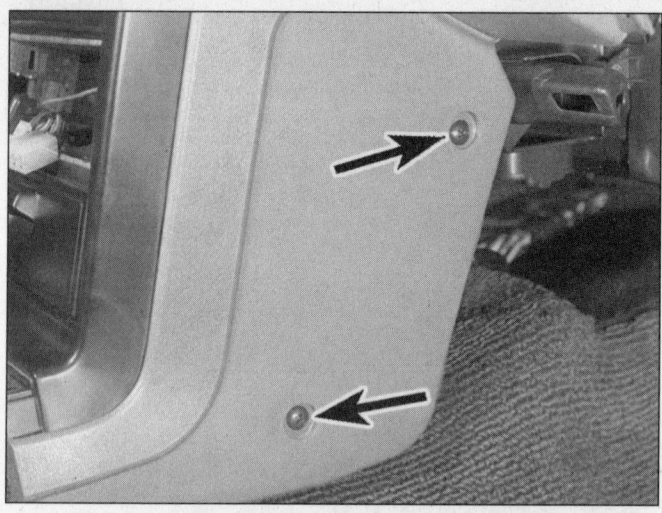

24.8 Remove the console side securing screws (arrowed)

24.9 Prise the ashtray moulding from the console

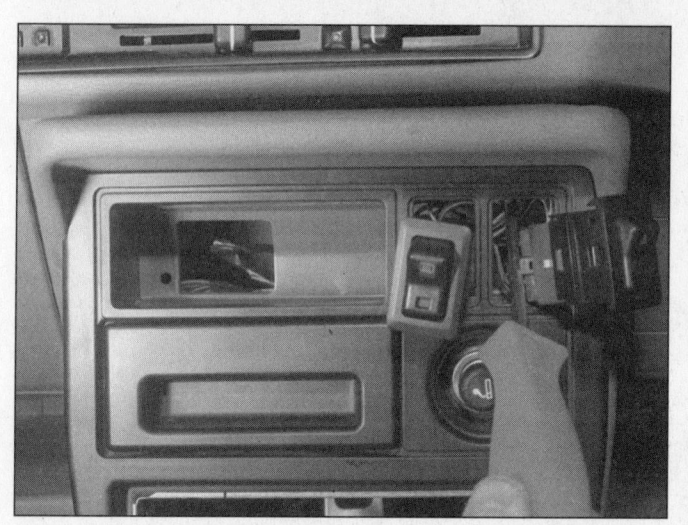

24.11 Remove the console to facia securing screws

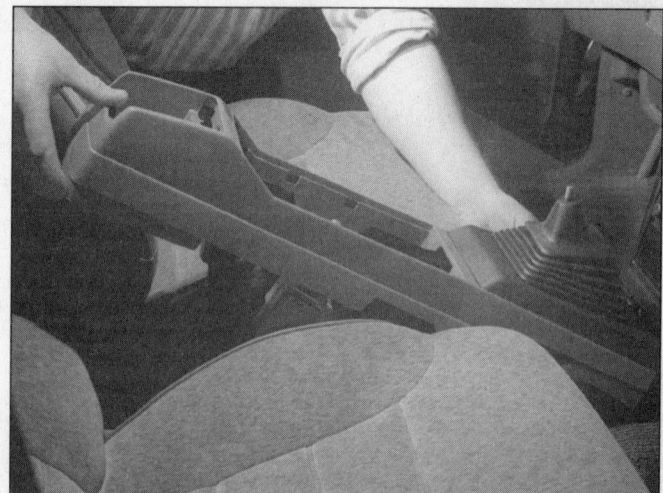

24.12 Carefully lift the console up and manipulate it over the gearchange/selector and handbrake lever

6 On models with manual transmission, unclip the gear lever gaiter surround from the top of the centre console.
7 On models with automatic transmission, unclip the selector lever cover from the centre console.
8 Remove the console side securing screws (see illustration).
9 Prise the ashtray moulding from the console (see illustration).
10 With reference to Chapter 12, remove the switch assemblies from the right hand side of the console.
11 Remove the console to facia securing screws (see illustration).
12 Draw the console assembly away from the facia, towards the rear of the vehicle. Carefully lift the console up and manipulate it over the gearchange/selector and handbrake lever (see illustration).

Refitting
13 Refitting is a reversal of removal, but ensure that the wiring plugs are correctly reconnected.

25 Facia - removal and refitting

Removal
1 Disconnect the battery negative cable and position it away from the terminal.
2 Refer to Chapter 10 and remove the steering wheel from the column.
3 Open the glovebox fully, then unclip their hinges from anchors by lifting the glovebox moulding upwards.
4 Detach the now exposed lap heater duct from the rear of the heater vents.
5 Remove the screws and detach the parcel tray from the underside of the facia.
6 Separate the lower shroud moulding from the steering column, after removing the securing screws.
7 With reference to Chapter 12, unplug the wiring from the rear of the steering column-mounted lighting and wiper switches.
8 Remove the steering column upper shroud moulding.
9 Detach the steering column cover panel from the lower edge of the facia, after removing the securing screws.
10 Refer to Chapter 12 and remove the instrument panel from the facia.
11 Undo the securing screws and separate the steering column bracket from the facia.
12 On the drivers side of the vehicle, remove the screws and lift off the corner section of the facia outer moulding.
13 With reference to Chapter 3, remove the

knobs from the heater control panel levers, then prise off the control panel front cover. Remove the screws that secure the heater control panel to the facia.
14 Remove the centre console (Section 24).
15 Slacken and remove the each of the securing nuts and bolts and carefully pull the facia away from the bulkhead. Unplug any remaining wiring from the rear of the facia, as the connector become exposed. Label each connector carefully, to aid correct refitting later.
16 Lift the facia moulding over the steering column and remove it from the vehicle or rest it on the front seats, as required.

Refitting

17 Refit the facia by following the removal procedure in reverse, noting the following points.

a) *Ensure that all wiring connections have been restored by checking the operation of all electrical accessories, before full tightening the facia fixings.*
b) *Ensure that all fresh air/heater ducting has been correctly refitted.*
c) *Securely tighten the facia-to-steering column bracket screws.*
d) *Refit the instrument panel with reference to Chapter 12.*

Chapter 12
Body electrical systems

Contents

Bulbs (exterior lights) - renewal 5
Bulbs (interior lights) - renewal 6
Electrical fault-finding - general information 2
Exterior light units - removal and refitting 7
Fuses and relays - general information 3
General information and precautions 1
Headlight beam alignment .... see Chapter 1
Horn - removal and refitting 9
Instrument panel - removal and refitting 8
Speedometer drive cable - removal and refitting 10
Switches - removal and refitting 4
Tailgate wiper motor - removal and refitting 13
Windscreen wiper motor and linkage - removal and refitting 12
Wiper arm - removal and refitting 11

Degrees of difficulty

| **Easy,** suitable for novice with little experience | **Fairly easy,** suitable for beginner with some experience | **Fairly difficult,** suitable for competent DIY mechanic | **Difficult,** suitable for experienced DIY mechanic | **Very difficult,** suitable for expert DIY or professional |

Specifications

Bulb ratings | Watts
Headlights 55/60
Front direction indicator light 21
Front sidelight 5
Front direction indicator repeater light 5
Stop light 21
Tail light 5
Rear direction indicator light 21
Reversing light 21
Rear foglight 21
Rear number plate light 10
Courtesy light 10
Load space light 5
Instrument pack lights 3.4

Torque wrench settings | Nm | lbft
Wiper motor securing nuts .... 7 | 5
Front wiper arm spindle nuts .... 15 | 11
Tailgate wiper arm spindle nut .... 8 | 6

1 General information and precautions

General information

1 The body electrical system consists of all lights, wash/wipe equipment, interior electrical equipment, and associated switches and wiring.
2 The electrical system is of the 12-volt negative earth type. Power to the system is provided by a 12-volt battery, which is charged by the alternator when the engine is running (see Chapter 5A).
3 The engine electrical system (battery, alternator, starter motor, ignition system, etc) is covered separately in Chapters 5A and 5B.

Precautions

Warning: *Before carrying out any work on the electrical system, read through the pre-cautions given in "Safety first!" at the beginning of this manual, and in Chapter 5. **Caution:** If the radio/cassette player fitted to the vehicle has an anti-theft security code, ensure that you have a copy of the code written down before disconnecting the battery.*

4 Prior to wiring on any component in the electrical system, the battery negative lead should first be disconnected, to prevent the possibility of electrical short-circuits and/or fires.

2 Electrical fault-finding - general information

Note: *Refer to the precautions given in "Safety first!" and in Section 1 of this Chapter before starting work. The following tests relate to testing of the main electrical circuits, and should not be used to test delicate electronic circuits (such as anti-lock braking systems), particularly where an electronic control module is used.*

General

1 A typical electrical circuit consists of an electrical component, any switches, relays, motors, fuses, fusible links or circuit breakers related to that component, and the wiring and connectors which link the component to both the battery and the chassis. To help to pinpoint a problem in an electrical circuit, wiring diagrams are included at the end of this manual.
2 Before attempting to diagnose an electrical fault, first study the appropriate wiring diagram, to obtain a more complete understanding of the components included in the particular circuit concerned. The possible sources of a fault can be narrowed down by noting whether other components related to the circuit are operating properly. If several components or circuits fail at one time, the problem is likely to be related to a shared fuse or earth connection.
3 Electrical problems usually stem from simple causes, such as loose or corroded connections, a faulty earth connection, a blown fuse, a melted fusible link, or a faulty relay (refer to Section 3 for details of testing relays). Visually inspect the condition of all fuses, wires and connections in a problem circuit before testing the components. Use the wiring diagrams to determine which terminal connections will need to be checked, in order to pinpoint the trouble-spot.
4 The basic tools required for electrical fault-finding include a circuit tester or voltmeter (a 12-volt bulb with a set of test leads can also be used for certain tests); a self-powered test light (sometimes known as a continuity tester); an ohmmeter (to measure resistance); a battery and set of test leads; and a jumper wire, preferably with a circuit breaker or fuse incorporated, which can be used to bypass suspect wires or electrical components. Before attempting to locate a problem with test instruments, use the wiring diagram to determine where to make the connections.
5 To find the source of an intermittent wiring fault (usually due to a poor or dirty connection, or damaged wiring insulation), a "wiggle" test can be performed on the wiring. This involves wiggling the wiring by hand, to see if the fault occurs as the wiring is moved. It should be possible to narrow down the source of the fault to a particular section of wiring. This method of testing can be used in conjunction with any of the tests described in the following sub-Sections.
6 Apart from problems due to poor connections, two basic types of fault can occur in an electrical circuit - open-circuit, or short-circuit.
7 Open-circuit faults are caused by a break somewhere in the circuit, which prevents current from flowing. An open-circuit fault will prevent a component from working, but will not cause the relevant circuit fuse to blow.
8 Short-circuit faults are caused by a "short" somewhere in the circuit, which allows the current flowing in the circuit to "escape" along an alternative route, usually to earth. Short-circuit faults are normally caused by a breakdown in wiring insulation, which allows a feed wire to touch either another wire, or an earthed component such as the bodyshell. A short-circuit fault will normally cause the relevant circuit fuse to blow.

Finding an open-circuit

9 To check for an open-circuit, connect one lead of a circuit tester or voltmeter to either the negative battery terminal or a known good earth.
10 Connect the other lead to a connector in the circuit being tested, preferably nearest to the battery or fuse.
11 Switch on the circuit, bearing in mind that some circuits are live only when the ignition switch is moved to a particular position.
12 If voltage is present (indicated either by the tester bulb lighting or a voltmeter reading, as applicable), this means that the section of the circuit between the relevant connector and the battery is problem-free.
13 Continue to check the remainder of the circuit in the same fashion.
14 When a point is reached at which no voltage is present, the problem must lie between that point and the previous test point with voltage. Most problems can be traced to a broken, corroded or loose connection.

Finding a short-circuit

15 To check for a short-circuit, first disconnect the load(s) from the circuit (loads are the components which draw current from a circuit, such as bulbs, motors, heating elements, etc).
16 Remove the relevant fuse from the circuit, and connect a circuit tester or voltmeter to the fuse connections.
17 Switch on the circuit, bearing in mind that some circuits are live only when the ignition switch is moved to a particular position.
18 If voltage is present (indicated either by the tester bulb lighting or a voltmeter reading, as applicable), this means that there is a short-circuit.
19 If no voltage is present, but the fuse still blows with the load(s) connected, this indicates an internal fault in the load(s).

Finding an earth fault

20 The battery negative terminal is connected to "earth" - the metal of the engine/transmission and the car body - and most systems are wired so that they only receive a positive feed, the current returning via the metal of the car body. This means that the component mounting and the body form part of that circuit. Loose or corroded mountings can therefore cause a range of electrical faults, ranging from total failure of a circuit, to a puzzling partial fault. In particular, lights may shine dimly (especially when another circuit sharing the same earth point is in operation), motors (eg wiper motors or the radiator cooling fan motor) may run slowly, and the operation of one circuit may have an apparently-unrelated effect on another. Note that on many vehicles, earth straps are used between certain components, such as the engine/transmission and the body, usually where there is no metal-to-metal contact between components, due to flexible rubber mountings, etc.
21 To check whether a component is properly earthed, disconnect the battery, and connect one lead of an ohmmeter to a known good earth point. Connect the other lead to the wire or earth connection being tested. The resistance reading should be zero; if not, check the connection as follows.
22 If an earth connection is thought to be faulty, dismantle the connection, and clean back to bare metal both the bodyshell and the wire terminal or the component earth connection mating surface. Be careful to remove all traces of dirt and corrosion, then use a knife to trim away any paint, so that a clean metal-to-metal joint is made. On reassembly, tighten the joint fasteners securely; if a wire terminal is being refitted, use serrated washers between the terminal and the bodyshell, to ensure a clean and secure connection. When the connection is remade, prevent the onset of corrosion in the future by applying a coat of petroleum jelly or silicone-based grease, or by spraying on (at regular intervals) a proprietary ignition sealer, or a water-dispersant lubricant.

3 Fuses and relays - general information

Fuses

1 Fuses are designed to break a circuit when a predetermined current is reached, in order to protect the components and wiring which could be damaged by excessive current flow. Any excessive current flow will be due to a fault in the circuit, usually a short-circuit (see Section 2).
2 The main fuses are located behind a cover panel, on the lower surface of the facia, adjacent to the steering column.
3 To gain access to the fuses, release the cover panel **(see illustrations)**.
4 A blown fuse can be recognised from its melted or broken wire **(see illustration)**.

Body electrical systems 12•3

3.3a Release the cover panel . . .

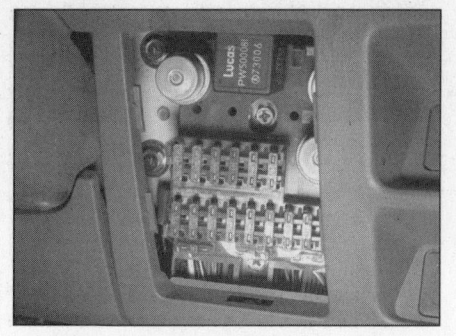

3.3b . . . to gain access to the fuses

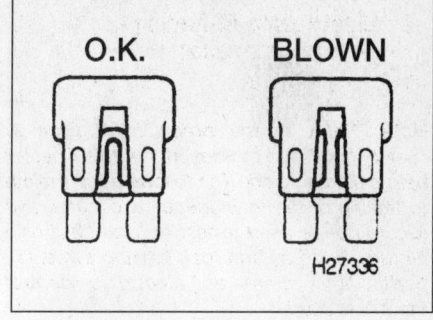

3.4 A blown fuse can be recognised from its melted or broken wire

5 To remove a fuse, first ensure that the relevant circuit is switched off.
6 Pull the fuse squarely from its socket **(see illustration)**.
7 Spare fuses are fitted in dummy sockets in the main fusebox.
8 Before renewing a blown fuse, trace and rectify the cause, and always use a new fuse of the correct rating (fuse ratings are specified on the inside of the fusebox cover flap). Never substitute a fuse of a higher rating, or make temporary repairs using wire or metal foil; more serious damage, or even fire, could result.
9 Note that the fuses are colour-coded as shown in the following table. Refer to the wiring diagrams for details of the fuse ratings used and the circuits protected.

Colour	Rating
Orange	5A
Red	10A
Blue	15A
Yellow	20A
Clear or White	25A
Green	30A

10 The radio/cassette player fuse is located in the rear of the unit, and can be accessed after removing the radio/cassette player - refer to Section 12 for greater detail.

Relays

11 Relays are electrical switches, operated indirectly by an electromagnetic solenoid. The internal workings are encapsulated in a single case, with the electrical terminals presented at the bottom of the case. They are used in preference to normal switches for the following reasons:
  a) A relay can be used to switch a heavy load current remotely, allowing the use of lighter-gauge wiring and contacts in the switching circuit.
  b) A relay can be activated by more than one control input, whereas a mechanically controlled switch can only act one a single input.
  c) A relay can manufactured to include a time delay function - for example, an intermittent wiper relay, or a direction indicator flasher unit.

12 The main and optional equipment relays are located in the fuse box. A number of additional relays may be fitted, depending on model and specification. These are generally mounted adjacent to the component being controlled; e.g. the radiator cooling fan relay(s) are mounted on a bracket next the cooling fan itself.
13 The direction indicator/hazard warning flasher unit is mounted in the fusebox.
14 If a circuit or system controlled by a relay develops a fault, and the relay is suspect, activate the system by operating the appropriate switch. If the relay is functioning, it should be possible to hear or feel it "click" as it is energised, by listening to it carefully or resting a finger tip on the relay case. If this is the case, the fault may lie with the components or wiring of the system. If the relay cannot be felt or heard to energise, then either the relay is not receiving a switching current, or the relay itself is faulty. Testing is by substitution of an identical unit that is known to be operating correctly. Exercise caution, though - while some relays are identical in appearance and in operation, others look similar but perform different functions. Check that you have the correct type of relay for the circuit you are dealing with.
15 To remove a relay, first ensure that the relevant circuit is switched off - the relay can then be pulled out from its socket as required. Note that some relays are secured to their sockets by a spring clip, or a screw.

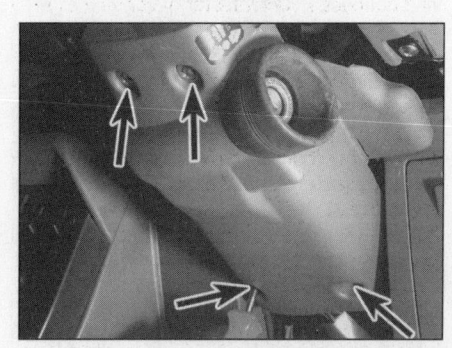

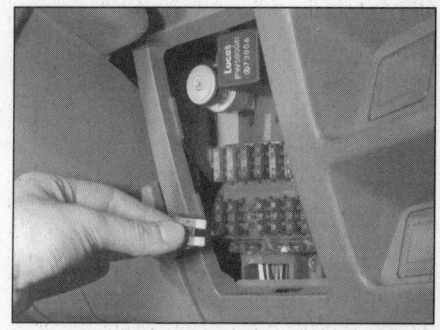

3.6 Pull the fuse squarely from its socket

4 Switches - removal and refitting

Steering column-mounted stalk switch

1 Disconnect the battery negative cable and position it away from the terminal. Turn the steering wheel so that the roadwheels are pointing in the straight-ahead position.
2 Refer to Chapter 10 and remove the steering wheel from the column.
3 Remove the screws and lift off the lower steering column shroud **(see illustration)**
4 Unplug the wiring from the switch at the connectors **(see illustration)**. Label each one to aid correct refitting later.

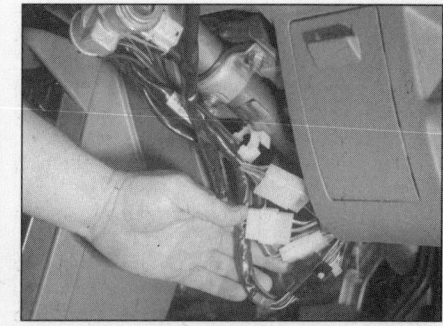

4.3 Remove the screws (arrowed) and lift off the lower steering column shroud

4.4 Unplug the wiring from the switch at the connectors

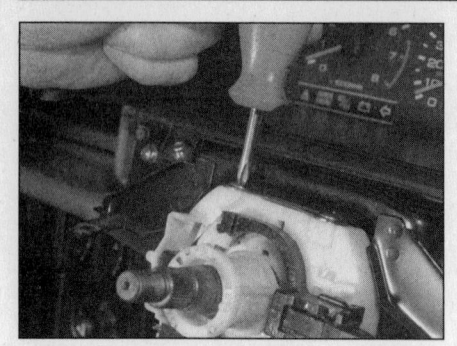

12•4 Body electrical systems

4.6 Slacken and withdraw the switch securing screws

4.7 Remove the switch unit from the steering column

4.8 Engage the metal bracket (arrowed) on the inside of the lower shroud with the mounting bracket on the steering column (arrowed)

5 Refer to the next sub-Section and remove the upper steering column shroud, together with the rotary switches.
6 Slacken and withdraw the switch securing screws, then release the clips at the side of the switch body **(see illustration)**.
7 Remove the switch unit from the steering column **(see illustration)**.
8 Refitting is reversal of removal, noting the following points:
  a) Ensure that the direction indicator cancelling collar is correctly positioned - check its operation before refitting the steering wheel.
  b) Ensure that the steering column/ roadwheels are still in the straight-ahead position, then refit the steering wheel with reference to Chapter 10.
  c) Engage the metal bracket on the inside of the lower shroud with the mounting bracket on the steering column **(see illustration)**.

Steering column-mounted rotary switches

9 The front/rear windscreen wiper/washer switch and the headlamp/sidelamp switches are housed in similar switch assemblies, on either side of the steering column upper shroud. The removal procedure is similar for both.
10 Disconnect the battery negative cable and position it away from the terminal.
11 Refer to Chapter 10 and remove the steering wheel .
12 With reference to the previous sub-Section, remove the screws and lift off the steering column lower shroud.
13 Remove the securing screws and detach the steering column upper shroud, complete with both switch assemblies **(see illustrations)**. Unplug the wiring at the connectors, as it becomes accessible.
14 To remove an individual switch, slide off the knob, then remove the screws and extract the switch body **(see illustrations)**.

Electric mirror adjustment switch

15 Disconnect the battery negative cable and position it away from the terminal.
16 Refer to Chapter 11 and remove the handbrake lever cover panel from the upper surface of the centre console.
17 Turn the panel over and unplug the wiring from the rear of the switch body at the connector.
18 Compress the clips at the side of the switch body, then carefully lever the switch body out of the cover panel **(see illustration)**.
19 Refitting is a reversal of removal.

Brake light switch

20 Refer to Chapter 9

Facia-mounted switches

21 The hazard lamp, rear windshield demister and fog lamp switches are all housed in similar switch assemblies, which are clipped into apertures in the facia.
22 To remove a switch of this type, first disconnect the battery negative cable and position it away from the terminal, to prevent accidental short circuits.

4.13a Remove the securing screws

4.13b ... and detach the steering column upper shroud, complete with both switch assemblies

4.14a To remove an individual switch, slide off the knob ...

4.14b ... then remove the screws (arrowed) ...

4.14c ... and extract the switch body

Body electrical systems 12•5

4.18 Mirror adjustment switch and wiring

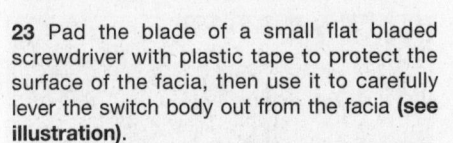

4.23 Removal of a facia-mounted rocker switch

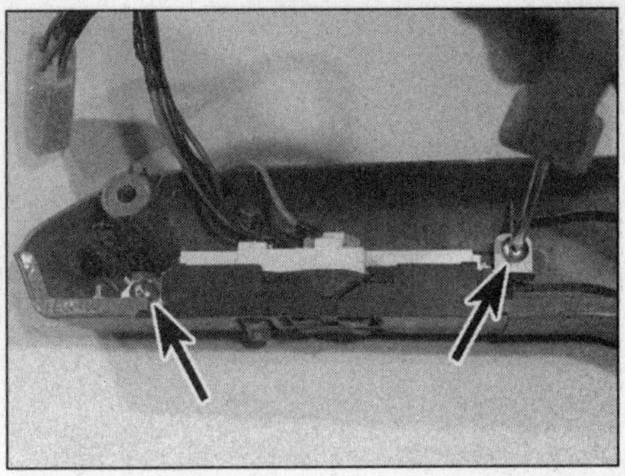

4.32a Remove the screws (arrowed) ...

23 Pad the blade of a small flat bladed screwdriver with plastic tape to protect the surface of the facia, then use it to carefully lever the switch body out from the facia **(see illustration)**.
24 Tape the wiring to the facia, to prevent it dropping inside, then unplug the wiring from the rear of the switch at the connector.
25 Refitting is a reversal of removal.

Door-mounted courtesy light switches

26 Disconnect the battery negative cable and position it away from the terminal.
27 Open the door to expose the switch body.
28 Peel off the rubber gaiter then remove the securing screw and withdraw the switch from the bodywork. Disconnect the wiring connector as it becomes accessible.

> **HAYNES HiNT**
> Tape the wiring to the door pillar, or tie a length of string to the wiring, to retrieve it if it falls back inside the bodywork.

29 Refitting is a reversal of removal, but ensure that the rubber gaiter is securely seated over the switch.

Electric window switches

30 Disconnect the battery negative cable and position it away from the terminal.
31 Refer to Chapter 11 and remove the arm rest moulding. Unplug the wiring from the switch, as it becomes exposed.

32 Remove the screws and lift the switch from the arm rest **(see illustrations)**.
33 Refitting is a reversal of removal

5 Bulbs (exterior lights) - renewal

General

1 Whenever a bulb is renewed, note the following points:
a) Ensure that the relevant electrical circuit is isolated before removing a bulb. If in doubt, disconnect the battery negative lead before starting work.
b) Remember that, if the circuit has just been in use, the bulb may be extremely hot.
c) Always check the bulb contacts and holder, ensuring that there is clean metal-to-metal contact between the bulb and its live contact(s) and earth. Clean off any corrosion or dirt before fitting a new bulb.
d) Wherever bayonet-type bulbs are fitted, ensure that the socket contacts bear firmly against the bulb contacts.
e) Always ensure that the new bulb is of the correct rating (see Specifications), and that it is completely clean before fitting it; this applies particularly to headlight/foglight bulbs (see following paragraphs).
f) Pay attention to the orientation when fitting multi-filament bulbs (e.g. combined

4.32b ... and lift the electric window switch from the arm rest

tail/brake light bulbs) - incorrect fitting will cause the filaments to illuminate in the wrong sequence.

Headlight

2 Open the bonnet. Ensure that the headlights and sidelights are turned off at the switch.
3 Unclip the cover from the rear of the headlight unit **(see illustration)**.
4 Pull the wiring plug from the rear of the bulb **(see illustration)**.
5 Squeeze the retaining spring-clip lugs, and release the clip from the rear of the bulb **(see illustration)**.
6 Withdraw the bulb **(see illustration)**.
7 When handling the new bulb, use a tissue or clean cloth, to avoid touching the glass with the fingers; moisture and grease from the skin can cause blackening and rapid failure of

5.3 Unclip the cover from the rear of the headlight unit

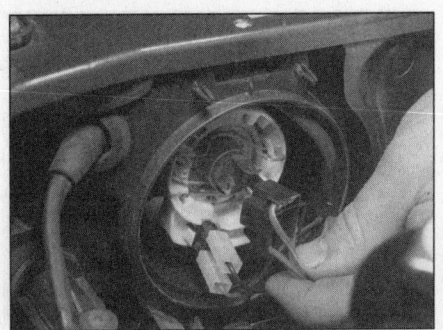

5.4 Pull the wiring plug from the rear of the bulb

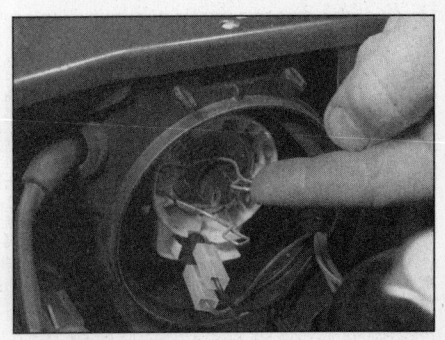

5.5 Release the clip from the rear of the bulb

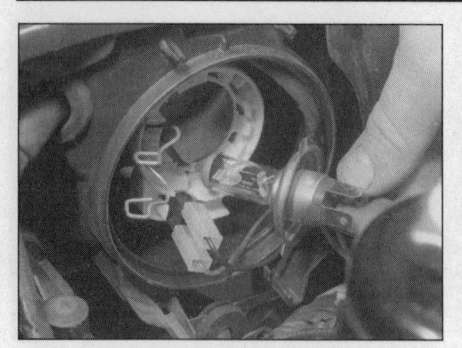

12•6 Body electrical systems

5.6 Withdraw the bulb

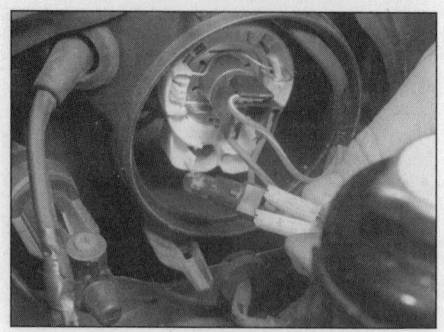

5.11 Pull the bulbholder from the rear of the headlight unit

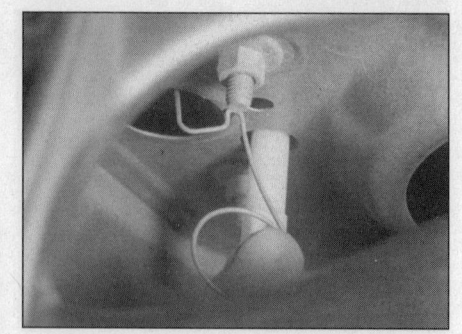

5.13 Unhook the light unit spring clip from the recess in the inner wing

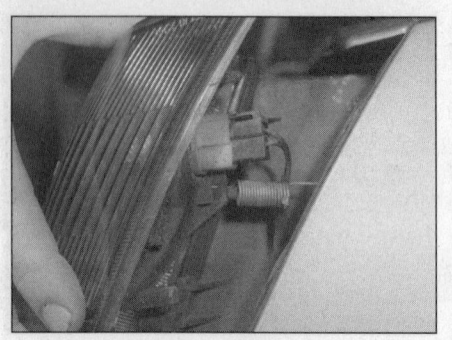

5.14 Pull the light unit forwards from its housing

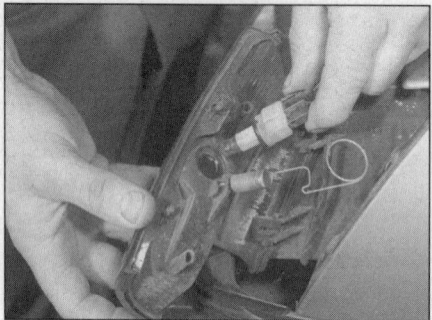

5.15 Twist the bulbholder anti-clockwise and withdraw it from the light unit

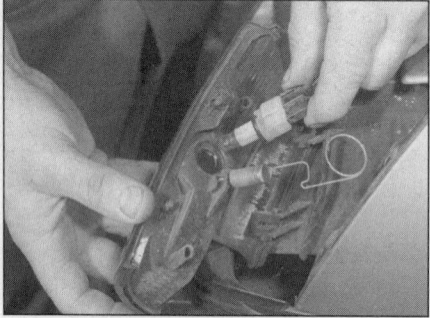

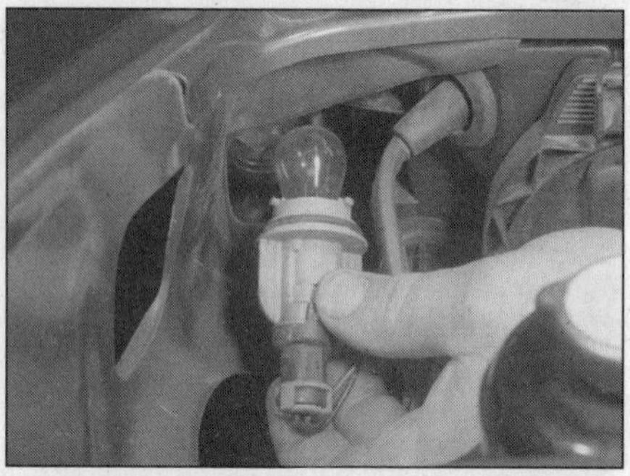

5.18 Twist the bulbholder anti-clockwise and withdraw it from the light unit

this type of bulb. If the glass is accidentally touched, wipe it clean using methylated spirit. Avoid knocking or shaking the bulb as this may weaken or even break the internal filament.
8 Install the new bulb, using a reversal of the removal procedure, ensuring that its locating tabs are correctly located in the light unit cut-outs.
9 Secure the bulb in position with the retaining clip and press the rubber boot back into position. Reconnect the wiring harness.

Sidelights

MPi models

10 Unclip the cover from the rear of the headlight unit.
11 Pull the bulbholder from the rear of the headlight unit, with the wiring still connected **(see illustration)**.

12 The bulb is a push fit in the bulbholder.

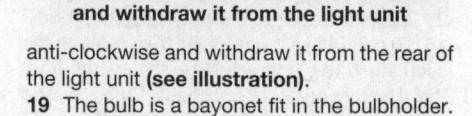

8 and 12 valve models

13 Open the bonnet. Unhook the light unit spring clip from the recess in the inner wing, directly behind the indicator light unit. **see illustration)**.
14 Pull the light unit forwards from its housing **(see illustration)**.
15 Twist the bulbholder anti-clockwise and withdraw it from the light unit **(see illustration)**.
16 The bulb is a bayonet fit in the bulbholder.
17 Fit the new bulb, then refit the light assembly using a reversal of the removal procedure. Hook the retaining spring clip securely into the recess in the inner wing.

Front direction indicator

MPi models

18 Open the bonnet. Twist the bulbholder

anti-clockwise and withdraw it from the rear of the light unit **(see illustration)**.
19 The bulb is a bayonet fit in the bulbholder.
20 Fit the new bulb, then refit the light assembly using a reversal of the removal procedure. Ensure that the locating pegs on the side of the light unit engage correctly. Tighten the securing screws securely.

8 and 12 valve models

21 Remove the screws and lift the lens panel from the front of the light unit **(see illustration)**.
22 Grip the bulb carefully and twist to release it from the bayonet mounting **(see illustration)**.
23 Refitting is a reversal of removal. Ensure that the lens seal is correctly seated.

Direction indicator side repeater

24 Slide the light unit towards the rear of the

5.21 Remove the screws and lift the lens panel from the front of the light unit

5.22 Grip the bulb carefully and twist to release it from the bayonet mounting

5.24a Slide the light unit towards the rear of the vehicle . . .

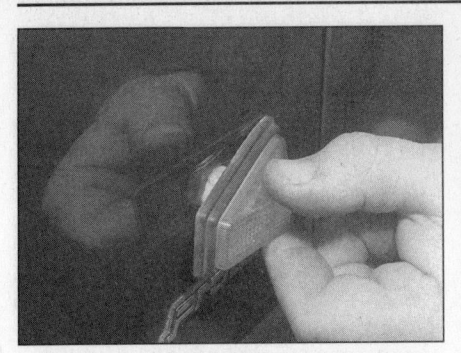

Body electrical systems 12•7

5.24b ... then lever it out of the wing aperture

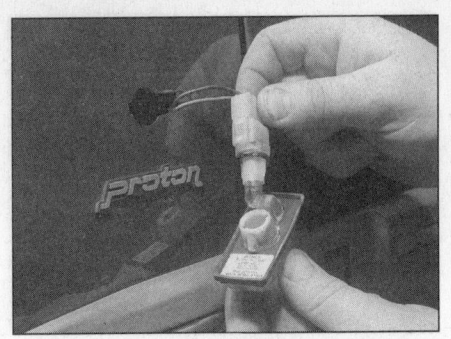

5.25 Twist the bulbholder to release it from the light unit

5.29 Prise off the plastic cover panel to expose the rear of the light cluster

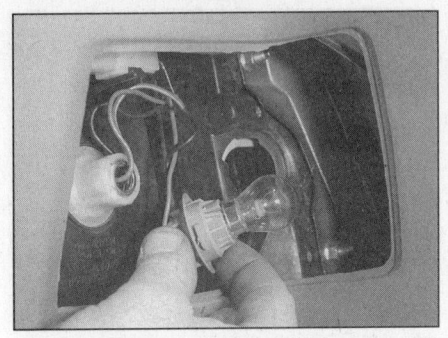

5.30 Then twist the bulbholder to release it from the rear of the light cluster

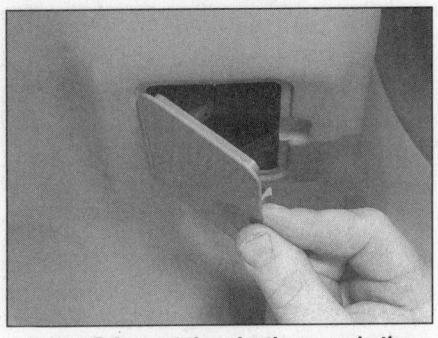

5.31a Prise out the plastic cover in the tailgate trim panel ...

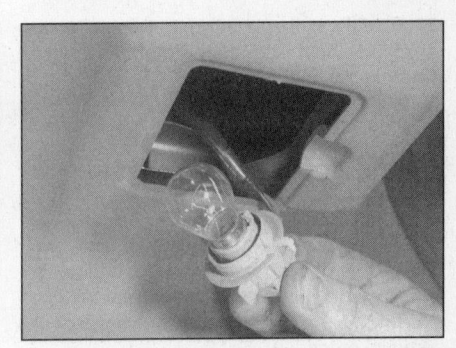

5.31b ... to gain access to the reversing light bulb

vehicle slightly, then insert a plastic implement behind the rear edge of the unit and lever it out of the wing aperture **(see illustration)**. Pad the blade of the instrument to prevent it damaging the paintwork.

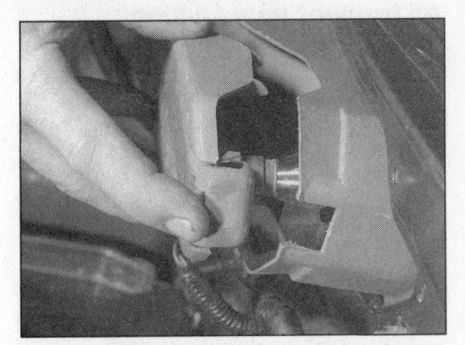

25 Withdraw the light unit, then twist the bulbholder anti-clockwise to release it from the light unit **(see illustration)**.
26 Release the bulb from the bulbholder.
27 Fit the new bulb using a reversal of the removal procedure.

Rear light cluster bulbs

28 Ensure that all exterior lighting is turned off the relevant switches.

Aeroback models

29 Open the tailgate. Working from within the loadspace, prise off the plastic cover panel to expose the rear of the light cluster **(see illustration)**.
30 The twist the relevant bulbholder to release it from the rear of the light cluster **(see illustration)**. Note that the stop/tail light bulb has offset locking pins, to ensure correct orientation.

31 Access to the reversing light bulb is via a plastic cover in the tailgate trim panel **(see illustrations)**.

Saloon models

32 Open the bootlid. Working from within the loadspace, unplug the wiring from the rear of the light cluster at the multiway connector.
33 Release the clip, then prise off the combined plastic cover panel and bulbholder **(see illustrations)**.
34 Release the relevant bulb by twisting it from its bayonet fit holder **(see illustration)**.
35 Fit the new bulb using a reversal of the removal procedure. Note that the stop/tail light bulb has offset locking pins, to ensure correct orientation.

Rear fog lights

36 Remove the screws and lift the lens panel away from the light unit **(see illustration)**.

5.33a Release the clip ...

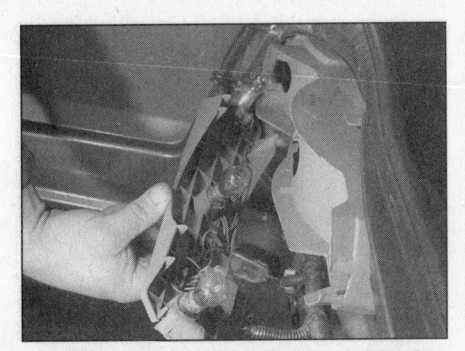

5.33b ... then prise off the combined plastic cover panel and bulbholder

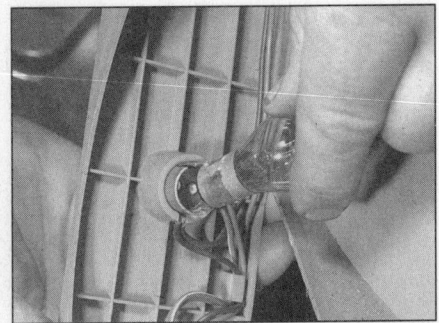

5.34 Release the bulb by twisting it from its bayonet fit holder

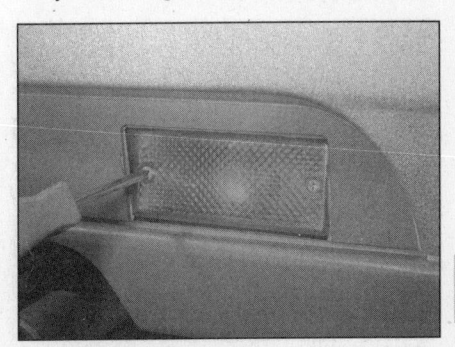

5.36 Remove the screws and lift the lens panel away from the light unit

12•8 Body electrical systems

5.37 Grip the bulb carefully and twist, to release it from the bayonet mounting

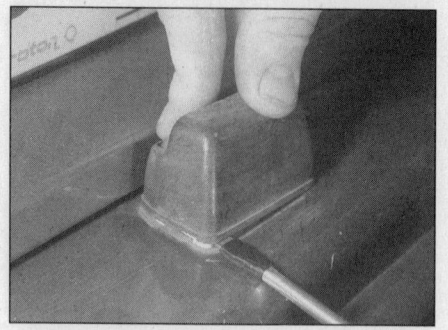

5.42 Unclip the cover from the light unit

5.43a Remove the securing screws...

37 Grip the bulb carefully and twist to release it from the bayonet mounting **(see illustration)**.
38 Refitting is a reversal of removal. Ensure that the lens seal is correctly seated.

Rear number plate light

Aeroback models
39 Remove the securing screws, and lower the light unit lens from the tailgate handle.
40 The bulb is a push fit in the light unit.
41 Fit the new bulb using a reversal of the removal procedure.

Saloon models
42 Unclip the cover from the light unit **(see illustration)**.
43 Remove the securing screws and lift the lens moulding from bulbholder **(see illustration)**.
44 The bulb is a push fit in the bulbholder **(see illustration)**.
45 Fit the new bulb using a reversal of the removal procedure.

6 Bulbs (interior lights) - renewal

General
1 Whenever a bulb is renewed, note the following points:
  a) Always ensure that the relevant electrical circuit is switched it off, before removing

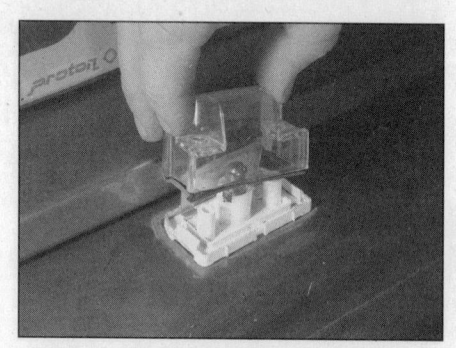

5.43b ...and lift the lens moulding from bulbholder

a bulb. If in doubt, disconnect the battery negative lead before starting work.
b) Remember that, if the light has just been in use, the bulb may be extremely hot.
c) Always check the bulb contacts and holder, ensuring that there is clean metal-to-metal contact between the bulb and its live contact(s) and earth. Clean off any corrosion or dirt before fitting a new bulb.
d) Wherever bayonet-type bulbs are fitted, ensure that the live contact(s) bear firmly against the bulb contact.
e) Always ensure that the new bulb is of the correct rating (see Specifications), and that it is completely clean before fitting it.

Courtesy light
2 Carefully prise the lens from the bezel, by inserting a flat bladed screwdriver into the slot at the side of the lens unit **(see illustration)**.
3 On Mpi models, twist the bulb to release it

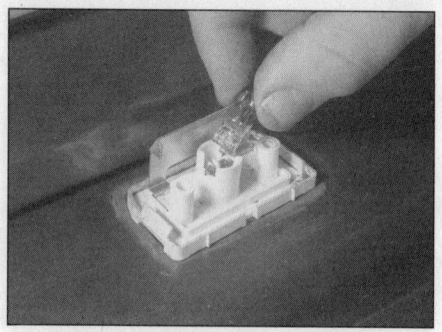

5.44 The bulb is a push fit in the bulbholder

from its bayonet-fit contacts. On 8 and 12 valve models, the bulb is push fit between the spring loaded contacts **(see illustration)**.
4 Fit the new bulb using a reversal of the removal procedure.

Instrument panel gauge illumination
5 Remove the instrument panel as described in Section 8.
6 The bulbs are a bayonet fit in the rear of the instrument pack **(see illustration)**. The colour of the bulb casing denotes its wattage - ensure that a replacement bulb of the correct rating is used.

Switch illumination
7 The bulbs that illuminate the facia and centre console-mounted switches are integral with the switch body and cannot be renewed separately.

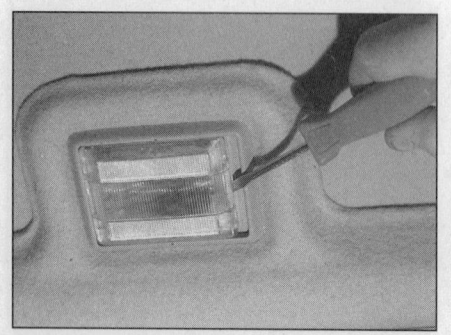

6.2 Prise the lens from the bezel, using a flat bladed screwdriver

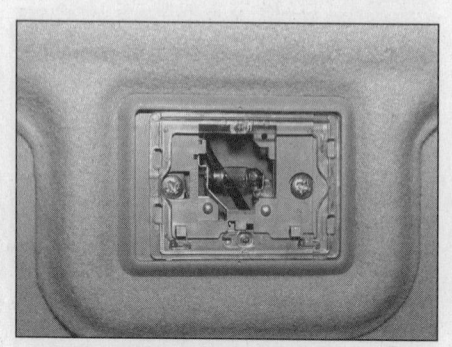

6.3 On 8 and 12 valve models, the bulb is push fit between the spring loaded contacts

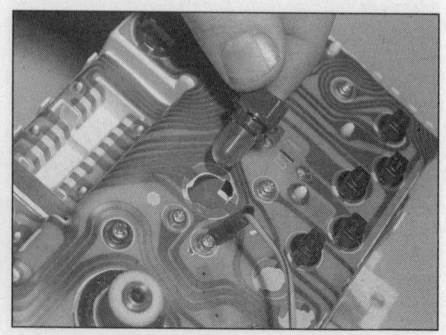

6.6 The bulbs are a bayonet fit in the rear of the instrument pack

Body electrical systems 12•9

7.4a Headlight unit inner securing screw (arrowed)

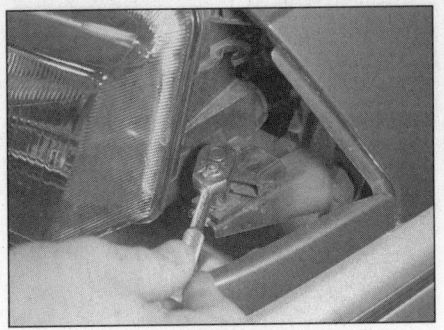

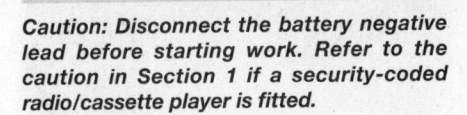

7.4b Remove the headlight unit outer securing screw

7.5 Withdraw the headlight unit from the vehicle

7 Exterior light units - removal and refitting

Caution: *Disconnect the battery negative lead before starting work. Refer to the caution in Section 1 if a security-coded radio/cassette player is fitted.*

Headlight

Removal

1 Refer to Chapter 11 and remove the radiator grille.
2 Remove the adjacent direction indicator light unit (Mpi models) / sidelight unit (8 and 12 valve models), as described in Section 5.
3 Disconnect all wiring from the rear of the light unit at the connectors. Label each carefully to aid correct refitting later.
4 Working at the front of the vehicle, remove the screws that secure the inner, outer and upper edges of the light unit to the bodywork (see illustrations).
5 Withdraw the headlight unit from the vehicle (see illustration).

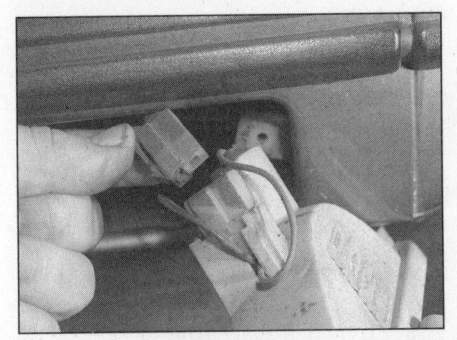

Refitting

6 Refitting is a reversal of removal. On completion, adjust the headlight beam alignment as described in Chapter 1, but have the alignment checked by a Proton dealer or auto-electrical specialist at the earliest opportunity.

Sidelight

Note: *Applies to 8 and 12 valve models only*
7 This procedure is described as part of the bulb renewal procedure, in Section 5. Note that the wiring harness can be disconnected from the light unit without removing the bulb holder.

Front direction indicator light

8 and 12 valve models

8 The procedure is described as part of the bulb renewal procedure in Section 5. Note that the wiring harness can be disconnected from the light unit without removing the bulb holder (see illustration).

Mpi models

9 Remove the bulbholder, as described in Section 5. Slacken and withdraw the securing screw, then withdraw the light unit from the bodywork (see illustrations).

Front direction indicator side repeater light

10 The procedure is described as part of the bulb renewal procedure in Section 5.

Rear light cluster

Note: *A new light unit sealing strip will be required on refitting.*

Removal

11 On Aeroback models, with reference to Section 5, remove the plastic cover to expose the rear of the light unit. Unplug the wiring at each of the connectors, making a careful note of their fitted positions.
12 On saloon models, remove the bulbholder assembly, as described for the bulb renewal procedure in Section 5.
13 Refer to Chapter 11 and remove the load space trim panel. Unplug the wiring from the rear of the cluster at the connector (see illustration).
14 Unscrew the light unit securing nuts and remove the mounting bracket. Pull the light unit away from the rear of the vehicle (see illustration). Note that the light unit is held in place with a self-adhesive sealing compound.

Refitting

15 Before refitting the light unit, clean all traces of the old sealant from the light unit and the wing panel.
16 Apply the new sealing compound to the rear of the light unit (the sealing strip is usually supplied in rolls, and will have to be trimmed to the required length).

7.8 Front direction indicator unit - 8 and 12 valve models

7.9a Slacken and withdraw the securing screw (arrowed) . . .

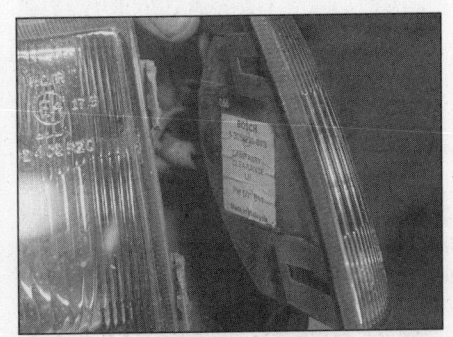

7.9b . . . then withdraw the light unit from the bodywork

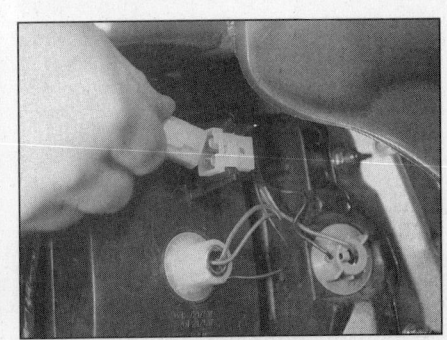

7.13 Unplug the wiring from the rear of the cluster at the connector

12•10 Body electrical systems

7.14 Unscrew the light unit securing nuts (arrowed)

17 Refit the light unit using a reversal of the removal procedure. Tighten the securing nuts securely and ensure that the wiring connectors are correctly refitted.

8 Instrument panel - removal and refitting

Removal

1 Disconnect the battery negative cable and position it away from the terminal.
2 Refer to Chapter 10 and remove the steering wheel.
3 Remove the steering column shroud panels, as described in Chapter 11.
4 Detach the hood from the instrument panel by removing the securing screws at the lower edge and then disengaging the clips at the upper edge (see illustrations).
5 Remove the instrument panel securing screws (see illustration).
6 Working in the engine compartment, disconnect the speedometer cable from the gearbox (see Section 10), then push the cable through the engine compartment bulkhead sufficiently to enable the instrument panel to be pulled forwards.
7 Pull the instrument panel forwards, and disconnect the wiring plugs and the speedometer cable from the rear of the panel (see illustrations). Withdraw the instrument panel from the facia aperture.

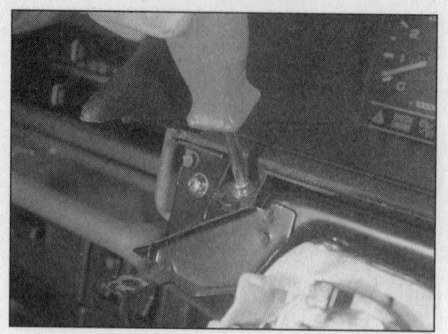

8.4a Detach the hood from the instrument panel by removing the securing screws at the lower edge . . .

Refitting

8 Refitting is a reversal of removal, bearing in mind the following points:
a) When reconnecting the speedometer cable, reconnect the cable to the speedometer, then pull the cable through the bulkhead, back into the engine compartment, until the instrument panel can be seated securely in the facia. Reconnect the speedometer to the gearbox with reference to Section 10.
b) Refit the steering wheel with reference to Chapter 10.

9 Horn - removal and refitting

Removal

1 Disconnect the battery negative lead.
2 Remove the front grille panel (Chapter 11).
3 Disconnect the wiring from the horn.
4 Unscrew the securing bolt(s), and withdraw the horn sounder(s), complete with the mounting bracket.
5 Note that the loudness of the horn can be altered by turning the hexagonal screw head at the rear of the horn sounder.

Refitting

6 Refitting is a reversal of removal.

8.4b . . . and then disengaging the clips at the upper edge

8.5 Remove the instrument panel securing screws (arrowed)

10 Speedometer drive cable - removal and refitting

Removal

1 Disconnect the battery negative cable and position it away from the terminal.
2 Working in the engine compartment, unscrew the sleeve securing the cable end to gearbox, then disconnect the cable from gearbox.
3 Remove the instrument panel (Section 7).
4 Where applicable, release the cable from the brackets in the engine compartment bulkhead, then pull the cable through the bulkhead grommet into the footwell.

Refitting

5 Refitting is a reversal of removal, bearing in

8.7a Disconnect the speedometer cable from the connector (arrowed) at the rear of the instrument panel

8.7b Disconnect the wiring plug from the rear of the instrument panel

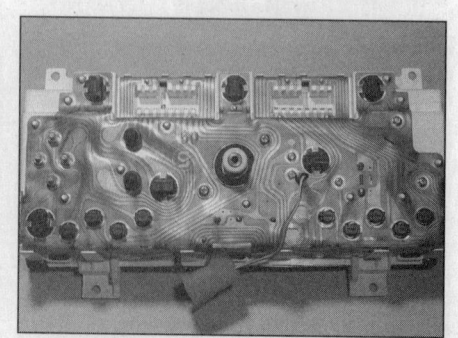

8.7c View of the rear surface of the instrument panel

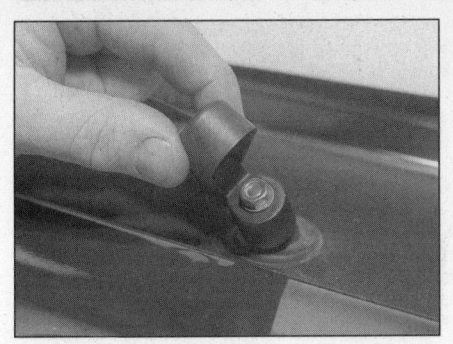

Body electrical systems 12•11

11.3a Lift up the wiper arm spindle nut cover...

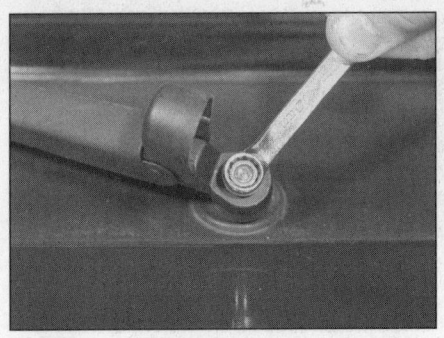

11.3b ...then slacken and remove the spindle nut

12.5 Wiper motor securing bolts (arrowed)

mind the following points:
a) Ensure that the bulkhead grommet is securely seated.
b) Pass the speedometer cable through the bulkhead grommet from inside the car, until the alignment marking on the outer surface of the cable can be seen from the engine bay side of the grommet.
c) Refit the instrument panel with reference to Section 9 - ensure that the connector sleeve at the end of the speedometer cable is pushed fully home.
d) Secure the cable to its mounting brackets in the engine bay, such that it is not kinked or forced to follow tight bends

11 Wiper arm - removal and refitting

Removal

1 Operate the wiper motor, then switch it off so that the wiper arm returns to the at-rest/parked position.
2 Stick a length of masking tape on the glass below the edge of the wiper blade, to use as an alignment aid on refitting.
3 Where applicable, lift up the wiper arm spindle nut cover, then slacken and remove the spindle nut **(see illustrations)**.
4 Lift the wiper blade off the surface of the glass, then counteract the tension of the hinge spring by pressing against the centre of the hinge. Lift the wiper arm squarely from the spindle. If necessary, the arm can be carefully levered off the spindle using a suitable flat-bladed screwdriver.
5 If both windscreen wiper arms are removed, note their locations, as different arms are fitted to the driver's and passenger's sides on certain models.

Refitting

6 Ensure that the wiper arm and spindle splines are clean and dry.
7 When refitting a windscreen or tailgate wiper arm, refit the arm to the spindle, aligning the wiper blade with the tape fitted before removal. If both windscreen wiper arms have been removed, ensure that the arms are refitted to

their correct positions as noted before removal.
8 Refit the spindle nut, tighten it securely, and where applicable, clip the nut cover back into position.
9 Operate the wipers and check that the swept area is satisfactory. If the tip of the blade wipes beyond the edge of the windscreen, the arm should be removed from the spindle, rotated by one spline and refitted.
10 Switch off the wipers and check that both wiper blades are level when at rest. If they are not, they may snag each other during operation and jam. Rectify this by adjusting the position of the wiper arms on their spindles, as described in the previous paragraph.

12 Windscreen wiper motor and linkage - removal and refitting

Removal

1 Disconnect the battery negative lead.
2 Remove both wiper arms (Section 11).
3 Where applicable, remove the securing screws and plastic clips, and withdraw the air inlet and bulkhead cowl panel at the rear of the engine bay.
4 Disconnect the wiper motor wiring plug.
5 Slacken and withdraw the motor and linkage securing bolts, then withdraw the assembly from the bulkhead **(see illustration)**.
6 If desired, the motor may be detached from the linkage by removing the securing screws, but note the correct operation of the automatic

blade parking mechanism depends on the angle between the linkage with and the wiper motor shaft being correctly set. Make alignment markings, before attempting disassembly

Refitting

7 Refitting is a reversal of removal, but ensure that the motor drive is in the "parked" position before reconnecting the crank arm (refer to paragraph 6).

13 Tailgate wiper motor - removal and refitting

Removal

1 Disconnect the battery negative lead.
2 Remove the tailgate inner trim panel, by carefully prising out each of the press stud fixings.
3 Remove the wiper arm (Section 11).
4 Working inside the tailgate space, unplug the tailgate wiper motor wiring at the connector.
5 Unscrew the bolts securing the motor mounting bracket to the tailgate **(see illustration)**.
6 Release the spindle grommet from the bodywork, then withdraw the motor assembly through the aperture in the tailgate and lift up the wiper **(see illustration)**.

Refitting

7 Refitting is a reversal of removal. Refit the wiper arm with reference to Section 11.

13.5 Unscrew the bolts securing the motor mounting bracket to the tailgate (arrowed)

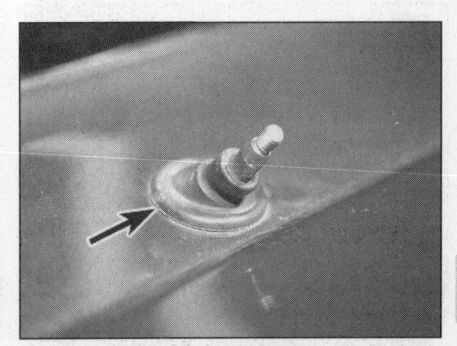

13.6 Release the spindle grommet (arrowed) from the bodywork

12•12 Wiring diagrams

Key to symbols

Symbol	Description
Bulb	
Switch	
Multiple contact switch (ganged)	
Fuse/fusible link	
Resistor	
Variable resistor	
Connecting wires	
Item no.	
Pump/motor	
Earth	
Gauge/meter	
Diode	
Line connector	
Solenoid actuator	

Cross sectional area and wire colour — 0.5B/R (0.5mm² black/red)

Connections to other circuits (e.g. diagram 3/grid location B2. Direction of arrow denotes current flow.)

Wire - permanent positive supply (double line)

Wire - permanent direct earth (thick line)

Wire - interconnecting (thin line)

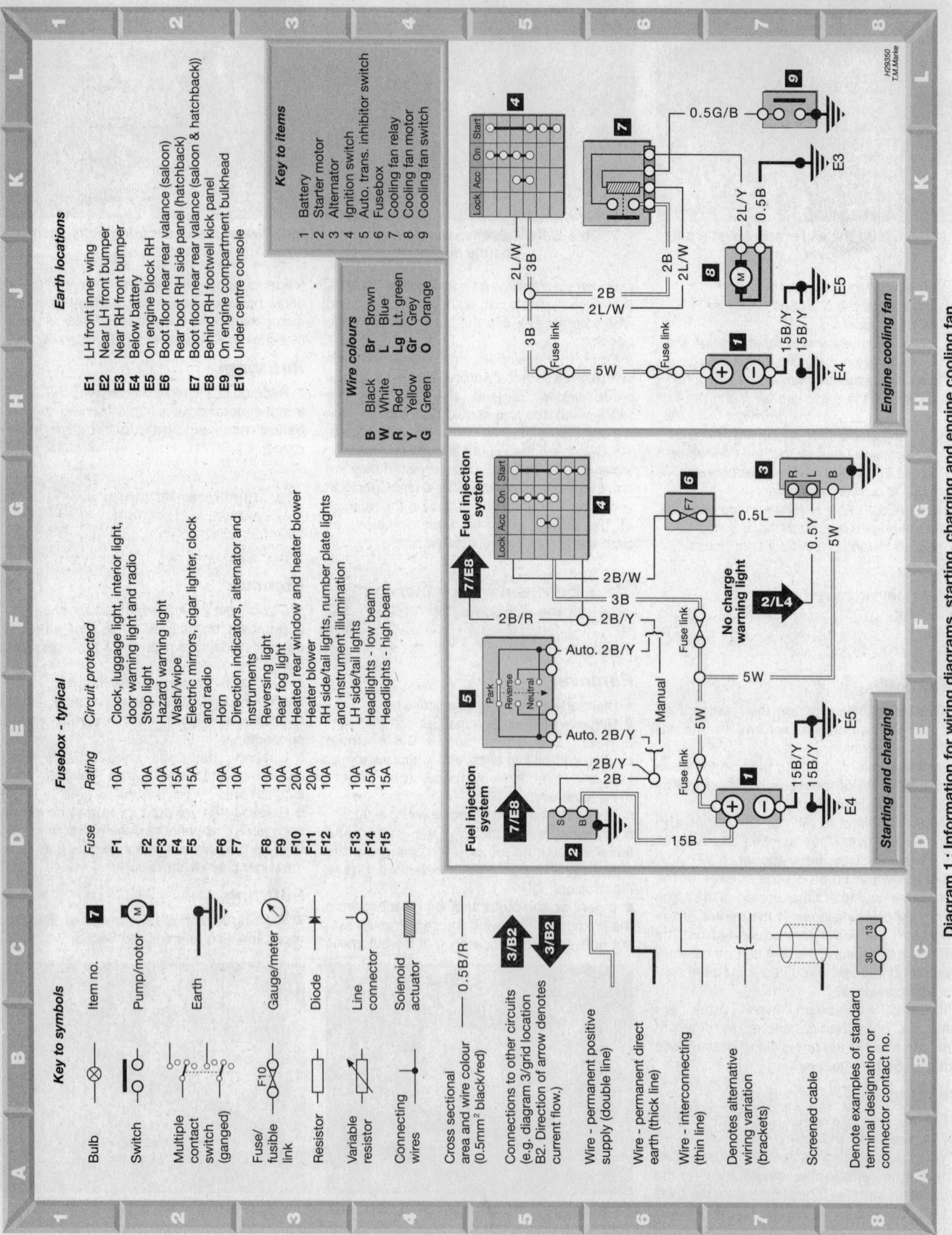

Denotes alternative wiring variation (brackets)

Screened cable

Denote examples of standard terminal designation or connector contact no.

Fusebox - typical

Fuse	Rating	Circuit protected
F1	10A	Clock, luggage light, interior light, door warning light and radio
F2	10A	Stop light
F3	10A	Hazard warning light
F4	15A	Wash/wipe
F5	15A	Electric mirrors, cigar lighter, clock and radio
F6	10A	Horn
F7	10A	Direction indicators, alternator and instruments
F8	10A	Reversing light
F9	10A	Rear fog light
F10	20A	Heated rear window and heater blower
F11	20A	Heater blower
F12	10A	RH side/tail lights, number plate lights and instrument illumination
F13	10A	LH side/tail lights
F14	15A	Headlights - low beam
F15	15A	Headlights - high beam

Key to items

1. Battery
2. Starter motor
3. Alternator
4. Ignition switch
5. Auto. trans. inhibitor switch
6. Fusebox
7. Cooling fan relay
8. Cooling fan motor
9. Cooling fan switch

Wire colours

B	Black	Br	Brown
W	White	L	Blue
R	Red	Lg	Lt. green
Y	Yellow	Gr	Grey
G	Green	O	Orange

Earth locations

E1	LH front inner wing
E2	Near LH front bumper
E3	Near RH front bumper
E4	Below battery
E5	On engine block RH
E6	Boot floor near rear valance (saloon)
E7	Rear boot floor near rear valance (hatchback)
E8	Boot floor near rear valance (saloon & hatchback)
E9	Behind RH footwell kick panel
E10	On engine compartment bulkhead
	Under centre console

Diagram 1 : Information for wiring diagrams, starting, charging and engine cooling fan

Engine cooling fan

Starting and charging

Wiring diagrams 12•13

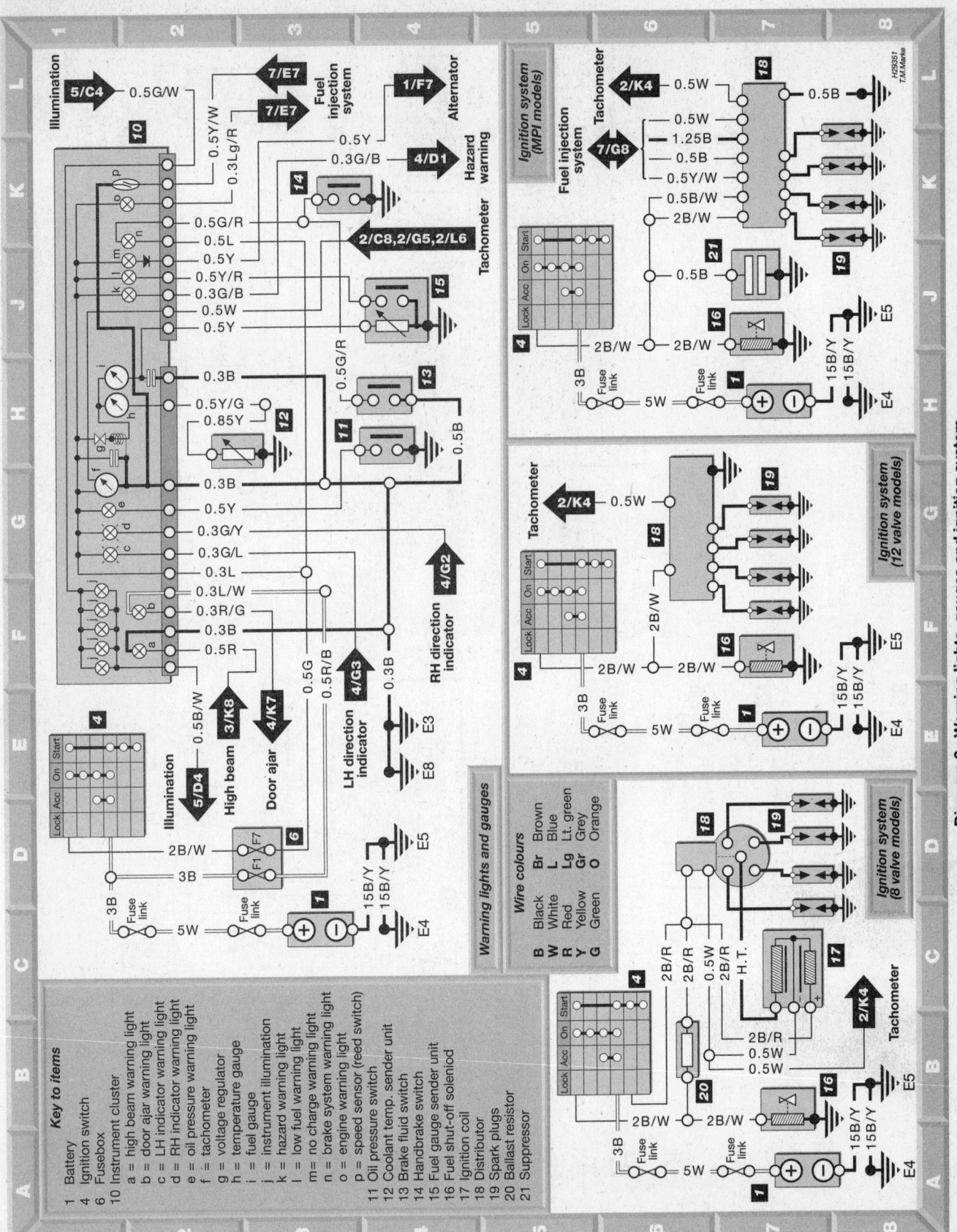

Diagram 2 : Warning lights, gauges and ignition system

12•14 Wiring diagrams

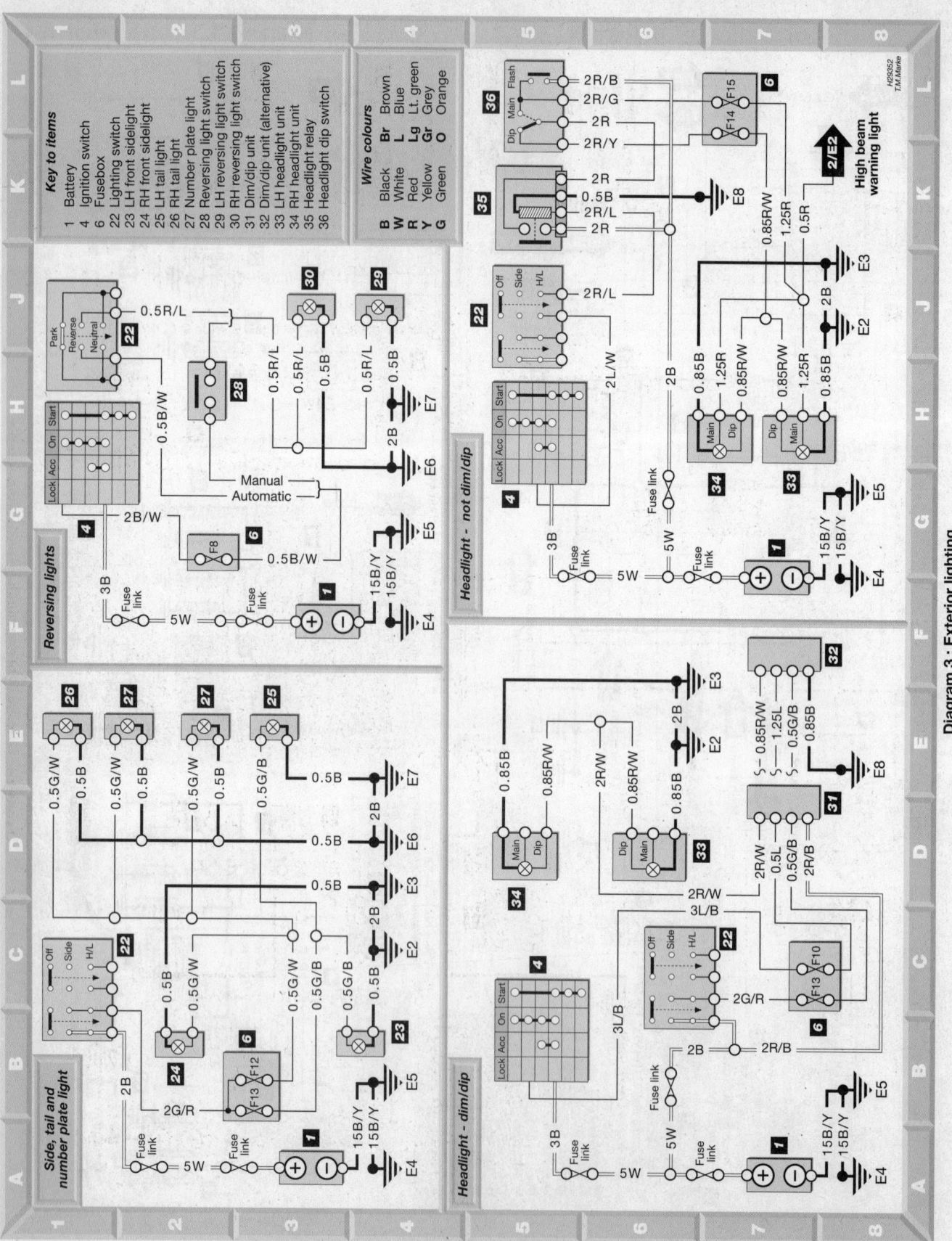

Key to items

1. Battery
4. Ignition switch
6. Fusebox
22. Lighting switch
23. LH front sidelight
24. RH front sidelight
25. LH tail light
26. RH tail light
27. Number plate light
28. Reversing light switch
29. LH reversing light switch
30. RH reversing light switch (alternative)
31. Dim/dip unit
32. Dim/dip unit (alternative)
33. LH headlight unit
34. RH headlight unit
35. Headlight relay
36. Headlight dip switch

Wire colours

B	Black	Br	Brown
W	White	L	Blue
R	Red	Lg	Lt. green
Y	Yellow	Gr	Grey
G	Green	O	Orange

Diagram 3 : Exterior lighting

Wiring diagrams 12•15

Diagram 4 : Exterior lighting continued and interior lighting

Rear fog lights

Interior lighting

Direction indicators and hazard warning

Stop lights

Key to items

1 Battery
4 Ignition switch
6 Fusebox
22 Lighting switch
37 LH direction indicator
38 LH rear direction indicator
39 LH direction indicator side repeater
40 RH direction indicator
41 RH rear direction indicator
42 RH direction indicator side repeater
43 Direction indicator flasher relay
44 Direction indicator switch
45 Hazard switch
46 Stoplight switch
47 LH stoplight
48 RH stoplight
49 Rear foglight switch
50 Rear foglight
51 Interior light
52 Interior light door switch
53 Luggage compartment light
54 Luggage compartment light switch

Wire colours

B	Black	Br	Brown
W	White	L	Blue
R	Red	Lg	Lt. green
Y	Yellow	Gr	Grey
G	Green	O	Orange

12

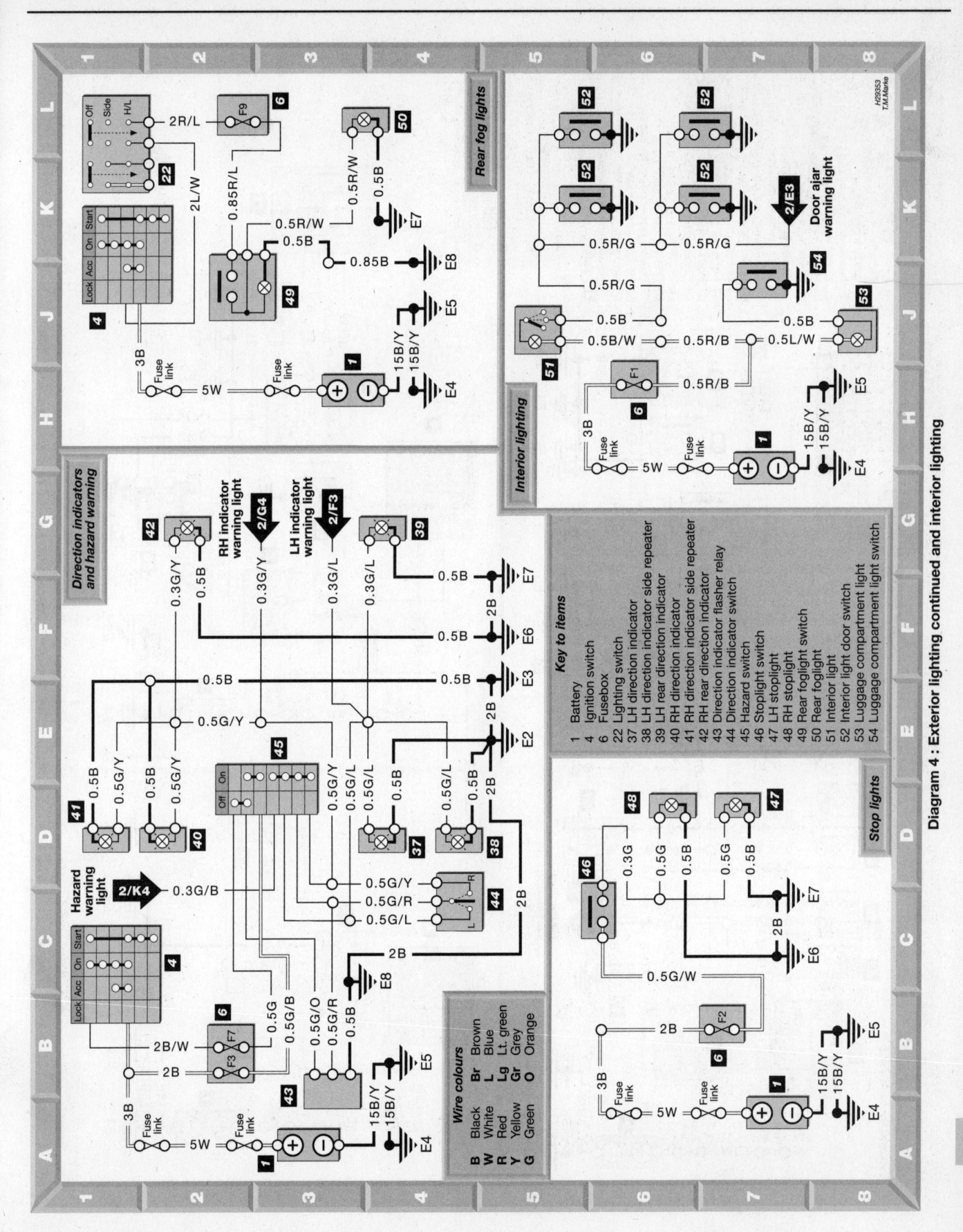

12•16 Wiring diagrams

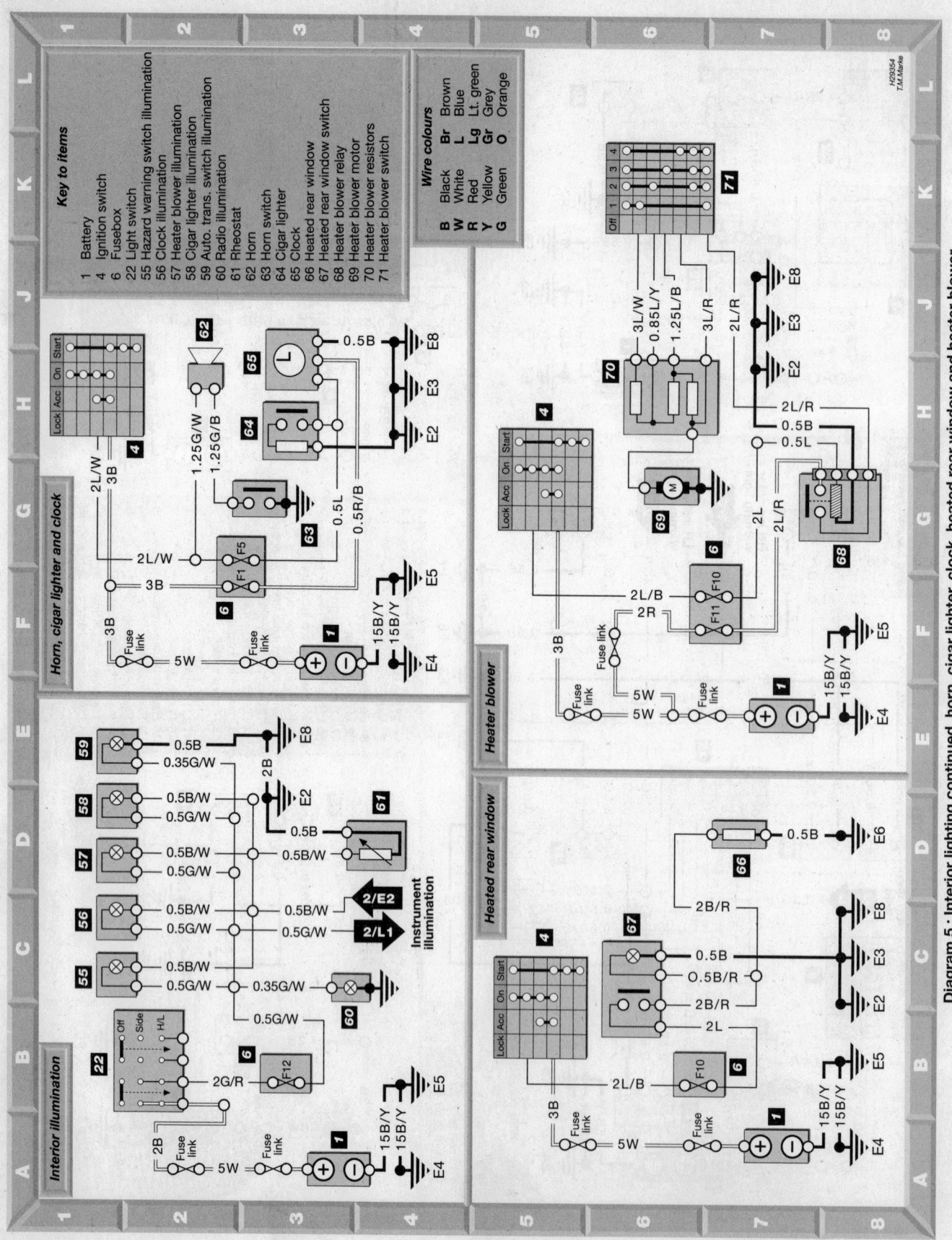

Key to items
1 Battery
4 Ignition switch
6 Fusebox
22 Light switch
55 Hazard warning switch illumination
56 Clock illumination
57 Heater blower illumination
58 Cigar lighter illumination
59 Auto. trans. switch illumination
60 Radio illumination
61 Rheostat
62 Horn
63 Horn switch
64 Cigar lighter
65 Clock
66 Heated rear window
67 Heated rear window switch
68 Heater blower relay
69 Heater blower motor
70 Heater blower resistors
71 Heater blower switch

Wire colours
B Black — Br Brown
W White — L Blue
R Red — Lg Lt. green
Y Yellow — Gr Grey
G Green — O Orange

Diagram 5 : Interior lighting continued, horn, cigar lighter, clock, heated rear window and heater blower

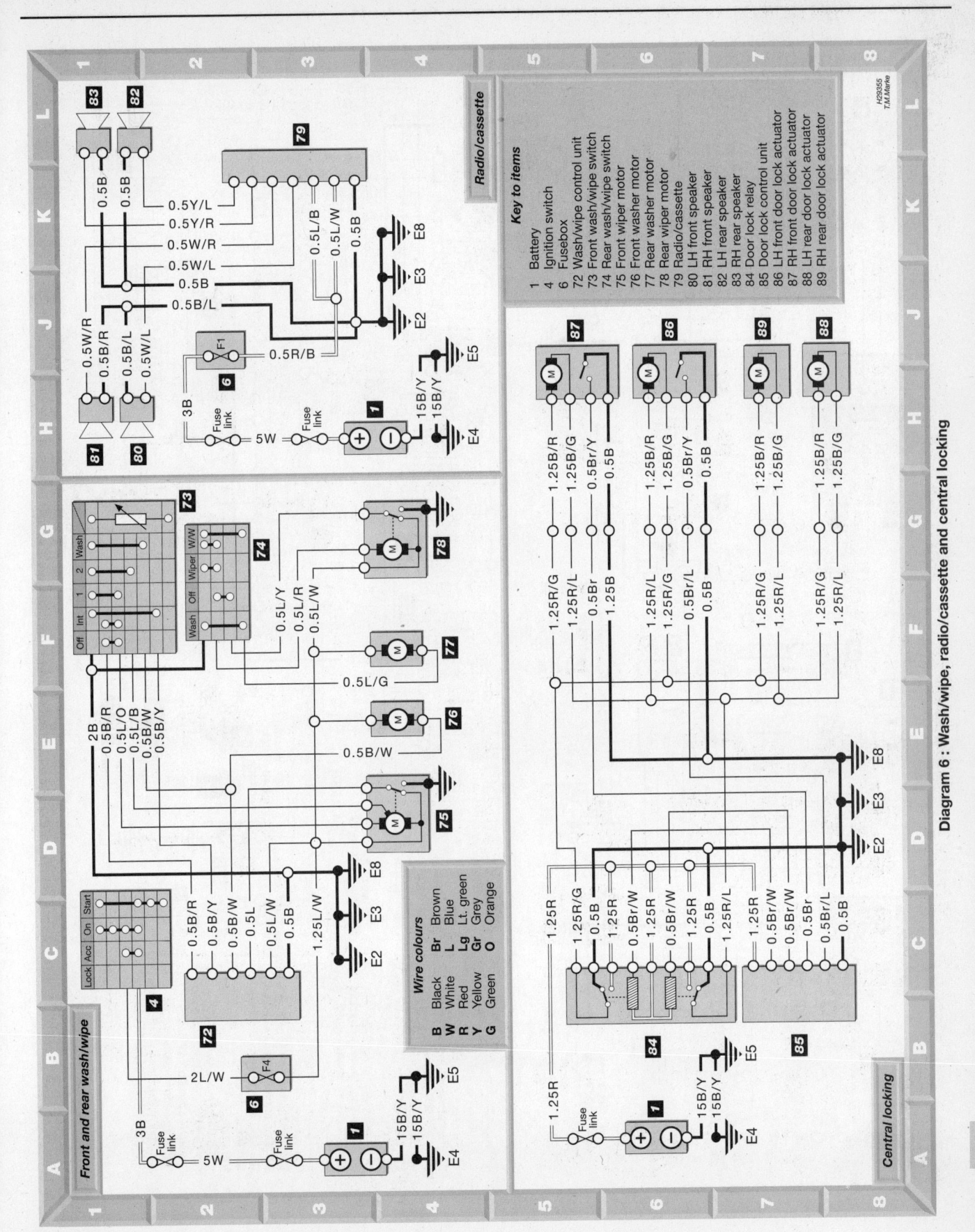

Wiring diagrams 12•17

Key to items

1 Battery
4 Ignition switch
6 Fusebox
72 Wash/wipe control unit
73 Front wash/wipe switch
74 Rear wash/wipe switch
75 Front wiper motor
76 Front washer motor
77 Rear wiper motor
78 Rear washer motor
79 Radio/cassette
80 LH front speaker
81 RH front speaker
82 LH rear speaker
83 RH rear speaker
84 Door lock relay
85 Door lock control unit
86 LH front door lock actuator
87 RH front door lock actuator
88 LH rear door lock actuator
89 RH rear door lock actuator

Wire colours

B	Black	Br	Brown
W	White	L	Blue
R	Red	Lg	Lt. green
Y	Yellow	Gr	Grey
G	Green	O	Orange

Diagram 6 : Wash/wipe, radio/cassette and central locking

12•18 Wiring diagrams

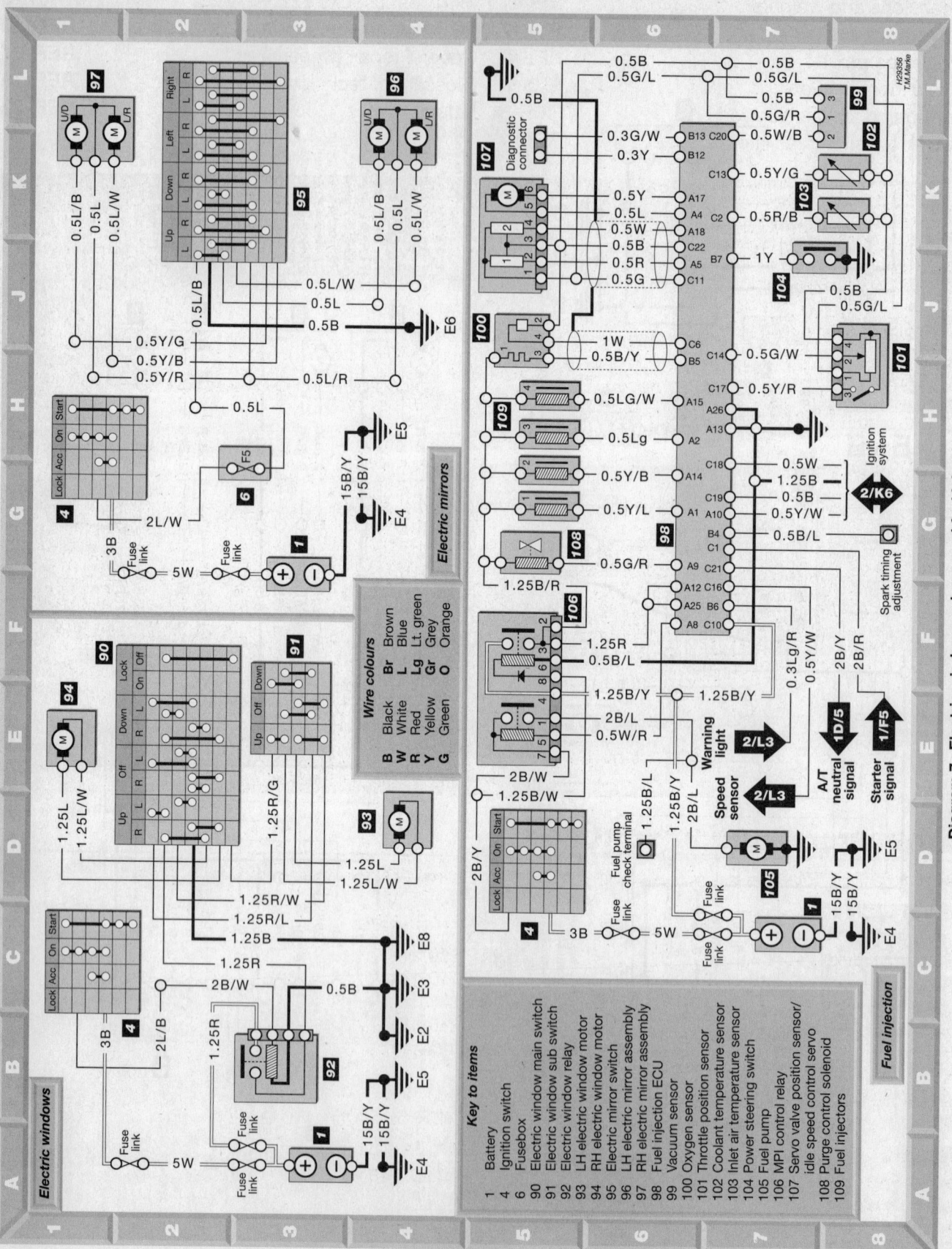

Diagram 7: Electric windows, mirrors and fuel injection

Wire colours
- B Black
- W White
- R Red
- Y Yellow
- G Green
- Br Brown
- L Blue
- Lg Lt. green
- Gr Grey
- O Orange

Key to items
- 1 Battery
- 4 Ignition switch
- 6 Fusebox
- 90 Electric window main switch
- 91 Electric window sub switch
- 92 Electric window relay
- 93 LH electric window motor
- 94 RH electric window motor
- 95 Electric mirror switch
- 96 LH electric mirror assembly
- 97 RH electric mirror assembly
- 98 Fuel injection ECU
- 99 Vacuum sensor
- 100 Oxygen sensor
- 101 Throttle position sensor
- 102 Coolant temperature sensor
- 103 Inlet air temperature sensor
- 104 Power steering switch
- 105 Fuel pump
- 106 MPI control relay
- 107 Servo valve position sensor/idle speed control servo
- 108 Purge control solenoid
- 109 Fuel injectors

Reference REF•1

Dimensions and weights . . . . REF•1
Conversion factors . . . . REF•2
Buying spare parts . . . . REF•3
Vehicle identification . . . . REF•3
Jacking and vehicle support . . . . REF•3
Tools and working facilities . . . . REF•4
MOT test checks . . . . REF•6
Fault finding . . . . REF•10
General repair procedures . . . . REF•17
Glossary of technical terms . . . . REF•18
Index . . . . REF•23

Dimensions and weights

Note: All figures are approximate, and may vary according to model. Refer to manufacturer's data for exact figures.

Dimensions

Overall length:
   Saloon models . . . . 4280 mm
   Aeroback models . . . . 4110 mm
Overall width . . . . 1655 mm
Overall height (unladen) . . . . 1360 mm
Wheelbase . . . . 2380 mm
Track
   Front . . . . 1390 mm
   Rear . . . . 1340 mm

Weights

Kerb weight . . . . 940 to 1015 kg*
Maximum payload . . . . 405 kg

Depending on model and specification.

Conversion factors

Length (distance)
Inches (in)	x 25.4	= Millimetres (mm)	x 0.0394	= Inches (in)
Feet (ft)	x 0.305	= Metres (m)	x 3.281	= Feet (ft)
Miles	x 1.609	= Kilometres (km)	x 0.621	= Miles

Volume (capacity)
Cubic inches (cu in; in^3)	x 16.387	= Cubic centimetres (cc; cm^3)	x 0.061	= Cubic inches (cu in; in^3)
Imperial pints (Imp pt)	x 0.568	= Litres (l)	x 1.76	= Imperial pints (Imp pt)
Imperial quarts (Imp qt)	x 1.137	= Litres (l)	x 0.88	= Imperial quarts (Imp qt)
Imperial quarts (Imp qt)	x 1.201	= US quarts (US qt)	x 0.833	= Imperial quarts (Imp qt)
US quarts (US qt)	x 0.946	= Litres (l)	x 1.057	= US quarts (US qt)
Imperial gallons (Imp gal)	x 4.546	= Litres (l)	x 0.22	= Imperial gallons (Imp gal)
Imperial gallons (Imp gal)	x 1.201	= US gallons (US gal)	x 0.833	= Imperial gallons (Imp gal)
US gallons (US gal)	x 3.785	= Litres (l)	x 0.264	= US gallons (US gal)

Mass (weight)
Ounces (oz)	x 28.35	= Grams (g)	x 0.035	= Ounces (oz)
Pounds (lb)	x 0.454	= Kilograms (kg)	x 2.205	= Pounds (lb)

Force
Ounces-force (ozf; oz)	x 0.278	= Newtons (N)	x 3.6	= Ounces-force (ozf; oz)
Pounds-force (lbf; lb)	x 4.448	= Newtons (N)	x 0.225	= Pounds-force (lbf; lb)
Newtons (N)	x 0.1	= Kilograms-force (kgf; kg)	x 9.81	= Newtons (N)

Pressure
Pounds-force per square inch (psi; lbf/in^2; lb/in^2)	x 0.070	= Kilograms-force per square centimetre (kgf/cm^2; kg/cm^2)	x 14.223	= Pounds-force per square inch (psi; lbf/in^2; lb/in^2)
Pounds-force per square inch (psi; lbf/in^2; lb/in^2)	x 0.068	= Atmospheres (atm)	x 14.696	= Pounds-force per square inch (psi; lbf/in^2; lb/in^2)
Pounds-force per square inch (psi; lbf/in^2; lb/in^2)	x 0.069	= Bars	x 14.5	= Pounds-force per square inch (psi; lbf/in^2; lb/in^2)
Pounds-force per square inch (psi; lbf/in^2; lb/in^2)	x 6.895	= Kilopascals (kPa)	x 0.145	= Pounds-force per square inch (psi; lbf/in^2; lb/in^2)
Kilopascals (kPa)	x 0.01	= Kilograms-force per square centimetre (kgf/cm^2; kg/cm^2)	x 98.1	= Kilopascals (kPa)
Millibar (mbar)	x 100	= Pascals (Pa)	x 0.01	= Millibar (mbar)
Millibar (mbar)	x 0.0145	= Pounds-force per square inch (psi; lbf/in^2; lb/in^2)	x 68.947	= Millibar (mbar)
Millibar (mbar)	x 0.75	= Millimetres of mercury (mmHg)	x 1.333	= Millibar (mbar)
Millibar (mbar)	x 0.401	= Inches of water (inH$_2$O)	x 2.491	= Millibar (mbar)
Millimetres of mercury (mmHg)	x 0.535	= Inches of water (inH$_2$O)	x 1.868	= Millimetres of mercury (mmHg)
Inches of water (inH$_2$O)	x 0.036	= Pounds-force per square inch (psi; lbf/in^2; lb/in^2)	x 27.68	= Inches of water (inH$_2$O)

Torque (moment of force)
Pounds-force inches (lbf in; lb in)	x 1.152	= Kilograms-force centimetre (kgf cm; kg cm)	x 0.868	= Pounds-force inches (lbf in; lb in)
Pounds-force inches (lbf in; lb in)	x 0.113	= Newton metres (Nm)	x 8.85	= Pounds-force inches (lbf in; lb in)
Pounds-force inches (lbf in; lb in)	x 0.083	= Pounds-force feet (lbf ft; lb ft)	x 12	= Pounds-force inches (lbf in; lb in)
Pounds-force feet (lbf ft; lb ft)	x 0.138	= Kilograms-force metres (kgf m; kg m)	x 7.233	= Pounds-force feet (lbf ft; lb ft)
Pounds-force feet (lbf ft; lb ft)	x 1.356	= Newton metres (Nm)	x 0.738	= Pounds-force feet (lbf ft; lb ft)
Newton metres (Nm)	x 0.102	= Kilograms-force metres (kgf m; kg m)	x 9.804	= Newton metres (Nm)

Power
Horsepower (hp)	x 745.7	= Watts (W)	x 0.0013	= Horsepower (hp)

Velocity (speed)
Miles per hour (miles/hr; mph)	x 1.609	= Kilometres per hour (km/hr; kph)	x 0.621	= Miles per hour (miles/hr; mph)

Fuel consumption*
Miles per gallon (mpg)	x 0.354	= Kilometres per litre (km/l)	x 2.825	= Miles per gallon (mpg)

Temperature
Degrees Fahrenheit = (°C x 1.8) + 32   Degrees Celsius (Degrees Centigrade; °C) = (°F - 32) x 0.56

It is common practice to convert from miles per gallon (mpg) to litres/100 kilometres (l/100km), where mpg x l/100 km = 282

Buying spare parts REF•3

Spare parts are available from many sources, including maker's appointed garages, accessory shops, and motor factors. To be sure of obtaining the correct parts, it may sometimes be necessary to quote the vehicle identification number. If possible, it can also be useful to take the old parts along for positive identification. Items such as starter motors and alternators may be available under a service exchange scheme - any parts returned should always be clean.

Our advice regarding spare part sources is as follows.

Officially-appointed garages

This is the best source of parts which are peculiar to your car, and are not otherwise generally available (eg badges, interior trim, certain body panels, etc). It is also the only place at which you should buy parts if the vehicle is still under warranty.

Accessory shops

These are very good places to buy materials and components needed for the maintenance of your car (oil, air and fuel filters, spark plugs, light bulbs, drivebelts, oils and greases, brake pads, touch-up paint, etc). Parts like this sold by a reputable shop are of the same standard as those used by the car manufacturer.

Motor factors

Good factors will stock all the more important components which wear out comparatively quickly and can sometimes supply individual components needed for the overhaul of a larger assembly. They may also handle work such as cylinder block reboring, crankshaft regrinding and balancing, etc.

Tyre and exhaust specialists

These outlets may be independent or members of a local or national chain. They frequently offer competitive prices when compared with a main dealer or local garage, but it will pay to obtain several quotes before making a decision. Also ask what 'extras' may be added to the quote - for instance, fitting a new valve and balancing the wheel are both often charged on top of the price of a new tyre.

Other sources

Beware of parts or materials obtained from market stalls, car boot sales or similar outlets. Such items are not invariably sub-standard, but there is little chance of compensation if they do prove unsatisfactory. In the case of safety-critical components such as brake pads there is the risk not only of financial loss but also of an accident causing injury or death.

Vehicle identification

Modifications are a continuing and unpublicised process in vehicle manufacture, quite apart from major model changes. Spare parts lists are compiled upon a numerical basis, the individual vehicle identification numbers being essential to correct identification of the component concerned.

When ordering spare parts, always give as much information as possible. Quote the car model, year of manufacture, body and engine numbers, as appropriate.

The chassis number is stamped on the rear of the engine compartment bulkhead. The Vehicle Identification Number (VIN) plate is riveted to the engine compartment bulkhead, and can be viewed once the bonnet is open. The plate carries the VIN, chassis number, vehicle weight information, and paint and trim colour codes (see illustration).

The Engine number is stamped on a machined surface on the front upper surface of the cylinder head, at the timing belt end (see illustration).

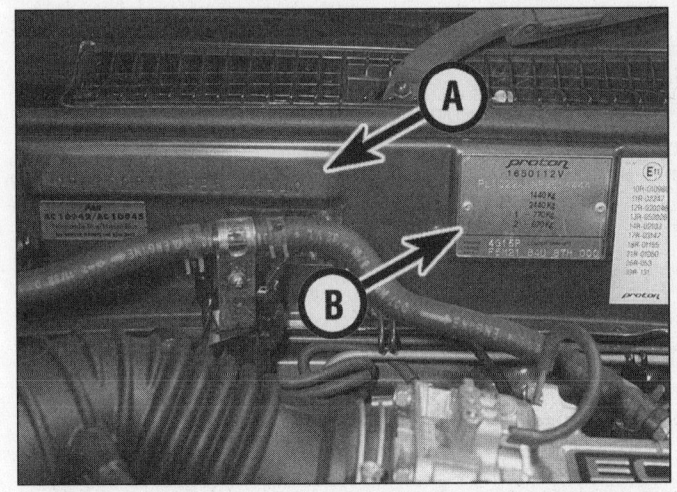

The chassis number and Vehicle Identification Number (VIN) plate are located to the rear of engine compartment bulkhead

A Chassis number   B VIN plate

The Engine number is stamped on a machined surface on the front upper surface of the cylinder head, at the timing belt end

Jacking and vehicle support

The jack supplied with the vehicle tool kit should only be used for changing the roadwheels - see "Wheel changing" at the front of this manual. When carrying out any other kind of work, raise the vehicle using a hydraulic (or "trolley") jack, and always supplement the jack with axle stands positioned under the vehicle jacking points.

When using a hydraulic jack or axle stands, always position the jack head or axle stand head under one of the relevant jacking points. **Do not** jack the vehicle under the sump or any of the steering or suspension components other than those indicated.

Never work under, around, or near a raised vehicle, unless it is adequately supported on stands.

REF•4 Tools and working facilities

Introduction

A selection of good tools is a fundamental requirement for anyone contemplating the maintenance and repair of a motor vehicle. For the owner who does not possess any, their purchase will prove a considerable expense, offsetting some of the savings made by doing-it-yourself. However, provided that the tools purchased meet the relevant national safety standards and are of good quality, they will last for many years and prove an extremely worthwhile investment.

To help the average owner to decide which tools are needed to carry out the various tasks detailed in this manual, we have compiled three lists of tools under the following headings: *Maintenance and minor repair*, *Repair and overhaul*, and *Special*. Newcomers to practical mechanics should start off with the *Maintenance and minor repair* tool kit, and confine themselves to the simpler jobs around the vehicle. Then, as confidence and experience grow, more difficult tasks can be undertaken, with extra tools being purchased as, and when, they are needed. In this way, a *Maintenance and minor repair* tool kit can be built up into a *Repair and overhaul* tool kit over a considerable period of time, without any major cash outlays. The experienced do-it-yourselfer will have a tool kit good enough for most repair and overhaul procedures, and will add tools from the *Special* category when it is felt that the expense is justified by the amount of use to which these tools will be put.

Maintenance and minor repair tool kit

The tools given in this list should be considered as a minimum requirement if routine maintenance, servicing and minor repair operations are to be undertaken. We recommend the purchase of combination spanners (ring one end, open-ended the other); although more expensive than open-ended ones, they do give the advantages of both types of spanner.

☐ Combination spanners:
  Metric - 8 to 19 mm inclusive
☐ Adjustable spanner - 35 mm jaw (approx.)
☐ Spark plug spanner (with rubber insert) - petrol models
☐ Spark plug gap adjustment tool - petrol models
☐ Set of feeler gauges
☐ Brake bleed nipple spanner
☐ Screwdrivers:
  Flat blade - 100 mm long x 6 mm dia
  Cross blade - 100 mm long x 6 mm dia
☐ Combination pliers
☐ Hacksaw (junior)
☐ Tyre pump
☐ Tyre pressure gauge
☐ Oil can
☐ Oil filter removal tool
☐ Fine emery cloth
☐ Wire brush (small)
☐ Funnel (medium size)

Repair and overhaul tool kit

These tools are virtually essential for anyone undertaking any major repairs to a motor vehicle, and are additional to those given in the *Maintenance and minor repair* list. Included in this list is a comprehensive set of sockets. Although these are expensive, they will be found invaluable as they are so versatile - particularly if various drives are included in the set. We recommend the half-inch square-drive type, as this can be used with most proprietary torque wrenches.

The tools in this list will sometimes need to be supplemented by tools from the *Special* list:

☐ Sockets (or box spanners) to cover range in previous list (including Torx sockets)
☐ Reversible ratchet drive (for use with sockets)
☐ Extension piece, 250 mm (for use with sockets)
☐ Universal joint (for use with sockets)
☐ Torque wrench (for use with sockets)
☐ Self-locking grips
☐ Ball pein hammer
☐ Soft-faced mallet (plastic/aluminium or rubber)
☐ Screwdrivers:
  Flat blade - long & sturdy, short (chubby), and narrow (electrician's) types
  Cross blade – Long & sturdy, and short (chubby) types
☐ Pliers:
  Long-nosed
  Side cutters (electrician's)
  Circlip (internal and external)
☐ Cold chisel - 25 mm
☐ Scriber
☐ Scraper
☐ Centre-punch
☐ Pin punch
☐ Hacksaw
☐ Brake hose clamp
☐ Brake/clutch bleeding kit
☐ Selection of twist drills
☐ Steel rule/straight-edge
☐ Allen keys (inc. splined/Torx type)
☐ Selection of files
☐ Wire brush
☐ Axle stands
☐ Jack (strong trolley or hydraulic type)
☐ Light with extension lead

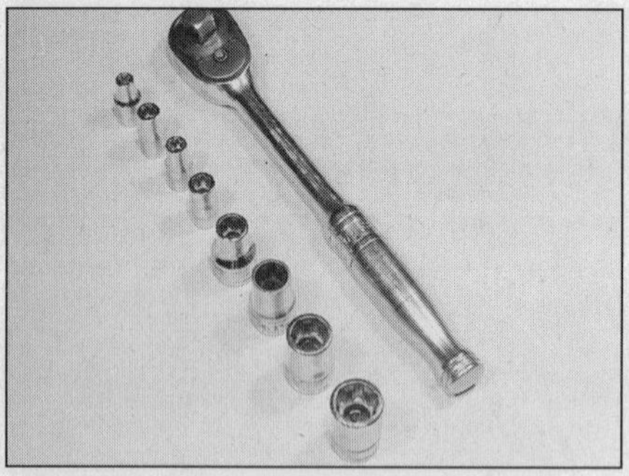

Sockets and reversible ratchet drive

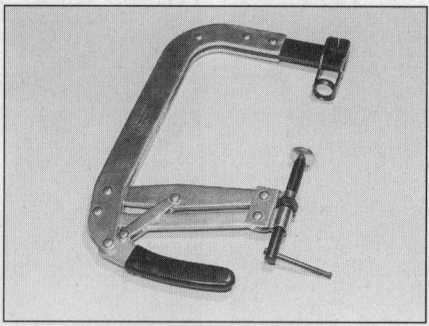

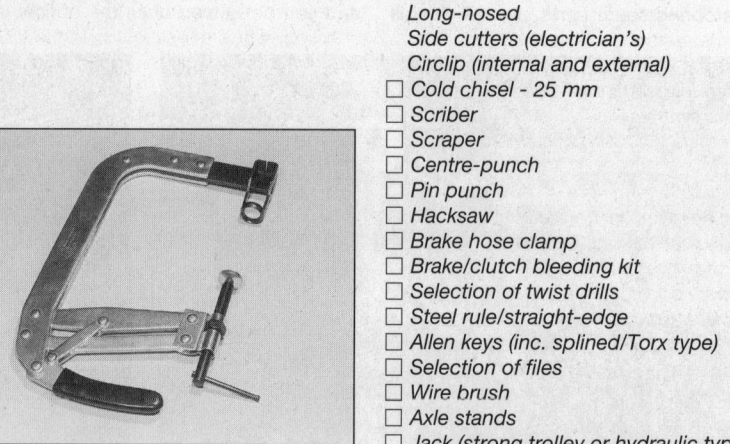

Valve spring compressor

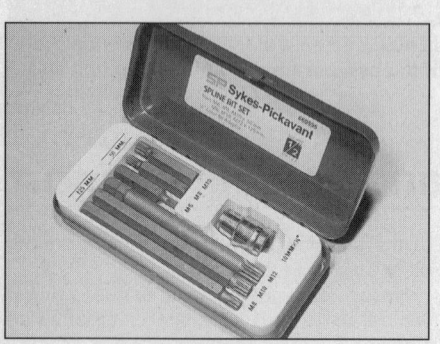

Spline bit set

Piston ring compressor

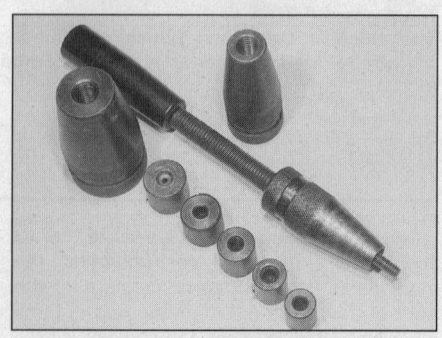

Clutch plate alignment set

Tools and working facilities REF•5

Special tools

The tools in this list are those which are not used regularly, are expensive to buy, or which need to be used in accordance with their manufacturers' instructions. Unless relatively difficult mechanical jobs are undertaken frequently, it will not be economic to buy many of these tools. Where this is the case, you could consider clubbing together with friends (or joining a motorists' club) to make a joint purchase, or borrowing the tools against a deposit from a local garage or tool hire specialist. It is worth noting that many of the larger DIY superstores now carry a large range of special tools for hire at modest rates.

The following list contains only those tools and instruments freely available to the public, and not those special tools produced by the vehicle manufacturer specifically for its dealer network. You will find occasional references to these manufacturers' special tools in the text of this manual. Generally, an alternative method of doing the job without the vehicle manufacturers' special tool is given. However, sometimes there is no alternative to using them. Where this is the case and the relevant tool cannot be bought or borrowed, you will have to entrust the work to a dealer.

☐ Valve spring compressor
☐ Valve grinding tool
☐ Piston ring compressor
☐ Piston ring removal/installation tool
☐ Cylinder bore hone
☐ Balljoint separator
☐ Coil spring compressors (where applicable)
☐ Two/three-legged hub and bearing puller
☐ Impact screwdriver
☐ Micrometer and/or vernier calipers
☐ Dial gauge
☐ Stroboscopic timing light
☐ Dwell angle meter/tachometer
☐ Universal electrical multi-meter
☐ Cylinder compression gauge
☐ Hand-operated vacuum pump and gauge
☐ Clutch plate alignment set
☐ Brake shoe steady spring cup removal tool
☐ Bush and bearing removal/installation set
☐ Stud extractors
☐ Tap and die set
☐ Lifting tackle
☐ Trolley jack

Buying tools

Reputable motor accessory shops and superstores often offer excellent quality tools at discount prices, so it pays to shop around.

Remember, you don't have to buy the most expensive items on the shelf, but it is always advisable to steer clear of the very cheap tools. Beware of 'bargains' offered on market stalls or at car boot sales. There are plenty of good tools around at reasonable prices, but always aim to purchase items which meet the relevant national safety standards. If in doubt, ask the proprietor or manager of the shop for advice before making a purchase.

Care and maintenance of tools

Having purchased a reasonable tool kit, it is necessary to keep the tools in a clean and serviceable condition. After use, always wipe off any dirt, grease and metal particles using a clean, dry cloth, before putting the tools away. Never leave them lying around after they have been used. A simple tool rack on the garage or workshop wall for items such as screwdrivers and pliers is a good idea. Store all normal spanners and sockets in a metal box. Any measuring instruments, gauges, meters, etc, must be carefully stored where they cannot be damaged or become rusty.

Take a little care when tools are used. Hammer heads inevitably become marked, and screwdrivers lose the keen edge on their blades from time to time. A little timely attention with emery cloth or a file will soon restore items like this to a good finish.

Working facilities

Not to be forgotten when discussing tools is the workshop itself. If anything more than routine maintenance is to be carried out, a suitable working area becomes essential.

It is appreciated that many an owner-mechanic is forced by circumstances to remove an engine or similar item without the benefit of a garage or workshop. Having done this, any repairs should always be done under the cover of a roof.

Wherever possible, any dismantling should be done on a clean, flat workbench or table at a suitable working height.

Any workbench needs a vice; one with a jaw opening of 100 mm is suitable for most jobs. As mentioned previously, some clean dry storage space is also required for tools, as well as for any lubricants, cleaning fluids, touch-up paints etc, which become necessary.

Another item which may be required, and which has a much more general usage, is an electric drill with a chuck capacity of at least 8 mm. This, together with a good range of twist drills, is virtually essential for fitting accessories.

Last, but not least, always keep a supply of old newspapers and clean, lint-free rags available, and try to keep any working area as clean as possible.

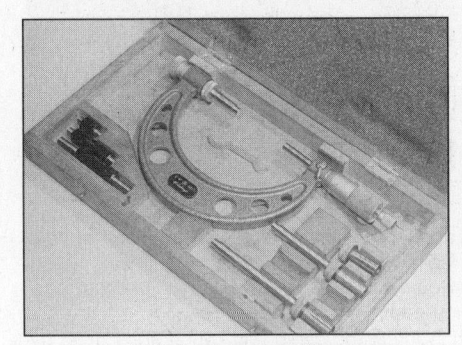

Micrometer set

Dial test indicator ("dial gauge")

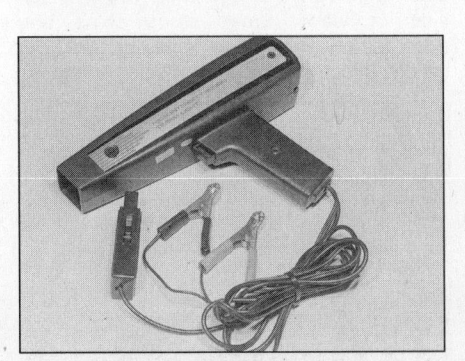

Stroboscopic timing light

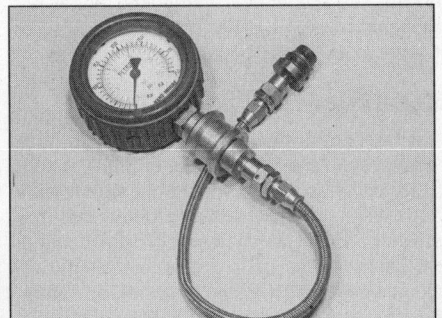

Compression tester

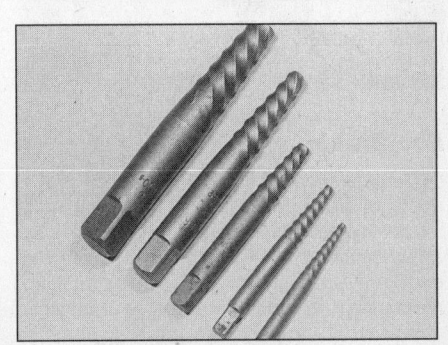

Stud extractor set

REF•6 MOT test checks

This is a guide to getting your vehicle through the MOT test. Obviously it will not be possible to examine the vehicle to the same standard as the professional MOT tester. However, working through the following checks will enable you to identify any problem areas before submitting the vehicle for the test.

Where a testable component is in borderline condition, the tester has discretion in deciding whether to pass or fail it. The basis of such discretion is whether the tester would be happy for a close relative or friend to use the vehicle with the component in that condition. If the vehicle presented is clean and evidently well cared for, the tester may be more inclined to pass a borderline component than if the vehicle is scruffy and apparently neglected.

It has only been possible to summarise the test requirements here, based on the regulations in force at the time of printing. Test standards are becoming increasingly stringent, although there are some exemptions for older vehicles. For full details obtain a copy of the Haynes publication Pass the MOT! (available from stockists of Haynes manuals).

An assistant will be needed to help carry out some of these checks.

The checks have been sub-divided into four categories, as follows:

1 Checks carried out **FROM THE DRIVER'S SEAT**

2 Checks carried out **WITH THE VEHICLE ON THE GROUND**

3 Checks carried out **WITH THE VEHICLE RAISED AND THE WHEELS FREE TO TURN**

4 Checks carried out on **YOUR VEHICLE'S EXHAUST EMISSION SYSTEM**

---

1 Checks carried out **FROM THE DRIVER'S SEAT**

Handbrake

☐ Test the operation of the handbrake. Excessive travel (too many clicks) indicates incorrect brake or cable adjustment.
☐ Check that the handbrake cannot be released by tapping the lever sideways. Check the security of the lever mountings.

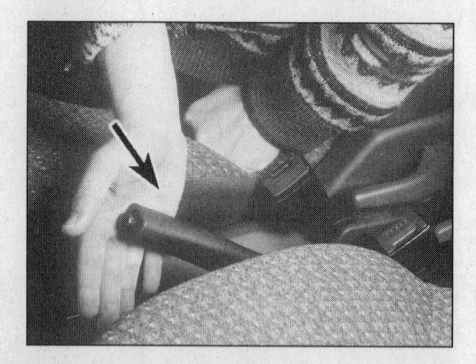

Footbrake

☐ Depress the brake pedal and check that it does not creep down to the floor, indicating a master cylinder fault. Release the pedal, wait a few seconds, then depress it again. If the pedal travels nearly to the floor before firm resistance is felt, brake adjustment or repair is necessary. If the pedal feels spongy, there is air in the hydraulic system which must be removed by bleeding.

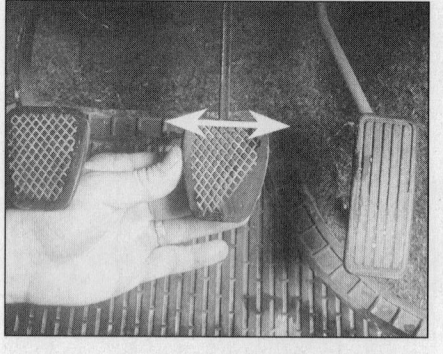

☐ Check that the brake pedal is secure and in good condition. Check also for signs of fluid leaks on the pedal, floor or carpets, which would indicate failed seals in the brake master cylinder.
☐ Check the servo unit (when applicable) by operating the brake pedal several times, then keeping the pedal depressed and starting the engine. As the engine starts, the pedal will move down slightly. If not, the vacuum hose or the servo itself may be faulty.

Steering wheel and column

☐ Examine the steering wheel for fractures or looseness of the hub, spokes or rim.
☐ Move the steering wheel from side to side and then up and down. Check that the steering wheel is not loose on the column, indicating wear or a loose retaining nut. Continue moving the steering wheel as before, but also turn it slightly from left to right.
☐ Check that the steering wheel is not loose on the column, and that there is no abnormal movement of the steering wheel, indicating wear in the column support bearings or couplings.

Windscreen and mirrors

☐ The windscreen must be free of cracks or other significant damage within the driver's field of view. (Small stone chips are acceptable.) Rear view mirrors must be secure, intact, and capable of being adjusted.

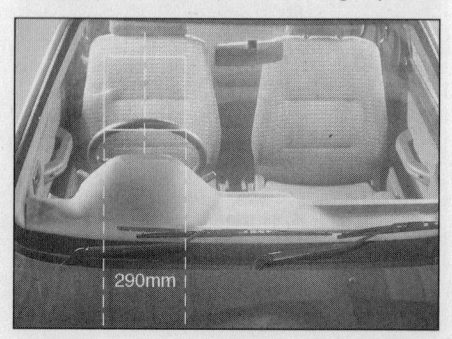

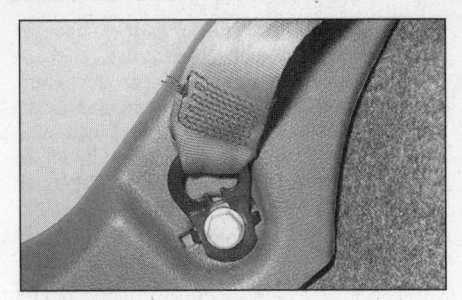

MOT test checks REF•7

Seat belts and seats

Note: *The following checks are applicable to all seat belts, front and rear.*

☐ Examine the webbing of all the belts (including rear belts if fitted) for cuts, serious fraying or deterioration. Fasten and unfasten each belt to check the buckles. If applicable, check the retracting mechanism. Check the security of all seat belt mountings accessible from inside the vehicle.

☐ The front seats themselves must be securely attached and the backrests must lock in the upright position.

Doors

☐ Both front doors must be able to be opened and closed from outside and inside, and must latch securely when closed.

2 Checks carried out WITH THE VEHICLE ON THE GROUND

Vehicle identification

☐ Number plates must be in good condition, secure and legible, with letters and numbers correctly spaced – spacing at (A) should be twice that at (B).

☐ The VIN plate and/or homologation plate must be legible.

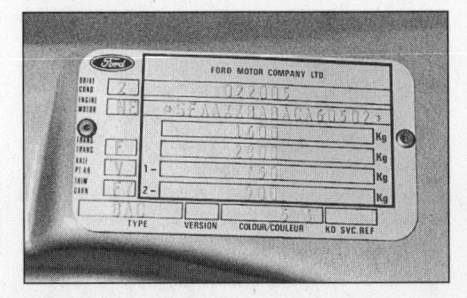

Electrical equipment

☐ Switch on the ignition and check the operation of the horn.

☐ Check the windscreen washers and wipers, examining the wiper blades; renew damaged or perished blades. Also check the operation of the stop-lights.

☐ Check the operation of the sidelights and number plate lights. The lenses and reflectors must be secure, clean and undamaged.

☐ Check the operation and alignment of the headlights. The headlight reflectors must not be tarnished and the lenses must be undamaged.

☐ Switch on the ignition and check the operation of the direction indicators (including the instrument panel tell-tale) and the hazard warning lights. Operation of the sidelights and stop-lights must not affect the indicators - if it does, the cause is usually a bad earth at the rear light cluster.

☐ Check the operation of the rear foglight(s), including the warning light on the instrument panel or in the switch.

Footbrake

☐ Examine the master cylinder, brake pipes and servo unit for leaks, loose mountings, corrosion or other damage.

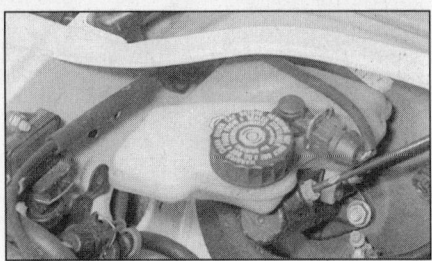

☐ The fluid reservoir must be secure and the fluid level must be between the upper (A) and lower (B) markings.

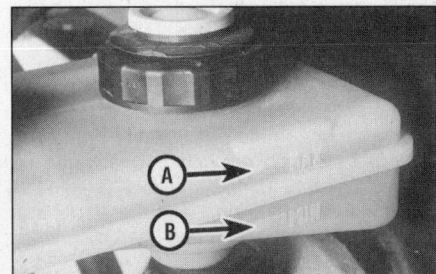

☐ Inspect both front brake flexible hoses for cracks or deterioration of the rubber. Turn the steering from lock to lock, and ensure that the hoses do not contact the wheel, tyre, or any part of the steering or suspension mechanism. With the brake pedal firmly depressed, check the hoses for bulges or leaks under pressure.

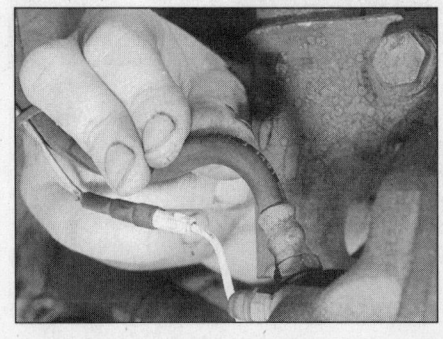

Steering and suspension

☐ Have your assistant turn the steering wheel from side to side slightly, up to the point where the steering gear just begins to transmit this movement to the roadwheels. Check for excessive free play between the steering wheel and the steering gear, indicating wear or insecurity of the steering column joints, the column-to-steering gear coupling, or the steering gear itself.

☐ Have your assistant turn the steering wheel more vigorously in each direction, so that the roadwheels just begin to turn. As this is done, examine all the steering joints, linkages, fittings and attachments. Renew any component that shows signs of wear or damage. On vehicles with power steering, check the security and condition of the steering pump, drivebelt and hoses.

☐ Check that the vehicle is standing level, and at approximately the correct ride height.

Shock absorbers

☐ Depress each corner of the vehicle in turn, then release it. The vehicle should rise and then settle in its normal position. If the vehicle continues to rise and fall, the shock absorber is defective. A shock absorber which has seized will also cause the vehicle to fail.

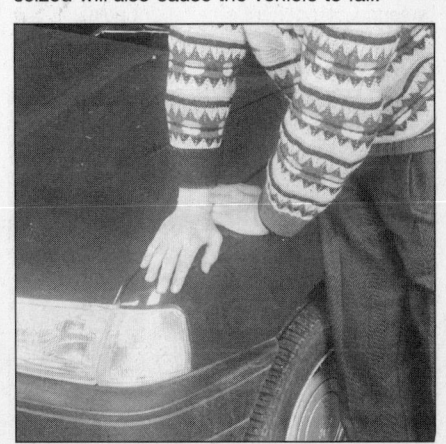

REF•8 MOT test checks

Exhaust system

☐ Start the engine. With your assistant holding a rag over the tailpipe, check the entire system for leaks. Repair or renew leaking sections.

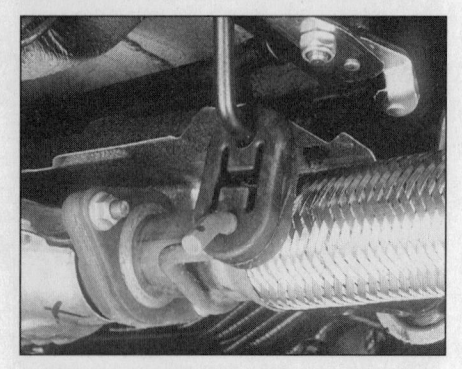

3 Checks carried out WITH THE VEHICLE RAISED AND THE WHEELS FREE TO TURN

Jack up the front and rear of the vehicle, and securely support it on axle stands. Position the stands clear of the suspension assemblies. Ensure that the wheels are clear of the ground and that the steering can be turned from lock to lock.

Steering mechanism

☐ Have your assistant turn the steering from lock to lock. Check that the steering turns smoothly, and that no part of the steering mechanism, including a wheel or tyre, fouls any brake hose or pipe or any part of the body structure.

☐ Examine the steering rack rubber gaiters for damage or insecurity of the retaining clips. If power steering is fitted, check for signs of damage or leakage of the fluid hoses, pipes or connections. Also check for excessive stiffness or binding of the steering, a missing split pin or locking device, or severe corrosion of the body structure within 30 cm of any steering component attachment point.

Front and rear suspension and wheel bearings

☐ Starting at the front right-hand side, grasp the roadwheel at the 3 o'clock and 9 o'clock positions and shake it vigorously. Check for free play or insecurity at the wheel bearings, suspension balljoints, or suspension mountings, pivots and attachments.

☐ Now grasp the wheel at the 12 o'clock and 6 o'clock positions and repeat the previous inspection. Spin the wheel, and check for roughness or tightness of the front wheel bearing.

☐ If excess free play is suspected at a component pivot point, this can be confirmed by using a large screwdriver or similar tool and levering between the mounting and the component attachment. This will confirm whether the wear is in the pivot bush, its retaining bolt, or in the mounting itself (the bolt holes can often become elongated).

☐ Carry out all the above checks at the other front wheel, and then at both rear wheels.

Springs and shock absorbers

☐ Examine the suspension struts (when applicable) for serious fluid leakage, corrosion, or damage to the casing. Also check the security of the mounting points.

☐ If coil springs are fitted, check that the spring ends locate in their seats, and that the spring is not corroded, cracked or broken.

☐ If leaf springs are fitted, check that all leaves are intact, that the axle is securely attached to each spring, and that there is no deterioration of the spring eye mountings, bushes, and shackles.

☐ The same general checks apply to vehicles fitted with other suspension types, such as torsion bars, hydraulic displacer units, etc. Ensure that all mountings and attachments are secure, that there are no signs of excessive wear, corrosion or damage, and (on hydraulic types) that there are no fluid leaks or damaged pipes.

☐ Inspect the shock absorbers for signs of serious fluid leakage. Check for wear of the mounting bushes or attachments, or damage to the body of the unit.

Driveshafts (fwd vehicles only)

☐ Rotate each front wheel in turn and inspect the constant velocity joint gaiters for splits or damage. Also check that each driveshaft is straight and undamaged.

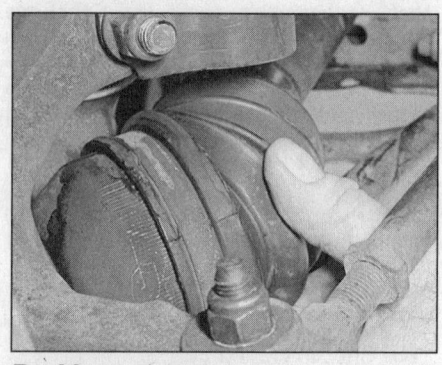

Braking system

☐ If possible without dismantling, check brake pad wear and disc condition. Ensure that the friction lining material has not worn excessively, (A) and that the discs are not fractured, pitted, scored or badly worn (B).

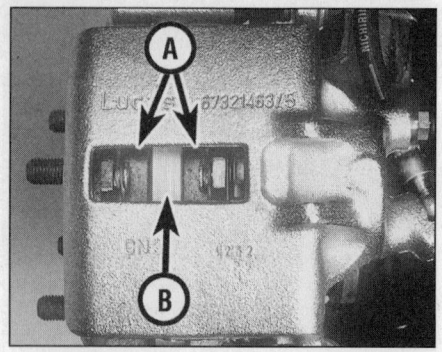

☐ Examine all the rigid brake pipes underneath the vehicle, and the flexible hose(s) at the rear. Look for corrosion, chafing or insecurity of the pipes, and for signs of bulging under pressure, chafing, splits or deterioration of the flexible hoses.

☐ Look for signs of fluid leaks at the brake calipers or on the brake backplates. Repair or renew leaking components.

☐ Slowly spin each wheel, while your assistant depresses and releases the footbrake. Ensure that each brake is operating and does not bind when the pedal is released.

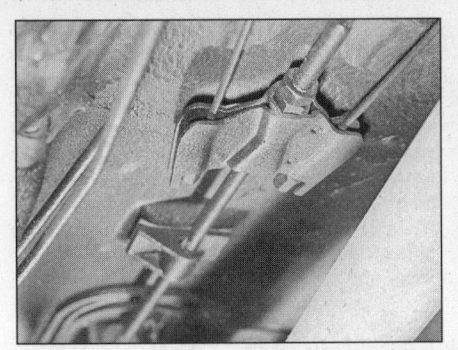

MOT test checks REF•9

☐ Examine the handbrake mechanism, checking for frayed or broken cables, excessive corrosion, or wear or insecurity of the linkage. Check that the mechanism works on each relevant wheel, and releases fully, without binding.

☐ It is not possible to test brake efficiency without special equipment, but a road test can be carried out later to check that the vehicle pulls up in a straight line.

Fuel and exhaust systems

☐ Inspect the fuel tank (including the filler cap), fuel pipes, hoses and unions. All components must be secure and free from leaks.

☐ Examine the exhaust system over its entire length, checking for any damaged, broken or missing mountings, security of the retaining clamps and rust or corrosion.

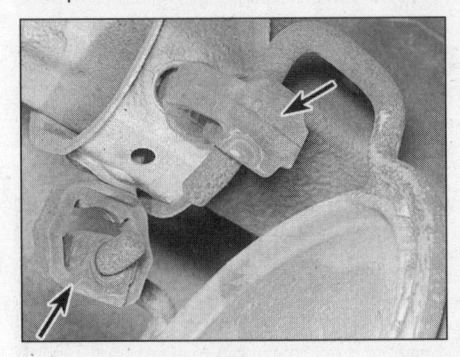

Wheels and tyres

☐ Examine the sidewalls and tread area of each tyre in turn. Check for cuts, tears, lumps, bulges, separation of the tread, and exposure of the ply or cord due to wear or damage. Check that the tyre bead is correctly seated on the wheel rim, that the valve is sound and properly seated, and that the wheel is not distorted or damaged.

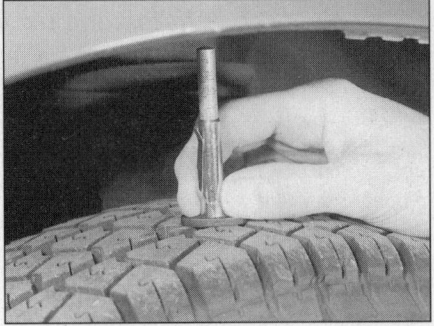

☐ Check that the tyres are of the correct size for the vehicle, that they are of the same size and type on each axle, and that the pressures are correct.

☐ Check the tyre tread depth. The legal minimum at the time of writing is 1.6 mm over at least three-quarters of the tread width. Abnormal tread wear may indicate incorrect front wheel alignment.

Body corrosion

☐ Check the condition of the entire vehicle structure for signs of corrosion in load-bearing areas. (These include chassis box sections, side sills, cross-members, pillars, and all suspension, steering, braking system and seat belt mountings and anchorages.) Any corrosion which has seriously reduced the thickness of a load-bearing area is likely to cause the vehicle to fail. In this case professional repairs are likely to be needed.

☐ Damage or corrosion which causes sharp or otherwise dangerous edges to be exposed will also cause the vehicle to fail.

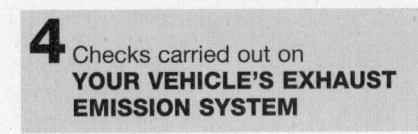

4 Checks carried out on YOUR VEHICLE'S EXHAUST EMISSION SYSTEM

Petrol models

☐ Have the engine at normal operating temperature, and make sure that it is in good tune (ignition system in good order, air filter element clean, etc).

☐ Before any measurements are carried out, raise the engine speed to around 2500 rpm, and hold it at this speed for 20 seconds. Allow the engine speed to return to idle, and watch for smoke emissions from the exhaust tailpipe. If the idle speed is obviously much too high, or if dense blue or clearly-visible black smoke comes from the tailpipe for more than 5 seconds, the vehicle will fail. As a rule of thumb, blue smoke signifies oil being burnt (engine wear) while black smoke signifies unburnt fuel (dirty air cleaner element, or other carburettor or fuel system fault).

☐ An exhaust gas analyser capable of measuring carbon monoxide (CO) and hydrocarbons (HC) is now needed. If such an instrument cannot be hired or borrowed, a local garage may agree to perform the check for a small fee.

CO emissions (mixture)

☐ At the time of writing, the maximum CO level at idle is 3.5% for vehicles first used after August 1986 and 4.5% for older vehicles. From January 1996 a much tighter limit (around 0.5%) applies to catalyst-equipped vehicles first used from August 1992. If the CO level cannot be reduced far enough to pass the test (and the fuel and ignition systems are otherwise in good condition) then the carburettor is badly worn, or there is some problem in the fuel injection system or catalytic converter (as applicable).

HC emissions

☐ With the CO emissions within limits, HC emissions must be no more than 1200 ppm (parts per million). If the vehicle fails this test at idle, it can be re-tested at around 2000 rpm; if the HC level is then 1200 ppm or less, this counts as a pass.

☐ Excessive HC emissions can be caused by oil being burnt, but they are more likely to be due to unburnt fuel.

Diesel models

☐ The only emission test applicable to Diesel engines is the measuring of exhaust smoke density. The test involves accelerating the engine several times to its maximum unloaded speed.

Note: *It is of the utmost importance that the engine timing belt is in good condition before the test is carried out.*

☐ Excessive smoke can be caused by a dirty air cleaner element. Otherwise, professional advice may be needed to find the cause.

REF•10 Fault finding

Engine
- [ ] Engine fails to rotate when attempting to start
- [ ] Engine rotates, but will not start
- [ ] Engine difficult to start when cold
- [ ] Engine difficult to start when hot
- [ ] Starter motor noisy or excessively-rough in engagement
- [ ] Engine starts, but stops immediately
- [ ] Engine idles erratically
- [ ] Engine misfires at idle speed
- [ ] Engine misfires throughout the driving speed range
- [ ] Engine hesitates on acceleration
- [ ] Engine stalls
- [ ] Engine lacks power
- [ ] Engine backfires
- [ ] Oil pressure warning light illuminated with engine running
- [ ] Engine runs-on after switching off
- [ ] Engine noises

Cooling system
- [ ] Overheating
- [ ] Overcooling
- [ ] External coolant leakage
- [ ] Internal coolant leakage
- [ ] Corrosion

Fuel and exhaust systems
- [ ] Excessive fuel consumption
- [ ] Fuel leakage and/or fuel odour
- [ ] Excessive noise or fumes from exhaust system

Clutch
- [ ] Pedal travels to floor - no pressure or very little resistance
- [ ] Clutch fails to disengage (unable to select gears)
- [ ] Clutch slips (engine speed increases, with no increase in vehicle speed)
- [ ] Judder as clutch is engaged
- [ ] Noise when depressing or releasing clutch pedal

Manual transmission
- [ ] Noisy in neutral with engine running
- [ ] Noisy in one particular gear
- [ ] Difficulty engaging gears
- [ ] Jumps out of gear
- [ ] Vibration
- [ ] Lubricant leaks

Automatic transmission
- [ ] Fluid leakage
- [ ] Transmission fluid brown, or has burned smell
- [ ] General gear selection problems
- [ ] Transmission will not downshift (kickdown) with accelerator fully depressed
- [ ] Engine will not start in any gear, or starts in gears other than Park or Neutral
- [ ] Transmission slips, shifts roughly, is noisy, or has no drive in forward or reverse gears

Driveshafts
- [ ] Clicking or knocking noise on turns (at slow speed on full-lock)
- [ ] Vibration when accelerating or decelerating

Braking system
- [ ] Vehicle pulls to one side under braking
- [ ] Noise (grinding or high-pitched squeal) when brakes applied
- [ ] Excessive brake pedal travel
- [ ] Brake pedal feels spongy when depressed
- [ ] Excessive brake pedal effort required to stop vehicle
- [ ] Judder felt through brake pedal or steering wheel when braking
- [ ] Brakes binding
- [ ] Rear wheels locking under normal braking

Suspension and steering systems
- [ ] Vehicle pulls to one side
- [ ] Wheel wobble and vibration
- [ ] Excessive pitching and/or rolling around corners, or during braking
- [ ] Wandering or general instability
- [ ] Excessively-stiff steering
- [ ] Excessive play in steering
- [ ] Lack of power assistance
- [ ] Tyre wear excessive

Electrical system
- [ ] Battery will not hold a charge for more than a few days
- [ ] Ignition/no-charge warning light remains illuminated with engine running
- [ ] Ignition/no-charge warning light fails to come on
- [ ] Lights inoperative
- [ ] Instrument readings inaccurate or erratic
- [ ] Horn inoperative, or unsatisfactory in operation
- [ ] Windscreen/tailgate wipers inoperative, or unsatisfactory in operation
- [ ] Windscreen/tailgate washers inoperative, or unsatisfactory in operation
- [ ] Electric windows inoperative, or unsatisfactory in operation
- [ ] Central locking system inoperative, or unsatisfactory in operation

Introduction

The vehicle owner who does his or her own maintenance according to the recommended service schedules should not have to use this section of the manual very often. Modern component reliability is such that, provided those items subject to wear or deterioration are inspected or renewed at the specified intervals, sudden failure is comparatively rare. Faults do not usually just happen as a result of sudden failure, but develop over a period of time. Major mechanical failures in particular are usually preceded by characteristic symptoms over hundreds or even thousands of miles. Those components which do occasionally fail without warning are often small and easily carried in the vehicle.

With any fault-finding, the first step is to decide where to begin investigations. Sometimes this is obvious, but on other occasions, a little detective work will be necessary. The owner who makes half a dozen haphazard adjustments or replacements may be successful in curing a fault (or its symptoms), but will be none the wiser if the fault recurs, and ultimately may have spent more time and money than was necessary. A calm and logical approach will be found to be more satisfactory in the long run. Always take into account any warning signs or abnormalities that may have been noticed in the period preceding the fault - power loss, high or low gauge readings, unusual smells, etc - and remember that failure of components such as fuses or spark plugs may only be pointers to some underlying fault.

Fault finding REF•11

The pages which follow provide an easy-reference guide to the more common problems which may occur during the operation of the vehicle. These problems and their possible causes are grouped under headings denoting various components or systems, such as Engine, Cooling system, etc. The Chapter and/or Section which deals with the problem is also shown in brackets. Whatever the fault, certain basic principles apply. These are as follows:

Verify the fault. This is simply a matter of being sure that you know what the symptoms are before starting work. This is particularly important if you are investigating a fault for someone else, who may not have described it very accurately.

Don't overlook the obvious. For example, if the vehicle won't start, is there fuel in the tank? (Don't take anyone else's word on this particular point, and don't trust the fuel gauge either!) If an electrical fault is indicated, look for loose or broken wires before digging out the test gear.

Cure the disease, not the symptom. Substituting a flat battery with a fully-charged one will get you off the hard shoulder, but if the underlying cause is not attended to, the new battery will go the same way. Similarly, changing oil-fouled spark plugs for a new set will get you moving again, but remember that the reason for the fouling (if it wasn't simply an incorrect grade of plug) will have to be established and corrected.

Don't take anything for granted. Particularly, don't forget that a "new" component may itself be defective (especially if it's been rattling around in the boot for months), and don't leave components out of a fault diagnosis sequence just because they are new or recently-fitted. When you do finally diagnose a difficult fault, you'll probably realise that all the evidence was there from the start.

Engine

Engine fails to rotate when attempting to start
- [ ] Battery terminal connections loose or corroded (Chapter 1).
- [ ] Battery discharged or faulty (Chapter 5).
- [ ] Broken, loose or disconnected wiring in the starting circuit (Chapter 5).
- [ ] Defective starter solenoid or switch (Chapter 5).
- [ ] Defective starter motor (Chapter 5).
- [ ] Starter pinion or flywheel/driveplate ring gear teeth loose or broken (Chapter 2A or 5).
- [ ] Engine earth strap broken or disconnected (Chapter 2A).
- [ ] Automatic transmission not in Park/Neutral position or starter inhibitor switch faulty (Chapter 7B).

Engine rotates, but will not start
- [ ] Fuel tank empty.
- [ ] Battery discharged (engine rotates slowly) (Chapter 5).
- [ ] Battery terminal connections loose or corroded (Chapter 1).
- [ ] Ignition components damp or damaged (Chapter 1 and 5).
- [ ] Broken, loose or disconnected wiring in the ignition circuit (Chapters 1 and 5).
- [ ] Worn, faulty or incorrectly-gapped spark plugs (Chapter 1).
- [ ] Carburettor/fuel injection system fault (Chapter 4A or 4B).
- [ ] Major mechanical failure (eg camshaft drive) (Chapter 2B).

Engine difficult to start when cold
- [ ] Battery discharged (Chapter 5).
- [ ] Battery terminal connections loose or corroded (Chapter 1).
- [ ] Worn, faulty or incorrectly-gapped spark plugs (Chapter 1).
- [ ] Choke mechanism faulty - carburettor models (Chapter 4A).
- [ ] Faulty fuel cut-off solenoid - carburettor models (Chapter 4A).
- [ ] Fuel injection system fault - fuel-injected models (Chapter 4B).
- [ ] Other ignition system fault (Chapters 1 and 5).
- [ ] Low cylinder compressions (Chapter 2A).

Engine difficult to start when hot
- [ ] Air filter element dirty or clogged (Chapter 1).
- [ ] Choke mechanism faulty - carburettor models (Chapter 4A).
- [ ] Faulty fuel cut-off solenoid - carburettor models (Chapter 4A).
- [ ] Fuel injection system fault - fuel-injected models (Chapter 4B).
- [ ] Ignition system fault (Chapters 1 and 5).
- [ ] Low cylinder compressions (Chapter 2A).

Starter motor noisy or excessively-rough in engagement
- [ ] Starter pinion or flywheel/driveplate ring gear teeth loose or broken (Chapter 2A or 5).
- [ ] Starter motor mounting bolts loose or missing (Chapter 5).
- [ ] Starter motor internal components worn or damaged (Chapter 5).

Engine starts, but stops immediately
- [ ] Loose or faulty electrical connections in the ignition circuit (Chapters 1 and 5).
- [ ] Vacuum leak at the carburettor/throttle body or inlet manifold (Chapter 4A or 4B).
- [ ] Faulty carburettor (Chapter 4A).
- [ ] Fuel injection system fault (Chapter 4B).

Engine idles erratically
- [ ] Air filter element clogged (Chapter 1).
- [ ] Vacuum leak at the carburettor/throttle body, inlet manifold or associated hoses (Chapter 4A or 4B).
- [ ] Worn, faulty or incorrectly-gapped spark plugs (Chapter 1).
- [ ] Uneven or low cylinder compressions (Chapter 2A).
- [ ] Camshaft lobes worn (Chapter 2A).
- [ ] Timing chain(s) incorrectly fitted (Chapter 2A).
- [ ] Faulty carburettor (Chapter 4A).
- [ ] Fuel injection system fault (Chapter 4B).

Engine misfires at idle speed
- [ ] Worn, faulty or incorrectly-gapped spark plugs (Chapter 1).
- [ ] Faulty spark plug HT leads (Chapter 1).
- [ ] Vacuum leak at the carburettor/throttle body, inlet manifold or associated hoses (Chapter 4A or 4B).
- [ ] Faulty carburettor (Chapter 4A).
- [ ] Fuel injection system fault (Chapter 4B).
- [ ] Distributor cap cracked or tracking internally (Chapter 1).
- [ ] Uneven or low cylinder compressions (Chapter 2A).
- [ ] Disconnected, leaking, or perished crankcase ventilation hoses (Chapter 4).

Engine misfires throughout the driving speed range
- [ ] Fuel filter choked (Chapter 1).
- [ ] Fuel pump faulty, or delivery pressure low (Chapter 4A or 4B).
- [ ] Fuel tank vent blocked, or fuel pipes restricted (Chapter 4A or 4B).
- [ ] Vacuum leak at the carburettor/throttle body, inlet manifold or associated hoses (Chapter 4A or 4B).
- [ ] Worn, faulty or incorrectly-gapped spark plugs (Chapter 1).
- [ ] Faulty spark plug HT leads (Chapter 1).
- [ ] Distributor cap cracked or tracking internally (Chapter 1).
- [ ] Faulty ignition coil (Chapter 5B).
- [ ] Uneven or low cylinder compressions (Chapter 2A).
- [ ] Faulty carburettor (Chapter 4A).
- [ ] Fuel injection system fault (Chapter 4B).

Engine hesitates on acceleration
- [ ] Worn, faulty or incorrectly-gapped spark plugs (Chapter 1).

REF•12 Fault finding

Engine (continued)

- [ ] Vacuum leak at the carburettor/throttle body, inlet manifold or associated hoses (Chapter 4A or 4B).
- [ ] Faulty carburettor (Chapter 4A).
- [ ] Fuel injection system fault (Chapter 4B).

Engine stalls

- [ ] Vacuum leak at the carburettor/throttle body, inlet manifold or associated hoses (Chapter 4A or 4B).
- [ ] Fuel filter choked (Chapter 1).
- [ ] Fuel pump faulty, or delivery pressure low (Chapter 4A or 4B).
- [ ] Fuel tank vent blocked, or fuel pipes restricted (Chapter 4A or 4B).
- [ ] Faulty carburettor (Chapter 4A).
- [ ] Fuel injection system fault (Chapter 4B).

Engine lacks power

- [ ] Fuel filter choked (Chapter 1).
- [ ] Fuel pump faulty, or delivery pressure low (Chapter 4A or 4B).
- [ ] Uneven or low cylinder compressions (Chapter 2A).
- [ ] Worn, faulty or incorrectly-gapped spark plugs (Chapter 1).
- [ ] Vacuum leak at the carburettor/throttle body, inlet manifold or associated hoses (Chapter 4A or 4B).
- [ ] Faulty carburettor (Chapter 4A).
- [ ] Fuel injection system fault (Chapter 4B).
- [ ] Brakes binding (Chapters 1 and 9).
- [ ] Clutch slipping - manual transmission models (Chapter 6).

Engine backfires

- [ ] Vacuum leak at the carburettor/throttle body, inlet manifold or associated hoses (Chapter 4A or 4B).
- [ ] Faulty carburettor (Chapter 4A).
- [ ] Fuel injection system fault (Chapter 4B).

Oil pressure warning light illuminated with engine running

- [ ] Low oil level, or incorrect oil grade (Chapter 1).
- [ ] Faulty oil pressure sensor (Chapter 5).
- [ ] Worn engine bearings and/or oil pump (Chapter 2A or 2B).
- [ ] Excessively high engine operating temperature (Chapter 3).
- [ ] Oil pressure relief valve defective (Chapter 2A).
- [ ] Oil pick-up strainer clogged (Chapter 2A).

Engine runs-on after switching off

- [ ] Excessive carbon build-up in engine (Chapter 2A or 2B).
- [ ] High engine operating temperature (Chapter 3).
- [ ] Faulty carburettor (Chapter 4A).
- [ ] Faulty fuel injection system fault (Chapter 4B).

Engine noises

Pre-ignition (pinking) or knocking during acceleration or under load

- [ ] Ignition timing incorrect/ignition system fault (Chapters 1 and 5).
- [ ] Incorrect grade of spark plug (Chapter 1).
- [ ] Incorrect grade of fuel (Chapter 1).
- [ ] Vacuum leak at carburettor/throttle body, inlet manifold or associated hoses (Chapter 4A or 4B).
- [ ] Excessive carbon build-up in engine (Chapter 2A or 2B).
- [ ] Faulty carburettor (Chapter 4A).
- [ ] Fuel injection system fault (Chapter 4B).

Whistling or wheezing noises

- [ ] Leaking inlet manifold or carburettor/throttle body gasket (Chapter 4A or 4B).
- [ ] Leaking exhaust manifold gasket or pipe-to-manifold joint (Chapter 4A or 4B).
- [ ] Leaking vacuum hose (Chapters 4A, 4B, 5B and 9).
- [ ] Blowing cylinder head gasket (Chapter 2A).

Tapping or rattling noises

- [ ] Worn valve gear or camshaft (Chapter 2A).
- [ ] Incorrect valve clearances (Chapter 1)
- [ ] Ancillary component fault (water pump, alternator, etc) (Chapters 3, 5A, etc).

Knocking or thumping noises

- [ ] Worn big-end bearings (regular heavy knocking, perhaps less under load) (Chapter 2B).
- [ ] Worn main bearings (rumbling and knocking, perhaps worsening under load) (Chapter 2B).
- [ ] Piston slap (most noticeable when cold) (Chapter 2B).
- [ ] Ancillary component fault (water pump, alternator, etc) (Chapters 3, 5A, etc).

Cooling system

Overheating

- [ ] Auxiliary drivebelt broken - or incorrectly adjusted (Chapter 1).
- [ ] Insufficient coolant in system (Chapter 1).
- [ ] Thermostat faulty (Chapter 3).
- [ ] Radiator core blocked, or grille restricted (Chapter 3).
- [ ] Electric cooling fan or thermostatic switch faulty (Chapter 3).
- [ ] Pressure cap faulty (Chapter 3).
- [ ] Ignition timing incorrect, or ignition system fault (Chapters 1 and 5).
- [ ] Inaccurate temperature gauge sender unit (Chapter 3).
- [ ] Airlock in cooling system (Chapter 1).

Overcooling

- [ ] Thermostat faulty (Chapter 3).
- [ ] Inaccurate temperature gauge sender unit (Chapter 3).

External coolant leakage

- [ ] Deteriorated or damaged hoses or hose clips (Chapter 1).
- [ ] Radiator core or heater matrix leaking (Chapter 3).
- [ ] Pressure cap faulty (Chapter 3).
- [ ] Water pump internal seal leaking (Chapter 3).
- [ ] Water pump seal leaking (Chapter 3).
- [ ] Boiling due to overheating (Chapter 3).
- [ ] Core plug leaking (Chapter 2B).

Internal coolant leakage

- [ ] Leaking cylinder head gasket (Chapter 2A).
- [ ] Cracked cylinder head or cylinder block (Chapter 2A or 2B).

Corrosion

- [ ] Infrequent draining and flushing (Chapter 1).
- [ ] Incorrect coolant mixture or inappropriate coolant type (Chapter 1).

Fault finding

Fuel and exhaust systems

Excessive fuel consumption
- [ ] Air filter element dirty or clogged (Chapter 1).
- [ ] Faulty carburettor (Chapter 4A).
- [ ] Fuel injection system fault (Chapter 4B).
- [ ] Ignition timing incorrect or ignition system fault (Chapters 1 and 5).
- [ ] Tyres under-inflated (Chapter 1).

Fuel leakage and/or fuel odour
- [ ] Damaged fuel tank, pipes or connections (Chapters 1 and 4).
- [ ] Faulty carburettor (Chapter 4A).

Excessive noise or fumes from exhaust system
- [ ] Leaking exhaust system or manifold joints (Chapters 1, 4A or 4B).
- [ ] Leaking, corroded or damaged silencers or pipe (Chapters 1, 4A or 4B).
- [ ] Broken mountings causing body or suspension contact (Chapter 4A or 4B).

Clutch

Pedal travels to floor - no pressure or very little resistance
- [ ] Broken clutch cable (Chapter 6).
- [ ] Incorrect clutch cable adjustment (Chapter 6).
- [ ] Broken clutch release bearing or fork (Chapter 6).
- [ ] Broken diaphragm spring in clutch pressure plate (Chapter 6).

Clutch fails to disengage (unable to select gears)
- [ ] Incorrect clutch cable adjustment (Chapter 6).
- [ ] Clutch disc sticking on splines (Chapter 8).
- [ ] Clutch disc sticking to flywheel or pressure plate (Chapter 8).
- [ ] Faulty pressure plate assembly (Chapter 8).
- [ ] Clutch release mechanism worn or incorrectly assembled (Chapter 8).

Clutch slips (engine speed increases, with no increase in vehicle speed)
- [ ] Incorrect clutch cable adjustment (Chapter 6).
- [ ] Clutch disc linings excessively worn (Chapter 6).
- [ ] Clutch disc linings contaminated with oil or grease (Chapter 6).
- [ ] Faulty pressure plate or weak diaphragm spring (Chapter 6).

Judder as clutch is engaged
- [ ] Clutch disc linings contaminated with oil or grease (Chapter 6).
- [ ] Clutch disc linings excessively worn (Chapter 6).
- [ ] Clutch cable sticking or frayed (Chapter 6).
- [ ] Faulty or distorted pressure plate or diaphragm spring (Chapter 6).
- [ ] Worn or loose engine or transmission mountings (Chapter 2A).
- [ ] Clutch disc hub or shaft splines worn (Chapter 6).

Noise when depressing or releasing clutch pedal
- [ ] Worn clutch release bearing (Chapter 6).
- [ ] Worn or dry clutch pedal bushes (Chapter 6).
- [ ] Faulty pressure plate assembly (Chapter 6).
- [ ] Pressure plate diaphragm spring broken (Chapter 6).
- [ ] Broken clutch disc cushioning springs (Chapter 6).

Manual transmission

Noisy in neutral with engine running
- [ ] Input shaft bearings worn (noise apparent with clutch pedal released, but not when depressed) (Chapter 7A).*
- [ ] Clutch release bearing worn (noise apparent with clutch pedal depressed, possibly less when released) (Chapter 6).

Noisy in one particular gear
- [ ] Worn, damaged or chipped gear teeth (Chapter 7A).*

Difficulty engaging gears
- [ ] Clutch fault (Chapter 6).
- [ ] Oil level low (Chapter 1).
- [ ] Worn or damaged gear linkage (Chapter 7A).
- [ ] Incorrectly-adjusted gear linkage (Chapter 7A).
- [ ] Worn synchroniser units (Chapter 7A).*

Jumps out of gear
- [ ] Worn or damaged gear linkage (Chapter 7A).
- [ ] Incorrectly-adjusted gear linkage (Chapter 7A).
- [ ] Worn synchroniser units (Chapter 7A).*
- [ ] Worn selector forks (Chapter 7A).*

Vibration
- [ ] Lack of oil (Chapter 1).
- [ ] Worn bearings (Chapter 7A).*

Lubricant leaks
- [ ] Leaking oil seal (Chapter 7A).
- [ ] Leaking housing joint (Chapter 7A).*
- [ ] Leaking input shaft oil seal (Chapter 7A).*

*Although the corrective action necessary to remedy the symptoms described is beyond the scope of the home mechanic, the above information should be helpful in isolating the cause of the condition, so that the owner can communicate clearly with a professional mechanic.

REF•14 Fault finding

Automatic transmission

Note: *Due to the complexity of the automatic transmission, it is difficult for the home mechanic to properly diagnose and service this unit. For problems other than the following, the vehicle should be taken to a dealer service department or automatic transmission specialist.*

Fluid leakage

☐ Automatic transmission fluid is usually deep red in colour. Fluid leaks should not be confused with engine oil, which can easily be blown onto the transmission by air flow.
☐ To determine the source of a leak, first remove all built-up dirt and grime from the transmission housing and surrounding areas, using a degreasing agent or by steam-cleaning. Drive the vehicle at low speed, so that air flow will not blow the leak far from its source. Raise and support the vehicle, and determine where the leak is coming from. The following are common areas of leakage.
 a) *Oil pan (Chapter 7B).*
 b) *Dipstick tube (Chapter 7B).*
 c) *Transmission-to-fluid cooler fluid pipes/unions (Chapter 7B).*

Transmission fluid brown, or has burned smell

☐ Transmission fluid level low, or fluid in need of renewal (Chapter 1).

General gear selection problems

☐ The most likely cause of gear selection problems is a faulty or poorly-adjusted gear selector mechanism. The following are common problems associated with a faulty selector mechanism.
 a) *Engine starting in gears other than Park or Neutral.*
 b) *Indicator on gear selector lever pointing to a gear other than the one actually being used.*
 c) *Vehicle moves when in Park or Neutral.*
 d) *Poor gear shift quality, or erratic gear changes.*
☐ Refer any problems to a Proton dealer, or an automatic transmission specialist.

Transmission will not downshift (kickdown) with accelerator pedal fully depressed

☐ Low transmission fluid level (Chapter 1).
☐ Incorrect selector cable adjustment (Chapter 7B).
☐ Incorrect kickdown cable adjustment (Chapter 7B).

Engine will not start in any gear, or starts in gears other than Park or Neutral

☐ Incorrect starter inhibitor switch adjustment (Chapter 7B).
☐ Incorrect selector cable adjustment (Chapter 7B).

Transmission slips, shifts roughly, is noisy, or has no drive in forward or reverse gears

☐ There are many probable causes for the above problems, but the home mechanic should be concerned with only one possibility - fluid level. Before taking the vehicle to a dealer or transmission specialist, check the fluid level and condition of the fluid as described in Chapter 1. Correct the fluid level as necessary, or change the fluid and filter if needed. If the problem persists, professional help will be necessary.

Driveshafts

Clicking or knocking noise on turns (at slow speed on full-lock)

☐ Lack of constant velocity joint lubricant, possibly due to damaged gaiter (Chapter 8).
☐ Worn outer constant velocity joint (Chapter 8).

Vibration when accelerating or decelerating

☐ Worn inner constant velocity joint (Chapter 8).
☐ Bent or distorted driveshaft (Chapter 8).

Braking system

Note: *Before assuming that a brake problem exists, make sure that the tyres are in good condition and correctly inflated, that the front wheel alignment is correct, and that the vehicle is not loaded with weight in an unequal manner.*

Vehicle pulls to one side under braking

☐ Worn, defective, damaged or contaminated front or rear brake pads/shoes on one side (Chapters 1 and 9).
☐ Seized or partially-seized front or rear brake caliper/wheel cylinder piston (Chapter 9).
☐ A mixture of brake pad/shoe lining materials fitted between sides (Chapter 9).
☐ Brake caliper mounting bolts loose (Chapter 9).
☐ Worn or damaged steering or suspension components (Chapters 1 and 10).

Noise (grinding or high-pitched squeal) when brakes applied

☐ Brake pad or shoe friction lining material worn down to metal backing (Chapters 1 and 9).
☐ Excessive corrosion of brake disc/drum - may be apparent after the vehicle has been standing for some time (Chapters 1 and 9).

Excessive brake pedal travel

☐ Inoperative rear brake self-adjust mechanism - rear drum brake models (Chapters 1 and 9).
☐ Faulty master cylinder (Chapter 9).
☐ Air in hydraulic system (Chapter 9).
☐ Faulty vacuum servo unit (Chapter 9).

Brake pedal feels spongy when depressed

☐ Air in hydraulic system (Chapter 9).
☐ Deteriorated flexible rubber brake hoses (Chapters 1 and 9).
☐ Master cylinder mountings loose (Chapter 9).
☐ Faulty master cylinder (Chapter 9).

Excessive brake pedal effort required to stop vehicle

☐ Faulty vacuum servo unit (Chapter 9).
☐ Disconnected, damaged or insecure brake servo vacuum hose (Chapters 1 and 9).
☐ Primary or secondary hydraulic circuit failure (Chapter 9).
☐ Seized brake caliper/wheel cylinder piston(s) (Chapter 9).
☐ Brake pads/shoes incorrectly fitted (Chapter 9).
☐ Incorrect grade of brake pads/shoes fitted (Chapter 9).
☐ Brake pads/shoes contaminated (Chapter 9).

Fault finding REF•15

Judder felt through brake pedal or steering wheel when braking
☐ Excessive run-out or distortion of brake disc/drum (Chapter 9).
☐ Brake pad/shoe linings worn (Chapters 1 and 9).
☐ Brake caliper/rear brake backplate mounting bolts loose (Chapter 9).
☐ Wear in suspension or steering components or mountings (Chapters 1 and 10).

Suspension and steering

Note: *Before diagnosing suspension or steering faults, be sure that the trouble is not due to incorrect tyre pressures, mixtures of tyre types, or binding brakes.*

Vehicle pulls to one side
☐ Defective tyre (Chapter 1).
☐ Excessive wear in suspension or steering components (Chapters 1 and 10).
☐ Incorrect front wheel alignment (Chapter 10).
☐ Accident damage to steering or suspension components (Chapters 1 and 10).

Wheel wobble and vibration
☐ Front roadwheels out of balance (vibration felt mainly through the steering wheel) (Chapter 10).
☐ Rear roadwheels out of balance (vibration felt throughout the vehicle) (Chapter 10).
☐ Roadwheels damaged or distorted (Chapter 10).
☐ Faulty or damaged tyre (Chapter 1).
☐ Worn steering or suspension joints, bushes or components (Chapters 1 and 10).
☐ Wheel bolts loose (Chapter 10).

Excessive pitching and/or rolling around corners, or during braking
☐ Defective shock absorbers (Chapters 1 and 10).
☐ Broken or weak coil spring and/or suspension component (Chapters 1 and 10).
☐ Worn or damaged anti-roll bar or mountings (Chapter 10).

Wandering or general instability
☐ Incorrect front wheel alignment (Chapter 10).
☐ Worn steering or suspension joints, bushes or components (Chapters 1 and 10).
☐ Roadwheels out of balance (Chapter 10).
☐ Faulty or damaged tyre (Chapter 1).
☐ Wheel bolts loose (Chapter 10).
☐ Defective shock absorbers (Chapters 1 and 10).

Excessively-stiff steering
☐ Lack of steering gear lubricant (Chapter 10).
☐ Seized track rod end balljoint or suspension balljoint (Chapters 1 and 10).
☐ Broken or incorrectly adjusted auxiliary drivebelt (Chapter 1).

Brakes binding
☐ Seized brake caliper/wheel cylinder piston(s) (Chapter 9).
☐ Incorrectly-adjusted handbrake mechanism (Chapter 9).
☐ Faulty master cylinder (Chapter 9).

Rear wheels locking under normal braking
☐ Rear brake shoe linings contaminated (Chapters 1 and 9).
☐ Faulty brake pressure regulator (Chapter 9).

☐ Incorrect front wheel alignment (Chapter 10).
☐ Steering rack or column bent or damaged (Chapter 10).

Excessive play in steering
☐ Worn steering column universal joint(s) (Chapter 10).
☐ Worn steering track rod end balljoints (Chapters 1 and 10).
☐ Worn rack-and-pinion steering gear (Chapter 10).
☐ Worn steering or suspension joints, bushes or components (Chapters 1 and 10).

Lack of power assistance
☐ Broken or incorrectly-adjusted auxiliary drivebelt (Chapter 1).
☐ Incorrect power steering fluid level (Chapter 1).
☐ Restriction in power steering fluid hoses (Chapter 1).
☐ Faulty power steering pump (Chapter 10).
☐ Faulty rack-and-pinion steering gear (Chapter 10).

Tyre wear excessive

Tyres worn on inside or outside edges
☐ Tyres under-inflated (wear on both edges) (Chapter 1).
☐ Incorrect camber or castor angles (wear on one edge only) (Chapter 10).
☐ Worn steering or suspension joints, bushes or components (Chapters 1 and 10).
☐ Excessively-hard cornering.
☐ Accident damage.

Tyre treads exhibit feathered edges
☐ Incorrect toe setting (Chapter 10).

Tyres worn in centre of tread
☐ Tyres over-inflated (Chapter 1).

Tyres worn on inside and outside edges
☐ Tyres under-inflated (Chapter 1).
☐ Worn shock absorbers (Chapters 1 and 10).

Tyres worn unevenly
☐ Tyres out of balance (Chapter 1).
☐ Excessive wheel or tyre run-out (Chapter 1).
☐ Worn shock absorbers (Chapters 1 and 10).
☐ Faulty tyre (Chapter 1).

Electrical system

Note: *For problems associated with the starting system, refer to the faults listed under "Engine" earlier.*

Battery will not hold a charge for more than a few days
☐ Battery defective internally (Chapter 5).
☐ Battery electrolyte level low - where applicable (Chapter 1).

☐ Battery terminal connections loose or corroded (Chapter 1).
☐ Auxiliary drivebelt worn - or incorrectly adjusted (Chapter 1).
☐ Alternator not charging at correct output (Chapter 5).
☐ Alternator or voltage regulator faulty (Chapter 5).
☐ Short-circuit causing continual battery drain (Chapters 5 and 12).

Fault finding

Electrical system (continued)

Ignition/no-charge warning light remains illuminated with engine running

- [ ] Auxiliary drivebelt broken, worn, or incorrectly adjusted (Chapter 1).
- [ ] Alternator brushes worn, sticking, or dirty (Chapter 5).
- [ ] Alternator brush springs weak or broken (Chapter 5).
- [ ] Internal fault in alternator or voltage regulator (Chapter 5).
- [ ] Broken, disconnected, or loose wiring in charging circuit (Chapter 5).

Ignition/no-charge warning light fails to come on

- [ ] Warning light bulb blown (Chapter 12).
- [ ] Broken, disconnected, or loose wiring in warning light circuit (Chapter 12).
- [ ] Alternator faulty (Chapter 5).

Lights inoperative

- [ ] Bulb blown (Chapter 12).
- [ ] Corrosion of bulb or bulbholder contacts (Chapter 12).
- [ ] Blown fuse (Chapter 12).
- [ ] Faulty relay (Chapter 12).
- [ ] Broken, loose, or disconnected wiring (Chapter 12).
- [ ] Faulty switch (Chapter 12).

Instrument readings inaccurate or erratic

Instrument readings increase with engine speed

- [ ] Faulty voltage regulator (Chapter 12).

Fuel or temperature gauges give no reading

- [ ] Faulty gauge sender unit (Chapters 3 and 4).
- [ ] Wiring open-circuit (Chapter 12).
- [ ] Faulty gauge (Chapter 12).

Fuel or temperature gauges give continuous maximum reading

- [ ] Faulty gauge sender unit (Chapters 3 and 4).
- [ ] Wiring short-circuit (Chapter 12).
- [ ] Faulty gauge (Chapter 12).

Horn inoperative, or unsatisfactory in operation

Horn operates all the time

- [ ] Horn contacts permanently bridged or horn push stuck down (Chapter 12).

Horn fails to operate

- [ ] Blown fuse (Chapter 12).
- [ ] Cable or cable connections loose, broken or disconnected (Chapter 12).
- [ ] Faulty horn (Chapter 12).

Horn emits intermittent or unsatisfactory sound

- [ ] Cable connections loose (Chapter 12).
- [ ] Horn mountings loose (Chapter 12).
- [ ] Faulty horn (Chapter 12).

Windscreen/tailgate wipers inoperative, or unsatisfactory in operation

Wipers fail to operate, or operate very slowly

- [ ] Wiper blades stuck to screen, or linkage seized or binding (Chapters 1 and 12).
- [ ] Blown fuse (Chapter 12).
- [ ] Cable or cable connections loose, broken or disconnected (Chapter 12).
- [ ] Faulty relay (Chapter 12).
- [ ] Faulty wiper motor (Chapter 12).

Wiper blades sweep over too large or too small an area of the glass

- [ ] Wiper arms incorrectly positioned on spindles (Chapter 1).
- [ ] Excessive wear of wiper linkage (Chapter 12).
- [ ] Wiper motor or linkage mountings loose or insecure (Chapter 12).

Wiper blades fail to clean the glass effectively

- [ ] Wiper blade rubbers worn or perished (Chapter 1).
- [ ] Wiper arm tension springs broken, or arm pivots seized (Chapter 12).
- [ ] Insufficient windscreen washer additive to adequately remove road film (Chapter 1).

Windscreen/tailgate washers inoperative, or unsatisfactory in operation

One or more washer jets inoperative

- [ ] Blocked washer jet (Chapter 1).
- [ ] Disconnected, kinked or restricted fluid hose (Chapter 12).
- [ ] Insufficient fluid in washer reservoir (Chapter 1).

Washer pump fails to operate

- [ ] Broken or disconnected wiring or connections (Chapter 12).
- [ ] Blown fuse (Chapter 12).
- [ ] Faulty washer switch (Chapter 12).
- [ ] Faulty washer pump (Chapter 12).

Washer pump runs for some time before fluid is emitted from jets

- [ ] Faulty one-way valve in fluid supply hose (Chapter 12).

Electric windows inoperative, or unsatisfactory in operation

Window glass will only move in one direction

- [ ] Faulty switch (Chapter 12).

Window glass slow to move

- [ ] Regulator seized or damaged, or in need of lubrication (Chapter 11).
- [ ] Door internal components or trim fouling regulator (Chapter 11).
- [ ] Faulty motor (Chapter 11).

Window glass fails to move

- [ ] Blown fuse (Chapter 12).
- [ ] Faulty relay (Chapter 12).
- [ ] Broken or disconnected wiring or connections (Chapter 12).
- [ ] Faulty motor (Chapter 11).

Central locking system inoperative, or unsatisfactory in operation

Complete system failure

- [ ] Blown fuse (Chapter 12).
- [ ] Faulty relay (Chapter 12).
- [ ] Broken or disconnected wiring or connections (Chapter 12).
- [ ] Faulty control unit (Chapter 11).

Latch locks but will not unlock, or unlocks but will not lock

- [ ] Faulty switch (Chapter 12).
- [ ] Broken or disconnected latch operating rods or levers (Chapter 11).
- [ ] Faulty relay (Chapter 12).
- [ ] Faulty control unit (Chapter 11).

One solenoid/motor fails to operate

- [ ] Broken or disconnected wiring or connections (Chapter 12).
- [ ] Faulty solenoid/motor (Chapter 11).
- [ ] Broken, binding or disconnected latch operating rods or levers (Chapter 11).
- [ ] Fault in door latch (Chapter 11).

General repair procedures

Whenever servicing, repair or overhaul work is carried out on the car or its components, observe the following procedures and instructions. This will assist in carrying out the operation efficiently and to a professional standard of workmanship.

Joint mating faces and gaskets

When separating components at their mating faces, never insert screwdrivers or similar implements into the joint between the faces in order to prise them apart. This can cause severe damage which results in oil leaks, coolant leaks, etc upon reassembly. Separation is usually achieved by tapping along the joint with a soft-faced hammer in order to break the seal. However, note that this method may not be suitable where dowels are used for component location.

Where a gasket is used between the mating faces of two components, a new one must be fitted on reassembly; fit it dry unless otherwise stated in the repair procedure. Make sure that the mating faces are clean and dry, with all traces of old gasket removed. When cleaning a joint face, use a tool which is unlikely to score or damage the face, and remove any burrs or nicks with an oilstone or fine file.

Make sure that tapped holes are cleaned with a pipe cleaner, and keep them free of jointing compound, if this is being used, unless specifically instructed otherwise.

Ensure that all orifices, channels or pipes are clear, and blow through them, preferably using compressed air.

Oil seals

Oil seals can be removed by levering them out with a wide flat-bladed screwdriver or similar implement. Alternatively, a number of self-tapping screws may be screwed into the seal, and these used as a purchase for pliers or some similar device in order to pull the seal free.

Whenever an oil seal is removed from its working location, either individually or as part of an assembly, it should be renewed.

The very fine sealing lip of the seal is easily damaged, and will not seal if the surface it contacts is not completely clean and free from scratches, nicks or grooves. If the original sealing surface of the component cannot be restored, and the manufacturer has not made provision for slight relocation of the seal relative to the sealing surface, the component should be renewed.

Protect the lips of the seal from any surface which may damage them in the course of fitting. Use tape or a conical sleeve where possible. Lubricate the seal lips with oil before fitting and, on dual-lipped seals, fill the space between the lips with grease.

Unless otherwise stated, oil seals must be fitted with their sealing lips toward the lubricant to be sealed.

Use a tubular drift or block of wood of the appropriate size to install the seal and, if the seal housing is shouldered, drive the seal down to the shoulder. If the seal housing is unshouldered, the seal should be fitted with its face flush with the housing top face (unless otherwise instructed).

Screw threads and fastenings

Seized nuts, bolts and screws are quite a common occurrence where corrosion has set in, and the use of penetrating oil or releasing fluid will often overcome this problem if the offending item is soaked for a while before attempting to release it. The use of an impact driver may also provide a means of releasing such stubborn fastening devices, when used in conjunction with the appropriate screwdriver bit or socket. If none of these methods works, it may be necessary to resort to the careful application of heat, or the use of a hacksaw or nut splitter device.

Studs are usually removed by locking two nuts together on the threaded part, and then using a spanner on the lower nut to unscrew the stud. Studs or bolts which have broken off below the surface of the component in which they are mounted can sometimes be removed using a stud extractor. Always ensure that a blind tapped hole is completely free from oil, grease, water or other fluid before installing the bolt or stud. Failure to do this could cause the housing to crack due to the hydraulic action of the bolt or stud as it is screwed in.

When tightening a castellated nut to accept a split pin, tighten the nut to the specified torque, where applicable, and then tighten further to the next split pin hole. Never slacken the nut to align the split pin hole, unless stated in the repair procedure.

When checking or retightening a nut or bolt to a specified torque setting, slacken the nut or bolt by a quarter of a turn, and then retighten to the specified setting. However, this should not be attempted where angular tightening has been used.

For some screw fastenings, notably cylinder head bolts or nuts, torque wrench settings are no longer specified for the latter stages of tightening, "angle-tightening" being called up instead. Typically, a fairly low torque wrench setting will be applied to the bolts/nuts in the correct sequence, followed by one or more stages of tightening through specified angles.

Locknuts, locktabs and washers

Any fastening which will rotate against a component or housing during tightening should always have a washer between it and the relevant component or housing.

Spring or split washers should always be renewed when they are used to lock a critical component such as a big-end bearing retaining bolt or nut. Locktabs which are folded over to retain a nut or bolt should always be renewed.

Self-locking nuts can be re-used in non-critical areas, providing resistance can be felt when the locking portion passes over the bolt or stud thread. However, it should be noted that self-locking stiffnuts tend to lose their effectiveness after long periods of use, and should then be renewed as a matter of course.

Split pins must always be replaced with new ones of the correct size for the hole.

When thread-locking compound is found on the threads of a fastener which is to be re-used, it should be cleaned off with a wire brush and solvent, and fresh compound applied on reassembly.

Special tools

Some repair procedures in this manual entail the use of special tools such as a press, two or three-legged pullers, spring compressors, etc. Wherever possible, suitable readily-available alternatives to the manufacturer's special tools are described, and are shown in use. In some instances, where no alternative is possible, it has been necessary to resort to the use of a manufacturer's tool, and this has been done for reasons of safety as well as the efficient completion of the repair operation. Unless you are highly-skilled and have a thorough understanding of the procedures described, never attempt to bypass the use of any special tool when the procedure described specifies its use. Not only is there a very great risk of personal injury, but expensive damage could be caused to the components involved.

Environmental considerations

When disposing of used engine oil, brake fluid, antifreeze, etc, give due consideration to any detrimental environmental effects. Do not, for instance, pour any of the above liquids down drains into the general sewage system, or onto the ground to soak away. Many local council refuse tips provide a facility for waste oil disposal, as do some garages. If none of these facilities are available, consult your local Environmental Health Department, or the National Rivers Authority, for further advice.

With the universal tightening-up of legislation regarding the emission of environmentally-harmful substances from motor vehicles, most vehicles have tamperproof devices fitted to the main adjustment points of the fuel system. These devices are primarily designed to prevent unqualified persons from adjusting the fuel/air mixture, with the chance of a consequent increase in toxic emissions. If such devices are found during servicing or overhaul, they should, wherever possible, be renewed or refitted in accordance with the manufacturer's requirements or current legislation.

OIL CARE — FOLLOW THE CODE
OIL BANK LINE
0800 66 33 66

Note: It is antisocial and illegal to dump oil down the drain. To find the location of your local oil recycling bank, call this number free.

Glossary of technical terms

A

ABS (Anti-lock brake system) A system, usually electronically controlled, that senses incipient wheel lockup during braking and relieves hydraulic pressure at wheels that are about to skid.

Air bag An inflatable bag hidden in the steering wheel (driver's side) or the dash or glovebox (passenger side). In a head-on collision, the bags inflate, preventing the driver and front passenger from being thrown forward into the steering wheel or windscreen.

Air cleaner A metal or plastic housing, containing a filter element, which removes dust and dirt from the air being drawn into the engine.

Air filter element The actual filter in an air cleaner system, usually manufactured from pleated paper and requiring renewal at regular intervals.

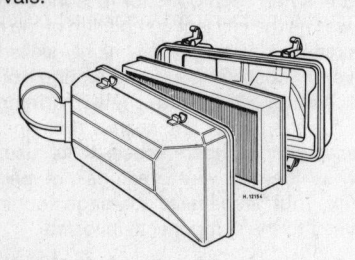

Air filter

Allen key A hexagonal wrench which fits into a recessed hexagonal hole.

Alligator clip A long-nosed spring-loaded metal clip with meshing teeth. Used to make temporary electrical connections.

Alternator A component in the electrical system which converts mechanical energy from a drivebelt into electrical energy to charge the battery and to operate the starting system, ignition system and electrical accessories.

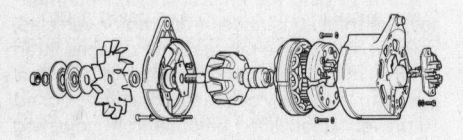

Alternator (exploded view)

Ampere (amp) A unit of measurement for the flow of electric current. One amp is the amount of current produced by one volt acting through a resistance of one ohm.

Anaerobic sealer A substance used to prevent bolts and screws from loosening. Anaerobic means that it does not require oxygen for activation. The Loctite brand is widely used.

Antifreeze A substance (usually ethylene glycol) mixed with water, and added to a vehicle's cooling system, to prevent freezing of the coolant in winter. Antifreeze also contains chemicals to inhibit corrosion and the formation of rust and other deposits that would tend to clog the radiator and coolant passages and reduce cooling efficiency.

Anti-seize compound A coating that reduces the risk of seizing on fasteners that are subjected to high temperatures, such as exhaust manifold bolts and nuts.

Anti-seize compound

Asbestos A natural fibrous mineral with great heat resistance, commonly used in the composition of brake friction materials. Asbestos is a health hazard and the dust created by brake systems should never be inhaled or ingested.

Axle A shaft on which a wheel revolves, or which revolves with a wheel. Also, a solid beam that connects the two wheels at one end of the vehicle. An axle which also transmits power to the wheels is known as a live axle.

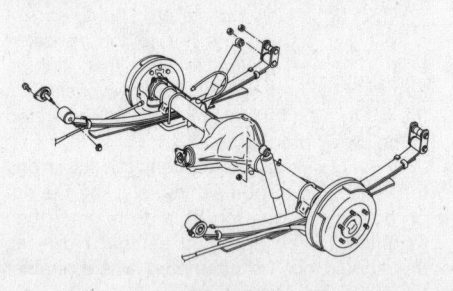

Axle assembly

Axleshaft A single rotating shaft, on either side of the differential, which delivers power from the final drive assembly to the drive wheels. Also called a driveshaft or a halfshaft.

B

Ball bearing An anti-friction bearing consisting of a hardened inner and outer race with hardened steel balls between two races.

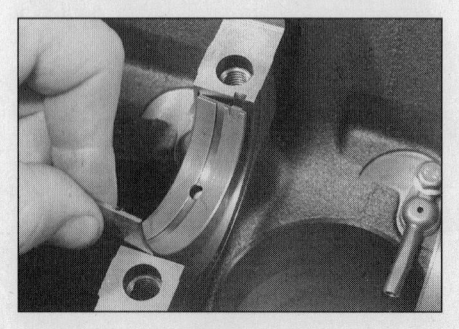

Bearing

Bearing The curved surface on a shaft or in a bore, or the part assembled into either, that permits relative motion between them with minimum wear and friction.

Big-end bearing The bearing in the end of the connecting rod that's attached to the crankshaft.

Bleed nipple A valve on a brake wheel cylinder, caliper or other hydraulic component that is opened to purge the hydraulic system of air. Also called a bleed screw.

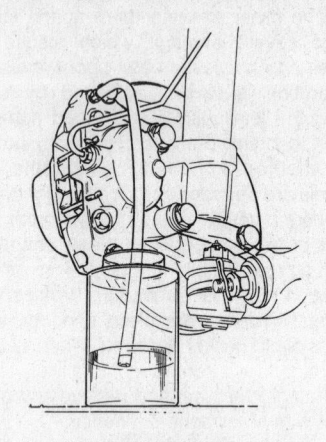

Brake bleeding

Brake bleeding Procedure for removing air from lines of a hydraulic brake system.

Brake disc The component of a disc brake that rotates with the wheels.

Brake drum The component of a drum brake that rotates with the wheels.

Brake linings The friction material which contacts the brake disc or drum to retard the vehicle's speed. The linings are bonded or riveted to the brake pads or shoes.

Brake pads The replaceable friction pads that pinch the brake disc when the brakes are applied. Brake pads consist of a friction material bonded or riveted to a rigid backing plate.

Brake shoe The crescent-shaped carrier to which the brake linings are mounted and which forces the lining against the rotating drum during braking.

Braking systems For more information on braking systems, consult the *Haynes Automotive Brake Manual*.

Breaker bar A long socket wrench handle providing greater leverage.

Bulkhead The insulated partition between the engine and the passenger compartment.

C

Caliper The non-rotating part of a disc-brake assembly that straddles the disc and carries the brake pads. The caliper also contains the hydraulic components that cause the pads to pinch the disc when the brakes are applied. A caliper is also a measuring tool that can be set to measure inside or outside dimensions of an object.

Glossary of technical terms REF•19

Camshaft A rotating shaft on which a series of cam lobes operate the valve mechanisms. The camshaft may be driven by gears, by sprockets and chain or by sprockets and a belt.

Canister A container in an evaporative emission control system; contains activated charcoal granules to trap vapours from the fuel system.

Canister

Carburettor A device which mixes fuel with air in the proper proportions to provide a desired power output from a spark ignition internal combustion engine.

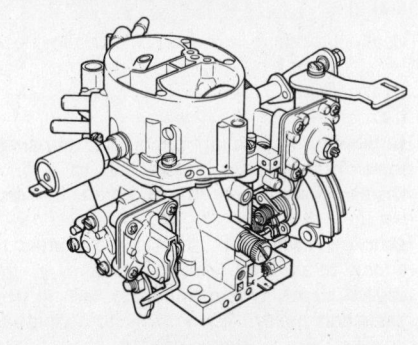

Carburettor

Castellated Resembling the parapets along the top of a castle wall. For example, a castellated balljoint stud nut.

Castellated nut

Castor In wheel alignment, the backward or forward tilt of the steering axis. Castor is positive when the steering axis is inclined rearward at the top.

Catalytic converter A silencer-like device in the exhaust system which converts certain pollutants in the exhaust gases into less harmful substances.

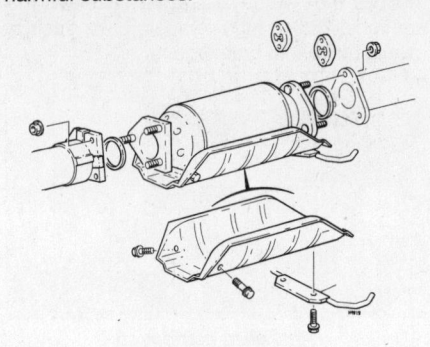

Catalytic converter

Circlip A ring-shaped clip used to prevent endwise movement of cylindrical parts and shafts. An internal circlip is installed in a groove in a housing; an external circlip fits into a groove on the outside of a cylindrical piece such as a shaft.

Clearance The amount of space between two parts. For example, between a piston and a cylinder, between a bearing and a journal, etc.

Coil spring A spiral of elastic steel found in various sizes throughout a vehicle, for example as a springing medium in the suspension and in the valve train.

Compression Reduction in volume, and increase in pressure and temperature, of a gas, caused by squeezing it into a smaller space.

Compression ratio The relationship between cylinder volume when the piston is at top dead centre and cylinder volume when the piston is at bottom dead centre.

Constant velocity (CV) joint A type of universal joint that cancels out vibrations caused by driving power being transmitted through an angle.

Core plug A disc or cup-shaped metal device inserted in a hole in a casting through which core was removed when the casting was formed. Also known as a freeze plug or expansion plug.

Crankcase The lower part of the engine block in which the crankshaft rotates.

Crankshaft The main rotating member, or shaft, running the length of the crankcase, with offset "throws" to which the connecting rods are attached.

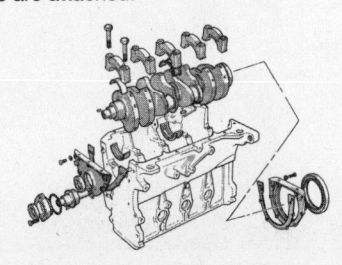

Crankshaft assembly

Crocodile clip See Alligator clip

D

Diagnostic code Code numbers obtained by accessing the diagnostic mode of an engine management computer. This code can be used to determine the area in the system where a malfunction may be located.

Disc brake A brake design incorporating a rotating disc onto which brake pads are squeezed. The resulting friction converts the energy of a moving vehicle into heat.

Double-overhead cam (DOHC) An engine that uses two overhead camshafts, usually one for the intake valves and one for the exhaust valves.

Drivebelt(s) The belt(s) used to drive accessories such as the alternator, water pump, power steering pump, air conditioning compressor, etc. off the crankshaft pulley.

Accessory drivebelts

Driveshaft Any shaft used to transmit motion. Commonly used when referring to the axleshafts on a front wheel drive vehicle.

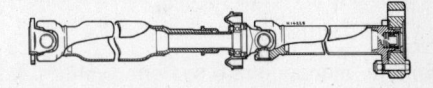

Driveshaft

Drum brake A type of brake using a drum-shaped metal cylinder attached to the inner surface of the wheel. When the brake pedal is pressed, curved brake shoes with friction linings press against the inside of the drum to slow or stop the vehicle.

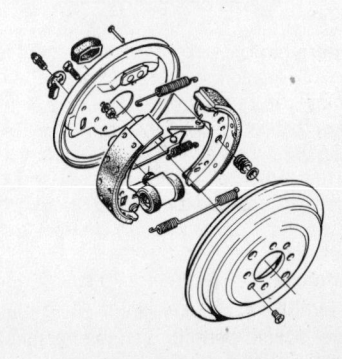

Drum brake assembly

REF•20 Glossary of technical terms

E

EGR valve A valve used to introduce exhaust gases into the intake air stream.

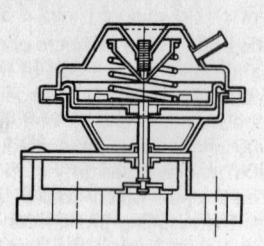

EGR valve

Electronic control unit (ECU) A computer which controls (for instance) ignition and fuel injection systems, or an anti-lock braking system. For more information refer to the Haynes Automotive Electrical and Electronic Systems Manual.

Electronic Fuel Injection (EFI) A computer controlled fuel system that distributes fuel through an injector located in each intake port of the engine.

Emergency brake A braking system, independent of the main hydraulic system, that can be used to slow or stop the vehicle if the primary brakes fail, or to hold the vehicle stationary even though the brake pedal isn't depressed. It usually consists of a hand lever that actuates either front or rear brakes mechanically through a series of cables and linkages. Also known as a handbrake or parking brake.

Endfloat The amount of lengthwise movement between two parts. As applied to a crankshaft, the distance that the crankshaft can move forward and back in the cylinder block.

Engine management system (EMS) A computer controlled system which manages the fuel injection and the ignition systems in an integrated fashion.

Exhaust manifold A part with several passages through which exhaust gases leave the engine combustion chambers and enter the exhaust pipe.

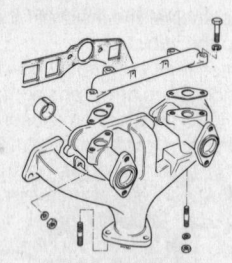

Exhaust manifold

F

Fan clutch A viscous (fluid) drive coupling device which permits variable engine fan speeds in relation to engine speeds.

Feeler blade A thin strip or blade of hardened steel, ground to an exact thickness, used to check or measure clearances between parts.

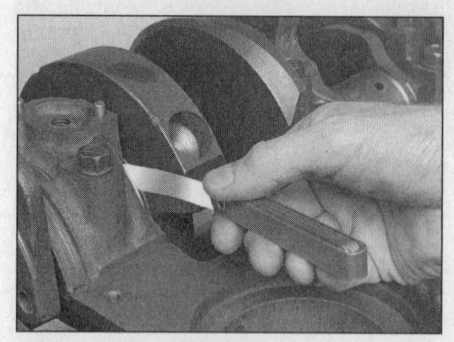

Feeler blade

Firing order The order in which the engine cylinders fire, or deliver their power strokes, beginning with the number one cylinder.

Flywheel A heavy spinning wheel in which energy is absorbed and stored by means of momentum. On cars, the flywheel is attached to the crankshaft to smooth out firing impulses.

Free play The amount of travel before any action takes place. The "looseness" in a linkage, or an assembly of parts, between the initial application of force and actual movement. For example, the distance the brake pedal moves before the pistons in the master cylinder are actuated.

Fuse An electrical device which protects a circuit against accidental overload. The typical fuse contains a soft piece of metal which is calibrated to melt at a predetermined current flow (expressed as amps) and break the circuit.

Fusible link A circuit protection device consisting of a conductor surrounded by heat-resistant insulation. The conductor is smaller than the wire it protects, so it acts as the weakest link in the circuit. Unlike a blown fuse, a failed fusible link must frequently be cut from the wire for replacement.

G

Gap The distance the spark must travel in jumping from the centre electrode to the side electrode in a spark plug. Also refers to the spacing between the points in a contact breaker assembly in a conventional points-type ignition, or to the distance between the reluctor or rotor and the pickup coil in an electronic ignition.

Gasket Any thin, soft material - usually cork, cardboard, asbestos or soft metal - installed between two metal surfaces to ensure a good seal. For instance, the cylinder head gasket seals the joint between the block and the cylinder head.

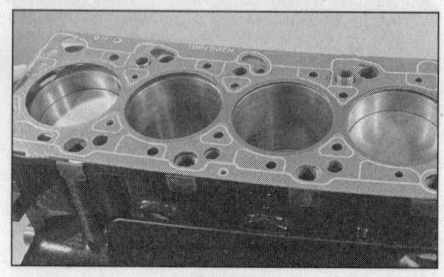

Gasket

Gauge An instrument panel display used to monitor engine conditions. A gauge with a movable pointer on a dial or a fixed scale is an analogue gauge. A gauge with a numerical readout is called a digital gauge.

H

Halfshaft A rotating shaft that transmits power from the final drive unit to a drive wheel, usually when referring to a live rear axle.

Harmonic balancer A device designed to reduce torsion or twisting vibration in the crankshaft. May be incorporated in the crankshaft pulley. Also known as a vibration damper.

Hone An abrasive tool for correcting small irregularities or differences in diameter in an engine cylinder, brake cylinder, etc.

Hydraulic tappet A tappet that utilises hydraulic pressure from the engine's lubrication system to maintain zero clearance (constant contact with both camshaft and valve stem). Automatically adjusts to variation in valve stem length. Hydraulic tappets also reduce valve noise.

I

Ignition timing The moment at which the spark plug fires, usually expressed in the number of crankshaft degrees before the piston reaches the top of its stroke.

Inlet manifold A tube or housing with passages through which flows the air-fuel mixture (carburettor vehicles and vehicles with throttle body injection) or air only (port fuel-injected vehicles) to the port openings in the cylinder head.

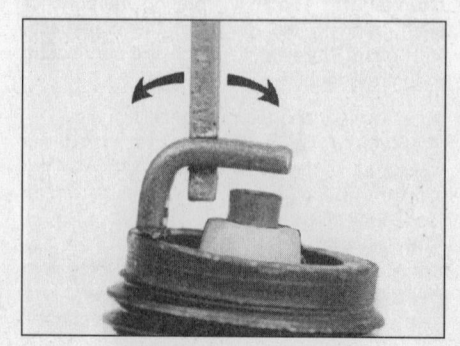

Adjusting spark plug gap

Glossary of technical terms REF•21

J

Jump start Starting the engine of a vehicle with a discharged or weak battery by attaching jump leads from the weak battery to a charged or helper battery.

L

Load Sensing Proportioning Valve (LSPV) A brake hydraulic system control valve that works like a proportioning valve, but also takes into consideration the amount of weight carried by the rear axle.

Locknut A nut used to lock an adjustment nut, or other threaded component, in place. For example, a locknut is employed to keep the adjusting nut on the rocker arm in position.

Lockwasher A form of washer designed to prevent an attaching nut from working loose.

M

MacPherson strut A type of front suspension system devised by Earle MacPherson at Ford of England. In its original form, a simple lateral link with the anti-roll bar creates the lower control arm. A long strut - an integral coil spring and shock absorber - is mounted between the body and the steering knuckle. Many modern so-called MacPherson strut systems use a conventional lower A-arm and don't rely on the anti-roll bar for location.

Multimeter An electrical test instrument with the capability to measure voltage, current and resistance.

N

NOx Oxides of Nitrogen. A common toxic pollutant emitted by petrol and diesel engines at higher temperatures.

O

Ohm The unit of electrical resistance. One volt applied to a resistance of one ohm will produce a current of one amp.

Ohmmeter An instrument for measuring electrical resistance.

O-ring A type of sealing ring made of a special rubber-like material; in use, the O-ring is compressed into a groove to provide the sealing action.

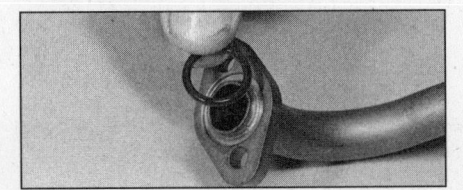

O-ring

Overhead cam (ohc) engine An engine with the camshaft(s) located on top of the cylinder head(s).

Overhead valve (ohv) engine An engine with the valves located in the cylinder head, but with the camshaft located in the engine block.

Oxygen sensor A device installed in the engine exhaust manifold, which senses the oxygen content in the exhaust and converts this information into an electric current. Also called a Lambda sensor.

P

Phillips screw A type of screw head having a cross instead of a slot for a corresponding type of screwdriver.

Plastigage A thin strip of plastic thread, available in different sizes, used for measuring clearances. For example, a strip of Plastigage is laid across a bearing journal. The parts are assembled and dismantled; the width of the crushed strip indicates the clearance between journal and bearing.

Plastigage

Propeller shaft The long hollow tube with universal joints at both ends that carries power from the transmission to the differential on front-engined rear wheel drive vehicles.

Proportioning valve A hydraulic control valve which limits the amount of pressure to the rear brakes during panic stops to prevent wheel lock-up.

R

Rack-and-pinion steering A steering system with a pinion gear on the end of the steering shaft that mates with a rack (think of a geared wheel opened up and laid flat). When the steering wheel is turned, the pinion turns, moving the rack to the left or right. This movement is transmitted through the track rods to the steering arms at the wheels.

Radiator A liquid-to-air heat transfer device designed to reduce the temperature of the coolant in an internal combustion engine cooling system.

Refrigerant Any substance used as a heat transfer agent in an air-conditioning system. R-12 has been the principle refrigerant for many years; recently, however, manufacturers have begun using R-134a, a non-CFC substance that is considered less harmful to the ozone in the upper atmosphere.

Rocker arm A lever arm that rocks on a shaft or pivots on a stud. In an overhead valve engine, the rocker arm converts the upward movement of the pushrod into a downward movement to open a valve.

Rotor In a distributor, the rotating device inside the cap that connects the centre electrode and the outer terminals as it turns, distributing the high voltage from the coil secondary winding to the proper spark plug. Also, that part of an alternator which rotates inside the stator. Also, the rotating assembly of a turbocharger, including the compressor wheel, shaft and turbine wheel.

Runout The amount of wobble (in-and-out movement) of a gear or wheel as it's rotated. The amount a shaft rotates "out-of-true." The out-of-round condition of a rotating part.

S

Sealant A liquid or paste used to prevent leakage at a joint. Sometimes used in conjunction with a gasket.

Sealed beam lamp An older headlight design which integrates the reflector, lens and filaments into a hermetically-sealed one-piece unit. When a filament burns out or the lens cracks, the entire unit is simply replaced.

Serpentine drivebelt A single, long, wide accessory drivebelt that's used on some newer vehicles to drive all the accessories, instead of a series of smaller, shorter belts. Serpentine drivebelts are usually tensioned by an automatic tensioner.

Serpentine drivebelt

Shim Thin spacer, commonly used to adjust the clearance or relative positions between two parts. For example, shims inserted into or under bucket tappets control valve clearances. Clearance is adjusted by changing the thickness of the shim.

Slide hammer A special puller that screws into or hooks onto a component such as a shaft or bearing; a heavy sliding handle on the shaft bottoms against the end of the shaft to knock the component free.

Sprocket A tooth or projection on the periphery of a wheel, shaped to engage with a chain or drivebelt. Commonly used to refer to the sprocket wheel itself.

Starter inhibitor switch On vehicles with an

Glossary of technical terms

automatic transmission, a switch that prevents starting if the vehicle is not in Neutral or Park.
Strut See MacPherson strut.

T

Tappet A cylindrical component which transmits motion from the cam to the valve stem, either directly or via a pushrod and rocker arm. Also called a cam follower.
Thermostat A heat-controlled valve that regulates the flow of coolant between the cylinder block and the radiator, so maintaining optimum engine operating temperature. A thermostat is also used in some air cleaners in which the temperature is regulated.
Thrust bearing The bearing in the clutch assembly that is moved in to the release levers by clutch pedal action to disengage the clutch. Also referred to as a release bearing.
Timing belt A toothed belt which drives the camshaft. Serious engine damage may result if it breaks in service.
Timing chain A chain which drives the camshaft.
Toe-in The amount the front wheels are closer together at the front than at the rear. On rear wheel drive vehicles, a slight amount of toe-in is usually specified to keep the front wheels running parallel on the road by offsetting other forces that tend to spread the wheels apart.
Toe-out The amount the front wheels are closer together at the rear than at the front. On front wheel drive vehicles, a slight amount of toe-out is usually specified.
Tools For full information on choosing and using tools, refer to the *Haynes Automotive Tools Manual*.
Tracer A stripe of a second colour applied to a wire insulator to distinguish that wire from another one with the same colour insulator.
Tune-up A process of accurate and careful adjustments and parts replacement to obtain the best possible engine performance.
Turbocharger A centrifugal device, driven by exhaust gases, that pressurises the intake air. Normally used to increase the power output from a given engine displacement, but can also be used primarily to reduce exhaust emissions (as on VW's "Umwelt" Diesel engine).

U

Universal joint or U-joint A double-pivoted connection for transmitting power from a driving to a driven shaft through an angle. A U-joint consists of two Y-shaped yokes and a cross-shaped member called the spider.

V

Valve A device through which the flow of liquid, gas, vacuum, or loose material in bulk may be started, stopped, or regulated by a movable part that opens, shuts, or partially obstructs one or more ports or passageways. A valve is also the movable part of such a device.
Valve clearance The clearance between the valve tip (the end of the valve stem) and the rocker arm or tappet. The valve clearance is measured when the valve is closed.
Vernier caliper A precision measuring instrument that measures inside and outside dimensions. Not quite as accurate as a micrometer, but more convenient.
Viscosity The thickness of a liquid or its resistance to flow.
Volt A unit for expressing electrical "pressure" in a circuit. One volt that will produce a current of one ampere through a resistance of one ohm.

W

Welding Various processes used to join metal items by heating the areas to be joined to a molten state and fusing them together. For more information refer to the *Haynes Automotive Welding Manual*.
Wiring diagram A drawing portraying the components and wires in a vehicle's electrical system, using standardised symbols. For more information refer to the *Haynes Automotive Electrical and Electronic Systems Manual*.

Index REF•23

Note: References throughout this index are in the form - "Chapter number" • "Page number"

A

Accelerator cable
 carburettor models - 4A•5
 fuel-injected models - 4B•2
Accelerator pedal
 carburettor models - 4A•5
 fuel-injected models - 4B•3
Air cleaner assembly
 carburettor models - 4A•2
 fuel-injected models - 4B•2
Air conditioning
 drivebelt - 1•11
 system check - 1•11
 system components - 3•8
Air filter element
 check - 1•12
 renewal - 1•18
Alternator
 drivebelt - 1•10
 removal and refitting - 5•7
 testing and overhaul - 5•7
Automatic transmission - 7B•1 et seq
Automatic transmission
 fluid level check - 1•16
 fluid renewal - 1•19
 overhaul - 7B•5
 removal and refitting - 7B•4
Auxiliary cooling fan - 3•4
Auxiliary drivebelt - 1•10
Axle, Rear - 10•9

B

Battery
 check - 0•15
 removal and refitting - 5•3
 testing and charging - 5•2
Bearings
 front hub - 10•2
 rear hub - 10•9
Bleeding
 brake hydraulic system - 9•2
 power steering system - 10•13
Body damage - 11•2, 11•3
Body electrical systems - 12•1 et seq
Bodywork and fittings - 11•1 et seq
Bonnet - 11•5
Boot lid (Saloon models)
 lock components - 11•12
 removal, refitting and adjustment - 11•11
Brake fluid level check - 0•12
Brake
 disc - 9•11
 drum - 9•12
 fluid renewal - 1•21
 pads - 9•4
 pedal adjustment - 9•6
 pedal freeplay - 1•11
 pipes and hoses - 9•4
 shoes - 9•6
Braking system - 9•1 et seq
Bulb and fuse check - 0•15
Bulbs
 exterior lights - 12•5
 interior lights - 12•8
 ratings - 12•1
Bumpers - 11•4
Buying spare parts - REF•3

C

Cables
 accelerator:
  carburettor models - 4A•5
  fuel-injected models - 4B•2
 bonnet release - 11•5
 clutch - 6•3
 handbrake - 9•17
 kickdown (automatic transmission) - 7B•3
 selector (automatic transmission) - 7B•2
 speedometer drive - 12•10
Camshaft - 2A•11
 oil seals - 2A•9
Capacities - 0•16
Carbon canister - 4C•4
Carburettor
 fault diagnosis, overhaul and adjustments:
  8-valve models - 4A•7
  12-valve models - 4A•10
 general information, - 4A•6
 removal and refitting - 4A•7
Catalytic converter - 4C•3, 4C•4
Central locking - 11•13
Centre console - 11•14
Charging system - 5•7
Clutch - 6•1 et seq
Clutch
 bleeding hydraulic system - 6•4
 cable - 6•3
 check and adjustment - 6•2
 fluid level check - 0•12
 master cylinder - 6•3
 pedal - 1•11, 6•5
 release mechanism - 6•7
 removal, inspection and refitting - 6•6
 slave cylinder - 6•4
Coil spring - 10•9
Compression test - 2A•3
Conversion factors - REF•2
Coolant
 level check - 0•11
 pump - 3•4
 renewal - 1•8
 temperature sensor - 4B•7
Cooling fan switch - 3•4
Cooling system hoses - 3•2
Cooling, heating and ventilation systems - 3•1 et seq
Courtesy light bulb - 12•8
Crank angle sensor - 4B•7
Crankcase emissions control - 1•14, 4C•2
Crankshaft
 inspection - 2B•12
 oil seals - 2A•15
 refitting - 2B•14
 removal - 2B•10

Constant velocity (CV) joint - 8•1
Cylinder block - 2B•10
Cylinder head
 cleaning and inspection - 2B•7
 dismantling - 2B•7
 reassembly - 2B•9
 removal, inspection and refitting - 2A•11
Cylinder head cover - 2A•4

D

Damper (shock absorber) - 10•9
Dashpot, carburettors - 4C•2
Dimensions - REF•1
Disc brake - 9•11
 pads - 9•4
Distributor - 5•4
Door - 11•6
 inner trim panel - 11•6
 latch, lock cylinder - 11•7
 handle components - 11•7
 switches - 12•5
 window glass and regulator - 11•9
Drivebelts
 air conditioning - 1•11
 auxiliary (alternator) - 1•10
 power steering pump - 10•14
Driveplate - 2A•15
Driveshaft gaiter
 check - 1•17
 removal and refitting - 8•3
Driveshafts - 8•1 et seq
Driveshafts
 removal and refitting - 8•1
 overhaul - 8•3

E

Electrical fault-finding - 12•2
Electrical systems, engine - 5•1 et seq
Electrical systems, body - 12•1 et seq
Electronic control unit (ECU) - 4B•7
Emission control components - 4C•2
Emission control systems - 4C•1 et seq
Engine removal, separation and refitting
 with automatic transmission - 2B•4, 2B•6
 with manual transmission - 2B•4
Engine electrical systems - 5•1 et seq
Engine in-car repair procedures - 2A•1 et seq
Engine
 initial start up after overhaul - 2B•18
 management relay - 4B•7
 mountings - 2A•16
 removal, separation and refitting
  automatic transmission - 2B•4, 2B•6
  manual transmission - 2B•4
 oil and filter renewal - 1•7
 oil level check - 0•11
 overhaul - 2B•7, 2B•13
Evaporative emissions control system - 4C•3
Exhaust gas recirculation - 4C•3

Index

Exhaust manifold
  carburettor models - 4A•13
  fuel-injected models - 4B•8
Exhaust system
  carburettor models - 4A•13
  fuel-injected models - 4B•9
  system check - 1•16
Exterior light units - 12•9
Exterior mirror - 11•13

F

Facia - 11•15
Facia mounted switches - 12•4
Fault finding - REF•10 et seq
Fault finding
  automatic transmission - REF•10, REF•14
  braking system - REF•10, REF•14
  clutch - REF•10, REF•13
  cooling system - REF•10, REF•12
  driveshafts - REF•10, REF•14
  electrical system - REF•10, REF•15
  engine - REF•10, REF•11
  fuel and exhaust systems - REF•10, REF•13
  manual transmission - REF•10, REF•13
  suspension and steering - REF•10, REF•15
Fluid cooler, automatic transmission - 7B•4
Fluid leak check - 1•16
Flywheel - 2A•15
Fog light bulb - 12•7
Front brake
  caliper - 9•13
  pad and disc check - 1•11
  pads, renewal - 9•4
Front bumper - 11•4
Front hub bearings - 10•2
Front suspension
  anti-roll bar - 10•8
  lower arm - 10•6
  lower arm balljoint - 10•8
  strut - 10•4
Front wheel alignment check - 1•17
Fuel and exhaust systems-
  carburettor models - 4A•1 et seq
  fuel-injected models - 4B•1 et seq
Fuel filter renewal - 1•18
Fuel gauge sender unit
  carburettor models - 4A•4
  fuel-injected models - 4B•4
Fuel injection system
  component removal and refitting - 4B•5
  depressurisation - 4B•3
  general information - 4B•3
  testing and adjustment - 4B•4
Fuel pressure regulator - 4B•6
Fuel pump
  carburettor models - 4A•3
  fuel-injected models - 4B•4
Fuel rail and injectors - 4B•5
Fuel tank
  carburettor models - 4A•4
  fuel-injected models - 4B•4
Fuses and relays - 12•2

G

Gaiters
  driveshaft - 8•3
  steering gear - 10•12
Gearchange
  cables - 7A•2
  lever - 7A•3
  mechanism - 7A•2
General engine overhaul procedures - 2B•1 et seq
General information
  air cleaner air temperature control system - 4A•3
  air conditioning system - 3•8
  automatic transmission - 7B•1
  body electrical systems - 12•1
  bodywork and fittings - 11•1
  braking system - 9•2
  carburettor - 4A•6
  clutch - 6•1
  cooling, heating and ventilation systems - 3•2
  driveshafts - 8•1
  electrical fault-finding - 12•2
  emission control systems - 4C•1
  engine electrical systems - 5•2
  engine in-car repair procedures - 2A•3
  exhaust system:
    carburettor models - 4A•13
    fuel-injected models - 4B•9
  fuel and exhaust systems:
    carburettor models - 4A•2
    fuel injected models - 4B•2
  fuel injection system - 4B•3
  fuses and relays - 12•2
  general engine overhaul - 2B•3
  ignition system - 5•3
  manual transmission - 7A•1
  routine maintenance - 1•6
  sunroof - 11•14
  suspension and steering - 10•2
General repair procedures - REF•17
Glossary of technical terms - REF•18

H

Handbrake
  cables - 9•17
  check - 1•11
  warning light switch - 9•18
Headlight - 12•9
  beam alignment check - 1•19
  bulb - 12•5
Heater assembly - 3•6
Heater
  blower motor - 3•7
  control unit - 3•6
  matrix - 3•7
Hinge and lock lubrication - 1•20
Horn - 12•10
Hose check - 1•16
Hub assembly
  front - 10•2
  rear - 9•12
Hydraulic pipes and hoses - 9•4
Hydraulic system, bleeding - 9•2

I

Identifying leaks - 0•9
Idle speed check and adjustment - 1•14
Idle speed control servo - 4B•7
If your car won't start - 0•6
Ignition HT coil - 5•4
Ignition switch - 10•10
Ignition system
  check - 1•13
  general information - 5•3
  testing - 5•3
Ignition timing - 1•19, 5•6
Indicator - 12•9
  bulb - 12•6
Inlet air temperature sensor - 4B•7
Inlet manifold
  carburettor models - 4A•13
  fuel injected models - 4B•7
Instrument panel - 12•10
  bulbs - 12•8
Intensive maintenance - 1•6
Introduction to the Proton - 0•4
Introduction to Weekly checks - 0•10

J

Jacking and vehicle support - REF•3
Jump starting - 0•7

K

Kickdown cable (automatic transmission) - 7B•3

L

Lubricants and fluids - 0•16
Light bulbs
  exterior lights - 12•5
  interior lights - 12•8
Light units - 12•9

M

Main and big-end bearings - 2B•12
Maintenance
  bodywork and underframe - 11•1
  routine - 1•1 *et seq*
  upholstery and carpets - 11•2
Maintenance procedures - 1•6
Maintenance schedule - 1•3
Major body damage - 11•3
Manifold absolute pressure sensor - 4B•7
Manual transmission - 7A•1 et seq
Manual transmission
  oil level check - 1•15
  oil renewal - 1•18
  overhaul - 7A•5
  removal and refitting - 7A•4
Master cylinder - 9•16
Minor body damage - 11•2
Mirror
  adjustment switch - 12•4
  removal and refitting - 11•13
Mixture (fuel) - 1•14
MOT test checks - REF•6

Index

N
Number plate bulb - 12•8

O
Oil capacities - 0•16
Oil pressure warning light switch - 5•8
Oil pump - 2A•13
Oil seals
   automatic transmission - 7B•4
   manual transmission - 7A•3
Oil types - 0•16

P
Pedal
   accelerator:
      carburettor models- 4A•5
      fuel-injected models - 4B•3
   brake - 9•6
   clutch - 6•5
Piston rings - 2B•13
Piston rod assembly - 2B•9, 2B•11, 2B•16
Power steering
   fluid level check - 0•13
   pump - 10•13
   pump drivebelt - 1•10, 10•14
   system bleeding - 10•13

R
Radiator - 3•2
   grille - 11•6
Rear axle - 10•9
Rear brake
   drum and hub assembly - 9•12
   pressure proportioning valve - 9•18
   shoe and drum check - 1•16
   shoes - 9•6
Rear bumper - 11•4
Rear hub bearings - 10•9
Rear light cluster - 12•9
   bulb - 12•7
Rear suspension components - 10•9
Rear wheel bearing
   lubrication - 1•20
   renewal - 10•9
Rear wheel cylinder - 9•15
Reference - REF•1 et seq
Relays
   engine management - 4B•7
   general - 12•2
Reversing light switch
   automatic transmission - 7B•4
   manual transmission - 7A•3
Road test - 1•12
Roadside repairs - 0•6
Rocker shafts and arms - 2A•9
Routine Maintenance and Servicing - 1•1 et seq

S
Safety First! - 0•5
Screen washer fluid level check - 0•12
Seats - 11•14
Selector cable - 7B•2
Selector lever assembly - 7B•3
Shock absorber - 10•9
Sidelight - 12•9
   bulb - 12•6
Solenoid control valve - 4C•4
Spark plugs
   check - 1•9
   renewal - 1•12
   type - 1•2
Specifications
   automatic transmission - 7B•1
   body electrical systems - 12•1
   bodywork and fittings - 11•1
   braking system - 9•1
   clutch - 6•1
   cooling, heating and ventilation systems - 3•1
   driveshafts - 8•1
   emission control systems - 4C•1
   engine electrical systems - 5•1
   engine in-car repair procedures - 2A•1
   engine overhaul procedures - 2B•1
   fuel and exhaust systems:
      carburettor models - 4A•1
      fuel-injected models - 4B•1
   manual transmission - 7A•1
   routine maintenance and servicing - 1•2
   suspension and steering - 10•1
Speedometer
   drive cable - 12•10
   drive:
      automatic transmission - 7B•4
      manual transmission - 7A•4
Starter inhibitor switch (automatic transmission) - 7B•4
Starter motor - 5•8
Starting system, testing - 5•7
Steering column - 10•11
   lock - 10•10
   switches - 12•3, 12•4
Steering gear - 10•11
   rubber gaiters - 10•12
Steering wheel - 10•10
Stop-light switch - 9•18
Sump - 2A•13
Sunroof - 11•14
Suspension and steering - 10•1 et seq
Suspension and steering check - 1•16
Switch
   illumination - 12•8
   ignition - 5•8, 10•10
   removal and refitting - 12•3

T
Tailgate (Aeroback models) - 11•11
   lock and handle components - 11•12
   wiper motor - 12•11
Temperature gauge coolant sensor - 3•6
Thermostat - 3•3
Throttle housing - 4B•4
Throttle position sensor - 4B•6
Timing belt
   check - 1•13
   removal and refitting - 1•21, 2A•5
   sprockets and tensioners - 2A•7
Tools and working facilities - REF•4
Top dead centre (TDC), locating - 2A•4
Top dead centre sensor - 4B•7
Towing - 0•9
Track-rod end - 10•13
Transmission -
   see Manual or Automatic transmission
Transmission overhaul
   manual transmission - 7A•5
   automatic transmission - 7B•5
Tyre condition and pressure check - 0•14
   pressures - 0•16

U
Underbody check - 1•17
Underbonnet check points - 0•10
Unleaded petrol, general information and usage
   carburettor models - 4A•6
   fuel-injected models - 4B•3

V
Vacuum servo unit - 9•17
   check valve - 9•17
Valve clearances - 1•13
Vehicle identification - REF•3
Vehicle speed sensor - 4B•7

W
Weekly checks - 0•10
Weights - REF•1
Wheel alignment check - 1•17
Wheel changing - 0•8
Wheel cylinder - 9•15
Window glass and regulator - 11•9
Window switches - 12•5
Windscreen wiper
   arm - 12•11
   blades check - 0•13
   motor and linkage - 12•11
Wiring diagrams - 12•12 et seq

Notes

Haynes Manuals – The Complete List

Title	Book No.
ALFA ROMEO	
Alfa Romeo Alfasud/Sprint (74 - 88)	0292
Alfa Romeo Alfetta (73 - 87)	0531
AUDI	
Audi 80 (72 - Feb 79)	0207
Audi 80, 90 (79 - Oct 86) & Coupe (81 - Nov 88)	0605
Audi 80, 90 (Oct 86 - 90) & Coupe (Nov 88 - 90)	1491
Audi 100 (Oct 76 - Oct 82)	0428
Audi 100 (Oct 82 - 90) & 200 (Feb 84 - Oct 89)	0907
AUSTIN	
Austin Ambassador (82 - 84)	0871
Austin/MG Maestro 1.3 & 1.6 (83 - 95)	0922
Austin Maxi (69 - 81)	0052
Austin/MG Metro (80 - May 90)	0718
Austin Montego 1.3 & 1.6 (84 - 94)	1066
Austin/MG Montego 2.0 (84 - 95)	1067
Mini (59 - 69)	0527
Mini (69 - 96)	0646
Austin/Rover 2.0 litre Diesel Engine (86 - 93)	1857
BEDFORD	
Bedford CF (69 - 87)	0163
Bedford Rascal (86 - 93)	3015
BL	
BL Princess & BLMC 18-22 (75 - 82)	0286
BMW	
BMW 316, 320 & 320i (4-cyl) (75 - Feb 83)	0276
BMW 320, 320i, 323i & 325i (6-cyl) (Oct 77 - Sept 87)	0815
BMW 3-Series (Apr 91 - 96)	3210
BMW 3-Series (sohc) (83 - 91)	1948
BMW 520i & 525e (Oct 81 - June 88)	1560
BMW 525, 528 & 528i (73 - Sept 81)	0632
BMW 5-Series (sohc) (81 - 93)	1948
BMW 1500, 1502, 1600, 1602, 2000 & 2002 (59 - 77)	0240
CITROEN	
Citroen 2CV, Ami & Dyane (67 - 90)	0196
Citroen AX Petrol & Diesel (87 - 94)	3014
Citroen BX (83 - 94)	0908
Citroen CX (75 - 88)	0528
Citroen Visa (79 - 88)	0620
Citroen Xantia Petrol & Diesel (93 - Oct 95)	3082
Citroen ZX Diesel (91 - 93)	1922
Citroen ZX Petrol (91 - 94)	1881
Citroen 1.7 & 1.9 litre Diesel Engine (84 - 96)	1379
COLT	
Colt 1200, 1250 & 1400 (79 - May 84)	0600
Colt Galant (74 - 78) & Celeste (76 - 81)	0236
DAIMLER	
Daimler Sovereign (68 - Oct 86)	0242
Daimler Double Six (72 - 88)	0478
DATSUN *(see also Nissan)*	
Datsun 120Y (73 - Aug 78)	0228
Datsun 1300, 1400 & 1600 (69 - Aug 72)	0123
Datsun Cherry (79 - Sept 82)	0679
Datsun Pick-up (75 - 78)	0277
Datsun Sunny (Aug 78 - May 82)	0525
Datsun Violet (78 - 82)	0430

Title	Book No.
FIAT	
Fiat 126 (73 - 87)	0305
Fiat 127 (71 - 83)	0193
Fiat 500 (57 - 73)	0090
Fiat 850 (64 - 81)	0038
Fiat Panda (81 - 95)	0793
Fiat Punto (94 - 96)	3251
Fiat Regata (84 - 88)	1167
Fiat Strada (79 - 88)	0479
Fiat Tipo (88 - 91)	1625
Fiat Uno (83 - 95)	0923
Fiat X1/9 (74 - 89)	0273
FORD	
Ford Capri II (& III) 1.6 & 2.0 (74 - 87)	0283
Ford Capri II (& III) 2.8 & 3.0 (74 - 87)	1309
Ford Cortina Mk III 1600 & 2000 (70 - 76)	0295
Ford Cortina Mk IV (& V) 1.6 & 2.0 (76 - 83)	0343
Ford Cortina Mk IV (& V) 2.3 V6 (77 - 83)	0426
Ford Escort (75 - Aug 80)	0280
Ford Escort (Sept 80 - Sept 90)	0686
Ford Escort (Sept 90 - 96)	1737
Ford Escort Mk II Mexico, RS 1600 & RS 2000 (75 - 80)	0735
Ford Fiesta (inc. XR2) (76 - Aug 83)	0334
Ford Fiesta (inc. XR2) (Aug 83 - Feb 89)	1030
Ford Fiesta (Feb 89 - 93)	1595
Ford Granada (Sept 77 - Feb 85)	0481
Ford Granada (Mar 85 - 94)	1245
Ford Mondeo 4-cyl (93 - 96)	1923
Ford Orion (83 - Sept 90)	1009
Ford Orion (Sept 90 - 93)	1737
Ford Sierra 1.3, 1.6, 1.8 & 2.0 (82 - 93)	0903
Ford Sierra 2.3, 2.8 & 2.9 (82 - 91)	0904
Ford Scorpio (Mar 85 - 94)	1245
Ford Transit Petrol (Mk 1) (65 - Feb 78)	0377
Ford Transit Petrol (Mk 2) (78 - Jan 86)	0719
Ford Transit Petrol (Mk 3) (Feb 86 - 89)	1468
Ford Transit Diesel (Feb 86 - 95)	3019
Ford 1.6 & 1.8 litre Diesel Engine (84 - 96)	1172
Ford 2.1, 2.3 & 2.5 litre Diesel Engine (77 - 90)	1606
Ford Vehicle Carburettors	1783
FREIGHT ROVER	
Freight Rover Sherpa (74 - 87)	0463
HILLMAN	
Hillman Avenger (70 - 82)	0037
Hillman Minx & Husky (56 - 66)	0009
HONDA	
Honda Accord (76 - Feb 84)	0351
Honda Accord (Feb 84 - Oct 85)	1177
Honda Civic 1300 (80 - 81)	0633
Honda Civic (Feb 84 - Oct 87)	1226
Honda Civic (Nov 91 - 96)	3199
JAGUAR	
Jaguar E Type (61 - 72)	0140
Jaguar MkI & II, 240 & 340 (55 - 69)	0098
Jaguar XJ6, XJ & Sovereign (68 - Oct 86)	0242
Jaguar XJ12, XJS & Sovereign (72 - 88)	0478
JEEP	
Jeep Cherokee Petrol (93 - 96)	1943

Title	Book No.
LADA	
Lada 1200, 1300, 1500 & 1600 (74 - 91)	0413
Lada Samara (87 - 91)	1610
LAND ROVER	
Land Rover 90, 110 & Defender Diesel (83 - 95)	3017
Land Rover Discovery Diesel (89 - 95)	3016
Land Rover Series IIA & III Diesel (58 - 85)	0529
Land Rover Series II, IIA & III Petrol (58 - 85)	0314
MAZDA	
Mazda 323 fwd (Mar 81 - Oct 89)	1608
Mazda 323 rwd (77 - Apr 86)	0370
Mazda 626 fwd (May 83 - Sept 87)	0929
Mazda B-1600, B-1800 & B-2000 Pick-up (72 - 88)	0267
Mazda RX-7 (79 - 85)	0460
MERCEDES-BENZ	
Mercedes-Benz 190 & 190E (83 - 87)	0928
Mercedes-Benz 200, 240, 300 Diesel (Oct 76 - 85)	1114
Mercedes-Benz 250 & 280 (68 - 72)	0346
Mercedes-Benz 250 & 280 (123 Series) (Oct 76 - 84)	0677
Mercedes-Benz 124 Series (85 - Aug 93)	3253
MG	
MGB (62 - 80)	0111
MG Maestro 1.3 & 1.6 (83 - 95)	0922
MG Metro (80 - May 90)	0718
MG Midget & AH Sprite (58 - 80)	0265
MG Montego 2.0 (84 - 95)	1067
MITSUBISHI	
Mitsubishi 1200, 1250 & 1400 (79 - May 84)	0600
Mitsubishi Shogun & L200 Pick-Ups (83 - 94)	1944
MORRIS	
Morris Ital 1.3 (80 - 84)	0705
Morris Marina 1700 (78 - 80)	0526
Morris Marina 1.8 (71 - 78)	0074
Morris Minor 1000 (56 - 71)	0024
NISSAN *(See also Datsun)*	
Nissan Bluebird 160B & 180B rwd (May 80 - May 84)	0957
Nissan Bluebird fwd (May 84 - Mar 86)	1223
Nissan Bluebird (T12 & T72) (Mar 86 - 90)	1473
Nissan Cherry (N12) (Sept 82 - 86)	1031
Nissan Micra (K10) (83 - Jan 93)	0931
Nissan Micra (93 - 96)	3254
Nissan Primera (90 - Oct 96)	1851
Nissan Stanza (82 - 86)	0824
Nissan Sunny (B11) (May 82 - Oct 86)	0895
Nissan Sunny (Oct 86 - Mar 91)	1378
Nissan Sunny (Apr 91 - 95)	3219
OPEL	
Opel Ascona & Manta (B Series) (Sept 75 - 88)	0316
Opel Ascona (81 - 88)	3215
Opel Astra (Oct 91 - 96)	3156
Opel Corsa (83 - Mar 93)	3160
Opel Corsa (Mar 93 - 94)	3159
Opel Kadett (Nov 79 - Oct 84)	0634
Opel Kadett (Oct 84 - Oct 91)	3196
Opel Omega & Senator (86 - 94)	3157

Title	Book No.
Opel Rekord (Feb 78 - Oct 86)	0543
Opel Vectra (88 - Oct 95)	3158
PEUGEOT	
Peugeot 106 Petrol & Diesel (91 - June 96)	1882
Peugeot 205 (83 - 95)	0932
Peugeot 305 (78 - 89)	0538
Peugeot 306 Petrol & Diesel (93 - 95)	3073
Peugeot 309 (86 - 93)	1266
Peugeot 405 Petrol (88 - 96)	1559
Peugeot 405 Diesel (88 - 96)	3198
Peugeot 505 (79 - 89)	0762
Peugeot 1.7 & 1.9 litre Diesel Engines (82 - 96)	0950
Peugeot 2.0, 2.1, 2.3 & 2.5 litre Diesel Engines (74 - 90)	1607
PORSCHE	
Porsche 911 (65 - 85)	0264
Porsche 924 & 924 Turbo (76 - 85)	0397
RANGE ROVER	
Range Rover V8 (70 - Oct 92)	0606
RELIANT	
Reliant Robin & Kitten (73 - 83)	0436
RENAULT	
Renault 5 (72 - Feb 85)	0141
Renault 5 (Feb 85 - 96)	1219
Renault 6 (68 - 79)	0092
Renault 9 & 11 (82 - 89)	0822
Renault 12 (70 - 80)	0097
Renault 15 & 17 (72 - 79)	0763
Renault 16 (65 - 79)	0081
Renault 18 (79 - 86)	0598
Renault 19 Petrol (89 - 94)	1646
Renault 19 Diesel (89 - 95)	1946
Renault 21 (86 - 94)	1397
Renault 25 (84 - 86)	1228
Renault Clio Petrol (91 - 93)	1853
Renault Clio Diesel (91 - June 96)	3031
Renault Espace (85 - 96)	3197
Renault Fuego (80 - 86)	0764
Renault Laguna (94 - 96)	3252
ROVER	
Rover 111 & 114 (95 - 96)	1711
Rover 213 & 216 (84 - 89)	1116
Rover 214 & 414 (Oct 89 - 92)	1689
Rover 216 & 416 (Oct 89 - 92)	1830
Rover 820, 825 & 827 (86 - 95)	1380
Rover 2000, 2300 & 2600 (77 - 87)	0468
Rover 3500 (76 - 87)	0365
Rover Metro (May 90 - 94)	1711
Rover 2.0 litre Diesel Engine (86 - 93)	1857
SAAB	
Saab 95 & 96 (66 - 76)	0198
Saab 99 (69 - 79)	0247
Saab 90, 99 & 900 (79 - Oct 93)	0765
Saab 9000 (4-cyl) (85 - 95)	1686
SEAT	
Seat Ibiza & Malaga (85 - 92)	1609

Title	Book No.
SIMCA	
Simca 1100 & 1204 (67 - 79)	0088
Simca 1301 & 1501 (63 - 76)	0199
SKODA	
Skoda 1000 & 1100 (64 - 78)	0303
Skoda Estelle 105, 120, 130 & 136 (77 - 89)	0604
Skoda Favorit (89 - 92)	1801
SUBARU	
Subaru 1600 (77 - Oct 79)	0237
Subaru 1600 & 1800 (Nov 79 - 90)	0995
SUZUKI	
Suzuki SJ Series, Samurai & Vitara (82 - 94)	1942
Suzuki Supercarry (86 - Oct 94)	3015
TALBOT	
Talbot Alpine, Solara, Minx & Rapier (75 - 86)	0337
Talbot Horizon (78 - 86)	0473
Talbot Samba (82 - 86)	0823
TOYOTA	
Toyota 2000 (75 - 77)	0360
Toyota Celica (78 - Jan 82)	0437
Toyota Celica (Feb 82 - Sept 85)	1135
Toyota Corolla (fwd) (Sept 83 - Sept 87)	1024
Toyota Corolla (rwd) (80 - 85)	0683
Toyota Corolla (Sept 87 - 92)	1683
Toyota Hi-Ace & Hi-Lux (69 - Oct 83)	0304
Toyota Starlet (78 - Jan 85)	0462
TRIUMPH	
Triumph Acclaim (81 - 84)	0792
Triumph GT6 (62 - 74)	0112
Triumph Herald (59 - 71)	0010
Triumph Spitfire (62 - 81)	0113
Triumph Stag (70 - 78)	0441
Triumph TR2, TR3, TR3A, TR4 & TR4A (52 - 67)	0028
Triumph TR7 (75 - 82)	0322
Triumph Vitesse (62 - 74)	0112
VAUXHALL	
Vauxhall Astra (80 - Oct 84)	0635
Vauxhall Astra & Belmont (Oct 84 - Oct 91)	1136
Vauxhall Astra (Oct 91 - 96)	1832
Vauxhall Carlton (Oct 78 - Oct 86)	0480
Vauxhall Carlton (Nov 86 - 94)	1469
Vauxhall Cavalier 1300 (77 - July 81)	0461
Vauxhall Cavalier 1600, 1900 & 2000 (75 - July 81)	0315
Vauxhall Cavalier (81 - Oct 88)	0812
Vauxhall Cavalier (Oct 88 - Oct 95)	1570
Vauxhall Chevette (75 - 84)	0285
Vauxhall Corsa (Mar 93 - 94)	1985
Vauxhall Nova (83 - 93)	0909
Vauxhall Rascal (86 - 93)	3015
Vauxhall Senator (Sept 87 - 94)	1469
Vauxhall Victor & VX4/90 (FD Series) (67 - 72)	0053
Vauxhall Viva HC (70 - 79)	0047
Vauxhall/Opel 1.5, 1.6 & 1.7 litre Diesel Engines (82 - 96)	1222
VOLKSWAGEN	
VW Beetle 1200 (54 - 77)	0036
VW Beetle 1300 & 1500 (65 - 75)	0039

Title	Book No.
VW Beetle 1302 & 1302S (70 - 72)	0110
VW Beetle 1303, 1303S & GT (72 - 75)	0159
VW Golf Mk 1 1.1 & 1.3 (74 - Feb 84)	0716
VW Golf Mk 1 1.5, 1.6 & 1.8 (74 - 85)	0726
VW Golf Mk 1 Diesel (78 - Feb 84)	0451
VW Golf Mk 2 (Mar 84 - Feb 92)	1081
VW Golf Mk 3 Petrol & Diesel (Feb 92 - 96)	3097
VW Jetta Mk 1 1.1 & 1.3 (80 - June 84)	0716
VW Jetta Mk 1 1.5, 1.6 & 1.8 (80 - June 84)	0726
VW Jetta Mk 1 Diesel (81 - June 84)	0451
VW Jetta Mk 2 (July 84 - 92)	1081
VW LT vans & light trucks (76 - 87)	0637
VW Passat (Sept 81 - May 88)	0814
VW Passat (May 88 - 91)	1647
VW Polo & Derby (76 - Jan 82)	0335
VW Polo (82 - Oct 90)	0813
VW Polo (Nov 90 - Aug 94)	3245
VW Santana (Sept 82 - 85)	0814
VW Scirocco Mk 1 1.5, 1.6 & 1.8 (74 - 82)	0726
VW Scirocco (82 - 90)	1224
VW Transporter 1600 (68 - 79)	0082
VW Transporter 1700, 1800 & 2000 (72 - 79)	0226
VW Transporter with air-cooled engine (79 - 82)	0638
VW Type 3 (63 - 73)	0084
VW Vento Petrol & Diesel (Feb 92 - 96)	3097
VOLVO	
Volvo 66 & 343, Daf 55 & 66 (68 - 79)	0293
Volvo 142, 144 & 145 (66 - 74)	0129
Volvo 240 Series (74 - 93)	0270
Volvo 262, 264 & 260/265 (75 - 85)	0400
Volvo 340, 343, 345 & 360 (76 - 91)	0715
Volvo 440, 460 & 480 (87 - 92)	1691
Volvo 740 & 760 (82 - 91)	1258
Volvo 850 (92 - 96)	3260
Volvo 940 (90 - 96)	3249
YUGO/ZASTAVA	
Yugo/Zastava (81 - 90)	1453
TECH BOOKS	
Automotive Brake Manual	3050
Automotive Electrical & Electronic Systems	3049
Automotive Tools Manual	3052
Automotive Welding Manual	3053
CAR BOOKS	
Automotive Fuel Injection Systems	9755
Car Bodywork Repair Manual	9864
Caravan Manual (2nd Edition)	9894
Ford Vehicle Carburettors	1783
Haynes Technical Data Book (87 - 96)	1996
In-Car Entertainment Manual (2nd Edition)	9862
Japanese Vehicle Carburettors	1786
Pass the MOT!	9861
Small Engine Repair Manual	1755
Solex & Pierburg Carburettors	1785
SU Carburettors	0299
Weber Carburettors (to 79)	0393
Weber Carburettors (79 - 91)	1784

All the products featured on this page are available through most motor accessory shops, cycle shops and book stores. Our policy of continuous updating and development means that titles are being constantly added to the range. For up-to-date information on our complete list of titles, please telephone: (UK) 01963 442030 • (USA) (805) 498-6703 • (France) (1) 47 03 61 80 • (Sweden) 018 124016

Preserving Our Motoring Heritage

The Model J Duesenberg Derham Tourster. Only eight of these magnificent cars were ever built – this is the only example to be found outside the United States of America

Almost every car you've ever loved, loathed or desired is gathered under one roof at the Haynes Motor Museum. Over 300 immaculately presented cars and motorbikes represent every aspect of our motoring heritage, from elegant reminders of bygone days, such as the superb Model J Duesenberg to curiosities like the bug-eyed BMW Isetta. There are also many old friends and flames. Perhaps you remember the 1959 Ford Popular that you did your courting in? The magnificent 'Red Collection' is a spectacle of classic sports cars including AC, Alfa Romeo, Austin Healey, Ferrari, Lamborghini, Maserati, MG, Riley, Porsche and Triumph.

A Perfect Day Out

Each and every vehicle at the Haynes Motor Museum has played its part in the history and culture of Motoring. Today, they make a wonderful spectacle and a great day out for all the family. Bring the kids, bring Mum and Dad, but above all bring your camera to capture those golden memories for ever. You will also find an impressive array of motoring memorabilia, a comfortable 70 seat video cinema and one of the most extensive transport book shops in Britain. The Pit Stop Cafe serves everything from a cup of tea to wholesome, home-made meals or, if you prefer, you can enjoy the large picnic area nestled in the beautiful rural surroundings of Somerset.

John Haynes O.B.E., Founder and Chairman of the museum at the wheel of a Haynes Light 12.

Graham Hill's Lola Cosworth Formula 1 car next to a 1934 Riley Sports.

The Museum is situated on the A359 Yeovil to Frome road at Sparkford, just off the A303 in Somerset. It is about 40 miles south of Bristol, and 25 minutes drive from the M5 intersection at Taunton.
Open 9.30am - 5.30pm (10.00am - 4.00pm Winter) 7 days a week, *except Christmas Day, Boxing Day and New Years Day*
Special rates available for schools, coach parties and outings Charitable Trust No. 292048